AIA

S T U D Y

T E X T

PAPER 2
BUSINESS ECONOMICS

In this 2020 edition

- A **user-friendly format** for easy navigation
- **Exam-centred topic coverage**, directly linked to AIA's syllabus
- **Exam focus points** showing you what the examiner will want you to do
- Regular **fast forward** summaries emphasising the key points in each chapter
- **Questions** and **quick quizzes** to test your understanding
- **Exam question bank** containing exam standard questions with answers
- **2 Mock exams** containing the November 2017 and May 2018 papers
- **A full index**

FOR EXAMS IN 2020

First edition April 2011
Eighth edition January 2020

ISBN 9781 5097 8717 3
(previous ISBN 9781 5097 2500 7)

eISBN 9781 5097 2847 3
(previous eISBN 9781 5097 2567 0)

British Library Cataloguing-in-Publication Data
A catalogue record for this book
is available from the British Library

Published by

BPP Learning Media Ltd
BPP House, Aldine Place
142-144 Uxbridge Road
London W12 8AA

www.bpp.com/learningmedia

Printed in the United Kingdom

Your learning materials, published by BPP Learning Media Ltd, are printed on paper obtained from traceable sustainable sources.

All rights reserved. No part of this publication may be reproduced, stored in a retrieval system or transmitted in any form or by any means, electronic, mechanical, photocopying, recording or otherwise, without the prior written permission of BPP Learning Media.

The contents of this book are intended as a guide and not professional advice. Although every effort has been made to ensure that the contents of this book are correct at the time of going to press, BPP Learning Media makes no warranty that the information in this book is accurate or complete and accept no liability for any loss or damage suffered by any person acting or refraining from acting as a result of the material in this book.

We are grateful to the Association of International Accountants for permission to reproduce past examination questions.

©
BPP Learning Media Ltd
2020

A note about copyright

Dear Customer

What does the little © mean and why does it matter?

Your market-leading BPP books, course materials and e-learning materials do not write and update themselves. People write them: on their own behalf or as employees of an organisation that invests in this activity. Copyright law protects their livelihoods. It does so by creating rights over the use of the content.

Breach of copyright is a form of theft – as well as being a criminal offence in some jurisdictions, it is potentially a serious breach of professional ethics.

With current technology, things might seem a bit hazy but, basically, without the express permission of BPP Learning Media:

- Photocopying our materials is a breach of copyright

- Scanning, ripcasting or conversion of our digital materials into different file formats, uploading them to Facebook or emailing them to your friends is a breach of copyright

You can, of course, sell your books, in the form in which you have bought them – once you have finished with them. (Is this fair to your fellow students? We update for a reason.) But the e-products are sold on a single user license basis: we do not supply 'unlock' codes to people who have bought them second hand.

And what about outside the UK? BPP Learning Media strives to make our materials available at prices students can afford by local printing arrangements, pricing policies and partnerships which are clearly listed on our website. A tiny minority ignore this and indulge in criminal activity by illegally photocopying our material or supporting organisations that do. If they act illegally and unethically in one area, can you really trust them?

Contents

Page

Introduction

The introduction pages contain lots of valuable advice and information. They include tips on studying for and passing the exam, also the content of the syllabus and what has been examined.

How the BPP Learning Media Study Text can help you pass – Help yourself study for your AIA exams – Syllabus – Command words and learning outcomes – The exam paper

Part A Introduction to economics
1 Introduction to economics 3

Part B Consumption, production and distribution
2 Price theory 23
3 Forms of enterprise 83
4 Theory of costs 119
5a Market structures – perfect competition and monopoly 145
5b Market structures – monopolistic competition, oligopoly and duopoly 173
6 Factor markets 189

Part C Household, corporate and finance sectors
7 Public policy and competition 211
8 Finance and financial intermediaries 227
9 Credit and banking 255

Part D Public sector and macro-economy
10 Macroeconomic theory 283
11 Inflation and unemployment 311
12 Macroeconomic policy 329

Part E The external sector
13 International trade – the foreign exchange market 375
14 International trade – the international economy 403

Answers to end of chapter questions 439
Exam question bank 463
Exam answer bank 473
Mock exam 1 491
Mock exam 2 505
Index 519

How the BPP Learning Media Study Text can help you pass

> It provides you with the knowledge and understanding, skills and application techniques that you need to be successful in your exams

This Study Text has been targeted at the **Business Economics** syllabus.

- It is **comprehensive**. It covers the syllabus content. No more, no less.
- It is written at the **right level**. Each chapter is written with AIA's syllabus in mind.
- It is aimed at the **exam**. We have taken account of recent exams, guidance the examiner has given and the assessment methodology.

> It allows you to study in the way that best suits your learning style and the time you have available, by following your personal Study Plan (see page vii)

You may be studying at home on your own or you may be attending a course. You may like to read every word, or you may prefer to do a fast read through and learn through doing practise questions the rest of the time. However you study, you will find the BPP Learning Media Study Text meets your needs in designing and following your personal Study Plan.

INTRODUCTION

Help yourself study for your AIA exams

Exams for professional bodies such as AIA are very different from those you have taken at college or university. You will be under **greater time pressure before** the exam – as you may be combining your study with work. Here are some hints and tips.

The right approach

1   **Develop the right attitude**

Believe in yourself	Yes, there is a lot to learn. But thousands have succeeded before and you can too.
Remember why you're doing it	You are studying for a good reason: to advance your career.

2   **Focus on the exam**

Read through the Syllabus	This tells you what you are expected to know and is supplemented by **Exam focus points** in the text.
Study the Exam paper section	Past papers are likely to be good guides to what you should expect in the exam.

3   **The right method**

See the whole picture	Keeping in mind how all the detail you need to know fits into the whole picture will help you understand it better. • The **Introduction** of each chapter puts the material in context. • The **Syllabus content** and **Exam focus points** show you what you need to **grasp**.
Use your own words	To absorb the information (and to practise your written communication skills), you need to **put it into your own words**. • **Take notes**. • Answer the **questions** in each chapter. • Draw **mind maps**. • Try **'teaching' a subject** to a colleague or friend.
Give yourself cues to jog your memory	The Study Text uses **bold** to **highlight key points**. • Try **colour coding** with a highlighter pen. • Write **key points** on cards.

4   **The right recap**

Review, review, review	Regularly reviewing a topic in summary form can **fix it in your memory**. The Study Text helps you review in many ways. • **Chapter roundups** summarise the 'Fast forward' key points in each chapter. Use them to recap each study session. • The **Quick quiz** actively tests your grasp of the essentials. • Go through the **Examples** in each chapter a second or third time.

Developing your personal Study Plan

BPP recommends that you follow a study plan. Planning and sticking to the plan are key elements of learning successfully.

There are five steps you should work through.

Step 1 **How do you learn?**

What types of intelligence do you display when learning? You might be advised to brush up on certain study skills before launching into this Study Text, but refer to the 'Tackling your studies' section below which will help.

Step 2 **What do you prefer to do first?**

If you prefer to get to grips with a theory before seeing how it is applied, we suggest you concentrate first on the explanations we give in each chapter before looking at the examples and case studies. If you prefer to see first how things work in practice, read through the detail in each chapter, and concentrate on the examples and case studies, before supplementing your understanding by reading the detail.

Step 3 **How much time do you have?**

Work out the time you have available per week, given the following.

- The standard you have set yourself
- The other exam(s) you are sitting
- Practical matters such as work, travel, exercise, sleep and social life

		Hours
Note your time available in box A.	A	

Step 4 **Allocate your time**

- Take the time you have available per week for this Study Text shown in box A, multiply it by the number of weeks available and insert the result in box B.   **B**
- Divide the figure in box B by the number of chapters in this text and insert the result in box C.   **C**

Remember that this is only a rough guide. Some of the chapters in this book are longer and more complicated than others, and you will find some subjects easier to understand than others.

Step 5 **Implement**

Set about studying each chapter in the time shown in box C, following the key study steps in the order suggested by your particular learning style.

This is your personal **Study Plan**. You should try to combine it with the study sequence outlined below. You may want to modify the sequence to adapt it to your **personal style**.

INTRODUCTION

Tackling your studies

The best way to approach this Study Text is to tackle the chapters in order. Taking into account your individual learning style, you could follow this sequence for each chapter.

Key study steps	Activity
Step 1 **Topic list**	This topic list helps you navigate each chapter; each numbered topic is a numbered section in the chapter.
Step 2 **Introduction**	This sets your objectives for study by giving you the big picture in terms of the context of the chapter. The content is referenced to the syllabus, and Exam guidance shows how the topic is likely to be examined. The Introduction tells you **why** the topics covered in the chapter need to be studied.
Step 3 **Fast forward**	Fast forward boxes give you a quick summary of the content of each of the main chapter sections. They are listed together in the roundup at the end of each chapter to help you review each chapter quickly.
Step 4 **Explanations**	Proceed methodically through each chapter, particularly focusing on areas highlighted as significant in the chapter introduction, or areas that are frequently examined.
Step 5 **Key terms and Exam focus points**	• Key terms can often earn you **easy marks** if you state them clearly and correctly in an exam answer. They are highlighted in the index at the back of this text. • Exam focus points state how the topic has been or may be examined, difficulties that can occur in questions about the topic, and examiner feedback on common weaknesses in answers.
Step 6 **Note taking**	Take brief notes, if you wish. Don't copy out too much. Remember that being able to record something yourself is a sign of being able to understand it. Your notes can be in whatever format you find most helpful; lists, diagrams, mind maps.
Step 7 **Examples**	Work through the examples carefully as they illustrate key knowledge and techniques.
Step 8 **Case studies**	Study each one, and try to add context to them from your own experience. They are designed to show how the topics you are studying come alive in the real world.
Step 9 **Questions**	Attempt each one, as they will illustrate how well you have understood what you have read.
Step 10 **Answers**	Check yours against ours, and make sure you understand any discrepancies.
Step 11 **Chapter roundup**	Review it carefully, to make sure you have grasped the significance of all the important points in the chapter.
Step 12 **Quick quiz**	Use the Quick quiz to check how much you have remembered of the topics covered and to practise questions in a variety of formats.
Step 13 **Question practice**	Attempt the Question suggested at the very end of the chapter. These are all AIA past exam questions, so provide an excellent indication of the type and standard of question that you can expect in your real exam. Some of these questions cover more than one subject area, which is a common feature of exam questions.

AIA Achieve

AIA provides an interactive course of study AIA Achieve, which offers students the tools, resources and learning environment to study for the exams. The study tools include a course of study e-book, marked practice questions, marked mock exam paper and feedback and technical advice via an e-Tutor. Contact the Study Support team at: Achieve@aiaworldwide.com

Moving on...

When you are ready to start revising, you should still refer back to this Study Text.

- As a source of **reference** (you should find the index particularly helpful for this)
- As a way to **review** (the Fast forwards, Exam focus points, Chapter roundups and Quick quizzes help you here)

INTRODUCTION

Syllabus

Aims

To examine the candidate's knowledge and understanding of:

- economic problems and possible solutions, together with a comprehension of the necessary tools for economic analysis and the relevant social and technological environments within which economic policies are applied

- the candidate's ability to apply knowledge of the analysis of particular economic situations in the United Kingdom, Europe and the Rest of the World including developing countries.

Learning Outcomes

After successfully completing this paper candidates should be able to:

- describe the nature and scope of economics

- explain economic problems and describe possible solutions

- identify and explain appropriate tools for economic analysis

- describe the social and technological environments within which economic policies are applied, and

- apply knowledge and the analysis of specified economic situations in the UK, Europe and developing countries

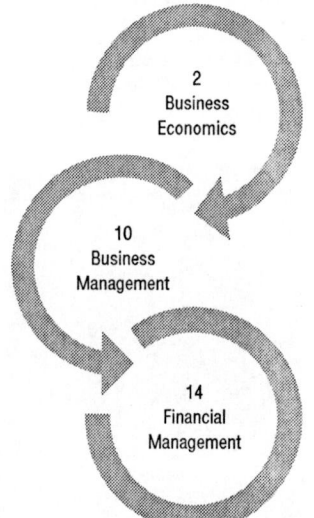

FIG. 2   INTER-RELATIONSHIP OF UNITS

2 Business Economics

10 Business Management

14 Financial Management

Structure of the Paper

- The three-hour 15 minute question paper will consist of two sections:

Section A

This section scores 60% of the overall marks for the paper and consists of two compulsory case study type questions, one on micro economics and the other macroeconomics including international economics of the External Sector. Each question is allocated 30 marks.

Section B

This section scores 40% of the overall marks for the paper and consists of two compulsory essay type questions, within the range of the Syllabus. Each question is allocated 20 marks and candidates are required to answer both of the questions.

Questions may be set which give candidates the opportunity to demonstrate their ability to discuss the relevance or application of principles to their homeland economies.

Syllabus

2.1 Introduction to Economics

Topic Weighting   10%

The nature and scope of economics:

- wealth and welfare
- scarcity and choice
- how an economy is organised
- natural resources
- the nature of the firm
- entrepreneurship
- the nature of profit
- opportunity cost

Relationship to other social sciences:

- the nature of accounting profit and economic profit

2.2 Consumption, Production and Distribution

Topic Weighting   25%

- demand and supply principles, price determination, partial equilibrium, price and other elasticities
- theories of consumer behaviour
- time periods, short and long run costs and opportunities
- the objectives and behaviour of firms under differing market conditions - competition, monopoly and oligopoly
- factor pricing, wages, interest, rent, profit
- productivity

2.3 Household, Corporate and Finance Sectors

Topic Weighting   25%

- household expenditure, price indices
- corporate decision making
- theory and practice
- agency theory, stakeholder theory and resource dependency theory
- corporate governance, board of directors and sub-committees of the board, audit, remuneration (or executive compensation), and nomination committees
- shareholder activism
- location, scale, merger and restrictive practice
- relationship of corporate sector to government
- industrial efficiency

INTRODUCTION

- the labour market
- money, its functions and dysfunctions
- the flow of money through the financial system
- monetarist theory and policy
- financial institutions including all banks
- the Central Bank
- the capital market

2.4 Public Sector and Macro economy

Topic Weighting   25%

- the major variables: national income, output, expenditure
- the circular flow of income; determination of national income
- consumption, saving and investment; their interaction and influence on employment
- fluctuations in national income and employment; regional problems
- inflation, deflation, reflation and disinflation
- government policies for managing the macro-economy, fiscal incomes, taxation and growth policies

2.5 The External Sector

Topic Weighting   15%

- elements of international trade theory
- the balance of payments, fixed and floating exchange rates, policies and effects
- the role of international organisations eg GATT, IMF, World Bank, the European Union and other regional trade organisations

Relationship to Overall Syllabus

Accountants need knowledge of the economic environment in which they operate. The decision making process often incorporates economic data: this applies in particular to the area of studies in the Business Management and Financial Management syllabuses. The syllabus for Business Economics provides the foundation to develop these further studies.

Ethics

Candidates are advised that the standards outlined in The Code of Ethics for Professional Accountants issued by the International Ethics Standards Board for Accountants (IESBA Code) are implicit in, and examinable throughout, the AIA syllabus. The Code can be accessed via the AIA website at www.aiaworldwide.com

Recommended Reading

AIA Magazine - International Accountant

ISSN: 1465 - 5144

AIA Text Book

Paper 2 Business Economics

Publisher: BPP Learning Media
ISBN: 9781 5097 8717 3
The e-Book is available at: exams@aiaworldwide.com

Contact our publisher BPP for information on purchasing a hard copy of the text book at: https://www.bpp.com/learning-media-listing/lmlist/6293

You can purchase any of the books listed below quickly and easily through the publisher's website or link stated below.

Corporate Governance (5th Edition)

Author: Mallin, C
Publisher: Oxford University Press
ISBN: 9780 1987 1802 4
Website: https://global.oup.com/academic/product/corporate-governance-9780198718024?cc=us&lang=en&

Journals

Corporate Governance: An International Review

Publisher: Wiley
ISSN: 1467 8683 (online)
Website: http://onlinelibrary.wiley.com/doi/10.1111/corg.v25.4/issuetoc

Command words and learning outcomes

The following list contains active command words and generic learning outcomes appropriate for use at each stage of the AIA qualification. Reference to the learning outcomes and use of the command words is essential to understanding how the assessment is applied in AIA exams.

Foundation Level Command Words

WORD	DEFINITION
ADVISE	To inform as necessary
CALCULATE	Work out a value mathematically
DEFINE	To state and or explain clearly
EXPLAIN	To make clear giving reasons for
EXPRESS	To present thoughts and ideas
DESCRIBE	To give an account of in words or formula including key features
IDENTIFY	Recognise and select
PLAN	Present a method or argument for doing or achieving a task
PREPARE	To make or get ready for use
SELECT	To choose in preference to another
STATE	Express fully and clearly the details/facts
TABULATE	Arrange in a table

The exam paper

Analysis of past papers

The analysis below shows the topics which have been examined in all sittings of the current syllabus from November 2008.

May 2018

Section A

1. Price elasticity of demand, complements and substitutes
2. Corporate governance (unitary and dual board structures), stakeholders

Section B

3. Fiscal policy, economic growth
4. G20, globalisation

November 2017

Section A

1. Remuneration committees and executive pay
2. Elasticity of demand (price, income, cross), complements and substitutes

Section B

3. GNP composition and difference to GDP
4. Forward rates and arbitrage

May 2017

Section A

1. Demand and supply curves; effect on price of reduction in supply; effect on price of increased supply in the long and short term
2. Three types of unemployment; reasons for job losses and unemployment; different sources of unemployment

Section B

3. Stakeholders; stakeholder theory; stakeholders in an airport
4. Three major types of exchange rate system and their advantages and disadvantages; effect of varying exchange rates on currency demand and supply

November 2016

Section A

1. Market clearing price and quantity; price elasticities of demand and supply; free market price; demand equation; price elasticity of domestic versus export demand; relationship between total demand and price
2. Separating ownership and control; principal v agent problem; management structures; characteristics of an effective board of directors; independent outsiders; composition of audit and remuneration committees; directors' share ownership

Section B

3   Total consumption; level of saving
4   Global financial institutions; World Bank; G20; functions of the IMF

May 2016

Section A

1   Scarcity; elasticity of demand; elasticity of supply; demand and price
2   Functions of banks; credit multiplier; causes and consequences of 2007-2010 financial crisis

Section B

3   Unemployment; government policy; Phillips curve
4   Floating exchange rates (and their advantages/disadvantages)

November 2015

Section A

1   Demand, and determinants of demand; derived demand
2   Exchange rates; free trade; protectionism

Section B

3   Central banks; money market; capital market
4   Macroeconomic policy; fiscal policy

May 2015

Section A

1   Directors' remuneration and corporate performance
2   Unemployment and the impact of wage levels on unemployment; minimum wages

Section B

3   Elasticity of demand (cross elasticity; income elasticity)
4   Comparative advantage and patterns of trade

November 2014

Section A

1   Price; supply and demand; income elasticity of demand
2   Private goods; market failure (externalities; subsidies; regulation)

Section B

3   Corporate social responsibility
4   Reasons for globalisation and foreign expansion

May 2014

Section A

1   Corporate performance measurement; corporate performance and directors' remuneration
2   Unemployment and the impact of wage levels on unemployment; minimum wages

Section B

3   Characteristics of monopolistic competition
4   Comparative advantage and patterns of trade

November 2013

Section A

1   The economic problem; price elasticity of demand; factors affecting price and demand
2   Negative externalities; market failure and indirect taxation

Section B

3   Comparative advantage and patterns of trade
4   Agency theory and stakeholder theory

May 2013

Section A

1   Auditors, audit committees and corporate governance
2   Price elasticity of demand

Section B

3   Globalisation and international expansion
4   Role and effectiveness of central banks

November 2012

Section A

1   Fiscal policy; management unemployment, economic growth, exports and aggregate demand
2   Demand, supply and price

Section B

3   Interest rates and the international economy
4   The economic problem

May 2012

Section A

1   Production possibility frontier, opportunity cost; demand and supply; oligopoly
2   Private goods; externalities; government intervention; subsidies; regulation and competition policy

Section B

3   Elasticity (cross elasticity; income elasticity); Oligopoly
4   Multiplier and its impact on the national economy
5   International organisations (the EU)

November 2011

Section A

1 Unemployment and the problems of unemployment
2 Production possibility frontier and opportunity cost

Section B

3 Remuneration and performance criteria
4 Opportunity cost
5 Specialisation and production costs; demand and revenue

May 2011

Section A

1 Scarcity; supply, demand and price; Price elasticity of demand
2 Externalities; indirect taxation

Section B

3 Inflation and the problems of inflation
4 International organisations (the EU)
5 Exchange rates; exchange rate policy and interest rates

November 2010

Section A

1 Principal-agent problem; executive remuneration.
2 Monopoly, and characteristics of monopolistic competition

Section B

3 Role of central bank; reserve ratios
4 Multinational corporations
5 Taxation and fiscal policies

May 2010

Section A

1 Price elasticity of demand
2 Fiscal policy and the circular flow of income

Section B

3 Opportunity cost
4 Role of central bank
5 Comparative advantage and terms of trade

November 2009

Section A

1 Impact of demand on price
2 Equilibrium employment and minimum wages

Section B

3 The economic problem
4 Central banks and credit creation
5 Impact of increased membership on a trading block

May 2009

Section A

1   Production possibility frontier
2   Diminishing marginal returns and marginal cost

Section B

3   Yield curves and investment
4   Interest rates and inflation
5   Globalisation

November 2008

Section A

1   Monopoly and takeovers
2   Impact of business cycle on business decisions

Section B

3   The role of the entrepreneur
4   Export led growth
5   Terms of trade

INTRODUCTION

Introduction to economics

Introduction to economics

Topic list	Syllabus reference
1 Economic systems	2.1
2 The production possibility frontier	2.1
3 Opportunity costs	2.1
4 Entrepreneurship and the separation of ownership from control	2.1
5 Exchange, specialisation and economic wealth	2.1

Introduction

This chapter introduces the basic concepts at the heart of the **economic problem**, which is: how to use scarce resources to achieve maximum benefits. This problem is solved by an **economic system**. The chapter reviews the nature of **the three main types of economic system**: command economies, market economies and mixed economies.

The **production possibility frontier** (or curve) depicts the choices open to an economy as a choice between two goods with limited resources available to produce either. This leads on to a definition of **efficiency in production**. Scarcity and choice give rise to **opportunity costs**, the cost of one decision expressed in terms of the benefits foregone from the next best alternative. The idea of scarcity also links to concepts of **exchange value** and **specialisation** we consider in the final section of the chapter.

Economics is a social science and as society changes, so must economic analysis. The role of the **entrepreneur** is discussed as are the implications of the **separation of ownership from control** in the modern business corporation.

1 Economic systems

1.1 The nature of an economic system

> **FAST FORWARD**
>
> Economics is concerned with **how** choices are made about the use of resources: **what** should be produced and **who** should consume it.

We are all economic agents, and economic activity is what we do to make a living.

Economists assume that **people behave rationally** at all times and always seek to improve their circumstances. This assumption leads to more specific assumptions.

- Producers will seek to maximise their profits.
- Consumers will seek to maximise the benefits (their 'utility') from their income.
- Governments will seek to maximise the welfare of their populations.

Both the basic assumption of rationality and these more detailed assumptions may be challenged, however. In particular, we will look again later at the assumption that businesses always seek to maximise their profits. A further complication is that concepts such as utility and welfare are not only open to interpretation, but also that the interpretation will change over time.

Economics studies the ways in which society decides **what** to produce, **how** to produce it, **who** to produce it for, and how to apportion it.

The way in which the choices about resource allocation are made, the way value is measured, and the forms of ownership of economic wealth will also vary according to the type of **economic system** that exists in a society.

1.2 Types of economic system

> **FAST FORWARD**
>
> Real world economies differ according to the extent of state involvement in providing goods and services. Economics simplifies this into **centrally planned economies** (or command economies), **market economies**, and **mixed economies**.

Key terms

> **Centrally planned economy**: an economy in which the government makes all major economic decisions.
>
> **Market economy**: an economy in which economic decisions are made by consumers, producers and owners of factors of production.
>
> **Mixed economy**: an economy in which both public and private enterprise engage in economic activity. All contemporary economic systems are mixed to some extent.

1.3 Centrally planned economic systems

> **FAST FORWARD**
>
> In a **centrally planned economy** the government decides what shall be made, who will make it, and who will receive it, based on the government's view of what is best for society.

In a centrally planned economy, the government decides the quantity of each good to be produced and the price at which it is sold. The government sets quotas for each individual production unit. It also decides the quantity of resources to be employed in producing the goods.

The state even decides how each worker is to specialise. The government in a country with a centrally planned economy believes that it knows how to organise, distribute and co-ordinate its country's resources to best advantage. Its objectives in doing this will depend upon its political or ideological framework. There is no private profit, however, because all resources are publicly owned.

The real-world economies of Communist countries – most notably China – have been likened to command economies. However, there are only a very small number of Communist countries left in the world now, and their economies often have some elements of a free market sector.

Other examples of centrally planned economic decisions may be seen in market economies during wartime or crisis. To mobilise economic resources in the national interest, governments take charge of production decisions, and consumer goods are rationed.

In a centrally planned economy, economic efficiency depends on the accuracy of the government's plan in forecasting society's wants and allocating resources to meet them. In such an economy, people have only limited freedom, if any, in their economic decisions, but in return they may have greater security and greater social equality. Basic necessities are intended to be made available to everyone at a price, fixed by the government, that they can all afford. However, in practice, planned economies suffer from shortages of consumer goods and services.

1.4 Market economic systems

FAST FORWARD

> In a **market economy** resources are allocated through a price mechanism governed by people's willingness to pay for things, and the pursuit of profits by firms.

A pure free market economy is a complete contrast to a centrally planned economy. In a pure free market economy, the state has no role in economic decisions, and price acts as a signal to both producers and consumers.

The **price mechanism** indicates what and how much firms should produce to maximise their profits, and how much consumers should buy to satisfy their wants. If the price is too low, consumers will demand more than is produced so the price will rise. Conversely, if the price is too high, consumers will demand less than producers produce, so the price will fall.

The price mechanism should ensure efficiency in the allocation and use of resources – because firms will always focus on producing what people want, as well as trying to make those products with the least resources in order to minimise their costs and so to maximise their profits.

Nevertheless, there can be **disadvantages to a free market system** in which the state plays no role in directing the allocation of resources.

(a) Since all resources are only available at their prevailing market prices, some members of the community might be badly deprived, unable to afford even the basic necessities of life.

(b) The free market society will result in an unequal distribution of income.

(c) Some vital services, for example police, fire services and armed forces would not be provided. These 'goods', whose benefits must be shared by society as a whole, are called **public goods**.

(d) Some other desirable goods or services, such as health care and education, might be provided in inadequate quantities in a completely free market economy, and provision of these **merit goods** by the state will be necessary.

(e) Some undesirable products may be produced, for example, recreational drugs.

(f) Competition may be eliminated by monopolies, oligopolies and restrictive practices, reflecting the disproportionate economic power of certain firms and groups in society.

(g) Where inequalities of wealth exist, resources may be allocated to producing luxury goods at the expense of producing necessities for the poor.

(h) Prices of some goods, for example agricultural goods, might be volatile (subject to big rises and falls) unless measures for price stabilisation are taken by the government.

1.5 The mixed economy

> **FAST FORWARD**
>
> In a **mixed economy** resources are allocated primarily through a price mechanism but the state will intervene to regulate the markets and to provide essential services.

Many of the disadvantages of the free market economy listed above indicate why the government may choose to intervene in the workings of the economy. In a mixed economy, market mechanisms exist, but the state also plays an important role. A government may intervene to:

(a) Restrain the unfair use of economic power by monopolies or other bodies which might be able to impose their wishes on the rest of society.

(b) Correct inequalities of the free market system, redistributing wealth between individuals and between regions.

(c) Provide goods and services that private enterprise would be reluctant or unable to provide in sufficient quantities and at an acceptable price.

(d) Remove socially undesirable consequences of private production – for example, pollution and regional imbalances in employment.

(e) Direct change in the structure of the nation's industries, by retraining programmes, aid to new industries, or investment in research and development, for example.

(f) Manage inflation rates, employment levels, the balance of payments and the economic growth rate in accordance with social objectives.

(g) Moderate the ups and downs in the trade cycle, by trying to stimulate economic activity during a recession, and to dampen demand when it is so high that steep price inflation occurs.

1.6 Scarcity of resources

> **FAST FORWARD**
>
> **Scarcity** of resources gives rise to the **economic problem** of allocating scarce resources between potentially unlimited wants.

It is a fact of life that the amount of resources available is limited. Economists describe this as the problem of **scarcity**.

Key term

> **Scarcity**: a situation when the amount of a resource available is inadequate to satisfy all the competing demands put upon it.

(a) For the individual **consumer**, the scarcity of goods and services might seem obvious enough. Most people would like to have more: perhaps a new car, or more clothes, or a house of their own. Examples of services which they would like more of include holidays, public passenger transport and concerts.

(b) For a **firm**, the scarcity of productive capacity (human resources, machinery available, selling space and so on) means it may have to turn away some customers in order to serve others.

(c) For the world as a whole, the resources available to serve human consumption are limited. For example, the supply of non-renewable energy resources such as coal and oil is, by definition, limited. The amount of many minerals which it is feasible to extract from the earth (for example, metals and ores of various kinds) is also limited.

This idea of scarcity is very important in economics, because it reminds us that producers and consumers have to make **choices** about what to produce or to buy.

Key term

> **Choice:** a process by which an economic actor allocates scarce resources between competing needs in order to maximise the attainment of their objectives.

Economists seek to describe the decisions of economic actors in terms of them being **rational choices** aimed at maximising the attainment of particular objectives.

(a) **Consumers and households** seek to allocate their scarce incomes between the purchase of alternative goods and services to maximise their total level of personal satisfaction.

(b) **Firms** allocate their productive resources between different products and customers to maximise the total profits of the business.

(c) **Governments** allocate national assets and taxation revenues between different uses to maximise the social benefit to the population.

1.7 Factors of production

FAST FORWARD

> Economic analysis classifies the resources of an economy into four **factors of production**. These are **land** (natural resources) **labour** (human resources), **capital** (man-made resources) and **enterprise** (the willingness to set up and run a business).

Economists we can identify four types of resource, which are input into the production process. These are known as **factors of production**.

Factor	Comment
Land	Land included not only land itself, but also all naturally occurring resources such as timber, minerals, water and oil.
Labour	Labour is the workforce of an economy, and covers all forms of human endeavour except enterprise (see below).
Capital	Capital relates to the stock of financial and physical resources (eg factories, offices, plant and machinery) which can be used to produce goods and services.
Enterprise or (entrepreneurship)	The entrepreneur organises production. This involves **organising** the resources (of land, labour and capital) as well as incurring the **risks** associated with running a business.

The factors of production are necessary for economic activity to take place. Economics is about the way these factors are used. Each of these factors of production has an associated reward which accrues to its owner when it is used.

(a) **Land** is rewarded with **rent**.

(b) **Labour** is rewarded with **wages** (including salaries).

(c) **Capital** is rewarded with **interest**.

(d) **Enterprise,** or entrepreneurship, creates new business ventures and the reward for the risk associated with this is **profit**.

PART A INTRODUCTION TO ECONOMICS

2 The production possibility frontier

FAST FORWARD Economists illustrate the choices open to an economy using a **production possibility frontier** that shows the maximum combinations of two goods that can be made using the resources available.

2.1 The production possibility frontier: illustrating the limits of production

We can approach the central question of scarcity in economics by looking first at decisions about what to produce and how much of a product to produce. the possibilities of production. Suppose, to take a simple example, that a society can spend its money on two products, digital versatile discs (DVDs) and books. The society's resources are limited. Therefore there are restrictions on the amount of DVDs and books that can be made, which can be shown by a production possibility frontier (or production possibility curve).

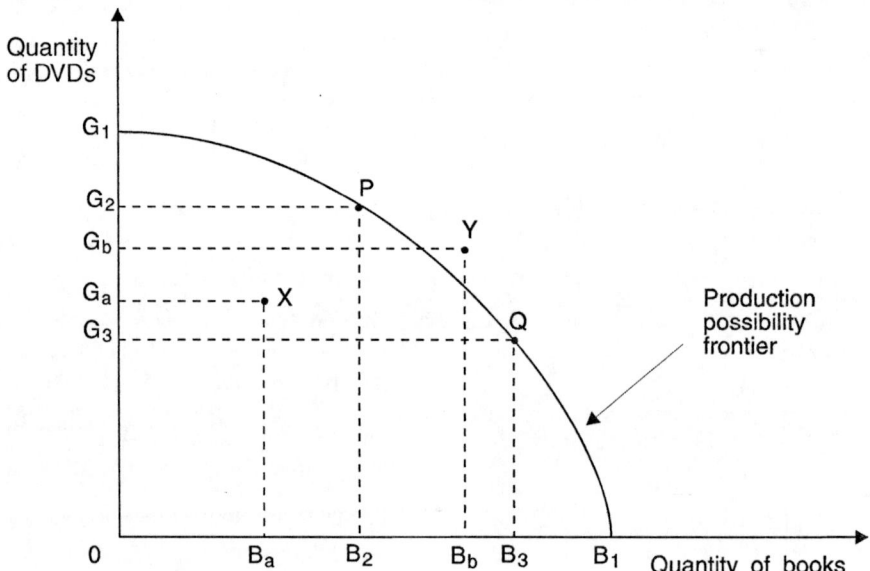

Figure 1 Production possibility frontier

The curve from G_1 round to B_1 in Figure 1 shows the various combinations of DVDs and books that a society can make, if it uses its limited resources efficiently.

(a) So, for example, society (or, more accurately, the firms in it) can choose to make up to:

 (i) G_1 units of DVDs and no books
 (ii) B_1 units of books and no DVDs
 (iii) G_2 units of DVDs and B_2 of books (point P on the curve)
 (iv) G_3 units of DVDs and B_3 of books (point Q on the curve)

(b) The combination of G_a units of DVDs and B_a units of books (plotted at point X) lies within the production possibility curve. More than these quantities could be made of either or both of DVDs and books given the resources available. Point X is therefore an **inefficient production point** for the economy, and if the society were to make only G_a of DVDs and B_a of books, it would be using its limited resources inefficiently.

 Production possibility frontier

What can you say about the combination of DVDs and books indicated by point Y in Figure 1?

Answer

Point Y lies outside the production possibility frontier. Even if the resources available are used efficiently, it is impossible to produce this combination of DVDs and books. To reach point Y either the amount of resources available must be increased or production methods must be improved, perhaps by developments in technology.

The production possibility frontier is an important idea in economics which illustrates the need to make a choice about what to produce when it is not possible to have everything – that is, when there is scarcity. Although we have characterised the products of our hypothetical economy as DVDs and books, we could generalise the production possibility frontier and show 'good X' on one axis and 'all other goods' on the other axis.

> **FAST FORWARD**
>
> Points on the production possibility frontier are points of **productive efficiency**: it is not possible to have more of one good without giving up some units of another.

Choice involves sacrifice. The production possibility frontier in Figure 1 illustrates that more DVDs can only be produced if fewer books are produced. Alternatively, consumers can only buy more DVDs if they buy fewer books. Following this logic, we can see that all choices of consumers, firms (producers) and governments involve an element of sacrifice.

This introduces an alternative way of looking at the cost of goods. Rather than merely focusing on the monetary cost of producing DVDs, a firm might also consider the amount of potential revenue they have sacrificed from the sale of books, in order to produce the DVDs instead of books.

2.2 Opportunity cost

The cost of an item, measured in terms of the benefits foregone from the best alternative, is called its **opportunity cost**. At a national level the opportunity cost of an investment in railways could be measured in terms of the number of miles of motorway that could have been built using the amount of resources which have been spent on the railways instead.

> **FAST FORWARD**
>
> The **opportunity cost** of an action is the value of the best alternative which has to be foregone in order to undertake that action.

A production possibility frontier therefore also illustrates opportunity costs. For example, in Figure 1, let us assume there is a decision to switch from making G_3 units of DVDs and B_3 units of books (point Q) to making in G_2 units of DVDs and B_2 units of books (point P). The opportunity cost of making $(G_2 - G_3)$ more units of DVDs would be the lost production of $(B_3 - B_2)$ units of books.

At the level of the firm, the production possibility frontier can be seen as showing the maximum output of different alternative goods which the firm can produce when all of its resources are fully used – for example, a firm might operate production lines capable of producing washing machines or refrigerators. Producing more washing machines bears the opportunity cost of a lower level of production of refrigerators.

2.3 Shifts in the production possibility frontier

When the availability of resources changes, the production possibility frontier may shift. Changes are made possible by developments such as a bigger labour force, more efficient methods of working, more efficient machinery (or the development of new technology), or a new discovery of natural resources, such as oil, natural gas or minerals.

(a) If the production possibility frontier moves outwards, to the right, this means that the economy is capable of producing more goods and services in total than it could before. This means there is **economic growth**.

(b) If the frontier moves to the left (inwards), this means that the economy cannot produce as much as before (for example because of a significant decline in population or the exhaustion of a natural resource).

In Figure 2, curve $G_{new} B_{new}$ represents greater production possibilities than the original production possibility frontier ($G_1 B_1$). Point Y, which was previously unattainable, can now be achieved.

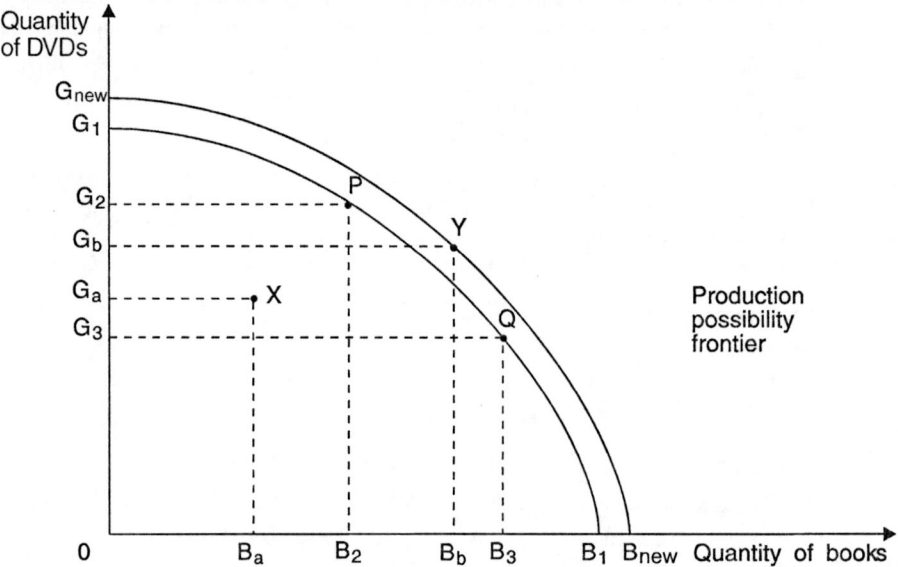

Figure 2 Shift in the production possibility frontier

3 Opportunity costs

FAST FORWARD

For **consumers** opportunity cost is expressed as the satisfaction foregone by not using scarce income to buy the next most preferred alternative product.

For **firms** opportunity cost is expressed as the revenue foregone by not using scarce factors of production to produce and sell the next most valuable alternative product.

For **governments** opportunity cost is expressed as the social satisfaction foregone by not using scarce resources to provide the next most socially beneficial good or service.

The previous section introduced opportunity cost in terms of the alternative bundles of goods and services available to a national economy from the use of its factors of production. The concept of opportunity cost has a wider use in economics though.

(a) For **consumers and households**: opportunity cost is the satisfaction foregone by deciding to spend scarce income on one product instead of others. It is measured as the satisfaction foregone by not consuming the **next most preferred alternative**. For example, a student sitting in a restaurant looking at a menu that offers pizza, burgers and sandwiches chooses between them. Let us assume the three items cost the same and the student ranks them in order of preference with pizza at the top and sandwiches at the bottom. If we assume they buy a pizza, the opportunity cost of the pizza will be the satisfaction they could have obtained from the next most preferred alternative meal they could have bought with the same money – a burger. Note, however, that the opportunity cost of the pizza does not include the satisfaction foregone from not buying a sandwich. The opportunity cost of the pizza reflects only the satisfaction foregone from not buying a burger.

(b) For **firms and businesses** opportunity cost is expressed in revenues foregone by using scarce factors of production to make one product rather than another. For example, a city centre hairdresser may decide to specialise in cutting women's hair and to only accept women customers. The alternatives are to cut men's hair, children's hair and so on. If we assume that men would pay more than children to have their hair cut, then the opportunity cost to the hairdresser of cutting women's hair is the revenue it could have obtained by using the same chairs, mirrors, staff and so on to cut men's hair – the best alternative foregone.

(c) For **governments**, opportunity cost is expressed as social satisfaction foregone by its decision to use its resources, such as taxation revenues, borrowed funds, public building and staff, to provide one set of services instead of an alternative one. For example, if a local authority faces a choice between building a new school or building a new health centre, the opportunity cost of building the school would be the social benefits which are foregone as a result of not having the new health centre.

4 Entrepreneurship and the separation of ownership from control

> **FAST FORWARD**
>
> Entrepreneurship (or enterprise) is the factor of production concerned with the **organisation of production** and with the **bearing of risk**. It is rewarded by **profit**.
>
> Modern business corporations feature a **separation between ownership and control** with the risks and profits being taken by **shareholders**, whilst the control is exercised by **paid managerial employees** who take the business decisions.

4.1 The entrepreneur (enterprise)

'Entrepreneur' is a term originally used by 18th century economists to describe the business people and factory owners who were emerging during the European industrial revolution. Entrepreneurs can still be seen in the 21st century business world; for example, as the owners of small, boutique shops or small service businesses such as beauty salons, or cafes. Increasingly, however, 21st century entrepreneurs are influenced by developments in IT as owners of online businesses.

An entrepreneur is responsible for paying all the costs of the business such as rent on premises, wages to employees, interest on any capital borrowed, as well as the costs of the materials used in making a product or providing a service.

The reward to the entrepreneur is **profit**. Profit is described as the **residual income** because it is the part of the firm's sales revenue left over after all its other costs have been paid. Profit is calculated at the end of a month, or a year, and it belongs to the owner, the entrepreneur, as a **factor reward** for their performance of two distinct functions: **organisation of production** (or decision-making), and the **bearing of risk**.

(a) **Organisation of production**: the entrepreneur assembles the other factors of production by recruiting labour, locating and renting premises, and borrowing money to buy machinery or equipment, or to fit out the business premises. The entrepreneur also decides what the firm will make, who it will serve, what it will charge, and so on. On a day-to-day basis, they issue instructions and make sure things get done.

(b) **Bearing of risk**: the entrepreneur may also have put their own money into the business such as investing savings into buying the first inventories for their shop, or borrowing against their home to buy a shop and fit it out. If they make poor decisions and things don't sell very well, or things happen beyond their control such as the economy suffering recession leading to a reduction in customer spending, it is the entrepreneur that will suffer. In the short run, revenues fall but the entrepreneur still has to pay the costs of the remaining factors of production and so their income, profit, will fall. Profits may even become negative (losses), requiring the entrepreneur to use more of their own money or to increase their borrowing just to pay the staff and suppliers. In the long run, the business may fail and they will lose their job, the money they invested and perhaps their home as creditors take legal action against them to obtain payment.

Economists recognise that entrepreneurs, small business-people, are a critical part of a growing economy. Entrepreneurs are often able to spot opportunities overlooked by large businesses. Because the entrepreneur takes the profits, and is acutely aware of the potential risks they face, they will be motivated to work hard and to make their business a success.

4.2 The joint-stock company and modern corporation

FAST FORWARD

Joint-stock companies are **owned** by their **shareholders**, while **control** is undertaken by **paid managers**. This means that the people controlling the business day-to-day may no longer be doing so to maximise profits.

Despite the importance of entrepreneurs to growth in 18th century Europe, by the end of that century the joint-stock company had been devised and has since grown into the major form of business enterprise around the world today.

A joint-stock company is a business entity which is **owned by shareholders**.

As such, the joint-stock company features a **separation of ownership from control**. This separation, in effect, splits the role of the entrepreneur between two different sets of people: shareholders, and management.

(a) **Ownership:** the entity is owned by its **shareholders**. In order to get large sums of investment needed for modern business the corporation sells shares, to investors. The money received from the sale of shares is used to invest in machines, buildings and so on. The investor, or shareholder, obtains the right to a portion of the corporation's profits each year, in the form of dividends. The shareholders also obtain some voting rights to influence the decisions of the corporation. The shareholder still bears the risk of good and bad profits and, in the event of the corporation going bankrupt and out of business, they might lose their original investment because their shares would be worthless.

(b) **Control:** the modern corporation can often be too large for individual investors to maintain personal control over day-to-day decisions. Instead, teams of paid **managers** run the business on the investors' behalf. Managers range from the Chief Executive and other directors, down through the ranks of department heads, to individual shop managers and assembly-line supervisors for example. These managers control the business and receive salaries or wages in return for their work and the responsibilities they take on.

4.3 Consequences of separation of ownership from control

Paid managers don't necessarily have the same interest in making a profit that the entrepreneur would have had. Making a bigger profit involves working harder and taking more risks. The paid manager – who receives a pre-determined salary – has no reason to want to work harder or take more risk because they won't receive the higher profit. [Note: In this analysis, we are ignoring bonuses and other incentives such as share options which might align the interests of managers more closely with those of owners (shareholders).]

1: INTRODUCTION TO ECONOMICS

FAST FORWARD

> The separation of ownership from control gives rise to economic study of the **principal-agent problem (agency theory)**, and of the adequacy of the arrangements of **corporate governance**, and the potential for **managerial enterprise**, that will be covered in later chapters.

This separation of ownership from control gives rise to several concepts that will be discussed later in this Study Text:

(a) The **principal-agent problem**. Another name for owner is 'principal'; so shareholders in a business are the principals. The principal is the person in whose interests the manager is supposed to be working. The 'agent' is employed by the principal to act on their behalf, and here the paid manager is the agent. For economists, a key question is how can a principal ensure that an agent really does work on their behalf, especially if the interests of the agent are selfish and they pursue their own agendas?

(b) **Corporate governance**. These are the legal and practical arrangements by which management are kept under control and the business is managed. Corporate governance includes the incentives and control structures that shareholders can use to keep a corporation's management acting in their (the shareholders') interests. Economists focus on the effectiveness of these controls and their implications for economic efficiency and for the decisions of firms in the marketplace.

(c) **Managerial enterprise and efficiency**. Entrepreneurs are assumed to steer their businesses to maximise profits because this will serve the self-interest of the entrepreneur. Managers are also self-interested and want the best for themselves – such as better salaries, career progression, prestige and so on. If control by shareholders is weak then the principal-agent problem raises the possibility that such managers will use their position in the corporation to steer the corporation to serve their own interests rather than those of the shareholders. The economist seeks to understand the impact of this on the efficiency of the business and its behaviour in the markets it serves.

We will look at the principal-agent problem and issues of corporate governance in more detail in Chapter 3 later in this Study Text.

5 Exchange, specialisation and economic wealth

5.1 Exchange value

FAST FORWARD

> **Exchange value** refers to the value something has on a market. It arises from the thing being **scarce** in relation to demand, rather than from its cost of production or from its being useful. Air and water are essential whereas oil paintings are not, but because oil paintings are scarce they have exchange value.

When a resource is scarce, it has an economic or exchange value. This is the basis on which producers will be prepared to pay for the natural resources, labour and equipment that they need to enable them to produce goods and services. Similarly, because those goods and services are scarce, consumers will be prepared to pay producers in exchange for receiving the goods and services.

In order for resources to have an exchange value, though, there is a presupposition that exchange can take place. If everyone were self-sufficient, producing goods only for their own individual needs, exchange would not be necessary. However, the vast range and complexity of goods and services in a modern society means that individuals cannot produce everything for themselves. They must specialise in one role and use their income from that role to purchase what they need. Exchange is thus fundamental to any economy and goes hand-in-hand with specialisation.

5.2 Specialisation

FAST FORWARD

Specialisation means allowing factors of production to concentrate on what they do best. In a traditional economy a household might try to build its own house, provide its own clothes and grow its own food. In a market economy the members of the household will specialise by seeking employment that uses their skills and use the money they earn to buy the things they need.

Specialisation is a system of organisation where economic resources (such as labour) are not self-sufficient, but concentrate on producing a limited range of goods and services and trading their output with others.

Specialisation enables the **division of labour** within an industry. Production is divided up so that employees can specialise in particular jobs or tasks, and can use their particular skills to the full. This increases the efficiency of operations and thus shifts the production possibility frontier to the right.

In practice, most workers sell their labour to a firm (or to the government) in exchange for monetary wages or salaries. Money is the medium of exchange which permits them to buy other goods and services.

Specialisation applies to land, capital and entrepreneurship, as well as to labour. Specialised machinery is a common feature of production; some entrepreneurs specialise in a certain type of industry or market, and land can have a specialised use.

Question — Drawbacks of specialisation

If specialisation increases efficiency, does it have any drawbacks?

Answer

If it is taken to extremes, it leads to boredom and frustration for the workers involved (due to the repetitiveness and lack of variety in their jobs). Also workers' ignorance of how their own contributions fit into the overall scheme can lead to inefficiencies.

5.3 Economic wealth

FAST FORWARD

Economic wealth refers to the **stock of assets** owned by an economy. This is the total of the assets owned by the households, firms and government within it.

Economics must take account of the processes by which wealth is created in an economy. Some economists are also concerned with the distribution of wealth in a society.

Economic wealth can be viewed as the stock of assets owned by households, firms and the state. Another way to consider economic wealth is in terms of the total stock of goods of a society at a given time. Four qualities can be specified in order to define the nature of such goods.

In order for goods to be considered as wealth, the following must apply.

(a) They must possess **utility**. In other words, they must be capable of yielding satisfaction.

(b) They must have a **monetary value**.

(c) They must be **limited in supply**. Goods are scarce in the sense that the resources available to society are insufficient to completely satisfy demand.

(d) **Ownership** must be possible. The ownership of such goods must be capable of being transferred from one person to another.

The definition of wealth implied by the above factors would exclude intangible things such as acquired skills. A craftsman, such as a carpenter, would count his tools as part of his personal stock of wealth, but would exclude his skill in using them, as skills are not transferable in the sense mentioned above. In speaking of a nation's wealth, however, it would be appropriate to include the quality of the labour as represented by the stock of human capital where maintenance is determined in part by the level of education and training. We can define economic wealth as the total stock of **tangible and intangible** possessions.

It is possible to distinguish three classes of ownership of wealth.

(a) **Personal wealth** comprises personal belongings such as cars, houses and consumer durables (for example electronic goods, or furniture).

(b) **Business wealth** comprises such things as factory buildings, machinery, raw materials and inventories of finished goods. These things also possess all the attributes of wealth, although they do not yield satisfaction for their own sake. They are derived merely to assist the production of other things and are usually termed **capital**.

(c) **Social wealth** consists of wealth owned collectively and includes all property owned by the national government and local authorities, for example the nationalised industries, roads, schools, public libraries and museums. It is possible to transfer wealth from the private sector to the social sector and *vice versa*. So, for instance, in the UK, railways, gas and electricity supplies were nationalised shortly after the Second World War, while during the 1980s, gas and electricity supply, telecommunications, and other forms of wealth owned by the state were transferred to the private sector under the UK government's privatisation programme.

PART A INTRODUCTION TO ECONOMICS

Chapter Roundup

- Economics is concerned with **how** choices are made about the use of resources: **what** should be produced and **who** should consume it.

- Real world economies differ according to the extent of state involvement in providing goods and services. Economics simplifies this into **centrally planned economies** (or command economies), **market economies**, and **mixed economies**.

- In a **centrally planned economy** the government decides what shall be made, who will make it and who will receive it based on its view of what is best for society.

- In a **market economy** resources are allocated through a price mechanism governed by people's willingness to pay for things, and the pursuit of profits by firms.

- In a **mixed economy** resources are allocated primarily through a price mechanism but the state will intervene to regulate the markets and to provide essential services.

- **Scarcity** of resources gives rise to the **economic problem** of allocating scarce resources between potentially unlimited wants.

- Economic analysis classifies the resources of an economy into four **factors of production**. These are **land** (natural resources), **labour** (human resources), **capital** (man-made resources) and **enterprise** (the willingness to set up and run a business).

- Economists illustrate the choices open to an economy using a **production possibility frontier** that shows the maximum combinations of two goods that can be made using the available resources of an economy.

- Points on the production possibility frontier are points of **productive efficiency**: it is not possible to have more of one good without giving up some units of another.

- The **opportunity cost** of an action is the value of the best alternative which has to be foregone in order to undertake that action.

- For **consumers** opportunity cost is expressed as the satisfaction foregone by not using scarce income to buy the next most preferred alternative product.

- For **firms** opportunity cost is expressed as the revenue foregone by not using scarce factors of production to produce and sell the next most valuable alternative product.

- For **governments** opportunity cost is expressed as the social satisfaction foregone by not using scarce resources to provide the next most socially beneficial good or service.

- **Entrepreneurship** (or enterprise) is the factor of production concerned with the **organisation of production** and with the **bearing of risk**. It is rewarded by **profit**.

- Modern business corporations feature a **separation between ownership and control** with the risks and profits being taken by **shareholders**, whilst the control is exercised by **paid managerial employees** who take the business decisions.

- Joint-stock companies are **owned** by their **shareholders**, while **control** is undertaken by **paid managers**. This means that the people controlling the business day-to-day may no longer be doing so to maximise profits.

- The separation of ownership from control gives rise to economic study of the **principal-agent problem (agency theory)**, and of the adequacy of the arrangements of **corporate governance**, and the potential for **managerial enterprise**, that will be covered in later chapters.

Chapter Roundup Cont'd

- **Exchange value** refers to the value something has on a market. It arises from the thing being **scarce** in relation to demand, rather than from its cost of production or from its being useful. Air and water are essential whereas oil paintings are not, but because oil paintings are scarce they have exchange value

- **Specialisation** means allowing factors of production to concentrate on what they do best. In a traditional economy a household might try to build its own house, provide its own clothes and grow its own food. In a market economy the members of the household will specialise by seeking employment that uses their skills and use the money they earn to buy the things they need.

- **Economic wealth** refers to the stock of assets **owned by an economy.** This is the total of the assets owned by the households, firms and government within it.

Quick Quiz

1. What is the essential feature of a command economy?

2. Which of the following is not recognised as a factor of production?

    A   Capital
    B   Management
    C   Land
    D   Labour

3. The cost of an item measured in terms of the resources used is called its opportunity cost. True or false?

4. What two functions does an entrepreneur (or enterprise) carry out?

5. What is meant by the separation of ownership from control in the modern business corporation?

PART A   INTRODUCTION TO ECONOMICS

Answers to Quick Quiz

1   Decisions about resources, production and prices are made by the government.

2   B   The fourth factor is enterprise or entrepreneurship.

3   False.   Opportunity cost is defined as the cost of an item in terms of the alternatives foregone. Cost in terms of resources used is a reasonable definition of the accounting concept of 'full cost'.

4   Entrepreneurship (enterprise) is the function of organising production and the bearing of risk.

5   The separation of ownership from control refers to the potential that the owners of a modern corporation will be shareholders seeking profit, whilst the controllers of the corporation will be paid managers.

End of chapter question

Scarcity (Nov 12)

'There are plenty of goods in our living world that we can enjoy. I enjoy my life and living environment. But I don't understand why people, even those who are very rich, would demand more things'.

Required

Critically comment on this statement from the viewpoint of an economist. **(20 marks)**

Consumption, production and distribution

Price theory

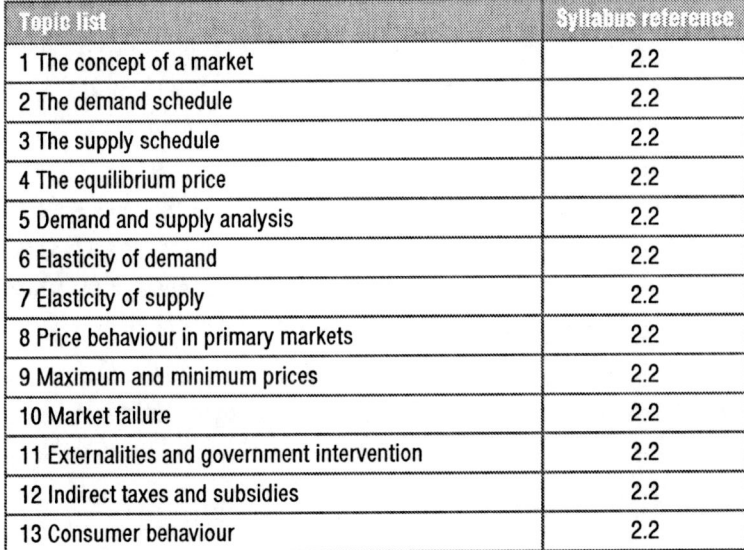

Topic list	Syllabus reference
1 The concept of a market	2.2
2 The demand schedule	2.2
3 The supply schedule	2.2
4 The equilibrium price	2.2
5 Demand and supply analysis	2.2
6 Elasticity of demand	2.2
7 Elasticity of supply	2.2
8 Price behaviour in primary markets	2.2
9 Maximum and minimum prices	2.2
10 Market failure	2.2
11 Externalities and government intervention	2.2
12 Indirect taxes and subsidies	2.2
13 Consumer behaviour	2.2

Introduction

In this chapter, we look in more depth at microeconomics: the study of the behaviour of individual firms, individual markets and consumers (or households) within the economy. This means looking at what influences the amount of a product demanded or supplied, and analysing how price and output are determined through the interaction of **demand** and **supply**.

We start by examining the concept of a market which, in economics, goes beyond the idea of a single geographical place where people meet to buy and sell goods.

PART B   CONSUMPTION, PRODUCTION AND DISTRIBUTION

1 The concept of a market

FAST FORWARD

In a free market, the **price mechanism** signals demand and supply conditions to producers and consumers. It therefore determines the activities of both producers and consumers, influencing the levels of demand for and the supply of goods.

1.1 What is a market?

FAST FORWARD

A **market** can be defined as a situation in which potential buyers and potential sellers (suppliers) of a good or service come together for the purpose of exchange.

Markets enable buyers and sellers to meet. For economists, a market is any convenient set of arrangements by which buyers and sellers can interact to exchange goods and services.

Examples of markets include:

(a) **Product markets**: this could include a street market selling fresh vegetables and the market for used furniture conducted in the back pages of the local newspaper. Increasingly, we can also see product markets operating online – for example, through sites such as Amazon.com.

(b) **Commodity markets**: these provide a marketplace for buying and selling primary (rather than manufactured) products. The New York Mercantile Exchange (NYMEX) is an example. Commodity markets deal in hard commodities (natural resources which have to be mined or extracted – such as gold, oil, or copper) and soft commodities (resources which are grown – such as agricultural products and livestock).

(c) **Financial markets**: this includes stock markets where shares in companies are traded, or money markets where banks trade loans using computer screens.

The discussion in this chapter will be restricted to product markets. In economics, suppliers and potential suppliers are referred to in economics as **firms**. The potential purchasers of consumer goods are known as **households**.

Price theory is concerned with how market prices for goods are arrived at, through the interaction of demand and supply.

[Note: Although economists often refer to 'goods', their analysis isn't only restricted to physical goods. In practice, the generic term 'goods' can usually be taken to mean goods and services.]

2 The demand schedule

2.1 The concept of demand

FAST FORWARD

Demand for a good or service is the quantity of that good or service that potential purchasers would be willing and able to buy, or attempt to buy, at any possible price.

The phrase 'willing and able to buy' in the Fast Forward above is very important. **Economic demand needs to be effective**. That is, it must be supported by available money (ie willing and able to buy), rather than just being a general desire for goods or services.

For example, a million households might wish that they owned a luxury yacht, but only one hundred households might actually be able to buy a luxury yacht at its given price. In this case, economic demand is one hundred, not one million.

2.2 The demand schedule and the demand curve

The relationship between demand and price is shown graphically as a **demand curve**. The demand curve of a single consumer or household is derived by estimating how much of the good the consumer or household would demand – be willing and able to buy – at various hypothetical market prices.

Suppose that the following **demand schedule** shows demand for biscuits by one household over a period of one month.

Price per kg $	Quantity demanded kg
1	9.75
2	8.00
3	6.25
4	4.50
5	2.75
6	1.00

Notice that we show demand falling as price increases. This is what normally happens with most goods, because purchasers have a limited amount of money to spend and must choose between goods that compete for their attention. When the price of one good rises, it is likely that other goods will seem relatively more attractive and so demand will switch away from the more expensive good to the cheaper alternative.

More generally, if the price of a good rises, but a household's income remains the same, the household will be able to buy less goods and services than before. This is because the price rise causes the household's real income to fall. (We will discuss this point – known as the income effect – in more detail later in the chapter.)

FAST FORWARD

The **law of demand** states that: as the price of a good falls then, other things remaining equal, the quantity demanded of the good increases.

We can illustrate the demand schedule graphically. Figure 1 is the household's demand curve for biscuits, based on the figures we have looked at above.

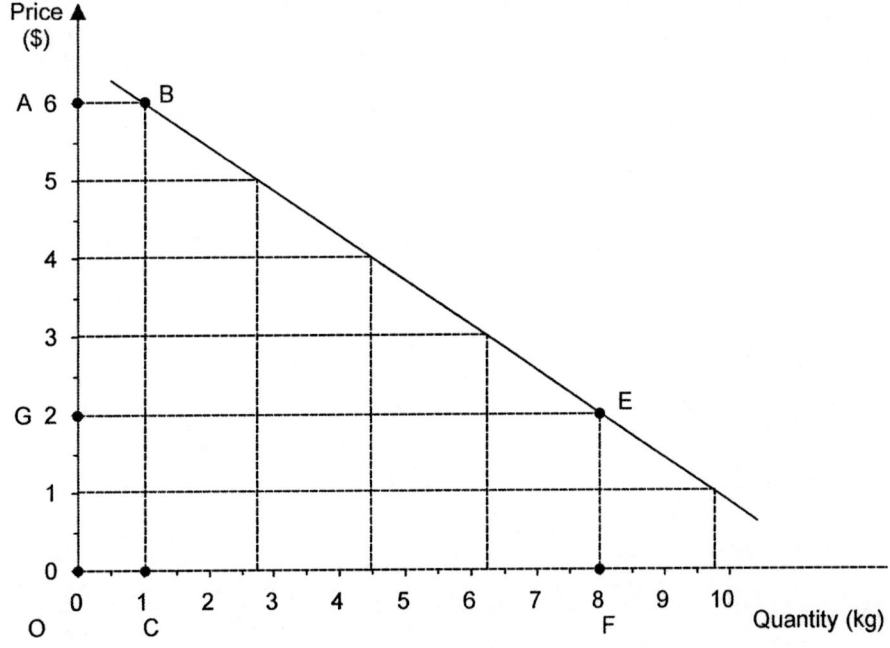

Figure 1 Graph of a demand schedule

The area of each rectangle in Figure 1 represents consumers' total money outlay at the price in question. For example, at a price of $6, demand would be 1 kilogram and total spending would be $6, represented by rectangle ABCO. Similarly, at a price of $2, demand would be 8 kilograms and the total spending of $16 is represented by rectangle GEFO.

> **Exam focus point**
>
> Drawing demand and/or supply curves is often required in exam questions.

In Figure 1, the demand curve happens to be a straight line. Straight line demand curves are often used as an illustration in economics because it is convenient to draw them this way. In reality, a demand curve is more likely to be a curved line convex to the origin.

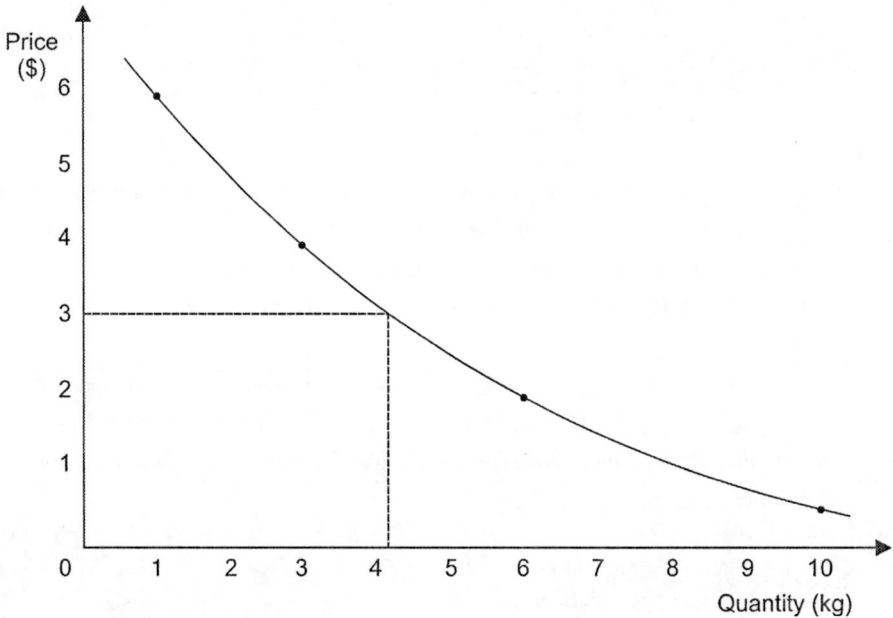

Figure 2 Demand curve convex to the origin

Example: Interpreting a demand curve

Refer to Figure 2. The price of the commodity is currently $3 per kilo, and demand is approximately 4 kilograms at that price. What would be the (approximate) demand for the commodity if the price fell to $2 per kilo? And what would be the demand if the price rose to $4 per kilo?

Solution

Demand rises to (approximately) 6 kilos at the reduced price of $2 per kilo. If price rises to $4 per kilo, demand falls to (approximately) 3 kilos.

Note that changes in demand caused by changes in price are represented by movements **along the demand curve,** from one point to another. These changes in quantity demanded in response to a change in price are called **expansions** or **contractions** in demand. The price has changed, and the quantity demanded changes (prompting a movement along the curve), but **the demand curve itself remains the same.**

2.3 The market demand curve

> **FAST FORWARD**
>
> The position of the **demand curve** is determined by the demand conditions, which include consumers' tastes and preferences, and consumers' incomes.

In our example of the demand for biscuits, we have been looking at the demand schedule of a single household. A **market demand curve** is a similar curve, but it expresses the expected total quantity of the good that would be demanded by **all consumers together**, at any given price.

Market demand is the total quantity of a product that **all** purchasers would be willing and able buy at each price level. A market demand schedule and a market demand curve are therefore simply the sum of all the individual demand schedules and demand curves put together. Market demand curves would be similar to those in Figures 1 and 2 – sloping downwards from left to right – but with quantities demanded (total market demand) being higher at each price level.

2.4 The conditions of demand

2.4.1 Factors affecting demand

Several factors influence the total market demand for a good. One of these factors is obviously its price. A demand curve shows how the quantity demanded will change in response to a change in price **provided that all other conditions affecting demand are unchanged** – that is, provided that there is no change in the prices of other goods, tastes, expectations or the distribution of household income.

(This assumption that 'all other things remain equal' is referred to, in economics, as *ceteris paribus*.)

2.4.2 Price of substitutes and complements

> **FAST FORWARD**
>
> **Substitute goods** are goods that are alternatives for each other, so that an **increase** in the demand for one is likely to cause a **decrease** in the demand for another. Switching demand from one good to another 'rival' good is substitution.
>
> **Complements** are goods that tend to be bought and used together, so that an **increase** in the demand for one is likely to cause an **increase** in the demand for the other.

Although the price of a good is one factor which affects demand for that good, it is by no means the only factors. Demand for a good can also be affected by the price of substitutes and complements. These are goods for which the market demand is inter-connected. A substitute is a good which can be replaced by another good, and so the two goods can be said to be in **competitive demand**.

Examples of substitute goods and services

- Rival brands of the same commodity, like Coca-Cola and Pepsi-Cola
- Supermarket 'own brand' products and branded products (eg supermarket 'own brand' Cola, as an alternative to either Coca-Cola or Pepsi-Cola)
- Self-catering holidays and hotel accommodation
- Tea and coffee

Substitution will take place when the price of one good rises relative to a substitute good.

By contrast, complements are goods **in joint demand**. In demanding one good, a consumer will also be likely to demand the other good.

Examples of complements

- Cars and petrol
- Tennis rackets and tennis balls
- DVDs and DVD players
- Washing machines and fabric conditioner

Example: Substitutes and complements

What might be the effect of an increase in the ownership of domestic deep freezers on the demand for perishable food products?

Solution

(a) Domestic deep freezers and perishable products are complements because people buy deep freezers to store perishable products.

(b) Perishable products are supplied either as fresh produce (for example, fresh meat and fresh vegetables) or as frozen produce, which can be kept for a short time in a refrigerator but for longer in a freezer. The demand for frozen produce will rise, while the demand for fresh produce will fall.

(c) Wider ownership of deep freezers is likely to increase bulk buying of perishable products. Suppliers can save some packaging costs, and can therefore offer lower prices for bulk purchases.

2.4.3 Household incomes

As you might imagine, an increase in their income will give households more to spend, so they will want to buy more goods at existing prices. However, a rise in household income will not increase market demand for all goods and services. The effect of a rise in income on demand for an individual good will depend on the nature of the good.

Demand and the level of income may be related in different ways.

(a) We might normally expect a rise in household income to lead to an increase in demand for a good, and goods for which demand rises as household income increases are called **normal goods**.

(b) Demand may rise with income up to a certain point but then fall as income rises beyond that point. Goods whose demand eventually falls as income rises are called **inferior goods**: examples might include public transport or cheap, unbranded clothing. The reason for falling demand is that as incomes rise, customers can afford to switch demand to superior products. For example, as their incomes rises, people may be able to afford their own cars which they will then use in preference to public transport; or they may start buying designer clothes instead of cheaper, unbranded clothes.

> **Normal goods** are goods for which demand **rises** when income rises.
>
> **Inferior goods** are goods for which demand **falls** when income rises.

2.4.4 Fashion and demand

A change in fashion or tastes will also alter the demand for a product. For example, if it becomes fashionable to wear a specific brand or item of clothing then demand for that brand or item – and expenditure on it – will increase. Tastes can be affected by advertisers and suppliers trying to 'create' demand for their products.

2.4.5 Expectations

If consumers believe that prices will rise, or that shortages of a good will occur, they may attempt to stock up on that good before these changes occur. Again, this could lead to increases in current demand, despite the price of the good remaining unchanged.

2.5 Shifts of the demand curve

Earlier in this chapter, we noted the way a change in price affects the quantity demanded – depicted as a movement **along** the demand curve. However, when there is a **change in the conditions of demand**, the quantity demanded will change even if price remains constant. In this case, there will be a different price/quantity demand schedule and so **a different demand curve**. We refer to such a change as a **shift of the demand curve**.

Figure 3 depicts a rise in demand at each price level, with the demand curve shifting to the right, from D_0 to D_1. For example, at price P_1, demand for the good would rise from X to Y. This shift could be caused by any of the following **conditions of demand**.

- A rise in **household income** (including a reduction in direct taxes)
- A rise in the price of **substitutes**
- A fall in the price of **complements**
- A change in **tastes** towards this product
- An **expected rise** in the price of the product
- An **increase** in population

Figure 3 shows an outward shift in the demand curve, but conversely a fall in demand at each price level would be represented by a shift in the opposite direction: a shift to the left of the original demand curve. Such a shift may be caused by the opposite of the conditions of demand shown above.

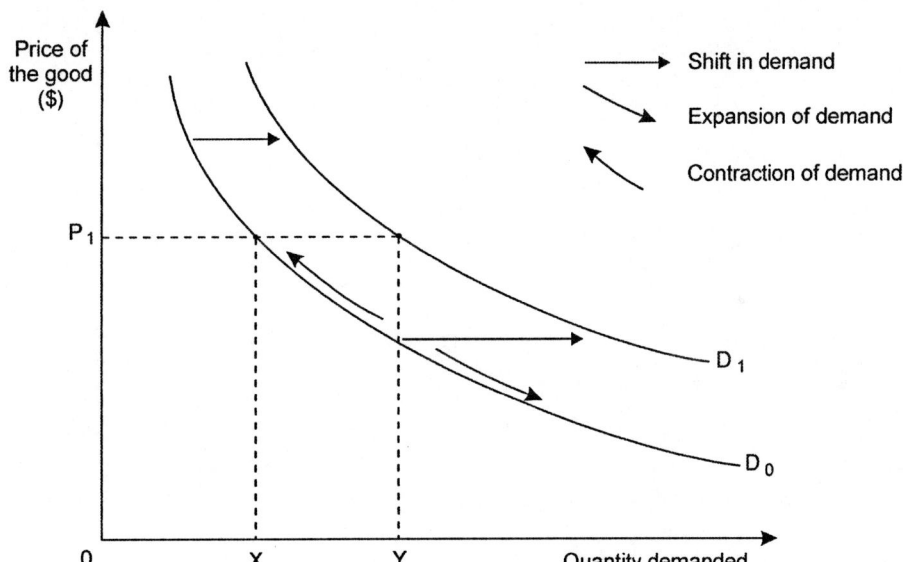

Figure 3 Changes in quantity demanded and outward shift of the demand curve

Exam focus point

The difference between a **change** in demand and a **shift** of the demand curve is of fundamental importance. Remember:

(a) Movements **along** a demand curve (contractions or expansions) for a good are caused solely by changes in its **price**

(b) Variations in the **conditions of demand** create **shifts** in the demand curve

Example: Substitutes and complements

In Country X, a recent fall in the price of DVDs has seen demand for DVDs increase significantly. However, cinema operators have reported a decline in customer numbers, and they believe this is due to people preferring to buy DVDs to watch rather than going to the cinema.

What effect is the fall in the price of DVDs likely to have on the demand curves for:

(a) DVD players
(b) Cinema tickets

Solution

(a) There is likely to have been an outward shift in the demand curve for DVD players. DVD players are complements to the DVDs themselves because people will need to buy the DVD players in order to watch their DVDs. So, the increased demand for DVDs is likely to lead to an increase in demand for DVD players even though their price may be unchanged. This results in an **outward shift** in their demand curve (a rise in demand).

(b) There is likely to be an inward shift in the demand curve for cinema tickets (a fall in demand). Even though the price of cinema tickets has not changed, people are demanding less of them because they are choosing to watch DVDs instead. Cinema tickets are a substitute product to DVDs, and a fall in the price of a substitute leads to an inward shift of the demand curve for a product.

3 The supply schedule

3.1 The concept of supply

FAST FORWARD

Supply refers to the quantity of a good that existing suppliers or would be suppliers would want to produce for the market at a given price.

As with demand, supply relates to a period of time – for example, we might refer to an annual rate of supply or to a monthly rate.

The quantity of a good supplied to a market varies up or down for two reasons.

(a) Existing suppliers may increase or reduce their output quantities.

(b) Firms may stop production altogether and leave the market, or new firms may enter the market and start to produce the good.

If the quantity that firms want to produce at a given price exceeds the quantity that households (consumers) would demand at that price, there will be an **excess of supply**, with firms competing to win what sales demand there is. Over-supply and competition would then be expected to result in price-competitiveness and **a fall in prices**.

As with demand, a distinction needs to be made.

(a) An individual firm's supply schedule is the quantity of a good that an individual firm would want to supply to the market at any given price.

(b) Market supply is the total quantity of a good that all firms in the market would want to supply at a given price.

3.2 The supply curve

A **supply schedule** and **supply curve** can be created both for an individual supplier and for all firms which produce the good. A supply schedule is a table which lists the quantities of a good that would be supplied at different prices. This data can then be shown graphically – as a supply curve.

The supply curve shows the quantity of a good suppliers are willing to produce at different price levels. It is an **upward sloping curve from left to right**, because greater quantities will be supplied at higher prices.

We usually assume that suppliers aim to maximise their profits, and the upward slope of the supply curve reflects this desire to make profit (ie they are prepared to supply more of something the higher the price that customers will pay for it).

> **FAST FORWARD**
>
> The **law of supply** states that: as price of a good rises, other things remaining equal, the quantity supplied of that good will increase.

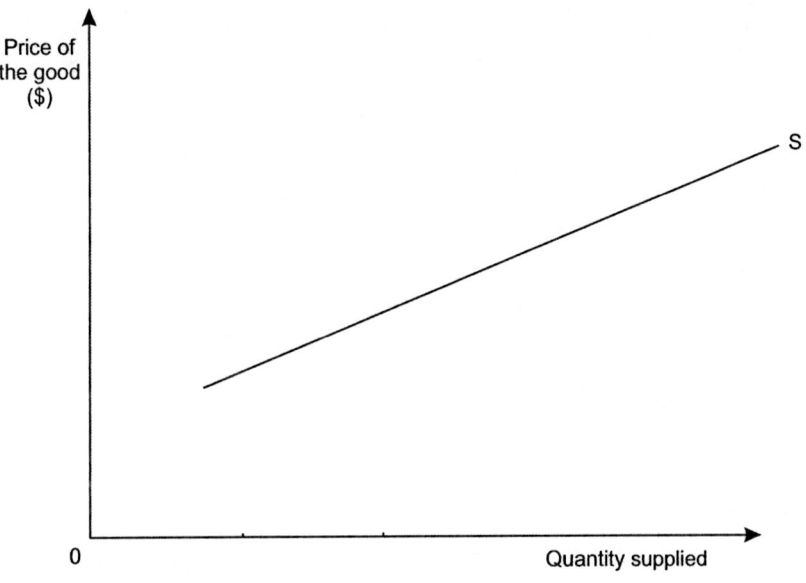

Figure 4 Supply curve

3.3 Factors influencing the supply quantity

> **FAST FORWARD**
>
> The position of a supply curve depends on the **conditions of supply**. These are costs of resources, prices of other products, indirect taxes and subsidies, expectations of market changes, and natural factors such as those affecting harvests.

The quantity supplied of a good depends, as you might expect, on prices and costs. More specifically, it depends on the following factors:

(a) The **costs of making the good**. These include raw materials costs, which ultimately depend on the prices of factors of production (wages, interest rates, rents and profit expectations).

(b) The **prices of other goods**. When a supplier can switch readily from supplying one good to another, the goods concerned are called **substitutes in supply**. An increase in the price of one such good would make the supply of another good whose price does not rise less attractive to suppliers. For example, if a car manufacturer makes two different types of car. If the price of one type of car increases, but the other one stays the same, the manufacturer will look to produce more of the car whose price has increased. If production capacity in the factory is limited, then supplies of the car whose price stayed the same will have to fall to compensate for the increase in the supply of the other type of car.

When a production process has two or more distinct and separate outputs, the goods produced are known as **goods in joint supply** or **complements in production**. Goods in joint supply include, for example, meat and hides. If the price of beef rises, more will be supplied and there will be an accompanying increase in the supply of cow hide.

(c) The application of **indirect taxes** and **subsidies** will affect prices. If the government applies an indirect tax on the producer, such as per litre of fuel oil, then the producer will treat this as an increase in cost and so will raise their price.

Alternatively if the government contributes a subsidy, say a sum of money per education course sold, then the supplier will reduce their prices, because, in effect, the subsidy reduces the cost to the course provider of running the course.

(d) **Expectations of price changes**. If a supplier expects the price of a good to rise, he is likely to try to reduce supply while the price is lower so that he can then supply more of the good once the price is higher.

(e) **Changes in technology**. Technological developments which reduce costs of production (and increase productivity) will raise the quantity of supply of a good at any given price.

(f) **Other factors**, such as changes in the weather (for example, in the case of agricultural goods), natural disasters or industrial disruption.

As with the demand curve, the supply curve shows how the quantity supplied will change in response to a change in price. If **supply conditions** alter, a different supply curve must be drawn. In other words, a change in the price of a good will cause a change in supply **along the supply curve**. A change in other supply conditions will cause a **shift in the supply curve itself**.

> **Exam focus point**
>
> This distinction between a movement along the supply curve and a shift in the supply curve is just as important as the similar distinction relating to the demand curve.

3.4 Shifts of the market supply curve

The **market supply curve** is the aggregate of all the supply curves of individual firms in the market. A shift of the market supply curve occurs when the conditions of supply (ie, factors other than the price of the good itself) change. Figure 5 shows a rightward shift in the supply curve from S_0 to S_1 and a leftward shift to S_2.

A **rightward** (or **downward**) shift of the curve shows an **expansion of supply** and may be caused by the factors below.

(a) A fall in the cost of factors of production, for example a reduction in the cost of raw material inputs

(b) A fall in the price of other goods. The production of other goods becomes relatively less attractive as their price falls. Firms are therefore likely to shift resources away from the goods whose price is falling and into the production of higher priced goods that offer increased profits. We therefore expect (*ceteris paribus*) that the supply of one good will rise as the prices of other goods fall (and *vice versa*)

(c) Technological progress, which reduces unit costs and also increases production capabilities

(d) Improvements in productivity or more efficient use of existing factors of production, which again will reduce unit cost

A shift of the supply curve is the result of changes in costs, either in absolute terms or relative to the costs of other goods. If the price of the good is P_1, suppliers would be willing to increase supply from Q_0 to Q_1 under the new supply conditions (see Figure 5).

Conversely, we might see a **leftward** (or **upward**) shift in the supply curve if the cost of supply increases. This would mean that at the existing price, a firm's output will decrease and less will be supplied. This is also illustrated on Figure 5. At price P_1, the quantity supplied now falls from Q_0 to Q_2, as the supply curve shifts from S_0 to S_2.

In order for the supplier to restore output levels to the original Q_0, price would have to increase to P_2.

A leftward (upward) shift ($S_0 \rightarrow S_2$) in supply could be caused by:

(a) An increase in the cost of factors of production (eg a rise in wages and salaries, which are the costs of labour)

(b) A rise in the price of other goods which would make them relatively more attractive to the producer

(c) An increase in indirect taxes, or a reduction in a subsidy, which would make supply at existing prices less profitable.

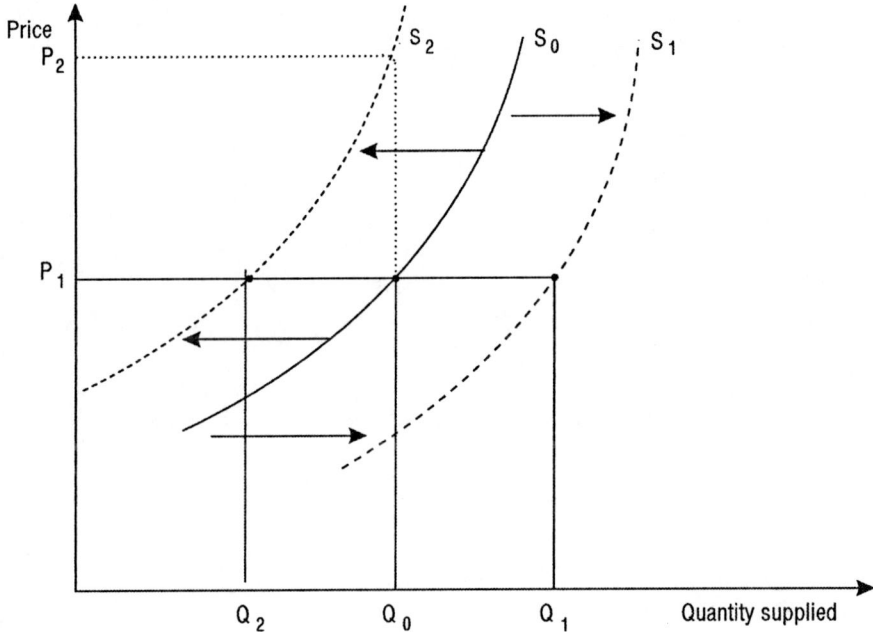

Figure 5 Shifts in the supply curve

Example: Quantity supplied

What effect will higher grain prices have on the supply curve of a cereal manufacturer who makes cereals from grain?

Solution

The higher price of grain will cause the supply curve to shift leftwards (or upwards). The increase in grain prices increase the cereal manufacturer's production costs, making supply at existing prices less profitable.

4 The equilibrium price

The **equilibrium price** is established by the price mechanism and is the price at which quantity demanded of a good equals quantity supplied of that good in a particular market.

4.1 Functions of the price mechanism

People only have a limited income and they must decide what to buy with the money they have. The prices of the goods they want will affect their buying decisions.

Firms' output decisions will be influenced by both demand and supply considerations.

(a) Market demand conditions influence the price that a firm will get for its output. Prices act as **signals** to producers, and changes in prices should stimulate a response from a firm to change the quantities of a good it is producing.

(b) Supply is influenced by production costs and profits. Remember that there is an underlying assumption that firms aim to maximise their profits, and in order to achieve this aim, firms respond to changes in price or cost by changing their production quantities. In this respect, price acts as an **incentive** to producers to change the quantity supplied, if doing so will increase their profits.

(c) In cases where demand is potentially greater then supply, the scarce supply must be **rationed-out** between the buyers. This is done by the price rising until only the keenest buyers can afford it.

> **FAST FORWARD**
> The **three functions of price** are **signalling**, **incentivising** and **rationing**.

4.2 The price mechanism and the equilibrium price

> **FAST FORWARD**
> The **price mechanism** brings demand and supply into equilibrium, and the **equilibrium price** for a good is the price at which the quantities demanded by consumers and the quantities that firms are willing to supply are the same. This is also known as the **market clearing price**, since at this price there will be neither surplus nor shortage in the market.

The way demand and supply interact to determine the equilibrium price can be illustrated by drawing the market demand curve and the market supply curve on the same graph (Figure 6).

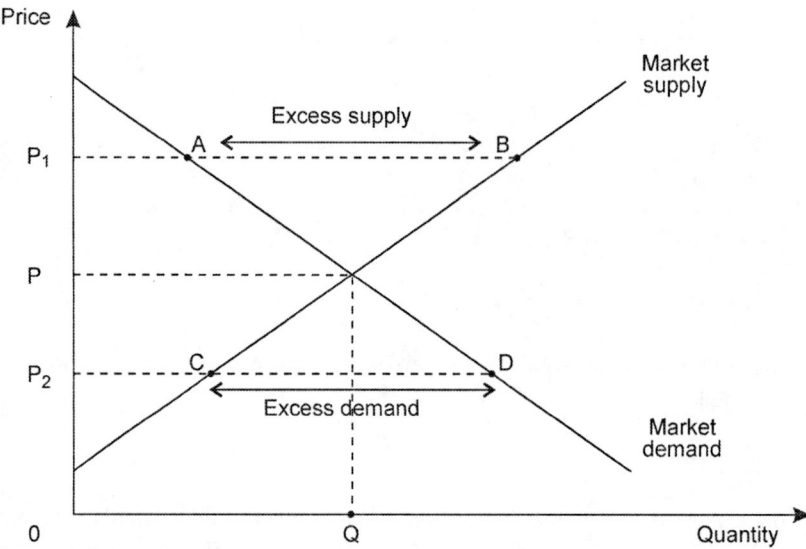

Figure 6 Market equilibrium

Excess supply – At price P_1 in Figure 6, suppliers want to produce a greater quantity than the market demands, meaning that there is excess supply, equal to the distance A-B. Suppliers would react as the stock of unsold goods accumulates:

(a) They would cut down the current level of production in order to sell unwanted inventories.
(b) They would also reduce prices in order to encourage sales.

Excess demand – By contrast, at price P_2 there is an excess of demand over supply shown by the distance C-D. In response to this, supply and price will both increase. Faced with an excess of demand, manufacturers would be able to raise their prices. This would make supplying the good more profitable and supply would increase.

Equilibrium – At price P, the amount that sellers are willing and able to supply is equal to the amount that customers are willing and able to buy. Consumers will be willing to spend a total of $(P \times Q)$ on buying Q units of the product, and suppliers will be willing to supply Q units to earn revenue of $(P \times Q)$. P is the **equilibrium price**.

The forces of supply and demand push a market to its equilibrium price and quantity. Note carefully the following key points.

(a) If there is no change in conditions of supply or demand, the **equilibrium price will prevail** in the market and will remain stable.

(b) If price is not at the equilibrium, the market is in **disequilibrium** and supply and demand will push prices towards the equilibrium price.

(c) In any market, there will only be one equilibrium position where the market is cleared.

(d) Shifts in the supply curve or demand curve will change the equilibrium price (and the quantity traded).

4.3 Calculating the equilibrium price and quantity

If the demand curve and the supply curve are straight lines, then it is possible to calculate the equilibrium position mathematically, and you could be asked to do this is an exam question.

When demand is linear, the equation for the demand curve is:

$Q_D = a - bP$

where Q_D = the quantity demanded

a = the quantity which would be demanded if price were zero

$b = \dfrac{\text{Change in quantity demanded}}{\text{Change in price}}$ (ie the gradient of the demand curve)

P = the price

Similarly, if supply is linear, the equation for the supply curve is:

$Q_S = a + bP$

where Q_S = the quantity supplied

a = the quantity which would be supplied if price were zero

b = the $\dfrac{\text{Change in quantity supplied}}{\text{Change in price}}$ ie the gradient of the supply curve)

P = the price

Note: the values for 'a' and 'b' will be different for the supply curve compared to the demand curve.

Note also the negative sign in front of 'bP' for the demand curve, indicating that as price increases quantity demanded will decrease. By contrast, the sign before 'bP' for the supply curve is positive, because supply will increase as price increases.

We know that the equilibrium price occurs when **supply = demand** ($Q_S = Q_D$), and this can be found by re-arranging values from the equations.

This may sound rather complicated in words, but it is easier to illustrate using an example.

4.3.1 Example: Equilibrium position

Statistical studies have shown that the supply curve for tablet computers in a country can be represented by $Q_S = 10,000 + 150P$ where Q_S is the quantity of tablets supplied, and P represents the price of a tablet (in $).

These studies have also shown that the demand curve for tablet computers in the country can be represented by $Q_D = 30,000 - 50P$ where Q_D is the quantity of tablets demanded, and P represents the price of a tablet (in $).

What are the equilibrium price and quantity for tablet computers in the country?

The equilibrium price occurs where $Q_S = Q_D$

Therefore, equilibrium occurs where: $10,000 + 150P = 30,000 - 50P$

Re-arrange the equation to find 'P': $150P + 50P = 30,000 - 10,000$ or $200P = 20,000$

Solve the equation: $200P = 20,000$; therefore $P = 100$.

The equilibrium price is $100 per tablet.

By substituting the equilibrium price into the equation for either supply or demand, we can then find the equilibrium quantity:

$Q_S = 10,000 + 150P$

So, if $P = 100$, $Q_S = 10,000 + (150 \times 100) = 25,000$

Therefore the market clearing quantity is 25,000.

We can confirm this by substituting $P = 100$ into the equation for demand:

$Q_D = 30,000 = 50P$

When $P = 100$, $Q_D = 30,000 - (50 \times 100) = 25,000$

At a price of $100 per tablet, supply and demand are both 25,000, meaning the market is in equilibrium.

5 Demand and supply analysis

5.1 Analysis

Petrol and cars are **complementary** products; demand for one is likely to affect demand for the other. Any change in the market for petrol (see Figure 7) would be expected to affect the market for second-hand cars. The demand for petrol, however, is likely to be relatively unresponsive to a change in price, so a change in price will only have a relatively small impact on the quantity of petrol demanded. Consequently, a major change in its price will be necessary to affect the demand for any complementary product (such as cars).

Figure 7 assumes that there is a large increase in the price of fuel (petrol).

(a)

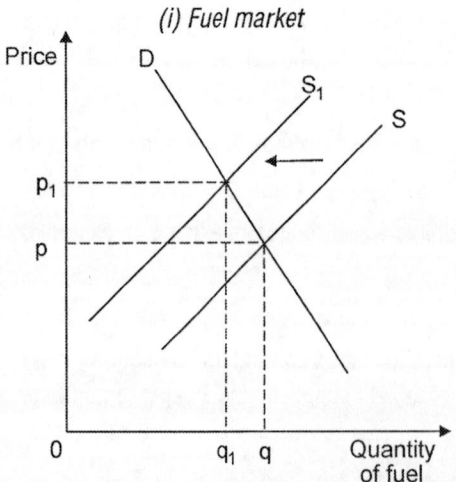 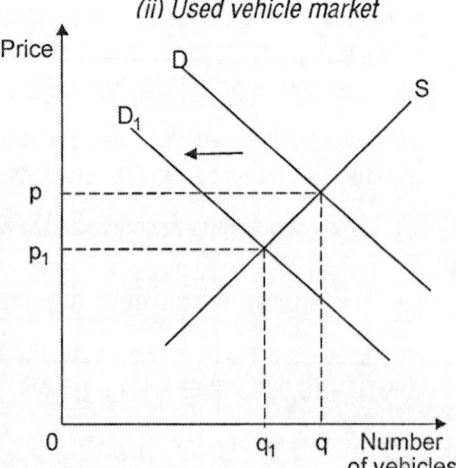

Figure 7 Complementary products

In this instance, we have assumed that the rise in the price of fuel results from a change in the conditions of supply, which have resulted in a leftward shift in the supply curve. This is illustrated in Figure 7(i), where the supply curve shifts from S to S_1. The resulting rise in the price of fuel represents a rise in the cost of owning and running a car. Consequently, there will be a fall in the demand for second-hand cars and a fall in the price and quantity sold (Figure 7 (ii)).

Similarly, we could look (Figure 8) at the relationship between the demand for new vehicles and the demand for used vehicles – which are **substitute** products. A consumer has a choice to buy either a new car or a used car. The consumer is likely to buy one or the other, not both.

(b)

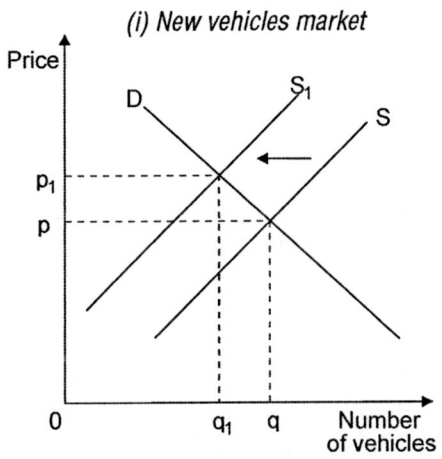 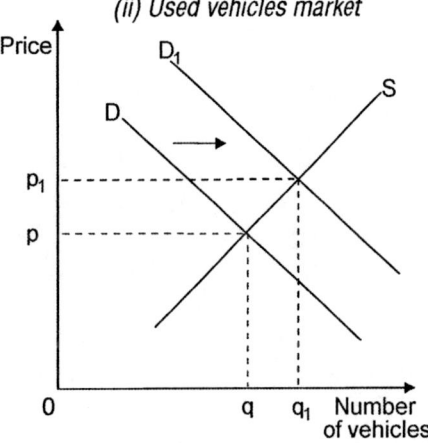

Figure 8 Substitute products

It is assumed that the increase in the price of new cars is the result of a major increase in supply costs. The rise in price causes a switch of demand into second-hand vehicles, so leading to an outward shift in the demand curve (from D to D^1) in Figure 8(ii).

Note, however, that the increase in demand for used vehicles (Figure 8(ii)) in turn also increases their price, reflecting the workings of the price mechanism.

Figure 9 looks at another 'product' which is in competition with second-hand cars: public transport. Figure 9 illustrates the likely impact on the used vehicle market following and outward shift in the supply of public transport services.

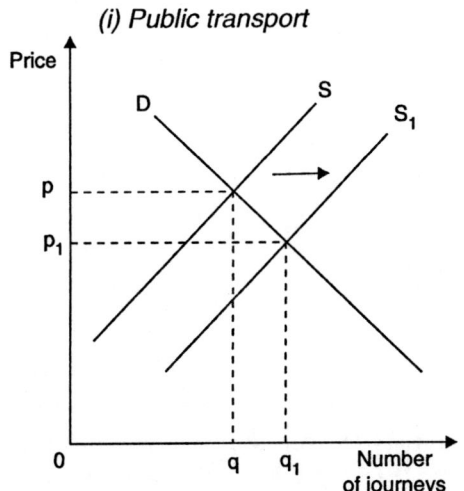 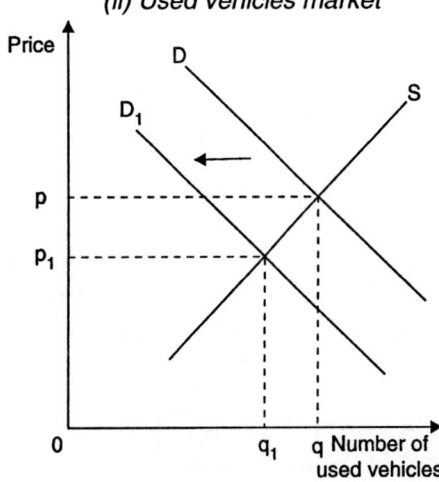

Figure 9 Substitute products and the impact of a shift in supply

PART B　CONSUMPTION, PRODUCTION AND DISTRIBUTION

The shift in the supply of public transport (Figure 9 (i)) leads to a fall in the price of public transport, which in turn leads to an expansion in demand for public transport. Since public transport is a substitute for used cars, the increased demand for public transport leads to a fall in the demand for second-hand cars falls (with a new demand line D_1 in Figure 9(ii)) along with a fall in price.

However, in practice, the relationship between public transport and the market for second-hand cars is likely to be a highly complex and indeterminate one. For example, although people might make greater use of public transport, car ownership and the demand for cars (including second-hand cars) might remain unchanged – if people want the option of being able to travel by car as well as by public transport. Similarly, if the population is increasing, demand for public transport and demand for cars might both increase at the same time.

6 Elasticity of demand

6.1 The price elasticity of demand

FAST FORWARD

> **Price elasticity of demand** (PED) is a measure of the extent of change in the market demand for a good in response to a change in its price.

The demand curve illustrates that the quantity demand of a good will vary according to the price of that good. However, if a firm is considering changes to the price of a good, a key factor in any such decision will be knowing how much the quantity demanded will change following the change in price. The answer to this depends on the price elasticity of demand for the good in question.

Elasticity, in general, refers to the relationship between two variables. Price elasticity of demand (PED) explains the relationship between **change in quantity demanded** and **changes in price**.

If prices went **up** by 10%, would the quantity demanded **fall** by the same percentage?

The coefficient of PED is measured as:

Formula to learn

> Percentage change in quantity demanded
> ──────────────────────────────────────
> Percentage change in price

Since demand usually increases when the price falls, and decreases when the price rises, elasticity has a negative value. **However, it is usual to ignore the minus sign**, and just describe the absolute value of the coefficient.

This can be expressed as:

$$\frac{\frac{\Delta Q}{Q} \times 100}{\frac{\Delta P}{P} \times 100}$$

where　Δ　is the symbol for 'change in'

　　　　Q　is the quantity demanded of the good

　　　　P　is the price of the good

If we are measuring the responsiveness of demand to a large change in price, we can measure elasticity between two points on the demand curve, and the resulting measure is called the **arc elasticity of demand**. We calculate the arc elasticity of demand from the percentage change in quantity relative to **average** quantity for the relevant range of output and from the percentage price change relative to the **average** of the corresponding price range.

If we wish to measure the responsiveness of demand at one particular point in the demand curve, we can calculate a **point elasticity of demand**, without averaging price and quantity over a range. In doing so, it is convenient to assume that the demand curve is a straight line unless told otherwise.

Example: Arc elasticity of demand

The price of a good is $1.20 per unit and annual demand is 800,000 units. Market research indicates that an increase in price of 10 cents per unit will result in a fall in annual demand of 70,000 units.

What is the price elasticity of demand measuring the responsiveness of demand over this range of price increase?

Solution

Annual demand at $1.20 per unit is 800,000 units.

Annual demand at $1.30 per unit is 730,000 units.

Average quantity over the range is 765,000 units.

Average price is $1.25.

% change in demand $\quad \dfrac{70{,}000}{765{,}000} \times 100\% = 9.15\%$

% change in price $\quad \dfrac{10c}{125c} \times 100\% = 8\%$

Price elasticity of demand = $\dfrac{-9.15}{8} = -1.14$

Ignoring the minus sign, the arc elasticity is 1.14.

The demand for this good, over the range of annual demand 730,000 to 800,000 units, is **elastic** because the price elasticity of demand is **greater than 1**.

Example: Arc elasticity of demand

If the price per unit of X rises from $1.40 to $1.60, it is expected that monthly demand will fall from 220,000 units to 200,000 units.

What is the arc price elasticity of demand over these ranges of price and output?

Solution

Monthly demand at $1.40 per unit = 220,000 units

Monthly demand at $1.60 per unit = 200,000 units

Average quantity = 210,000 units

Average price = $1.50

% change in demand $\quad \dfrac{20{,}000}{210{,}000} \times 100\% = 9.52\%$

% change in price $\quad \dfrac{20}{150} \times 100\% = 13.33\%$

Arc price elasticity of demand = $\dfrac{-9.52}{13.33} = -0.71\%$

Ignoring the minus sign, the arc elasticity is 0.71.

Demand is **inelastic** over the demand range considered, because the price elasticity of demand (ignoring the minus sign) is **less than 1**.

Example: Point elasticity of demand

The price of a good is $1.20 per unit and annual demand is 800,000. Market research indicates that an increase in price of 10 cents per unit will result in a fall in annual demand for the good of 70,000 units.

Required

Calculate the elasticity of demand at the current price of $1.20.

Solution

We are asked to calculate the elasticity at a particular price. We assume that the demand curve is a straight line.

At a price of $1.20, annual demand is 800,000 units. For a price rise:

% change in demand $\quad \dfrac{70{,}000}{800{,}000} \times 100\% = 8.75\%$ (fall)

% change in price $\quad \dfrac{10c}{120c} \times 100\% = 8.33\%$ (rise)

Price elasticity of demand at price $1.20 = $\dfrac{-8.75}{8.33} = -1.05$

Ignoring the minus sign, the price elasticity at this point is 1.05. Demand is **elastic** at this point, because the elasticity is **greater** than 1.

Example: Point elasticity of demand

If the price per unit of X rises from $1.40 to $1.60, it is expected that monthly demand will fall from 220,000 units to 200,000 units.

What is the point price elasticity of demand when the price is $1.40?

Solution

We assume that the demand curve is a straight line.

At a price of $1.40, demand is 220,000 units.

For a price rise of 20 cents to $1.60:

% change in demand $\quad \dfrac{20{,}000}{220{,}000} \times 100\% = 9.09\%$ (fall)

% change in price $\quad \dfrac{20c}{140c} \times 100\% = 14.29\%$ (rise)

Price elasticity of demand = $\dfrac{9.09}{-14.29} = -0.64$

or 0.64 ignoring the minus sign.

Demand is **inelastic** at this point, because it is **less than 1**.

6.2 Price elasticity of demand at a single point

As well as asking you to calculate the price elasticity of demand in relation to a change in price, the examiner could also ask you to calculate elasticity of demand at a specific point on the demand curve.

In this situation, you are not able to calculate a changes in quantity or price by reference to values before and after a price change. However, the gradient of the demand curve provides you with an alternative way of identifying how the quantity demanded changes in response to a change in price. (If you remember, in Section 4.3 we identified the equation for a straight line demand curve as $Q_D = a - bQ$. In effect, the gradient of the curve ('b') represents its elasticity – the ratio of change in quantity to the change in price.)

Price elasticity of demand (PED) at a specific point on the demand curve is calculated as:

$$PED = \frac{P}{Q} \times \frac{\Delta Q_D}{\Delta P}$$

where P = price at the given point

Q = quantity demanded

$\frac{\Delta Q_D}{\Delta P}$ = the gradient of the demand curve

Example: Calculating elasticity of demand at a single point

The demand curve for a product can be shown as: $Q_D = 4,000 - 256P$.

The equilibrium price for the product is $3.50 per unit, and the equilibrium quantity is 3,104.

What is the product's price elasticity of demand at the equilibrium point?

Solution

We use the demand curve to find the price elasticity of demand, applying the formula:

$$PED = \frac{P}{Q} \times \frac{\Delta Q_D}{\Delta P}$$

$$= \frac{3.50}{3,104} \times -256$$

$$= -0.29$$

6.3 Elastic and inelastic demand

FAST FORWARD

Price elasticity of demand (PED) is expressed as a co-efficient and can have a value between zero and infinity. A value of zero means that quantity demanded did not change at all when price changed and demand is **perfectly inelastic**. Values **between zero and one** are described as price **inelastic** demand. Values **in excess of one** denote price **elastic** demand.

The value of demand elasticity may be anything from zero to infinity.

- Demand is **inelastic** if the absolute value is less than 1
- Demand is **elastic** if the absolute value is greater than 1

Think about what this means if there is an increase in price. Where demand is **inelastic**, the quantity demanded falls by a **smaller** percentage than the rise in price. Where demand is **elastic**, demand falls by a **larger** percentage than the rise in price. As we will see shortly, this has important implications for the relationship between the price of a good and the revenue a firm can earn from sales of that good.

6.4 Price elasticity varies along the demand curve

Generally, demand curves slope downwards. Consumers are willing and able to buy more at lower prices than at higher prices. Except in certain special cases (which we look at below), **elasticity will vary in value along the length of a demand curve**.

The ranges of price elasticity (η) at different points on a downward sloping straight line demand curve are illustrated in Figure 10.

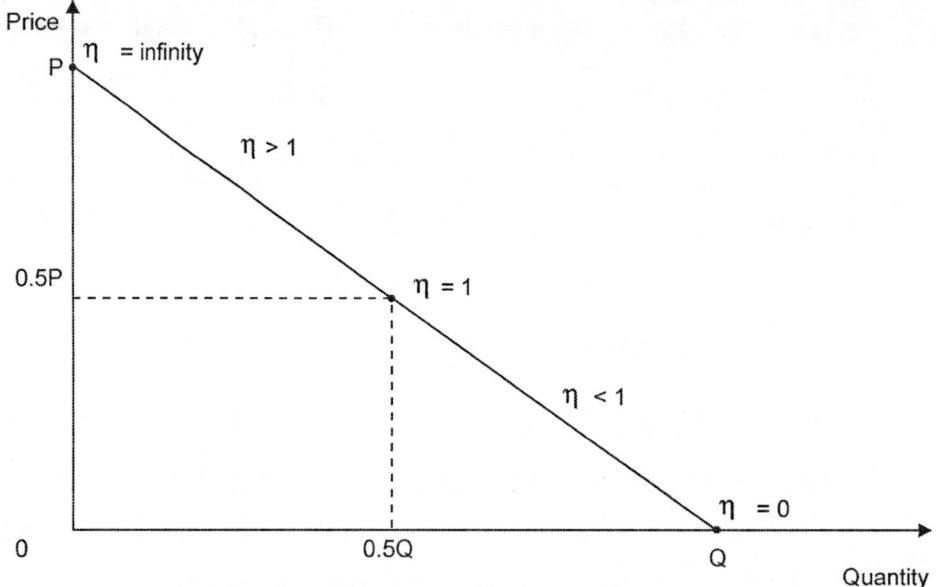

Figure 10 Ranges of price elasticity of demand

At **higher prices** on a straight line demand curve (the top of the demand curve), small percentage price reductions can bring **large percentage** increases in quantity demanded. This means that demand is **elastic** (PED >1) over these ranges.

At **lower prices** on a straight line demand curve (the bottom of the demand curve), **large percentage** price reductions will lead to smaller percentage increases in quantity. This means that demand is **inelastic** (PED <1) over these price ranges.

6.5 Special values of price elasticity of demand

There are three special values of price elasticity of demand: 0, 1 and infinity.

(a) **Demand is perfectly inelastic**: $\eta = 0$. There is no change in quantity demanded, regardless of the change in price. In this case, the demand curve is a **vertical straight line**.

(b) **Perfectly elastic demand**: $\eta = \infty$ (infinitely elastic). Consumers will want to buy an infinite amount, but only up to a particular price level. Any price increase above this level will reduce demand to zero. In this case, the demand curve is a **horizontal straight line.**

(c) **Unit elasticity of demand**: $\eta = 1$. Total revenue for suppliers (which is the same as total spending on the product by households) does not change regardless of how the price changes. The demand curve of a good whose price elasticity of demand is 1 over its entire range is a **rectangular hyperbola** (Figure 11).

In Figure 11, rectangles OABC, ODEF and OGHJ all have the same area, since the areas of these rectangles represent total spending by customers at each price.

(i) If the selling price were D, total demand would be F and total spending on the product would be D × F (rectangle ODEF).

(ii) If the selling price were A, total demand would be C, and total spending on the product would be A × C (rectangle OABC).

(iii) If the selling price were G, total demand would be J and total spending on the product would be G × J (rectangle OGHJ).

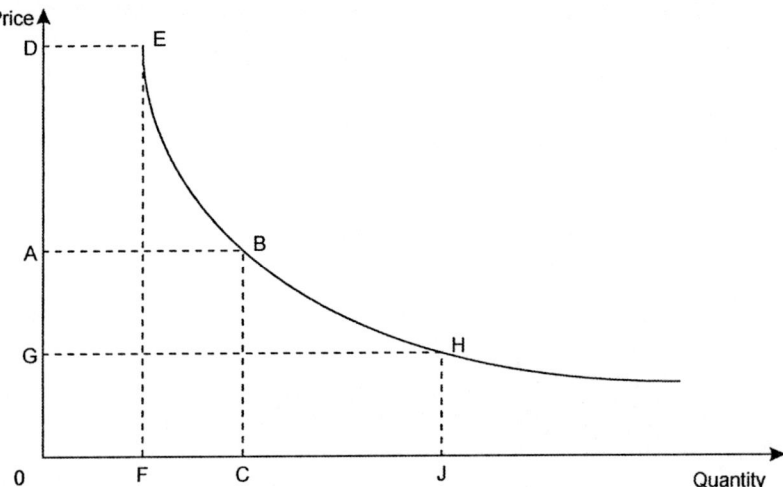

Figure 11 Unit elasticity of demand

In practice, it is unusual to find goods with perfectly elastic or perfectly inelastic demand. However, the table below summarises the different price elasticities of demand.

Level of elasticity	Coefficient value	Type of good	Real world examples
Perfectly inelastic	0 (zero)	–	–
Relatively inelastic	Between 0 – 1	Necessity	Fuel; basic foodstuffs (eg bread)
Unit elasticity	1	–	–
Relatively elastic	>1	Luxury	Holidays; luxury cars
Perfectly elastic	∞ (infinity)	–	–

6.6 The significance of price elasticity of demand

Exam focus point

You need to be able:

- To understand the **factors influencing elasticity**
- To **measure** price elasticity from given price and demand data, and to draw appropriate conclusions from such information
- To draw the correct implications for the **total revenue** of the producer of changes in the price of the product

FAST FORWARD

If demand is **price inelastic**, a **rise in price** will lead to a rise in total expenditure on the good and therefore a **rise in the firm's total revenue** from selling the good. If demand is price elastic, a **fall** in price will lead to a **rise in revenue** for the firm from selling the good.

The price elasticity of demand has important implications for total spending on a good or service. Total expenditure is a matter of interest to both suppliers, to whom sales revenue accrues, and to government, who may receive a proportion of total expenditure in the form of taxation.

By definition, if a good is price elastic, a change in price will lead to a **greater than proportional change** in the quantity of it demanded. Therefore, when is demand is **elastic,** an **increase in price** will result in a greater than proportional fall in the quantity demanded. As a result, the increase in price will lead to **a fall in total expenditure** on the good (or the total revenue received from sales of that good).

In Figure 12, total expenditure at price P_A is represented by the area OP_AAQ_A and total expenditure at price P_B is represented by the area OP_BBQ_B. Area OP_AAQ_A is greater than area OP_BBQ_B. This can be seen by observing that area Y (expenditure lost on a rise in price from A to B) is greater than area X (expenditure gained).

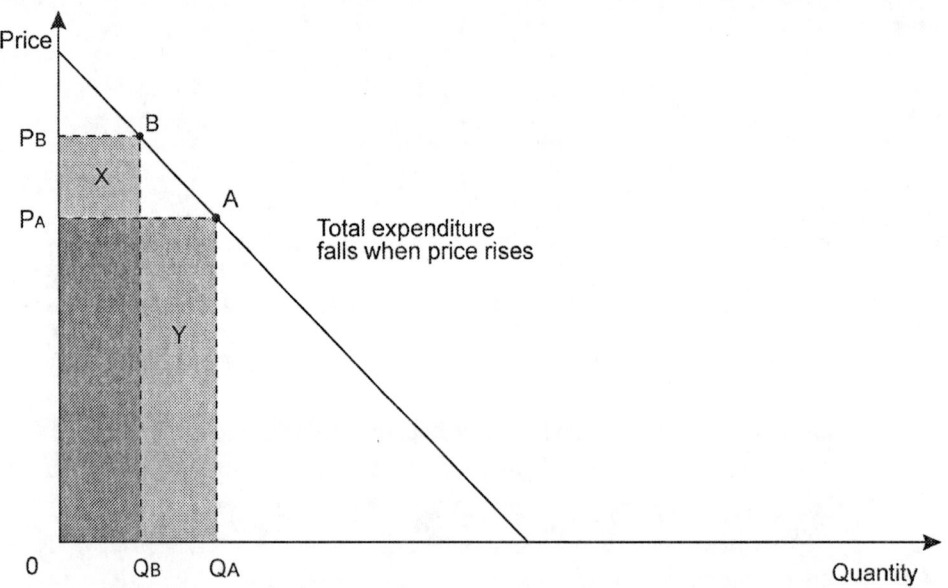

Figure 12 Elastic demand

When demand is **inelastic,** an increase in price will still result in a fall in quantity demanded, but the fall in quantity demanded will be less than proportional to the rise in price. Therefore, **total expenditure will rise**. In Figure 13, area X (expenditure gained following an increase in price from P_A to P_B) is greater than area Y (expenditure lost).

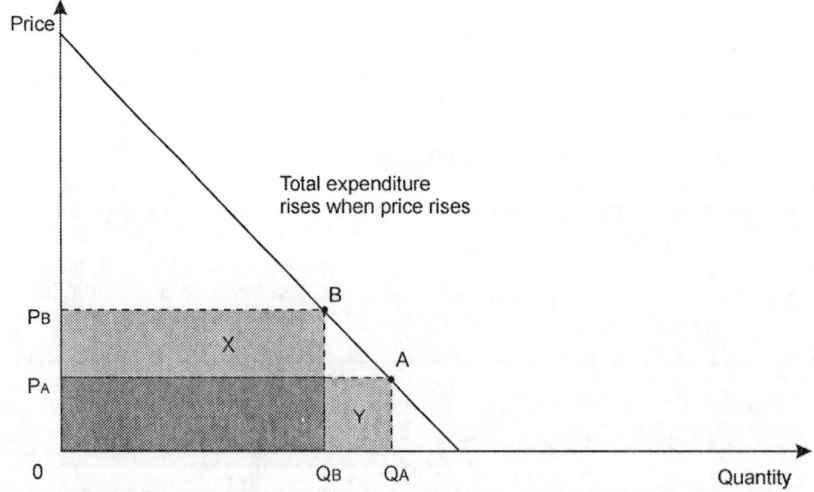

Figure 13 Inelastic demand

With **unit elasticity, expenditure will stay constant** regardless of a change in price. In Figure 14, area X and area Y are the same.

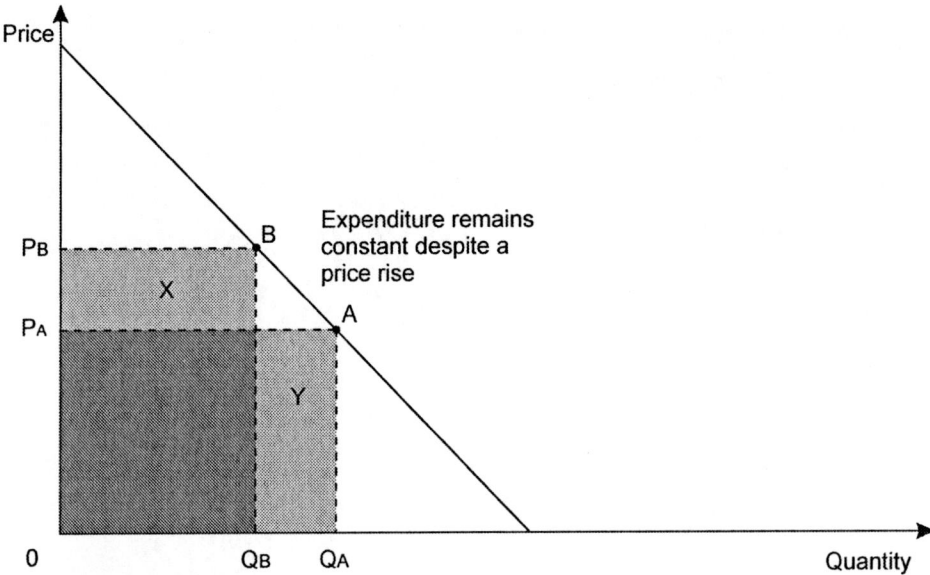

Figure 14 Unit elasticity

6.7 Information on price elasticity of demand

Understanding price elasticity of demand for a product is important for firms because it gives them an indication of how consumers are likely to respond to different prices or changes in price. Similarly, this will help firms assess the likely impact that a price change will have on its revenues and profits (and therefore whether a potential price change is likely to be beneficial or not).

Information on price elasticities of demand could also be useful to a business which needs to know the price decrease necessary to clear a surplus (excess supply) or the price increase necessary to eliminate a shortage (excess demand).

Government policy makers can also use information about elasticity, for example when making decisions about indirect taxation. Items with price inelastic demand – such as cigarettes and alcohol – tend to be useful targets for taxation, because by increasing taxes on these governments can increase their total revenue.

At the same time, governments may also want to discourage the consumption of harmful goods which cause increased expenditure in other areas (eg consumption of 'sugary' foods increases obesity, which in turn can lead to medical problems and increased demands on health services). In this case, governments might prefer these goods to be price elastic – because then increasing the tax on them will have a greater than proportional reduction in demand.

Question — Elasticity and total revenue

Suppose that there are two products, A and B.

Product A currently sells for $5, and demand at this price is 1,700 units. If the price fell to $4.60, demand would increase to 2,000 units.

Product B currently sells for $8 and demand at this price is 9,500 units. if the price fell to $7.50, demand would increase to 10,000 units.

In each of these cases (and using the 'point' method), calculate:

(a) The price elasticity of demand (PED) of the products in relation to the price changes given
(b) The effect of the change in price on total revenue, if demand is met in full at both the old and the new prices.

Answer

(a) Product A

At price $5:

Change in quantity $\quad \dfrac{300}{1,700} = 17.7\%$

Change in price $\quad \dfrac{40c}{\$5} = 8\%$

PED $= -\dfrac{17.7\%}{8\%} = -2.2$. (Ignoring the minus sign = 2.2, and so > 1.)

Demand is elastic and a fall in price should result in a greater than proportional increase in quantity demanded, meaning that total revenue will rise.

	$
Revenue at old price of $5 (× 1,700)	8,500
Revenue at new price of $4.60 (× 2,000)	9,200
Increase in total revenue	700

(b) Product B

At price $8:

Change in quantity $\quad \dfrac{500}{9,500} = 5.3\%$

Change in price $\quad \dfrac{50c}{\$8} = 6.25\%$

PED $= -\dfrac{5.3\%}{6.25\%} = -0.85$. (Ignoring the minus sign = 0.85, and so < 1.)

Demand is inelastic and a fall in price should result in a less than proportional increase in quantity demanded. As a result, total revenue will fall following the price reduction.

	$
Revenue at old price of $8 (× 9,500)	76,000
Revenue at new price of $7.50 (× 10,000)	75,000
Fall in total revenue	1,000

6.8 Factors influencing price elasticity of demand for a good

FAST FORWARD

Price elasticity of demand is affected by the **determinants of price elasticity of demand**. It will be reduced by having low **percentage of income** spent on the good, few **substitutes** available, the good being a **necessity** not a luxury, it being a **habitual purchase**, and a **short period of time** having elapsed since the price changed.

6.8.1 Percentage of income spent on the good

If expenditure on a good only constitutes a small proportion of a consumer's income, then a change in the price of that good will not have much impact on the consumer's overall real income. Therefore demand for low price goods (such as safety matches) is likely to be inelastic. By contrast, demand is likely to be elastic for expensive goods.

6.8.2 Availability of substitutes

The more substitutes there are for a good, especially close substitutes, the more elastic the price elasticity of demand for the good will be. For example, the elasticity of demand for a particular brand of breakfast cereal will be much greater than the elasticity of demand for breakfast cereals as a whole, because the former have both more, and also closer, substitutes. A rise in the price of a particular brand of cereal is likely to result in customers switching their demand to a rival brand. **Availability of substitutes is probably the most important influence on price elasticity of demand.**

6.8.3 Definition of the market

If a market is narrowly defined (for example, breakfast cereals) there will be a number of competing brands and substitute products available so these brands will be price elastic. If a market is only broadly defined (for example, food) there will be fewer generic alternatives and so demand will tend to be inelastic.

This links to the point, above, about availability of substitutes.

6.8.4 Necessity

Demand for goods which are necessary for everyday life (for example, basic foodstuffs) tends to be relatively inelastic while demand for luxury goods tends to be elastic. If a good is a luxury and its price rises, the rational consumer may well decide he or she no longer needs that good and so demand for it will fall. However, if a good is a necessity, the consumer will have to continue buying it even though its price has increased.

6.8.5 The time horizon

If the price of a good is increased, there might initially be little change in demand because the consumer may not be fully aware of the increase, or may not have found a suitable substitute for the product. Then, as consumers adjust their buying habits in response to the price increase, demand might fall substantially. The time horizon influences elasticity largely because the longer the period of time which we consider, the greater the **knowledge** of substitution possibilities by consumers and the **provision** of substitutes by producers. Therefore, elasticity tends to increase as the time period increases.

6.8.6 Competitor pricing

If the response of competitors to a price increase by one firm is to keep their prices unchanged, the firm raising its prices is likely to face elastic demand for its goods at higher prices. If the response of competitors to a reduction in price by one firm is to match the price reduction themselves, the firm is likely to face inelastic demand at lower prices. This is a situation which faces many large firms with one or two major competitors. We will look at this situation in more detail later in this Study Text when we consider the characteristics of oligopolies.

6.8.7 Habit-forming

Goods which are habit-forming tend to be inelastic, because the consumer 'needs' the goods despite their increase in price. This pattern can be seen with addictive products such as cigarettes or alcohol (which again explains why these products are seen as lucrative targets for indirect taxation.)

6.9 Further elasticities of demand

6.9.1 Income elasticity of demand

It is possible to construct other elasticity measures, and an important one which you need to know about is the income elasticity of demand. The income elasticity of demand for a good indicates the responsiveness of demand to changes in household incomes.

Income elasticity of demand = % change in quantity demanded / % change in household income

(a) Demand for a good is **income elastic** if income elasticity is greater than 1. This means that quantity demanded rises by a larger percentage than the rise in income. For example, if the demand for high definition televisions rises by 10% following a rise in household income of 7%, we would say that the demand for high definition televisions is income elastic.

(b) Demand for a good is **income inelastic** if income elasticity is between 0 and 1. This means that the quantity demanded rises less than proportionally to the increase in income. For example, if the demand for books rises by 6% following an increase in household income of 10%, we would say that the demand for books is income inelastic.

Goods whose demand is income elastic or income inelastic are said to be **normal goods**, which means that demand for them will rise when household income rises, and so they have a positive income elasticity of demand. If income elasticity is less than 0, income elasticity is negative and the goody is said to be an **inferior good** since demand for it falls as income rises.

For most goods, an increase in income will lead to an increase in demand. However, the exact effect on demand will depend on the type of product. For example, the demand for some products like bread will not increase much as income rises. Therefore, bread has a low income elasticity of demand. In contrast, the demand for luxuries increases rapidly as income rises. Therefore luxury goods are likely to have a high income elasticity of demand.

6.9.2 Cross elasticity of demand

Cross elasticity of demand refers to the responsiveness of demand for one good to changes in the price of another good.

Cross elasticity of demand = % change in quantity of good A demanded* / % change in the price of good B

*(given no change in the price of A)

The cross elasticity of demand depends on the degree to which goods are substitutes or complements.

(a) If the two goods are **substitutes**, cross elasticity will be **positive**, since a fall in the price of one will reduce the amount demanded of the other.

(b) If the goods are **complements**, cross elasticity will be **negative**, since a fall in the price of one will increase demand for the other.

Cross elasticity involves a comparison between two products. Cross elasticity is significant where the two goods are close substitutes for each other, so that a rise in the price of foreign holidays, for example, is likely to result in an increase in the demand for domestic holidays. The cross elasticity of demand between two complementary products can also be significant because, for example, a rise in the price of beef burgers would result in some fall in demand for bread buns (to put the burgers in) because of the underlying fall in demand for the burgers. The concept of cross elasticity is a useful one in the context of considering substitutes and complementary products.

7 Elasticity of supply

7.1 Price elasticity of supply

FAST FORWARD

The **price elasticity of supply** indicates the responsiveness of supply to a change in price.
Price elasticity of supply refects the willingness and ability of firms to increase output as price rises.

Formula to learn

$$\text{Elasticity of supply} = \frac{\%\text{ change in quantity supplied}}{\%\text{ change in price}}$$

Where the supply of goods is **fixed** whatever price is offered, for example in the case of antiques, vintage wines and land, supply is **perfectly inelastic** and the elasticity of supply is **zero. The supply curve is a vertical straight line.**

Where the supply of goods **varies proportionately** with the price, **elasticity of supply equals one** and the supply curve is a straight line **passing through the origin**. (Note that a demand curve with unit elasticity along all of its length is **not** a straight line, but a supply curve with unit elasticity **is** a straight line.)

Where the producers will **supply any amount at a given price** but none at all at a slightly lower price, elasticity of supply is infinite, or **perfectly elastic. The supply curve is a horizontal straight line.**

Perfectly inelastic supply, unit elastic supply and perfectly elastic supply are illustrated in Figure 15.

Figure 15 Elasticity of supply (i)

FAST FORWARD

The values of price elasticity of supply vary between zero and infinity. A value of zero denotes a situation of **perfectly price inelastic supply** in which supply is fixed and cannot be increased as price rises. A value of infinity denotes **infinitely (or perfectly) price elastic supply.**

Note that a supply curve with unit elasticity can have many different gradients. The key feature that identifies unitary elasticity is not the gradient of the curve, but the fact that it passes through the origin.

Supply is **elastic** (greater than 1) when the percentage change in the amount producers want to supply is greater than proportional to the percentage change in price.

Supply is **inelastic** (less than 1) when the amount producers want to supply changes by a smaller percentage than the percentage change in price.

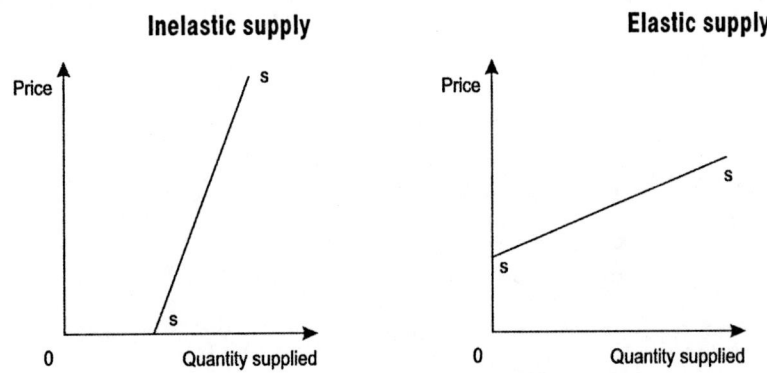

Figure 16 Elasticity of supply (ii)

Note: If the supply curve 'cuts' across the quantity supplied axis, supply is inelastic (< 1). If the supply curve 'cuts' across the price axis, supply is elastic (> 1).

7.2 Factors affecting elasticity of supply

FAST FORWARD

Price elasticity of supply will be lower, more inelastic, for a price rise if **inventories** of goods to sell are low, if labour or other **factors in short supply**, if there is an absence of spare **production capacity**, if there are **barriers to enty** stopping new firms joining, or if there has only been a **short length of time** since the price rose.

Elasticity of supply is a measure of firms' ability to adjust the quantity of goods they supply in response to a change in price. A firm's ability to adjust the quantity of goods it suppliers depends on a number of factors.

7.2.1 Existence of inventories of finished goods

If a firm has large inventories of finished goods, it can draw on these to increase supply following an increase in the price of the good. So supply will be relatively elastic. Perishability or shelf life are important considerations here though.

7.2.2 Availability of labour

When unemployment is low it may be difficult to find workpeople with the appropriate skills. If a firm is unable to recruit additional staff, this may prevent it from increasing its output, even if it would like to, following an increase in price.

7.2.3 Spare capacity

If a firm has spare capacity (eg machinery which is not being fully utilised) it can quickly and easily increase supply following an increase in price. In this way, spare capacity is likely to increase elasticity of supply.

7.2.4 Availability of raw materials and components

The existence and location of inventories of raw materials and components is important, just as inventories of finished goods are. If a firm has readily available inventories of raw materials, it can use these to increase production following an increase in price.

7.2.5 Barriers to entry

Barriers to entry are covered in more detail later in this Study Text. Here it is sufficient to point out that if firms can move into the market easily and start supplying quickly, elasticity of supply in that market will be increased.

7.2.6 Time scale

This is dealt with in the next paragraph.

7.3 Elasticity of supply and time

As with elasticity of demand, **the elasticity of supply of a product varies according to the time period over which it is measured**. For analytical purposes, four lengths of time period may be considered.

(a) **The market period** is so short that supplies of the commodity in question are limited to existing inventories. In effect, supply is fixed.

(b) **The short run** is a period long enough for supplies of the commodity to be altered by increases or decreases in current output, but not long enough for the fixed equipment (plant, machinery and so on) used in production to be altered. This means that suppliers can increase their output only if they are not already operating at full capacity. However, they could reduce output fairly quickly; for example, through redundancies or laying-off staff.

(c) **The long run** is a period sufficiently long to allow firms' fixed equipment to be altered. There is time to build new factories and machines, and time for old ones to be closed down. New firms can enter the industry in the long run.

(d) **The secular period** is so long that underlying economic factors such as population growth, supplies of raw materials (such as oil) and the general conditions of capital supply may alter. The secular period is ignored by economists except in the theory of economic growth.

In general, supply tends to be **more elastic** in **longer time periods**.

7.4 Response to changes in demand

The price elasticity of supply can be seen, in effect, as a measure of the readiness with which an industry responds following a shift in the demand curve.

Suppose that there is an increase in the demand for restaurant meals in a city, shown by the rightward shift in the demand curve in Figure 17 from D_1 to D_2. The capacity of the industry is limited in the short run by the number of restaurants in operation. The restaurants can be used more **intensively** to a certain extent, and so supply (S_1) is not perfectly inelastic, but there is a limit to this process. As a result, in the short run there is a large increase in the price from P_1 to P_2.

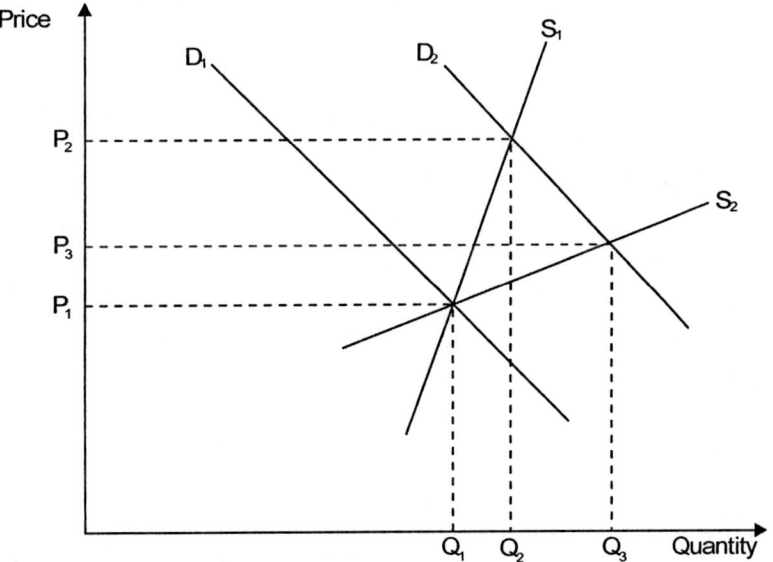

Figure 17 Response to a shift in the demand curve

The rise in price in the **short run** will encourage entrepreneurs to open new restaurants to take advantage of the profits to be earned. In the **long run**, supply is consequently **more elastic** and is shown by supply curve S_2. The expanded output in the industry leads to a new equilibrium at a lower price P_3 with the new level of output being Q_3.

PART B   CONSUMPTION, PRODUCTION AND DISTRIBUTION

Question   Elasticity of supply

Which diagram shows perfectly elastic supply?

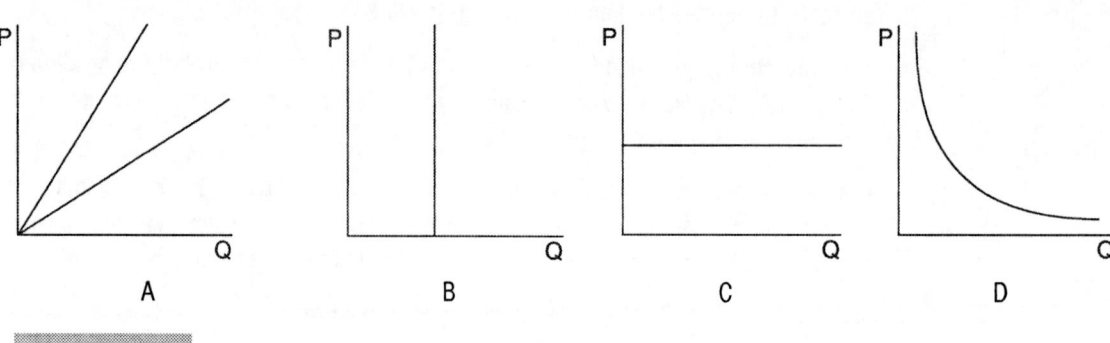

Answer

C   A is unit elastic supply (two examples). B is perfectly inelastic supply (or demand), D is unit elastic demand. C shows perfectly elastic supply.

7.5 Price elasticity of supply at a single point

In the same way that the examiner could ask you to calculate the price elasticity of demand at a specific point on the demand curve, you could also be asked to calculate the price elasticity of supply at a specific point on the supply curve.

In this situation, you can use the gradient of the supply curve to calculate price elasticity of supply (similar to the way you can use the gradient of the demand curve to calculate price elasticity of demand.) Again, if you remember, in Section 4.3 we identified the equation for a straight line supply curve as $Q_S = a + bQ$, meaning that, in effect, the gradient of the curve ('b') represents its elasticity.

Price elasticity of supply (PES) at a specific point on the supply curve is calculated as:

$$PES = \frac{P}{Q} \times \frac{\Delta Q_S}{\Delta P}$$

where p = price at the given point

q = quantity supplied

$\frac{\Delta Q_S}{\Delta P}$ = the gradient of the supply curve

Example: Calculating elasticity of supply at a single point

The supply curve for product can be shown as: $Q_S = 1,200 + 225P$.

The equilibrium price for the product is $3.20 per unit, and the equilibrium quantity is 1,920.

What is the product's price elasticity of supply at the equilibrium point?

Solution

We use the supply curve to find the price elasticity of supply, applying the formula:

$$PES = \frac{P}{Q} \times \frac{\Delta Q_S}{\Delta P}$$

$$= \frac{3.20}{1,920} \times 225$$

$$= 0.375$$

8 Price behaviour in primary markets

8.1 Weather and agricultural output

Agriculture is particularly subject to the influence of the weather. In temperate climates, levels of production can vary quite markedly from year to year. Paradoxically, a good growing season does not usually mean a good trading year for farmers, whilst poor weather can often lead to better trading conditions for them. This is because demand for agricultural produce is quite **inelastic** overall: people's choices of individual foodstuffs are affected by their relative prices, but their total consumption does not vary very much.

Earlier in this chapter we discussed **the effect of a rise in price when demand is inelastic** and we showed that total revenue would rise. This is the situation farmers which find themselves in when harvests generally are bad: the supply curve shifts to the left, with less being offered at any price, so **prices go up**.

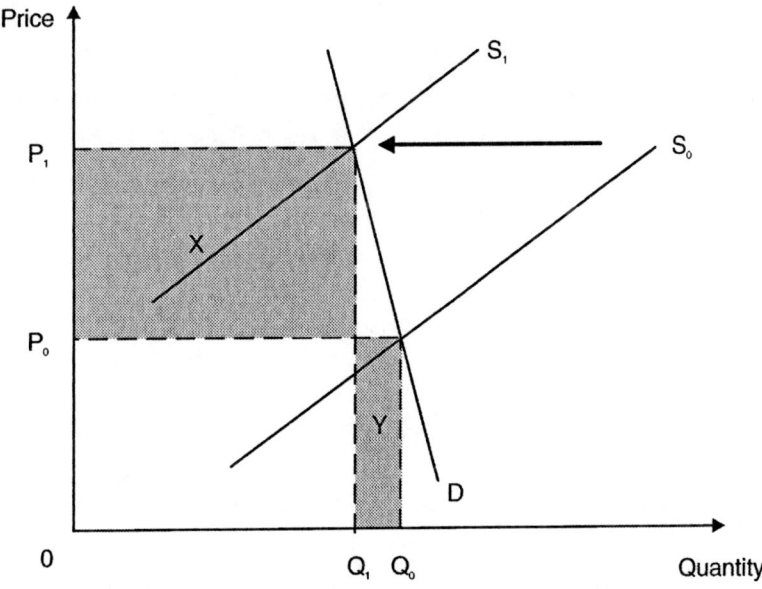

Figure 18 The effect of a poor harvest

Figure 18 shows the effect of the overall shift in the supply curve resulting from a poor harvest. At time 0, supply was at S_0 and price was at P_0. The next harvest was poor and by time 1, the supply curve has shifted to the left (S_1). The quantity sold, Q_1, is not very much reduced below Q_0 because demand is inelastic, but there has been a marked increase in price from P_0 to P_1. Total revenue equal to area Y has been lost, but this is more than compensated for by extra revenue equal to area X.

It is easy to see that in years when harvests are generally good, the opposite effect will be apparent: the supply curve will shift to the right, prices will fall, but the amount of extra units sold will be less than proportional to the fall in price so total revenue will fall.

Ironically, when harvests generally have been good and there is an abundance of supply, farmers find their incomes falling. Conversely, when harvests are poor and prices rise, farmers will have higher incomes. Therefore there is considerable potential for instability and insecurity of supply in agriculture, in that a series of good harvests can lead to lack of investment, exit from the industry and even financial failure among farmers.

To prevent fluctuations in the price of primary products (raw materials), some of the world's main suppliers have formed cartels and developed a system of **buffer stocks**. In this way, they can intervene in the markets and control the open market price at a relatively constant price.

If there are large surpluses of supply over demand which threaten to depress prices, the cartel will buy up the surplus – thereby creating artificial demand and holding up price.

Then if there is a shortage of natural supply onto the market so that prices seem likely to rise, the suppliers can release some of their buffer stock onto the market to stabilise the market.

The buffer stock scheme is an example of a market intervention which helps to stabilise price for both consumers and producers.

8.2 Government response to agricultural price instability

Historically, governments have been willing to intervene in agricultural markets. Such intervention can take several forms, including **direct payments** to producers, **subsidies** for producing particular crops, and **government purchase of surpluses.**

Unfortunately, there are disadvantages to all forms of intervention and there is therefore a strong case to be made against it.

(a) It is extremely difficult to decide the price at which the market should be stabilised.

(b) Intervention has costs, to public funds, to consumers or to both.

(c) Intervention tends to protect inefficient producers against efficient ones and domestic producers against foreign ones: the effects on less-developed countries are particularly harmful.

(d) Purchase of surpluses represents a shift of the demand curve to the right: as a result, production expands, tending to produce very large surpluses. The EU has a bad record for dumping its surpluses on the world market, further depressing the prospects of producers in less developed countries.

8.2.1 Common Agricultural Policy

The Common Agricultural Policy (CAP) established by the European Union is an example of a **buffer stock system**, combined with an **external tariff**.

The external tariff protects European farmers from foreign competition, while the EU sets target prices for farm produce to **guarantee a minimum price** for the farmers. If market forces dictate that the market price will be less than the target at any given level of supply, the EU intervenes and buys up the excess output to guarantee the target price is achieved.

The **target price** (in effect, the minimum price) is set above the world market price, with the result that higher quantities are supplied than would be the case under market forces.

CAP gives European farmers the benefit of a stable, higher prices for their produce than they would achieve in the free market. But this also created the now infamous 'wine lakes' and 'butter mountains' in the 1980s, because the amounts being supplied were greater than the market demands at the target price. The EU has attempted to control the excess by imposing quotas to restrict the amounts farmers can produce, and introducing **set-aside** conditions – actually paying farmers who would normally grow crops on their land not to use that land for any agricultural purposes.

While the CAP benefits European farmers, it is disadvantageous to consumers who have to pay a price above the free market price, as figure 19 illustrates.

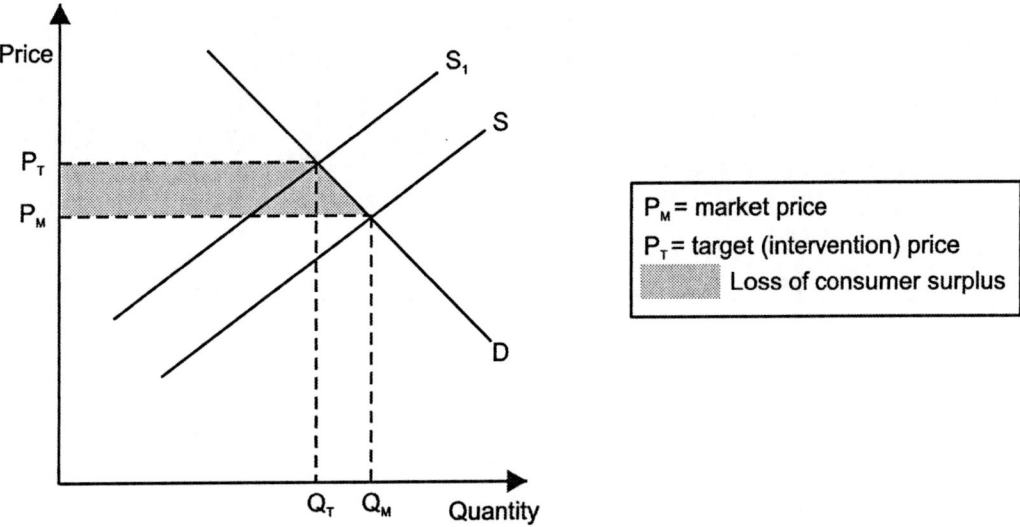

Figure 19 Common Agricultural Policy and price intervention

(Note: **Consumer surplus** is the difference between the value consumer would be prepared to pay for a good and what they actually have to pay for it.)

9 Maximum and minimum prices

9.1 Price regulation

The regulation of prices provides an illustration of how demand and supply analysis can be applied. Governments might try to control prices in two ways.

(a) They might set a **maximum price** (or **price ceiling**) for a good, perhaps as part of an anti-inflationary economic policy.

(b) They might set a **minimum price** (or **price floor**) for a good. The EU Common Agricultural Policy (CAP) is an example of a price floor, designed to ensure that farmers receive at least the minimum prices for their produce.

FAST FORWARD

Where **maximum prices** are imposed, there will be excess demand: rationing may be necessary, and black marketeers may seek to operate. Where **minimum prices** are imposed, producers will make excess supply.

9.2 Maximum prices

The government may try to prevent prices of goods rising by establishing a price ceiling **below** the equilibrium price. (Note: the price ceiling has to be below the equilibrium price. If the price ceiling is higher than the equilibrium price, a price ceiling will have no effect on the operation of market forces. Make sure that you understand why this is so.)

If the maximum price, M, is lower than the equilibrium price would be, there will be an excess of demand over supply (Figure 20). The low price attracts customers, but deters suppliers. Because the price ceiling is below the equilibrium price, P, the amount producers will be prepared to supply to the market falls, from Q to A. However, the quantity demanded will increase from Q to B, because of the lower price. The excess quantity demanded is AB.

Because the market is now in disequilibrium, the limited supply has to be allocated by a means other than price.

To prevent an unfair allocation of the units of the good that are available, the government might have to introduce **rationing** or a **waiting list** (as for state housing). However, the imposition of maximum prices can also lead to the emergence of black markets. Rationing and **black marketers** tend to go together. In Figure 20 consumers demand quantity B but can only get A. However, for quantity A they are prepared to pay price Z, which is well above the official price, M. The black marketers step in to exploit the gap. The commodity may be sold on ration at the official price M, but black marketers may sell illicit production at price Z.

Note also that maximum prices can lead to a misallocation of resources. Producers will reduce output of the products subject to price controls because they are now relatively less profitable to produce than those products which are not subject to price controls.

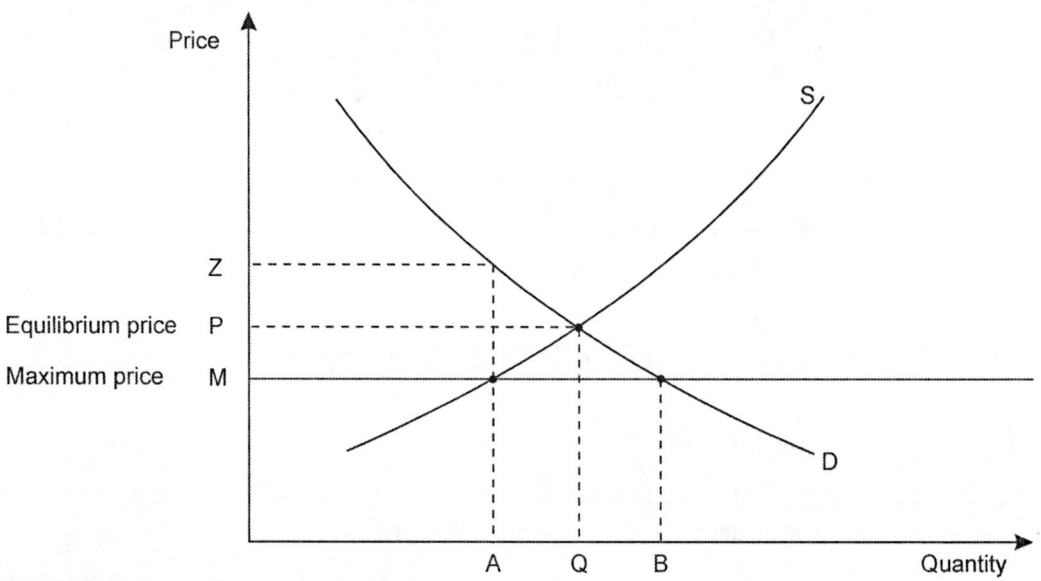

Figure 20 Maximum price below equilibrium price

Equilibrium

Supply of and demand for good Q are initially in equilibrium as shown in the diagram below.

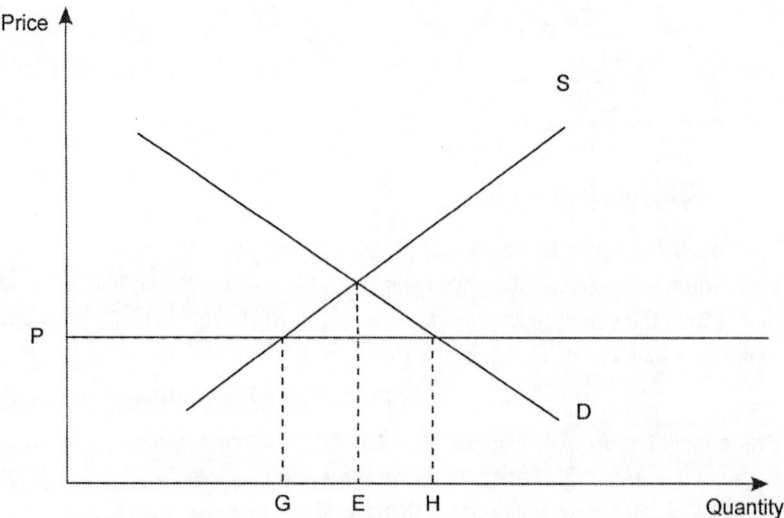

The government introduces a maximum price P. What effect will this have on the quantity of good Q purchased?

A   It will rise from G to E
B   It will rise from E to H
C   It will fall from H to G
D   It will fall from E to G

Answer

D   The initial equilibrium quantity is E (where the supply and demand curves intersect). Quantity demanded at the controlled price P will be H. However, only quantity G will be supplied and purchases will therefore be limited to this amount. Therefore, the quantity purchased will fall from E to G due to the shortage of supply available.

9.3 Minimum prices

Minimum price legislation aims to ensure that suppliers earn a guaranteed minimum price (or floor price) for each unit of output they sell.

If the minimum price is set below the market equilibrium there is no effect. But if it is set above the market price, it will cause an excess supply (see surplus 'AB' in Figure 21). As we mentioned earlier, this was a major problem with the Common Agricultural Policy (CAP) in the 1980s, where minimum prices – guaranteed by agricultural subsidies – resulted in surplus production, and the creation of the so-called 'butter mountains' and 'wine lakes.'

In Figure 21, the minimum price, Z, is set above the equilibrium price, P. As a result, the quantity demanded falls from Q to A but the quantity supplied increases to B because the higher price encourages suppliers to supply more. There is excess supply equal to the quantity AB. As such, the floor price leads to a misallocation of resources.

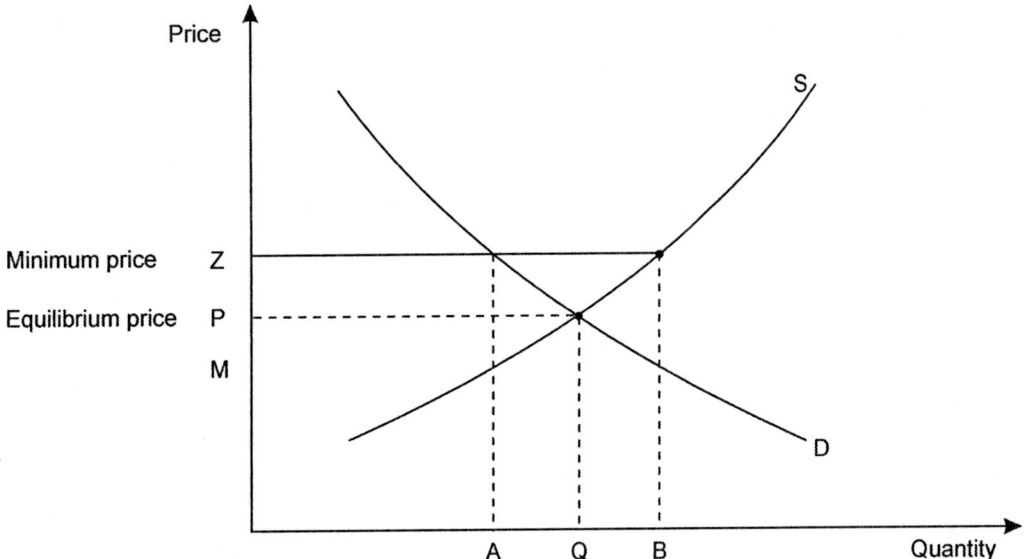

Figure 21 Minimum price above equilibrium price

To try to prevent over-supply and 'dumping' of excess supply at low prices, a system of **production quotas** might be introduced whereby each supplier is only allowed to produce up to a maximum quantity and no more.

9.3.1 Minimum wages

As well as being applied to goods or services, minimum prices can also be applied to labour – through minimum wage legislation.

Introducing a statutory minimum wage is likely to have two main effects:

(a) **Increases pay of workers.** If the minimum wage is higher than the current market price, then workers will receive a higher price for supplying their labour (ie their wages will increase).

(b) **Create a surplus of labour (unemployment).** As in Figure 21 above, imposing a minimum wage, higher than the equilibrium wage, will lead to an increase in supply of labour but a reduction in demand for labour. This will lead to an excess supply of labour: unemployment.

If Figure 21 related to the introduction of a minimum wage, the overall excess supply of labour would be represented by B to A. However, the increase in unemployment caused by the minimium wage itself is only Q – A (because the equilibrium point prior to the minimum wage was Q).

In practice, this situation may lead to informal arrangements whereby workers agree to work for less than the minimum wage.

10 Market failure

> **FAST FORWARD**
>
> **Market failure** occurs when a free market mechanism fails to produce the most efficient allocation of scarce resources.

Remember, the idea of how resources are used lies at the heart of economics. The central economic problem is how scarce resources should be allocated in order to satisfy human wants and needs. Therefore, market failure – and the inefficient allocation of resources – is also a very important issue, because it means these human wants and needs are not being met as efficiently as they could be.

Market failure is caused by a number of factors.

- Imperfections in a market
- Immobility of factors of production – for example: (i) occupational immobility, where there are barriers preventing people moving between different jobs or different industries; (ii) geographical immobility, where there are barriers preventing people moving to different locations
- Divergence between private costs and social costs (**externalities**)
- The need to provide public goods
- The need to consider non-market goals, such as the consumption of merit goods

10.1 Market imperfections

The following are examples of market imperfections.

(a) If a monopoly firm controls a market, it might prevent other firms from entering the market (for example by claiming patent rights, or launching a strong marketing campaign with the intention of keeping customers away from the new firms). By restricting supply in this way, the monopolist may keep prices higher than they would be in a competitive market. (We will look at monopolies in more detail in a later chapter.)

(b) Just as monopolies are firms which dominate supply to a market, **monopsony buyers** are large individual buyers who dominate demand in a market. **Monopsonists** may exert control over the market, exacting low prices or other favourable conditions from suppliers.

(c) Consumers may make bad purchasing decisions because they do not have complete and accurate information ('perfect information') about all goods and services that are available.

(d) It takes time for the price mechanism to work. Firms cannot suddenly enter a new market or shut down operations. The slow response of the price mechanism to changes in demand creates some short term inefficiency in resource allocation.

11 Externalities and government intervention

Key terms

- **Market failure**: the failure of a market to produce a satisfactory allocation of scarce resources.
- **Social costs**: the total costs to society as a whole of using economic resources.
- **Social benefits**: the total gains to society as a whole flowing from an economic decision.
- **Public goods**: goods which cannot be provided privately because if they are, everyone will benefit from them; regardless of whether they have paid for them or not. As a result, individuals would have no incentive to pay for these goods.
- **Merit goods**: goods which need to be provided in the long-term public interest, but which would be under-provided by the market mechanism.

11.1 Social costs and private costs

In a free market, decisions taken by firms and households about how much to supply and how much to consume are determined by their own private benefits. In turn, these decisions determine how the economy's scarce resources will be allocated to production and consumption. Therefore, in a free market, private costs and private benefits determine which goods are made and bought, and in what quantities.

However, these private costs and benefits are not necessarily the same as the social costs and benefits from using the resources (ie the costs and benefits to **society as a whole**).

- **Private cost** measures the cost **to a firm** of the resources it uses to produce a good.
- **Social cost** measures the cost **to society as a whole** of the resources that a firm uses.
- **Private benefit** measures the benefit obtained directly by a supplier or by a consumer from a transaction.
- **Social benefit** measures the total benefit to society from a transaction.

It can be argued that a free market system would result in a satisfactory allocation of resources, **provided that** private costs are the same as social costs and private benefits are the same as social benefits. In this situation, suppliers will maximise profits by supplying goods and services that benefit customers, and that customers want to buy. By producing their goods and services, suppliers are giving benefit to both themselves and the community.

However, there are other possibilities.

(a) Members of the economy (suppliers or households) may do things which give benefit to others, but yield no reward to themselves.

(b) Members of the economy may do things which are harmful to others, but which have no cost to themselves.

When private benefit is **not** the same as social benefit, or when private cost is **not** the same as social cost, an allocation of resources which only reflects private costs and benefits **may not be socially acceptable** or desirable.

Here are some examples of situations where **private cost** and **social cost** differ.

(a) A firm produces a good and, during the production process, pollution is discharged into the air. The private cost to the firm is the cost of the resources needed to make the good. The social cost consists of the private cost plus the additional 'costs' incurred by other members of society, who suffer from the pollution.

(b) The private cost of transporting goods by road is the cost to the haulage firm of the resources to provide the transport. The social cost of road haulage would consist of the private cost plus the cost of repairs and maintenance of the road system (which sustains serious damage from heavy goods vehicles) plus any environmental costs, such as harm to wildlife habitats from road building or pollution emitted by the transport lorries.

11.2 Private benefit and social benefit

Here are some examples of situations where **private benefit** and **social benefit** differ.

(a) Customers at an open air café benefit from the entertainment provided by professional musicians, who are hired by the café. The customers of the café are paying for the service in the prices they pay, and they obtain a private benefit from it. At the same time, other people passing by, who are not customers of the café, might stop and listen to the music. They will obtain a benefit, but at no cost to themselves. They are **free riders**, taking advantage of the service without contributing to its cost. The social benefit from the musicians' service is greater than the private benefit to the café's customers.

(b) Suppose that a large firm pays for the training of employees as accountants, expecting a certain proportion of these employees to leave the firm in search of a better job once they have qualified. The private benefits to the firm are the benefits of the training of those employees who continue to work for it. The total social benefit includes the enhanced economic output resulting from the training of those employees who go on to work for other firms.

11.3 Externalities

FAST FORWARD

> **Externalities** are the spill-over effects of a transaction which extend beyond the parties to the transaction and affect society as a whole. In other words, externalities are the differences between the **private** and the **social** costs, or benefits, arising from an activity.

An 'externality' is a cost or benefit which the market mechanism fails to take into account, because the market responds purely to private signals.

So far we have looked at the price mechanism as being driven purely by the costs and benefits accruing to the parties to the transaction. However, if pricing policy is to maximise **net social benefit** then it also needs to include externalities when calculating costs.

We can use demand and supply analysis to illustrate the consequences of externalities. If an adverse externality exists, (the social cost of supplying a good is greater than the private cost to the supplier firm), then a supply curve which reflects total social costs will be above the (private cost) market supply curve.

Figure 22 shows two possibilities.

(a) If a free market exists, the amount of the good produced will be determined by the interaction of demand (curve D) and supply curve S. Here, output would be Y, at price P_y.

(b) If social costs are taken into account, and the market operates successfully, the supply curve should shift leftwards, and the amount of the good produced should be X, at price P_x.

As we will see in detail in a later chapter, the profit maximising level of production for a firm (and therefore the level of production a firm will aim for) is that where marginal cost equals marginal revenue. Marginal cost is the increase in total cost which results from producing one extra unit of output. Marginal revenue is the increase in total revenue which results from selling one extra unit of a good.

If a firm's private costs are adjusted to take account of social costs, its optimum level of production will still occur when MC = MR, but now marginal cost also includes the cost to society of producing an extra unit of output. This is the concept of **social marginal costs**.

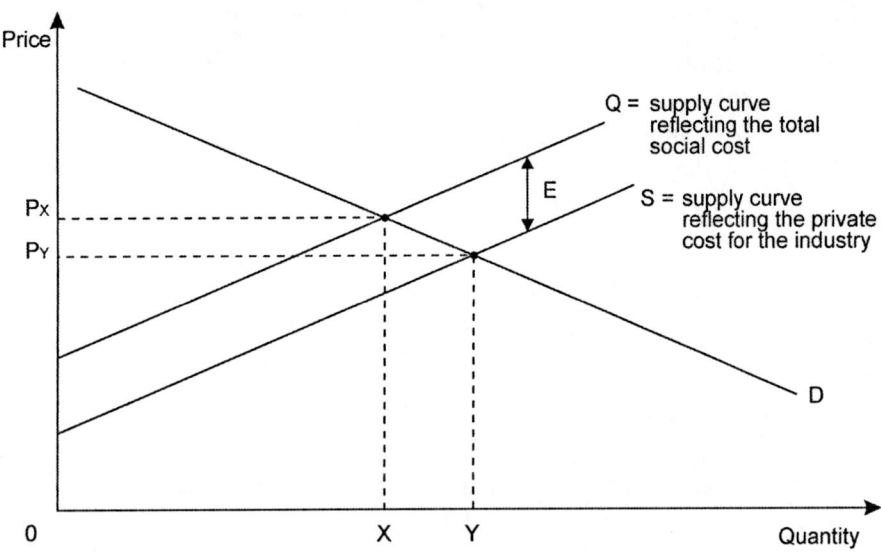

Figure 22 Externalities

Given a free market, output of the good will exceed what it ideally should be (by Y – X in Figure 22 above), and so resources will have been over-allocated to production of this particular good.

11.4 Public goods

Attention!

> Some goods, by their very nature, involve so much 'spill-over' of externalities that they are difficult to provide except as **public goods** whose production is organised by the government.

In the case of public goods, the consumption of the good (or service) by one individual or group **does not significantly reduce the amount available for others**. Furthermore, it is often difficult or impossible to **exclude** anyone from its benefits, once the good has been provided. In other words, the good is **non-exclusive**. As a result, in a free market, individuals benefiting from the good would have no economic incentive to pay for them, since they might as well be **free riders**, enjoying the benefits of the good while others pay for it.

National defence is perhaps the most obvious examples of a public good. It is clearly not practicable for individuals to buy their own defence systems. Equally, if some people paid for the service, they couldn't stop others who hadn't paid for it from benefiting from it. Hence the government provides defence at zero price at the point of consumption, although taxpayers indirectly fund its provision through their tax payments. Street lighting and policing are sometimes cited as other examples of public goods, although the growth of private security firms in the private sector illustrates how some areas of policing are now becoming privatised.

11.5 Merit goods

The existence of market failure and of externalities suggests the need for intervention in markets by the government, in order to improve the allocation of resources. Another possible reason for intervention is to **increase** the consumption of **merit goods**.

Attention!

> **Merit goods** are considered to be worth providing to everyone irrespective of whether everyone can afford to pay for them, because their consumption is in the long-term public interest. Education is one of the chief examples of a merit good; health services are another.

Merit goods are different from public goods in that they are **divisible**. For example, some consumers possess the means to buy merit goods, such as education and healthcare, and they are willing to do so. However, while the people who choose to pay for the good will benefit from it, in doing so they will use up the supply of the good, so that free riders cannot also benefit from it.

Although national governments provide a service of merit goods in the interests of the nation's well-being, the private sector provides an alternative supply of them – for example, in the UK there are private schools, and private health care schemes which consumers pay to use. However, what distinguishes a merit good from a public good is that where people have elected for a private supply the benefit is restricted to them. Thus only people who pay for private schools or private health care will benefit from them.

Because merit goods provided by the state are offered on a large scale, governments can achieve economies of scale in their provision. Governments also provide merit goods (such as education and health) because it is in the nation's interests as a whole that such things are provided.

On the other hand, many governments want to see less consumption of certain **demerit goods**, such as tobacco.

Apart from providing public goods and merit goods, a government might choose to intervene in the workings of markets by other methods.

(a) **Controlling the means of production** (for example, through state ownership of industries)

(b) **Influencing markets** through legislation and regulation (regulation of monopolies, bans on dangerous drugs, enforcement of the use of some goods such as car seat belts, laws on pollution control and so on) or by persuasion (for example, using anti-tobacco advertising)

(c) **Redistributing wealth**, perhaps by taxing relatively wealthy members of society and redistributing this tax income so as to benefit the poorer members

(d) **Influencing market supply and demand** through:

   (i) Price legislation
   (ii) Indirect taxation
   (iii) Subsidies

(e) **Creating a demand for output that creates employment**. A free market system would match supply with demand. Demand would thus lead to **employment** because of the needs of suppliers, but the level of demand might not be high enough to ensure **full employment**. Governments might therefore wish to intervene to create a demand for output in order to create more jobs.

Some externalities, particularly the problems of pollution and the environment, appear to call for co-operation between governments. The Kyoto Protocol adopted in 1997, aimed to stabilise the levels of greenhouse gases in the atmosphere to control the threat of global warming.

Example: Externalities

An industrial company alters its production methods to reduce the amount of waste discharged from its factory into the local river. What will be the effect (increase or decrease) on:

(a) Private costs
(b) External benefits

Solution

(a) Private costs of the company will presumably increase: the anti-pollution measures will have involved a financial outlay. (However, if the changes to the company's production methods mean they become more efficient generally, in the longer term the change could help to reduce the company's costs as a result of this increased efficiency.)

(b) External benefits will presumably increase: the public will benefit from a cleaner river.

11.6 Pollution policy

One area which is often discussed in relation to externalities is that of pollution. If polluters take little or no account of their actions on others, this generally results in the output of polluting industries being greater than is optimal for society. If polluters were forced to pay for any externalities they imposed on society, then they would almost certainly reduce production or change their production techniques so as to minimise pollution. Equally, consumers would be likely choose to consume less of those goods which cause pollution because the producers are likely to pass the cost of any changes on to the consumers (by increasing the price of the goods.)

One solution to reflect the social cost of polluting activity is to impose a tax on polluters equal to the cost of removing the effect of the externality they generate. This is called the **'polluter pays' principle**. This approach is generally held to be preferable to regulation, as regulation can be difficult to enforce and provides less incentive to reduce pollution levels permanently.

Examples of polluter pays (also known as extended polluter responsibility (EPR)) include:

(a) Taxation of airports for the noise and pollution caused by jets during take-off and landing

(b) Requirements for firms producing, using and selling packaging such as wood, and paper, and plastic to demonstrate that they have paid for the reclaiming and recycling of an equivalent quantity during the year

(c) Requirements that manufacturers of electronic goods and cars have facilities for their goods to be reclaimed and recycled at their end of lifecycle

Apart from the imposition of a tax, there are a number of other measures open to governments in attempting to reduce pollution. One of the main measures available is the application of subsidies which may be used either to persuade polluters to reduce output and hence pollution, or to provide financial assistance towards expenditure on production processes (such as new machinery and air cleaning equipment) which reduce levels of pollution.

A problem with using subsidies is that, unlike taxes, they do not provide an incentive to reduce pollution any further. Indeed, profits are increased under subsidies which may have the perverse effect of encouraging more pollution to be generated in order to qualify for a subsidy. In addition, this is likely to be an expensive option for governments, whereas imposing a tax actually provides them with additional revenue. We look at subsidies in more detail in the next section.

Two other options which could be considered to help deal with externalities are:

Government regulation	Governments could set limits for the maximum permitted levels of emissions, or for minimum levels of environmental quality. Firms which breach these limits could then be fined.
Tradable permits	Maximum permitted levels are set for specific pollutants and a firm (or country) is given a permit to emit up to that level of pollution. If the firm (or country) emits below its limit, it is given a credit for the difference which it can then sell to a firm (or country) which needs to go above its permitted levels.
	Tradable permits are used in relation to carbon dioxide emissions, with the result that firms can now engage in **carbon trading**.

PART B CONSUMPTION, PRODUCTION AND DISTRIBUTION

12 Indirect taxes and subsidies

12.1 Indirect taxes

FAST FORWARD

Indirect taxes are levied on expenditure on goods or services as opposed to direct taxation which is applied to incomes. A **selective** indirect tax is imposed on some goods but not on others (or is imposed at a higher rate on some goods than on others).

We looked at the effects of one form of government intervention in markets – price regulation – earlier. An alternative form of price and output regulation is **indirect taxation**.

Indirect taxation may be used to improve the **allocation of resources** when there are damaging externalities.

If an indirect tax is imposed on a good, the tax will shift the supply curve **upwards** (leftwards) by the amount the tax adds to the price of each item. This is because although the price to **consumers** includes the tax, the revenue the suppliers receive is only the **net-of-tax price**. For example, in Figure 23:

(a) The supply curve without any tax is S_0
(b) The supply curve including the cost of the tax is S_1
(c) The tax is equal to $P_1 - P_2$ or the distance A – B.

Before the tax was imposed, quantity supplied and demanded was X_0, but once the tax has been imposed, the equilibrium quantity is only X_1.

At this point (demand = X_1), the price the **consumer pays** is P_1, but the amount that the **supplier receives** is only P_2. $P_1 - P_2$ is the amount of tax payable.

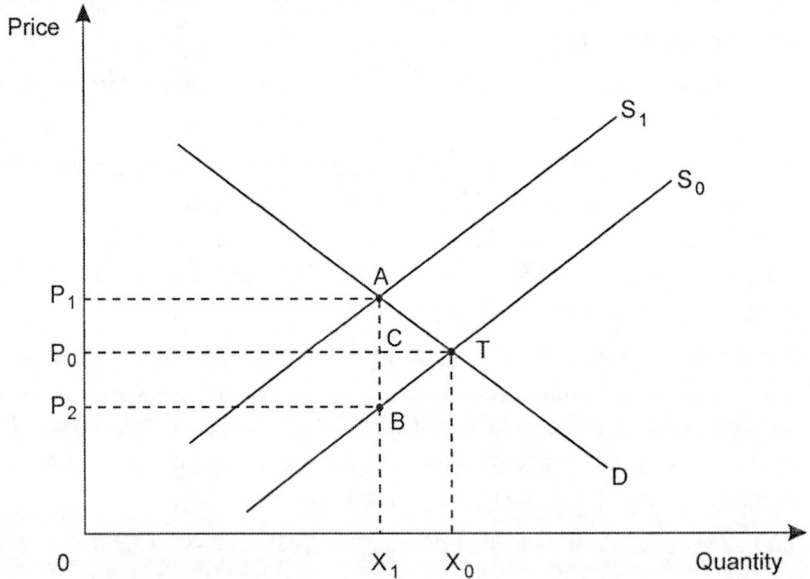

Figure 23 The effect of an indirect tax

Without the tax, output would be X_0 and price P_0. Total expenditure (before the tax was imposed) can be shown by the rectangle OP_0TX_0.

(a) After the tax has been imposed, output falls to X_1 and price with tax rises to P_1. Total expenditure is OP_1AX_1, of which P_2P_1AB is tax revenue and OP_2BX_1 is producers' total revenue.

(b) A new price equilibrium arises at point A.

    (i) Price to the customer has risen from P_0 to P_1.

    (ii) Average revenue received by producers has fallen from P_0 to P_2.

    (iii) The tax burden is **shared** between the producers and consumers, with CB borne by the supplier and AC borne by consumers.

Consumers pay P_0P_1AC of total tax revenue and producers pay P_2P_0CB.

12.2 Elasticity effects

The proportion of the tax which is passed on to the consumer rather than being borne by the supplier depends upon the elasticities of demand and supply in the market.

Figures 24(a) and 24(b) illustrate the extreme cases of perfectly elastic demand and perfectly inelastic demand respectively.

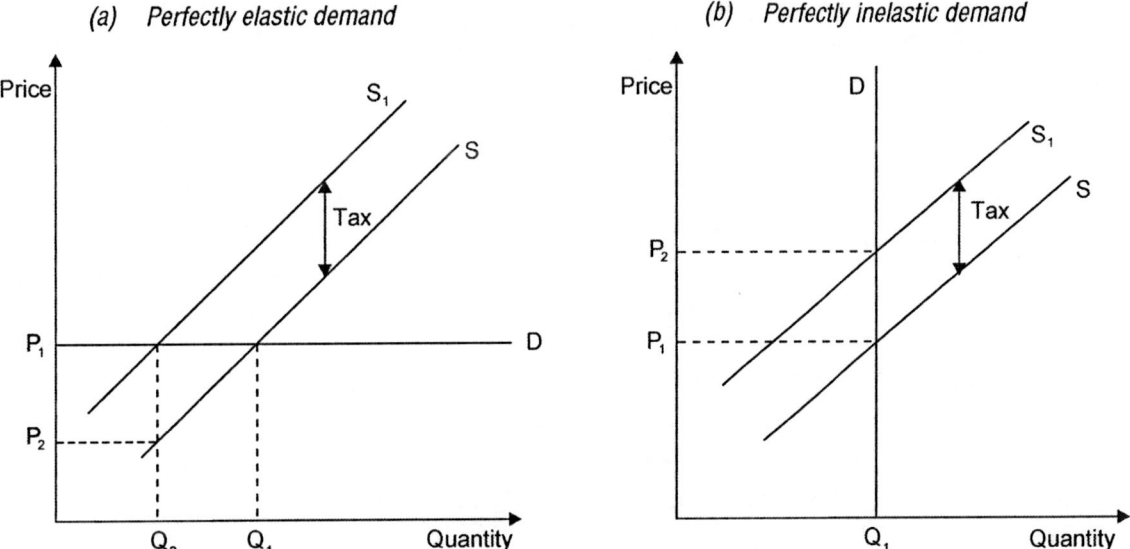

Figure 24 Impact of elasticity of demand on the burden of taxation

Exercise: Burden of taxation

Try to work out yourself (from general principles, or from study of Figure 24) who bears the burden of taxation in each of these extreme cases.

Solution

In Figure 24(a), with perfectly elastic demand, demand falls to zero if the price is raised. Consequently, the supplier must bear the full burden of the tax. In spite of the imposition of the tax, the market price has to remain the same but there is a fall in the quantity supplied from Q_1 to Q_2, following the shift in the supply curve from S to S_1. The supplier only receives P_2 after paying $P_1 - P_2$ in tax.

In the case of perfectly inelastic demand (Figure 24(b)), the supplier can pass on the full amount of the tax to the consumer by increasing the price from P_1 to P_2. Demand is not reduced at all by the increase in price. Because the supplier can charge a higher amount to compensate for the tax payable, the quantity supplied remains unchanged.

The elasticity of supply is also relevant. Figure 25 shows that for a given demand curve, the more inelastic the supply curve, the greater the proportion of the tax that is borne by the supplier.

(a) Figure 25(a) shows a relatively inelastic supply curve (S). Imposition of the tax shifts the supply curve upwards to S_1 and the equilibrium price rises from P_1 to P_2. The price to the consumer rises by AB per unit, while the net revenue received by the producer falls by BC per unit. Thus, the greater tax burden is borne by the supplier (because the distance BC is greater than the distance AB).

(b) By contrast, Figure 25(b) shows a relatively elastic supply curve S. With the imposition of the tax, the supply curve shifts to S_1 and the equilibrium price rises to P_2. The price to the consumer rises by AB per unit, and the net revenue received by the producer falls by BC per unit. The greater tax burden is borne by the consumer (because AB is greater than BC).

So, Figure 25 shows that the consumer bears a greater proportion of the tax burden the more elastic the supply curve is. Figure 25 also shows that, for any given demand curve, the price rise and the fall in the equilibrium quantity will also both be greater when the supply cu

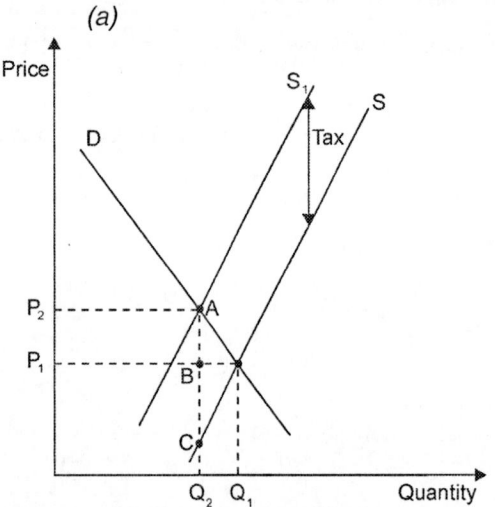
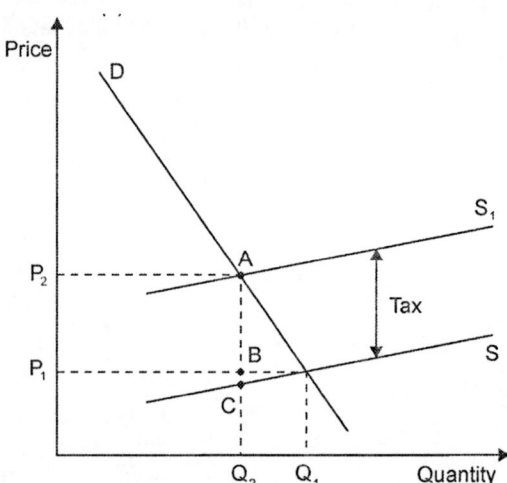

Figure 25 The effect of elasticity illustrated

It is also important to consider the relationship between the elasticity of demand and the elasticity of supply when assessing how the burden of tax will be split between producer and consumer.

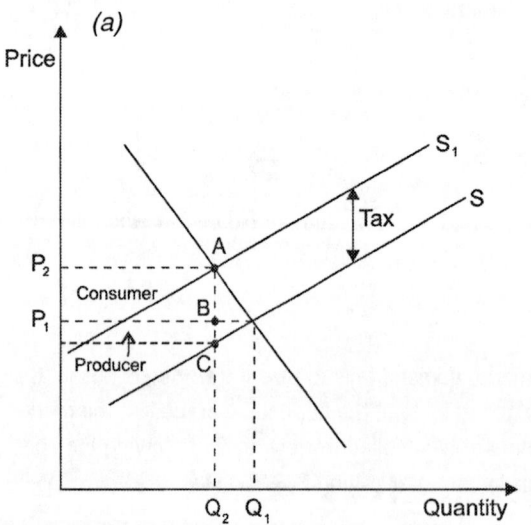
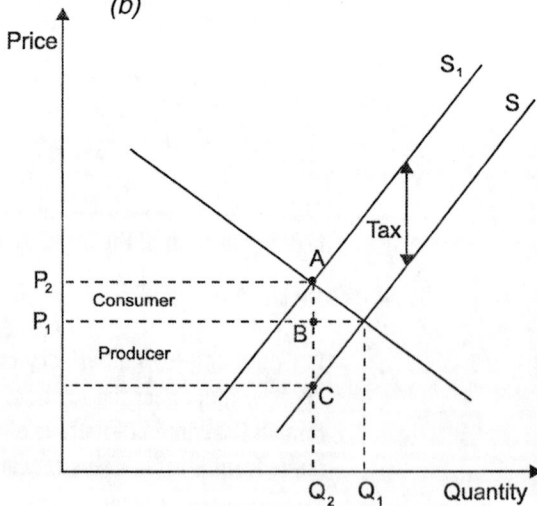

Figure 26 (a) Inelastic demand, elastic supply   Figure 26 (b) Elastic demand, inelastic supply

If demand is less elastic than supply – Figure 26(a) – the consumer will bear the greater proportion of the tax burden.

If demand is more elastic than supply – Figure 26(b) – the producer will bear the greater proportion of the tax burden.

As a final point on this topic, though, be aware that while an indirect tax can help adjust for externalities, it could affect the competiveness of individual firms or industries. **Since such a tax reduces output, it may be harmful to an industry**. For some companies, the reduction in quantities produced may lead to significant rises in the unit costs of production. This could have adverse consequences on the competitive position of the firm, if it competes (either domestically or internationally) with foreign firms which are not subject to the same tax.

12.3 Subsidies

A subsidy is a payment to the supplier of a good by the government. The payment may be made for a variety of reasons:

(a) **To encourage more production of the good**, by offering a further incentive to suppliers

(b) **To keep prices lower for socially desirable goods** whose production the government wishes to encourage

(c) **To protect a vital industry** such as agriculture, when demand in the short term is low and threatening to cause an excessive contraction of the industry.

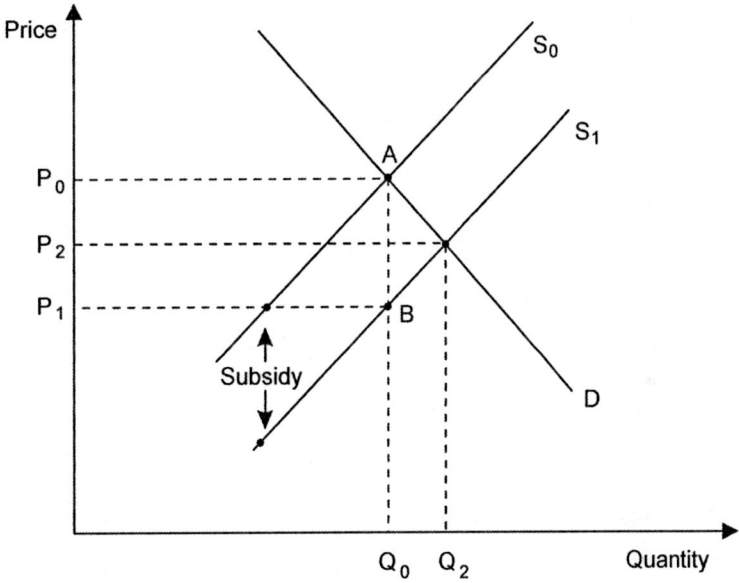

Figure 27 The effect of a subsidy

A subsidy is rather like indirect taxation in reverse.

- In Figure 27, supply curve S_0 indicates what the level of supply would be if no subsidy existed.
- Payment of the subsidy moves the supply curve downwards (outwards) to S_1.

If there were no subsidy, the free market equilibrium price would be P_0, and output would be Q_0. A subsidy per unit equivalent to AB is introduced, such that suppliers would now be willing to produce Q_0 at a lower price (P_1 rather than at P_0). As a result of the outward shift in the supply curve, there will also be a shift in the equilibrium quantity produced – to Q_2, which can be sold on the market for P_2. Thus, the subsidy will have two effects:

- The amount supplied in equilibrium will increase (from Q_0 to Q_2).

- The price will fall (from P_0 to P_2), but the decrease in price will be less than the value of the subsidy itself ($P_0 - P_1$).

Question

Incidence of a subsidy

By reference to Figure 27, analyse the extent to which the benefit of the subsidy falls to:

(a) The consumer
(b) The supplier

Who bears the cost of the subsidy?

Answer

The benefit of the subsidy will be shared between the consumer and the supplier.

(a) Consumers benefit by the lowering of prices from P_0 to P_2.
(b) Suppliers benefit because although they receive a lower price, P_2, they receive the subsidy AB per unit.

The cost of the subsidy is borne by the **government** (in effect, the taxpayer).

13 Consumer behaviour

13.1 The individual's demand curve

> **FAST FORWARD**
>
> **Consumer behaviour theory** seeks to explain the response of demand to changes in price by reference to the rational consumer seeking to **maximise total utility** (or satisfaction) they can obtain from spending their scarce income.

The law of demand states that as price falls, other things remaining constant, the quantity demanded of a product will increase. Consumer behaviour theory seeks to explain this in terms of the decision process of the individual consumer.

Two approaches are used:

(a) **Cardinalist approach**: this describes a measurable thing called **marginal utility** and suggests that consumers balance this marginal utility, the happiness they get from consuming an extra unit of the product, against the price they must pay.

(b) **Ordinalist approach:** this approach abandons the idea of measuring utility, and instead uses **indifference curves** that show how consumers rank alternative combinations products into bundles of greater and lesser **satisfaction**.

13.2 The marginal utility approach to explaining consumer behaviour

> **FAST FORWARD**
>
> **Marginal utility** is defined as the increase in total utility (or consumer happiness) resulting from the consumption of one extra unit of a product.
>
> The **law of diminishing marginal utility** states that: as a consumer's total consumption of a product increases, the marginal utility they obtain from extra units fall continuously and may eventually become negative.

Utility is a 19th century term for 'usefulness' or 'happiness'. This was the era in which Cardinalist economists like Walras sought to measure the enjoyment consumers obtained from consuming goods using 'cardinal' numbers. However, one limitation of the Cardinalist approach has been that, to date, it has not been possible to arrive at a numerical measure of happiness.

The following table summarises the approach of the Cardinalists. It shows the utility that an individual gets from drinking additional cans of soft drink on a hot day. (Assume utility can be measured in Utils.)

Total cans consumed	Total utility of the consumer (Utils)	Marginal utility per can (Utils)
1	10	10
2	15	5
3	17	2
4	17	0
5	14	-3

The first can is very welcome and gives the consumer refreshment and 10 Utils of pleasure. The second can is also welcome and increases the consumers pleasure to 15 Utils. The second can **adds** 5 Utils of pleasure. This extra 5 Utils is the **marginal utility** of the second can.

Having consumed two cans the individual is not really thirsty anymore. The third can has marginal utility of 2 and the consumer really doesn't want the fourth can and so its marginal utility is 0 Utils.

The effect of drinking a fifth can is to reduce the total satisfaction of the individual. Having drunk it they feel bloated and rather ill perhaps. This fifth can has a negative marginal utility: of -3 Utils.

FAST FORWARD

Principle of equi-marginal utility: Cardinalists predict that consumers will allocate their income between products to obtain the same **marginal utiltity per dollar** from each.

Consumers have a limited income, and rational consumers will seek to spend their income in a way which maximises their total utility. They do this by considering the **marginal utility per dollar** they obtain. The following table shows the principle:

	Good A	Good B
Total consumption (Units)	4	3
Price	$20	$40
Marginal utility	10	10
Marginal utility / Price	0.5	0.25

The consumer is currently getting a higher marginal utility per $ from Good A than Good B. If the consumer buys additional units of Good A, by transferring income from buying Good B, they will increase their total utility (happiness).

However, as they buy additional units of Good A the marginal utility they receive from it will fall. At the same time, as they consume less of Good B, the marginal utility of Good B will rise.

Assume that an additional fifth unit of Good A yields 6 Utils, while forgoing a unit of Good B means the marginal utility of the second unit is 12 Utils. The table will appear as follows:

	Good A	Good B
Total consumption (Units)	5	2
Price	$20	$40
Marginal utility	6	12
Marginal utility / Price	0.3	0.3

Here the consumer has achieved **equi-marginal utility**. The utility per $ is the same for both products, meaning that the marginal utility is directly proportional to the price they paid for each product.

If the price of one of the products falls then it will represent better **value for money** because it will provide a higher marginal utility per $. The consumer will buy more of it. The table below shows the effect of a fall in price of Good A, from $20 to $10, and shows the consumer able to enjoy a higher marginal utility per $ from buying extra units of Good A.

	Good A	Good B
Total consumption (Units)	5	2
Price	$10	$40
Marginal utility	6	12
Marginal utility/Price	0.6	0.3

The consumer will buy extra units of Good A and forego units of Good B until they achieve equi-marginal utility once more.

	Good A	Good B
Total consumption (Units)	16	1
Price	$10	$40
Marginal utility	5	20
Marginal utility/Price	0.5	0.5

In a long-winded way, the Cardinalists have shown that the fall in price of Good A has led to a rise in the quantity demanded. The fall in price from $20 to $10 led to a rise in quantity demanded from 5 units to 16 units.

13.3 The indifference curve approach to explaining consumer behaviour

FAST FORWARD

Indifference curves are an Ordinalist approach to explaining consumer behaviour. They show alternative bundles of goods which the consumer can buy which will yield the same satisfaction.

The basis of the Ordinalist approach is the Indifference Map shown in Figure 28:

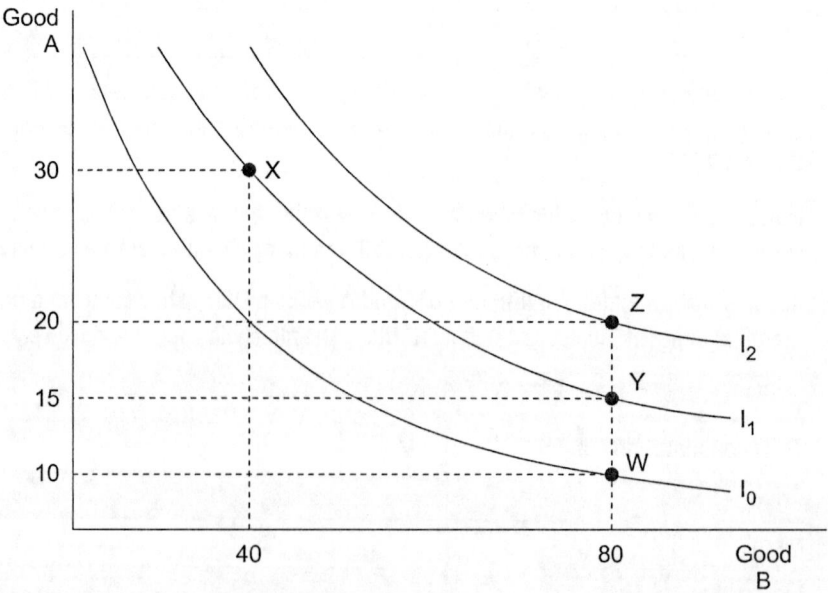

Figure 28 Indifference map

In Figure 28, a consumer presently enjoys 30 units of Good A and 40 units of Good B, as indicated at point X on indifference curve I_1.

Imagine you bargain with this consumer by taking away units of Good A and offering to compensate them with extra units of Good B. You would move them down indifference curve I_1 to point Y where they could enjoy 80 units of Good B and 15 units of Good A. They would only accept the combination at point Y if they were **equally satisfied**; ie, in effect, 40 extra units of Good B is enough to compensate for the loss of 15 units of Good A. However, in such a case, the consumer is said to be **indifferent** between points X and Y – they don't prefer one point over the other.

Starting from point Y

- A move to point X would leave them equally satisfied

- A move to point Z would increase their satisfaction. This is because they could keep consuming 80 units of Good B but also increase consumption of Good A from 15 to 20 units. An assumption of indifference curve analysis is that consumers always prefer more of a good to less of a good.

- A move to point W would reduce their satisfaction. This is because they would still have 80 of Good B but would have to give up 5 units of Good A, because they can now only afford 10 units of Good A.

Therefore indifference curves further to the right indicate higher total satisfaction.

> **FAST FORWARD**
>
> **Budget constraints** are a straight line showing the maximum of each good that can be consumed using the individual's fixed income.

Figure 29 shows the equilibrium of the consumer:

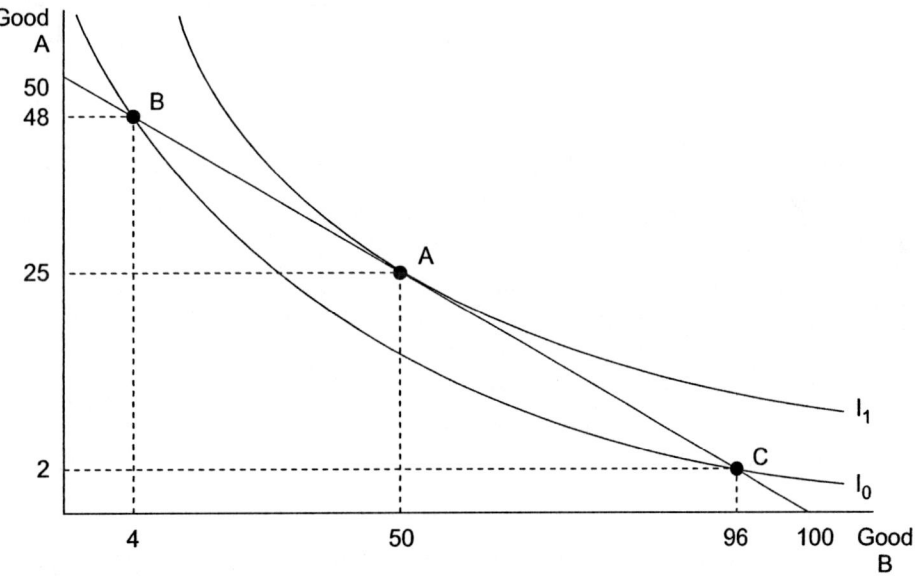

Figure 29 Consumer equilibrium with budget constraint

Assume the consumer has $100 to spend and that Good A costs $2 a unit and Good B costs $1 per unit. In Figure 29 the budget constraint shows that the consumer can buy either 50 units of Good A **or** 100 units of Good B, or combinations of the two goods (say 40 units of A and 20 units of B and so on).

The consumer will be in equilibrium at point A **where the budget constraint is tangential to the highest attainable indifference curve** I_1. Here the consumer is enjoying 25 units of A and 50 units of B, and is spending all their income (25 × $2 + 50 × $1 = $100). Points B and C are also affordable to the consumer but will not be chosen because they are on a lower indifference curve I_0.

13.4 Change in the price of the product

FAST FORWARD

Changing price is shown by a pivot of the budget constraint and will lead a consumer to increase their consumption of a good whose price has fallen.

Figure 30 analyses the effect of a fall in price of Good B. Here the price has fallen from $1 to $0.50 per unit. This is shown as a pivot of the budget constraint to denote that the consumer can now afford to buy a maximum of 200 units of Good B with their $100 income.

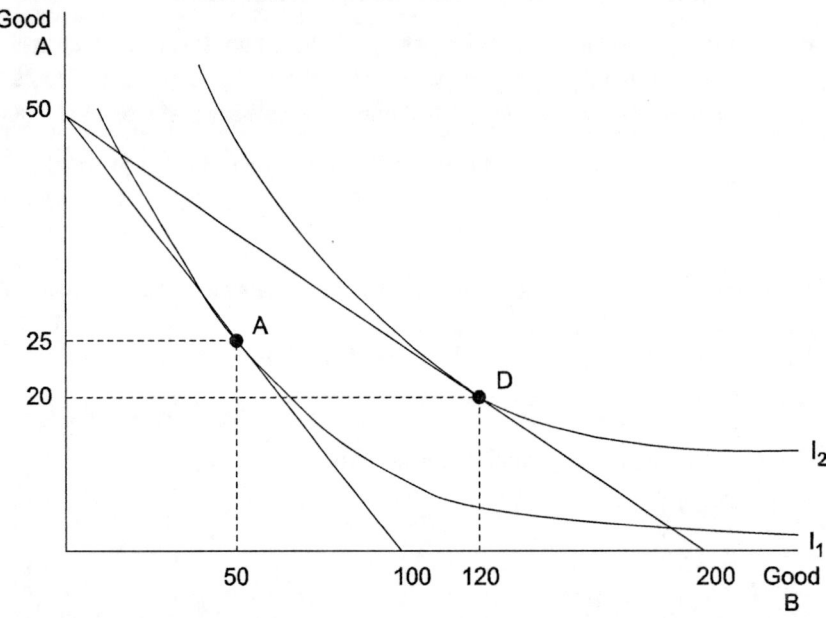

Figure 30 Fall in price of Good B

The fall in price means the consumer's equilibrium point moves to point D: the consumer increases their consumption of B from 50 to 120, while reducing their consumption of A from 25 to 20. They have increased demand of the good whose price has fallen. However, it is also noticeable that they have moved to a higher indifference curve, I_2. This indicates that their **total satisfaction** (utility) **has increased.**

13.5 Change in total income

FAST FORWARD

Changing income is shown as a parallel shift of the budget constraint. A rise in income shifts the budget constraint to the right.

Figure 31 analyses the effect of a rise in income from $100 to $150 when the prices were at their original values of $2 per unit of A and $1 per unit of B.

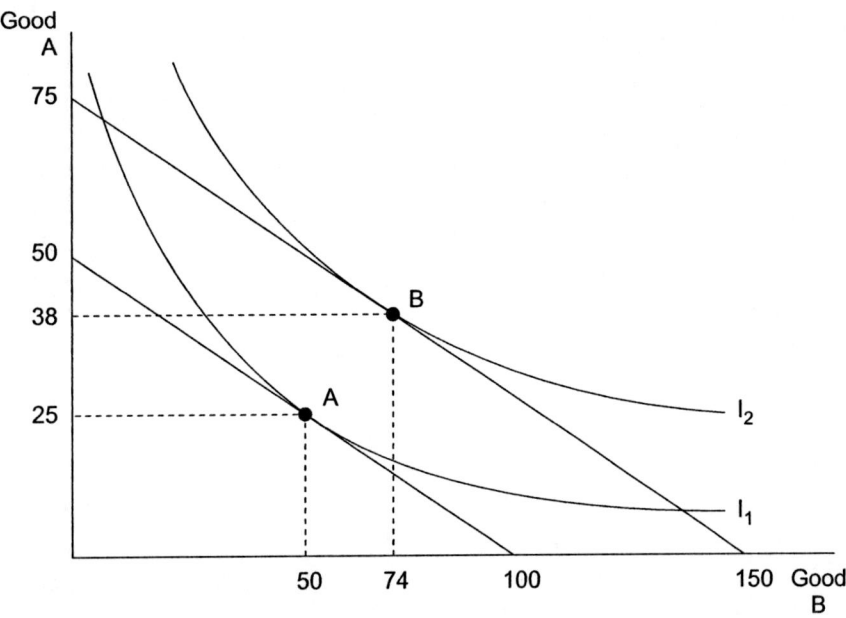

Figure 31 Rise in income

The rise in income leads to a higher budget constraint showing that the consumer can now buy either 75 units of A or 150 units of B.

The consumer's equilibrium point has moved from point A to point B, increasing the consumption of both products. There are two points to notice:

- The rise in income has led to a rise in the consumption of both goods. This means that both goods are **normal goods** ie that demand rises as income rises
- The consumer has now attained a higher level of welfare because they are enjoying more of both goods. This is denoted by the higher indifference curve I_2.

13.6 Income and substitution effects

FAST FORWARD

Substitution effects are the changes in demand for a good because its relative price has changed.

Income effects are the changes in demand for a good because the consumer's income has changed.

The two effects are distinguished by drawing a new budget line tangent to the original indifference curve. This is called a Hicksian Compensating Variation.

Returning to Figure 30 it can be seen that the effect of the price fall was to allow the consumer to move to a higher indifference curve. Some economists, notably Hicks, argued that this reflected a higher level of real income. Hicks makes the point that when prices, fall a given level of income can buy more products and so the **real income** of the consumer increases.

The difference in the amount of money a consumer would need to achieve the same level of utility following a change in prices, is known as the **compensating variation**.

Figure 32 analyses the effect of a fall in price of B from £1 to $0.50 in more detail.

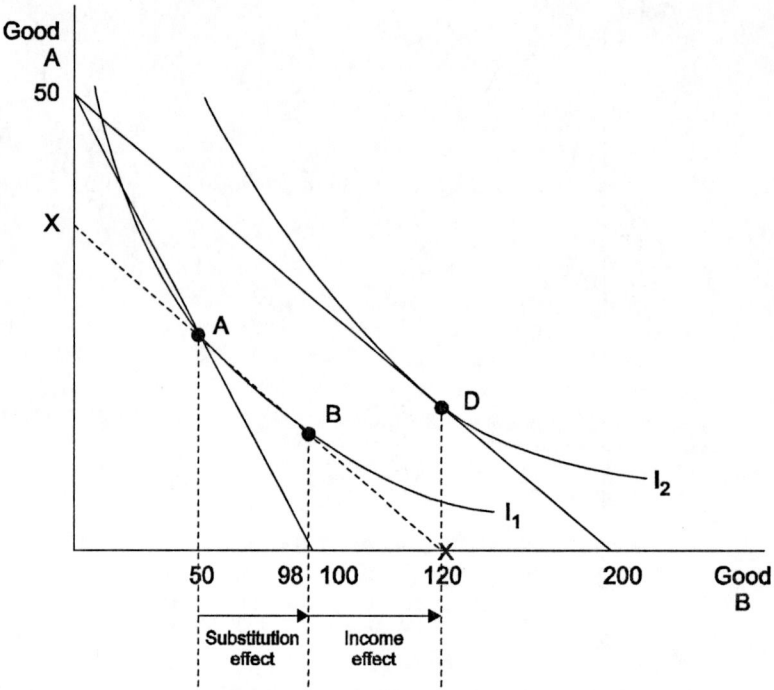

Figure 32 Income and substitution effects of a price change

The fall in the price of Good B is shown as a pivot in the budget constraint as it was in Figure 30. The consumer increases consumption of Good B from 50 to 120 as before and moves to the higher indifference curve, I_2, at point D.

Hicks compensates for the income rise by drawing a new budget constraint, labelled XX in Figure 32. This new compensated budget constraint has the same slope as the budget constraint following the price fall (ie the shallower one following the fall in price of Good B to only $0.50 per unit) and therefore denotes that Good B has become relatively cheaper compared to Good A. However this new budget constraint, XX, is drawn **tangential to the original indifference curve** I_1 to put the consumer back at their original level of welfare. In other words the welfare effects of a higher real income have been removed by this new budget constraint XX.

Figure 32 shows that the rise in demand from 50 to 98 units (point A to point B) was due to the new lower price of Good B relative to Good A, such that the consumer **substituted** Good B for Good A. The rise in demand for Good B from 98 to 120 (point B to point D) was an **income effect** and was due to the rise in the consumer's real income following the fall in the price of Good B.

A noticeable effect is that in moving from point B to point D as real income rose, the consumer also bought more of Good A. This shows that both Good A and Good B are normal goods (because consumption of both of them increased following a rise in the consumer's real income).

Chapter Roundup

- In a free market, the **price mechanism** signals demand and supply conditions to producers and consumers. It therefore determines the activities of both producers and consumers, influencing the levels of demand for and the supply of goods.

- A **market** can be defined as a situation in which potential buyers and potential sellers (suppliers) of a good or service come together for the purpose of exchange.

- **Demand** for a good or service is the quantity of that good or service that potential purchasers would be willing and able to buy, or attempt to buy, at any possible price.

- The **law of demand** states that: as the price of a good falls then, other things remaining equal, the quantity demanded of the good increases.

- The position of the **demand curve** is determined by the demand conditions, which include consumers' tastes and preferences, and consumers' incomes.

- **Substitute goods** are goods that are alternatives for each other, so that an **increase** in the demand for one is likely to cause a **decrease** in the demand for another. Switching demand from one good to another 'rival' good is substitution.

- **Complements** are goods that tend to be bought and used together, so that an **increase** in the demand for one is likely to cause an **increase** in the demand for the other.

- **Normal goods** are goods for which demand **rises** when income rises.

- **Inferior goods** are goods for which demand **falls** when income rises.

- **Supply** refers to the quantity of a good that existing suppliers or would be suppliers would want to produce for the market at a given price.

- The **law of supply** states that: as price of a good rises, other things remaining constant, the quantity supplied of that good will increase.

- The position of a supply curve depends on the **conditions of supply**. These are costs of resources, prices of other products, indirect taxes and subsidies, expectations of market changes, and natural factors such as those affecting harvests.

- The **equilibrium price** is established by the price mechanism and is the price at which quantity demanded equals quantity supplied of a good in a particular market.

- The **three functions of price** are **signalling**, **rewarding** and **rationing**.

- The **price mechanism** brings demand and supply into equilibrium, and the **equilibrium price** for a good is the price at which the volume demanded by consumers and the volume that firms would be willing to supply is the same. This is also known as the **market clearing price**, since at this price there will be neither surplus nor shortage in the market.

- **Price elasticity of demand** (PED) is a measure of the extent of change in the market demand for a good in response to a change in its price.

Chapter Roundup Cont'd

- Price elasticity of demand (PED) is expressed as a co-efficient and can have a value between zero and infinity. A value of zero means that quantity demanded did not change when price changed and demand is **perfectly inelastic**. Values **between zero and one** are described as price **inelastic** demand. Values in **excess of one** denotes price **elastic** demand.

- If demand is **price inelastic**, a **rise in price** will lead to a rise in total expenditure on the good and therefore a **rise in the firm's total revenue** from selling the good. If demand is price elastic a **fall** in price will lead to a **rise in revenue** for the firm from selling the good.

- Price elasticity of demand is affected by the **determinants of price elasticity of demand**. It will be reduced by having low **percentage of income** spent on the good, few **substitutes** available, the good being a **necessity** not a luxury, it being a **habitual purchase**, and a **short period of time** having elapsed since the price changed.

- The **price elasticity of supply** indicates the responsiveness of supply to a change in price. Price elasticity of supply refects the willingness and ability of firms to increase output as price rises.

- The values of price elasticity of supply vary between zero and infinity. A value of zero denotes a situation of **perfectly price inelastic supply** in which supply is a fixed quantity and cannot be increased as price rises. A value of infinity denotes **infinately (or perfectly) price elastic supply.**

- Price elasticity of supply will be lower, more inelastic, for a price rise if **inventories** of goods to sell are low, labour or other **factors in short supply**, if there is an absence of spare **production capacity**, if there are **barriers to enty** stopping new firms joining, or if there has only been a **short length of time** since the price rose.

- Where **maximum prices** are imposed, there will be excess demand: rationing may be necessary, and black marketers may seek to operate. Where **minimum prices** are imposed, producers will make excess supply.

- **Market failure** occurs when a free market mechanism fails to produce the most efficient allocation of scarce resources.

- **Externalities** are the spill-over effects of a transaction which extend beyond the parties to the transaction and affect society as a whole. In other words, externalities are the differences between the **private** and the **social** costs, or benefits, arising from an activity.

- **Indirect taxes** are levied on expenditure on goods or services as opposed to direct taxation which is applied to incomes. A **selective** indirect tax is imposed on some goods but not on others (or is imposed at a higher rate on some goods than on others).

- **Consumer behaviour theory** seeks to explain the response of demand to changes in price by referenece to the rational consumer seeking to **maximise total utility** (or satisfaction) obtained from spending their scarce income.

- **Marginal utility** is defined as the addition to total utility (or consumer happiness) resulting from the consumer's increasing total consumption of the product by one unit.

- The **law of diminishing marginal utility** states that: as a consumer's total consumption of a product increases the marginal utility they obtain from extra units fall continuously and may eventually become negative.

- **Principle of equi-marginal utility**: Cardinalists predict that consumers will allocate their income between products to obtain the same **marginal utiltity per dollar** from each.

- **Indifference curves** are an Ordinalist approach to explaining consumer behaviour. They show alternative bundles of goods that the consumer can say will yield the same satisfaction.

Chapter Roundup Cont'd

- **Budget constraints** are a straight line showing the maximum of each good that can be consumed using the individual's fixed income.
- **Changing price** is shown by a pivot of the budget constraint and will lead the consumer to increase their consumption of the good whose price has fallen.
- **Changing income** is shown as a parallel shift of the budget constraint. A rise in income shifts the budget constraint to the right.
- **Substitution effects** are the change in demand for a good because its relative price has changed.
- **Income effects** are the change in demand for a good because the consumer's income has changed.
- The two effects are distinguished by drawing a new budget line tangent to the original indifference curve. This is called a Hicksian Compensating Variation.

Quick Quiz

1. What factors influence demand for a good?
2. What are (a) substitutes and (b) complements?
3. What factors affect the supply quantity?
4. What is meant by equilibrium price?
5. A demand curve is drawn on all **except** which of the following assumptions?

    A   Incomes do not change.
    B   Prices of substitutes are fixed.
    C   Price of the good is constant.
    D   There are no changes in tastes and preferences.

6. The diagram shown relates to the demand for and supply of Scotch whisky. The market is initially in equilibrium at point X. The government imposes a specific tax on Scotch while at the same time, the price of Irish whiskey (a substitute for Scotch whisky) rises. Which point, A, B, C or D represents the new market equilibrium?

    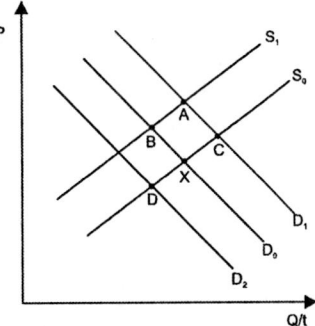

7. A price ceiling set above the equilibrium market price will result in:

    A   Market failure
    B   Excess supply over demand
    C   Market equilibrium
    D   Excess demand over supply

PART B   CONSUMPTION, PRODUCTION AND DISTRIBUTION

8   Which one of the following would normally cause a rightward shift in the demand curve for a product?

   A   A fall in the price of a substitute product
   B   A reduction in direct taxation on incomes
   C   A reduction in price of the product
   D   An increase in the price of a complementary product

9   What is an inferior good?

   A   A good of such poor quality that demand for it is very weak
   B   A good of lesser quality than a substitute good, so that the price of the substitute is higher
   C   A good for which the cross elasticity of demand with a substitute product is greater than 1
   D   A good for which demand will fall as household income rises

10 In traditional theory, which of the following best describes a firm's short run supply curve:

   A   Its marginal cost curve where price is less than average variable costs
   B   Its marginal cost curve where price is greater than average variable costs
   C   Its average cost curve where price is less than marginal cost
   D   Its average cost curve where price is greater than marginal cost

11 What is the general case in favour of allowing a free market to operate?

12 What is market failure, and what are its main causes?

13 What is an externality?

14 List the various forms of government intervention in markets.

15 Which of the following are imperfections in a market?

   1   Consumer brand loyalty to a firm's branded goods, regardless of price

   2   The lack of completely accurate information for consumers about all goods and services available

   3   The slow response of firms to price changes and the relatively inelastic supply of a good in the short run

   A   Items 1 and 2 only
   B   Items 2 and 3 only
   C   Items 1 and 3 only
   D   Items 1, 2 and 3

16 Which of the following are weaknesses of a completely free-enterprise economic system?

   1   It only reflects private costs and private benefits
   2   It may lead to serious inequalities in the distribution of income and wealth
   3   It may lead to production inefficiencies and a wastage of resources

   A   1 and 2 only
   B   2 and 3 only
   C   1 and 3 only
   D   1, 2 and 3

17 Muddy Waters Co is an industrial company which has altered its production methods so that it has reduced the amount of waste discharged from its factory into the local river. Which of the following is most likely to be reduced?

   A   Total private costs
   B   Social costs
   C   External benefit
   D   Variable costs

18 Much Wapping is a small town where a municipal swimming pool and sports centre have just been built by a private firm, Builder Co. Which of the following is an external benefit of the project?

- A The increased trade of local shops
- B The increased traffic in the neighbourhood
- C The increased profits for the firm operating the sports centre
- D The increased building on land which was previously open space

19 The government has just increased the tax on tobacco. Assuming that the demand for cigarettes is completely inelastic, who pays the tax?

- A It is shared between supplier and consumer in proportions equal to the relative prices before and after the increase.
- B The supplier
- C The consumer
- D It is shared between supplier and consumer in proportions equal to the relative quantities sold before and after the increase.

20 Which of the following statements is **always** true if an indirect tax is imposed on a good or service:

- A The price will rise by an amount equal to the tax
- B The producer will bear more of the tax than the consumer
- C The price rise will be smaller the greater the price elasticity of demand
- D The price rise will be greater the greater the price elasticity of demand

PART B   CONSUMPTION, PRODUCTION AND DISTRIBUTION

Answers to Quick Quiz

1. The price of the good
   The price of other goods
   Household income
   Taste and fashion

2. Substitutes are goods that are alternatives to each other (for example, Coca-Cola and Pepsi)

   Complements are goods which are bought and used together (for example, cars and petrol)

3. The price obtainable for the good
   The prices obtainable for other goods, particularly goods in joint supply
   The costs of making the good
   Disruptions such as bad weather and strikes

4. The price at which the volume of demand and the volume of supply are equal; there is neither surplus nor shortage.

5. C   Demand curves express the quantity demanded at each given market price. Non-price determinants such as income must be held constant when looking at the effect of price movements in isolation.

6. A   Supply shifts from S_0 to S_1, reflecting the per-unit tax. Demand shifts from D_0 to D_1 as the price of a substitute (Irish whiskey) rises.

7. C   If the price ceiling is above the equilibrium market price, it will not interfere with the working of the price mechanism. The market will not be forced from its current equilibrium. A price ceiling only affects the workings of the price mechanism if the ceiling is set **below** the equilibrium price.

8. B   A reduction in income tax will increase 'real' household income, and so demand for normal products will shift to the right, ie quantity demanded will be greater at any given price.

   A fall in the price of a substitute good would entice consumers away from the original good. This would cause a leftward shift in the demand curve.

   A change in the price of the good itself does not cause a shift in the curve but a movement along it.

   Complementary products tend to be bought and used together, so an increase in the price of one will lead to a reduction in demand for the other, reflected in a leftward shift in the demand curve.

9. D   Inferior goods are defined in terms of the relationship between quantity demanded and income. The issue of substitutes is not relevant.

10. B   The marginal cost curve represents the firm's supply curve, but a firm will only continue to supply in the short run provided that the selling price covers its variable costs and therefore allows it to make a contribution to covering fixed costs.

11. Free markets are efficient in that they adjust quickly to changing demand and supply and they operate automatically, without need for direction or control.

12. Market failure occurs when a free market mechanism produces an allocation of resources which can be criticised on efficiency, social or political grounds.

13. An externality is an effect caused by an economic transaction which extends beyond the parties to the transaction.

14. Controlling the means of production
    Legal regulation of products and prices
    Indirect taxation
    Subsidies
    Redistributing income via taxation and welfare payments

2: PRICE THEORY

15	D	Brand loyalty can make consumers pay more for a good, without getting any greater total satisfaction from consuming it. Lack of information to consumers will result in 'bad' purchasing decisions. The slowness to price changes is a further market imperfection.
16	D	The need to limit or avoid these weaknesses is the chief argument in favour of some government involvement in the allocation of economic resources – ie in favour of a mixed economy or even a command economy.
17	B	Social cost is the sum of the private cost to a firm plus the external cost to society as a whole. Here, social cost is the sum of production costs (private costs) plus the cost of pollution (external cost). The firm's private costs might have been increased by the measures to reduce pollution, but the external costs will have fallen, so that total social costs should have fallen too.
18	A	This is correct because the benefits to local shops are additional to the private benefits of the sports firm and as such are external benefits.
		B is an external cost of the project, since increased volumes of traffic are harmful to the environment.
		C is a private benefit for the firm.
		D would only be an external benefit if a building is better for society than the use of open land, which is unlikely.
19	C	As the consumer's consumption is not altered by the price rise (demand is completely inelastic), the supplier can pass the price rise on in full.
20	C	The price rise will be lower for products with a higher price elasticity of demand. In the extreme case, if demand is perfectly elastic, there will be no increase in the price at all.
		Option A would be true if the good or service had a perfectly inelastic demand, but that is the only condition under which it would be true. Equally, Option B would be true if demand was relatively more elastic than supply, but it will not always be true.

PART B CONSUMPTION, PRODUCTION AND DISTRIBUTION

End of chapter question

Elasticity and pricing (May 2013)

In June 2007 the English Beef and Lamb Executive (EBLEX) produced a report on the price elasticity of demand for beef. This report provided estimates of the price elasticity of demand for different cuts of beef. Data was also produced for beef from various countries of supply (see the table below). Using the data, the National Beef Association (NBA) then controversially argued that farm suppliers and supermarkets of beef in the UK could benefit from a rise in beef prices. The UK is around 70% self-sufficient in beef. Imports are required throughout the year, in particular between November and March, when domestic consumption most exceeds supply.

The main argument in the report was that the price of most cuts of English beef (roasting joints excepted) could be increased to generate more revenue both from supermarkets and for farmers. The gain in revenue from a price increase would be less than the fall in sales due to customers switching to beef elsewhere, to other types of meat or buying less English beef. The NBA's view was that English beef is 'undervalued and undersold'. A rise in English beef prices would benefit British farmers and supermarkets, and, in turn, would contribute to the national economy and, in particular, the English livestock sector.

Beef Products	Price elasticity of demand	Cuts of English beef	Price elasticity of demand
English beef	-0.9	Beef mince	-0.17
Home produced beef (incl. Scotland)	-1.2	Stewing steak	-0.32
Irish beef	-2.0	Sirloin steak	-0.38
Other imported beef	-2.1	Roasting joints	-1.61

Required

Discuss the extent to which you agree with the NBA's argument that British beef suppliers should raise their prices, using the data provided by EBLEX in the table. **(30 marks)**

Forms of enterprise

Topic list	Syllabus reference
1 Organisations	2.1
2 The objectives of firms	2.1
3 Corporate governance	2.3
4 Businesses and their environments	2.2 & 2.3

Introduction

Most major industrialised countries have mixed economies, with both a large private sector and also a substantial public (or government) sector. Developing countries feature additional forms such as co-operatives, joint ventures and corporations owned wholly or partly by the government (parastatal organisations).

In this chapter we will look more carefully at the kinds of organisations that undertake economic activity and their objectives in doing so.

We will also look at some of the key structures and mechanisms which control the way organisations operate – corporate governance.

PART B   CONSUMPTION, PRODUCTION AND DISTRIBUTION

1 Organisations

FAST FORWARD

> The ownership of an organisation affects the goals that it will pursue. A significant distinction is made between **public sector** organisations, which belong to the state, and **private sector** organisations which are owned by private individuals. Private sector organisations are assumed to be **profit maximisers** whereas public sector organisations pursue **not-for-profit objectives.**

1.1 The public and private sectors

The economy of a developed country can usually be divided into two sectors: the public sector and the private sector. Private sector organisations, also called businesses, are owned and operated by private individuals or institutions, while organisations in the public sector are owned by the state.

1.2 Private sector organisations

There are two main types of private sector organisations: those that **seek profit** for their owners, and those that have **other objectives**. The latter are known as non-profit making or **not-for-profit** organisations. However, the majority of organisations in the private sector are businesses which aim to make profits for their owners (shareholders).

1.2.1 Not-for-profit organisations

FAST FORWARD

> Not-for-profit organisations include **clubs and associations,** associations owned by members such as **mutuals** and **co-operatives,** as well as **charitable groups, trade unions,** and **professional associations** including the Association of International Accountants.

This terminology is a little misleading, since 'not-for-profit' organisations can sometimes engage in profitable trade and they would not be able to continue operating if they consistently ran at a loss. The essence of their status as 'not-for-profit' organisations is not that they seek to avoid generating a surplus of funds, but that the generation of wealth for their owners is **not the primary purpose** of their existence. Not-for-profit organisations still aim to operate as **efficiently** as possible, but their primary objective is to provide a service or benefit, rather than to maximise profit. Not-for-profit organisations include co-operatives and mutual organisations; charities; and unincorporated clubs, societies and associations.

Not-for-profit organisations use the surplus they generate to further their other objectives.

Clubs and associations exist to provide some kind of benefit to their members.

Charities and **voluntary organisations** generally exist to provide some kind of benefit to society at large. For example, sports clubs provide their members the opportunities to participate in sporting activities. This enables them to benefit from concessions not available to profit seeking organisations. These benefits may include exemption from a requirement to pay taxes on earnings and access to special funding.

Mutual organisations are a special case in the private sector. The **co-operative** is a leading example of this sector. Co-operatives are commercial operations **owned by their members,** typically farmers, lenders or customers, rather than having external shareholders for whom they have to earn profit.

This means that their customers benefit both from the **services** the mutuals provide to them as well as from the **trading surplus** they make by doing so. It is also possible for the managers of mutuals to pursue **purposes other than profit**. These can include a high level of charitable giving, the promotion of community interests, and a high quality of service; such pursuits may well provide a high degree of intangible benefit to members. Mutuals thus resemble both non-profit-making organisations and profit-seeking companies.

3: FORMS OF ENTERPRISE

Although not-for-profit organisations are not profit seekers, they still use economic factors of production to produce goods or services. Therefore they need to be efficiently managed so that their resources are used **effectively** to meet the objectives of the organisation whilst not making a financial loss.

The reference to effectiveness is very important here. Being **cost effective** is one of the key economic aims of not-for-profit organisations.

1.2.2 Profit seeking organisations

FAST FORWARD

Profit seeking organisations are divided into **sole-traders, partnerships**, and **corporations** (or **companies**). Companies are denoted as **public companies** and **private companies** according to whether the general public is allowed to own shares in them.

The economy in most countries is driven primarily by the profit-seeking part of the private sector. It is profit-seeking businesses that undertake the most enterprising aspects of economic activity, provide the bulk of employment opportunities and tax revenue, and create the growth needed to enhance economic welfare. Remember also the point we made in Chapter 1: that economists assume that producers will seek to maximise their profits.

Businesses are of two main types, distinguished by the extent to which the owners are liable for the debts of the undertaking.

(a) An individual may set up business on his or her own account, as a **sole trader** or in **partnership** with others. In either case, the law will not distinguish between the private assets and liabilities of the owners and those of the enterprise. Crucially, this means that the owners have **unlimited liability** for the debts of their businesses.

(b) The degree of risk attached to 'unlimited liability' is unattractive to many potential investors. Therefore, to attract investors to invest, and thus to release more funds for wealth-producing enterprise, the legal systems of most countries provide for some form of **limited liability** enterprise. Such businesses are referred to as corporations or **companies**.

Under UK company law, there are two forms of limited liability company. They both limit the liability of investors to the nominal value of their share holdings; however, they differ in the extent to which they are permitted to solicit investment from the general public. **Private limited companies** may not offer their securities to the public; a **public limited company** (plc) may. When the shares of plcs are regularly bought and sold on a stock exchange, they may be referred to as **quoted companies**, because the current price of their shares will be quoted in a journal of record.

Attention!

Note carefully the confusing terminology here: **public limited companies** are owned by **private** investors (shareholders); they are **not** part of the **public sector**.

1.2.3 Joint ventures

These are separate organisations owned in common by two or more businesses. For example two telecommunications firms may decide to collaborate to exploit an opportunity by forming a new company in which each takes a 50% shareholding. This means they can share the rewards and risks equally, and to pool finance and skills.

1.3 Public sector organisations

Traditionally, economists have divided public sector organisations into **two main groups**: those that **provide public services** – such as hospitals, schools, the police and the armed forces – and **state-owned industries**. This distinction has become less clear, as governments have privatised state-owned industries, and sought to **reform the public sector** by involving private companies in the provision of public services.

The objective has been to **curb waste** of public money and **improve efficiency** by importing the disciplined cost control that is required in the private sector if profit is to be created.

Many states have moved away from being direct providers of public services, such as hospitals and schools, and transport, and are now involved in different forms of **public-private partnership**. In such partnerships, the private sector provides funds for public sector purposes such as education, health or infrastructure projects.

Public sector bodies are all, ultimately, **responsible to government** for their activities, and their purposes are defined in the laws that establish them. They have a range of possible aims and objectives: rarely will they set out to trade at a profit. Nevertheless, their managers will be expected to exercise **good stewardship** and **prevent waste of resources**. The objectives of public sector bodies will usually be defined in terms of the **provision of a service** that is deemed to be beneficial to society.

It is an important feature of public sector bodies that (unless they engage in trade of some kind) they have little control over their incomes; they depend upon government for the funds they need to operate. The funds they receive will be influenced by a large number of forces, including current public opinion, government aspirations, the skill of their leaders in negotiation, the current state of the public finances overall and the current economic climate.

Alongside public sector organisations there are also quasi autonomous non-governmental organisations (QUANGOs), which are private organisations independent of the government but to which governments have devolved the authority for running public services.

2 The objectives of firms

2.1 The firm

> **FAST FORWARD**
>
> **Firm** is the term used in economics for any organisation that carries on a business. Economists assume that the objective of firms is to **maxmise profits**.

In Chapter 1, we identified entrepreneurship as one of the four factors of production – the entrepreneur organises **production** and bears **risk**, and is rewarded for this by earning **profit**.

In the real world of the 21st century it is hard to identify an entrepreneur behind many businesses. Instead they are owned by shareholders and managed by paid employees. This is described as the **separation of ownership from control**. (We will look at this point in more detail later in this chapter, in relation to **agency theory**.)

2.2 Profit maximisation and other objectives

Profit maximisation is usually assumed to be the goal of the firm. However, this assumption pre-supposes both that the owners of the firm are in control of the everyday management of it, and also that the owners want to achieve the highest profits that they can.

If these two conditions are not met, then the logic behind the assumption of the profit maximising firm is flawed.

The profit maximising assumption is not universally accepted: the great management thinker Peter Drucker said that a business exists 'to create a customer', by which he meant that its activities were best explained in terms of marketing activity. Other writers have suggested that **survival** is the main long-term aim of businesses.

Where the entrepreneur is in full managerial control of the firm, as in the case of a small owner-managed company or partnership, the profit maximisation assumption would seem to be very reasonable. However, some companies have considerations that constrain their ability to maximise profits. These include the demands of **ethics** in pharmaceutical and medical companies, the requirement to provide a **public service** where specific subsidies are received, and the demands of safety – in shipping and airline companies, for example. The process of incorporating UK companies may define its particular **type of business**, though it is possible to incorporate as a 'general commercial company', which makes it legal for the company to undertake any kind of legal business activity.

2.3 Corporate social responsibility and ethics

> **FAST FORWARD**
>
> Corporate social responsibilty (CSR) is the requirement that organisations behave as good neighbours by taking into account the impact of their actions on society as a whole rather than solely on the profits of their owners.

Seeking to maximise profits can lead to corporations behaving selfishly. By considering corporate social responsibility (CSR), firms and their managers are reminded of their potential for doing **social good** and for causing **social harm**. CSR should encourage a firm to maximise the positive impact it has on society, the environment and the economy, whilst also trying to minimising the negative effects of its actions.

Examples of where firms can do social good include:

(a) Provision of essential and desirable products
(b) Providing jobs and training to their workforce
(c) Improving the built environment by having attractive buildings and spaces
(d) Providing taxes to government from their profits
(e) Improving the opportunities for different sorts of minorities through their hiring and promotion policies
(f) Improving or caring for the natural environment through energy efficiency and careful waste disposal
(g) Providing money, products or the time of staff to community projects and other good works.

Firms can also cause social harm, for example:

(a) Producing undesirable and harmful products which can endanger human life or pollute the natural environment
(b) Excessive waste emissions of heat, noise, or non-degradable materials
(c) Closing operations and causing unemployment and deprivation in a region
(d) Adopting unsafe working practices
(e) Exploiting workers with low pay and poor conditions
(f) Producing unsafe products
(g) Becoming involved in political manipulation and bribery that undermines democratic rule

Failure to act in a socially responsible manner can lead a firm to incur fines, bad publicity and may lead to harsh new laws.

The ideas of social responsibility may cause some firms to adopt **profit satisficing** strategies instead of **profit maximisation.** Such firms seek to balance the obligations upon them by making an adequate profit for their shareholders (profit satisficing) but also leaving money and resources available for CSR work too.

PART B   CONSUMPTION, PRODUCTION AND DISTRIBUTION

> **FAST FORWARD**
>
> **Corporate ethics** concern the morality of the behaviour of a business such as its honesty in dealings and its care for human life.

Ethics are based in the principles of good moral behaviour. These include values such as fairness, honesty, duty and justice. We generally expect the people that run businesses to honour these principles in their private lives and in their work lives.

Examples of unethical business practices include:

(a) Making misleading statements to sell products or win contracts
(b) Overcharging by having hidden charges or taking advantage of a desperate customer
(c) Unfair competition such as artificially dropping price simply to force a rival out of business
(d) Making and selling a product that is not safe
(e) Discrimination between customers or staff based on gender, race, religion or age
(f) Hiding or denying errors or mistakes that affect society
(g) Bribing government employees to win contracts or gain influence

There are overlaps between CSR and ethics. However, social responsibility and ethical behaviour are not the same thing.

Business ethics is concerned with the standards of behaviour in the conduct of business. **CSR** reflects an organisation's obligation to maximise positive stakeholder benefits while minimising the negative effects of its actions.

Importantly, **CSR includes economic and legal issues, as well as ethical ones**: reflecting the whole range of stakeholders who have an interest in an organisation.

In this respect, CSR requires an organisation to go beyond simply adhering to minimum ethical standards. 'Ethics' concerns issues such as justice, fairness and honesty, which are fundamental, unchanging values that have implications for business. However, CSR is also more closely associated with contemporary business issues, and concerns organisations giving something back to society, and being good citizens. Therefore, in contrast to ethics, CSR is socially mediated and likely to be specific to the time and culture in which it is considered, and in which an organisation is operating.

Firms can take a number of **policy stances** on CSR and ethics.

(a) **Resistance**: here the firm tries to argue against the need to change its ways, for example by spending money on a campaign to convince people that following a socially responsible route is misguided. An example of this is the tobacco industry which tries to argue that regulations against smoking are a denial of personal freedom.

(b) **Compliance**: the firm will ensure that it stays within the law but will not go any further until the law changes and forces it to.

(c) **Engagement**: the firm will seek to understand the thinking behind the CSR issues and will seek to gain a competitive advantage by being (seen to be) the more socially responsible. Deliberate stocking of Fair Trade products is an example of this.

(d) **Philanthropy**: here the firm will channel money to good causes, employ staff who might otherwise be unemployed, and will pay more than it needs to for factors of production in order to help the poor.

(e) **Social engineering**: the firm might use its position to bring about a profound change for the better in society. Some large firms deliberately build better housing and schools in the countries they have factories in.

2.4 Stakeholder theory

Stakeholder theory highlights that firms need to be accountable to a wide range of stakeholder groups, and not just to their shareholders.

The notion of corporate social responsibility (CSR) highlights that, when making business decisions, firms need to consider the implications of those decisions on a range of different stakeholders – not just for their shareholders.

This idea is captured more generally through the notion of stakeholder theory. Stakeholder theory highlights that the extent of the impact firms have on society is so significant that firms need to **be accountable to many more groups in society (stakeholder groups) than just their shareholders**.

The traditional, shareholder-based, view of the firm argues that a firm's primary objective is to meet the needs of its owners (shareholders) and to generate value for them.

However, stakeholder theory argues that there is a much wider range of parties (stakeholders) who have legitimate interests in a firm, and who can affect it or are affected by it. Consequently, a firm's management needs to give due consideration to the interests of those groups. Potential stakeholder groups in a firm include employees, customers, suppliers, banks and other finance providers, local communities, government or government bodies, trades unions, and environmental agencies – as well as the firm's shareholders.

Consequently, the logic of stakeholder theory suggests that, instead of viewing business as a way of creating value solely for shareholders, we should see business as a way of **creating value for the much wider range stakeholders**. Importantly, in the context of business economics, stakeholder theory suggests that a firm's business decisions cannot be seen simply in terms of maximising profits for its shareholders, but also in relation to considering the needs of other stakeholder groups – for example, managing relationships with customers and suppliers, and maintaining employee motivation.

In the stakeholder model, business decisions also need to consider the following sorts of question: If this course of action is taken, for whom does it create value and for whom does it destroy value? How benefits from the decision and who is harmed by it? Once again, this emphasises that business decisions can no longer be taken purely on the basis of the value they generate for shareholders.

2.4.1 Stakeholder theory, CSR and ethics

The potential links to CSR should also be apparent here, because the stakeholder view acknowledges the increased social impact that businesses have on local communities and the natural environment.

In their text *Stakeholder Theory: The State of the Art*, Freeman *et al* highlight this point when they note that we can no longer separate the economics of value creation from the ethics of value creation; with the consequence that decision-makers need to take account of sustainability and social responsibility when making business decisions.

This recognition that **business decisions can no longer be detached from ethical issues** is also crucial in stakeholder theory. Freeman *et al* argue that although it is fallacy to assume that business decisions can be separate from ethical issues. Almost any business decision has some ethical content, while ethical questions cannot be ignored in business decisions. Consequently, it makes no sense to talk about business without also talking about ethics. Perhaps equally importantly, it also makes no sense to talk about either business or ethics without also talking about human beings. So, for example, when thinking about the decisions firms might take in order to maximise their profits, it is also important to consider the impact those decisions will have on people as well as profit.

2.4.2 Stakeholder theory and firms' objectives

Stakeholder theory has particularly important implications for our understanding of firm's objectives. As we have noted earlier in this chapter, economists assume that firms will seek to maximise their profits. However, stakeholder theory challenges that this position. When a firm seeks to maximise profits above all else, it is fulfilling its duties to its shareholders, but not necessarily to any other stakeholders.

By contrast, when the managers of a firm take account of all the stakeholders who are affected by an organisation's activities before taking decisions, **those decisions may not be taken purely on the basis of the level of profit they will generate**. For example, while it may be profitable to sell a new kind of product, a firm may decide not to do so if the production process needed to make that product creates a high level of pollution for the surrounding environment.

In this respect, it is also important to consider the potential links between stakeholder theory and the idea of market failure we discussed in Chapter 2. Market failure occurs when resources are not allocated as efficiently as they could be, and we highlighted that the divergence between private costs and social costs (externalities) is one cause of market failure. However, by considering the range of stakeholders affected by its actions, a firm should be more aware of the **social costs** of its action. Consequently, a firm may **'internalise' these externalities** when making business decisions, which in turn should reduce the risk of them contributing to market failure.

2.5 Agency theory and the principal-agent problem

> The **separation of ownership from control** arises from shareholders, the firm's **principals**, being different people from the firm's managers, the paid **agents** of the shareholders.

Nowadays, very few large businesses are managed by their owners. In the case of larger companies, there are large numbers of shareholders and they are unlikely to wish to take part in the management of the company, viewing it simply as a vehicle for investment. Even where ownership is concentrated, large companies tend to be managed mostly by professional managers who have little ownership interest, if any. This **separation of ownership from control** has arisen for several reasons.

(a) Limited liability structure does not give shareholders power to manage the company (unless they are also managers); their influence normally extends only to proposing and voting on resolutions at company meetings.

(b) It is impracticable for a large number of shareholders to exercise managerial powers jointly; to be effective, power must be concentrated.

(c) Many shareholders are not interested in being managers, and are content to employ professional managers, so long as their investment prospers.

(d) Many organisations are so large or complex, or deal with such advanced technology, that they can only be managed effectively by well-qualified professionals.

Separation of ownership from control has been a feature of business for over a century and brings with it a recurring problem: the business should be managed so as to promote the economic interest of its owners (shareholders) as a body, but the power to manage the business lies in the hands of people who may use it to promote their own interests. How can the managers be made to favour the interest of the owners rather than their own?

This question provides the context of agency theory. **Agency theory** is concerned with resolving the problems between principals (such as shareholders) and agents (such as company executives.)

A following key concepts are vital in understanding agency theory:

(a) An **agent** is employed by a **principal** to carry out a task on their behalf. The relationship between a principal and their agent is known as agency.

(b) **Accountability** – By agreeing to undertake a task on their behalf, an agent becomes accountable to the principal by whom they are employed. So, in the context of a firm, the executives and managers of the firm are accountable to the shareholders to act in their best interests.

(c) **Agency costs** are incurred by principals in ensuring that agents act in the best interests of the principal. So, in the context of a firm, shareholders will provide reward incentives (such as performance bonuses or share options) to try to ensure that agents execute their duties in a way which increases shareholder value, thereby aligning the interests of principals and agents.

Agency theory addresses two key problems:

(a) The problems which arise when the **objectives or goals of the principal and the agent differ**, or are in conflict, and it is difficult or expensive for the principal to verify what the agent is actually doing. For example, the managers in a company may be motivated to grow a company in a way which maximises their personal power and wealth, rather than in a way which generates value for the shareholders.

(b) The problems which arise when principals and agents have **different attitudes to risk** and therefore may be inclined to take different actions, or to think that different courses of action are acceptable.

More generally, the issues of agency and accountability highlight the **need for effective corporate governance** in firms, and we will consider corporate governance in more detail in the next section of this chapter.

However, the problems addressed in agency theory are not confined only to the management of companies: they are the general problems of the **agency relationship**, and occur whenever one person (the **principal**) gives another (the **agent**) power to deal with their affairs. This separation of ownership from control is known as a **principal-agent problem**.

2.5.1 Resolving the agency problem

> **FAST FORWARD**
>
> The **agency problem** refers to the problem that agents will pursue their personal interests, sometimes at the expense of making profits for the principals. This can be addressed by **incentivisation**, basing the earnings of agents on the profits given to principals.

A common approach to ensuring that company managers act in the owners' interest is to offer them **reward incentives** that depend on the achievement of ownership goals. Thus, it is common for the remuneration of a CEO to depend, at least in part, on satisfactory achievement in such matters as profit and share price. At lower levels, **bonus schemes** can be based on achieving targets that support good overall performance, such as improved sales or reduced costs. **Profit sharing schemes** that provide shares to large numbers of employees are intended to align employees' interests with those of the wider body of shareholders.

Unfortunately, these types of approach can be flawed in that they have to be designed – and the designers themselves are in an agency relationship with the owners, such that their objectives may conflict with the owners' (shareholders') objective of profitability. Thus executive remuneration schemes have been criticised for emphasising the wrong targets or for setting the targets too low.

Critics of bonus schemes based on annual profits argue that such bonuses may encourage short-term, risky behaviour which maximises profits in the short term but could potentially be loss-making in the longer term.

We will discuss issues surrounding executive remuneration (or 'executive compensation') more generally in Section 3 of this chapter, when we look at remuneration in relation to corporate governance and the role of the **remuneration committee** in controlling executive remuneration.

2.6 Alternative managerial goals

Under the conditions of the agency relationship between owners and managers, the goal of profit maximisation might not fully explain management behaviour, because managers have interests of their own.

Managers will not necessarily make decisions that will maximise profits.

(a) They may have no **personal interests** at stake in the size of profits earned, except in so far as they are accountable to shareholders for the profits they make.

(b) There may be a **lack of competitive pressure** in the market to be efficient, minimise costs and maximise profits, for example where there are few firms in the market.

It has been suggested that price and output decisions will be taken by managers with **managerial objectives** in mind. Rather than seeking to **maximise** profits, managers may choose to achieve a **satisfactory** profit for a firm: this is called **satisficing**. Satisficing is also a common managerial response when there are multiple objectives, such as boosting share price, and achieving revenue growth. Similarly, if directors' remuneration schemes are based on non-financial criteria such as growth in market share or improving CSR performance, then they are unlikely to make the maximisation of profit their sole objective.

2.7 Baumol's sales maximisation model

One managerial model of the firm – Baumol's sales maximisation model – assumes that the firm acts to **maximise sales revenue** rather than profits. The management of a firm might opt for sales revenue maximisation in order to maintain or increase its market share, ensure survival, and discourage competition. Managers benefit personally because of the prestige of running a large and successful company, and also because salaries and other perks are likely to be higher in bigger companies than in smaller ones.

2.8 Williamson's management discretion model

Another managerial model – Williamson's **management discretion model** – assumes that managers act to further their own interests and so **maximise** their own **utility** (or satisfaction), subject to a minimum profit requirement. Utility may be thought of in terms of prestige, influence and other personal satisfactions. The profit aimed for will not be maximum profit, because of management's wish for expenditure on themselves and their staff, and the privileges of management.

2.9 A behavioural theory of the firm

Cyert and March suggested that a firm is an **organisational coalition** of shareholders, managers, employees and customers, with each group having different goals, so there is a need for **political compromise** in establishing the goals of the firm. Each group must settle for less than it would ideally want to have. Shareholders must settle for less than maximum profits; managers for less than maximum utility; and so on.

Despite the range of these theories, the ultimate goal of many managers is simply **survival**.

2.9.1 Stakeholder theory and agency theory

By highlighting the range of stakeholders who can all shape the goals of a firm, Cyert and March's behavioural theory of the firm also has some echoes of stakeholder theory.

However, looking at the ideas of stakeholder theory and agency theory also identifies another complication companies and their managers face.

The logic of agency theory is that agents (managers) have a duty to act in the best interests of the principals (shareholders). Yet this effectively suggests a shareholder view of a firm, in which the objectives of the firm a primarily aimed at generating value for shareholders. Stakeholder theory challenges this approach, though, and argues that firms need to recognise the interests of a much wider group of stakeholders. In turn, this suggests that the managers in a firm have a duty to this wider group of stakeholders and not just the firm's shareholders.

2.10 Resource dependency theory

So far, when we have been considering firms and the ways they are managed, we have tended to treat them as self-contained, stand-alone entities.

However, resource dependency theory (RDT) challenges this approach. Instead of characterising firms as autonomous units, it argues should view firms as being **constrained and affected by inter-dependencies with other organisations and the context of their external environment**.

RDT highlights the influence of external factors (such as external resources) on firms' behaviour, and emphasises the need for firms to respond to their external environments. However, RDT also identifies that despite firms and managers being constrained by their context, they can nevertheless act to reduce environmental uncertainty and dependence.

In this context, the concept of **power** is very important, particularly in relation to the control over vital resources. RDT suggests that when explaining a firm's strategy, power may often be more important than profit.

Power and resource dependence are directly linked, with Firm A's power over Firm B being proportional to Firm B's dependence on Firm A's resources. With this in mind, firms will attempt to reduce others' power over them, while often attempting to increase their own power over others.

Two particularly important aspects of resources are **criticality** (how critical a resource is) and **scarcity** (how easily available the resource is, or not). Critical resources are those which a firm must have in order to operate. (For example, a petrol station cannot operate with a supply of petrol). However, a firm can adopt different strategies to deal with this criticality – on the one hand it may develop links with more suppliers, or it may integrate vertically or horizontally.

While this emphasis on power relationships is one of the hallmarks of RDT, it also marks a fundamental distinction between RDT and economists' theories of the firm which are based around costs and revenues, and the key assumption that firms seek to maximise their profit.

In this next chapter of this text we look at costs in more detail, and we also look at the ideas of growth and economies of scale. Economists consider that one of the key drivers for acquisitions and alliances is that they enable costs to be reduced – it will be cheaper to provide a good or service within the firm than having to buy it through the market.

However, RDT argues that acquisitions and alliances are primarily a means of reducing uncertainty and interdependence, rather than being driven by transaction costs. Pfeffer (who played a key role in developing RDT) suggests three reasons why firms may make acquisitions:

(a) To reduce competition by absorbing an important competitor (thereby increasing the **relative power** of the firm making the acquisition)

(b) To **manage interdependence** with either sources of inputs or purchases or output. (For example, if the firm acquires a supply, it can guarantee its supply of materials from them rather than being reliant on buying them through the market place.)

(c) To diversify operations and thereby **lessen dependence** on the other firms with which it exchanges.

2.10.1 Resource dependency theory and boards of directors

Resource dependency theory can also be useful when assessing the **size and composition of a company's board** of directors (something we will consider in more detail in the context of corporate governance, in the next section of this chapter.)

The size and composition of a board indicate the board's ability to provide strategic management resources to a firm. One of the main benefits which directors bring to organisations is the information they offer, in the form of advice or recommendations.

Pfeffer suggests that board size and composition are not random or independent factors, but rather, are rational organisational responses to the external environment. As such, he suggests that firms with higher degrees of interdependence also require a higher ratio of 'outsider' (non-executive) directors with relevant experience.

'Insiders' are members of firm's top management who also serve on the board of directors. 'Outsiders' are members of the board of directors who are not otherwise employed by the firm. 'Independent outsiders' are outsiders who have no business connections with the firm.

Another perspective is that the number of other directorships each director holds can also be benefit, suggesting that 'resource-rich' directors (who have experience from sitting on the boards of a number of companies) can share their experience from one company to another. As such, it is not the just the number, but the type of directors which is important.

Similarly, if firms are able to attract powerful members of the community onto their boards, this can help to acquire critical resources from the environment.

3 Corporate governance

> **FAST FORWARD**
>
> Corporate governance refers to the systems by which a firm is managed and controlled.

3.1 Management accountability

According to the Cadbury Report (a UK Report about the way companies' boards and accounting systems should be structured in order to mitigate corporate governance risks and failures) corporate governance is 'the system by which organisations are directed and controlled'.

The UK Corporate Governance Code also identifies that 'the purpose of corporate governance is to facilitate **effective, entrepreneurial and prudent management that can deliver the long-term success of the company.**'

However, although governance is mostly discussed in relation to large quoted companies, it is an issue for all corporate bodies, whether they are commercial or not-for-profit (NFP).

3.1.1 Elements of corporate governance

There are a number of key elements in corporate governance:

(a) The management and **reduction of risk** is a fundamental issue in all definitions of good governance; whether explicitly stated or merely implied.

(b) The notion that overall performance is enhanced by good **supervision and management** within set best practice guidelines underpins most definitions of corporate governance

(c) Good governance provides a **framework** for an organisation to pursue its strategy in an **ethical and effective** way from the perspective of **all stakeholder groups** affected, and offers safeguards against misuse of resources, physical or intellectual.

(d) Good governance is not just about externally established codes, it also requires a willingness to **apply the spirit** as well as the letter of the law.

(e) **Accountability** is generally a major theme in all governance frameworks.

Good corporate governance involves managing risk and internal control, being **accountable to shareholders** and other stakeholders, and conducting business in an ethical and effective way.

Directors' accountability to 'other stakeholders' beyond 'shareholders' not only highlights the importance of dealing with interests of stakeholders but also highlights the link between stakeholder management, ethics and corporate social responsibility which we have looked at earlier in this chapter.

3.1.2 OECD Principles of Corporate Governance

The Organisation for Economic Co-operation and Development (OECD) first developed its Principles of Corporate Governance in 1998, and they were revised in 2015. These principles are not legally binding, but they are intended to assist governments in their efforts to evaluate and improve the legal, institutional and regulatory framework for corporate governance in their countries. They are also intended to provide guidance to stock exchanges, investors and companies.

The OECD principles are grouped into six broad areas:

(a) **Ensuring the basis for an effective corporate governance framework**

The corporate governance framework should promote **transparent** and **fair markets**, and the **efficient allocation of resources**. It should be consistent with the prevailing laws, and should support effective supervision and enforcement.

The reference to the efficient allocation of resources is particularly relevant in the context of business economics, since (as we discussed in Chapter 1) the fundamental economic problem is how to make the best use of scarce resources.

(b) **The rights and equitable treatment of shareholders**

Shareholders should have the right to **participate and vote in general meetings** of the company, **elect** and **remove members of the board** and **obtain relevant and material information** on a timely basis.

All shareholders of the same class of shares should be **treated equally**, including minority and foreign shareholders. All shareholders should have the opportunity to obtain effective redress for violation of their rights.

(c) **Institutional investors, stock markets and other intermediaries**

The corporate governance framework should provide sound economic incentives throughout the investment chain, and enable stock markets to function in a way that contributes to good corporate governance.

This principle highlights that, in many cases, the reality of corporate governance and ownership is no longer characterised by a simple relationship between the performance of a company and the income of the ultimate beneficiaries of shareholdings. Instead, **intermediaries** (in particular, institutional investors, such as pension funds, insurance companies and hedge funds) stand between the company and the ultimate beneficiary. As a result, these intermediaries could have a significant influence on corporate governance. Consequently, in order for the corporate governance framework to work effectively, institutional investors (acting in a fiduciary capacity on behalf of their clients) need to make informed use of their shareholder rights and to disclose this to their clients.

Equally, advisors, brokers and other agencies that provide analysis and advice that is relevant to investors need to disclose and minimise any **conflicts of interest** that may compromise the integrity of that advice.

(d) **The role of stakeholders in corporate governance**

Rights of stakeholders should be recognised, and the corporate governance framework should encourage active co-operation between corporations and stakeholders in creating wealth, jobs, and the sustainability of financially sound enterprises.

All stakeholders (including employees, customers, and suppliers) should have **access to relevant information** on a regular and timely basis.

Performance-enhancing mechanisms for employee participation should be permitted to develop. Corporations need to recognise that the contributions of stakeholders constitute a valuable resource for future competitiveness. Therefore, it is in the long-term interest of corporations to foster wealth-creating co-operation among stakeholders.

Stakeholders, including employees, should be able to freely communicate their concerns about illegal or unethical relationships to the board.

(e) **Disclosure and transparency**

Timely and accurate disclosure must be made of all material matters regarding the company, including the financial situation, performance and results, goals and objectives, foreseeable risk factors, ownership, and issues regarding employees and other stakeholders. The company's approach to disclosure should promote the provision of analysis or advice that is relevant to decisions by investors.

Importantly, disclosure is not restricted to financial information. Companies are increasingly publishing **non-financial information** in their management reports and in corporate social responsibility reports, in response to market demand for these disclosures.

(f) **The responsibilities of the board**

The board is responsible for the **strategic guidance** of the company, and for the **effective monitoring** of management. However, the board should also be accountable to the company and its shareholders.

Board members should act on a fully informed basis, in good faith, with due diligence and care and in the **best interests of the company and its shareholders**. They should treat **all shareholders fairly**.

The board should be able to exercise **independent judgement**; this includes assigning independent non-executive directors to appropriate tasks (such as remuneration, audit and risk management).

3.2 Management accountability

> **FAST FORWARD**
> All managers have a **duty of faithful service** to the owners of a firm.

As the agents of its owners, a company's managers are **collectively responsible** for the conduct of its affairs. This is true of organisations generally, whatever their nature and whether or not they seek profit. There is a **chain of authority and accountability** that runs hierarchically up and down the organisation. Junior managers are accountable to more senior ones and so on up the chain until the most senior managers are reached. The question then arises: who are these senior managers accountable to for the activities of the organisation as a whole? As a matter of principle, we can say that there should be some **external entity** on behalf of which the most senior managers control the organisation and to which they are accountable.

Question

Accountability

Who are the senior managers of the following organisations and to whom are they accountable?

(a) A charity
(b) The government of a democracy
(c) A trade union

Answer

(a) The senior management of a charity is likely to be similar in nature to the board of a company, consisting of heads of departments (such as fundraising and operations) together with non-executive directors. Their collective responsibility is likely to be to subscription-paying members of the institution assembled in a general meeting, where these exist, or possibly to a supervisory board, or even to a court of law. In any event, the actions of the managers in dealing with the **interests of those the charity is intended to benefit** will be the main concern.

(b) The senior management of a democratic government is called the Cabinet and, again, consists of senior politicians with functional and advisory roles. The external body to which it is responsible is the **electorate** (the members of the public), who have the power collectively to expel the government from office and install a completely different one.

(c) The senior management of a trade union will consist of senior executives and, depending on its constitution, is likely to be responsible to the **membership of the union**. The extent of this responsibility will depend on local law and tradition and may be discharged for example, through postal ballots or, less satisfactorily, through mass meetings.

In a company, although the shareholders own the company, the responsibility for directing and controlling the company rests largely with the **board of directors**. The respective power and key responsibilities of shareholders and directors are summarised in the following table:

Shareholders	Board of directors
Appoint the directors	Determine the strategy of the company
	Oversee the management of the company and its performance in achieving strategy and objectives
	Report to shareholders on the performance of the company
Appoint the auditors	
Assure themselves that the system of corporate governance is appropriate and effective	Ensure suitable internal controls are in place and the company complies with laws and regulations.

3.3 Fiduciary responsibility

The essence of all these examples of **external accountability** is that organisations are **not autonomous**: that is to say, they do not exist to serve their own purposes or those of their senior managers. They exist to serve some external purpose and their managers have a duty to run them in a way that serves that purpose, whether it be to relieve distress (a charity), to keep the peace and manage the economy (a government), to promote the interests of its members (a trade union), or to make a profit (a business). Managers have a **fiduciary responsibility** (or duty of faithful service) in this respect and their behaviour must always reflect it.

The concept of fiduciary responsibility highlights that directors must try to act in a way which is most likely to promote the success of the company for the benefit of the shareholders. This needs to consider a number of factors, including the long-term consequence of decisions, the firm's reputation and the interests of other stakeholders, such as employees and the community.

In the UK, the Companies Act (2006) identifies that directors have a duty to:

(a) Promote the success of the company
(b) Exercise reasonable care, skill and diligence
(c) Avoid conflicts of interest or of duties

This duty to 'promote the success of the company' could have important implications in the context of an organisation's business strategy:

(a) Directors need to consider the consequences of any strategic decisions for both the long term and the short term

(b) Directors need to consider how different stakeholder groups can affect the company's success; for example, the company's relationships with its employees, suppliers, customers, the local community and the environment. Once again, this highlights the importance of **stakeholder management** (stakeholder theory) as a key element of business strategy, as well as the underlying goal of profit maximisation in commercial organisations.

3.4 The objectives of commercial organisations

We implied earlier that the objective of a commercial organisation is to make a profit. However, stakeholder theory and the 'stakeholder view' identify that wider objectives should be acknowledged, and that the interests of people other than the owners should also be served.

Nevertheless, whatever an organisation's objectives may be, it is the duty of its managers to seek to attain them. Many senior figures in the world of business have given the impression that the organisations they run exist to serve their own personal purposes. This is not the case and managers at all levels must be aware of this.

3.5 Personal motivation and corruption

Although, as the corporate scandals noted in the next section illustrate, there are occasions when individuals deliberately act corruptly, we must emphasise that managers need not be corrupt in order to fail in their fiduciary duty. The CEO who sets in motion a takeover bid that will enhance his prestige; the head of department who 'empire builds'; and the IT manager who buys an unnecessarily sophisticated enterprise resource management system are all failing in their fiduciary duty even though they receive no material benefit themselves.

3.6 Failures of corporate governance

> **FAST FORWARD**
>
> The main **failures of corporate governance** have come from allowing **dominant individuals**, **poor board** involvement, lack of **control** and scrutiny, **lack of independent scrutiny**, and the exclusion of **shareholders** from information and involvement.

Though mostly discussed in relation to large quoted companies, governance is an issue for all bodies corporate, regardless of whether they are commercial or not-for-profit organisations.

A number of **high profile corporate scandals** and collapses have raised questions about further measures that may be necessary to improve corporate governance. These cases have also highlighted the need for guidance to tackle the various **risks and problems** that can arise in organisations' systems of governance.

3.6.1 Domination by a single individual

A feature of many corporate governance scandals has been boards dominated by a single senior executive doing what that executive wants, with other board members merely acting as a rubber stamp. Sometimes the single individual may even bypass the board to action his own interests.

The presence of non-executive directors on the board is felt to be an important safeguard against domination by a single individual.

3.6.2 Lack of involvement of board

Boards that meet irregularly or fail to consider systematically the organisation's activities and risks are clearly weak. Sometimes the failure to carry out proper oversight is due to a **lack of information** being provided.

3.6.3 Lack of adequate control function

An obvious weakness is a **lack of internal audit,** since this is one of the most important aspects of internal control.

Another important control weakness is **lack of adequate technical knowledge** in key roles, for example in the audit committee or in senior compliance positions. A rapid turnover of staff involved in accounting or control may suggest inadequate resourcing, and will make control more difficult because of lack of continuity.

3.6.4 Lack of supervision

Employees who are not properly supervised can create large losses for the organisation through their own incompetence, negligence or fraudulent activity.

3.6.5 Lack of independent scrutiny

External auditors may not carry out the necessary questioning of senior management because of fears of losing the audit, and internal audit do not ask awkward questions because the chief financial officer determines their employment prospects. Often corporate collapses are followed by criticisms of external auditors.

3.6.6 Lack of contact with shareholders

Often board members may have grown up with the company but lose touch with the **interests and views** of shareholders. One possible symptom of this is the payment of remuneration packages that do not appear to be warranted by results. Equally, the directors may choose to pursue their own interests and ignore the requirements of the shareholders.

3.6.7 Emphasis on short-term profitability

Emphasis on short-term results can lead to the **concealment** of problems or errors, or **manipulation** of accounts to achieve desired results.

3.6.8 Misleading accounts and information

Often misleading figures are symptomatic of other problems (or are designed to conceal other problems) but in many cases, poor quality accounting information is a major problem if markets are trying to make a fair assessment of the company's value.

3.7 Benefits of improving corporate governance

> **FAST FORWARD**
> The benefits of improved corporate governance are **risk reduction**, improved **business performance**, and greater **external support**, most notably from investors.

3.7.1 Risk reduction

Clearly, the ultimate risk is of the organisation **making such large losses** that **bankruptcy** becomes inevitable. The organisation may also be closed down as a result of **serious regulatory breaches,** for example misapplying investors' monies. Proper corporate governance reduces such risks by aligning directors' interests with the company's strategic objectives, and by providing for measures to reduce fraud.

3.7.2 Performance

Performance should improve if accountabilities are made clear and directors' motivation is enhanced by **performance-related remuneration**. Also, the extra breadth of experience brought by non-executive directors, and measures to prevent domination by a single powerful figure, should improve the quality of decision-making at board level.

3.7.3 External support

External perceptions of the company should be enhanced through having a robust system of corporate governance. This can have wide-ranging benefits:

(a) Improved ability to raise finance
(b) Improved corporate image with public and government
(c) Improved relations with stakeholders such as customers and employees

3.8 Main provisions of good corporate governance

> **FAST FORWARD**
> The **Board of Directors** plays a crucial role in the **corporate governance** of an organisation. Key areas of governance include: the composition of the Board, its accountability, remuneration and the Board's relationship with an organisation's shareholders and auditors.

One benchmark code of corporate governance designed to bring corporations under the control of shareholders is the UK Corporate Governance Code. This sets out principles of best practice in relation to issues such as the composition of the Board of Directors, their remuneration, their accountability, and their relationship with a company's shareholders and its auditors.

3.8.1 The role of the Board of Directors

Given its focus on management and control systems in an organisation, it should not be surprising that a large element of corporate governance focuses on the Board of Directors and their role in organisations.

The 2018 UK Corporate Governance Code (Financial Reporting Council, 2018) suggests that the role of the board should be to promote the long-term sustainable success of a company, generating value for shareholders and contributing to wider society.

This will involve establishing the company's overall strategy, establishing appropriate targets and ensuring that the necessary resources are provided. The board should also make sure that it engages with key stakeholders, notably its workforce and its shareholders.

The board is also responsible for establishing policies and procedures for addressing the key areas of governance that are described in the following sections.

3.8.2 Key areas of governance

The UK Corporate Governance Code (Financial Reporting Council, 2018) identifies a number of key areas of governance which should be addressed by the board:

(a) **Division of responsibilities** – Every board should include a strong element (at least 50%) of independent non-executive directors who should constructively criticise and help develop proposals on strategy, as well as scrutinising management's performance in meeting agreed objectives.

The roles of chairman and chief executive are the two leading management roles in a company, with the chairman responsible for running the board and the CEO responsible for running the company including, for example, encouraging debate at board level. As such, there needs to be a clear **division of responsibility** between them so that there is a balance of power, and no single individual has unfettered powers of decision-making in the company.

(b) **Composition, selection and evaluation** – The board and its committees should have an appropriate balance of **skills, experience** and **knowledge** to enable them to carry out their respective duties and responsibilities effectively.

There should be a formal and rigorous procedure for appointing new directors to the board organised by the nomination committee (see later), and all directors must be able to allocate sufficient time to the company to carry out their responsibilities effectively.

The board should undertake a rigorous, formal **evaluation of its own performance**, and the performance of its committees and individual directors on an annual basis.

All directors should be submitted for re-election at regular intervals, provided they subject to continued satisfactory performance.

Selection of the Chair and non-executive directors should be conducted by open advertising or an external search agency.

The annual report should also report on the composition of the board in terms of its ethnicity and gender balance.

(c) **Accountability** – The board should present a fair, balanced and understandable assessment of the company's current position and its future prospects. This will require the establishment of an Audit Committee (see later) to ensure the integrity of the company's financial reporting.

The board should determine the nature and extent of the principal risks it is willing to take in achieving the company's objectives, and should also maintain sound risk management and internal control systems within the company.

(d) **Remuneration** – Directors' remuneration should be designed to promote the long-term sustainable success of the company. Performance-related elements of remuneration should be transparent, stretching and rigorously applied. Non-executive director remuneration should not include performance related elements, including share options.

There should be a formal and transparent procedure for developing a company's policy on executive remuneration, and no director should be involved in deciding their own remuneration (see remuneration committee later).

(e) **Relationship with shareholders** – The board collectively has responsibility for ensuring that a satisfactory **dialogue** takes place with shareholders, based on a mutual understanding of the company's objectives. If 20% or more of votes have been cast against a board recommendation at a general meeting then the board should consult with dissenting shareholders and report on the action taken as a result of this consultation.

(f) **Relationships with stakeholders** – the board should engage with key stakeholders. The workforce should be represented at board level, and should be able to raise any matters of concern.

> **Exam focus point**
> You are not expected to know the detail of the Corporate Governance Codes in specific countries. We use the UK Corporate Governance Code here to highlight the key features which corporate governance – and corporate governance codes in general – should be expected to address.

3.8.3 Unitary and dual board structures

Under a **unitary** board structure there is a single board consisting of executive and non-executive directors, which controls a company's activities. This is the predominant structure in the UK and the USA.

A **dual board** system consists of a **supervisory board** and a **management board**. The supervisory board oversees the long-term direction of the business, whilst the day to day running of the company is the responsibility of the separate management board (members of one board can't be members of the other).

A range of different stakeholder groups are represented on the supervisory board. Shareholders appoint a significant proportion of the members of the supervisory board. Employees also appoint a significant proporation of the supervisory board. Other stakeholders (for example banks, and sometimes key suppliers or customers) will also have a degree of representation.

The supervisory board appoints the members of the management board.

The dual structure is common in many European countries (but not in the UK).

The dual system has the advantage of there being a more distinct and formal separation between the supervisory body and those being 'supervised', because of the separate management board and supervisory board structures. Key stakeholders, such as employees, are represented on the supervisory board which should help to ensure that a company's activities bring benefits to a wide variety of stakeholder groups, not just shareholders.

The unitary approach has the advantage of there being a closer relationship and better information flow as all directors, both executive and non-executive, are on the same single board.

However, stakeholder representation can also be achieved within a unitary board structure. The 2018 UK Corporate Governance code (Financial Reporting Council, 2018) has brought in a requirement that, in order to ensure engagement with the workforce, listed companies must use one of the following approaches.

- Designate a non-executive director to represent workforce concerns
- Create a formal employee advisory council
- Appoint an employee to represent workforce interests at board level.

The remainder of the discussion of corporate governance assumes that a unitary (single) board structure is being used, as is the case in the UK.

> **Exam focus point**
> A question on the May 2018 paper required an awareness of the different types of board structures.

3.8.4 Executive Committee

Although the Board of Directors overall controls a business, it delegates day to day responsibility to the executive management team (or the 'Executive Committee'). The Executive Committee will be made up of the Chief Executive, the other executive directors on the Group Board, plus any senior executives of subsidiary companies.

The purpose of the Executive Committee is to undertake:

(a) The development and implementation of **strategy**, operational plans, policies, procedures and targets

(b) The monitoring of operating and financial **performance**

(c) The assessment and control of **risk**
(d) The prioritisation and allocation of **resources** in order to achieve objectives and targets

Sub-committees of the Board

The overall Board of Directors also delegates specific tasks to three sub-committees:

(a) Nominations Committee
(b) Remuneration Committee
(c) Audit Committee

3.8.5 Nominations committee

The key principle of 'effectiveness' highlights the importance of a company's Directors having an appropriate balance of skills and experience. The nominations committee plays a key role in ensuring that balance because it oversees the process for board appointments and makes recommendations to the board.

The UK Corporate Governance Code recommends that a majority of the committee members should be independent non-executive directors.

When considering board appointments, the nomination committee needs to consider the balance between executives and independent non-executives, the existing **skills and knowledge** possessed by the board, the need for continuity and succession planning, and the desirable **size** of the board.

Recent corporate governance guidance has laid more stress on the need to attract board members from a **diversity** of backgrounds. This includes gender diversity – in other words, increasing the number of female directors. However, the nomination committee should ensure that appointments to the board are made on merit, using **objective criteria**.

3.8.6 Executive remuneration and the remuneration committee

Attention!

> The syllabus for this Paper refers to "the remuneration (or executive compensation) committee." As such it is important that you understand that some organisations may have an **executive compensation committee**, rather than a remuneration committee.
>
> Some companies refer to the 'executive **remuneration**' they pay their directors, and in these companies the committee which designs and managers this remuneration is known as the remuneration committee. However, other companies refer to 'executive **compensation**' packages they award their directors – in which case, these compensation packages are designed and managed by the executive compensation committee.
>
> The purpose of the committees is the same – it is just the name which varies from company to company. In this text we refer to remuneration and the remuneration committee, but these references could equally be changed to 'executive compensation'.

Executive remuneration and the procedures for determining executive remuneration is another key aspect of corporate governance – in particular the need to prevent executive directors from setting their own remuneration.

Executive remuneration is another area where the **principal-agency problem** is evident, since directors and senior managers have a vested interest in maximising their remuneration, yet the value they create for shareholders may not justify the levels of remuneration which management receive, or think they should receive. Complaints over the level of directors' remuneration are frequently a feature of debate about corporate governance. However, these complaints focus not only on remuneration levels themselves, but also on the unwillingness of those who can challenge remuneration packages (eg non-executive directors, institutional shareholders) to do so.

Various problems have been highlighted:

(a) **Remuneration levels** that are **excessive** per se, and are not justified by the contribution directors have made

(b) Directors being **rewarded for failure**, for example receiving bonuses when their companies have performed poorly and receiving **significant compensation payments** when they lose office

(c) **Remuneration arrangements** providing incentives for directors to allow risk-taking beyond levels that would be deemed acceptable by many shareholders

(d) **Remuneration arrangements** being based on targets and objectives that highlight the differences between directors' and shareholders' interests. Many shareholders will be primarily interested in the creation of long-term wealth, but it may be difficult for directors to create this wealth or show that they have done it. Basing remuneration on objectives such as increasing sales revenues or short-term profits may be more popular with the directors.

Remuneration policy

Directors being paid excessive salaries and bonuses has been seen as one of the major corporate abuses for a large number of years. It is thus inevitable that the corporate governance provisions have targeted it.

The **Greenbury committee** in the UK set out principles which are a good summary of what remuneration policy should involve.

(a) Directors' remuneration should be set by **independent members** of the board (the remuneration committee)

(b) Any form of bonus should be related to **measurable performance** or enhanced shareholder value

(c) There should be **full transparency of directors' remuneration** including pension rights in a company's annual accounts

One of the dilemmas faced when setting directors' remuneration is that the levels of remuneration need to be sufficient to attract, retain and motivate directors of the quality required to run the company successfully, but, at the same time, a company should avoid paying more than is necessary for this purpose.

Similarly, it is important that remuneration reflects performance – both by the company and individual directors. As such, it is recommended that a significant proportion of directors' remuneration should be performance-related. However, as the 'Remuneration' element of the UK Corporate Governance Code suggests, performance targets should be linked to long-term success (as well as short-term performance); so the remuneration committee should consider different kinds of long-term incentives schemes as well as annual bonuses.

When setting any performance-related targets, it is also important that they should be stretching.

3.8.7 The remuneration committee

Executive directors should not be involved in setting their own remuneration. Therefore, the remuneration committee, staffed by independent non-executive directors, plays the key role in establishing remuneration arrangements in an organisation.

In order to be effective, the remuneration committee needs to determine both the organisation's **general policy** on the **remuneration of executive directors,** and also **specific remuneration packages** for each director. These packages could include cash and non-cash elements (such as shares and share options).

Measures to ensure that the committee is **independent** include not just requiring that the committee is staffed by non-executive directors, but also placing limits on the members' connection with the organisation. Measures to ensure independence include stating that the committee should have no personal interests other than as shareholders, no conflicts of interest and no day-to-day involvement in running the business.

3.8.8 Establishing executive remuneration arrangements

As we noted earlier, remuneration packages need to be sufficient to **attract, retain and motivate directors** of sufficient quality, whilst at the same time taking into account shareholders' interests as well. However, assessing executive remuneration in an imperfect market for executive skills may prove problematic.

The **link between remuneration and company performance** is particularly important. Recent UK guidance has stressed the need for the performance-related elements of executive directors' remuneration to be stretching, **designed to align their interests with those of shareholders** and **promote the long-term success of the company. Share options** are often used as a way of aligning directors' interests more closely with those of shareholders.

Remuneration incentives should be **compatible with risk policies and systems** and **criteria for paying bonuses** should be **risk-adjusted.** Discussion is often in terms of designing a remuneration package that encourages directors to avoid excessive risks. However, directors' remuneration can also be designed to encourage cautious directors to take more risks. Shareholders, who hold diversified portfolios, may be keener that a company undertakes a risky investment than its directors, whose livelihood may be threatened if the investment is not a success.

The remuneration committee must also consider the **balance** between the different elements of the package, the balance between **basic rewards** and **incentives** (eg performance-related bonuses). A well-balanced package should aim to **reduce agency costs** by ensuring that directors' (agents) interests are aligned with shareholders' (principals). This means the package should reward directors who meet targets that further the interests of shareholders, for example by including a bonus based on achievement of targets that are consistent with enhanced shareholder value.

Remuneration schemes should promote long-term shareholdings. In the 2018 UK Corporate Governance Code it is recommended that share awards to directors should be held for a minimum of five years and should be recoverable by the company if the director is shown to have acted inappropriately.

3.9 Shareholder activism

Although directors' remuneration is determined by the remuneration committee, in recent years, there have been an increasing number of instances where a company's shareholders have rejected the directors' proposed remuneration packages – with the shareholders arguing that the amounts being proposed are excessive or unduly generous.

Case Study

In July 2014, investors at fashion house Burberry rejected the chief executive's remuneration package, with 52% of shareholders voting not to support the remuneration report.

The chief executive has a remuneration package worth up to £10 million a year, but – although Burberry admitted this is a lot of money – the company said the amount was justified to retain the chief executive, arguing that he had been offered a higher salary by another company.

Also, Burberry pointed out that much of the package is performance-related, and therefore the chief executive would only receive it if the company performed strongly – which would also benefit shareholders. However, investors expressed concern at the 1.35m shares the chief executive had been allocated before his appointment, which had no performance criteria attached to them.

Burberry said the vote was disappointing. However, it was not binding, so the company was not forced to change its remuneration policy.

Nonetheless, the shareholders' actions at Burberry can be seen as example of shareholder activism.

3.9.1 Purpose of shareholder activism

Shareholder activism is 'the way shareholders can assert their power as owners of the company to influence its behaviour.' [European Corporate Governance Institute].

Activism covers a broad spectrum of activities, and isn't limited to voting against remuneration packages. The overriding rationale behind shareholder activism is to make companies more accountable to shareholders, and to increase shareholders' influence over a company's strategy more generally.

(Note: In this context, the shareholders we are considering are external investors; not directors who hold shares in a company, for example as a result of their share options maturing).

Although shareholders don't run a company, there are still ways for them to influence its board of directors and senior management. In some cases shareholders may engage in dialogue with a company's management to raise concerns they have about a particular issue, while in other cases formal proposals are voted on at an annual general meeting.

The notion of shareholders (as owners of a company) wanting to assert their power is not new, but historically they had done so in private – through discussions with management behind closed doors. However, shareholder activism has become more apparent to the outside world as shareholders have adopted higher profile tactics in their efforts to determine a company's course of action or strategy.

In addition, the profile of shareholder activism has also been heightened by the increased use of social media. For example, blogs and Twitter messages allow shareholder activists to have a public voice, and to publicise their issues or concerns about a company's performance or about management's performance.

3.9.2 Drivers for shareholder activism

Shareholder activists can be motivated by many different reasons. The UK Institutional Shareholders' Committee has identified a number of reasons why shareholders might want to intervene:

(a) To raise concerns about the strategy being pursued, in terms of products, markets and investments, and/or to ensure a different strategy is pursued in order to improve performance and profitability

(b) To influence the outcome of a takeover or other merger and acquisition activity

(c) Poor operational performance, particularly if one of more key business segments (or business units) has persistently underperformed. (In this respect, shareholders may also seek the disposal of under-performing assets).

(d) Major failures in internal controls; particularly in sensitive areas such as health and safety, pollution or quality.

(e) Poor attitudes towards corporate social responsibility; for example, poor working conditions in a company's factories, or across its supply chain

(f) Failure to comply with laws and regulations, or corporate governance codes

(g) The company's management is being dominated by a small group of executive directors, and the non-executive directors are failing to hold management to account

(h) Excessive levels of directors' remuneration, or concerns that directors' remuneration packages do not reward value creation

(i) To ensure changes to a company's board – either removing individual directors, or replacing the board as a whole.

3.9.3 Implications of shareholder activism

Despite the potential reasons for it, shareholder activism remains controversial. Proponents argue that companies with active and engaged shareholders are more likely to be successful in the long term than those whose shareholders are passive and do not hold the board to account for a company's performance. For example, by forcing a debate about a company's strategy and leadership, shareholder activism could potentially help to improve the company's performance.

Opponents of shareholder activism say that it is disruptive, arguing that the uninformed actions of unruly shareholders, and their hostility to management, can weaken strong companies. Also, some critics view shareholder activists as 'corporate raiders' who aren't interested in the long term future of the company, but buy shares in a company they perceive to be undervalued and then push through changes in order to increase share value. This then enables them to generate a massive return on their shares.

Ultimately, though, the issues around shareholder activism again link back to the agency problem. Although shareholders do not run the company, to what extent should they be able to influence the board of directors and the company's management? This question becomes even more important if a company (or its management) is under-performing. If shareholders feel a company is underperforming – and not maximising the value it generates for them as owners – why should they not be entitled to voice their concerns about this?

In this respect, discussions around shareholder activism perhaps also highlight the need for improved relations and communications between boards and shareholders – and this also has potential implications for corporate governance.

3.10 Accountability, audit and the audit committee

Accountability is identified in the UK Corporate Governance Code as a key area of corporate governance. The Code identifies the following responsibilities for a company's Board of Directors:

(a) The board must present a balanced and understandable assessment of the company's position and its prospects

(b) The board must determine the nature and extent of the risks it is willing to take in achieving its strategic objectives. The board must also maintain sound risk management and internal control systems within the company

(c) The board must establish formal and transparent arrangements for considering how to apply the corporate reporting, risk management and internal control principles, and for maintaining an appropriate relationship with the company's auditor.

This last point has two important implications:

(a) First, it identifies the important role which **auditors** have to play in maintaining good corporate governance. If information is disclosed and audited to a high quality, the reliability and comparability of reporting will be increased, and investors (ie the company's owners) will be able to make better investment decisions.

(b) Second the relationship between a company and its auditors introduces the role of the **audit committee**.

The audit committee

There should be **formal and clear arrangements** with the **company's auditors**, and for applying the financial reporting and internal control principles. Companies should have an **audit committee** consisting of independent non-executive directors.

At least one member of the audit committee must also have recent and relevant **financial experience**.

The main role and responsibilities of the audit committee include the following:

(a) To monitor **the integrity of the financial statements** of the company and any formal announcements relating to the company's financial performance, reviewing significant financial reporting issues and judgements contained in them. Where requested by the board, the audit committee should provide advice on whether the annual report and accounts, taken as a whole, are fair, balanced and understandable, and provide the information necessary for shareholders to assess the company's performance, business model and strategy.

(b) To review the company's **internal financial controls** and, unless expressly addressed by a separate board risk committee composed of independent directors, or by the board itself, the company's control and risk management systems

(c) To monitor and review the effectiveness of the company's **internal audit function.** Where there is no internal audit function, the audit committee should consider annually whether there is a need for an internal audit function, and should make a recommendation to the board accordingly.

(d) To make recommendations to the board, for it to put to the shareholders for their approval in general meeting, in relation to **the appointment, reappointment or removal of the external auditor** and to approve the **remuneration** and terms of engagement of the external auditors

(e) To review and monitor the **external auditor's independence and objectivity** and **the effectiveness of the audit process**, taking into consideration relevant professional and regulatory requirements

(f) To develop and implement policy on the engagement of the external auditor to supply non-audit services, taking into account relevant ethical guidance regarding the provision of non-audit services (eg consultancy services) by the external audit firm, and to report to the board, identifying any matters in respect of which it considers that action or improvement is needed and making recommendations as to the steps to be taken.

A lot of guidance around corporate governance has been concerned with defining effective internal control. Inevitably many companies involved in scandals have had obvious weaknesses in internal control, weaknesses that have not been picked up by those monitoring control.

Lack of adequate internal control functions – An obvious weakness is a **lack of internal audit**. Another important control is **lack of adequate technical knowledge** in key roles, for example in the audit committee or in senior compliance positions. A rapid turnover of staff involved in accounting or control may suggest inadequate resourcing, and will make control more difficult because of lack of continuity.

Lack of independent scrutiny – External auditors may not carry out the necessary questioning of senior management because of fears of losing the audit. Often corporate collapses are followed by criticisms of external auditors, and suggestions that poorly planned or poorly performance audit work failed to identify control weaknesses or other issues within an organisation.

3.10.1 Audit and the external auditor

The objective of an **audit** of financial statements is to enable the auditor to express an opinion on whether the financial statements are prepared, in all material respects, in accordance with an applicable financial reporting framework. An audit of financial statements is an example of an assurance engagement. The purpose of an external audit is to enable auditors to **give an opinion** on the financial statements.

While an audit might produce by-products such as advice to the directors on how to run the business, and areas of control weakness which should be addressed, its objective is **solely to report to the shareholders.**

The accounting and auditing professions have been under the public spotlight for many years now, and as a result of certain events, many changes have occurred in relation to audit and assurance engagements.

 **Case Study**

As a result of the stock market bubble of the late 1990s and speculation over the future of 'dotcom' companies, many countries experienced huge **corporate financial scandals and frauds**. The bubble burst in 2000, followed by a revelation that senior management at **Enron**, a US energy company, had been deceiving investors by fraudulently overstating profitability. Its auditor, **Arthur Andersen**, was shown to have lacked objectivity in evaluating Enron's accounting methods. This led to the collapse of Arthur Andersen in 2002.

Other companies that were also involved in corporate frauds included WorldCom, Parmalat, Cable & Wireless and Xerox, to name but a few. The subsequent fallout of these frauds was a lack of confidence in the way companies were run and audited. In the USA, this resulted in the **Sarbanes-Oxley Act 2002** which has not only radically changed the **regulation** of the accounting profession in the USA but also influenced such issues worldwide.

In September 2008 Lehman Brothers, a global financial services firm, filed for bankruptcy in the US triggering a severe world-wide financial crisis. Lehman had expanded aggressively into property-related investments, including so called sub-prime mortgages (loans to people on low incomes or with poor credit histories). In subsequent reports it was claimed that Lehman Brothers covered up the extent of their irrecoverable debts using an accounting manoeuvre known as 'Repo 105', which involves loaning 'bad' assets to other firms in exchange for short-term financing. Lehman's auditors had issued a clean audit report on the accounts to 30 November 2007 and the Accountancy and Actuarial Discipline Board (AADB), an independent investigative and disciplinary body in the UK, commenced an investigation in 2010 into the conduct of the auditors of Lehman Brothers International Europe.

Following the collapse of Lehman Brothers, other banks failed worldwide and many needed government support to continue. There was a knock on effect in the wider economy in many countries in 2008 and 2009 with many business struggling or failing altogether. The aftermath of the global financial crisis also saw nations (such as Greece and Portugal) in danger of defaulting on their debts, and needing to be bailed out by the European Union.

In light of this global financial crisis, regulators have again been considering the effectiveness of the audit and the auditor's role in helping to prevent, or at least provide warning of, corporate and financial institution collapses in the future.

One important area being focused on is the importance of **professional scepticism** for audit quality. Regulators have been trying to stimulate debate about what actions may be needed to ensure the appropriate degree of scepticism is applied by auditors in practice.

3.11 Limitations of corporate governance

Whilst this section of the chapter, as a whole, has highlighted how corporate governance plays a beneficial role in risk management and control within organisations, corporate governance could nevertheless have some less favourable implications in relation to business strategy:

(a) Governance increases **shareholders' power** and prioritises shareholders' interests, potentially at the expense of other stakeholder groups.

(b) The increased scrutiny to which results are exposed (particularly in listed companies) may encourage a focus on short-termism and **short term results** rather than long term plans.

(c) The increased emphasis on risk management and risk reduction may make directors feel that they should accept lower risk (and lower return) projects in favour of ones which might generate higher returns (but which might also carry higher risk).

3.12 Performance measurement

In our discussion of executive remuneration earlier we highlighted the need for remuneration to be linked to performance.

We also highlighted the importance of performance measures being linked to the long-term success of a company as well as short-term performance. However, we have also noted one of the potential limitations of corporate governance is that it could lead to an increased scrutiny on short-term results.

As such, an important consideration in relation to performance measurement is selecting which aspects of performance to measure. We can identify two common types of performance measures: accounting-based, and market-based.

Accounting-based measures include:

- Profit-based measures (such as earnings before interest and tax (EBIT)
- Return on capital employed (ROCE)
- Earnings per share. Investors look for growth; a company's earnings levels need to be sustained in order to pay dividends and invest in the business.

$$\text{Earnings per share (EPS)} = \frac{\text{Profits distributable to ordinary shareholders}}{\text{Number of ordinary shares issued}}$$

Critics of accounting-based measures argue that these encourage a bias towards shot-term performance.

As such, they could mean that managers' interests are not aligned with the interest of shareholders who are more interested in the long term. For example, earnings per share, for example, could be reduced, in the short term, by capital-building investments in research and development and in marketing, even though these will generate value in the longer term. Similarly, critics of measures such as ROCE argue that they discourage asset replacement – even though this could impede growth and innovation in the future.

One solution could be to measure profit-based performance over a longer period (for example three to five years) rather than on an annual basis, to try to encourage a sustained improvement in performance.

More generally, a **shareholder value approach** to performance measurement involves moving the focus away from short-term profits to a **longer-term view of value creation**, the motivation being that it will help the business stay ahead in an increasingly competitive world.

In this respect, it is important to include market-based performance measures alongside accounting-based ones when assessing executives' performance.

Remember that earlier in the chapter we also mentioned the potential importance of aligning directors' interests with those of shareholders, and the use of **share options** as one way of helping to achieve this. Using market-based performance measures will also help to reiterate the importance of shareholder value in performance measurement.

Market-based performance measures include:

- Share price
- Shareholder return. Analysts can use the following ratios to measure shareholder returns: price-earnings (P/E) ratio; market to book value; dividend yield and total shareholder return.

The **P/E ratio** reflects the market's confidence in a company's earnings growth in the future:

$$\text{P/E ratio} = \frac{\text{Market price per share}}{\text{EPS}}$$

Dividend yield shows the return achieved from dividends as a percentage of the market price of a share:

$$\text{Dividend yield} = \frac{\text{Dividend per share}}{\text{Market price per share}} \%$$

Total shareholder return (TSR) represents the value a company's financial performance has created for an investor. It measures the total percentage return to shareholders over a given period, and is calculated using the formula:

$$\frac{\text{Dividend per share + Movement in share price}}{\text{Share price at the start of the period}}$$

4 Businesses and their environments

> **FAST FORWARD**
>
> The **business environment** refers to all the factors affecting a business that are not under the control of its managers.

4.1 Elements in the business environment

The factors influencing a business can be **internal** or **external**. The internal factors are its factors of production and these are under the control of management.

The external factors are such things as the behaviour of competitors, the state of the economy and market, and advances in technology. These are its business environment. Managers cannot control the business environment and instead they must respond to it.

4.1.1 The STEEPLE model

> **FAST FORWARD**
>
> The **STEEPLE model** of the business environment stands for Social, Technological, Economic, Ecological/ethical, Political and LEgal factors.

One model of the business environment is STEEPLE, a mnemonic that stands for:

Social/cultural factors: these include fashion, changing patterns of population, and changing lifestyles.

Technological factors: including availability of advanced communications technologies, cures for illnesses, and faster air transport.

Economic factors: the extent to which trade is global, whether the economy is growing richer or poorer, and the behaviour of important factors such as interest rates, exchange rates and price levels.

Ecological and ethical factors: growing concern, and policy, to prevent carbon emissions, dumping of waste, and using up non-renewable resources like fossil fuels. The treatment of workers from poorer countries and trading with countries that deny human rights are part of ethical concern.

Political/Legal factors: laws for and against free trade with a country, the policy of governments to encourage or discourage growth of particular industries, taxation law and the possibility of radical swings of government policy.

4.2 Responding to the business environment

FAST FORWARD
> The business environment is both a source of **opportunities** and a source of **threats** to a firm. Management seeks to grasp opportunties and to avoid threats.

The business environment contains the **factors of production** that the firm seeks to buy-in to make its products. It also contains the **markets and customers** that will buy its products. Finally it contains its **competitors** that rival it for these factors of production and for the same customers.

4.3 Impacts of uncertainty

FAST FORWARD
> **Uncertainty** refers to the problems management has in **making reliable assumptions about the future**.

As we have already mentioned several times, economics assumes that firms seek to maximise profits. However, this assumption could overlook the problems management faces in predicting how its decisions will turn out . The business environment is not predictable.

This has led economists to recognise a number of behaviours that management adopt that can appear to conflict with simple profit maximisation.

4.3.1 Bounded rationality

FAST FORWARD
> Managers recognise uncertainty and the **bounded rationality** of the decisions they make and instead seek to make **satisfactory profits** rather than maximium profits, and develop **risk reducing** and **collaborative** strategies in relation to other firms.

The American social scientist Herbert Simon suggested that management seek to take rational decisions within the framework of the information they have available. However, this information, including information about the environment and future events, is imperfect.

This situation in which management's decisions are limited by the information they have, as well as other constraints – such as the shortage of time available to analyse the information before making a decision – is known as bounded rationality.

Bounded rationality can lead to two potential outcomes:

1. **Faulty decisions**: decisions may be taken which, on the basis of the information available, were intended to lead to maximum profits. However, subsequent unanticipated changes to the environment mean that the effects of the decision did not maximise profits. With the benefit of hindsight an alternative decision would have generated maximum profits.

2. **Satisficing behaviour**: management recognises that they suffer bounded rationality and uncertainty. Instead of taking risks to maximise profit they follow conservative and cautious strategies that will bring about a satisfactory profit at less risk.

4.3.2 Vertical integration

Vertical integration refers to firms taking over responsibility for business downstream, nearer to its customer or upstream, towards the source of its supplies.

Management may decide to use vertical integration to eliminate the risk of trade customers ceasing to buy its products, or component manufacturers raising prices or failing to supply. By bringing it all in-house this risk is reduced. This may not be consistent with profit maximisation because it may increase costs, but it does reduce risk.

4.3.3 Resource dependency theory

The importance of appreciating the context and environment in which a firm is operating – and the uncertainties it presents – resonates the ideas of resource dependency theory which we discussed earlier in this chapter.

Resource dependency theory argues that firms are as much **externally controlled by their environment** as internally controlled by their management. This is due to the firm's dependence on resources provided to them by other firms in their environments.

A steel producing firm depends on an electricity generating firm for the power it needs. The electricity generating firm depends on the steel producing firm for someone to sell its power to.

This is a contrast to the conventional notion of a market for electricity in which two profit maximisers battle each other, the generating firm pushing the price up and the steel producer beating the price down. Instead, according to resource dependency theory, both sides are aware of dependence on the other and will seek to establish a satisfactory price and terms of business that keeps them both making adequate profits for their shareholders.

Chapter Roundup

- The ownership of an organisation affects the goals that it will pursue. A significant distinction is made between **public sector** organisations, which belong to the state, and **private sector** organisations which are owned by private individuals. Private sector organisations are assumed to be **profit maximisers**, whereas public sector organisations pursue **not-for-profit objectives.**

- Non-profit organisations include **clubs and associations**, associations owned by members such as **mutuals** and **co-operatives**, as well as **charitable groups**, **trade unions**, and **professional associations**, including the Association of International Accountants.

- Profit seeking organisations are divided into **sole-traders, partnerships**, and corporations (or companies). Companies are denoted as **public companies** and **private companies** according to whether the general public is allowed to own shares in them.

- **Firm** is the term used in economics for any organisation that carries on a business. Economists assume that the objective of firms is to **maxmise profits**.

- **Corporate social responsibilty (CSR)** is the requirement that organisations behave as good neighbours by taking into account the impact of their actions on society as a whole rather than just on the profits of their owners.

- **Corporate ethics** concern the morality of the behaviour of a business such as its honesty in dealings and its care for human life.

- **Stakeholder theory** highlights that firms need to be accountable to a wide range of stakeholder groups, and not just to their shareholders.

- The **separation of ownership from control** arises from shareholders, the firm's **principals**, being different people from the firm's managers, the paid **agents** of the shareholders.

- The **agency problem** refers to the problem that agents will pursue their personal interests, sometimes at the expense of making profits for the principals. This can be addressed by **incentivisation** basing the earnings of agents on the profits given to principals.

- **Corporate governance** refers to the systems by which a firm is managed and controlled.

- All managers have a **duty of faithful service** to the owners of a firm.

- The main **failures of corporate governance** have come from allowing **dominant individuals, poor board** involvement, lack of **control** and scrutiny, **lack of independent scrutiny**, and the exclusion of **shareholders** from information and involvement.

- The benefits of improved corporate governence are **risk reduction**, improved **business performance**, and greater **external support**, most notably from investors.

- The **Board of Directors** plays a crucial role in the **corporate governance** of an organisation. Key areas of governance include: the composition of the Board, its accountability, remuneration and the Board's relationship with an organisation's shareholders and auditors.

- The **business environment** refers to all the factors affecting a business that are not under the control of its managers.

- The **STEEPLE model** of the business environment stands for **S**ocial, **T**echnological, **E**conomic, **E**cological/ethical, **P**olitical and **LE**gal factors.

Chapter Roundup Cont'd

- The business environment is both a source of **opportunities** and a source of **threats** to a firm. Management seeks to grasp opportunties and to avoid threats.

- **Uncertainty** refers to the problems management has in **making reliable assumptions about the future.**

- Managers recognise uncertainty and the **bounded rationality** of the decisions they make and instead seek to make **satisfactory profits** rather than maximium profits, and develop **risk reducing** and **collaborative** strategies in relation to other firms.

Quick Quiz

1 Who proposed a model of business based on the objective of maximising sales?

    A   Drucker
    B   Williamson
    C   Ansoff
    D   Baumol

2 What does the term 'stakeholders' mean?

3 Which one of the following is not a stakeholder for a mutual organisation?

    A   Customers
    B   Staff
    C   Shareholders
    D   Directors

4 In a modern business corporation, who are the agents and who are the principals?

5 Suggest three reasons why shareholders may not be able to control the decisions of the firms they have invested in.

6 Suggest three ways in which shareholders can regain control over firms.

7 What is meant by the 'business environment'?

8 What is bounded rationality?

Answers to Quick Quiz

1. D   Baumol

2. The stakeholders of an organisation are people or organisations who have a legitimate interest in the strategy and behaviour of that organisation.

3. C   By definition, mutual organisations do not have shareholders, because they are owned collectively by their customers.

4. The agents are the paid managers of the business who are supposed to be acting in the best interests of their principals. The principals are the shareholders of the business.

5. Shareholders may be unable to control firms due to infrequent shareholder meetings, lack of information from management about what the firm is doing, and the desire of managers to do things to benefit themselves rather than the things that will benefit the shareholders.

6. Shareholders can regain control by more effective scrutiny of management decisions, providing incentives to management linked to profits, and by strengthening some of the measures of corporate governance.

7. The business environment is the factors that influence a business that are beyond management control – sometimes remembered using the STEEPLE model.

8. Bounded rationality refers to fact that management can only take rational decisions within the constraints of the information they have at the time. If this information is faulty then the decisions they take will not maximise profits.

End of chapter question

Performance and directors' remuneration (May 2014)

The debate on executive directors' remuneration has rumbled on through the last decade. However with the increase in institutional investor activism and the scandals and subsequent collapses associated with a number of large corporations in the UK, US, and elsewhere, the focus is well and truly on curtailing excessive and undeserved remuneration packages but left shareholders with little reward in terms of company's performance. The recent financial crisis has accelerated the debate by the view that directors in financial industry are overpaid to the detriment of the shareholders, the employees, and the company as a whole.

The emphasis of the debate is on remuneration committees to try to ensure that executive directors' remuneration packages are fairly and appropriately constructed, taking into account long-term objectives. Central to this aim is the use of performance indicators which will incentivise directors but at the same time align their interests with those of shareholders, to the long-term benefit of the company. It is argued that there should be a clear link between the remuneration top managers receive and the performance of the business. However, it is found that this correlation between reward and performance is far from clear (Leaver, A. et al., *Financialisation and Strategy*, Routledge, 2006).

Required

(a) Identify at least four common corporate performance measurements, including two market-based and two accounting-based indicators. **(7 marks)**

(b) Critically discuss those performance criteria identified in part (a) that may be used in determining executive directors' remuneration. **(23 marks)**

(Total 30 marks)

PART B CONSUMPTION, PRODUCTION AND DISTRIBUTION

Theory of costs

Topic list	Syllabus reference
1 Costs of production	2.2
2 Average costs, marginal costs and diminishing returns	2.2
3 Economies of scale and long run costs	2.2
4 Growth of firms	2.3

Introduction

In this chapter we look at the costs of production for an individual firm and how these are affected by both short run and long run factors.

We contrast the concept of **opportunity cost** (which we introduced in Chapter 1), with **financial cost** as seen from the accountant's point of view.

The aggregate amount of goods supplied by every individual firm adds up to the market supply. By studying an individual firm we are looking at the 'building blocks' of market supply.

However, we also examine how individual firms look to grow in order to benefit from cost savings and efficiencies.

PART B CONSUMPTION, PRODUCTION AND DISTRIBUTION

1 Costs of production

Although we have identified that there are a range of organisations with differing objectives, we focus now on organisations which seek to make a profit. It is widely accepted that this will enable us to give a useful explanation of the way firms behave. The basic condition for profitability is very simple: **overall revenues must exceed overall costs**.

> **Key term**
>
> **Profit** is equal to **total revenue minus total cost** of any level of output.

In order to understand how firms go about seeking profit, therefore, we must examine the ways in which costs and revenues arise. We will start by considering the costs incurred by a firm that makes and sells goods, and will define some key concepts about costs in economics.

1.1 Short run and long run costs

> **FAST FORWARD**
>
> A firm's output decisions can be examined in the **short run**, (when at least one factor of production is fixed) and in the **long run**, (when all factors of production can be varied).
>
> Total costs can be divided into **fixed** and **variable** elements. These elements have different effects on total cost as output is increased.

Production is carried out by firms using the **factors of production** which must be paid or rewarded for their use. The cost of production is the cost of the factors used.

Factor of production	Its cost
Land	Rent
Labour	Wages
Capital	Interest
Enterprise	Normal profit

Notice that normal profit is viewed here as a cost. This may seem odd to an accountant, who thinks of profit as the excess of revenues over cost, but normal profit is the amount of profit necessary to keep an entrepreneur in his or her present activity. In other words, normal profit is the **opportunity cost** of preventing the entrepreneur investing elsewhere.

> **Key term**
>
> **Normal profit** is the minimum amount of profit a firm must make from the production of a good to prevent the firm moving its economic resources to the production of another good.

> **Attention**
>
> It is very important to note that normal profit is not the same as accounting profit, because normal profit takes account of opportunity cost whereas accounting profit does not.

Any profit earned in excess of this normal profit is known as **supernormal, abnormal, or excess profit**.

Whether a firm can maintain these profits in the long run will depend on the nature of the industry it is operating in. We will return to this point later in this Study Text when we look at the differences between perfect competition and monopoly.

> **Key terms**
>
> The **short run** is a time period in which the amount of at least one factor of production (land, labour, capital or enterprise) is fixed.
>
> The **long run** is a period sufficiently long to allow full flexibility in all the factors of production used.

120

1.2 Fixed costs and variable costs

In the **short run**, certain costs are **fixed** because the availability of factors of production is restricted. Decisions must therefore be taken for the short run within the restriction of having some resources in fixed supply. In the **longer run**, however, most costs are **variable**, because the supply of skilled labour, machinery, buildings and so on can all be increased or decreased. Decisions in the long run are therefore subject to fewer restrictions about resource availability.

Inputs are variable at the decision of management. For example, management might decide to buy more raw materials, hire more labour, start overtime working and so on.

(a) Labour is usually considered to be variable in the short run. Inputs which are treated as **fixed** in the short run are likely to include **capital items**, such as buildings and machinery, for which a significant lead time might be needed before their quantities are changed. There could also be constraints around **technology** which could limit the productivity of other factors of production.

(b) **All inputs are variable in the long run.** A decision to change the quantity of an input variable which is fixed in the short run will involve a change in the **scale of production**.

1.3 Short run costs: total costs, average costs and marginal costs

Let us now turn our attention to short run costs. Note, however, that in economics the 'short run' is not a time period which can be measured in days or months. The critical determinant of a time period being 'short' is that **at least one factor of production is fixed**.

Key terms

- **Total cost** (TC). Total cost is the cost of all the resources needed to produce a given level of output. Total cost comprises total fixed cost (TFC) and total variable cost (TVC).
- **Fixed costs** are costs which do not change when levels of production change, for example, the rent of premises.
- **Variable costs** are costs which change according to the level of output, for example, raw material costs.
- **Average cost** (AC). Average cost for a given level of output is the total cost divided by the total quantity produced.

    Average cost is made up of an **average fixed cost** per unit plus an **average variable cost** per unit.

    $$AC = \frac{TC}{N} = \frac{TFC}{N} + \frac{TVC}{N}$$

    $$AC = AFC + AVC$$

    Average fixed cost per unit (AFC) – total fixed costs divided by the number of units – will get smaller as the number of units produced (N) increases. This is because total fixed costs remain the same amount regardless of the volume of output, so as N gets bigger, AFC must get smaller.

    Average variable costs per unit (AVC) – total variable costs divided by the number of units – will also change as output volume increases, but may rise as well as fall.

- **Marginal cost** (MC). This is the extra cost (incremental cost) of producing one more unit of output. For example, the marginal cost for a firm of producing the 50th unit of output is the total cost of making 50 units minus the total cost of making the first 49 units.

PART B CONSUMPTION, PRODUCTION AND DISTRIBUTION

Question

Costs

To test your understanding of these concepts, look at the three definitions given below. Which one(s) of them, if any, correctly describes the marginal cost of producing one extra unit of output?

(a) MC = increase in total cost of production
(b) MC = increase in variable cost of production
(c) MC = increase in average cost of production

Answer

(a) and (b) are both correct; (c) is incorrect. An example might help. Suppose a firm has made 100 units of output, and now goes on to produce one more. The costs might be as follows.

	Cost of 100 units $	Cost of 101 units $
Total variable cost	200	202
Total fixed cost	100	100
Total cost	300	302
Average cost	$3.00	$2.99

Marginal cost = $302 – $300 = $2.

Because fixed costs have not changed, the marginal cost is both the increase in the total cost of production and the increase in the total variable cost of production.

Figure 1 shows how the various elements of cost vary as output changes.

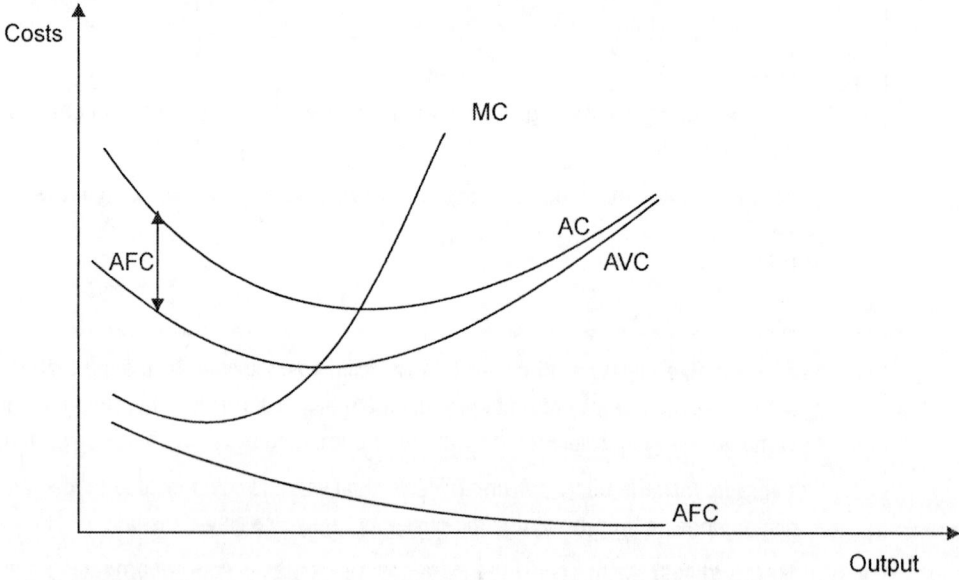

Figure 1 Components of a firm's short run costs

Exam focus point The diagram in Figure 1 is a very important diagram in economics. Make sure you know what each of the curves are, and what each curve represents.

1.4 Numerical illustration

Let us suppose that a firm employs a given amount of capital which is a fixed (invariable) input in the short run. The firm may combine different amounts of labour with this capital, and we assume labour is a variable input in the short term. Thus fixed capital and variable labour can be combined to produce different levels of output.

Here is an illustration of the relationship between the different definitions of the firm's costs. (The figures used are hypothetical.)

Units of output n	Fixed costs FC $	Variable costs VC $	Total cost TC $	Average cost AC $	Marginal cost MC $	
1	0.80	0.30	1.10	1.10	1.10	
2	0.80	0.80	1.60	0.80	0.50	(1.60 – 1.10)
3	0.80	0.95	1.75	0.58	0.15	(1.75 – 1.60)
4	0.80	1.20	2.00	0.50	0.25	(2.00 – 1.75)
5	0.80	1.70	2.50	0.50	0.50	(2.50 – 2.00)
6	0.80	2.32	3.12	0.52	0.62	(3.12 – 2.50)
7	0.80	3.19	3.99	0.57	0.87	(3.99 – 3.12)
8	0.80	4.32	5.12	0.64	1.13	(5.12 – 3.99)
9	0.80	5.50	6.30	0.70	1.18	(6.30 – 5.12)
10	0.80	7.20	8.00	0.80	1.70	(8.00 – 6.30)

(a) **Total cost** is the sum of capital costs (fixed costs) plus labour costs (variable costs), since these are the only two inputs in this example.

(b) **Average cost** is the cost per unit of output, ie $AC = \dfrac{TC}{output} = \dfrac{TC}{n}$

(c) **Marginal cost** is the total cost of producing n units minus the total cost of producing one less unit, ie (n – 1) units.

Note the following points on this set of figures.

(a) **Total cost.** Total costs of production carry on rising as more and more units are produced.

(b) **Average cost.** AC changes as output increases. It starts by falling, reaches its lowest level when 4 or 5 units are produced, and then starts rising again.

(c) **Marginal cost.** The MC of each extra unit of output also changes with each unit produced. It too starts by falling, fairly quickly reaches its lowest level (when 3 units are produced), and then starts rising.

(d) **AC and MC compared.** At lower levels of output, MC is less than AC. At higher levels of output, though, MC is higher than AC. There is a 'cross-over' point, where MC is exactly equal to AC. In this example, it is at 5 units of output.

1.5 Economists' and accountants' concepts of cost

FAST FORWARD

Economic costs are different from accounting costs, and represent the opportunity costs of the factors of production that are used.

As we have already mentioned, to an economist cost includes an amount for normal profit which is the reward for entrepreneurship. **Normal profit is the opportunity cost of entrepreneurship**. The opportunity cost of entrepreneurship is the amount of profit that an entrepreneur could earn elsewhere and so must be foregone to undertake the current project. In this situation, normal profit is the profit the entrepreneur must earn to persuade him to keep on with his investment in his current enterprise. If he could earn more by undertaking a different enterprise, as a rational decision-maker he will choose to invest in the other enterprise instead.

To put this another way, the **economic cost of production** for a firm is the **opportunity cost of production**.

A second feature of an accountant's concept of costs is that they can be divided into fixed costs and variable costs. Total fixed costs per period are a given amount, regardless of the volume of production and sales. Cost accountants usually assume that the variable cost per unit is a **constant amount,** so that the total **variable cost** of sales is directly proportional to the **volume** of sales.

Economists do not take this approach. In the short run, there are **fixed costs** and **variable costs**, but the variable cost of making an extra unit of output need not be the same for each extra unit that is made. As a result, the **marginal cost** of **each extra unit** is not constant either.

Accounting profits consist of sales revenue minus the **explicit costs** of the business. Explicit costs are those which are clearly stated and recorded, for example:

- Materials costs – prices paid to suppliers
- Labour costs – wages paid
- Depreciation costs on non-current assets
- Other expenses, such as rates and building rental

Economic profit consists of sales revenue minus both the explicit costs and the **implicit costs** of the business. Implicit costs are benefits foregone by not using the factors of production in their next most profitable way (opportunity costs).

It is a well-established principle in both accounting and economics that relevant costs for decision-making purposes are **future costs incurred as a consequence of the decision**. Past or 'sunk' costs are not relevant to our decisions now, because we cannot change them: they have already been incurred. Relevant future costs are the **opportunity costs** of the input resources to be used.

1.6 Example: economic profits and opportunity costs

Suppose that a sole trader sells goods worth $200,000. He incurs materials costs of $70,000, hired labour costs of $85,000, and other expenses of $20,000. He has no non-current assets other than the building from which he trades, on which depreciation is not charged. In accounting terms, his profit would be as follows.

	$	$
Sales		200,000
Materials	70,000	
Labour	85,000	
Other expenses	20,000	
		(175,000)
Profit		25,000

But suppose the buildings the trader uses in his business could have been put to another use to earn $15,000, and his own labour as business manager could get him a job with a salary of $20,000. The position of the business in economic terms would be as follows.

	$
Sales less explicit costs	25,000
Opportunity costs ($15,000 + $20,000)	(35,000)
Loss	(10,000)

In economic terms, the business has made a loss. It would pay the trader to put his buildings and capital to the alternative use, and employ his own labour another way, working for someone else at a salary of $20,000.

Question: Accounting profit and economic profit

Wilbur Proffit set up his business one year ago. In that time, his firm has earned total revenue of $160,000, and incurred costs of $125,000, including his own salary of $12,000. Before, he had been a salaried employee of Dead End Ventures, earning an annual salary of $20,000.

To finance the business, Wilbur had to sell his investment of $200,000 in government securities which earned interest of 10% pa. He used $80,000 of this to buy a warehouse, whose annual commercial rental value would be $11,000 pa. The remaining $120,000 has been used to finance business operations.

Required

Calculate:

- The accounting profit earned by Wilbur in the last year
- The economic profit or loss earned

Answer

Accounting profit

	$
Revenue	160,000
Costs	125,000
Profit	35,000

Economic profit

	$	$
Revenue		160,000
Accounting costs	125,000	
Opportunity cost of owner's time – extra salary foregone from alternative employment (20,000 – 12,000)	8,000	
Rental of factory (opportunity cost of commercial rental foregone)	11,000	
Opportunity cost of other capital tied up in the business (10% of $120,000)	12,000	
		156,000
Economic profit		4,000

2 Average costs, marginal costs and diminishing returns

FAST FORWARD If the cost of producing one extra unit of a good is different to the current average cost, producing the extra unit will cause the average cost to change.

2.1 The relationship between average cost and marginal cost

In our key terms earlier in this chapter we have defined **average cost** as the total cost for a given level of output divided by the quantity of output, while **marginal cost** is the incremental cost of producing an additional unit of output.

Both of these terms are very important in their own right, but the relationships between average and marginal costs are equally important.

(a) **When the average cost curve is rising, the marginal cost will always be higher than the average cost.** If the cost of making one extra unit of output exceeds the average cost of making all the previous units, then making the extra unit will clearly cause an increase in the average unit cost.

(b) In our numerical example in section 1.4 of this chapter, the average cost schedule rises from six units of output onwards and MC is higher than AC at all these levels of output (6 – 10 units).

(c) **When the average cost curve is falling, marginal cost lies below it.** This follows similar logic. If the cost of making an extra unit is less than the average cost of making all the previous units, the effect of making the extra unit must be a reduction in average unit cost. In our example in section 1.4, this happens between production of one and four units.

(d) **When the average cost curve is horizontal, marginal cost is equal to it.** In our example in section 1.4, when there are five units of output, the average cost stays at $0.50 and the marginal cost of the fifth unit is also $0.50.

The relationship between marginal costs and average costs means that the marginal cost curve **always** cuts through the average cost curve at the **lowest point of the average cost curve** (see Figure 1 earlier).

Question — Cost curves

(a) It is possible for the average total cost curve to be falling while the average variable cost curve is rising. True or false?

(b) Marginal fixed costs per unit will fall as output increases. True or false?

Answer

(a) True. Average total cost (AC) comprises average fixed cost (AFC) and average variable cost (AVC). AFC falls as output rises, and the fall may be sufficient to outweigh a possible increase in AVC. In such a case, AC will fall while AVC rises.

(b) False. It is **average** fixed costs per unit that fall as output increases. **Marginal** fixed costs = 0, because fixed costs do not change when one extra unit of output is produced.

2.2 U-shaped short run average cost curve

FAST FORWARD — A firm's short run average cost (SRAC) curve is U-shaped, due to **diminishing returns** beyond a certain output level.

The short run average cost curve (AC in Figure 1) **is U-shaped**. We now consider why.

Fixed costs per unit of output (ie average fixed costs) will fall as the level of output rises. Thus, if fixed costs are $20,000 and we make 10,000 units, the average fixed cost (AFC) will be $2 per unit. If output increases to 12,500 units the AFC will fall to $1.60 (20,000 ÷ 12,500) and if output increases to 15,000 units, the AFC will fall again to $1.33 (20,000 ÷ 15,000), and so on. Spreading fixed costs over a larger amount of output is a major reason why short run average costs per unit fall as output increases.

Variable costs are made up from the cost of the factors of production whose use can be varied in the short run – for example wages, fuel and raw material purchases. **Total variable costs therefore vary with output in the short run as well as in the long run.**

(a) The accountant's assumption about short run variable costs is that **up to a certain level of output, the variable cost per unit is more or less constant** (eg wages costs and materials costs per unit of output are unchanged). If the average fixed cost per unit is falling as output rises, and the average variable cost per unit is constant, it follows that the average total cost per unit will also be falling as output increases.

(b) However, there are other reasons for the initial fall in average total cost. The first is the effects of the **division of labour** and **specialisation**. Imagine a small but fully equipped factory, with a variety of machinery and equipment and a workforce of, say, ten. If each person attempts to perform all the operations on a single item, production is likely to be low.

(i) They will be unable to develop a high level of skill at every one of the jobs

(ii) Time will be lost as they move from machine to machine

(iii) Individual variability will produce a high rate of defects, perhaps with each person tending to produce different faults

(iv) Individuals will work at different rates on different operations: as a result, queues will form at some machines and others will be under-utilised

If there is a degree of specialisation, expertise and speed will rise, machines will be run at optimum rates and output will rise. Average costs will therefore fall.

(c) **The second reason for the initial fall in average total cost is the utilisation of indivisibilities.** If a machine has an output capacity of 100 units per day but is only used to produce 50 units per day, the machinery cost of each of those 50 units will be twice as high as it would be if the machine was used to capacity. Operation of a plant below normal output is uneconomical, so there are cost savings as production is increased up to capacity level.

2.3 The law of diminishing returns

Key term

> The **law of diminishing returns** says that if one or more factors of production are fixed, but the input of another is increased, the extra output generated by each extra unit of input will eventually begin to fall.

The **law of diminishing returns** states that, given the present state of technology, as more units of a variable input factor are added to input factors that are in fixed supply in the **short run**, the resulting increments to total production will eventually start to decline. In other words, as more units of a variable factor (eg labour) are added to a quantity of a fixed factor (eg a factory), there may initially be some increasing returns or constant returns as more units of the variable factor are added, but eventually, diminishing marginal returns will set in. Putting more people to work in a factory will increase the yield up to a point, but eventually marginal output will fall, and will ultimately even become negative. In our factory example, if too many extra workers are employed in a factory:

- Queues could start forming at the machines
- People could find it harder to co-ordinate work
- Machinery may start to break down through over-use
- There may simply not be enough space for everyone to work efficiently.

It is important that you appreciate that diminishing returns set in once the **rate** at which the increase in productivity from adding an extra unit of a factor of production starts to fall. This does not necessarily mean, however, that total output has started to fall.

We can illustrate this with a simple example:

Workers	Total output	Marginal output	Average output
1	5	5	5.0
2	11	6	5.5
3	18	7	6.0
4	24	6	6.0
5	29	5	5.8
6	32	3	5.3
7	33	1	4.7
8	32	−1	4.0

In this example, diminishing returns set in once the fourth worker is employed (because the marginal output of adding a fourth worker (6) is lower than the marginal output from adding a third worker (7)). However, total output continues to rise as workers four to seven are added, and only starts to fall when the eighth worker is added.

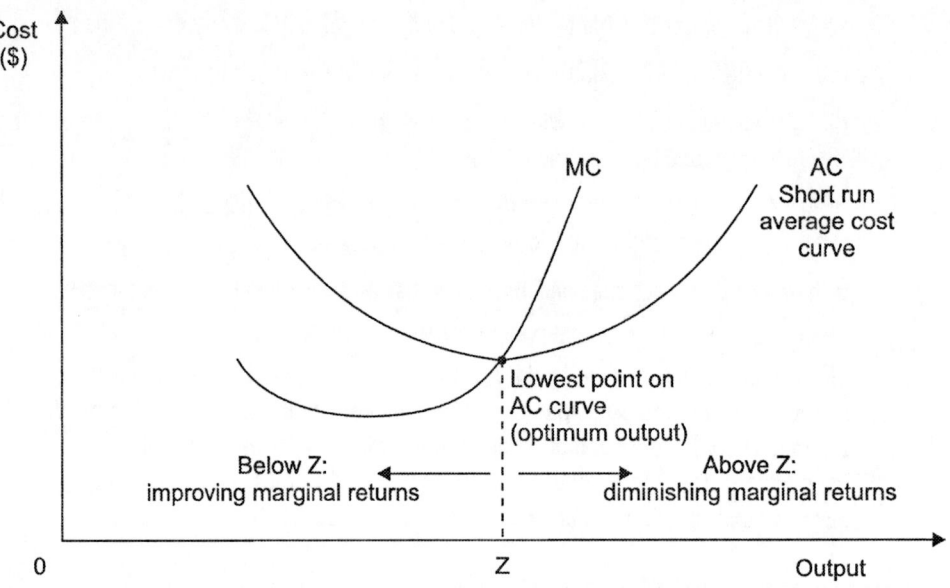

Figure 2 U shaped short run cost curve and the relationship of AC to MC in the short run

Exam focus point

Remember that the law of diminishing returns is a **short run** phenomenon; the diminishing returns are caused by the fact that at least one factor of production is fixed.

The law of diminishing returns is expressed in production quantities, but it obviously has direct implications for short run average and marginal **costs**. Resources cost money, and the average and marginal costs of output will depend on the quantities of resources needed to produce the given output.

In our simple example earlier, the marginal output from adding an extra worker increased for workers 1–3, perhaps because adding extra workers means that each worker can now specialise in specific tasks.

This increasing productivity means it will cost less to produce an extra unit of output, therefore the marginal cost of producing an extra unit of output falls.

However, once diminishing returns set in, the marginal cost of producing an additional extra unit of output will increase, because trying to add extra workers will now have proportionally less impact on output: for example, because the factory may be getting over-crowded and workers are having to wait for machines to become available for them to use.

A firm operates at **maximum efficiency** when average cost is at its minimum (output Z on Figure 2 above). Remember, this optimum output point (the bottom point of the AC cost curve) is always found where the **marginal cost curve intersects the average cost curve**.

4: THEORY OF COSTS

Question — Diminishing returns

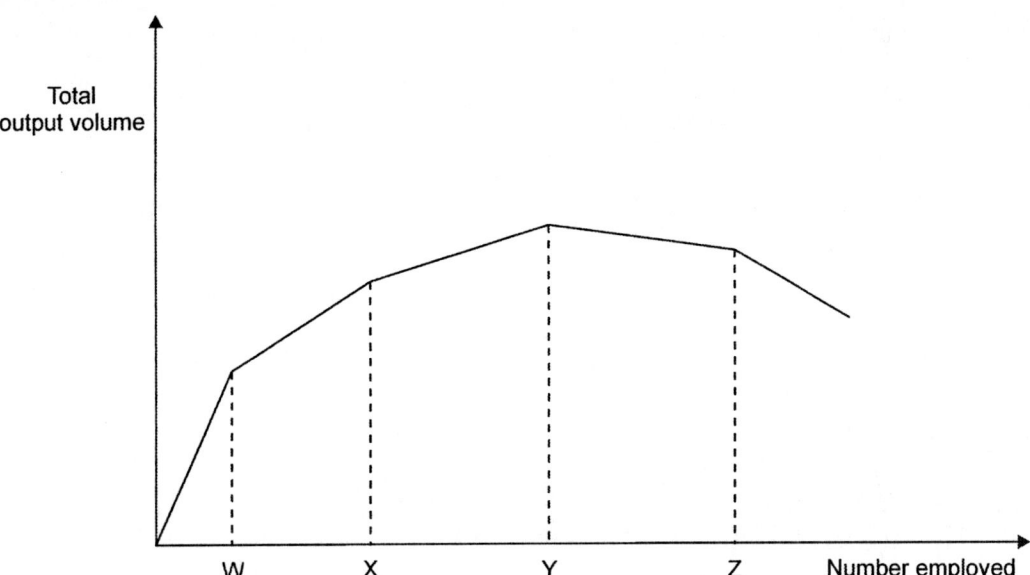

In the diagram above, from what level of employment do diminishing returns start to occur?

Answer

Diminishing returns occur when the **marginal** physical product of extra units of labour starts to decline. This begins to happen at W, because the rate of increase in total output starts to slow while the number employed continues to increase. Note this is a theory of diminishing **marginal** returns, it does not relate to a decline in total output (which occurs at Y).

3 Economies of scale and long run costs

FAST FORWARD

Once all the factors of production become variable, a firm's short run average cost (SRAC) curve can be shifted, and a firm's minimum achievable average costs at any level of output can be depicted by a **long run average cost (LRAC) curve**.

3.1 Costs in the long run

We have not yet considered a firm's long run costs of output. In the long run, all factors of production are, by definition, variable.

There are two direct consequences of this.

(a) Since there are no fixed factors, there can be no fixed costs in the long run.

(b) Because all factors of production are variable, a firm can change its **scale of production** significantly.

These two direct consequences then also generate a third difference between the short run and the long run. Because all inputs are variable in the long run, the problems associated with the diminishing returns for variable factors constrained by fixed factors of production cannot arise. In other words, the **law of diminishing returns applies only to short run costs**, and cannot apply to long run costs.

However, whereas short run output decisions are concerned with diminishing returns, long run output decisions are concerned with **economies (and diseconomies) of scale**.

Output will vary with variations in inputs, such as labour and capital.

(a) If output increases in the **same proportion** as inputs (for example, doubling all inputs doubles output) there are said to be **constant returns to scale**.

(b) If output increases **more than in proportion** to inputs (for example, doubling all inputs trebles output) there are beneficial **economies of scale**. Economies of scale mean that the long run average costs of production will fall as the volume of output rises.

(c) If output increases **less than proportionally** to inputs (for example, trebling all inputs only doubles output) there are said to be **diseconomies of scale**. Diseconomies of scale mean that the long run average costs of production will rise as output volume rises.

Returns to scale are, for example, concerned with improvements or declines in productivity **by increasing the scale of production**, for example by mass-producing instead of producing in small batch quantities.

3.2 Constant returns to scale

The key feature of constant returns to scale is that **long run** average costs and marginal costs per unit remain constant. For example:

Output	Total cost (with constant returns) $	Average cost per unit $	Marginal cost per unit $
1	6	6	6
2	12 (2 × 6)	6	6
3	18 (3 × 6)	6	6
4	24 (4 × 6)	6	6

In the real world, the duplication of all inputs might be impossible if one incorporates qualitative as well as quantitative characteristics in inputs. One such input is entrepreneurship. Doubling the size of the firm does not necessarily double the inputs of organisational and managerial skills, even if the firm does hire extra managers and directors. The input of entrepreneurship might be intangible and indivisible.

3.3 Economies of scale

Key term

Economies of scale: Reductions in cost per unit, in the long run, due to an increase in the size of the firm or its industry.

The effect of economies of scale is to shift the whole cost structure downwards and to the right on a graph showing costs and output. A **long run average cost curve (LRAC)** can be drawn as the 'envelope' of all the short run average cost curves (SRAC) of firms producing on different scales of output. Each SRAC shows a different scale of production and, once diminishing returns start to occur, the firm varies its factors of production – thereby shifting the SRAC to a new position.

Remember the distinction between the 'long run' and the 'short run' in economics. In the short run, at least one factor of production is fixed. However, in the long run, all the factors of production are variable.

The LRAC is tangential to each of the SRAC curves. Figure 3 shows the shape of such a long run average cost curve if there are increasing returns to scale – economies of scale – up to a certain output volume and then constant returns to scale thereafter.

4: THEORY OF COSTS

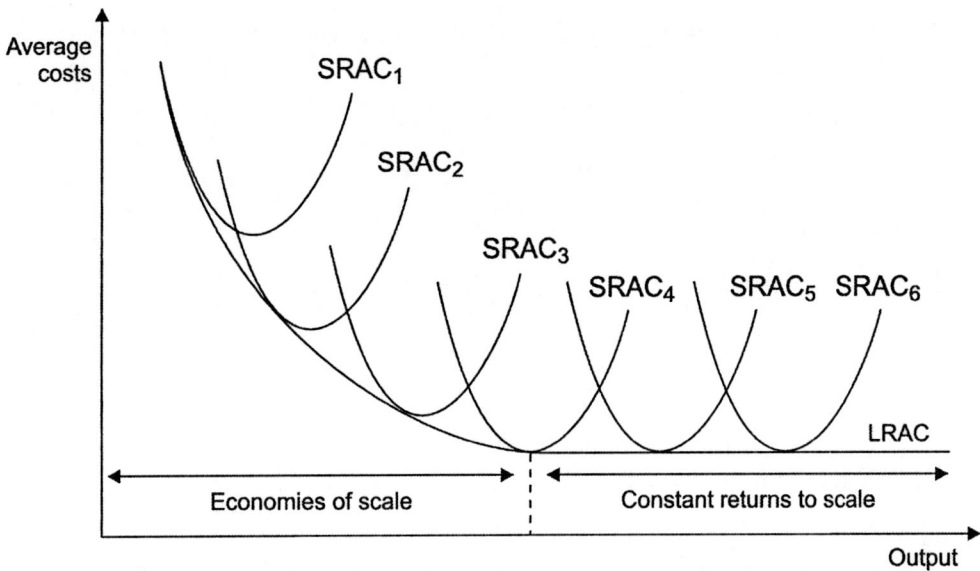

Figure 3 Economies of scale

> **FAST FORWARD**
>
> The shape of the LRAC depends on whether there are **increasing, constant** or **decreasing returns to scale**. Even if increasing returns to scale are not achievable indefinitely as output rises, up to a certain **minimum efficient scale of production** (MES) there will be **increasing returns to scale**. Firms will reduce their average costs by producing on a larger scale up to the MES.

3.4 Reasons for economies of scale

The economies of scale attainable from large scale production fall into two categories.

(a) **Internal economies**: economies **arising within** the firm from the organisation of production

(b) **External economies**: economies attainable by the firm because of the **growth of the industry as a whole**

3.5 Internal economies of scale

3.5.1 Technical economies

Technical economies arise in the production process. They are also called **plant economies of scale** because they depend on the size of the factory or piece of equipment.

Large undertakings can make use of **larger and more specialised machinery**. If smaller undertakings tried to use similar machinery, the costs would be excessive because the machines would become obsolete before their physical life ends (that is their economic life would be shorter than their physical life). Obsolescence results from falling demand for the product made by the machine, or from the development of newer and better machines.

A large firm also benefits from economies of scale by overcoming **indivisibilities**. For example, a manufacturing company will need a factory unit in which to manufacture its goods. The factory space is a single, indivisible unit, and so the associated costs of the factory (eg depreciation or rent) are the same whatever the level of output. Consequently the manufacturing cost per unit will be reduced as production output increases.

We can also see the interaction of economies of scale and indivisibilities in the context of advertising. An advertising campaign would not be worth considering unless there is a certain level of output against which to charge the cost and justify the campaign.

Dimensional economies of scale arise from the relationship between the volume of output and the size of equipment (eg storage tanks) needed to hold or process the output. The cost of a container for 10,000 gallons of product is likely to be much less than 10 times the cost of a container for 1,000 gallons.

3.5.2 Commercial or marketing economies

Buying economies may be available, reducing the cost of material purchases through bulk purchase discounts. Similarly, **inventory holding** becomes more efficient. The most economic quantities of inventory to hold increase with the scale of operations, but at a lower proportionate rate of increase.

Also, bulk selling will enable a large firm to make relative savings in **distribution** costs, and **advertising** costs.

Large firms can potentially also benefit from **economies of scope**. Economies of scope refer to cost savings which can be achieved by offering a wider range of products; for example, a sales team could offer a wider range of products without incurring significant extra costs.

3.5.3 Organisational economies

When the firm is large, centralisation of functions such as administration, R&D and marketing may reduce the burden of overheads (ie the indirect costs of production) on individual operating locations. The need for management and supervisory staff does not increase at the same rate as output.

Equally, large firms can also employ specialist staff in IT, HR, accountancy etc and their skills can be fully utilised in their specialist areas.

3.5.4 Financial economies

Large firms may find it easier to borrow money than smaller firms and they may also obtain loan finance at more attractive rates of interest, due to their reputation and asset base. Quoted public limited companies can also raise finance by selling shares to the public via a stock exchange.

Question — Economies of scale

The above list of sources of economies of scale is not exhaustive. Can you add to it?

Answer

(a) Large firms attract **better quality employees** if the employees see better career prospects in a large firm than in a small firm.

(b) Specialisation of labour applies to management, and there are thus **managerial economies**; the cost per unit of management will fall as output rises.

(c) **Marketing economies** are available, because a firm can make more effective use of advertising, specialist salesmen, and specialised channels of distribution.

(d) Large companies are able to devote more resources to **research and development** (R & D). In an industry where R & D is essential for survival, large companies are more likely to prosper.

3.6 External economies of scale

Whereas internal economies of scale accrue to an individual firm, it is also possible for general advantages to be enjoyed by all of the firms in an industry. These are known as external economies of scale.

External economies of scale occur as an **industry** grows in size. Here are two examples.

(a) **A large skilled labour force is created** and educational services can be geared towards training new entrants.

(b) **Specialised ancillary industries will develop** to provide components, transport finished goods, trade in by-products, provide special services and so on. For instance, law firms may be set up to specialise in the affairs of the industry.

3.7 The effect of size

The extent to which both internal and external economies of scale can be achieved will vary from industry to industry, depending on the conditions in that industry. In other words, large firms are better suited to some industries than others.

(a) **Internal economies of scale** are potentially more significant than external economies to a supplier of a product or service for which there is a large consumer market. It may be necessary for a firm in such an industry to grow to a certain size in order to benefit fully from potential economies of scale, and thereby be cost-competitive and capable of making profits and surviving.

(b) **External economies of scale** are potentially significant to smaller firms who specialise in the ancillary services to a larger industry. For example, the development of a large world-wide industry in drilling for oil and natural gas off-shore has led to the creation of many new specialist supplier firms, making drilling rigs, and various types of equipment. Thus, a specialist firm may benefit more from the market demand created by a large customer industry than from its own internal economies of scale.

3.8 Diseconomies of scale

It may be that a firm never reaches the level of output at which its LRAC becomes flat. Equally, however, firms may expand to such a size that they start to encounter diseconomies of scale. Diseconomies of scale might arise when a firm gets so large that it cannot operate efficiently or it is too large to manage efficiently, such that average costs begin to rise.

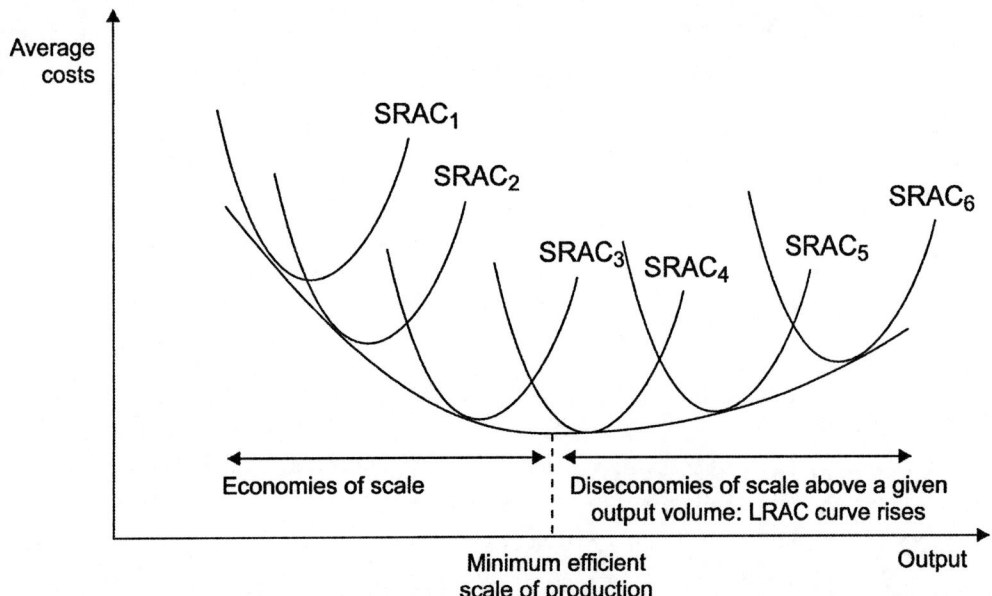

Figure 4 Long run average cost curve and diseconomies of scale

A firm should try to minimise its average costs in the long run, and to do this it ought to try to produce output on a scale where the LRAC curve is at its lowest point. This indicates its **minimum efficient scale**

of production (MES). While there are economies of scale, a firm should always be trying to grow until it reaches its minimum efficient scale of production.

If a firm is suffering diseconomies of scale, in theory it should look to reduce production levels back to its MES, or else seek a more efficient combination of its factors of production.

Economic theory predicts that there will be **diseconomies of scale** in the long run costs of a firm once the firm gets beyond an ideal size. The main reasons for possible diseconomies of scale are human and behavioural problems of managing a large firm. In a large firm employing many people, with many levels in the hierarchy of management, there may be a number of undesirable effects:

(a) Communicating information and instructions may become difficult.

(b) Chains of command may become excessively long, and management will become too remote, and lose control over operations.

(c) Morale and motivation amongst staff may deteriorate, and there may be conflicts between different departments which have different objectives.

(d) Senior management may have difficulty in assimilating all the information they need in sufficient detail to make good quality decisions.

(e) There may be increased levels of bureaucracy.

A firm may also experience **technical** diseconomies of scale. For example, increasing the size of the plant and equipment may create large administrative overheads (thereby increasing total average costs) even though the direct production cost itself is lowered.

These are all **internal** diseconomies of scale. However, there may also be **external diseconomies of scale** which affect all firms in an industry as the industry grows. For example, if a natural resource such as oil or gas is over-used then shortages may result. In turn, this would increase the average cost of production.

The implication of diseconomies of scale is that companies should achieve a certain size to benefit fully from scale economies, but should not become too big, because if they do cost controls might slacken and organisational inefficiency may be likely to result.

3.9 X-inefficiency

Large firms have the potential to have lower costs than smaller firms through the enjoyment of economies of scale. However they may lack the incentive to do so.

This inability of large firms to achieve technical efficiency was termed X-inefficiency by Liebenstein.

According to Liebenstein managers in large firms lack the motivation to reduce costs for two reasons:

1 **Lack of internal motivation**: individual managers are just one person within a huge team of managers. Their efforts to reduce costs and increase profits will not be noticed and will not bring them career success. Neither would anyone notice if they relaxed and allowed costs to rise.

2 **Lack of external motivation**: large firms are insulated from the competitive pressures suffered by smaller firms. They can use market dominance to raise prices in order to increase profits. Therefore improving profits does not require the firm's management to pay attention to costs.

Key term

> **X-inefficiency**: the amount by which actual average cost exceeds the technically feasible average cost at a given level of output.

3.10 Minimum efficient scale

Key term

> Given the idea of economies of scale, it is generally accepted that in any industry there is a **minimum efficient scale** of production which is necessary for a firm to achieve the full potential economies of scale.

The level of the **minimum efficient scale** (MES) will vary from industry to industry. In the paint manufacturing industry, for example, it might be necessary to have a 15% share of the market in order to achieve maximum scale economies, whereas in frozen food production, a 25% share of the market might be necessary, and so on. If a firm has a production capacity below the minimum economic scale, its unit costs of production will be higher than the unit costs of its bigger competitors, and so it will not compete successfully and it will make lower profits, or even losses. A profit maximising firm should be attempting to reduce its unit costs (given that 'profit' is revenue less cost), and this means striving to maximise the economies of scale it can achieve.

Question — Economies of scale and diminishing marginal returns

Explain the difference between diminishing marginal returns and economies of scale.

Answer

Diminishing marginal returns. In the short run, some factors of production are fixed, and some are variable. This means that although a firm can increase the volume of its output in the short run, it can only do so within the constraint of having some fixed factors. As a result, the short run average cost curve is U shaped, because of increasing and then diminishing marginal returns. Diminishing marginal returns occur within a given production capacity limit.

Economies of scale. In the long run, all factors of production are variable and so a firm can increase the scale of its output without any constraints of fixed factors. By increasing output capacity in this way, a firm might be able to reduce its unit costs, for example by mass-producing with bigger and more efficient machines or with more specialised machines. These cost reductions are economies of scale.

Crucially, diminishing marginal returns can only occur in the short run, because they result from the constraints imposed by having at least one fixed factor of production. However, economies of scale occur in the long run.

3.11 Short-run and long-run production decisions

There are some occasions when it is beneficial for a firm to carry on producing even though it is making a loss.

In the short run, a firm will have to pay its fixed costs even though it may not be producing any output. However, it only incurs variable costs once it starts producing output. Therefore, in the short run, a firm will carry on producing provided its **total revenue exceeds total variable costs** because this means it is making a **contribution towards fixed costs**.

If total revenue is less than total variable costs, the firm would be better off not producing any output and just paying its fixed costs.

Alternatively, we could look at this short run cut-off point as being where average revenue (price) is greater than or equal to average variable cost.

However, this cut-off point needs revisiting in the long run.

In the long run, by definition, there are no fixed costs, so all costs are variable. Therefore, in the long run a firm will only carry on producing if **total revenue** is greater than or equal to **total cost**, or if average revenue (price) is greater than or equal to average cost. This means that, in the long run, a firm will only carry on producing if it is **making at least a normal profit**. If we remember what normal profit is, then this long run production decision is exactly as it should be. Normal profit is the opportunity cost of enterprise. So if an entrepreneur is making less profit by using his resources in their current way than he could by using them elsewhere, the rational decision will be to shift them to the alternative use which could generate higher profits.

4 Growth of firms

FAST FORWARD

Firms seek to grow in order to improve their relationship with their owners and to achieve **economies of scale**. If there are significant economies of scale to be earned, there is a strong argument in favour of growth. The two methods of growth are **organic** (internal growth) and by **mergers and acquisitions** (external growth). Growth may take the form of **vertical** or **horizontal integration** or **conglomerate diversification**.

4.1 Forms of growth

The possibility of achieving economies of scale through expansion should encourage firms to try to grow in size. There are two broad methods of obtaining growth.

(a) **Organic growth** (internal growth), which is growth through a gradual build-up of the firm's own resources: developing new products, acquiring more plant and machinery, hiring extra labour and so on. Organic growth is often a slow but steady process.

(b) **Growth through mergers and acquisitions** (external growth), which is the combination of two or more firms into one. An acquisition is often a **hostile form** of takeover, in which one business acquires ownership of another without the agreement or full approval of the target firm's directors. A **merger** is usually a **mutual agreement**, where the two firms agree to form a new company.

4.2 Mergers and acquisitions

The nature of a merger or acquisition can be categorised according to which firms are coming together: Are they in exactly the same line of business? Are they in very similar businesses? Are they in related businesses, but operating in different stages of the production and selling process? Are they in unrelated lines of business?

Key terms

Horizontal integration. When two firms in the same business merge, there is horizontal integration. Horizontal integration tends to create monopolies. For example, if All-England Chocolate Co with a 15% share of the UK chocolate market were to merge with British Choc Co which has a 20% share of the UK market, the enlarged company might expect to hold a 35% share of the market.

Vertical integration. Two firms operating at different stages in the production and selling process might merge. When they do, vertical integration occurs. For example a company which operates exclusively in oil refining might take over an oil shipping company, and perhaps an oil extraction company too. This would be **backward vertical integration**, moving back through stages in production towards the raw material growing/extracting stage. The same company might take over a company with a distribution fleet of petrol tanker lorries, and perhaps a chain of petrol stations too. This would be **forward vertical integration**: integrating forward through stages in production and selling towards the end consumer sales stage.

> **Conglomerate diversification.** A company might take over or merge with another company in a completely different business altogether. This form of merger is diversification, and a group of diversified companies is referred to as a conglomerate organisation.

The advantages and disadvantages of these different types of business expansion are summarised in the table below.

Horizontal expansion or integration	
Advantages	**Disadvantages**
• Economies of scale from larger production quantities, ie lower costs. 　– Technical economies (use of larger machines or more specialised machines) 　– Managerial economies (greater specialisation of middle managers) 　– Commercial economies (bulk buying and selling) 　– Financial economies (ability to borrow money more cheaply) 　– Risk-bearing economies (some greater spread of products made within the same general market should help the firm to spread its risks) 　– Knowledge economies (consolidating research and development facilities to advance technical knowledge) • To increase market share with the possibility of achieving monopoly or oligopoly status, and so having greater influence in the market and chance to earn supernormal profits and raise prices.	• Top management might be unable to handle the running of a large firm efficiently, ie there might be management diseconomies of scale. • The creation of a monopoly (or a reduction in the level of competition in an industry) is likely to be unacceptable to government.

Vertical integration	
Advantages	**Disadvantages**

• Gives the firm greater control over its sources of supply (**backward** vertical integration) or over its end markets (**forward vertical** integration).
  – This should improve cost efficiency between the various stages of production, because there are no longer third parties trying to make a profit
  – It should also increase the reliability of supplies (which is an important requirement for flexible manufacturing techniques)
• By increasing control over the sources of supplies and/or the sales and distribution network, a firm can increase barriers to entry stopping new entrants joining the industry.
• Achieves financial economies of scale and possibly some commercial economies. Otherwise few economies of scale unless production now becomes better co-ordinated through its various stages.
	• Possible management diseconomies of scale, owing to lack of familiarity with businesses acquired.

Diversification	
Advantages	**Disadvantages**
• Risks are spread by operating in several industries. If one industry declines, others may thrive. • Economies of scale in finance and administration. • Expertise can be shared across areas which would previously have been unconnected.	• No technical or commercial economies of scale. • Possible management diseconomies of scale, owing to lack of familiarity with businesses acquired.

4.3 Market concentration and market structure

As firms grow and merge, individual markets are more likely to be dominated, or controlled, by a few large firms.

Market concentration is the extent to which supply to a market is provided by a small number of firms. The market concentration ratio of an industry is used as an indicator of the relative size of individual firms to the size of the industry as a whole.

Often a four- or five-firm concentration ratio is used, and this shows the percentage market share of the four (or five) largest firms in the industry.

For example, if an industry has total annual sales of $100m, and the four largest firms in the industry have annual sales $25m, $22m, $17m and $15m respectively, the four-firm concentration is 79%.

The market concentration ratio may also assist in determining the market form of the industry.

Market forms can be classified by the concentration ratio. In ascending order of their concentration ratio they would be:

(a) Perfect competition (a larger number of small firms share the market)
(b) Monopolistic competition
(c) Oligopoly
(d) Duopoly
(e) Monopoly (a single firm supplies the whole market)

We will look at all of these market structures in more detail in Chapters 5a and 5b of this Study Text.

4.4 Advantages of small firms

If there are economies of scale, it is reasonable to ask why small firms continue to prosper. In some industries and professions, small firms predominate while in others, small and large firms co-exist. The number of small firms in the UK has grown in recent years, particularly with the increasing number of internet start-up businesses. The reasons for the survival of the small firm may be divided into three categories.

(a) **Diseconomies of scale in large firms**, meaning that small firms face lower costs

(b) **Economic advantages of small firms**

(c) **Financial and managerial challenges of expansion**. Entrepreneurs may be unwilling to use outside capital as this erodes their autonomy, while their business may not generate enough funds to pay for expansion. Also, they may be temperamentally unsuited to management by delegation, preferring to make all decisions themselves; this will place a limit on their firms' expansion.

Small firms have certain advantages over large firms which may outweigh economies of scale.

(a) Since they are small, they are more likely to operate in **competitive markets**, in which prices will tend to be lower and the most efficient firms will survive at the expense of the inefficient.

(b) They are more likely to be **risk takers**, investing 'venture capital' in projects which might yield high rewards. Innovation and entrepreneurial activity are important ingredients for economic recovery or growth.

(c) **Management-employee relations** are more likely to be **co-operative**, with direct personal contacts between managers at the top and all their employees.

(d) Small firms tend to **specialise**, and so **contribute efficiently** towards the division of labour in an economy.

(e) The structure of a small firm may allow for **greater flexibility** (eg an employee or manager can switch from one task to another much more readily). There is also likely to be **less bureaucracy** in small firms compared to larger firms. So, small firms may be able to respond to opportunities more quickly than larger firms.

(f) Small firms often sell to a **local market**; large firms need wider markets, and may incur relatively higher costs of transport.

(g) **Managerial economies** can be obtained by hiring expert consultants, possibly at a cheaper cost than having to employ permanent management specialists.

(h) Some small firms act as **suppliers** or **sub-contractors** to larger firms. Market demand may be insufficient to justify large scale production.

The **growth of the internet** has also helped provide new opportunities for small firms. Through the internet, small firms can reach a much wider potential customer base than they were able to through direct selling alone. For example, an online retailer has a much wider potential customer base than a retailer who has a single high street shop. The online retailer also has a lower cost base – for example, because they do not need physical shop space (with the associated rental costs, and heat and light) that the high street shop needs.

4.4.1 Outsourcing

Outsourcing can also be a strategy which helps smaller firms to survive in competitive markets.

Outsourcing refers to the transfer of an activity previously carried out internally by the firm itself to an outside contractor.

When supplying products to a market, a firm has to undertake a number of different activities; for example, an internet shopping firm must develop and maintain its website, purchase inventory, provide warehousing, operate a home delivery service etc. In the same way that firms as a whole has a minimum efficient scale (MES), each of these activities will also have their own MES.

If a firm's competitiveness is being reduced as a result of the high cost of one of its activities, it may be able to reduce its costs by outsourcing that activity to a contractor. The contractor can perform the activity at lower cost because it combines the work of the firm with work from other clients, which allows it to achieve economies of scale and obtain the minimum efficient scale.

For example, a small online retail company, can use an external logistics company to deliver goods to its customers, rather than operating its own in-house delivery service (employing its own delivery staff, and having to purchase and maintain its own delivery vehicles).

Chapter Roundup

- A firm's output decisions can be examined in the **short run**, (when at least one factor of production is fixed), and in the **long run**, (when all factors of production can be varied).

- Total costs can be divided into **fixed** and **variable** elements. These elements have different effects on total cost as output is increased.

- **Economic costs** are different from **accounting costs**, and represent the **opportunity costs of the factors of production** that are used.

- If the cost of producing one extra unit of a good is different to the current average cost, producing the extra unit will cause the average cost to change.

- A firm's short run average cost (SRAC) curve is U shaped, due to **diminishing returns** beyond a certain output level.

- Once all the factors of production become variable, a firm's short run average cost (SRAC) curve can be shifted, and a firm's minimum achievable average costs at any level of output can be depicted by a **long run average cost (LRAC) curve**.

- The shape of the LRAC depends on whether there are **increasing**, **constant** or **decreasing returns to scale**. Even if increasing returns to scale are not achievable indefinitely as output rises, up to a certain **minimum efficient scale of production** (MES) there will be **increasing returns to scale**. Firms will reduce their average costs by producing on a larger scale up to the MES.

- Firms seek to grow in order to improve their relationship with their owners and to achieve **economies of scale**. If there are significant economies of scale to be earned, there is a strong argument in favour of growth. The main methods of growth are **organic** (internal growth) and by **mergers and acquisitions** (external growth). Growth may take the form of **vertical** or **horizontal integration** or **conglomerate diversification**.

Quick Quiz

1 Explain the distinction between short run and long run costs.

2 What is the law of diminishing returns?

3 Why might there be diseconomies of scale?

4 Which of the following is an example of an external economy of scale?

    A   Increased wage costs due to falling unemployment in the region.

    B   The employment of specialist managers by a firm to cope with higher output levels.

    C   The extension of low-cost telecommunication links to an area of the country not previously served by such links.

    D   Cheaper finance in recognition of the firm's increased share of the market and therefore its stability.

5 Which of the following cannot be true? In the short run, as output falls:

    A   Average variable costs falls
    B   Average total cost falls
    C   Average fixed cost falls
    D   Marginal costs falls

PART B CONSUMPTION, PRODUCTION AND DISTRIBUTION

6 The tendency for unit costs to fall as output increases in the short run is due to the operation of:

    A   Economies of scale
    B   The experience of diminishing marginal returns
    C   Falling marginal revenue
    D   Increasing marginal returns

7 Which THREE of the following are internal economies of scale for a firm?

    A   The firm is able to reduce administration costs per unit of output when it opens a second production plant

    B   The firm can buy raw materials at lower prices than smaller firms are able to because it buys in bulk

    C   The firm benefits from working with marketing firms which specialise in advertising and selling products similar to the firm's

    D   The firm can obtain finance at lower interest rates than smaller firms which banks think are more likely to default on their loans

    E   The firm's training costs are reduced because it can draw on a pool of highly skilled labour available in its region

8 Harold Ippoli employs 30 people in his factory which manufactures sweets and puddings. He pays them $5 per hour and they all work maximum hours. To employ one more person he would have to raise the wage rate to $5.50 per hour. If all other costs remain constant, the marginal cost of labour is:

    A $20.50
    B $15.00
    C $5.50
    D $0.50

Answers to Quick Quiz

1. The distinction between the short run and the long run is that in the long run all factors of production (land, labour, capital, entrepreneurship) are variable. In the short run, at least one factor of production is fixed. In practice, often only the amount of labour input is variable.

2. If one or more factors of production are fixed, but the input of another is increased, the extra output generated by each extra unit of input will eventually begin to fall. (Note: the law of diminishing returns relates to the marginal output generated by adding an extra unit of input: it does not mean that total output starts to decline.)

3. Diseconomies of scale are problems of size and tend to arise when the firm grows so large that it cannot be managed efficiently. Communications may become difficult, motivation may deteriorate because of alienation and senior management may find it difficult to identify the information they need in the vast volumes available.

4. C   This is an external economy of scale.

    A is a diseconomy of scale.
    B is an internal economy of scale.
    D is an internal economy of scale.

5. C   If output falls, fixed costs are divided over a smaller number of units, therefore average fixed costs will rise. (It may help you to draw a diagram of the cost curves, to illustrate this.)

6. D   The benefits of specialisation and the division of labour could allow increasing marginal returns

    Economies of scale only operate in the long run.
    B results in rising unit costs in the short run.
    C is nothing to do with costs.

7. A, B, D   Internal economies of scale occur when a firms costs fall as a result of it expanding in size.

    The distinction between internal and external economies of scale is that internal economies are due to the size of the individual firm, whereas external economies arise as a result of the growth of an industry as a whole. External economies of scale can benefit all the firms in an industry, rather than being restricted to a single firm.

    The availability of labour with specific skills, and the existence of marketing firms which specialise in selling a certain type of product are both factors which relate to the industry as a whole, and so are external – not internal – economies of scale.

    Although financial economies of scale (such as Option D) don't relate directly to the firm's operations and production, they are still internal economies of scale because the lower interest rate is a function of the firm's own size, not the size of the industry.

8. A

	$
Cost of 31 people (at $5.50 per hour)	170.50
Cost of 30 people (at $5.00 per hour)	150.00
Marginal cost	20.50

    Note that by increasing the wage for the 31st person to $5.50 per hour, the employer also had to increase the wage for the existing 30 people to $5.50 per hour.

PART B CONSUMPTION, PRODUCTION AND DISTRIBUTION

End of chapter question

Scale of operations

A local entrepreneur has built up a successful business which is still growing. They are aware that the increasing scale of operations has a number of cost advantages but is finding the administration of the organisation more and more difficult. They have asked you, a trainee accountant studying economics, to explain the relative merits of expanding the size of their business still further.

Write the entrepreneur a brief paper on this subject. (30 marks)

Market structures – perfect competition and monopoly

Topic list	Syllabus reference
1 The firm's output decision	2.2
2 Equilibrium under perfect competition	2.2
3 Equilibrium for a monopoly	2.2
4 More about monopoly	2.2

Introduction

A key decision for a firm is how much to produce. The outcome of this decision will depend on the firm's revenues and costs. However, the firm's revenues themselves will be dependent on the structure and nature of the market in which it operates.

To understand the immediate environment within which a business operates, you need to be aware of the different **market structures** in which it might be operating. We look at these different market structures in this part of the Study Text.

The purpose of this chapter is to consider output decisions by firms which operate in the forms of market structure characterised as **perfect competition** and **monopoly**. (These are the two most extreme types of market structure.)

We will then look at other forms of market structure in Chapter 5b.

PART B CONSUMPTION, PRODUCTION AND DISTRIBUTION

1 The firm's output decision

FAST FORWARD

> The assumption that firms seeks to **maximise their profits** provides a basis for beginning to look at the output decisions of individual firms. A firm will maximise its profits by producing and selling the quantity of output at which its marginal costs equal marginal revenue (**MC = MR**).

1.1 Total revenue, average revenue and marginal revenue

There are three aspects of revenue to consider.

(a) **Total revenue** (TR) is the total income obtained from selling a given quantity of output. We can think of this as quantity sold multiplied by the price per unit.

(b) **Average revenue** (AR) is the total revenue divided by the number of units sold. We can think of this as the **price** per unit sold.

(c) **Marginal revenue** (MR) is the **addition to total revenue** earned from the sale of **one extra unit** of output. We can think of this as the incremental revenue earned from selling the last unit of output.

1.2 The average revenue curve

When a firm can sell all its extra output at the same price, the AR 'curve' will be a straight horizontal line on a graph. The **marginal revenue** per unit from selling extra units at a fixed price must be the same as the **average revenue** (see Figure 1).

If the price per unit must be lowered in order to sell more units, then the **marginal revenue** per unit obtained from selling extra units will be less than the previous price per unit (see Figure 2). In other words, when the AR is falling as more units are sold, the MR must be less than the AR.

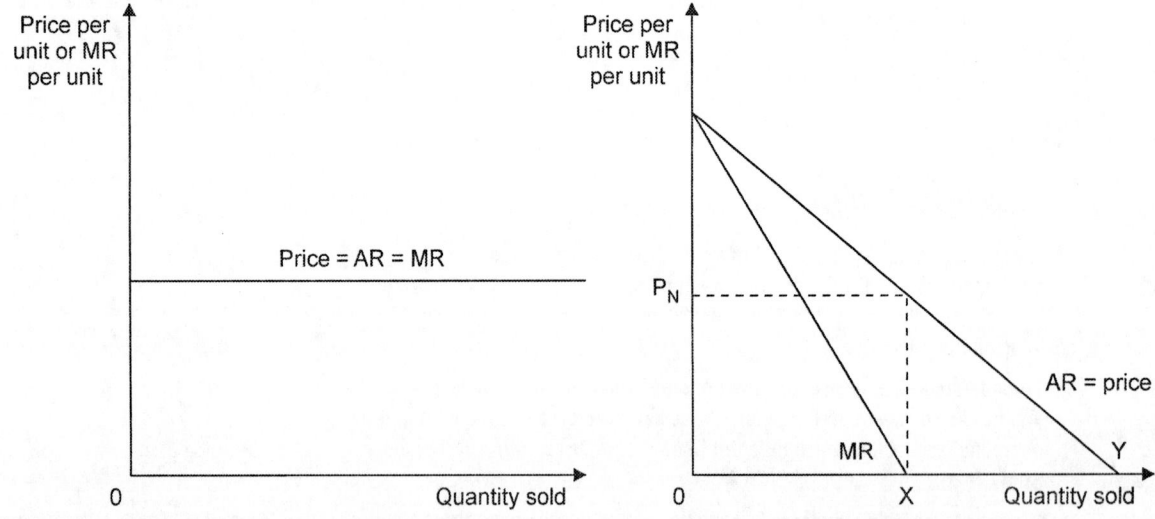

Figure 1: Demand curve when AR = MR   Figure 2: Downward-sloping demand

In Figure 2, with straight line MR and AR curves, the length OX is exactly half of the length OY (ie the gradient of MR is twice as steep of the gradient of AR.)

Exam focus point

Figure 2 is a very important diagram and forms the basis of other more detailed illustrations. Make sure you understand the principles behind Figure 2.

Note that in Figure 2, at any given level of sales, all units are sold at the same price. The firm has to reduce its selling price to sell more, but the **price must be reduced for all units sold**, not just for the extra units.

This is because we are assuming that all output is produced for a single market, where a single price will prevail.

When the price per unit has to be reduced in order to increase the firm's sales, the marginal revenue can become negative. This happens in Figure 2 at prices below P_N when a reduction in price does not increase output sufficiently to earn the same total revenue as before. In this situation, demand would be **price inelastic**.

We can illustrate this by using an example. The figures below illustrate the relationship between price (average revenue), total revenue and marginal revenue. Note that although reducing the price from 5 to 4 generates an additional unit of sales (from 6 to 7), the fact that the sale price of all the initial 6 units has also been reduced from 5 to 4 means that total revenue falls as a result (from 30 to 28).

Average revenue (AR) price	Units sold	Total revenue (TR)	Marginal revenue (MR)
11	0	0	0
10	1	10	10
9	2	18	8
8	3	24	6
7	4	28	4
6	5	30	2
5	6	30	0
4	7	28	−2

1.3 Profit

We have defined profit as total revenue (TR) minus total cost (TC).

(a) Figure 3 shows, in simplified form, how TR and TC vary with output. As you might expect, TC increases as output rises. The effect of increasing marginal cost (caused by diminishing returns) is that the rise in TC accelerates as output increases and so the TC curve becomes steeper.

(b) Conversely, the gradient of the TR curve reduces as output and sales increase. This is because most firms operate under the conditions illustrated in Figure 2. That is to say, they must reduce their prices in order to sell more. Therefore the rate of growth of TR declines as more units are sold.

(c) Notice carefully that the vertical axis of Figure 3 shows total values whereas in Figures 1 and 2, it shows value per unit.

(d) Profits are at a maximum where the vertical distance AB between the TR and TC curves is greatest (at output 'M' in Figure 3.)

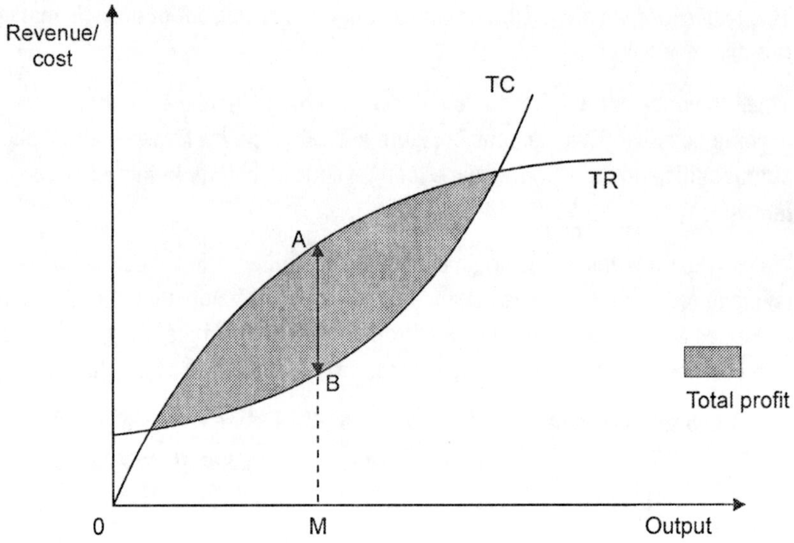

Figure 3 Profit maximisation

1.4 Profit maximising position

As a firm produces and sells more units, its total costs will increase and its total revenues will also increase (unless demand is price inelastic and MR has become negative).

(a) Provided that the **extra cost** of making an extra unit is **less than** the **extra revenue** obtained from selling it, the firm will increase its profits by making and selling that extra unit.

(b) If the **extra cost** of making an extra unit of output **exceeds** the **extra revenue** obtained from selling it, the firm's profits would be reduced by making and selling that extra unit.

(c) If the **extra cost** of making an extra unit of output is **exactly equal** to the **extra revenue** obtained from selling it, bearing in mind that economic cost includes an amount for normal profit, it will be worth the firm's while to make and sell the extra unit. However, since the extra cost of a further additional unit would be higher due to the law of diminishing returns, whereas extra revenue per unit from selling extra units is never higher: this extra unit would generate a loss. Therefore, **the profit-maximising output is reached where MC = MR.**

> **Exam focus point**
>
> The identification of the profit-maximising output (**MC = MR**) is a crucial concept in economics. Make sure you remember this.

(d) Figures 4 and 5 show the profit maximising output quantity M for the two types of firm shown in Figures 1 and 2. In both cases, the firm increases its profit with each extra item it produces until output M is reached, because MC < MR when output is less than M. At output M, the MC and MR curves cross (ie MC = MR). The addition to total revenue from additional units sold will be less than the increase in total cost which they cause (ie at quantities greater than M, MC > MR). Therefore output M is the profit-maximising level of output. This level of output, M, in Figures 4 and 5 corresponds to the level M shown in Figure 3.

5a: MARKET STRUCTURES – PERFECT COMPETITION AND MONOPOLY

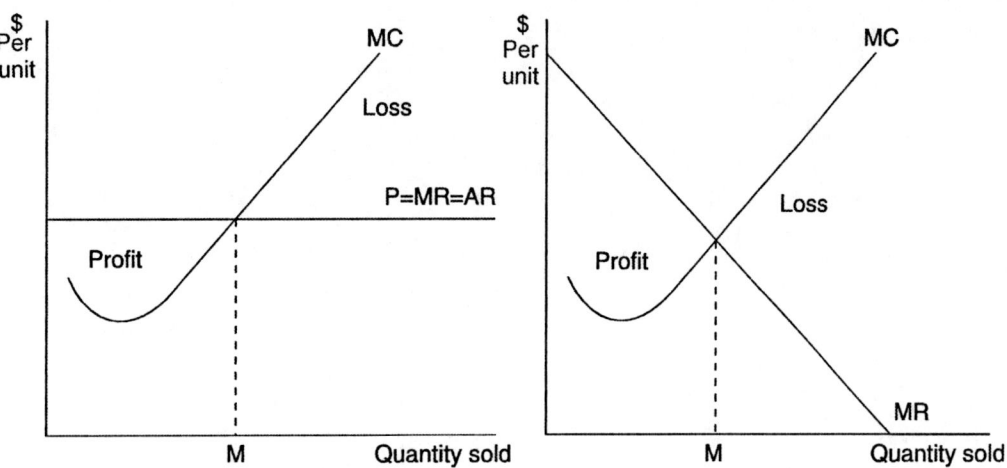

Figure 4 Profit maximisation   *Figure 5 Profit maximisation*

In other words, given the objective of profit maximisation there are **three possibilities**:

(a) If **MC is less than MR**, profits will be increased by **making and selling more**.

(b) If **MC is greater than MR**, a firm will look to **reduce output**. Profit will fall if more units are made and sold beyond M. Therefore a profit-maximising firm would not make this extra output.

(c) If **MC = MR, the profit-maximising output has been reached**, and so this is the output quantity that a profit-maximising firm will decide to produce and sell.

Question — Revenue and costs

The following data refer to the revenue and costs of a firm.

Output	Total revenue $	Total costs $
0	–	110
1	50	140
2	100	162
3	150	175
4	200	180
5	250	185
6	300	194
7	350	229
8	400	269
9	450	325
10	500	425

Required

(a) Calculate the marginal revenue for the firm.

(b) Calculate the firm's fixed costs and the marginal cost at each level of output.

(c) What level of output will the firm aim to produce and what amount of profit will it make at this level?

PART B CONSUMPTION, PRODUCTION AND DISTRIBUTION

Answer

Output	Total revenue (TR) $	(a) Marginal revenue $TR_n - TR_{(n-1)}$ $	Total costs (TC) $	(b) Marginal costs $TC_n - TC_{(n-1)}$ $	Total profit TR – TC $
0	–	–	110	–	(110)
1	50	50	140	30	(90)
2	100	50	162	22	(62)
3	150	50	175	13	(25)
4	200	50	180	5	20
5	250	50	185	5	65
6	300	50	194	9	106
7	350	50	229	35	121
8	400	50	269	40	131(max)
9	450	50	325	56	125
10	500	50	425	100	75

(a) Marginal revenue is the incremental revenue which results from the sale of the last unit of output.

The figures in the table above show that marginal revenue is a constant $50 at all levels of output given. This means that average revenue (price) must also be a constant $50.

(b) The fixed costs of the firm are those costs which do not vary with output. The level of fixed costs are therefore the total costs of $110 at the output level of zero.

Marginal cost is the change in total cost arising from the production of the last unit of output. The marginal cost for each level of output is shown in the table.

(c) The firm will seek to maximise profits by producing at a level of output at which marginal cost equals marginal revenue ($50). It can be seen from the table that this will occur somewhere between output level 8 (marginal cost $40) or 9 (marginal cost $56).

Whether the firm can product partial units of output will depend on the nature of the product. However, for whole units of output, total profit (total revenue minus total cost) is maximised at an output of 8.

Therefore the firm should aim to product 8 units, and its total profit at this level will be $131.

1.5 Breakeven analysis

So far we have been looking at the conditions under which a firm maximises its profit.

However, a firm may also want to identify the level of output required for it to breakeven.

Breakeven occurs where total revenue equals total cost, and therefore by extension, average revenue equals average cost.

We can illustrate the breakeven point graphically by adding the average revenue and average cost lines to the Figure 5 we showed earlier.

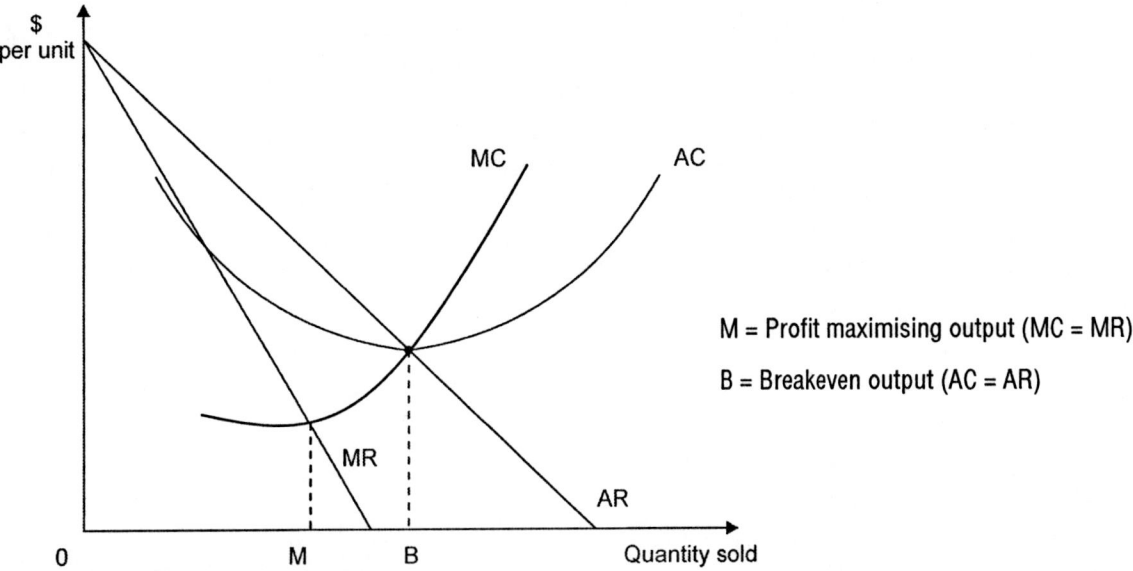

Figure 6 Profit maximising position and breakeven position

In economic terms, the **breakeven point** also represents the point at which a firm is making a **normal profit**.

Ultimately, the amount of profit a firm makes, and whether it is normal or supernormal, depends on the **market structure** in which the firm is operating, and the **time period** (short run or long run) under review.

We shall return to both of these points about market structure and time period later.

2 Equilibrium under perfect competition

In a **perfectly competitive market**, firms are **price takers**, and so their decisions are concerned only with what **output level** will maximise profits. In **imperfect competition**, firms can influence the market price, and so their decisions are about what **price to set** as well as what quantity of output to produce. **Pure monopoly** is an extreme form of **imperfect competition**.

2.1 Perfect competition

Key term

Perfect competition: a theoretical market structure in which no supplier has an advantage over another.

Perfect competition acts as a useful theoretical benchmark with which to start our review of market structures.

(a) We can use it to **judge or predict what firms might do** in markets where competition shows some or most of the characteristics of being perfect.

(b) We can also **contrast the behaviour of firms in less perfect markets**. We shall be looking later in this chapter and in the next chapter at imperfect types of market structure – namely monopoly, duopoly, monopolistic competition and oligopoly.

Characteristics of perfect competition

(a) There are a large number of buyers and sellers in the market.

(b) Firms are '**price takers**': they are unable to influence the market price individually. Buyers and sellers can trade as much as they want at the prevailing market price, as determined by the interaction of supply and demand.

PART B CONSUMPTION, PRODUCTION AND DISTRIBUTION

(c) Producers and consumers have the same, **perfect, information** about the product and the market.

(d) The product is **homogeneous**: one unit of the product is the same as any other unit.

(e) There is free entry of firms into and free exit of firms out of the market: there are **no barriers to entry** or exit. There are also no restrictions on the mobility of factors of production.

(f) Producers and consumers **act rationally**. This means that producers will always try to maximise profits.

(g) **Normal profits** are earned in the long run.

Exam focus point You need to be familiar with the assumptions of the 'perfect competition' model for your assessment.

Question Perfect market?

Think about the market for a particular product – say motor cars. To what extent is this market 'perfect', as defined by the criteria above?

Answer

(a) There is a huge number of buyers, and many sellers too.

(b) For any given model of car, a particular dealer is likely to be a price taker. However, vehicle manufacturers (eg Toyota, Ford, Fiat etc.) are likely to be able to influence price.

(c) Communication is generally good. Product features are well known and list prices are freely available. And discount levels too are widely commented on, in the press and by word of mouth.

(d) The product is very far from homogeneous though: different makes and models of car differ significantly from one another.

(e) Entry to the market is not easy, whether we are talking about manufacturers of cars (very high start-up costs), or dealerships.

(f) Consumers don't always act rationally. Some might be attracted to a car with a higher price (for example, due to brand loyalty), even if it is no better than other cheaper cars. Some may not shop around at different dealers even though doing so could save them money.

(g) Manufacturers can sustain large accounting profits in the long run, so it is likely these are supernormal economic profits.

2.2 Equilibrium in the short run

How are price and output determined in the case of the profit-maximising firm operating under conditions of perfect competition in the short run?

We assume that in the short run the number of firms in the market is **temporarily fixed**. In these circumstances it is possible for firms to make supernormal profits or losses.

2.3 Diagrammatic explanation

Figure 7 shows the cost and demand curves of a firm in the short run making supernormal profits. The demand curve is the horizontal line D_1 at price P_1. The demand curve in perfect competition is a horizontal line indicating that **the firm has to accept the price that the market as a whole fixes** for it. If the firm were to charge a higher price it would lose all its sales because customers, acting rationally and with perfect information, would buy the identical good from another supplier at a lower price. There is no point charging a lower price than the market price because the firm can sell all its output at the given price. Thus the demand curve for the firm is **perfectly elastic** at price P_1.

7price P_1 increases total revenue by the same amount, P_1.

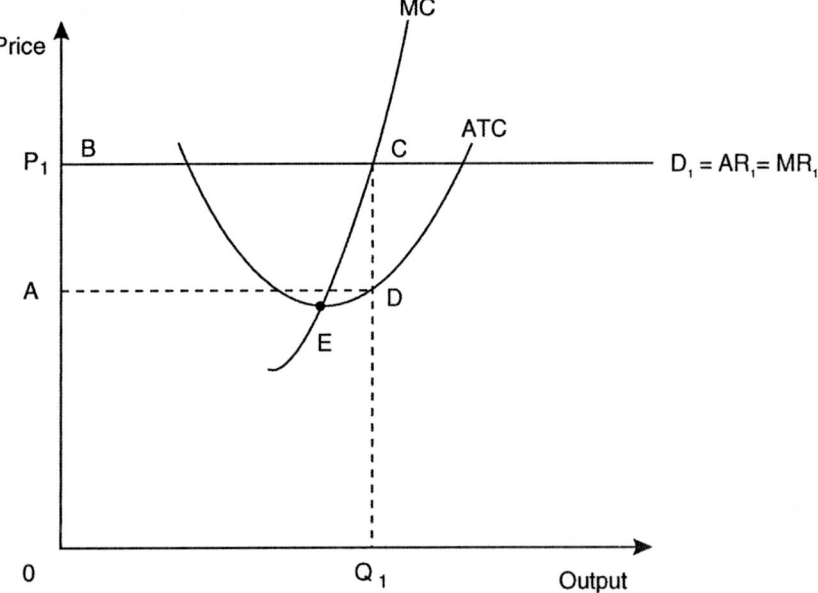

Figure 7 Supernormal profits in the short run

Figure 7 also shows the average total cost curve (ATC) and the marginal cost curve (MC), with the MC cutting the ATC at the lowest point of the ATC. Given these cost curves and the demand curve D_1, the firm will produce the output Q_1, where the MC curves cuts the MR horizontal curve at the point C. This is the **profit maximising level of output** (MC = MR).

Note, however, that the profit maximising level of output is not the same as the level of **technical efficiency**. This would occur at point E, where average cost (ATC) is at its minimum. By definition, technical efficiency is achieved when a firm is producing the level of output at which its **average costs are minimised**.

At Q_1, on Figure 7, average revenue is greater than average cost, so the firm is making **supernormal profits** indicated by the rectangle ABCD.

However, one of the characteristics of perfect competition is that there are **no barriers to entry**. These supernormal profits will therefore attract **new firms** into the industry and the price will be bid down. This new position is illustrated in Figure 8, where the new price is P_2. Here, instead of making a profit, the firm makes a **loss** shown by the rectangle WXYZ. Once again the firm produces where MC = MR giving an output of Q_2. (A firm could choose to do this for a short period so long as revenues covered its **variable costs**.) In this case, MC = MR is the loss minimising position rather than the profit maximising position.

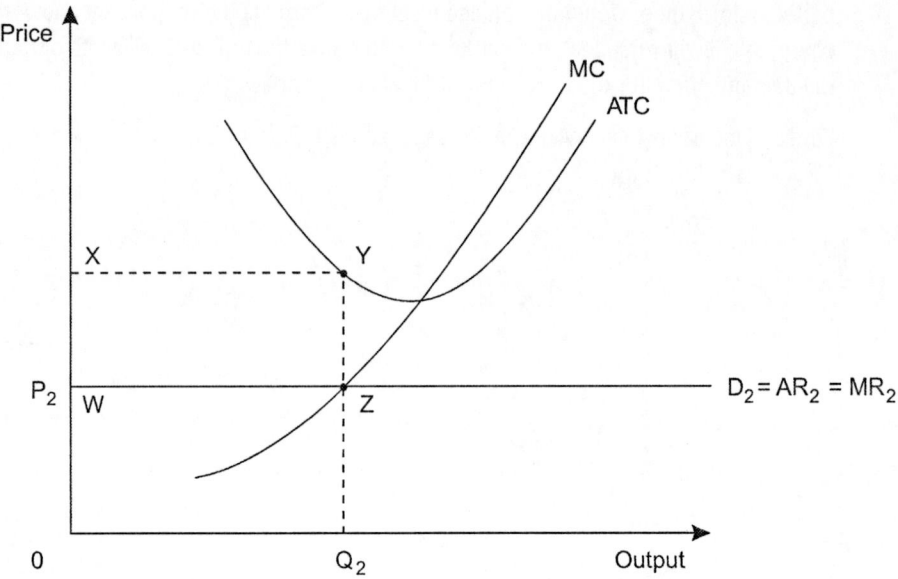

Figure 8 Losses in the short run

In the long run, whenever profits are being made, new firms will enter the industry increasing supply and causing the price will fall. Similarly, when losses are made, because there are no barriers to exit, firms will leave the industry and the price will rise. If profits are not 'normal', they act as a signal to producers to transfer resources into, or out of, an industry.

Question — Perfect competition

In conditions of perfect competition, the demand curve for a firm's product is:

(a) Identical to the firm's marginal revenue curve. True or false?
(b) Perfectly inelastic. True or false?

Answer

(a) True. The firm can sell whatever output it produces at the market price. (D = AR = MR)
(b) False. (a) above implies that the demand curve is perfectly **elastic**.

Importantly though, it is only the demand curve for the **firm** which is horizontal because of the firm's position as a price taker. The **demand curve facing the industry** may not be horizontal. Its elasticity will vary according to the industry, but it is usually drawn as the normal downward-sloping demand curve.

Similarly, market supply is shown in the traditional way, as an upward-slowing curve.

The demand and supply diagram for the **industry** is shown as Figure 9 below.

5a: MARKET STRUCTURES – PERFECT COMPETITION AND MONOPOLY

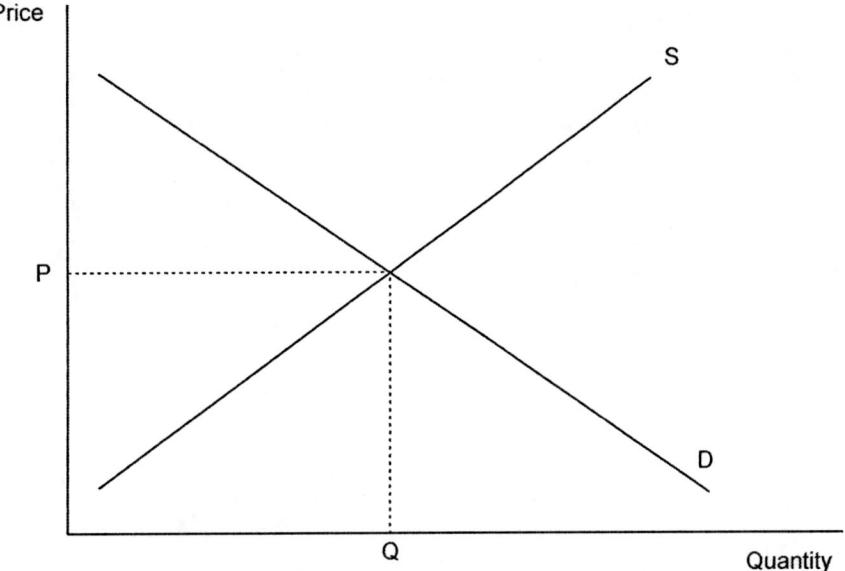

Figure 9 Supply and demand in a perfectly competitive industry

The industry supply and demand model also explains why a firm in a perfectly competitive industry can go from making a supernormal profit to making a loss (Figures 7 and 8 above) as new firms enter the industry.

The introduction of new producers leads to an outward shift in the industry supply curve from S to S_1 (Figure 10). This shift causes price to fall from P_1 to P_2 meaning that the individual firm, which takes the market price, moves from making a supernormal profit (Figure 7) to a loss (Figure 8).

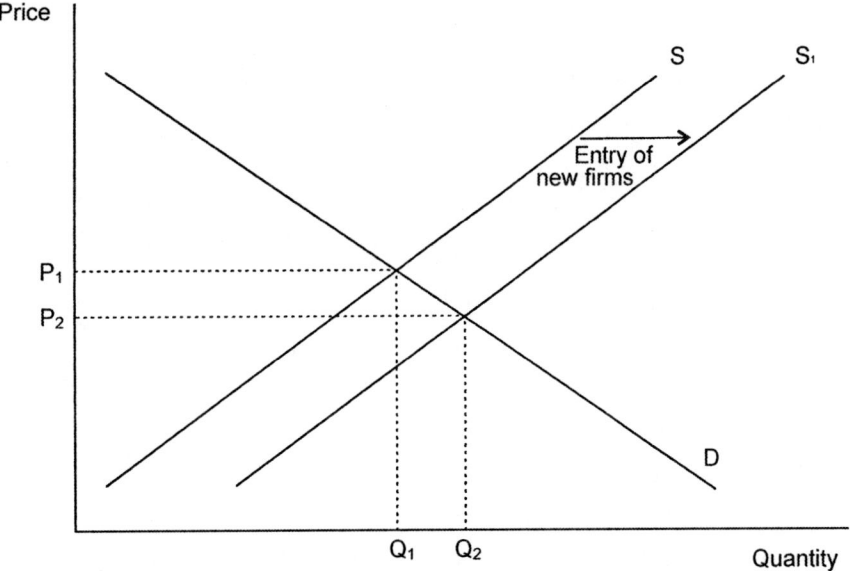

Figure 10 Impact of new entrants on industry supply

2.4 Equilibrium in the long run

In a perfectly competitive market in the **long run**, the firm **cannot influence** the market price and its average revenue curve is horizontal. The firm's average cost curve is U shaped.

We saw that in the short run, firms would enter the industry to secure a share of supernormal profits, and leave the industry in times of loss. However, in the long run these movements are eradicated, and a long-run equilibrium will be established where there is just enough profit (normal profit) to keep existing firms in the industry. There is no incentive for firms to enter or leave the industry.

This long-term position is illustrated in Figure 11. Note the following points about Figure 11.

(a) The market price, P, is the price which all individual firms in the market must take.

(b) If the firm must accept a given MR (as it must in conditions of perfect competition) and it sets MR = MC, then **the MC curve is in effect the individual firm's supply curve** (Figure 11(b)). The **market supply curve** in Figure 11(a) is derived by aggregating the individual supply curves of every firm in the industry.

(c) Consumer surplus for the market as a whole is represented by the area to the left of the demand curve above price P. (Remember, consumer surplus is the difference between the amount consumers are willing and able to pay for a good, and the market price they actually have to pay for it. Diagramatically, consumer surplus is shown as the area under the demand curve but above the equilibrium price.)

(d) The firm is operating at its most **cost-effective point** (the lowest point on the AC curve).

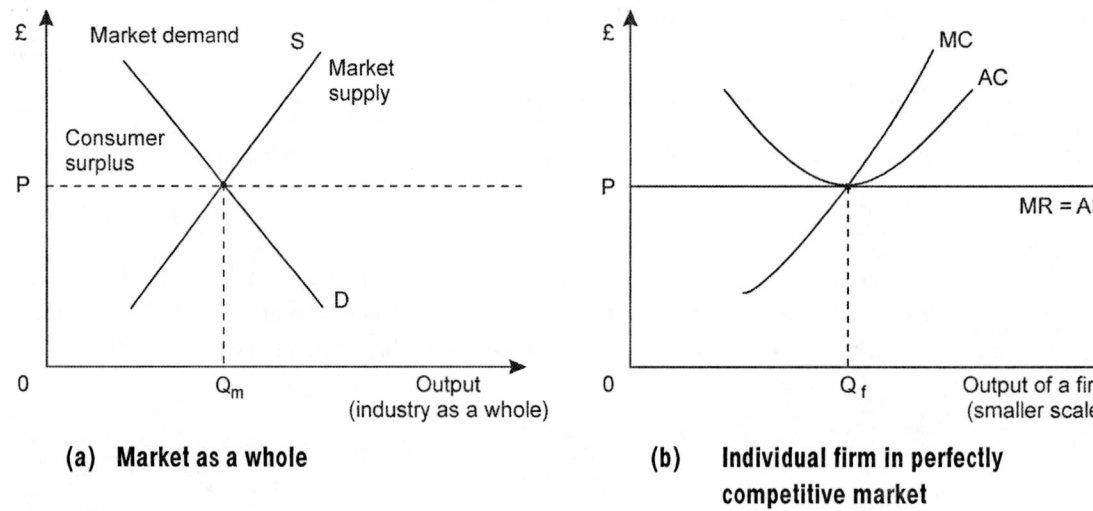

(a) Market as a whole   (b) Individual firm in perfectly competitive market

Figure 11 Equilibrium positions in the long run

Figure 11(b) also shows us that the individual firm's equilibrium position occurs where **price equals marginal cost (P=MC)**. Since price is a measure of the value of the good to a consumer, and marginal cost measures the cost to the producer of attracting resources from alternative uses, then the price of the last unit of output is equal to the opportunity cost of its production. This signifies that **allocative efficiency** is being achieved. (We will look at allocative efficiency again later in the Chapter; but the crucial point to note is that allocative efficiency is only achieved at the level of output where price equals marginal cost.)

The long-run equilibrium position under perfect competition is unique because it is the only market condition which achieves allocative efficiency.

In the **long run**, all firms in the industry will have MR = MC = AC = AR = price, as at output Q_f in Figure 11(b). Because this position earns the entrepreneur the desired return on their capital (normal profit), ensures allocative efficiency, and means that firms operate their most cost-effective point, long-run equilibrium under perfect competition is held to be a desirable model for an economy.

Exam focus point

This explanation of long run equilibrium under perfect competition and the accompanying diagrams are fundamental knowledge.

5a: MARKET STRUCTURES – PERFECT COMPETITION AND MONOPOLY

Question
Small firm

A small, perfectly competitive firm manufactures 200 wooden garden benches each month which it sells for $40 each. The table below shows the firm's costs.

Total variable cost	$7,200
Marginal cost	$40
Total fixed cost	$1,800

What should the firm do in the short term?

A Increase output
B Cease production
C Lower its price
D Maintain output at its present level

Answer

D The firm is producing and selling at a level of output where marginal cost ($40) is equal to marginal revenue ($40). It is therefore already maximising its profit or minimising its loss. Its monthly total revenue is $40 × 200 units = $8,000. This covers the variable costs and makes a contribution of $800 towards its fixed costs. Ceasing production would cause this contribution to be lost. There would be no point to reducing price since under perfect competition it can sell as much as it can produce at the prevailing market price. Equally, there would be no point increasing output, because if the firm increased production, it would find that its marginal cost rose. Therefore, the firm should remain in the market and should continue producing and selling at its present level.

3 Equilibrium for a monopoly

FAST FORWARD

Firms will generally try to earn **supernormal profits** if they can. Competition, though, tends to erode supernormal profits, and firms may have to be satisfied, when equilibrium is reached, with earning **normal profits**. The ability to sustain supernormal profits depends on the nature of competition in the industry.

3.1 The monopoly market

Key term

In a **monopoly**, there is only one firm which is the sole producer of a good or service, and which has no closely competing substitutes.

Whereas perfect competition represents one extreme of the market spectrum (characterised by a large number of small suppliers), monopoly represents the other end of that spectrum.

In theory, a monopoly is a market in which there is a **single supplier**, and many consumers. The single supplier controls market supply, and can control price.

In practice, legislation often deems a firm in the private sector to be a monopoly once its market share exceeds a certain level. In the UK, a firm is deemed to hold a monopoly if its market share exceeds 25%. (However, this definition can be problematic in economics, because it would also include duopolists and some oligopolists.)

A firm's monopolistic position may result from some natural factor which makes it too costly for another firm to enter the industry. For example, in the domestic water supply industry it will normally be too costly for a second firm to lay a second water supply system to compete for part of the business of an existing sole supplier. In such a case, the sole supplier enjoys a **natural monopoly**.

In other cases, a monopoly may be formed by mergers of a number of firms in an industry. However it is formed, a **monopoly can only exist if potential competitors are kept out of the market by barriers to entry**. (We will look at potential barriers to entry later.) For a monopoly, because there is only a single firm in the market, the total market supply is identical to the firm's supply, and the average revenue curve in monopoly is the same as the total market demand curve.

A monopolist can either be a price maker (and thus a quantity taker) or set quantity (and take the equilibrium price which results). However, it cannot fix both price and quantity because it cannot control market demand.

As price has to be reduced to increase unit sales, average revenue will also fall and marginal revenue will always be lower than average revenue. If the monopolist increases output by one unit, the price per unit received will fall, so the **extra revenue** generated by the sale of the extra unit of the good is **less** than the **price** of that unit. The monopolist therefore faces a **downward-sloping AR curve** with an MR curve below the AR curve (Figure 12). For any given price, AR is double the MR on straight-line average revenue curves. (Remember, the gradient of the MR curve is twice as steep as that of the AR curve.)

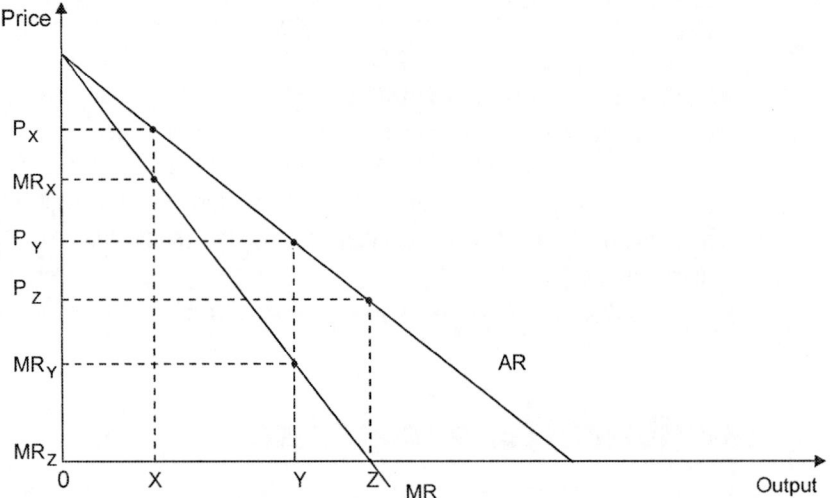

Figure 12 A monopolist's average revenue (AR) and marginal revenue (MR) curves

Marginal revenue can be negative. This occurs when demand is price inelastic and, although lowering the price increases sales demand, the volume increase is proportionately less than the decrease in price and so total revenue falls.

Question — Price and output level

Study the diagram in Figure 12 above. At what price and output level would the firm maximise its sales revenue?

Answer

At the point where MR = 0, price P_Z and output Z. Further sales will lead to negative MR, and hence a reduction in total revenue.

It is important that you understand what the MR and AR (demand) curves are showing us in Figure 12.

(a) At output quantity X, the marginal revenue earned from the last unit produced and sold is MR_X, but the price at which all the X units would be sold is P_X. This is found by looking at the price level on the AR curve associated with output X.

(b) Similarly, at output quantity Y, the marginal revenue from the last unit produced and sold is MR_Y, but the price at which all Y units would be sold on the market is, from the AR curve for Y output, P_Y.

(c) At output Z, the marginal revenue from the last unit produced is zero, and the price at which all Z units would be sold is P_Z. **Total revenue** will be maximised at Z. If any more units are sold, MR will be negative, thereby reducing total revenue.

3.2 Profit-maximising equilibrium of a monopoly

The condition for profit maximisation is, as we have seen, that marginal cost should equal marginal revenue (MC = MR). This is true for any firm. As long as marginal revenue exceeds marginal cost, an increase in output will add more to revenues than to costs, and therefore increase profits.

A monopolist will have U-shaped cost curves, because it will experience diminishing marginal returns in the short run, or economies (and diseconomies) of scale in the long run, just like any other producer.

3.3 Monopolist earning normal profits

Figure 13 shows a monopoly equilibrium where the AC curve touches the AR curve at a tangent, at exactly the same output level where MC = MR (output Q). Since AC = AR and AC includes normal profits, the monopolist will be earning **normal profits** but no supernormal profits.

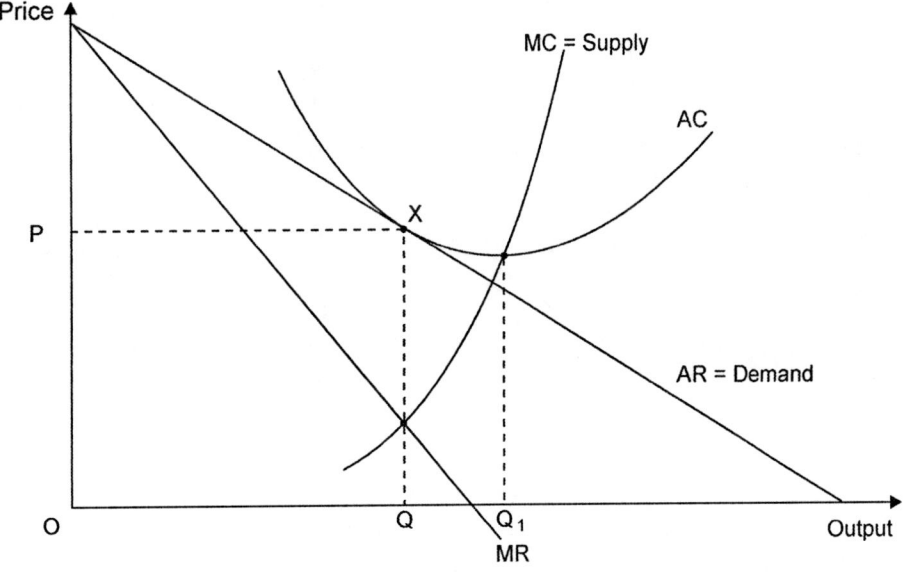

Figure 13 Equilibrium of a monopoly firm earning normal profits

In this situation, the monopoly will make a loss by producing at output higher than Q, and so it will have to produce at an output level which is well below the capacity at which its average costs are minimised (output Q_1).

Monopolies are usually able to earn 'monopoly' or supernormal profits in the **long run** as well as the short run, and the situation illustrated in Figure 13 will be **rare** for a monopoly, although (as we shall see later in this Study Text) this is a long-run equilibrium situation for firms in the type of market structure known as monopolistic competition.

In perfect competition, a firm will not be able to earn supernormal profits in the long run because they would be 'competed away' by new entrants to the industry. However, a monopoly firm can earn

supernormal profits in the long run as well as in the short run, because there are **barriers to entry** which prevent rivals entering the market.

3.4 Monopolist earning supernormal profits

Figure 14 shows the position of the monopolist earning supernormal profits in the short run. SMC is the short-run marginal cost curve and SAC represents short-run average costs.

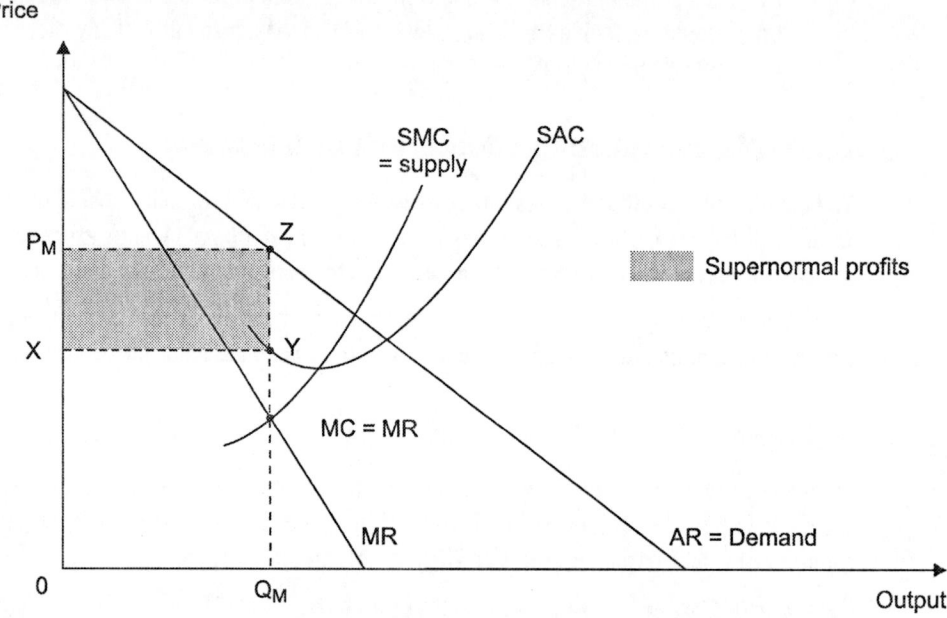

Figure 14 Monopolist's short-run equilibrium

In Figure 14, the monopolist's profit is maximised at output Q_M, where marginal cost (MC) equals marginal revenue (MR), and the price charged is the average revenue P_M. The monopolist is earning supernormal profits represented by the rectangular area $P_M ZYX$.

3.5 Prices and output

If (as in Figure 15) we superimpose the perfect competition demand curve onto the monopolist's demand curve we can see a further potential effect of monopoly on economic welfare.

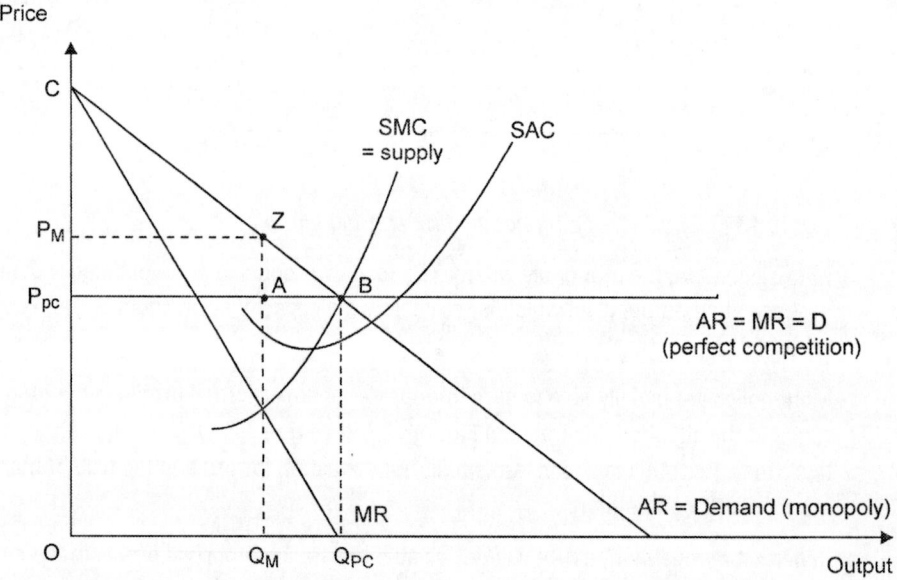

Figure 15 Monopoly and perfect competition compared

The monopoly **restricts output** and **raises price** compared to levels under perfect competition.

Given that firms will always try to produce where MC = MR, under perfect competition output of Q_{PC} would be produced at a price of P_{PC}. Under monopoly, however, output of Q_M would be produced at a price of P_M.

Under perfect competition, the area CBP_{pc} would constitute consumer surplus. Under monopoly, with price P_M being charged, consumer surplus is reduced to CZP_M. Part of the consumer surplus has been transformed into super-normal profit for the monopolist.

The small triangular area ZBA is called the **dead weight loss** due to monopoly, since it is a benefit totally lost.

4 More about monopoly

FAST FORWARD

Monopolists are able to use **price discrimination** to sell the same product at different prices in different markets.

4.1 Price discrimination

Price discrimination occurs when a firm sells the **same product** at **different prices** in **different markets**.

Question — Price discrimination

You are likely to have encountered examples of price discrimination in practice. Can you recall any?

Answer

You might have thought of:

- Rail travel (there are many different tickets you can buy for the same route)
- Package holidays (the same holidays are often more expensive during school holidays)
- Restaurants offering students a discount

Four basic conditions are necessary for price discrimination to be effective and profitable.

(a) The seller must be able to **control the supply of the product** and keep out any competitors who could undercut the premium price. To this extent, the market must be imperfect.

(b) There must be at **least two distinct markets** with no cross-over between them. For example, a rail fare will either be for a peak time or off-peak. If a customer buys an off-peak fare he or she cannot use it during a peak period.

(c) The seller must be able to **prevent the resale of the good** by one buyer to another. The markets must, therefore, be clearly separated so that those paying lower prices cannot resell to those paying higher prices. The ability to prevent resale tends to be associated with the character of the product, or the ability to classify buyers into readily identifiable groups. Services are less easily resold than goods, while transportation costs, tariff barriers or import quotas may separate classes of buyers geographically and thus enable price discrimination.

(d) There must be significant differences in the willingness to pay among the different classes of buyers. In effect this means that the **elasticity of demand must be different in at least two of the separate markets** so that total profits may be increased by charging different prices.

A monopolist can increase its supernormal profit by selling more of its output in the market which is most inelastic.

We can illustrate this as in Figure 16 below. The diagram on the left illustrates a market with inelastic demand, the diagram on the right illustrates a market with elastic demand.

In each market, the profit maximising output is determined by MC = MR, and costs are assumed to be the same in both markets.

Price (P_1) is higher in Market 1 because demand is more inelastic than in Market 2, and the supplier makes more profit in Market 1 than Market 2.

This is part of the logic behind price discrimination. Separating a product into different markets with different elasticities allows the monopolist to increase profits by charging **higher prices in the market with inelastic demand**.

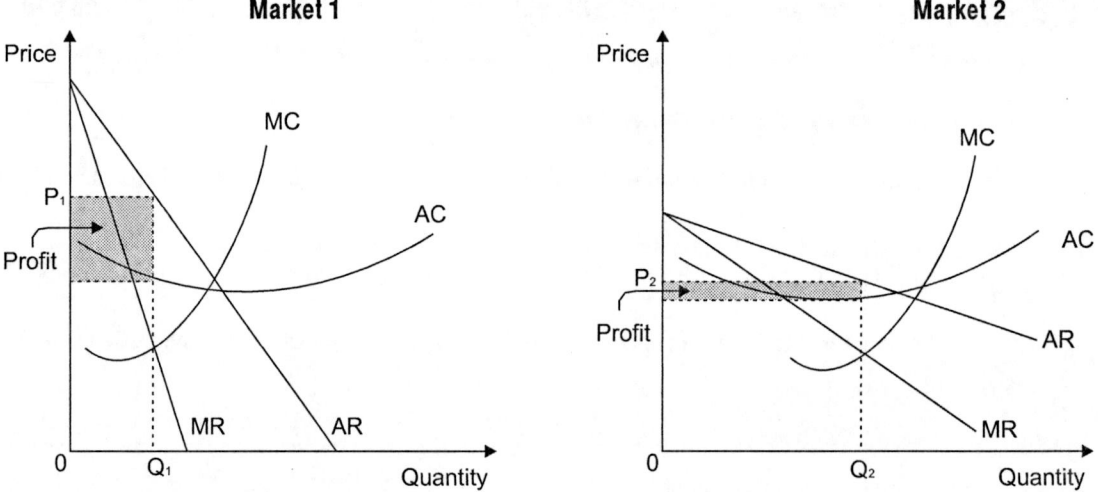

Figure 16 Price discrimination and elasticity

4.2 Diagrammatic explanation

We can use a diagram to illustrate how a monopolist seller practising price discrimination can maximise revenue.

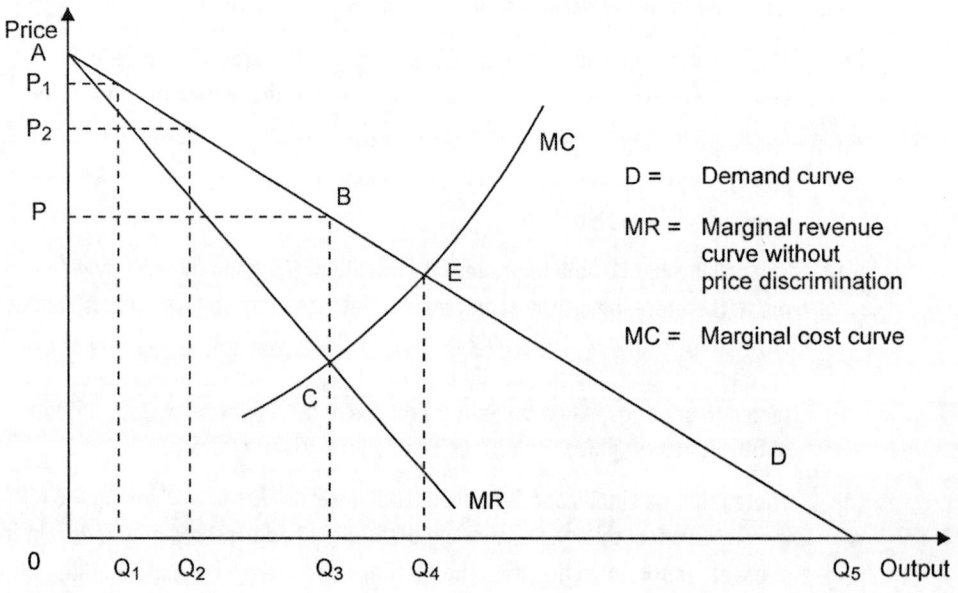

Figure 17 Price discrimination

Figure 17 demonstrates first the equilibrium position of a monopolist who does not discriminate. He produces at the point C where marginal cost equals marginal revenue, producing output Q_3 and selling at price P. His total revenue is given by the rectangle $OPBQ_3$.

However, the monopolist can improve on this position, both from the point of increased revenue and increased profits. **The discriminating monopolist does not charge the same price for all units sold.** If we assume that the monopolist can discriminate **perfectly**, then they can sell each unit for a different price as indicated on the demand curve. Thus they can sell the first unit Q_1 at the price P_1, and the second unit Q_2 at the price P_2. This follows for all units sold so that the **demand curve now becomes the marginal revenue curve**; each extra unit sold is sold for the price indicated on the demand curve, each previous unit being sold for the higher price relevant to that unit.

The perfectly discriminating monopolist will still maximise profits by producing at the level of output where MC = MR, but the **marginal revenue curve is the demand curve D**. The perfectly discriminating monopolist therefore produces at the point E where marginal cost equals the new marginal revenue, producing Q_4 units.

Recall that the total revenue for the non-discriminating monopolist by producing at the level of output was equivalent to area $OPBQ_3$. The **additional** revenue of the discriminating monopolist is represented by the areas APB plus Q_3BEQ_4. The discriminating monopolist has thus maximised his revenue (consistent of course with maximising his profit). If the monopolist did not wish to maximise profit but wished simply to maximise revenue he would expand production to the point Q_5 when his total revenue would be the area OAQ_5.

Take care not to confuse maximising revenue with maximising profit, though. Increasing output beyond Q_4, in the example of Figure 17, will not increase profit as marginal costs exceed marginal revenue for each additional unit sold.

4.3 Examples of price discrimination

Various examples show that the conditions necessary for price discrimination can be met. However, there tend to be four main ways in which price discrimination is applied.

Time – Markets may be separated by a **time barrier**. For example, rail operating companies charging cheaper rates for off peak travel, and holiday companies charge higher prices for a given holiday at certain times of the year. These are examples of services which cannot be transferred from the cheaper to the more expensive market, because they are defined by the time period to which they relate.

User groups – Price discrimination also occurs where it is possible to separate customers into clearly defined **groups**. Industrial users of gas and electricity are able to purchase these fuels more cheaply than are domestic users. Similarly milk is sold more cheaply to industrial users, for example for making into cheese or ice cream, than to private households.

Income – A third way price discrimination can be applied is on the basis of **income** (for example, concessionary travel fares offered to students).

Place – Finally, price discrimination could be applied according to **place** – for example, banks offering different interest rates for online-only accounts, compared accounts operated by the branch network.

Question | Price discrimination

Explain why it is possible for a railway or airline to charge different fares for passengers using the same service.

PART B   CONSUMPTION, PRODUCTION AND DISTRIBUTION

Answer

(a) **The nature of the good**. Prices can be varied according to the time of day or day of the week because there are distinct business and leisure markets. Many customers will be forced to travel at peak times and pay top prices and some will switch to travelling at a cheaper time when the railway or airline has spare capacity. Demand for journeys at peak times will be **relatively inelastic**, since demand will be from commuters who must travel in these periods in order to reach their workplace on time. Demand for leisure journeys is much more elastic.

(b) **The seller can prevent the resale of tickets**. A cheaper rate might be offered to children. Since a child cannot transfer his ticket to an adult there is no danger that adults can buy cheaper tickets by using children to obtain tickets on their behalf.

(c) **Geographical separation of market segments**: a railway can sell cheap travel to customers travelling from say, Manchester to London, but still charge full rates to customers travelling from London to Manchester.

4.4 Are monopolies beneficial or harmful?

FAST FORWARD

> **Monopolies** may be **beneficial** (because of economies of scale) or **harmful** (because they restrict output and raise prices). Government policies have been directed at the harmful aspects of monopoly. Rather than keeping nationalised monopolies in public ownership, the UK government has privatised them, setting up **consumer watchdog bodies** to regulate the newly privatised industries.

We have identified two key characteristics of monopolies:

(a) A monopolist is likely to produce less output but charge a higher price for it than a comparable firm operating in conditions of perfect competition – unless the monopolist can achieve economies of scale that a smaller firm could not. This restriction in output leads to the monopolist earning extra profits and also a social cost or **deadweight burden** of monopoly.

(b) Monopolists can practise price discrimination.

These two points might suggest that monopolies are a bad thing. But there are economic arguments both for and against monopolies.

4.5 Arguments in favour of monopolies

A firm might need a monopoly share of the market if it is to achieve maximum economies of scale. Economies of scale mean lower unit costs, and lower marginal costs of production. Therefore we could argue that monopoly provides a better utilisation of resources and technical efficiency even though it is not operating at the level of allocative efficiency. The consumer is likely to benefit from these cost efficiencies through lower prices from the monopoly supplier. Economies of scale shift the firm's cost curves to the right, which means that it will maximise profits at a higher output level, and quite possibly at a **lower selling price** per unit too.

So-called **natural monopolies** exist because of a very high ratio of fixed costs to variable costs. Think, for example, of the network of pylons needed to supply electricity via a national grid. Such a cost structure makes it very likely that significant **economies of scale** will exist. Therefore a monopoly would be the most cost-effective way of organising production. (This also links back to the idea of minimum efficient scale which we considered in the previous chapter, because natural monopolies are most likely to occur where the **minimum efficient scale of production** is very high relative to the total quantity supplied or demanded in an industry.)

Monopolies can afford to spend more on research and development, and are able to exploit innovation and technological progress much better than small firms and they can safeguard the rewards of their risks through securing **patent rights**.

Monopolies may find it easier than small firms to raise new capital on the capital markets, and so they can finance new technology and new products. This may help a country's economy to grow.

Monopolies will make large profits in the short term, but in many cases their profits will eventually encourage rival firms to break into their market, by developing rival products which might have a better design, better quality or lower price. It can therefore be argued that **temporary monopolies can stimulate competition**, and are in the longer term interests of consumers.

4.6 Arguments against monopolies

> **FAST FORWARD**
>
> It may be that monopolies encourage **complacency about costs** (X-inefficiency) and may produce **allocative** and **technical inefficiency**. Goals other than profit maximisation pursued in large companies could also result in inefficiencies.

Arguments against monopolies include the following.

(a) The profit-maximising output of a monopoly is at a point where **total market output is lower and prices are higher** than they would be under perfect competition. Consumer surplus is also reduced under monopoly compared to perfect competition, suggesting that the monopolist is benefiting privately at the expense of society as a whole.

(b) Monopolies do not achieve **allocative efficiency** since the prices they charge are greater than marginal cost.

(c) **Monopolies do not use resources in the most efficient way possible** (technical efficiency). Efficient use of resources can be defined as combining factors of production so as to minimise average unit costs. The profit-maximising output of a monopoly is not where **average costs (AC) are minimised**, and so monopolies are not efficient producers.

(d) Monopolists can carry out restrictive practices, such as **price discrimination**, to increase their supernormal profits.

(e) The higher prices and supernormal profits encourage firms in competitive markets to want to become monopolies, and they can do this by trying to create **product differentiation**, by introducing differences between their own products and the products of rival competitors. These differences might be real product design or quality differences, or imaginary differences created by a brand name and a brand image. This can be beneficial for producers, but at the expense of consumers.

(f) Because they are not threatened by competition and can earn supernormal profits, **monopolies might become slack about cost control**, so that they fail to achieve the lowest unit costs they ought to be capable of. They may also adopt a **complacent attitude to innovation**. Because a monopolist is able to maintain supernormal profits in the long run (due to barriers to entry) it has less need to innovate than a firm operating in a more competitive market would have.

(g) Monopolies might **stifle competition**, by taking over smaller competitors who try to enter the market or by exploiting barriers to entry against other firms trying to enter the market.

(h) If a monopoly controls a vital resource, it might make decisions which are damaging to the public interest. This is why the government often chooses to put vital industries under state control (for example, health care, the fire service and the nuclear power industry in the UK at the time of writing).

(i) There might be diseconomies of scale in a large monopoly firm.

4.7 Barriers to entry

Key term

> **Barriers to entry**: factors which make it difficult for suppliers to enter a market, and therefore allow supernormal profits to be maintained in the long run.

Barriers to entry can be classified into several groups.

(a) **Product differentiation barriers**. An existing monopolist would be able to exploit its position as supplier of an established product so that the consumer can be persuaded to believe it is a top quality product. A new entrant to the market would have to design a better product, or convince customers of the product's qualities, and this might involve spending substantial sums of money on research and development, advertising and sales promotion.

(b) **Exclusive control barriers**. These exist where an existing monopolist (or oligopolist) has access to, and exclusive control over, cheaper raw material sources or know-how that the new entrant would not have. This gives the existing monopolist an advantage because his input costs would be cheaper in absolute terms than those of a new entrant.

(c) **Economies of scale**. These exist where the long run average cost curve for firms in the market is downward sloping, and where the minimum level of production needed to achieve the greatest economies of scale is at a high level. New entrants to the market would have to be able to achieve a substantial market share before they could gain full advantage of potential scale economies, and so the existing monopolist would be able to produce its output more cheaply.

(d) The amount of **fixed costs** that a firm would have to sustain, regardless of its market share, could be a significant entry barrier.

(e) **Legal barriers**. These are barriers where a monopoly is fully or partially protected by law. For example, there are some legal monopolies (nationalised industries perhaps) and a company's products might be protected by patent (for example computer hardware or software).

(f) **Cartel agreements**. If firms work together and agree to co-operate rather than compete they can, in effect, form a monopoly. Such collusion can take the form of **price fixing**. (We will look at the idea of cartels in more detail in relation to oligopolies in the next chapter.)

(g) **Geographical barriers**. In remote areas, the transport costs involved for a supplier to enter a market may prevent it from entering that market. For example, in the UK, local village shops have historically had a local monopoly, although the barriers to entry to such a market have been weakened by the growth of the internet and online shopping.

4.8 Allocative inefficiency, technical inefficiency and X-inefficiency

One of the arguments against monopolies is that they are inefficient compared with firms operating under perfect competition because, unlike perfectly competitive firms, they do not produce at an output where price equals marginal costs. Instead, they restrict production and raise price to the level that maximises profit. As a result, less is produced and consumed than would be the case under perfect competition. The resources that would have been used are diverted elsewhere to produce things that households actually want less than the monopolist's product. This implies **that monopolies are inefficient in allocating resources**. This is called **allocative inefficiency**. Allocative efficiency is only achieved by producing at the point where **price equals marginal cost (P = MC)**.

Also, because a monopolist does not produce at the lowest point on its average cost curve, it is producing at a level of **technical inefficiency**.

Another criticism of monopolies is that they are wasteful of costs, and spend more than they need to. The lack of competition, perhaps, makes monopolies **complacent**, so they do not use resources **with**

maximum efficiency. This type of over-spending inefficiency is called **X–inefficiency**. (This was discussed in Chapter 4.)

The difference between technical inefficiency and X-inefficiency is illustrated in Figure 18.

(a) **Figure 18(a)**. If a monopolist maximises profit at output level Q_2, there is technical inefficiency because the firm would produce more at lower cost at output Q_1, where it achieves the lowest possible cost per unit of output.

(b) **Figure 18(b)**. If a monopolist has an average cost curve AC_1, when it ought to use resources more efficiently and have an average cost curve AC_2, there is X-inefficiency. The problem is that the **whole cost curve is too high**, rather than the firm is producing at the wrong level of output.

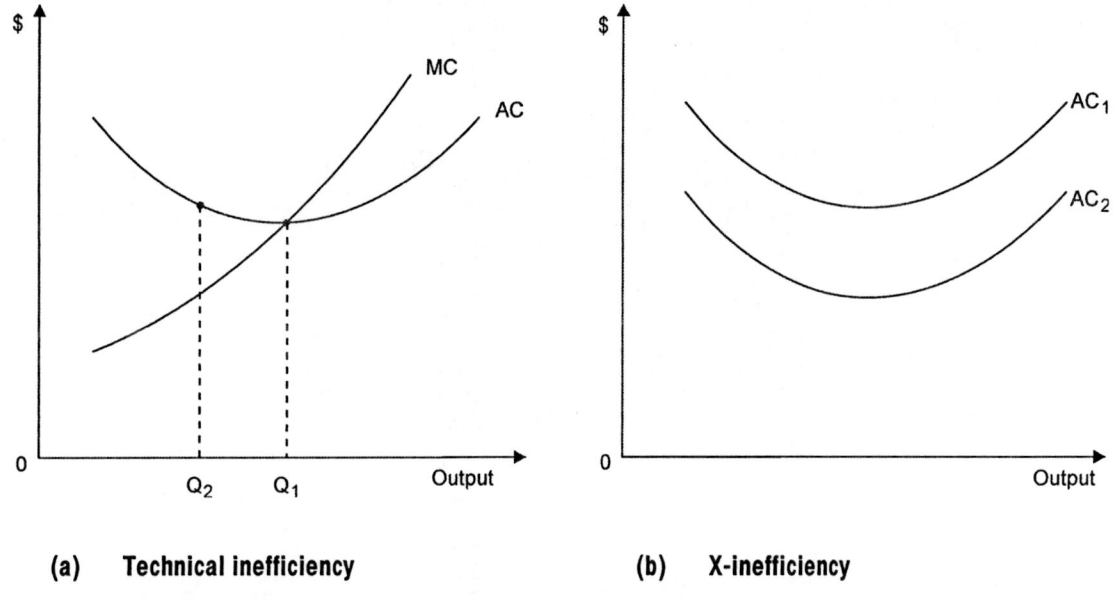

(a) Technical inefficiency (b) X-inefficiency

Figure 18

All monopolies might be accused of some X-inefficiency, but there has been a view that **state-owned monopolies** have a tendency to be more X-inefficient than monopolies which are private companies. This may be because state-owned monopolies have different objectives from those of private sector organisations.

PART B CONSUMPTION, PRODUCTION AND DISTRIBUTION

Chapter Roundup

- The assumption that firms seek to **maximise their profits** provides a basis for beginning to look at the output decisions of individual firms. A firm will maximise its profits where its marginal costs equal marginal revenues (**MC = MR**).

- In a **perfectly competitive market**, firms are **price takers**, and so their decisions are concerned only with what **output level** will maximise profits. In **imperfect competition**, firms can influence the market price, and so their decisions are about what **price to set** as well as what volumes of output to produce. **Pure monopoly** is an extreme form of **imperfect competition**.

- Firms will generally try to earn **supernormal profits** if they can. Competition, though, tends to erode supernormal profits, and firms may have to be satisfied, when equilibrium is reached, with just **normal profits**. The ability to sustain supernormal profits depends on the nature of competition in the industry.

- Monopolists are able to use **price discrimination** to sell the same product at different prices in different markets.

- **Monopolies** may be **beneficial** (because of economies of scale) or **harmful** (because they restrict output and raises prices). Government policies have been directed at the harmful aspects of monopoly. Rather than keeping nationalised monopolies in public ownership, the UK government has privatised them, setting up **consumer watchdog bodies** to regulate the newly privatised industries.

- It may be that monopolies encourage **complacency about costs** (X-inefficiency) and may produce **allocative** and **technical inefficiency**. Goals other than profit maximisation pursued in large companies could also result in inefficiencies.

Quick Quiz

1 Which of the following correctly describes a way in which a monopoly differs from perfect competition?

   In a monopoly:

   A   Products are differentiated
   B   Supernormal profit is possible in the short run
   C   There are barriers to entry
   D   There are economies of scale

2 How can a firm in perfect competition make supernormal profits?

3 What is price discrimination?

4 The necessary conditions for a firm to be able to discriminate on price are:

   (i)   The firm is a price setter
   (ii)   The markets are kept separate
   (iii) Price elasticity of demand is different in each market
   (iv)   Customers in each market are not aware of the prices charged in other markets

   A   (i), (ii) and (iii) only
   B   (i), (ii) and (iv) only
   C   (ii), (iii) and (iv) only
   D   All of them

5   Which of the following defines the long-run equilibrium position of a firm operating under conditions of perfect competition?

   A   MC = MR, AC < AR, MR < AR
   B   MC = MR, AC = AR, MR < AR
   C   MC > MR, AC = AR, MR = AR
   D   MC = MR, AC = AR, MR = AR

6   Selling the same good at different prices to different customers is termed:

   A   Monopolistic exploitation
   B   Protectionism
   C   Price discrimination
   D   Non-price competition

7   In the diagram the firm is currently producing at output level E.

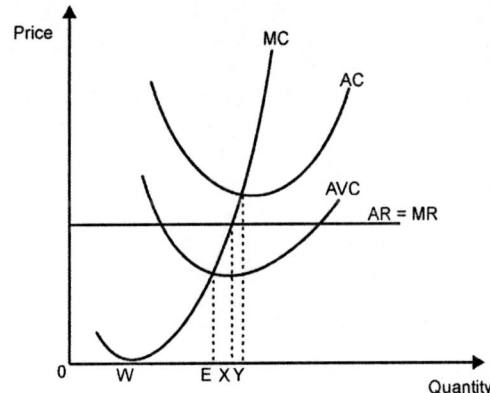

   The firm will seek to:

   A   Leave the industry because AC > MR at all outputs and so losses are inevitable
   B   Increase output to point Y in order to maximise profits
   C   Reduce output to point W in order to maximise profits
   D   Increase output to point X in order to maximise profits

8   The diagram shows the cost curves and revenue curves for Hans Tordam Co, a firm of tulip growers. Which of the following statements is true?

   1   Price P and output Q are the profit-maximising price and output levels for the firm.
   2   Price P and output Q are price and output levels at which the firm makes normal profits.
   3   Price P and output Q are the revenue-maximising price and output levels.

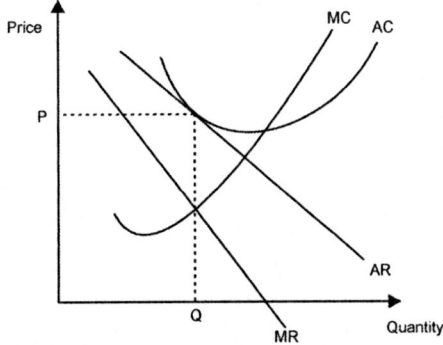

   A   Statement 1 only is correct
   B   Statements 1 and 2 only are correct
   C   Statements 2 and 3 only are correct
   D   Statements 1, 2 and 3 are correct

PART B   CONSUMPTION, PRODUCTION AND DISTRIBUTION

9   The diagram shows the revenue and cost curves for a profit-maximising monopoly firm, Lord and Masters Co. Which of the following statements are correct?

1   If the firm has zero marginal costs and 100% fixed costs, its profit-maximising output would be OZ;

2   At profit-maximising output OY, supernormal profits for Lord and Masters Co are STWX;

3   If the firm's fixed costs increased, so that the AC curve rose to a level where it is at a tangent to the AR curve at point W, it would cease to make supernormal profit.

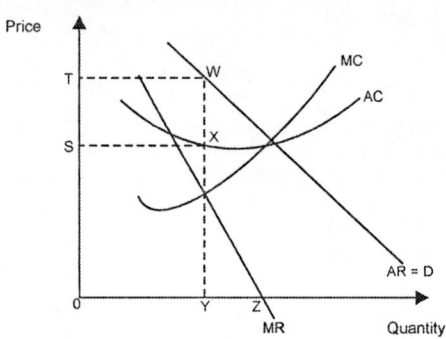

A   Statements 1 and 2 are correct
B   Statements 2 and 3 are correct
C   Statements 1 and 3 are correct
D   Statements 1, 2 and 3 are all correct

10   These diagrams show long term equilibrium under perfect competition for both the firm and the industry.

Label these diagrams using options A to F listed below.

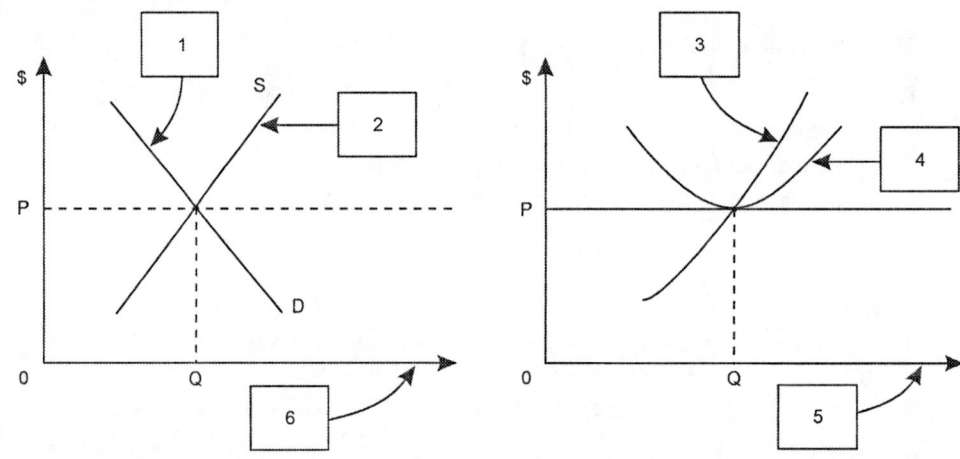

A   Firm's average cost
B   Output of the firm
C   Market supply
D   Firm's marginal cost
E   Market demand
F   Total industry output

11   Which one of the following is unlikely to act as a barrier to entry for a new firm wishing to enter an industry?

A   Significant economies of scale
B   High fixed costs
C   Perfect information
D   Product differentiation and brand loyalty

12   Why are perfectly competitive markets said to achieve allocative efficiency?

Answers to Quick Quiz

1. **C** All firms produce homogenous goods under perfect competition. Under a monopoly there is only one producer so the concept of product differentiation is not applicable. Both market forms permit supernormal profit in the short run, (however, only the monopoly can make supernormal profit in the long run). Economies of scale may be possible under any market form, though they are, perhaps, less likely under perfect competition.

2. In the short run, the number of firms in the market is fixed. If the prevailing market price is above the lowest point on a firm's average total cost curve, it will make supernormal profits. This will continue until new entrants are attracted into the market and drive the market price down by increasing supply.

3. Price discrimination exists when the same product is sold at different prices in different markets or market segments.

4. **A** To be able to discriminate on price a firm must be a price setter, must have at least two separate markets, and the price elasticity of demand must be different in each market. Although customers may be aware of different prices in other markets, because the markets are separate they have to take the price prevailing in their market. (iv) is incorrect.

5. **D** For long run equilibrium, MC = MR = AC = AR = Demand.

6. **C** Price discrimination occurs when a firm sells the same product at different prices in different markets.

7. **D** The firm will aim to produce where MR = MC.

8. **B** 1. Profit is maximised at price P and output Q, because this is where MC = MR; 2. At this price/output level, average cost equals average revenue. Normal profit is included in cost, and so the firm is making normal profits only, but no supernormal profits; 3. Total revenue is not being maximised because this price/output level is not where MR = 0.

9. **D** Statement 1 is correct, because if MC = 0, profits would be maximised where MC = MR, which would be at output OZ, where MR = 0. Statement 2 is correct. Supernormal profits per unit are the difference between AR and AC (price and average cost). This is (W – X) or (T – S). Total supernormal profits for output OY are therefore illustrated by area STWX. Statement 3 is probably more difficult to understand but is also correct. If fixed costs increase, but variable costs remain the same, the MC curve will be unchanged, and so the profit-maximising price will still be OT and the profit-maximising output OY. But if higher fixed costs have raised average costs (AC) to point W, at this price and output level AR = AC, and so there will be no supernormal profits.

10.
    1. E
    2. C
    3. D The profit maximising level of output is where marginal costs equals marginal revenue.
    4. A Long-term equilibrium is at an output where average cost equals marginal cost and marginal revenue.
    5. B
    6. F

11. **C** If consumers had perfect information this would mean they were aware of all new entrants to the industry as potential alternative suppliers to the existing producers in the industry. The fact that consumers are aware of the new suppliers removes a barrier to entry rather than creating one.

12. Allocative efficiency is only achieved if a firm produces at the point where price equals marginal cost.

    Profit maximising firms will seek to produce where MC = MR. Under perfect competition, because price (AR) = MR, price also equals MC.

End of chapter questions

Perfect competition and market failure

It is often argued by economists and politicians that if goods and services are produced by private enterprise in a free market, then everyone will benefit. Prices will be kept as low as possible, by competition between producers, and goods and services will, as a result, be produced efficiently.

The above claim however, rests on the assumptions of perfect competition and does not consider the possibility of market failure.

(a) State the assumptions of perfect competition and explain briefly why individual producers will be under pressure to sell at the market price. **(8 marks)**

(b) Explain why market failure may occur. **(12 marks)**

(Total 20 marks)

Monopolies and public interest

(a) Explain how prices and output are determined under conditions of monopoly, illustrating your answer with an appropriate diagram. **(10 marks)**

(b) Evaluate the argument that monopolies are always against the public interest. **(10 marks)**

(Total 20 marks)

Market structures – monopolistic competition, oligopoly and duopoly

Topic list	Syllabus reference
1 Monopolistic competition and non-price competition	2.2
2 Oligopoly	2.2
3 Duopoly	2.2
4 Contestable markets	2.2

Introduction

Economic theorists have noted that actual market structures very rarely correspond with the extreme cases of perfect competition and monopoly which we examined in Chapter 5a.

Moving away from these extremes leads to the analysis of other forms of imperfect market structure, including monopolistic competition, oligopoly and duopoly, which we will now consider.

These different market structures are defined largely by the number of suppliers in the market. However, in each of the markets, the firm is a price searcher – searching for the price which will maximise profits, given the conditions in the market.

By the time you have finished Chapters 5a and 5b you should have an understanding of the different models of market structure.

PART B CONSUMPTION, PRODUCTION AND DISTRIBUTION

1 Monopolistic competition and non-price competition

FAST FORWARD

When **price competition** is restricted, firms usually go in for other forms of competition, such as **sales promotion** and **product differentiation**.

1.1 Monopolistic competition

Key term

Monopolistic competition is a market structure in which firms' products are comparable rather than homogeneous. **Product differentiation** gives the products some market power by acting as a barrier to entry. Monopolistic competition is a market structure which combines features of perfect competition and monopoly.

A firm operating in conditions of **monopolistic competition** has a downward sloping demand curve like a monopoly: the quantity of output customers demand responds to the price at which the firm is prepared to sell. The downward sloping demand curve is possible because of **product differentiation** created by the firm. However, unlike a monopoly firm, a firm operating under monopolistic competition is unable to utilise barriers to entry against other firms. Indeed, the firm already competes with rivals, which can take retaliatory competitive action if the firm makes big profits. (Remember, the absence of barriers to entry is a feature of perfect competition, and so firms operating under either perfect competition or monopolistic competition will **not be able to maintain supernormal profits in the long run**.)

Firms in monopolistic competition (as well as in oligopoly, which we discuss later in this chapter) will **try to avoid competition on price** in order to preserve their position as price maker. As a result, they will often resort to **non-price competition**, perhaps through advertising and sales promotion, or through **product differentiation**. With product differentiation, suppliers try to create differences between their products and those of their competitors – for example, due to the design or quality of their products.

Establishing a strong **brand image** is also important in product differentiation – for example, leading consumers to choose one brand of clothing in preference to another, or to favour one brand of drink over another.

However, one of the key features of monopolistic competition is that there are **no significant barriers to entry**.

1.2 Profit-maximising equilibrium

A firm which operates in conditions of monopolistic competition will have a **short-run** equilibrium in which it can make **supernormal profits**, and a **long-run** equilibrium in which it cannot. In the **long run**, the monopolistic competitor **cannot** earn supernormal profits since there are no **entry barriers**. Its short-run supernormal profits will be **competed away** by new entrants. As a result of competition, the **demand curve will move to the left** and the firm will eventually be able to achieve normal profits only.

However, in the short run, a firm in monopolistic competition is very similar to a monopoly.

The **short-run equilibrium** for a firm in monopolistic competition is illustrated in Figure 1 below. This is the same as the equilibrium of a monopoly firm **earning supernormal profits**. The firm makes supernormal profits of $(P - A) \times Q$ units, shown by the area of the rectangle PQBA.

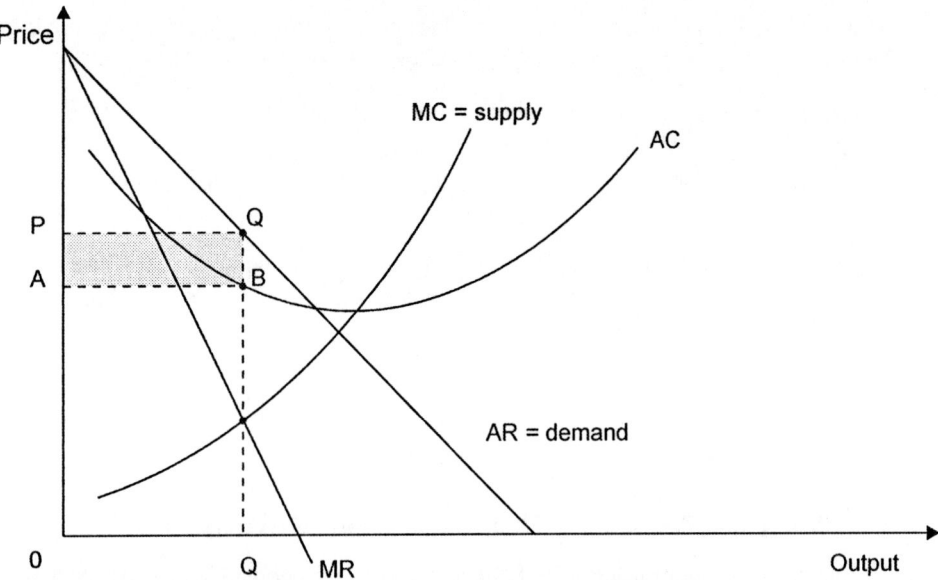

Figure 1 The short-run equilibrium of a firm in monopolistic competition

Note that although the short-run equilibrium of a firm in monopolistic competition resembles that of a monopolist's, the demand curve (average revenue curve) for the firm in monopolistic competition is likely to be **more elastic**. This is because the customer in the market has a choice between products, and can be tempted to move between products by advertising campaigns (which are a feature of this type of market structure).

The **long-run equilibrium** for a firm in monopolistic competition is illustrated by Figure 2. This is the same as the equilibrium of a monopoly firm which earns no supernormal profits, but **normal profits only**. The supernormal profits earned in the short run have attracted new market entrants and so have been competed away.

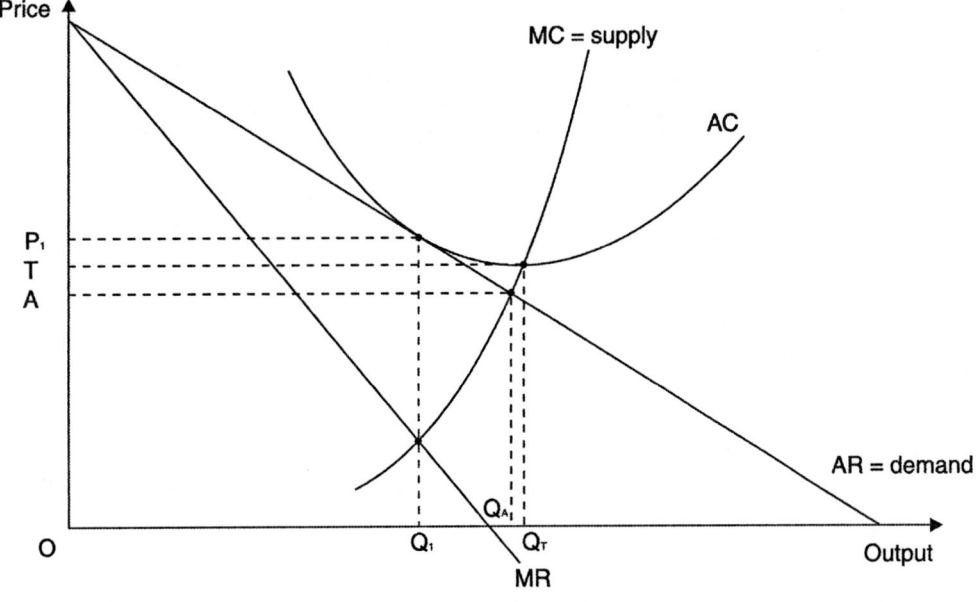

Figure 2 The long-run equilibrium of a firm in monopolistic competition

The competitive rivalry resulting from the new entrants to the market causes the firm to lose some of its customers, but not all. This is an important point: because the firm has established a **brand loyalty** it will be able to retain some of its customers despite the entry of the new competitors into the market.

However, the loss of customers is reflected in a leftward shift of the demand curve, and the reduction of profit levels to normal profit only.

However, although monopolistic competition creates **normal profit** in the long run like perfect competition, unlike perfect competition it **does not achieve allocative or technical efficiency**.

Allocative efficiency occurs where price equals marginal cost. However, as Figure 2 illustrates, price (P_1) is higher than marginal cost at output level Q_1 (where MC = MR). This means that output could be increased so some people could be made better off without others suffering. Allocative efficiency would be achieved at quantity Q_A and price A.

Technical efficiency is not achieved because the average cost of the equilibrium output is not at the lowest point on the average cost curve (T). This would be achieved where output quantity equals Q_T. Figure 2 also illustrates that the firm has excess capacity, because output at the level of technical efficiency (Q_T) is greater than current output of Q_1.

As a result of the allocative and technical inefficiency, monopolistic competition still gives rise to higher prices and lower outputs than perfect competition.

1.3 Implications of monopolistic competition

Because profit-maximising output under monopolistic competition is lower than it would be under perfect competition and is at a point where average costs are not minimised, monopolistic competition, like monopoly, is arguably more **wasteful of resources** than perfect competition.

Since firms in monopolistic competition cannot expand their output to the level of minimum average cost output without making a loss, the **excess capacity theorem** predicts that industries marked by monopolistic competition will always tend to have excess capacity. (Check this in Figure 2: profit is maximised at output Q_1 but output Q_1 is lower than the output level where AC would be minimised (Q_T). However, at the lowest point on the AC curve, AC > AR. The firm will be loss-making at this point (Q_T) so a rational, profit-maximising firm will not produce here.)

It can also be argued that it is wasteful to produce a wide variety of differentiated versions of the same product. If a single version of the same product were made, firms might be able to achieve economies of scale with large-volume production (and so shift their cost curves to the right).

Some methods that are used to create product differentiation are a waste of resources. Advertising costs are arguably an example of this, although some people would argue that promotional activity actually adds utility to a product. Similarly, it is debatable how much value packaging adds to a product, although packaging helps distinguish one brand from another.

Nonetheless, while there are some indications that monopolistic competition is wasteful, there are other reasons to argue that monopolistic competition is **not** so wasteful of resources.

(a) Some product differentiation is 'real', where there are technical differences between similar goods from rival firms. In such situations, consumers therefore have more options to choose from when there is product differentiation and this means their requirements are likely to be satisfied better than if there were just a single, basic, low-price good available, without any choice.

(b) If product differentiation is entirely imaginary, created by brand image and advertising when the goods of rival firms are exactly the same, rational consumers should opt for the least-cost good anyway.

2 Oligopoly

FAST FORWARD

Oligopolists might collude and make a formal or informal **cartel** agreement on the price for the industry and output levels for each firm. The **kinked oligopoly demand curve** helps to explain why there is price stability (and non-price competition) in many oligopoly markets.

2.1 The nature of oligopoly

Key term

An **oligopoly** is a market structure in which a few large suppliers dominate the market.

Oligopoly differs from **monopoly** in that there is more than one firm in the market and from **monopolistic competition** because in oligopoly the number of rival firms is small. The UK supermarket industry can be seen as an oligopoly, because it is dominated by a small number of key players.

Case Study

As of March 2017, the two largest supermarket chains in the UK, Tesco and Sainsbury's, together held 43.7% of the UK grocery market. Prior to the increased popularity of discount chains, such as Aldi and Lidl, the UK grocery retail market was dominated by the 'big four' supermarkets: Tesco, Sainsbury's, Asda and Morrisons. Consumer behaviour has now shifted in favour of cheaper stores, and supermarkets have had to lower their prices and are now spending heavily on promotion to try to protect their market shares. In January 2017, Aldi overtook the Co-operative to become the fifth largest supermarket in the UK.

The size of the existing firms in an oligopoly is likely to act as a **barrier to entry** to potential new entrants, and can allow oligopolists to **sustain abnormal profits** in the long run.

Oligopolists may produce a homogeneous product (oil, for example) or there may be **product differentiation** (cigarettes and cars, for example). An oligopoly will exhibit **both price and non-price competition** between firms.

Another key feature of oligopoly is that **firms' production decisions are interdependent**. One firm cannot set price and output without considering how its rivals' response will affect its own profits. An oligopolist's pricing and output decisions will usually depend on what assumptions they make about their competitors' behaviour.

Exam focus point

This **interdependence of decision-making** is fundamentally important to any discussion of oligopoly.

One strategy which an oligopolist might adopt is to co-operate with other firms, and such a strategy will give rise to a cartel.

2.2 Price cartels by oligopolist producers

A **price cartel** or **price ring** is created when a group of oligopoly firms combine to **agree** on a price at which they will sell their product to the market. The market might be willing to demand more of the product at a lower price, while the cartel attempts to impose a higher price (for higher unit profits) by restricting supply to the market.

Each oligopoly firm could increase its profits if all the firms together control prices and output as if the market were a monopoly, and split the output between them. This is known as **collusion**, which can either be tacit or openly admitted. Collusion usually leads to higher prices and lower outputs than the free market equilibrium, and so **reduces consumer surplus** and **consumer sovereignty**.

Cartels are illegal but difficult to prevent. There might still be price leadership. This occurs when all firms realise that one of them is initiating a price change that will be of benefit to them all, and so follow the leader and change their own price in the same way.

Figure 3 shows that in a competitive market, with a market supply curve S_1 and demand curve D, the price would be P_1 and output Q_1. A cartel of producers might agree to fix the market price at P_2, higher than P_1. But to do so, the cartel must also agree to cut market supply from Q_1 to Q_2, and so fix the market supply curve at S_2.

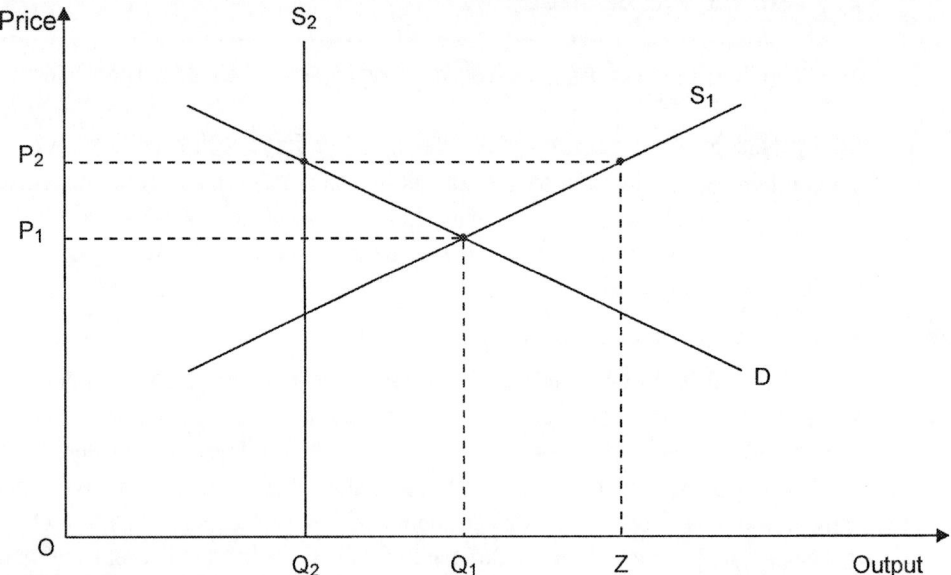

Figure 3 Price cartel

2.3 Establishing a cartel

Establishing a cartel depends on two things.

- The firms in the cartel must be able to control supply to the market.
- The firms must agree on a price and on the output each should produce.

In Figure 3, if the market price is fixed at P_2, firms would want to supply output Z in a free market. This cannot be allowed to happen; otherwise market price P_2 could not be sustained.

The main **weakness** with cartels is that each firm is still seeking the best results for itself, and so there is an incentive for an individual firm to break the cartel agreement by secretly increasing its output and selling it at the fixed cartel price. However, if all firms increased their output in this way, the cartel would collapse because the high price could not be sustained without a restricted output, and excess supply on the market would force down the price.

This has been the common experience of the oil-producing nations who are members of the Organisation of Petroleum Exporting Countries (OPEC). Attempts to agree on a restricted output quota for each country in order to push up oil prices have often broken down because some member countries exceeded their quota, or sold below the cartel's agreed price.

The **success** of a price cartel will depend on several factors.

(a)   Whether it consists of most or all of the **producers** of the product.

(b)   Whether or not there are **close substitutes** for the product. For example, a price cartel by taxi drivers might lead to a shift in demand for buses and trains, because these are possible substitutes for taxis.

(c) The ease with which supply can be **regulated**. In the case of primary commodities, such as wheat, rice, tea and coffee, total supply is dependent on weather conditions and even political events in the producing country.

(d) The **price elasticity** of demand for the product. Cartels are likely to be most effective for goods which are inelastic. An attempt to raise prices by cutting output of an elastic good might result in such a large a fall in demand and such a small rise in price that the total income of producers also falls.

(e) Whether producers can agree on their **individual shares** of the total restricted supply to the market. This is often the greatest difficulty of all.

2.4 The kinked oligopoly demand curve

Price cartels do not always exist in an oligopoly market. So how does an oligopoly firm which is **competing** with rival oligopoly firms decide on its price and output level? Remember, a feature of oligopoly markets is that each firm's pricing and output decisions are influenced by what its rivals might do.

When demand conditions are stable, the major problem confronting an oligopolist in fixing their price and output is judging the response of their competitors to the prices they have set. An oligopolist is faced with a downward sloping demand curve, but the nature of the demand curve is dependent on the reactions of their rivals. Any change in price will invite a competitive response. This situation is described by the **kinked oligopoly demand curve**, shown in Figure 4.

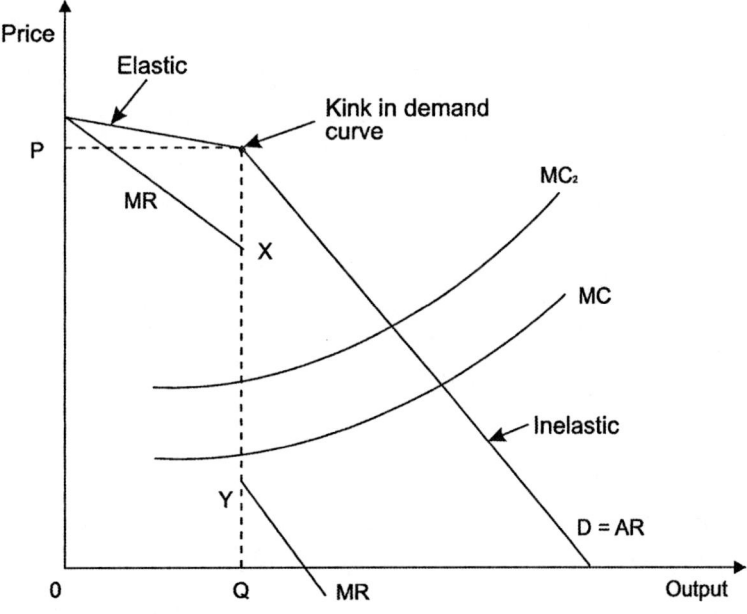

Figure 4 Kinked oligopoly demand curve

The kinked demand curve is used to explain how an oligopolist might have to **accept** price stability in the market.

Let us assume that the oligopolist is currently charging price P, and producing output Q, meaning they are producing at the 'kink' on the demand curve.

(a) If the oligopolist were to **raise** their prices above P, their competitors are likely to keep their price **lower** so that many consumers would buy from the competitors instead. An example is the difficulty which individual petrol companies have in raising the price of petrol at garages. If competitors do not raise their prices too, the firm usually soon has to restore its prices to their previous level. In other words, the demand curve would be quite **elastic** at these increased prices, because consumers will switch to an alternative supplier.

(b) If, on the other hand, the oligopolist were to **reduce** their prices below P, competitors would probably **do the same**. Total market demand might rise, but the increase in demand for the individual oligopolist's products would probably be quite low. Demand is thus likely to be **inelastic** at prices below P, hence the 'kink' in the demand curve, with the curve being **elastic** at prices **above** P and **inelastic** at prices **below** it.

The marginal revenue (MR) curve is **discontinuous** at the output level where there is the kink in the demand curve. The kink in the demand curve explains the nature of the marginal revenue curve MR. At price P, output OQ, the MR curve falls vertically because at higher prices the MR curve is based on the more elastic demand curve, and at prices below P the MR curve is based on the less elastic demand.

2.5 Profit maximisation

Oligopolists, like any other firms, will maximise their profits at the point where MR = MC. However, the discontinuity in the MR curves means that there will be a number of points where MR = MC (represented by the range XY on Figure 4). Thus there are a wide range of possible positions for the MC curve that produce the same profit maximising level of output.

The oligopolist's cost structure can change, with worsening or improved efficiencies, but as long as the MC curve cuts the MR curve through its vertical portion XY, the oligopolist's price and output decision should not alter. If the MC curve (in Figure 4) shifts from MC to MC_2, price (P) and quantity (Q) remain unchanged. The important implication of this is that there will be **price and output stability**: although changes in costs may affect an oligopolist's MC curve, they will not affect output and price. The discontinuity in the MR curve resulting from the kinked demand curve causes the price stability, because there are a range of points where MC = MR. **This situation is unique to an oligopoly**.

Only if marginal costs rise far enough for the MC curve to pass through the MR curve above point X in Figure 4 is there a case for raising price, and only if MC falls far enough to pass through the MR curve below point Y is there a case for lowering price.

In general, oligopoly prices will only rise if all the firms follow the lead of a rival in raising its price, so that the AR curve shifts outwards. The kink rises to the new common price level, which is again stable. The converse holds for price falls, with all prices being reduced to a new level, perhaps due to technological advances reducing costs in the industry.

2.6 Price leadership and price wars

In oligopoly markets there is a tendency for one firm to set the general industry price, with the other firms following suit. This is called **price leadership**.

If rivals follow suit when a price leader increases price, then the consumer will suffer because the market effectively becomes a monopoly with prices raised above the initial equilibrium level.

However, if the price leader cuts prices (perhaps to try to increase market share) but rivals follow suit, then a **price war** could be created. Each firm is prepared to cut its own prices in order to preserve its share of the market. In this case, customers will benefit from the action, as prices will fall across the market as a whole.

However, although the effect of price wars is usually beneficial to consumers, such periods of price cutting are usually of limited duration because it is not in the interests of oligopolists to sustain them for long.

Economists sometimes model the strategies of oligopolists and market participants in other types of market structure using **game theory**, which involves examining participants' strategies according to what they stand to gain or lose from each strategy.

2.7 Game theory and oligopoly

Economists sometimes model the strategies of oligopolists and market participants in other types of market structure using **game theory**, which involves examining participants' strategies according to what they stand to gain or lose from each strategy.

2.8 Price stability and non-price competition

In Figure 4, we illustrated how the kinked demand curve creates price stability in an oligopoly market. However, this price stability means that oligopolists have to try to influence demand for their goods or services without changing the price of those goods or services.

They are likely to turn to methods of non-price competition instead:

- Advertising and promotions
- Special offers (such as buy one, get one free)
- Loyalty schemes
- Extended guarantees and warranties
- Levels of after-sales service
- Elaborate presentation and packaging.

The presence of these aspects of non-price competition is a common feature of oligopoly markets.

Question — Cartels and oligopoly

(a) Draw a diagram to show the effect of a cartel on price and output to the market.
(b) Draw a diagram to show a kinked oligopoly demand curve.

Compare your diagrams with Figures 3 and 4 respectively in this chapter.

3 Duopoly

FAST FORWARD

A **duopoly** is an oligopoly market structure containing only two firms. The two firms can either collude or compete. If they compete, one firm can only gain at the expense of the other firm.

Duopoly is a useful model for analysing oligopoly behaviour, especially the interdependence between firms.

In a duopoly, if the firms compete, then, assuming the market size remains constant (*ceteris paribus*), the gains of one firm must be matched exactly by the losses of the other firm. So a firm must decide whether to try to increase its market share or to allow market share to remain constant.

This decision can be considered as **game theory**.

3.1 Game theory example

FAST FORWARD

Game theory is an attempt to explain the decisions of firms by developing simulations that examine participants' strategies according to what they stand to gain or lose from each strategy.

There are four strategies about pricing which an oligopolist might adopt:

(a) Co-operate with the other large firms to agree a common policy on pricing and market sharing. This is a **collusive oligopoly**.

(b) Make their own decisions and ignore rivals (to become a price leader). The effect of this will depend on how rivals react, as illustrated by the kinked demand curve.

(c) Become a price follower (price taker) and respond to the actions of a price leader.

(d) Do nothing. The firm may feel it would be disadvantageous to change its price, again based on the kinked demand curve it faces.

Exercise: Game theory

Two firms, A and B, share the market for soft drinks in a country. Firm A is considering launching a major advertising campaign. The nature of the market, as a duopoly, means that Firm A's actions will not only increase its own sales and profit, but will also reduce those of its rival (B). However, once B becomes aware of A's campaign, B is likely to take a counter action and launch a campaign of its own to restore its market share.

At the moment – before any advertising campaigns – both A and B make profits of $250m per year. A and B are both thinking of spending $50m each on their respective advertising campaigns. Each campaign will generate $150m for the firm running the campaign by taking customers from the other firm, meaning that B will suffer a reduction in profit of $150m during A's campaign. However, the net benefit to the advertiser is only $100m ($150m revenue less $50m cost).

Even if both Firm A and Firm B advertise, it is anticipated that overall market sales will remain largely the same. Consequently, if both firms advertise, profits for each firm will fall by the costs of their advertising campaigns (ie $50m).

What are the potential outcomes of the decisions to advertise or not?

Solution

Option	A's profit	B's profit	Industry profit
Currently (no advertising)	$250m	$250m	$500m
A advertises but B does not	$350m	$100m	$450m
B advertises but A does not	$100m	$350m	$450m
Both advertise	$200m	$200m	$400m

Interestingly, if both firms advertise then they will both be worse off than if neither of them had advertised.

The potential outcomes of the decision to advertise or not lead to the following terminology (as seen from A's point of view)

Win/Lose scenario	A advertises and B doesn't. A will gain $100m
Lose/Win scenario	A doesn't advertise but B does. A will lose $150m
Lose/Lose scenario	A and B both advertise. Both lose $50m
Win/Win scenario	Neither advertises.

The figures show that although one firm can gain in the short run from a competitive strategy, in the long run both firms are likely to be better off by working together and not advertising (colluding) rather than competing with each other.

However, game theory presupposes that the firms do not have a collusive agreement and do not know what the other is going to do. So A and B must select their strategies based solely on the outcome which is best for them regardless of the decision made by their rival.

Under these circumstances, both firms will choose to advertise. Individually, they hope to increase profitability $100m by advertising. But, collectively, this course of action causes them both to lose $50m.

[Note, however, that this example assumes that there is no increase to the overall size of the market following the advertising campaigns. In practice this may not be the case though. The advertising campaigns might encourage additional people to start drinking soft drinks, although they had previously bought neither Firm A nor Firm B's drink.]

Example: Winning and losing

Two firms, X and Y compete in the same market and sell their product for $10. Each sells 10m units a year. Both are considering increasing price from $10 to $11. Their economic advisors have told them that customers would be willing to pay the extra $1 without reducing the number of units sold. However if one firm were to raise its price by $1 it would lose 30% of its customers to its rival if the rival did not increase their price.

Model the four possible outcome as seen from X's point of view.

Solution

Each firm presently receives revenue of $100m a year (10m units at $10 each).

Win/Lose scenario	X does not raise price but Y does.
	X will receive $130m a year (13m @ $10)
	Y will receive $77m (7m @ $11)
Lose/Win scenario	X raises price but Y does not.
	X will receive $77m (7m @ $11)
	Y will receive $130m a year (13m @ $10)
Lose/Lose scenario	Neither raises price
	Both continue to receive £100m a year each
Win/Win scenario	Both raise prices
	Both will receive $110m (10m @ $11)

Game theory illustrates the key problem of interdependent decision-making in duopoly and oligopoly. In the examples above the decisions are one-off decisions in which each decision maker has no previous knowledge on which to base their judgement of what the other might do. Neither wishes to be the one who doesn't act and is therefore left as the loser.

More complex versions of game theory are called **iterative game theory**. Here the decision makers learn from previous experience what their rivals tend to do (such as whether they do raise prices or advertise) and then adjust their behaviour accordingly.

4 Contestable markets

A firm in a **contestable market**, in which there are low barriers to entry, will only earn normal profit and no supernormal profit.

4.1 The theory of contestable markets

The theory of contestable markets argues that although there might be just a **few firms** in the market, the market might operate more efficiently than an oligopoly (or monopolistic competition). The key feature of contestable market is that **entry** and **exit costs** are **relatively low** making it easy for new firms to enter a market, and then leave it again. In equilibrium, a firm in a **perfectly contestable market** will earn **normal profits only** (rather than supernormal profits) and produce at an output level where AC is minimised. Thus the firm will be at equilibrium MR = MC = AC = AR, just as in perfect competition, regardless of how many firms exist in the industry.

Here is an exercise to help you to refresh your memory.

PART B CONSUMPTION, PRODUCTION AND DISTRIBUTION

> **Question** — Long-run equilibrium
>
> Draw a diagram to show the long-run equilibrium position for a firm in a perfectly competitive market. Include on your diagram marginal cost (MC), average cost (AC), marginal revenue (MR) and average revenue (AR).
>
> Once you have drawn your diagram, compare it with Figure 11(b) in Chapter 5a: that is what your diagram should look like.

Firms in contestable markets are forced into having to accept normal profits because of the absence of barriers to entry and exit which can help sustain supernormal profits.

If the firms were to be inefficient and produce at a level where AC is not minimised, or if they were to raise prices to earn supernormal profits, other firms would quickly enter the market to skim off any excess profits knowing they could leave just as easily if supernormal profits were to be eroded by the extra competition.

Thus, the theory of contestable markets shows that it is not necessary to have many firms supplying to a market for conditions similar to perfect competition to apply. It is enough for the few firms in the market to know that many more firms could enter the market, skim off supernormal profits and then leave the industry again, for the few firms to act in a similar way to firms in the perfect competition model.

Chapter Roundup

- When **price competition** is restricted, firms usually go in for other forms of competition, such as **sales promotion** and **product differentiation**.

- **Oligopolists** might collude and make a formal or informal **cartel** agreement on the price for the industry and output levels for each firm. The **kinked oligopoly demand curve** may explain why there is price stability (and non-price competition) in many oligopoly markets.

- A **duopoly** is an oligopoly market structure containing only two firms. The two firms can either collude or compete; and if they compete one firm can only gain at the expense of the other firm.

- **Game theory** is an attempt to explain the decisions of firms by developing simulations that examine participants' strategies according to what they stand to gain or lose from each strategy.

- A firm in a **contestable market**, in which there are low barriers to entry, will only earn normal profit and no supernormal profit.

Quick Quiz

1. What is meant by non-price competition?

2. What are the implications of the kinked oligopoly demand curve for price and output by an oligopoly firm?

3. What is meant by the term 'contestable market'?

4. Which of the following statements best describes long run equilibrium in a market where there is monopolistic competition?

    A Marginal revenue equals average cost
    B There is excess capacity in the industry since firms can reduce average costs by expanding output
    C Firms will earn supernormal profits because price exceeds marginal cost
    D Price equals marginal cost, but does not equal average cost

5. Which one of the following statements about price discrimination is NOT correct?

    A Dumping is a form of price discrimination.

    B For price discrimination to be possible, the seller must be able to control the supply of the product.

    C Price discrimination is only profitable where the elasticity of demand is different in at least two of the markets.

    D An example of price discrimination is the sale of first class and second class tickets on an aeroplane journey.

6. The oligopolist is **least** likely to compete through:

    A Advertising
    B Improving product quality
    C Cutting price
    D Providing incidental services as an 'add-on' to the basic good

PART B CONSUMPTION, PRODUCTION AND DISTRIBUTION

7   This question consists of two statements. Which, if either, is correct?

   1   In conditions of **monopolistic competition**, firms will eventually reach an equilibrium output which is less than the output level at which average total cost is at a minimum.

   2   In **perfect competition**, at the output level where marginal revenue equals marginal cost, a firm's average variable costs are minimised.

   A   Both statements are correct
   B   The first statement is correct but the second statement is false
   C   The first statement is false but the second statement is correct
   D   Both statements are false

8   Which of the following factors would weaken the long-term survival of a cartel?

   A   Greater price elasticity of demand for the product in the long run
   B   A high concentration of production in the hands of a few firms
   C   Substantial costs associated with entry into the industry
   D   Broadly similar cost structures between industry members

9   Which one of the following is NOT normally a characteristic of an oligopolistic market?

   A   There is interdependence of decision making
   B   Low barriers to entry
   C   Price stability
   D   Non-price competition

10 What is a duopoly?

Answers to Quick Quiz

1. Non-price competition occurs when firms attempt to increase their sales by product differentiation or various forms of promotion, but without reducing the price of the goods or service.

2. The kinked demand curve illustrates the tendency to stability of prices in oligopoly markets. Oligopolists avoid price competition since a price cut will be matched by competitors and produce little lasting benefit.

3. A contestable market is one in which just a few firms operate but there are no barriers to entry or exit. Firms therefore tend to operate as under perfect competition since they know that any abnormal profits will attract new entrants very rapidly.

4. **B** For long run equilibrium in monopolistic competition, MR = MC and AR = AC, but it is wrong to say that MR = AC or that AR = MC. Since AR = AC, the firm does not earn any supernormal profits. There is excess capacity because at the profit-maximising output, average cost is not at a minimum. AC is minimised at a higher output. Since firms could produce more output at a lower AC, we would say that there is excess capacity in the industry.

5. **D** First and second class tickets are not an example of price discrimination, because even though they are tickets for the same aeroplane journey, they are different products – eg in terms of service and travel comfort – rather than the same product being sold at two or more different prices. All the other statements are true.

6. **C** Oligopoly is usually characterised by price stability, as illustrated by the so-called kinked oligopoly demand curve. Oligopolists are unlikely to cut prices, and are more likely to resort to non-price competition such as advertising and sales promotion, innovation and technical differences and incidental services.

7. **B** In monopolistic competition, a firm's equilibrium is where MR = MC, and this is at an output level below minimum AC. Statement 2 is false because although average total cost is minimised, average variable costs are not at a minimum and diminishing returns already apply.

8. **A** Few suppliers, barriers to entry and similar cost structures are prerequisites for an effective collusive oligopoly. Greater elasticity of demand for a product in the long run would affect the cartel's ability to charge a higher price while maintaining the same volume of sales. This would lead to firms leaving the cartel and cutting prices in order to sell more of their own production.

9. **B** Oligopolies usually contain a small number of large firms. The size of these existing firms (and the economies of scale they enjoy) will act as a barrier to entry for potential new entrants.

10. A duopoly is a market structure containing only two firms. If the firms choose to complete, and the size of the market remains constant, one firm can only gain directly at the expense of the other (as illustrated by game theory).

End of chapter question

Oligopoly

(a) Using an appropriate model, describe the main features of an oligopolistic market with particular emphasis on the concepts of uncertainty and interdependence. **(14 marks)**

(b) Explain why oligopolistic industries are often characterised by heavy expenditure on advertising. **(6 marks)**

(Total 20 marks)

Factor markets

Topic list	Syllabus reference
1 Basic features of factor markets	2.2
2 Capital and interest	2.2
3 Labour and wages	2.2
4 Land and rent	2.2
5 Entrepreneurship and profit	2.2
6 Transfer earnings and economic rent	2.2

Introduction

The four factors of production – **capital, labour, land** and **entrepreneurship** – have been mentioned already in this Study Text already.

Now we look at them in more detail, however, analysing the markets for each of them in terms of demand and supply. This involves a broadly similar approach to that we used in looking at product markets (markets for goods and services) in Chapter 2.

However, the key point about demand for factors of production is that it is a **derived demand**. For example, a firm's demand for labour is determined by the quantity of goods and services it needs labour to produce.

PART B CONSUMPTION, PRODUCTION AND DISTRIBUTION

1 Basic features of factor markets

> **FAST FORWARD**
>
> **Factor prices** are market prices for the four factors of production: interest, wages, rent and profit.

1.1 The four factors of production

Each scarce economic resource has a value, and the owner of the resource or factor of production is rewarded for giving it up to someone else. Firms are rewarded for the goods and services they produce by the price customers will pay for them. The resources used in production are also rewarded, by the price that firms pay to use them.

(a) **Capital** is rewarded with **interest**. In manufacturing firms, capital is used to purchase machinery and other **capital goods** and to provide **working capital** to finance inventories and receivables. If we assume that the original capital sum was borrowed, possibly from the owner of the business, we can see that **interest** is the cost of providing both working capital and capital goods. In some industries, such as banking, capital as money is the basic raw material of the business.

(b) **Labour** is rewarded with **wages** (including 'salaries'). Labour consists of both the mental and the physical resources of human beings.

(c) **Land** is rewarded with **rent**. Land includes the **natural resources** of the soil and woodlands, as well as extracted minerals such as coal.

(d) **Entrepreneurship** or enterprise is a fourth type of factor of production. An entrepreneur is someone who undertakes the task of organising the other three factors of production in a business enterprise and, in doing so, bears the risk of the venture. The entrepreneur creates new business ventures and the reward for the risk the entrepreneur takes is **profit**.

1.2 Factor prices

The prices paid to each factor of production are sometimes referred to as factor prices. The prices for land, labour and capital are determined by supply and demand. Entrepreneurship and profit are rather different, and these will be discussed later.

1.3 Factor demand as a derived demand

> **FAST FORWARD**
>
> **Derived demand** means that the demand for factors of production depends on the demand for, and the profits from, the goods and services they can produce.

The demand for factors of production is a derived demand.

Key term

> By **derived demand** we mean that the factors of production are not demanded for their own sake. They are demanded because a firm needs them to make goods, which are then sold to households. Demand for the factors of production is ultimately determined by households' demand for the goods.

Firms want to make goods because of the revenue they get from selling them, and the profit that they can make by doing so. Firms will not want to pay for factors of production if their marginal cost (and so the marginal cost of producing the good) exceeds the marginal revenue that can be earned from selling a good.

Question: Factor rewards

Think carefully about what is, and what is not, a factor reward. Which of the following are factor rewards?

(a) Commission charges earned by an insurance salesman.
(b) Dividends received on shares.
(c) Cash paid to a window cleaner.
(d) The army pension earned by an ex-army officer now working for a security firm.

Answer

All of these are factor rewards, with the exception of (d). The pension relates to a former employment. The wages earned from the security firm are the reward for the officer's current labour.

Having set out some basic points about the markets for factors of production, we now look at each in turn.

2 Capital and interest

FAST FORWARD

The **rate of interest** comes from the demand for capital. Capital will be demanded until it is marginally efficient, that is, until the cost of borrowing is equal to the profit from employing the most recent item of capital equipment.

2.1 The role of interest

Interest is the reward for capital. The rate of interest, according to traditional economic theory, is determined by supply and demand for capital.

(a) The demand for capital comes from firms, which expect to invest in inventories and equipment so as to create more output, make more sales and earn more profit.

(b) The supply of capital (finance to acquire inventories, equipment and so on) comes from investors.

Firms will only demand capital if they can make an adequate return: the return must exceed the cost of obtaining the capital. Investors will only supply capital if the interest rates they are paid makes it worth their while to invest.

2.2 The marginal efficiency of capital

The demand by firms to borrow capital is explained in traditional (Keynesian) economic theory by the marginal efficiency of capital (MEC). Marginal efficiency of capital theory suggests that the level of investment is inversely related to the price of capital (ie the rate of interest).

Firms should always seek to invest in the opportunities that offer the highest returns. Once these have been invested in, remaining opportunities will not offer such high returns. As more and more investments are made, the returns from additional capital investments will gradually decline. This changing return is the marginal efficiency of capital.

This can be illustrated by a marginal efficiency of capital curve as shown in Figure 1. The MEC curve is, in effect, a demand curve for capital.

PART B CONSUMPTION, PRODUCTION AND DISTRIBUTION

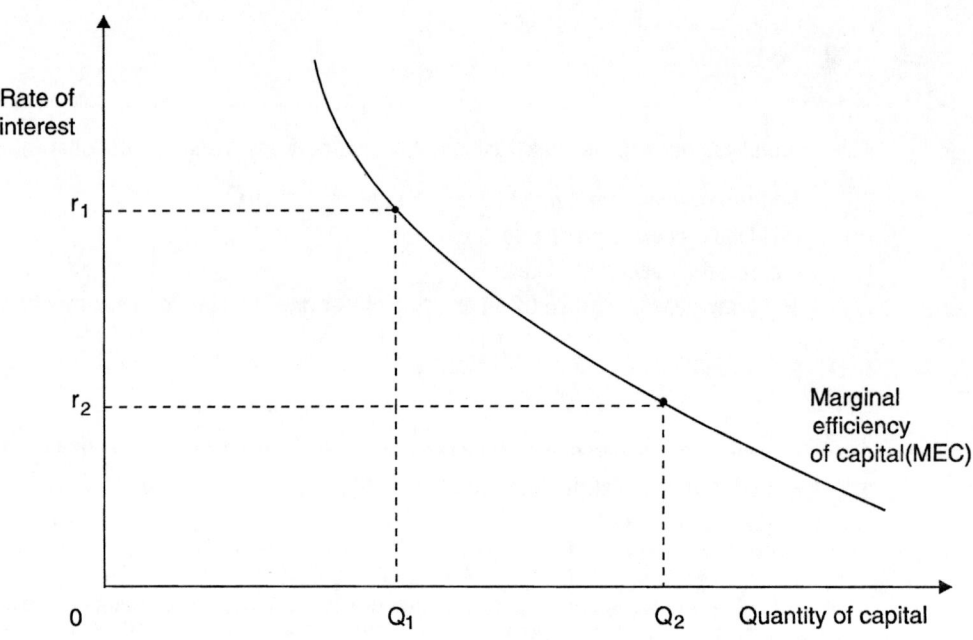

Figure 1 Marginal efficiency curve of capital, which is the demand curve for capital

Firms should be willing to borrow capital up to the point where MEC is equal to the interest rate the firm has to pay for that capital. In Figure 1, if the interest rate is r_1, firms should be willing to borrow up to Q_1 of capital to invest.

Question
MEC curve

Remembering the basic principles of supply and demand, how would an increased demand by firms (interest rates remaining unchanged) be represented on the above diagram?

Answer

The increase in demand would be represented by a rightward shift in the MEC curve.

The MEC curve for all the firms in an industry is the industry's demand curve for capital, and it is the sum of the demand curves (MEC curves) of all the individual firms in the industry. An industry's MEC curve and an individual firm's MEC curve have the same basic shape, as shown in Figure 1.

The assumption that firms are profit maximisers ensures that the rate of interest becomes an important determinant in an investment decision, because it represents the cost to the firm of the investment capital. It only makes sense for firms to use capital to finance an investment project if the returns from that project are greater than the cost of the finance.

When interest rates are high, say at r_1 in Figure 1, few investments will earn adequate return to cover such high costs and yield a profit and the demand for funds will therefore be relatively low at Q_1. However, when interest rates are lower, say at r_2 (in Figure 1), more investments will become profitable, and therefore demand for capital will increase (Q_2 in Figure 1).

2.3 The supply of capital

The rate of interest also depends on the supply of capital from investors, and the interaction of supply and demand for capital establishes interest rates. The supply of capital comes from savers. Savings lead to investment and the creation of capital, but savings are only made by sacrificing some current consumption.

Savers choose to save in order to make possible the consumption of even more outputs in the future, and so the amount of savings is determined by comparing:

(a) What the available wealth could be used to obtain now from the current consumption; and
(b) How much extra wealth will be obtained in the future from saving.

This extra wealth in the future, which makes savers prefer to save rather than consume their wealth now, is represented by the interest they earn on their savings. Higher interest will make saving more attractive, and the supply of savings will therefore increase.

The price of capital (the interest rate) should therefore be determined by the interaction of supply (savings) and demand (marginal efficiency of capital). In Figure 2, the equilibrium interest rate would be r, with quantity Q of capital supplied by savers and demanded by firms.

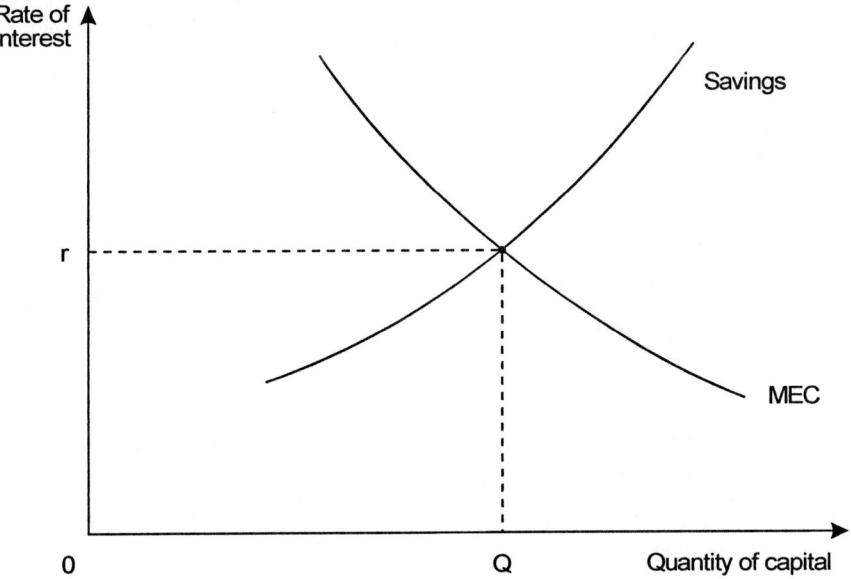

Figure 2 Demand for and supply of capital

2.4 Differences in interest rates

In practice, different rates of interest apply to different firms. This is mainly because there are different levels of risk involved for the lender. A lender will usually expect a higher rate of interest from lending to a newer, small company than from lending to a large, long-established company in the same industry, because there is an increased risk that the small company will be liquidated and the debt not repaid in full. Another factor affecting the price of capital (the rate of interest) is the economies of scale which a lender can gain from larger scale lending, which makes such lending cheaper.

2.5 Imperfections in the market for capital

In reality, the interest rate for capital is not determined just by the free market forces of supply and demand operating as we have suggested so far. Several imperfections in the capital market affect savings, investment decisions and interest rates.

(a) **Monetary factors**. Interest rates are probably influenced not just by investment factors and savings versus consumption factors, but by monetary factors too – such as levels of debt and lending, and growth in the money supply. (Keynes' theory about the influence that demand for money has on interest rates is described in a later chapter.)

(b) **Investment factors**. The theory of the marginal efficiency of capital does not properly explain the pattern of investments made by firms.

   (i) Investments cover a period of several years into the future. The returns from an investment cannot be predicted with much certainty over a long period of time. A firm may even decide to invest in a project in anticipation of future profitability, even though at present short-term and long-term interest rates would counsel against such an investment. **Expectations** therefore play an important role in the decision to invest.

   (ii) Some firms have better access to finance than others: for example, large firms can usually borrow more easily than small firms as they are considered less risky.

   (iii) The level of investment undertaken by a firm will depend on the age of its capital stock. A company with a high proportion of old capital equipment which needs renewing will tend to spend more on investment than a firm which already has modern machinery.

   (iv) A firm which is operating close to full capacity will need to invest in order to continue to expand, whereas investment may be largely unnecessary for a firm working at half capacity, because it can meet the increased demand by making use of its spare capacity.

(c) **Savings factors**. Savings decisions are not just a simple choice between saving and consumption.

   (i) Many savings decisions are made by the management of firms **on behalf of shareholders**, by retaining profits for future investment.

   (ii) The division of national income between high and low income families could be significant, because low income families need to spend more of their income on basic living expenses and hence have a preference for consumption over saving, whereas high income families are more inclined (and more able) to save. (This introduces the idea of a household's 'propensity to save' – a concept which we will look at in more detail in Chapter 10 later in this Study Text.)

   (iii) Consumption and savings patterns are influenced by social attitudes towards thrift. A government might also make saving unattractive by taxing interest earnings at a high rate. Therefore it does not necessarily follow that a rise in interest rates will lower consumption and increase savings.

3 Labour and wages

> **Wages** will be equal to the profit made from employing the marginal worker, called its marginal revenue product.

3.1 The demand for labour and marginal productivity theory

A similar demand and supply analysis can be made for labour and the price of labour (wages), as for capital and interest.

(a) Like the demand for capital, the demand for labour by firms is a derived demand, arising from consumer demand for a firm's output. If the demand for a firm's product increases, it follows that the firm will need to recruit extra staff in order to produce the extra units of the product demanded.

(b) Labour is employed to help to make the goods and services of the firm, and the more labour that is employed, the greater the total volume of goods or services the firm should be able to product.

(c) However, with labour the **law of diminishing marginal returns** applies, in the short run at least, because as more and more labour is hired, the productivity of the extra workforce will gradually decline.

In our basic analysis below, we shall assume that labour is a variable factor of production and all other factors are fixed.

Key term

> The **marginal revenue product (MRP)** of labour is the extra revenue that a firm would obtain from the extra output provided by each extra recruit to the workforce.

The MRP of labour is similar in concept to the MEC of capital. It also represents the demand curve for labour by a firm (or by firms in the industry as a whole). Firms should be willing to pay for labour provided that the marginal revenue product of labour exceeds the cost of employing the labour.

Put simply, if a firm can make an extra £150 per week from hiring an extra employee, it should be willing to hire the employee provided that the employee's weekly wage cost does not exceed £150. In Figure 3, if the MRP of labour for a certain type of job, job type A, is as shown, and the wage level for job type A is W, then the industry would want to employ X employees in job type A, because the MRP of labour exceeds the wage rate up to X.

In contrast, job type B has a higher marginal productivity value than job type A, and so the industry would be willing either:

(a) To pay a higher wage (V) for the same quantity of employees as job type A; or
(b) To employ more employees (Y) into job type B than job type A if the wage rate for both were W.

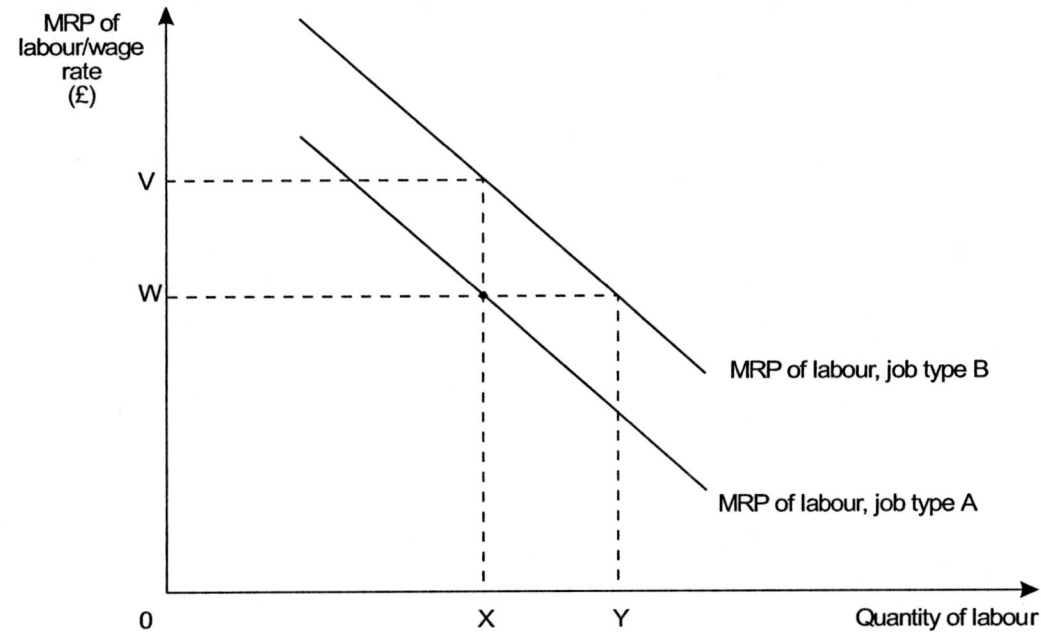

Figure 3 Marginal revenue product of labour

Key term

> The **marginal productivity theory of wages** states that the demand for labour is determined by the additional output resulting from the employment of an additional worker. At a given wage level, the entrepreneur will hire additional labour until the revenue contribution of the last additional worker employed equals the wage paid. As the theory assumes that the level of wages is 'given', it ignores the supply side of wage determination.

3.2 The supply of labour

Since the above analysis of the MRP of labour only considers the demand by firms for labour of different types and skills, we should now consider the supply of labour.

Higher wages will attract more people willing to do the work. The supply curve for labour can therefore be shown as the marginal cost of the labour; in other words the extra total wage payments needed to increase total labour supply.

When higher wages must be paid to attract more labour:

(a) the supply curve for labour, which is the marginal cost curve for labour (MC_L), will be rising
(b) MC_L will be higher than the wage level – that is, higher than the average cost of labour AC_L.

We therefore have wage levels determined by the interaction of supply and demand, which is where the MC_L curve intersects with the marginal revenue product curve for labour (MRP_L) – Figure 4.

The wage level also depends on whether industry and labour market are:

(a) **Perfectly competitive**, and firms can obtain extra quantities of labour freely at a constant wage rate, so that the average cost of labour and marginal cost of labour are the same ($AC_L = MC_L$); or

(b) **Imperfectly competitive**, for example dominated by a single firm who can only obtain more labour by paying higher wages. In this situation, the supply curve for labour that faces the firm will be upward-sloping.

Figure 4 shows that an individual firm will continue to hire more labour at wage rate W until the MRP of labour falls to this level. The individual firm will therefore hire L_f units of labour. Total employment in the industry (L_i) is the sum of the employment of labour by the individual firms.

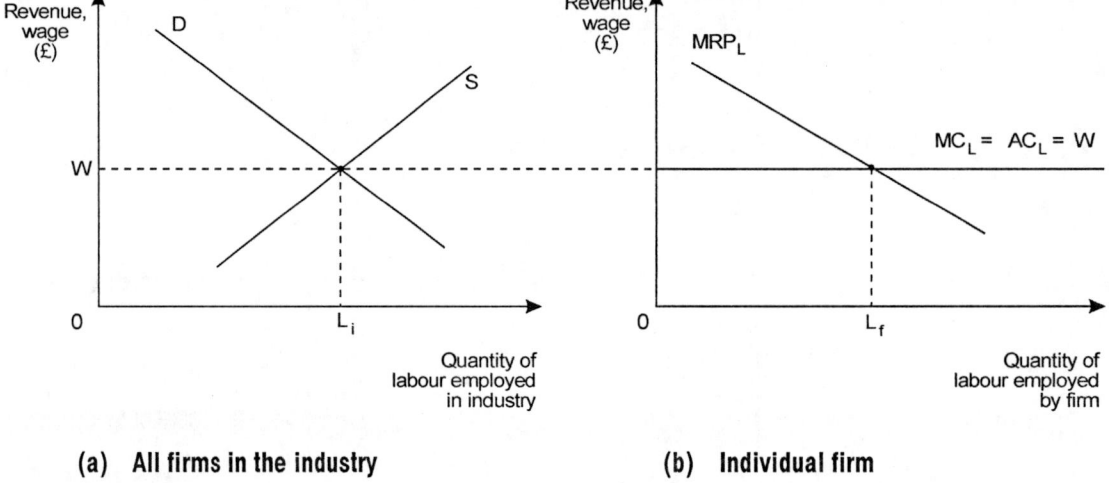

(a) All firms in the industry   (b) Individual firm

Figure 4 Competition among firms for labour

Wage level = W; employment level in the industry = L_i and in an individual firm = L_f.

3.3 Limitations of marginal productivity theory

The marginal productivity theory of wages cannot account wholly for the determination of wage rates and wage differentials because the assumptions on which it is based do not apply in reality.

(a) It is often difficult to calculate the marginal productivity of labour, especially in administrative work or service industries.

(b) Marginal productivity theory for labour assumes that all other factors of production are held in constant supply. This is unlikely to be so, especially in the case of capital. As the amount of labour employed changes, so too would the amount of capital. (There is substitutability between labour and capital; alternatively more capital might be combined with more labour to increase total output.) If other factors of production are not held constant, it becomes difficult, if not impossible, to measure MRP, and so an MRP curve could not be drawn with accuracy.

(c) A further assumption is that labour is free to enter the market or leave it for alternative employment elsewhere. In practice, this might not be the case.

3.4 Imperfections in the labour market

> **FAST FORWARD**
>
> **Labour market imperfections** are things that stop wages equalling their marginal revenue product, such as artifical restrictions on the supply of workers or lack of labour mobility.

In a perfect labour market, the supply of labour would shift rapidly to whatever use provides the highest reward. Factor mobility is the term used to describe the readiness and speed with which a factor of production can switch from one use to another. Labour immobility is an imperfection in the labour market which helps to explain pay differentials between different industries, jobs and regions.

In a perfect market, labour would move from regions with low wage rates to regions with high wage rates until equilibrium was achieved and wage levels in all regions were the same. Similarly, the supply of labour should move from lower paid occupations to higher paid occupations.

In practice, there are restrictions which create a certain amount of labour immobility, so that:

(a) The level of unemployment may vary regionally; and

(b) In the same region, there may be job vacancies for some types of worker but excess supply and unemployment among others.

You are probably aware of many of the causes of labour immobility, for example:

(a) Professional barriers, where **professional associations** maintain standards by means of examinations.

(b) **Lack of information** about employment opportunities.

(c) **Lack of provision of training and education** to give people access to alternative jobs.

(d) A **housing system** which makes moving between regions difficult, for example where there are high costs of housing in regions with better job opportunities.

(e) **Non-monetary considerations** (for example, friends, social life outside work) which make individuals reluctant to move to a different region.

(f) High **natural ability** required in certain labour markets, barring people without the necessary ability or skills.

(g) **Linguistic and cultural differences**, making some jobs more socially acceptable than others for some people.

(h) **Discrimination** in the allocation of jobs, such as illegal discrimination on the basis of sex, race or age.

The problem of the geographical immobility of labour could be alleviated by encouraging jobs to go to the regions with unemployment rather than expecting labour to go to the jobs. This is also the logic of schemes such as the EU European Regional Development Fund (ERDF) which aims to support projects and activities which stimulate economic development and increase employment in areas which have previously found it difficult to attract private investment. In this way, the ERDF tries to help these areas improve their economic competitiveness, which should in turn increase the number of jobs available in them.

However, government retraining schemes and a job-oriented education policy might also be necessary to overcome the problems of occupational immobility of labour. But a problem with such policies is that trainees would become disillusioned quite rapidly if they were unable to find a job after retraining, and the government would have to co-ordinate training programmes with the demands of industry for skilled workers.

3.5 Barriers to entry into labour markets

In some labour markets there are barriers to entry, such as requirements for lengthy training or relevant experience. Barriers to entry prevent the supply curve from shifting far to the right.

3.6 Wage differentials

Wage differentials are differences in the rate of pay between one type of job and another. Some jobs are more attractive than others or pay more because certain skills are required.

Skilled workers are more productive and add more to a firm's marginal revenue product than unskilled workers. Skilled workers expect to be paid more for their skills. In order to attract a bigger supply of skilled workers, with more people willing to acquire the necessary training, skills and qualifications, higher wages must be paid. The supply of skilled workers will also be more inelastic, because the barriers to entry (such as the need to obtain suitable training and qualifications) are higher, or the availability of individuals with suitable talent will be restricted. As a consequence, there will be a wage differential between the skilled and the unskilled workers.

How might wage differentials be eliminated? If a group of low-paid workers wished to eliminate the wage differentials between themselves and more highly paid skilled workers, they might try strike action, or even ask for government support (minimum pay legislation, or income controls). However, according to marginal productivity theory, the solution would be to increase productivity. If unskilled labour can become more productive, they can justify higher wages. Wage differentials with other workers would be reduced and perhaps eliminated. This is why, in some highly profitable industries, unskilled workers might have such a high MRP that they earn higher wages than skilled workers in an unprofitable industry.

Marginal productivity theory is not the only way to explain wage differentials. Other factors affecting labour supply might help to influence wage levels for skilled workers – such as the willingness of some skilled labour to work for low wages, despite their skills and training (for example, nurses and social workers).

3.7 Trade unions and the bargaining theory of wages

Although we have looked at marginal productivity theory and the view that wage levels are set by demand and supply factors, it should also be recognised that trade unions try to negotiate higher wages for labour. There is a 'bargaining theory' of wages which states that wage levels are set by negotiation between unions and management.

Collective bargaining is a term which refers to the process by which unions negotiate and reach agreements with employers. It is common for collective bargaining to involve a single monopolist seller of labour (the trade union) and one buyer or monopsonist (a single firm or an employers' federation).

The role of trade unions, in economic terms, has two aspects. Unions try to:

(a) Erect and maintain barriers to entry into jobs in the industry, thus ensuring high earnings for the existing members.

(b) Monopolise the supply of labour in the industry. If the supply of labour is in the hands of a collective body as opposed to individuals, this can influence the price at which it can be sold.

By restricting entry to the labour force, trade unions might force wages to increase from W_0 to W_1 by effectively changing the supply curve from S_0 to S_1 in Figure 5. This will however result in fewer jobs. The number employed will fall from L_0 to L_1.

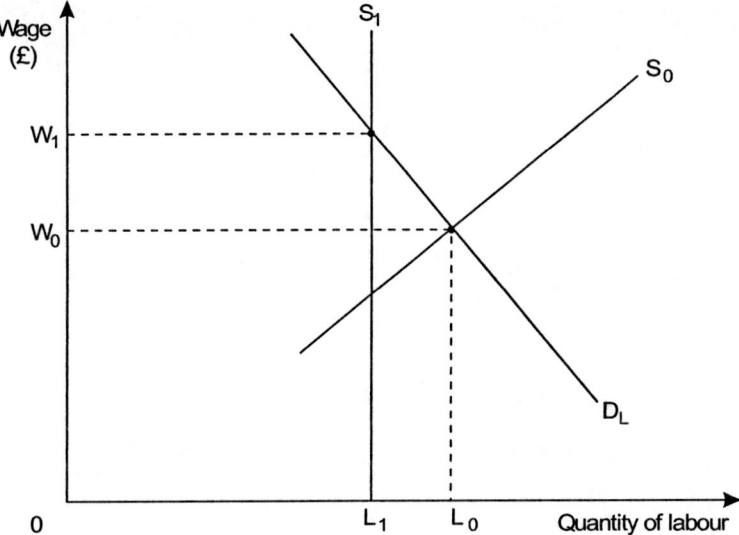

Figure 5 The effect of unionisation

However, once wage rates have been given an initial increase by the unionisation of the work force, any further pay rises, given no change in the marginal revenue product (MRP) of labour, will probably reduce the total demand for labour by employers.

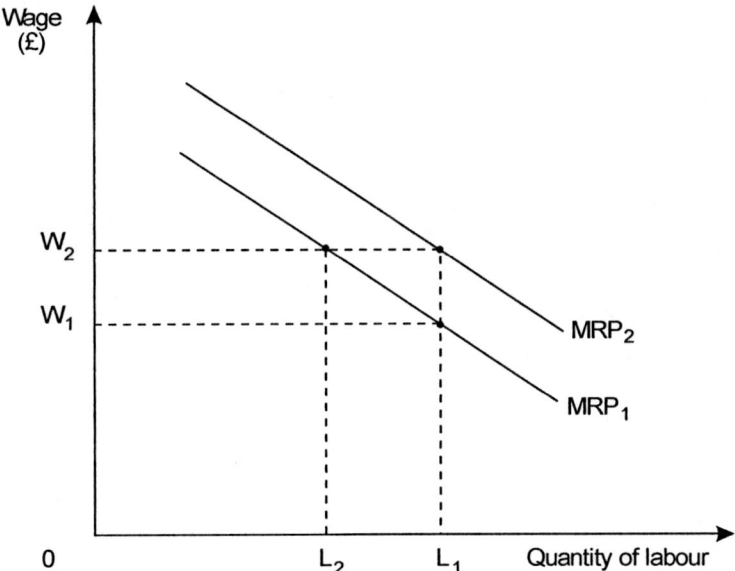

Figure 6 Wage increase

When wages rise from W_1 to W_2, the demand for labour will fall from L_1 to L_2 (Figure 6), given no change in the MRP of labour (initially MRP_1). However, if the labour force agrees to an improvement in productivity so that the marginal revenue product of labour shifts to MRP_2, an increase in wages from W_1 to W_2 could be achieved without changing the total workforce employed from L_1.

PART B CONSUMPTION, PRODUCTION AND DISTRIBUTION

3.8 Minimum wages

FAST FORWARD

> **Minimum wage legislation** is designed to ensure a fair deal for workers. However, it can also lead to persistant unemployment as firms reduce the number of staff they hire but more workers seek jobs at the higher pay rates.

Many countries have minimum wage legislation. The purpose of a minimum wage is to ensure that low-paid workers earn at least enough in wages to have a certain standard of living.

If a minimum wage is enforced by legislation (a statutory minimum wage) or negotiated nationally for an industry by a trade union the minimum wage will probably be above the current wage level for the jobs concerned. The consequences of a minimum wage would then be to:

(a) Raise wage levels for workers employed to a level above the equilibrium wage rate
(b) Reduce the demand for labour and so cause job losses

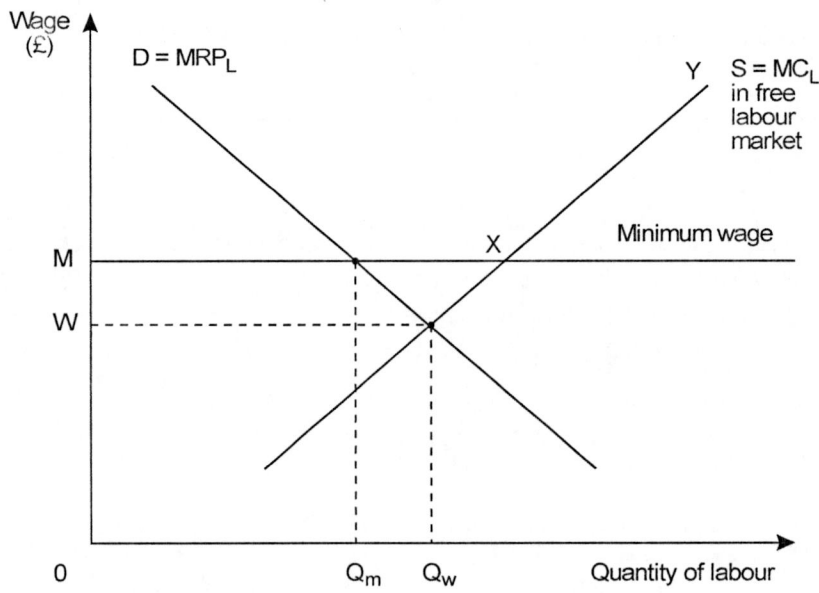

Figure 7 Minimum wage

Without a minimum wage, Q_w workers would be employed at wage rate W (Figure 7).

Question

By reference to Figure 9, work out what happens when a minimum wage M, higher than the existing rate W, is imposed.

Answer

The supply curve for labour is now the line MXY. Demand for labour from employers will fall to Q_m, but the workers who are actually employed will earn a higher wage.

It is probably fair to conclude that the bargaining theory of wages is consistent with marginal productivity theory and the principles of demand and supply. The level of wages bargained by unions will help to determine employment levels and when conditions in the industry favour the employer with labour having low marginal revenue productivity, unions will find it difficult to bargain for higher wages or to preserve jobs in the industry.

3.9 Imperfections in labour supply: conclusion

In spite of imperfections in the labour markets, there is a lot of common sense in the general principle that the willingness of firms to hire workers and the willingness of workers to accept jobs will depend largely on wage levels.

3.10 The substitutability of capital for labour

Substitution between factors of production (for example, between labour and capital) will take place:

(a) **Provided that substitution is practical or technologically feasible** (for example, machines can be made to do the work previously carried out by labour, or that labour can physically do the work of machines);

(b) **When the price or productivity of one factor of production rises relative to another.** If wages go up, the marginal cost of labour will rise, and firms will want less labour at this higher cost. Labour will also become more expensive in relation to capital, and there will be some substitution of capital for labour. The net result of an increase in wages will be a reduction in the quantity of labour employed – unless the productivity of labour can be increased at the same time, to strengthen the demand for labour.

Key term

Labour productivity can be defined as the output per worker over a given period of time and is indicated by the average product of labour.

4 Land and rent

FAST FORWARD

Rent is the return to land. Because land is in fixed supply, the level of rent is entirely set by the level of demand for land and for what it can produce.

4.1 Rent

The price of land (ie the earth and its natural resources), which is rent, is also determined by supply and demand. (It is also common to speak of renting a house or a car. This is 'commercial rent' though, and is not the same. The more specific concept of economic rent is dealt with later.)

4.2 The price of land

In the 19th century, David Ricardo argued that:

(a) The total amount of land available is fixed, therefore the supply of land is inelastic, regardless of how much rent is paid for it;

(b) Since the supply of land is inelastic, the amount of rent will be determined by the price of the goods produced from the land for sale to markets.

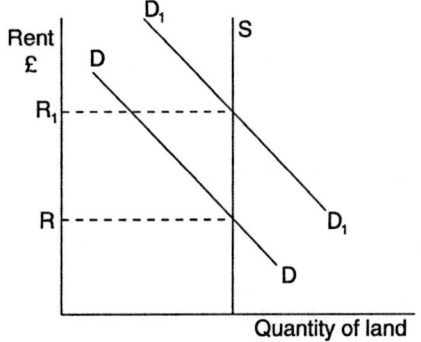

Figure 8 The level of rents

The total amount of land is fixed therefore the supply curve is vertical in Figure 8. The demand for land is determined by the use which can be made of it and the profit this brings. Thus, with a downward sloping demand curve DD, rent is at level R. If the profitability of using land increases the demand curve will shift to the right (D_1); more will be demanded at any price. Since the supply is fixed, the new equilibrium is at increased rent R_1.

4.3 The price of land for specific uses

We can extend this principle to cover the situation where the supply of land is not perfectly inelastic (Figure 9). This situation arises where we are considering the supply of land for a particular purpose, for example, office development or agricultural use. Since it is usually possible to change the use of a piece of land, the supply of land for a particular purpose should not normally be considered fixed. If the price of agricultural land in the UK went up we would expect a transfer of land from (say) the domestic housing sector to the agricultural sector. In fact, the supply curve of agricultural land slopes upward from left to right. The equilibrium price and quantity of agricultural land are determined by the intersection of the demand curve (derived from the price of goods produced on the land) and the supply curve (derived from the price which prevents a quantity of land being transferred to any other use).

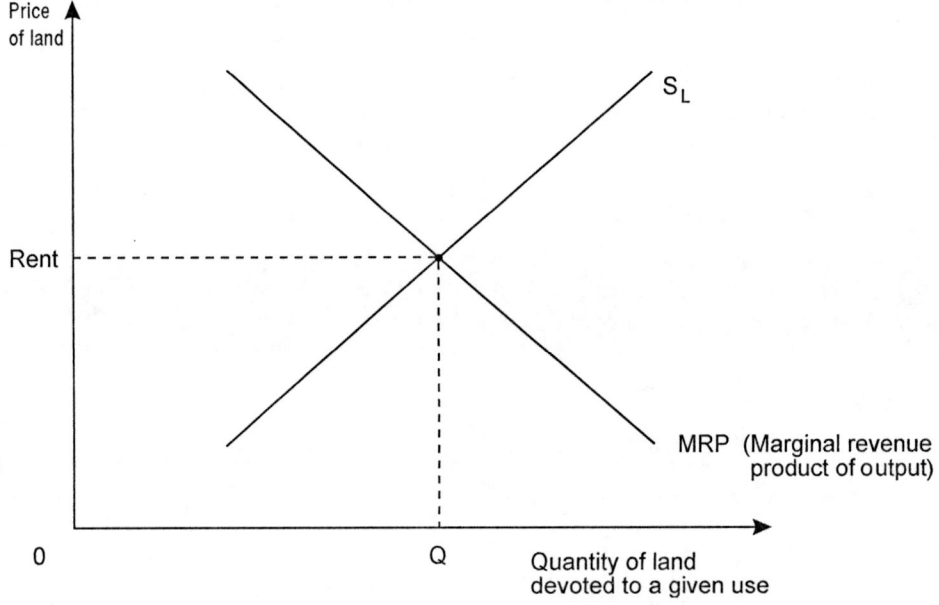

Figure 9 Price of land in a specific use

5 Entrepreneurship and profit

FAST FORWARD

Profit is the return to the entrepreneur. It is what is left over after all other costs have been paid. It is divided into normal profit and supernormal profit.

5.1 The function of the entrepreneur

The entrepreneur:

(a) Organises production and makes decisions about new business ventures;
(b) Earns the reward of profit.

These dual aspects of entrepreneurship are possibly most apparent in partnerships and small private limited companies, where the owners of the business are often also the senior managers. They organise production, make the decisions, and earn the profits for themselves.

5.2 The nature of profit

Unlike land, labour and capital, which are rewarded by rents, wages and interest respectively, the entrepreneur cannot be sure of gaining a reward (making a profit) because his business might make unanticipated losses.

5.3 Supernormal profits

When total revenues exceed the total opportunity costs of input resources, the firm will be earning profit in excess of normal profits, and so resources are earning more than they could in an alternative occupation.

Supernormal profits indicate to entrepreneurs the best markets for new investments or for a switch of their existing investments. When a firm makes supernormal profits, however, other firms will want to enter the industry if they can, to grab a share of the high profits that are available. In competitive industries, supernormal profits therefore tend to be temporary, because they are eventually eroded by competition.

5.4 Normal profit, risk and uncertainty

Firms in high risk industries should expect to earn a higher return than firms in low risk industries. The higher the risk, the higher the risk premium required. (Risk premium can be defined as the additional return needed to compensate an investor for making the risky investment.) Thus, normal profit will be higher in a more risky market than in a less risky market.

6 Transfer earnings and economic rent

FAST FORWARD

> **Economic rent** is a general description of the portion of a factor's income that arises from its relative scarcity.
>
> **Transfer earnings** refers to the portion of a factor's income that is the minimum necessary to keep it in its present line of employment.

We have discussed the supply and price of each factor. We will now consider some principles of factor pricing which may be applied to every factor of production.

The owners of factors of production will transfer their factors to another use unless the present usage provides the greatest rewards. This reward may be divided into two parts.

Key terms

> **Transfer earnings** are the reward the factor would receive in its next best employment, ie its opportunity cost. Transfer earnings are therefore the amount needed to keep the factor in its present employment.
>
> **Economic rent** is the difference between its transfer earnings and its actual reward for its present use, ie it is the surplus in excess of transfer earnings.

If a football player can earn a salary of $375,000, while his next best alternative employment would be as a salesman earning $35,000 (transfer earnings), the 'rent' paid to him as a football player is $340,000. If working as a salesman is the only alternative, any payment above $35,000 should be sufficient to keep the person as a football player.

To measure the contribution of transfer earnings and economic rent to the reward for factors it is necessary to study the elasticity of supply because the size of the economic rent is determined by the elasticity of supply of the factor of production.

PART B CONSUMPTION, PRODUCTION AND DISTRIBUTION

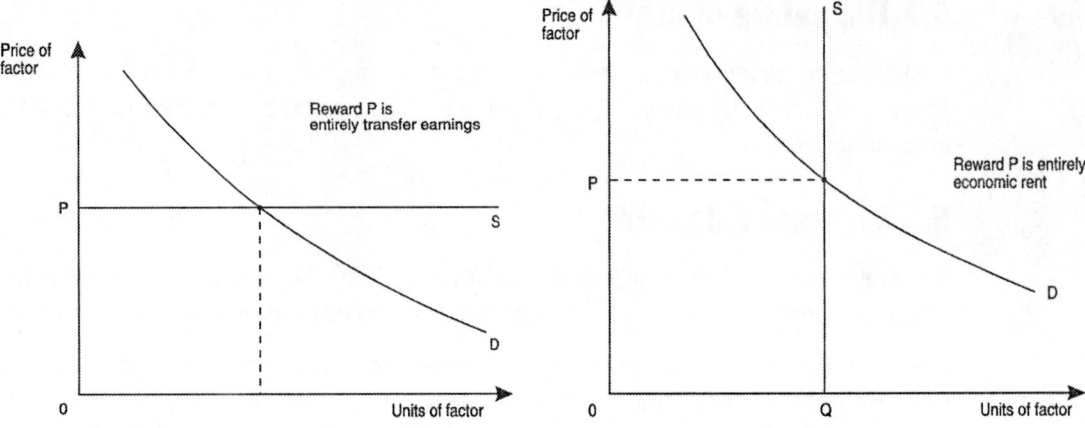

Figure 10 (a) Perfectly elastic supply   (b) Perfectly inelastic supply

Where the supply is perfectly elastic (Figure 10 (a)), all income is transfer earnings. If the price is not paid for the factor the whole supply will move to a new use. On the other hand, where the supply of a factor is fixed and has only one use (Figure 10 (b)), the reward may be entirely economic rent. The factor cannot transfer to another use; therefore there are no transfer earnings.

Where the elasticity of supply is nearer to unit elasticity it is possible to measure the transfer earnings by considering the payment of each unit on the supply curve.

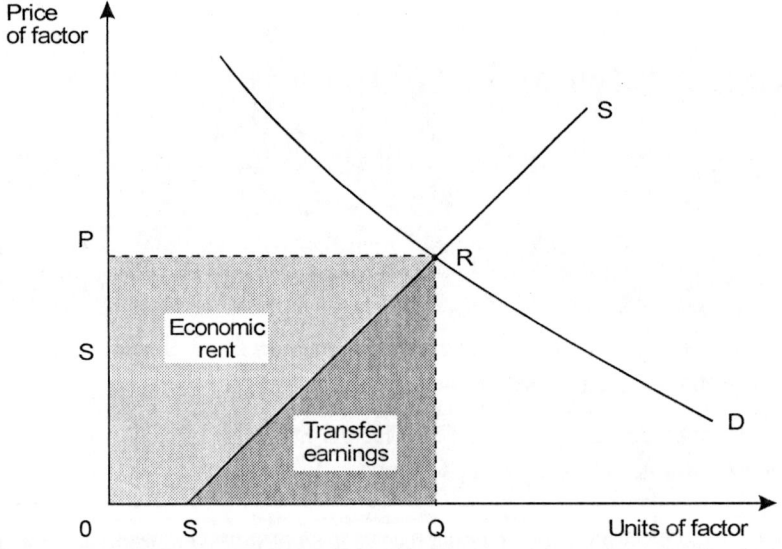

Figure 11 Economic rent and transfer earnings

In Figure 11, the area OPRQ represents the total income earned by the factor. The area within OPRQ but below the supply curve (SRQ) represents the transfer earnings and the area above the supply curve (OPRS) represents the economic rent.

Thus the more elastic the supply curve becomes, the less economic rent is paid. The more inelastic the supply curve becomes, the less transfer earnings are paid.

Exam focus point

Do not confuse **transfer earnings** and **transfer payments**. Transfer earnings were defined above. Transfer payments are grants or other payments not made in return for a productive service (for example, state pensions, unemployment benefit and charitable donations by companies).

Chapter Roundup

- **Factor prices** are market prices for the four factors of production: wages, interest, rent and profit.
- **Derived demand** means that the demand for factors of production depends on the demand for, and profits from, the goods and services they can produce.
- The **rate of interest** comes from the demand for capital. Capital will be demanded until it is marginally efficient, that is, until the cost of borrowing is equal to the profit from employing the most recent item of capital equipment.
- **Wages** will be equal to the profit made from employing the marginal worker, called its marginal revenue product.
- **Labour market imperfections** are things that stop wages equalling their marginal revenue product such as artificial restrictions on the supply of workers or lack of labour mobility.
- **Minimum wage legislation** is designed to ensure a fair deal for workers. However, it can also lead to persistent unemployment as firms reduce the numbers of staff they hire but more workers seek jobs at the higher pay rates.
- **Rent** is the return to land. Because land is in fixed supply, the level of rent is entirely set by the level of demand for land and for what it can produce.
- **Profit** is the return to the entrepreneur. It is what is left over after all other costs have been paid. It is divided into normal profit and supernormal profit.
- **Economic rent** is a general description of the portion of a factor's income that arises from its relative scarcity.
- **Transfer earnings** refers to the portion of a factor's income that is the minimum necessary to keep it in its present line of employment.

Quick Quiz

1. What is derived demand?
2. What is the demand curve for capital?
3. List as many imperfections in the market for capital as you can.
4. What is the MRP of labour?
5. Show how wage and employment levels are determined, according to marginal productivity theory, in a perfectly competitive market?
6. What is likely to be the consequence for employment of minimum wage levels in an industry?
7. What is rent and how is it determined?
8. Outline the function of the entrepreneur and the nature of his or her reward.
9. What is meant by the entrepreneur's 'risk premium'?
10. What are (a) transfer earnings and (b) economic rent?

Answers to Quick Quiz

1. Derived demand means that the demand for factors depends on the demand for, and profits from, what they can produce.

2. The Marginal efficiency curve of capital

3. You answer may include: monetary factors such as interest rates, investment patterns (based on expectations in uncertain environments, access to finance and soon) and savings factors (wealth distribution, social attitudes, and business policies are significant factors).

4. The marginal revenue product (MRP) of labour is the extra revenue that firms would obtain from the extra output provided by each extra recruit to the workforce.

5. In a perfectly competitive market firms can obtain extra quantities of labour freely at a constant wage rate, so that the average cost of labour and marginal cost of labour are the same.

6. Unemployment, as firms reduce hiring but more workers seek jobs at the higher pay rates.

7. Rent is the return to land, and it is determined by the level of demand for land and for what it can produce.

8. The entrepreneur organises production and makes decisions about new business ventures and earns the reward of profit.

9. Risk premium can be defined as the additional return needed to compensate an investor for making the risky investment.

10. Transfer earnings refers to the portion of a factor's income that is the minimum necessary to keep it in its present line of employment.

    Economic rent is a general description of the portion of a factor's income that arises from its relative scarcity.

End of chapter question

Labour mobility

(a) Explain how the demand for a factor of production is a **derived** demand. **(6 marks)**

(b) According to theory, the supply of labour moves to whatever use provides the highest reward, but in practice this does not happen.

Explain why labour immobility occurs and what can be done to improve the efficiency of the labour market. **(14 marks)**

(Total 20 marks)

PART B CONSUMPTION, PRODUCTION AND DISTRIBUTION

PART C

Household, corporate and finance sectors

Public policy and competition

Topic list	Syllabus reference
1 Government regulation and privatisation	2.3
2 Public policy towards monopolies	2.3

Introduction

There is a potential role for government in the regulation of private markets where these fail to bring about an efficient use of resources.

We now examine this role of government in relation to monopolies and other aspects of competition.

Since monopolies have both economic disadvantages and economic advantages, there are reasons why a government might wish either to restrict or to encourage the development of private enterprise monopolies within its country.

PART C HOUSEHOLD, CORPORATE AND FINANCE SECTORS

1 Government regulation and privatisation

1.1 Market failure and regulation

> **FAST FORWARD**
>
> **Market failure** is said to occur when the market mechanism fails to result in economic efficiency, and therefore the outcome is sub-optimal.

In response to the existence of market failure, and as an alternative to taxation and public provision of production, the state often resorts to regulation of economic activity in a variety of ways. Of the various forms of market failure, the following are the cases where regulation of markets can often be the most appropriate policy response.

Market failure	Regulation
Imperfect competition	Where monopoly power is leading to inefficiency, the state will intervene through controls on, say, prices or profits in order to try to reduce the effects of the monopoly.
Externalities	A possible means of dealing with the problem of external costs and benefits is via some form of regulation. Regulations might include, for example, controls on emissions of pollutants, restrictions on car use in urban areas, the banning of smoking in public buildings, compulsory car insurance and compulsory education.
Imperfect information	Regulation is often the best form of government action whenever informational inadequacies are undermining the efficient operation of private markets. This is particularly so when consumer choice is being distorted. Examples here would include legally enforced product quality/safety standards, consumer protection legislation, and the provision of job centres and other means of improving information flows in the labour market.
Equity	The government may also resort to regulation for social reasons. For example, legislation to prevent racial, sexual or age discrimination in the labour market; regulation to ensure equal access to goods such as health care, education and housing; minimum wage regulations and equal pay legislation.

1.2 Types of regulation

Regulation can be defined as any form of state interference in the operation of the free market. This could involve regulating demand, supply, price, profit, quantity, quality, entry, exit, information, technology, or any other aspect of production and consumption in the market.

With specific reference to competition and free market economics, there are two aspects which government will regulate.

(a) Mergers or acquisitions which would create monopolies.
(b) Restrictive trade practices which reduce competition in a market, for example price fixing.

1.3 Self-regulation

Bear in mind that in many markets the participants (especially the firms) may decide to maintain a system of voluntary self-regulation, possibly in order to try to avert the imposition of government controls. Self-regulation often exists in the professions (eg the Association of International Accountants (AIA), the Law Society, the British Medical Association and other professional bodies).

1.4 Costs of regulation

Potential costs of regulation

(a) **Enforcement costs.** Direct costs of enforcement include the setting up and running of the regulatory agencies. Indirect costs are those incurred by the firms being regulated in conforming to the restrictions. These requirements will add to the firms' costs of production and ultimately to their prices.

(b) **Regulatory capture** refers to the process by which the regulator becomes dominated and controlled by the regulated firms, such that it acts increasingly in the latter's interests, rather than those of consumers and other stakeholders.

Case Study

In the aftermath of the Deepwater Horizon oil spill (in 2010) the Minerals Management Service (MMS) – which had regulatory responsibility in the US for offshore oil drilling at the time – was widely cited as an example of regulatory capture. It had granted BP and many other companies licences to drill for oil in the Gulf of Mexico without them providing environmental impact statements or assessing the risks and potential consequences of an oil spill.

(c) **Unintended consequences of regulation.** Firms will not react passively to regulatory constraints on their behaviour; they will instead try to limit the effectiveness of the constraints. In general, theory and observation suggest that firms will substitute away from the regulated activity towards those which are less constrained or completely unregulated.

1.5 Deregulation

Deregulation can be defined as the removal or weakening of any form of statutory (or voluntary) regulation of free market activity. Deregulation allows free market forces more scope to determine the outcome.

There was a shift in policy in the 1980s in the UK and in the USA towards greater deregulation of markets, in the belief that this would improve efficiency. Indeed, many politicians and commentators believed that it was over-regulation of British industry that was largely responsible for Britain's comparatively uncompetitive and inefficient performance in the preceding years.

A rational assessment of deregulation should weigh the potential **social** benefits against the **social** costs. If there will be a net gain to society, we can say that the deregulation should proceed. It would be simplistic to contend that **all** regulation is detrimental to the economy. As we have seen, where there is a clear case of market failure, then state regulation may be required.

1.6 Advantages and disadvantages of deregulation

Deregulation measures, whose main aim is to introduce more competition into an industry by removing statutory or other entry barriers, are also known as **liberalisation**. The benefits of liberalising an industry include the following.

(a) **Improved incentives for internal/cost efficiency.** Greater competition compels managers to try harder to keep down costs.

(b) **Improved allocative efficiency.** Competition keeps prices closer to marginal cost, and firms therefore produce closer to the socially optimal output level.

PART C HOUSEHOLD, CORPORATE AND FINANCE SECTORS

In some industries, liberalisation could have certain disadvantages.

(a) **Loss of economies of scale**. If increased competition means that each firm produces less output on a smaller scale, unit costs will be higher.

(b) **Lower quality or quantity of service**. The need to reduce costs may lead firms to reduce quality or eliminate unprofitable but socially valuable services.

(c) **Need to protect competition**. It may be necessary to implement a regulatory regime to protect competition where inherent forces have a tendency to eliminate it, for example if there is a dominant firm already in the industry, such as BT (formerly British Telecom) in the telecommunications industry in the UK. In this type of situation, effective regulation for competition will be required; in other words, there will need to be regulatory measures aimed at maintaining competitive pressures, whether existing or potential.

1.7 Deregulation and liberalisation in the UK

In the UK, deregulation and liberalisation have taken place in the areas of financial markets, broadcasting, transport and the professions.

(a) **The 1986 'Big Bang' in the Stock Exchange** abolished the old system of separate jobbers and brokers, and fixed brokerage commissions. Barriers to the entry of new firms were also lifted. One result of this was the merging of many broking and jobbing firms in the City into larger groupings, owned in most cases by 'outside' financial institutions.

(b) The Cable and Broadcasting Act (1984) laid the groundwork for both **cable and direct satellite broadcasting** (eg Sky) to develop, in competition with the existing over-the-air BBC and ITV transmissions.

(c) Liberalisation of **road passenger transport** – both buses (stage services) and coaches (express services) – was brought about by the Transport Acts of 1980 and 1985. There is now effective free entry into both markets (except in London where Transport for London (TFL) still controls the bus services).

(d) The monopoly position enjoyed by some **professions** has been removed; for example, opticians' supply of spectacles and solicitors' monopoly over house conveyancing have been removed. In addition, the controls on advertising by professionals have been loosened.

A further instance of liberalisation was the introduction of **compulsory competitive tendering** into public sector organisations. Both local authorities (eg refuse collection, office cleaning and management of leisure facilities) and health authorities (eg hospital cleaning, laundry and catering) have had to **contract out** the supply of these services, where private sector firms have offered to provide the services at a lower price than their own internal producers.

1.8 Privatisation and denationalisation

Key term

Privatisation is the transfer by government of state owned activities to the private sector.

Privatisation as originally envisaged takes three broad forms.

(a) The **deregulation of industries**, to allow private firms to compete against state owned businesses where they were not allowed to compete before (for example, deregulation of bus and coach services; deregulation of postal services).

(b) **Contracting out** work to private firms, where the work was previously done by government employees – for example, refuse collection or hospital laundry work.

(c) **Transferring the ownership of assets** from the state to private shareholders, for example in the UK the denationalisation of British Gas, BT and many other enterprises.

Case Study

The UK government, like many other governments of developed countries, has carried out a policy of denationalisation. British Gas, British Rail, BT, the regional water authorities, much of the electricity industry, and – more recently – Royal Mail are among the enterprises which have been privatised in the UK. Many of the utility industries which have been privatised are still subject to regulations though; for example, the water regulator (OFWAT) sets limits on the prices water companies can charge for water and sewerage services.

The Private Finance Initiative

A fourth type of privatisation has been established in the UK since the 1990s. The **Private Finance Initiative** (PFI) enlists private sector **capital** and **management expertise** to provide public services at reduced cost to the public sector budget. The capital aspect of the scheme has been particularly welcome to government as it allows for expansion of public services without an increase in the Public Sector Net Cash Requirement. These have been extended to other countries where they are also known as Public Private Partnerships (PPP).

A typical PFI/PPP contract would involve a consortium of private companies which undertakes to design, finance, build and manage a facility such as a school or hospital over a long term contract, typically 30-60 years. The consortium accepts the **risk** of the project and takes its **returns** in the form of **periodic fees**. Because they usually involve the provision of services, PFI contracts tend to be very complex in order to ensure that performance standards are rigorously defined.

Perceived advantages of PFI

(a) Government is able to finance improved provision of goods and services for the public without increasing its borrowing.

(b) Risks are transferred to the private sector.

(c) Private sector qualities of efficiency and innovation are brought into the public sector.

Criticisms of PFI

(a) Public projects will be more expensive because a private company cannot borrow as cheaply as the government.

(b) There is often no real transfer of risk, as the government will be forced to support projects that suffer financial failure, or bail out the private companies which are managing them.

(c) Cost savings have been made to the detriment of quality of service. For example, in the UK, there have been claims that the standard of cleaning in NHS hospitals has deteriorated after cleaning contracts were awarded to private companies.

1.9 Arguments for and against privatisation

The following are **possible advantages of privatisation**.

(a) Privatised companies may be **more efficient** than state monopolies and private sector managers are likely to try to reduce costs and strip out unproductive labour. Private companies may also provide **better quality** because they will have to compete to survive. The threat of competition may also lead to innovation.

(b) Denationalisation provides an immediate **source of money** for the government, through the sale of assets or businesses.

(c) Privatisation **reduces bureaucratic and political meddling** in the industries concerned.

(d) Privatised companies may have a **more flexible** and **profit-oriented management culture**.

(e) There is a view that **wider share ownership** should be encouraged. Denationalisation is one method of creating wider share ownership, as the sale of BT, British Gas and Royal Mail, for example, have shown in the UK. The logic behind this argument is that if workers own shares in their company, they are more likely to want it to be successful.

There are arguments against privatisation too.

(a) State owned industries are more likely to respond to the **public interest**, ahead of the profit motive. For example, state-owned industries are more likely to cross-subsidise unprofitable operations from profitable ones.

Case Study

When it was a state-owned company, the Post Office in the UK had an obligation to provide a 'universal service' – in other words to deliver post to all UK residents, including those in remote locations (such as the isles of Scotland) where the service might be very unprofitable. The Post Office was privatised in 2013, although the Postal Services Act (2011) guaranteed that Royal Mail would continue to provide a universal service until at least 2021.

(a) Encouraging private competition to state-run industries might be inadvisable where **significant economies of scale** can be achieved by monopoly operations.

(b) Government can **provide capital more cheaply** than the market to industries whose earning potential is low, but which are deemed to be of strategic importance, such as aircraft manufacture. Opponents of privatisation suggest that the very idea of privatising a strategic industry is spurious.

(c) State-owned industries can be run in a way that **protects employment**, as was the case in the UK coal industry, for instance. The problem with this is that the taxpayer is effectively **subsidising technical inefficiency**.

(d) Surpluses from state-run industries can be used for **public welfare** rather than private wealth. However, the problem here is that points (a) and (d) above tend to preclude the creation of surpluses.

1.10 Privatisation, efficiency and competition

The inefficiency associated with monopolies in general was discussed earlier and could be said to be of three types.

(a) **Technical inefficiency**. A firm is only technically efficient when it uses the **least-cost combination of productive resources** for a given level of output. Failure to do this leads to its not operating at the lowest possible cost per unit of output. (This is also known as **productive** inefficiency.)

(b) **Allocative inefficiency**. Secondly, there is allocative inefficiency where price is higher than marginal cost such that the good or service is under-produced and under-consumed.

(c) **X-inefficiency**. The monopolist's privileged position relieves it of the need to exert constant effort to keep costs down. The resulting rise in costs is called X-inefficiency.

The contention that privatisation will lead to efficiency improvements is based on a number of assumptions. The most important assumption is that privatisation will place the industry in a market subject to **competitive pressures** approaching the perfectly competitive ideal. In practice, however, there are few examples of perfectly competitive markets and the likelihood is of restricted competition between a small number of large firms, with a degree of inefficiency persisting. If there are no legal restrictions, it is also possible that state monopolies will merely become private monopolies with even less regard than before for the consumer.

Another assumption of the privatisation analysis is that there are no economies of scale. Where there are significant economies of scale there may be a **natural monopoly**, with room in the market for one firm only, and monopoly may be productively more efficient than a market with competing firms.

It is believed that **management and working practices** will be changed under private sector control. Management will become largely free of interference from the government, working practices should become more efficient and trade union power may be reduced.

It is claimed that with the central objective of profit maximisation, privatised firms will be **responsive to the wants of consumers**, as revealed by market research and signalled by the operation of the price mechanism. The profit objective induces firms to innovate and to seek out new markets, a process which promotes the efficient allocation of resources.

Where privatisation increases competition, the **greater competition** is likely to make firms produce output more cheaply and to sell it at a lower price. Nationalised organisations have often acted as monopolists, with the consequences of higher prices and lower output characteristic of non-competitive markets.

1.11 Privatisation in practice

In the UK, there has been only a limited increase in competition following some privatisations. Indeed, some organisations have been sold as monopolies to increase their attractiveness to shareholders in effect transferring a public monopoly to a private monopoly. As monopolies, they would aim to produce at the profit maximising level of output, which leads to higher prices than perfect competition, and does not create technical or allocative efficiencies like perfect competition does.

To try to avoid creating private sector monopolies, the government has tried to create competition alongside privatisation.

Case Study

The example of British Telecom (BT) in the UK – when it was first privatised in the 1980s – can be used to illustrate the attempt to encourage competition along with privatisation. First, BT's pricing was regulated by a 'Retail Prices Index minus x percent' formula. Second, a relatively small competitor, Mercury, a subsidiary of Cable and Wireless, was licensed to compete for part of BT's activities. However, these were relatively minor restrictions on a company with great market power. Since the mid-1990s, new operators have entered the market as competitors, and with the growth of mobile phone usage (and companies like EE, O2, Three and Vodafone) BT's share of the overall telecommunications market in the UK has reduced significantly.

The alternative strategy, adopted in the USA for the telecommunications giant AT&T, was to break down its operations into smaller units which could compete with one another.

Privatisation alone is often not sufficient to improve the performance of a monopoly and other steps may need to be taken to increase competition. On the other hand, improvements to the competitive environment might equally be achieved without privatisation.

1.12 Criticisms of privatisation

There are also a number of criticisms of privatisation in practice.

- Critics argue that privatisation **has not enhanced competition**, and in some cases it has merely transferred a public monopoly to a **private monopoly**.

- **Quality of service has diminished** where privately owned companies have tried to cut costs on services previously provided centrally.

- In some cases, level of service has been reduced and prices raised as private companies do not want to operate loss-making services (for example, on rural rail routes in the UK). Whereas nationalised organisations were prepared to cross-subsidise loss-making elements of their business, private sector companies are less likely to be prepared to do this. They are more likely to focus on the profitable elements of their business and discontinue the less profitable elements.
- The assets sold by governments have been **undervalued** and this allowed private investors to make large capital gains by acquiring the assets.
- In some industry sectors, privatisation has been **selective**, and only the profitable parts of the sector have been sold off. This means the unprofitable areas remain in the public sector, and are a drain on public funds.
- Top executives of privatised companies have been granted very **large salaries and share options**, which looks insensitive in the context of trying to improve employee efficiency and competitiveness.

Question — Benefits of privatisation

Can you identify three possible benefits of privatisation?

Answer

Any three of:

- Improved efficiency of production in privatised companies
- Reduces bureaucracy and political interference in the industries concerned, so producers have greater economic freedom
- Private companies have a more profit-oriented management culture
- Encourages wider share ownership

2 Public policy towards monopolies

FAST FORWARD

You should understand the various arguments in favour of **public (or 'nationalised') ownership of production** concerning public goods, merit goods and natural monopoly. You should also be aware of the **efficiency arguments** against public ownership.

2.1 The public sector

Public sector organisations are all ultimately responsible (accountable) to government, and their purposes are defined in the laws that established them.

Public sector bodies' objectives will usually be defined in terms of the provision of goods or services which are beneficial to society, rather than in terms of the profit maximising objectives of private sector firms.

2.2 Public policy towards monopolies

Monopolies might be harmful or beneficial to the public interest.

(a) A beneficial monopoly is one that succeeds in achieving economies of scale in an industry where the minimum efficiency scale is at a level of production that would mean having to achieve a large share of the total market supply.

(b) A monopoly would be detrimental to the public interest if cost efficiencies are not achieved. Oliver Williamson suggested that monopolies might be inefficient if 'market power provides the firm with the opportunity to pursue a variety of other-than-profit objectives'. For example, managers might instead try to maximise sales, or try to maximise their own prestige.

2.3 Methods of government control

There are several different ways in which a government can attempt to control monopolies.

(a) It can stop them from developing, or it can break them up once they have been created. Preventing monopolies from being created is the reason why a government might have a public policy on mergers.

(b) It can take them over. **Nationalised industries** are often government-run monopolies, and central and/or local government also have virtual monopolies in the supply of other services, such as health, the police, education and social services. Government-run monopolies or nationalised industries are **potentially advantageous**.

   (i) They need not have a profit-maximising objective so that the government can decide whether or not to supply a good or service to a household on grounds other than cost or profit. In this way, **services which provide a social benefit** rather than an economic profit will be provided, whereas they would not be under free market forces.

   (ii) The government can regulate the quality of the good or service provided more easily than if the industry were operated by private firms. The government can also keep strategic control over provision of the goods and services, and can maintain strategic control over key resources.

   (iii) **Key industries** can be protected (for example, health, education), and **capital** can be made available for investment where it might not be in the private sector.

   (iv) Nationalised industries may benefit from **economies of scale**, particularly if they require significant investment in infrastructure.

   (v) The government can **protect employment** and reduce social costs related to unemployment. This argument was used to justify keeping 'uneconomic' coal mines open in the UK. If the mines were closed, as free market economics would dictate, this would reduce production, but it would also increase unemployment and the related costs of unemployment benefits and social unease.

   (vi) Nationalised industries may also promote a fairer distribution of wealth, since economic surpluses can be reinvested for the benefit of society rather than being related as profit by capitalist entrepreneurs.

(c) It can allow monopolies or oligopolies to operate, but try to control their activities in order to protect the consumer. For example, it can try to prohibit the worst forms of restrictive practice, such as price cartels. Or it may set up regulatory 'consumer watchdog' bodies to protect consumers' interests where conditions of natural monopoly apply, as in the privatised utility industries of the UK.

Control over markets can arise by firms eliminating the opposition, either by merging with or taking over rivals or stopping other firms from entering the market. When a single firm controls a big enough share of the market it can begin to behave as a monopolist even though its market share is below 100%.

Several firms could behave as monopolists by agreeing with each other not to compete. This could be done in a variety of ways – for example, by exchanging information, by setting common prices or by splitting up the market into geographical areas and operating only within allocated boundaries.

In a perfect monopoly, there is only one firm that is the sole producer of a good that has no closely competing substitutes, so that the firm controls the supply of the good to the market. The definition of a monopoly in practice is wider than this, because governments seeking to control the growth of monopoly firms will probably choose to regard any firm that acquires a certain share of the market as a potential monopolist.

2.4 Pricing in nationalised industries

Nationalised industries are monopolies, and so if they operated like private-sector monopolies they would earn supernormal profits by producing where MC = MR.

However, the logic of public sector organisations is different to the private sector; an alternative requirement of public sector monopolies in the UK was that they produced at breakeven levels. (Remember, breakeven occurs where total cost equals total revenue, and therefore also where average cost equals average revenue.)

Figure 1 below illustrates monopoly output under breakeven pricing.

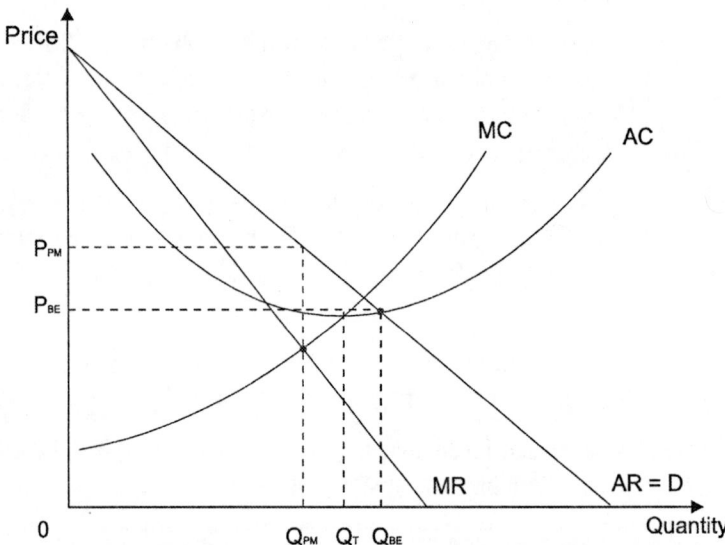

Figure 1 Breakeven pricing in a monopoly

The breakeven output (Q_{BE}) is greater than it would have been under a profit maximising monopolist (Q_{PM}) and price is lower (P_{BE} versus P_{PM}). However, the public sector monopoly is still neither technically or allocatively efficient.

For technical efficiency to be achieved, output quantity would need to be Q_T, so that the firm is producing at the lowest point on its average cost curve.

A second option would be for a nationalised industry to produce at the level of allocative efficiency (Price = MC) but this could cause it to make a loss, if marginal cost (and therefore price) are less than average cost.

However, nationalised monopolies do still have the option to discriminate on price to increase profits. In the UK, when railway services were run by a nationalised company – British Rail – price discrimination was applied to charge commuters different (higher) fares to leisure travellers.

2.5 Regulation and Competition Policy

There are two main aspects of government policy investigating:

- Mergers and acquisitions which might lead to the creation of a monopoly
- Restrictive trade practices in a market (for example, collusion by suppliers) which undermine competition and consumer sovereignty in the market

UK competition legislation

In the UK, there are two main laws designed to maintain competition in the market place: the **Competition Act 1998** and the **Enterprise Act 2002**.

The **Competition Act 1998** prohibits any agreements between businesses which are anti-competitive, or any other business practices which have a damaging effect on competition. So, for example, the Act prohibits business agreeing price rises with their competitors, or agreeing with competitors to limit supply of a product in order to increase price.

The law is directed mainly at agreements between businesses with a significant market share, and who therefore have more ability to influence price than smaller firms. However, the law applies to all businesses, so even small businesses must avoid anti-competitive agreements, like price fixing.

The Act also prohibits the abuse of a dominant market position – which is a measure designed to deal with any anti-competitive conduct by monopolies. As such, the Act created the Competition Commission as an authority for monitoring and preventing anti-competitive activity which is against the public interest.

The **Enterprise Act (2002)** focuses on one specific anti-competitive structure: cartels. The Act prohibits certain aspects of cartel conduct, and firms founds to be engaging in any of these activities can face large fines. The prohibited activities include: fixing prices; firms agreeing to split markets between themselves (rather than competing for market share); and limiting production.

In addition to the overall competition legislation, the UK government has also established **specific industry regulators** to monitor the activities of private companies in industries which had previously been nationalised. For example, OFTEL was established to regulate the telecommunications market, while OFGAS regulates the gas industry.

The regulators have two roles, both of which are designed to promote competition.

First, they can impose price caps and performance standards on the firms in their industries. Second, they can demand the removal of barriers to entry which stop new firms entering the market, for example requiring BT to allow potential new entrants to the telephone market to have access to its network.

Enterprise and Regulatory Reform Act (2013)

In 2012, the UK government announced proposals for strengthening competition and competition policy in the through the creation of the Competition and Markets Authority (CMA) as a successor to the Office of Fair Trading (OFT) and the Competition Commission. The formation of the CMA was officially enacted in the Enterprise and Regulatory Reform Act 2013.

The CMA is an independent, non-ministerial government department, whose primary duty is to promote competition, both within and outside the UK, for the benefit of consumers. According to its website, the CMA's aim is 'to make markets work well for consumers, businesses and the economy as a whole.'

2.6 The Competition and Markets Authority

Exam focus point

The Competition and Markets Authority is specific to the UK, so you shouldn't be asked questions specifically about it. However, you could still be set questions about public control of monopolies, or the purpose of regulating businesses more generally.

The activity of the Competition and Markets Authority in the UK is a good example of the way governments may approach the problem of monopoly, or other anti-competitive market structures.

Its responsibilities include:

- Investigating mergers which could **restrict competition**.

- Conducting market studies and investigations in markets where there may be competition and consumer problems.

- Investigating individual businesses to determine whether they have breached UK or EU prohibitions against **anti-competitive agreements** and abuses of dominant positions under the Competition Act 1998.

- Bringing criminal proceedings against individuals who commit **cartel offences** under the Enterprise Act 2002.

- Enforcing consumer protection legislation to tackle practices and market conditions that make it **difficult for consumers to exercise choice**; including brining criminal proceedings against businesses who engage in unfair trading.

- Conducting regulatory appeals and references in relation to price controls, terms of licences, or other regulatory arrangements in relation to sector specific legislation (gas, electricity, water, post, communications, aviation, rail and health).

2.7 Competition policy in the EU

European Union (EU) competition policy is intended to ensure free and fair competition in the EU. The **Commission of the European Union** has authority under the Treaty of Rome (Articles 81 to 89) to **prohibit price fixing** and other uncompetitive arrangements, including limiting production or seeking to exclude competitors from a market.

The Commission also has authority to prevent national governments within the EU offering subsidies or other **state aid** to firms in their countries which will distort competition across the wider market.

Chapter Roundup

- **Market failure** is said to occur when the market mechanism fails to result in economic efficiency, and therefore the outcome is sub-optimal.
- You should understand the various arguments in favour of **public (or 'nationalised') ownership of production** concerning public goods, merit goods and natural monopoly. You should also be aware of the **efficiency arguments** against public ownership.

Quick Quiz

1. In what circumstances might government regulation of markets have an economic justification?
2. What different forms can privatisation take?
3. Why might a government wish to control monopolies?
4. How might a government be able to control monopolies?
5. Which one of the following statements is incorrect?

    A   Privatisation can be a means of widening share ownership
    B   Privatising a public sector industry will permit economies of scale
    C   Denationalisation provides a source of money for the government
    D   Privatising a public sector industry is likely to make it more responsive to the profit motive

6. Which of the following are arguments in favour of a policy of privatisation?

    (i)   It reduces X-inefficiency because competition is always introduced
    (ii) It raises useful short term funds for the government
    (iii) It encourages a more profit-oriented management culture

    A   (i) and (ii)
    B   (i) and (iii)
    C   (ii) and (iii)
    D   All of them

Answers to Quick Quiz

1. The undesirable effects of various forms of market failure can be reduced by government action. Monopoly power can be attacked by regulation of price or profit or even the break-up of the monopoly firm. Externalities can be reduced by bans on some forms of behaviour, such as dangerous pollution, and by levying taxes on others such as the consumption of alcohol. Where imperfect information distorts consumer choice, legally enforceable product standards and disclosure requirements can improve the operation of the market. Finally, governments may intervene for social and political reasons, banning racial discrimination and enforcing a minimum wage, for example.

2. Privatisation can take three forms.
   - Deregulation allows private firms to compete against state owned organisations.
   - Work done by government employees may be contracted out.
   - State owned businesses may be sold to private shareholders.

3. There are arguments both for and against monopolies. Monopolies are detrimental to the public interest when they are inefficient in their allocation of resources and their operations generally. They may also be objected to on the grounds that they charge higher prices, and hence earn higher profits, than would be possible in a competitive market; and they restrict choice.

4. Governments can regulate monopolies, particularly their prices and the quality of their goods and services; prevent them from developing; break them up; or take them into public ownership.

5. B Privatisation often leads to smaller firms as public sector monopolies are broken up into smaller companies. Although privatisation may be seen as a way of increasing competitiveness, it does not do so through promoting economies of scale.

6. C Selling off nationalised industries can raise useful funds for the government, and private companies are likely to have a more profit-oriented management culture than state-owned monopolies. However, competition is not always introduced following privatisation. A firm could simply be transferred from being a state-owned monopoly to being a private sector monopoly: this would not reduce X-inefficiency.

7: PUBLIC POLICY AND COMPETITION

End of chapter question

Takeover declined (Nov 2008)

A company has been told by the relevant Government agency that it cannot take over one of its competitors on the basis that this will increase the monopoly power of the combined company if the takeover goes ahead.

Required

(a) Show diagrammatically how a monopoly increases prices and reduces output compared to what it would do if the company was operating in a perfectly competitive market. **(15 marks)**

(b) What is the other concern about X-inefficiency with respect to monopolies in the diagram? **(6 marks)**

(c) What type of merger is suggested by the question and why? **(3 marks)**

(d) How might the company be able to persuade the Government agency to allow the takeover to take place? **(6 marks)**

(Total 30 marks)

PART C HOUSEHOLD, CORPORATE AND FINANCE SECTORS

Finance and financial intermediaries

Topic list	Syllabus reference
1 Functions of money	2.3
2 The need for financial intermediation	2.3
3 Firms	2.3
4 Governments	2.3
5 The flow of funds	2.3
6 Financial markets	2.3
7 The main financial intermediaries	2.3
8 The insurance market	2.3

Introduction

So far in this Study Text we have concentrated on the way business and consumers operate in particular markets. However, we will now turn to look at how financial system and institutions help meet the financial needs of these businesses and consumers.

A national economy depends on a vast network of economic relationships. Among the most important are those that facilitate the flow of value between households, firms and governments. In this chapter we look at the institutions that perform this function and how they do it.

PART C   HOUSEHOLD, CORPORATE AND FINANCE SECTORS

1 Functions of money

FAST FORWARD

Money has four functions: to act as a medium of exchange; a store of value; a unit of account; and a standard for deferred payment.

Within any economy, some people, firms and organisations will have money which is surplus to their needs, while others have less money than they need for their spending requirements. **Credit** involves lending money, and the transfer of money (usually in return for interest payments) from surplus units to deficit units.

1.1 The functions and qualities of money

One of the key features of all economies is the existence of money.

Money, and other related financial instruments in the economy, are managed through the **financial system**. However, before we look at the way the financial system operates, we will first consider some the qualities of money itself.

At the most basic level, we can think of money as any asset that **is generally accepted** in exchange as payment for goods and services. Nowadays we think of money as notes, coins, or cheques but any asset could serve as money as long as it is accepted as a medium of payment throughout an economy. The asset does not need to be legal tender provided it is acceptable to both parties to a transaction.

There are **four main functions of money**.

(a) To act as a **medium of exchange**. Money allows buyers and sellers a medium of exchange through which to trade. Money is accepted throughout an economy as a means of payment for goods and services. Buyers acquire goods by giving up money. Sellers receive money for selling their wares. Without money, they would have to use a system of bartering in order to manage these exchanges, and this could prove problematic if the needs and wants of the buyer were not matched with those of the seller, or if the buyer and seller could not agree on the value of the items being bartered.

(b) To act as a **store of value**. People may not want to spend their money as soon as they receive it, so money needs to store value so that it can be used to purchase the same quantity of goods and services in future as it could today. In practice, inflation means that often money does not perform this function very well.

(c) To act as a **unit of account**. Money is used to designate the prices of goods and services, and it allows their relative values to be compared by reference to a common denomination which everybody understands.

(d) A standard of **deferred payment**. Money is used to designate and determine the value of future payments, such as those for loan repayments. The use of money as a standard of deferred payment is a natural result of it being the standard unit of account, and acting as a store of value.

Throughout history, different economies have used many different items as money. Some have tended to work better than other, and those that best performed the function of money had certain key characteristics.

1.1.1 Qualities of money

(a) **Durability**. It is important that money does not deteriorate physically, especially as it is a medium for storing value over time. Durability is one reason that metals, such as gold and silver, have been used as money.

(b) **Acceptability**. For money to act as a medium of exchange, it must be acceptable to both the buyer and seller in a transaction, in return for the goods or services being traded.

(c) **Divisibility**. To be generally accepted as a medium of exchange, money needs to be exchangeable for both large items and small items.

(d) **Transportability**. Similarly, because transactions can take place at many different locations, money must be easily portable from one location to another.

(e) **Stable value**. Money must retain a stable value and purchasing power otherwise it cannot act as a store of value or a standard of deferred payment.

(f) **Not easily counterfeited**. Money that is easily counterfeited would quickly lose its value in exchange because anyone could create their own money.

The most important function of money is usually considered to be as a **medium of exchange**. Another important characteristic associated with this is **liquidity**: the ease with which a financial asset can be turned into a form that can be used as a medium of exchange.

However, one function of money which has caused most problems within economies is the requirement to act as a **store of value**, and to retain a stable value. Money can only do this if there is no **inflation**.

Inflation, by definition, leads to a decline in the **purchasing power of money**, and thereby means that money cannot perform its functions of storing value and acting as a standard of deferred payment. This will consequently make it less acceptable as a medium of exchange. Therefore inflation, especially high inflation or hyper-inflation, will undermine the qualities of money and the workings of the financial system.

Inflation is also a secondary reason (behind interest rates) why an investor will prefer to receive a payment of a fixed amount of money today rather than an equal amount in the future. This is known as the **time value of money presumption**.

1.1.2 Inflation and the value of money

Inflation can be defined as a persistent increase in the average price level in the economy.

It is measured by the inflation rate, the annual percentage change in a price index such as the **consumer price index** (CPI), or the gross domestic product **(GDP) price deflator**. The CPI measures the rate of change in consumer prices, while the GDP deflator measures the rate of change in the price of all the goods and services produced in an economy.

Indices such as the CPI are constructed by selecting a base year against which prices changes are measured, selecting the 'basket' of goods and services to be included in the index, and then weighting each of the items in the basket according to their relative importance.

The rate of inflation can then be calculated by comparing the index for one period with another, and working out the rate of change. Inflation is usually calculated on an annual basis.

The Office for National Statistics in the UK publishes monthly and annual inflation figures, by comparing the CPI against a base level. Recent annual figures (for the UK) are shown below.

Year		CPI	% inflation
2005	(base level)	100.0	-
2006		103.2	3.2
2007		106.2	2.9
2008		110.2	3.8
2009		109.9	-0.3
2010		111.7	1.6
2011		115.2	3.1
2012		117.6	2.1
2013		119.3	1.5
2014		121.2	1.6
2015		121.4	0.2
2016		122.5	0.9

PART C HOUSEHOLD, CORPORATE AND FINANCE SECTORS

1.2 The flow of funds

Within any economy, there is a flow of between people or institutions in the economic system. For example, individuals pay for goods and services supplied by firms, and firms pay rent on land or wages to individuals who provide labour.

If we begin by ignoring imports and exports and foreign investments, we can start to build up a picture of the flow of funds by identifying three main sectors in the economy that make payments and receipts.

(a) Households and individuals or the **personal sector**

(b) Firms or the **business sector** – ie companies and other businesses

(c) Governmental organisations or the **government sector** – ie central government, local government and public corporations

Within each of these three sectors, there is a continual movement of funds, payments and receipts on a short-term, medium and long-term basis.

Importantly though, within any economy, some people, firms and organisations will have money which is surplus to their needs, while others will have less money than they need for their spending requirements. As such, people or firms which need money have to **borrow** it from those who have surplus funds (and are prepared to **lend** it).

Key term

> **Financial intermediaries:** The role of **financial intermediaries** such as banks and building societies in an economy is to provide the means by which funds can be transferred from **surplus units** in the economy to **deficit units**. Financial intermediaries develop the facilities and **financial instruments** which make lending and borrowing possible.

2 The need for financial intermediation

FAST FORWARD

> **Financial intermediaries** are institutions, such as banks and building societies, which help to provide credit, by channelling funds from savers (with surplus funds) to borrowers (who need additional funds).

A consequence of the functions of money is that income can be separated from expenditure. In a barter economy, income and expenditure are simultaneous because they are two sides of the same transaction. However, in a money-based economy, a flow of income no longer has to be the same as a flow of expenditure, and they do not have to occur at the same time either.

This means that individuals, businesses and governments can all have cash inflows which are not the same as their cash outflows in any given time period. In other words, there can be a **lack of synchronisation between receipts and payments**. This applies equally to the short, medium and long term, although the nature of the receipts and payments will vary according to the time period involved.

An important consequence of this is that in any one period there will be net **savers** (whose inflows exceeds their expenditures) and net **borrowers** (who have expenditures which exceed incomes).

As a result, market economies need to have effective mechanisms to enable the surplus funds of net savers to be transferred to the net borrowers in a way which is appropriate to their requirements.

This is the rationale for the **financial intermediaries** (such as banks) who provide the link which enables money to be transferred from savers to borrowers. This transfer process is known as **financial intermediation**.

We will look at financial intermediaries and the benefits of financial intermediation in more detail in Section 5 of this chapter.

2.1 Households

FAST FORWARD

Credit for households comes from a variety of sources including credit agreements, bank loans and mortgages.

Households and individuals receive income from employment, savings and investments, and social security and pensions. They will need to use these to finance both their short term needs for food, shelter and clothing and also their longer term needs such as buying a house or buying a car.

However, the timings of the inflows are unlikely to match the expenditures. Therefore households will need to develop ways of dealing with this lack of synchronisation.

They can do this in a number of ways.

Time Frame	Ways to deal with lack of synchronisation
Short term (routine transactions)	• Retain cash in hand to meet day-to-day expenditure needs • Use short term credit functions, such as credit cards and bank overdrafts • Make savings in periods of net surplus (when receipts exceed payments) in order to finance periods of net deficit
Medium term (infrequent purchases of more expensive items, such as cars or holidays)	• Save over a period of time prior to expenditure, for example using a deposit account at a bank • Borrow money to fund the purchase and then repay over a period of time, for example through taking out a bank loan, or through hire purchase or lease finance arrangements.
Long term (for example, buying a house, or retirement planning)	• Need very long-term financial instruments, for example mortgages or pension funds • Mortgages are loans used to acquire an asset, typically a property. The asset is conveyed to the lender as security for the loan and ownership only passes to the buyer once the mortgage is repaid in full.

In all of the time frames, the households use financial intermediaries to provide the facilities they need to match their income with their expenditure.

3 Firms

Businesses, like households, will find that flows of payments and receipts rarely match.

A business will have **receipts** from several sources, which might include sales, investment income and proceeds from the disposal of non-current assets.

A firm's **payments** include purchases of raw materials or inventory, and payment of wages and salaries, rent and utility bills. For its medium and long term needs the company will need to purchase assets such as premises, machinery and equipment.

In order to achieve profit and function as a going concern, most companies will need funding over and above that contributed by shareholders.

The need for finance for firms arises for two main reasons. First, production takes place before products are sold. A firm has to finance production (labour, raw material, inventory) before any receipts accrue and therefore needs funds in the form of working capital in order to operate. This type of finance is a bridging type and is short term.

A second reason for a firm to need funds is for investment purposes. A business that needs to expand or replace its plant and equipment may need funds far in excess of the income that it earns from its daily operating activities. These types of funds are typically long-term.

Businesses have three main sources of long-term finance:

- Equity capital (through issuing shares)
- Internally generated funds (retained profits)
- Debt capital (such as bank loans and corporate bonds)

3.1 Sources of finance for companies

FAST FORWARD

> A company must have **capital** to carry out its operations. Many companies start in a small way, often as family businesses, then grow to become **public companies**, which can invite the public to subscribe for shares.

New capital enables the firm to expand its activities and achieve the advantages of large-scale production.

Credit may be short-term, medium-term or long-term. The **length of credit ought to match the life of the assets** they finance, and should not exceed the asset's life.

(a) The amount of short-term credit taken by a firm should be limited by considerations of liquidity. The firm must have the cash to pay creditors on time, and so short-term credit should not become excessive in relation to current assets, which are short-term sources of cash.

(b) The amount of long-term credit is effectively measured by the gearing ratio, which should remain at an acceptable level.

Principal sources of short-term finance

(a) **Credit agreements** allow businesses to borrow money for the immediate purchase of goods or services and to pay for them over an extended period of time. These agreements take a variety of forms including short-term **bank loans**, overdraft facilities, credit card, trade credit, hire purchase and short-term **lease finance**. (Note: Loans and leases can also be used as a source of long-term finance).

(b) **Bank overdrafts** are a short-term facility which allow businesses to borrow money up to an agreed limit. The bank will charge interest on the amount overdrawn, but the overdraft can be a valuable means of overcoming a short-term cash flow problem or working capital shortage.

(c) **Bills of exchange** are a means of one business providing credit to another business for a short period, usually for three months. The lender makes up the bill for a specified sum payable at a future date and the borrower accepts the bill by signing it. Once the loan has been made there may be secondary trading in the bill, that is the loan will be sold on to a third party. The bill will be bought from the drawer at a discount from the face value of the loan, this discount representing an interest charge on the amount owed.

(d) **Commercial paper**. Banks and companies with good credit ratings raise funds by issuing unsecured promissory bearer notes that can be interest-bearing or discounted. These notes usually have short lives of up to 270 days.

(e) **Retained cash**. A business can also solve the short term mismatch of payments and receipts (the cash flow problem) by retaining a reserve of cash in its bank accounts to use in periods where expenditure exceeds income.

Principal sources of long-term finance

(a) **Issued share capital.** Share capital might be in the form of ordinary shares (**equity**) or preference shares. Bear in mind that only the ordinary shareholders are owners of the company, and preference shares are comparatively rare.

(b) **Retained profits and other reserves.** Retained profits are profits that have been kept within the company, rather than paid out to shareholders as dividends. These provide a source of **internally generated funds**.

(c) **Borrowing and long-term loans.** Companies borrow from banks and from private or institutional investors. Investors might purchase debt securities issued by the company. The company promises to repay the debt at a date in the future, and until then, pays the investors interest on the debt. **Debt capital** includes debentures and, for larger companies, eurobonds and commercial paper.

Debentures and other loan stock are **long-term loans**, the terms of which are set out in a debenture trust deed. Debentures issued by large companies are traded on the stock market.

Bonds are financial securities issued by government or businesses to provide them with long-term borrowing. The bonds bear a fixed nominal (or coupon) rate of interest. The market in secondary dealings for bonds involves selling the bonds at various prices in order to keep the effective interest rate in line with current interest rates. **Eurobonds** are bonds sold outside the jurisdiction of the country in whose currency the bond is denominated.

(d) **Venture capital.** Venture capitalists are prepared to finance risky ventures such as start ups. Because they accept a high degree of risk (with many of their ventures producing little or no return) they require a very high return from the ones that do succeed. They also require a clear exit route that allows them to realise their capital, such as a public flotation issue of shares.

Question — Long term funding

What are the main types of long-term funding for businesses?

Answer

The four main sources of long-term funding are:

- Equity (share capital)
- Retained profits (internally generated funds)
- Debt (borrowing)
- Venture capital

Mezzanine finance

In general, there are main two sources of external finance: debt and equity. However, in some circumstances firms can obtain **mezzanine finance** which, in effect, combines aspects of both debt and equity finance. Although the financing is initially given as a loan (debt capital), the lender has the right to convert to an equity interest in the company if the loan is not paid back on time and in full.

3.2 Raising capital

If a company wants to raise new capital from sources other than retained profits, it should establish whether it needs long-term (usually meaning three years or longer) or short-term capital. Short-term capital can be obtained either by taking longer credit from suppliers, or by asking the company's bank for a short-term loan or bigger overdraft facility. Ideally, a company should use long-term finance to finance commitments with a long payback period, such as fixed assets or research and development.

Raising more long-term capital would require the issue of more share capital or more debt. The ability to raise capital by issuing new shares will depend on the status of the company. A **listed company** (for example, in the UK, a company listed on the Stock Exchange or AIM) could go to the market to raise funds. A **private company** would have to try to raise new share capital privately, without being able to use the institutions of an organised market place. The task of raising share capital is therefore much more difficult for private companies than for listed ones.

A large public limited company (plc) is usually in a better position to raise capital than smaller companies, private companies and non-incorporated businesses.

(a) The high standing of plc's makes investors and other prospective creditors more willing to offer finance.

(b) There is a well established machinery for raising capital through the Stock Exchange. A share issue will be organised for a firm by an investment bank (known as an issuing house) or similar organisation.

(c) The limited liability of company shareholders usually makes large companies more willing to borrow, in contrast to small company owner-directors, sole traders and partners, who accept greater personal financial risks when they borrow large amounts of capital.

The main source of external lending to companies, both long and short-term, is the banks. New debenture (loan) stock is not often issued by companies to raise new funds because this stock must compete with government loan stock (gilts) to attract investors, and because they are higher risk, company debentures must generally offer a higher rate of interest than the interest rate on gilts.

3.3 Retained earnings

Advantages of funds generated from retained earnings

- Absence of brokerage costs
- Simplicity and flexibility
- All gains from investment will accrue to existing shareholders

Disadvantages

(a) Shareholders' expectation of dividends may present a problem, particularly for a public company quoted on the Stock Exchange.

(b) Insufficient earnings may be available.

3.4 Difficulties in raising finance

Despite the existence of various capital markets and money markets, it is not necessarily easy for firms to raise new capital, except by drawing on retained profits. Small firms in particular find it difficult to attract investors without surrendering a measure of **control**, with the banks remaining the major source of funds for such companies. The capital markets are dominated by institutional investors who have tended to channel their funds into safe investments such as 'blue chip' stocks and shares which are traded on the major stock markets (such as the New York, London, or Tokyo Stock Exchanges), as well as government securities. The venture capital providers take a more adventurous approach, although it should be noted that some of the venture capital organisations have been set up by the large institutional investors.

4 Governments

4.1 Government payments and receipts

> **FAST FORWARD**
>
> During any given period of time **governments** need to spend money on outlays of a **short**, **medium** and **long-term** nature. To pay for these outlays governments collect **taxes**.

4.1.1 Government payments

Governments need to spend money on a number of outlays of a current or long term nature. These can be analysed into the following categories:

(a) **Government purchases of goods and services**

   Short term: Expenditure on current goods and services such as:

   (i) Salaries of government employees
   (ii) Repairs, maintenance of public buildings
   (iii) Payments for goods and services needed to carry on daily government activities (eg heat and light)

   Medium and long term: Investment on infrastructure such as building roads, schools and hospitals.

(b) **Transfer payments**

   These are payments made for which the government received no goods or services in return. Examples include:

   (i) Unemployment and welfare payments
   (ii) Other social security payments
   (iii) State pension

4.1.2 Government receipts

To pay for expenditure governments collect revenues, mainly taxes. There are four main types of government revenues.

(a) **Taxes on income and capital gains**

   (i) Taxes paid by individuals (income tax)
   (ii) Taxes paid by companies such as corporation tax

(b) **Indirect taxes on expenditure** or **sales taxes** whereby consumers pay a tax on their consumption of goods and services. In the UK, the main sales taxes are **excise duties** (for example, on tobacco, alcohol and petrol) and **value added tax**.

(c) **Social security contributions**

   In the UK these are a fixed percentage of a worker's salary up to a certain ceiling and they are matched by contributions from the employer (national insurance contributions).

(d) **Other revenues**

   One of the main elements of this category is income from government corporations such as the United States Postal Service (USPS), or Saudi Aramco (the Saudi Arabian Oil Company). In the UK, the proportion of total revenues coming from this source fell significantly after the privatisations of the late 1980s and early 1990s.

PART C   HOUSEHOLD, CORPORATE AND FINANCE SECTORS

4.1.3 Matching Government payments and receipts

Governments, like households and businesses, find that their payments are not synchronised with their receipts. Receipts from tax can be very uneven during a year, but social security payments to unemployed people are required regularly throughout the year.

Governments may also have to spend more in some years than others, for example, an increase in government spending may be required to boost demand in the economy during a recession. In such cases, it is also likely that government spending will increase while government receipts from taxation are decreasing.

Therefore governments also have to find ways of dealing with the problem of synchronisation.

Time Frame	Consequence
Short term (social security payments and pensions; payment of wages and salaries to government employees; payments to providers of routine goods and services)	• If expenditure exceeds revenue, government needs short term credit, which is usually provided by the **central bank**. • One of the central bank's functions is to act as banker to government.
Medium term (public sector investment activities, such as construction of schools, hospitals or roads)	• Governments may allocate more funds to one year rather than another as part of their fiscal policy to manage economic growth. In this case, government spending is likely to be counter-cyclical with the economic cycle, and will be highest in those years when tax revenues are lowest. • Governments may run **budget deficits**, to be funded by borrowing from the private sector. • Governments can raise funds by **issuing bonds** and securities.
Long term (investment projects to develop infrastructure)	• Governments can continue to borrow in the long term provided there is sufficient taxation revenue to fund the resulting debt. • Amounts borrowed through budget deficits aggregate to form the **national debt**. • In practice, the national debt will never be entirely repaid.

4.2 Government deficits/surpluses

The government budget deficit is the **difference** between government **expenditures** and **revenues** in any one period, normally a year referred to as a fiscal year.

Key term

A **fiscal year** is the period over which the government revises its revenue and expenditure plans.

Government expenditure is very unlikely to be equal to government revenues in each fiscal year, and so a government is likely to have either a budget surplus or a budget deficit.

When revenues exceed outlays there is a **budget surplus**. When outlays exceed revenues there is a **budget deficit**.

The deficit can therefore be represented as

Budget deficit = government expenditures − government revenues
= government purchases (P) + transfers (TR) + net interest (INT) − government revenues (T)
= P + TR + INT − T

When governments spend more than they raise in taxes and therefore incur a budget deficit, they have to borrow.

Governments borrow by issuing debt. In the UK, government debt is referred to as gilt edged securities. These will be discussed later.

4.3 Government deficit and government debt

FAST FORWARD

The **government deficit** in any one fiscal year represents the **new borrowing** that the government needs to undertake.

It is important to understand the distinction between government deficit and government debt.

The government **deficit** represents the excess of government spending over government revenues in any one period. As such, the government deficit is a flow concept, just like the profit and loss is a flow concept in the financial statements of a company.

In any one year, the budget deficit represents the amount of **new borrowing** that the government must undertake. (The amount that the government must borrow in a year is known as the **public sector net cash requirement** (PSNCR) in the UK. We will look at the PSNCR again in Chapter 12 in the context of macroeconomic policy.)

Government **debt** is the accumulation of government deficits over time and represents all the debt issued to fund the deficits. Since deficits in the UK are funded by issuing government bonds (known as gilts), government debt is the total outstanding amount of gilts issued.

5 The flow of funds

FAST FORWARD

Finance can either be obtained directly, from **financial markets**, or indirectly through **financial intermediaries**.

Having discussed the main units of the economy and the reasons why there is a demand and supply of funds to the economy, we discuss now how **surplus units** are able to transfer surplus funds to **deficit units**, and how the deficit units can raise the requisite funds.

There are two ways in which the transfer of funds takes place. First, there is the direct way, in which economic units transact directly in an organised market. There are many markets that cater for all the needs of the economic units in terms of maturity or currency. A schematic approach of the flow of funds is shown as

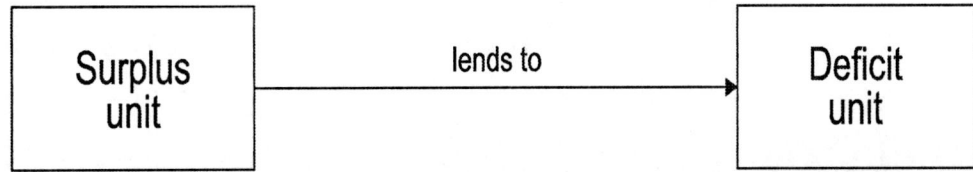

The second way of bringing together surplus and deficit units is through a **financial intermediary**. The intermediary provides a service to both the surplus unit and the deficit unit, by accepting surplus funds and making these funds available to a deficit unit.

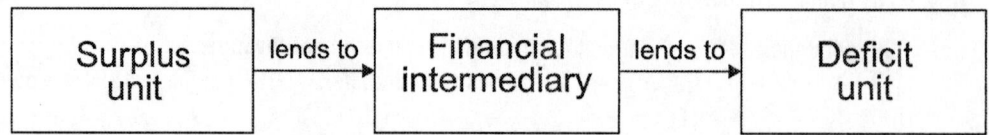

The main advantage of financial intermediation is that it provides a way of channelling funds for large and small economic units. For example, a person might deposit savings with a bank, and the bank might use its collective deposits of savings to provide a loan to a company.

The two methods of channelling funds are shown schematically below.

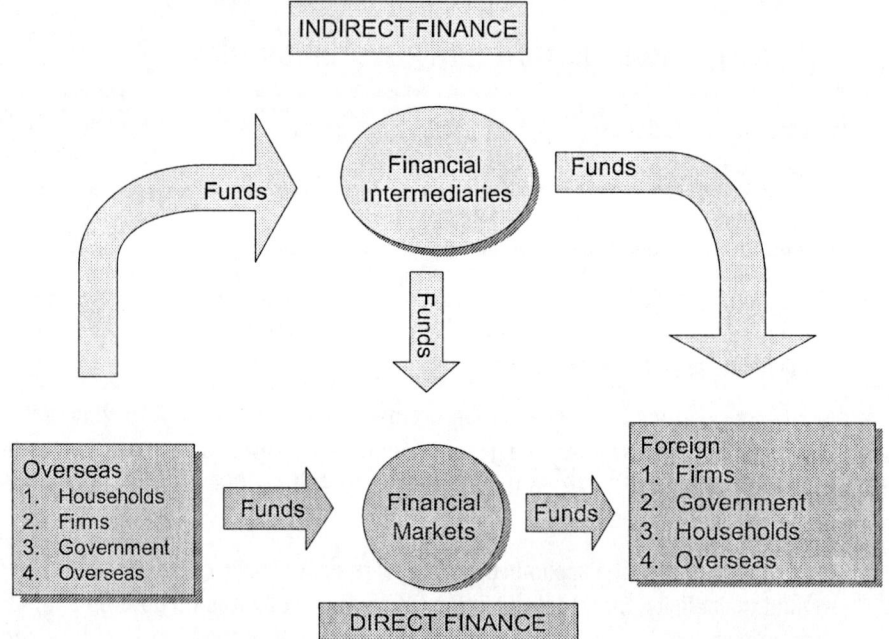

Figure 1 Flow of funds in an open economy, showing the role of financial intermediation

In the next sections we shall discuss the main financial intermediaries and financial markets in the financial system.

5.1 Financial intermediaries

Financial intermediaries are institutions which channel funds from savers to borrowers. In doing so, the intermediaries provide a link between savers and borrowers, meaning that individual savers and borrowers do not have to make individual arrangements between themselves.

In the UK, we can identify three different groups of financial intermediaries:

(a) Banks
(b) Building societies
(c) Insurance companies, pension funds, unit trust companies and investment trust companies

All of these are supervised by the central bank which, in the UK, is the Bank of England.

In spite of competition from building societies, insurance companies and other financial institutions, banks arguably remain the major financial intermediaries in the UK.

5.1.1 Benefits of financial intermediation

(a) **Ease of saving**. Financial intermediaries provide obvious and convenient ways in which a saver can **save money**. Instead of having to find a suitable borrower for his money, the saver can deposit his money with a financial intermediary that offers a financial instrument to suit his requirements. So the financial intermediary acts as a conduit to **channel funds** from net savers to net borrowers. It also pays interest on the savings so the saver earns a return on his money.

(b) **Source of funds**. They provide a **ready source of funds for borrowers**. Even when money is in short supply, a borrower will usually find a financial intermediary prepared to lend some. Intermediaries are an efficient, and often cost-effective, source of money for borrowers.

(c) **Aggregation**. They can package up the amounts lent by savers and lend on to borrowers in bigger amounts (a process called **aggregation**). Without aggregation, a borrower would either have to find a lender who is prepared to lend the amount he wants to borrow, or else would need to use a number of different lenders in order to raise the amount of funds he wants to borrow.

(d) **Maturity transformation**. Financial intermediaries bridge the gap between the wish of most lenders for liquidity and the desire of most borrowers for loans over longer periods. They do this by providing investors with financial instruments which are liquid enough for the investors' needs and by providing funds to borrowers in a different longer term form (for example, mortgages). This process of managing the different time preferences of savers and borrowers is known as **maturity transformation**.

(e) Provided that the financial intermediary is itself financially sound, **the lender's capital is secure**. Bad debts would be borne by the financial intermediary in its re-lending operations.

(f) **Risk transformation**. An individual saver may not wish to lend to an individual borrower, considering that borrower to be a bad debt risk. However, the financial intermediary can borrow from a number of different savers and then provide funds to the borrowers with minimal risk to any single saver. This is known as **risk transformation**.

5.2 Types of financial market

Financial markets can be classified into two groups, according to whether they deal with long-term or short-term capital.

(a) **Capital markets** are financial markets for **raising** and **investing** largely **long-term** capital.
(b) **Money markets** are financial markets for lending and borrowing largely **short-term** capital.

What do we mean by **long-term** and **short-term** capital?

(a) By **short-term capital**, we mean usually capital that is lent or borrowed for a period which might range from as short as overnight up to about one year, and sometimes more.

(b) By **long-term capital**, we mean capital invested or lent and borrowed for a period of about five years or more, but sometimes less.

(c) There is a **grey area** between long-term and short-term capital, which is lending and borrowing for a period from about one to two years up to about five years (**medium-term** capital).

There are a large number of different types of financial instrument for businesses to choose from when looking to raise finance.

However, businesses should always try to **match the time-scale of the instrument to the funding needs**, so that short-term instruments are used for short-term (working capital) financing requirements, and long-term instruments are used to fund long-term investments, or acquisitions.

The table below shows a summary of the main financial instruments.

Time scale	Financial instruments
Short term (Provided through **money markets**)	Short-term bank loans and overdrafts
	Trade credit (ie purchasing goods on credit)
	Bills of exchange
	Commercial paper
	Leasing and hire purchase
Long term (Available through **capital markets**)	Equity finance • Ordinary shares • Preference shares (which are hybrid securities with characteristics of both debt and ordinary shares) • Convertible securities (these also combine debt and equity, with the debt-holder having an option to convert to equity) Debt finance, including • Bonds • Debentures (loans secured by fixed or floating charges over a firm's property or assets)

5.2.1 Primary and secondary markets

A **primary market** is a part of the capital market, dealing with the **issue of new securities**. A company's new shares are issued by an issuing house with the help and advice of a stockbroker.

A company can also offer a rights issue on a primary market. This allows existing shareholders to subscribe for new shares in proportion to their existing shareholding.

A **secondary market** is a market where the instruments are brought and sold by investors after they have been issued. This is important because having a means of buying and selling existing shares makes them more **liquid**.

5.2.2 Exchanges

Most financial markets are organised as exchanges in which trading takes place either face to face or most commonly electronically. Examples of exchanges include the London Stock Exchange and the New York Stock Exchange.

5.2.3 Over-the-counter markets

Shares and other financial instruments are also bought and sold outside the supervised and regulated official exchanges in the over-the-counter (OTC) markets. OTC market prices are negotiated rather than set by auction, as is the case in most stock exchanges. In the USA, OTC market prices are reported via the National Association of Securities Dealers Automatic Quotation (NASDAQ) system. Most OTC trading deals with shares that are not quoted on any public stock exchange.

6 Financial markets

FAST FORWARD

Firms may obtain long-term or medium-term capital as **share capital (equity finance)** or as **debt finance**. Debentures, loan stock, and bonds are all types of debt finance.

In this section we discuss short-term instruments which can be traded in the **money markets**, and long-term instruments such as bonds and shares (which are available through the **capital markets**).

6.1 Money market instruments

As we have mentioned earlier, money markets are the markets **for short-term finance**.

The UK money markets are operated by the **banks** and other financial institutions. Although the money markets largely involve wholesale borrowing and lending by banks, some large companies and the government are also involved in money market operations. The money markets are essentially shorter term debt markets, with short-term loans and other products being offered for a specified period at a specified rate of interest.

Discount houses act as market makers for the short term **treasury bills** and **commercial bills**.

When the government issues treasury bills to make good a shortfall between government expenditure and reserves, any excess supply of bills in the market will be bought by the discount houses.

The price which the discount house pays for the bill reflects the market rate of interest.

A similar discounting process occurs for commercial bills, whereby a financial intermediary will discount a bill on issue, knowing that it will receive its full value at a later date. Again, the difference between the two indicates the market interest rate.

The money markets operate both as a **primary market**, in which new financial claims are issued, and as a **secondary market**, where previously issued financial claims are traded.

Amounts dealt in are relatively large, generally being above £50,000 in the UK and often in millions of pounds. Loans are transacted on extremely 'fine' terms – ie with small margins between lending and borrowing rates – reflecting the **economies of scale** involved. The emphasis is on liquidity: the efficiency of the money markets can make the financial claims dealt in virtually the equivalent of cash.

There are various markets, including the following.

(a) On **the primary market** (as already described), companies, governments or public sector institutions obtain funding through the sale of a new stock or bond issue.

(b) **The interbank market** is the market in which banks lend short-term funds to one another. The principal interest rate in this market is the London Inter-Bank Offer Rate (LIBOR), which is used by individual banks to establish their own base interest rates and interest rates for wholesale lending to large borrowers.

(c) **The certificate of deposit market** is a market for trading in **certificates of deposit**, a form of deposit which can be sold by the investor before maturity. A certificate of deposit (CD) is a certificate (a paper asset) issued by a bank that shows a specific amount of money has been deposited at the issuing institution. The CD bears a specific maturity date, interest rate, and denomination, and so banks can issue them to depositors who are willing to leave their money on deposit for a specified period of time. CDs are issued by banks to access funds (cash) for their finance and lending activities.

Other markets include the local authority debt market, the finance house market, the inter-company market and the sterling commercial paper market. The growth of these markets has reflected the increased deregulation of the financial markets.

A distinction is sometimes made between the **primary market** and all the other money markets which are referred to collectively as the **parallel money markets** or 'unofficial' markets.

6.2 The stock market

In our discussion of financial intermediaries, we highlighted the importance of financial markets for bringing together net savers with net borrowers.

Stock markets are a particular type of financial market which enable the trading of company stock (shares) and derivatives. Major stock markets include the New York Stock Exchange, the London Stock Exchange, the Tokyo Stock Exchange (Nikkei) and the Deutsche Börse.

We will use the London Stock Exchange as an example here.

The **London Stock Exchange** (LSE) is an organised capital market based in London which plays an important role in the functioning of the UK economy. It is the main capital market in the UK.

(a) It makes it easier for large firms and the government to raise long-term capital, by providing a market place for borrowers and investors to come together.

(b) The Stock Exchange publicises the prices of quoted (or 'listed') securities, which are then reported online, and in the financial press, meaning that investors can monitor the value of their shares, and make buying and selling decisions accordingly.

(c) The Stock Exchange tries to enforce certain rules of conduct for its listed firms and for operators in the market, so that investors have the assurance that companies whose shares are traded on the Exchange and traders who operate there are reputable. Confidence in the Stock Exchange will make investors more willing to put their money into stocks and shares.

Alongside the main market, the London Stock Exchange also contains the **Alternative Investment Market** (AIM). The AIM is a market where smaller companies which cannot meet the more stringent requirements needed to obtain a full listing on the Stock Exchange can raise new capital by issuing shares. Like the Stock Exchange main market, the AIM is also a market in which investors can trade in shares already issued. It is regulated by the Stock Exchange.

The price of shares on a stock market fluctuate up and down.

(a) The price of shares in a **particular company** might remain unchanged for quite a long time; alternatively, a company's share price might fluctuate continually throughout each day.

(b) The **general level** of share prices, as measured by share price indices such as the All-Share Index and the FTSE 100 Index, may go up or down each minute of the day.

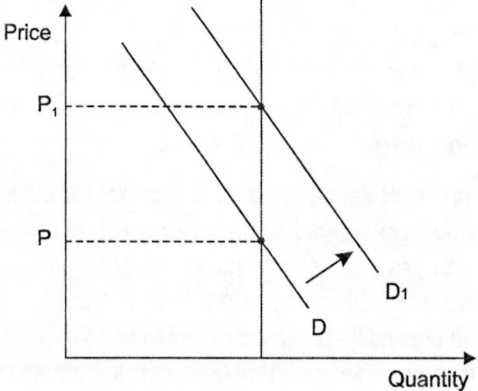

Figure 2 Impact of changes in demand on share prices

In essence, share prices on a stock market reflect the equilibrium between supply and demand in the same way that any other prices do.

For example, if a company announces very good results, demand for its shares may increase (an outward shift in its demand curve) causing share prices to rise (as in Figure 1).

Equally, a company may wish to issue new shares to generate extra capital. This new share issue represents an outward shift in the supply curve, and so, *ceteris paribus,* will lead to a fall in share price (as illustrated in Figure 3).

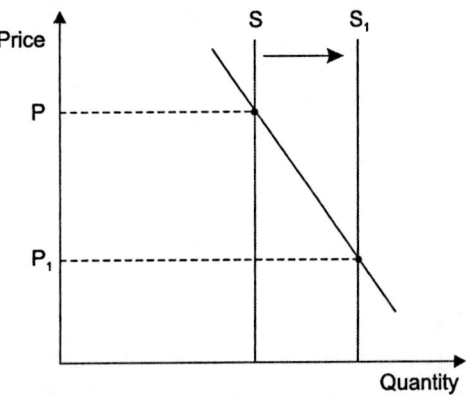

Figure 3 Impact of a new share issue on share prices

The indices of share prices on the Stock Exchange act as indicators of the state of **investor confidence** in the country's economy. For example, if investors believe that interest rates are too low to curb inflation, they may sell shares and move their funds to other countries, causing a decline in share prices. Although in theory a stock market should be an example of a perfectly competitive market, with large numbers of buyers and sellers reacting to perfect knowledge, in practice this is not the case. Factors which are not related to the market itself – such as concerns about political instability or general confidence in the economy – will affect share prices. Therefore the share price of a company may not truly reflect the value or performance of that company.

Question — Share prices

From your reading of the business pages of the newspapers (which should be a central feature in anyone's study of economics) what factors have you noticed as having an influence on share prices?

Answer

Share prices respond to:

(a) Factors related to the circumstances of individual companies – eg news of a company's annual profits, or a proposed takeover bid

(b) Factors related to the circumstances of a particular industry – eg new government legislation or regulations for an industry, such as new laws on pollution controls or customer protection measures

(c) Factors related to the circumstances of the national economy – eg optimism about economic growth, changes in interest rates, the latest official figures for the balance of trade, or price inflation

Exam focus point

You should be aware of the types of factors set out in the question above, but detailed knowledge of theories of share price behaviour is not expected for your exam.

6.3 Bond markets

The bond market is a capital market in which debt securities are issued and traded. These are typically in the form of bonds (fixed interest securities).

The bond market includes government-issued securities and corporate debt. The goal of the bond market is to provide long-term funding for public and private expenditures (eg government projects, or business expansions).

As with other markets, participants can issue new debt in the primary market, while existing debt securities are traded in the secondary market.

6.4 Foreign exchange markets

The globalisation of financial markets, and the growth of multinational companies has reinforced the importance of foreign exchange markets, which facilitate the sale and purchase of foreign exchange.

Foreign exchange markets serve to finance international trade, but also allow companies to manage their foreign exchange risk and deal in foreign exchange so that they can benefit from changes in exchange rates.

Funds available on the international financial markets can, like funds available on other markets, be grouped by timescale.

Timescale	Category of funds	Used for
Short	Eurocurrency	Funding working capital requirements
Medium	Eurocredit	Working capital and investment purposes
Long (> 5 years)	Eurobonds	Investment purposes and funding acquisitions

Note: Eurocurrency does not simply refer to deposits made in euros. Eurocurrency refers to **any** currency deposited by companies or governments into banks outside their own country. For example, a deposit denominated in US dollars residing in a UK bank is a Eurocurrency deposit. (The same rules apply for Eurocredits and Eurobonds.)

7 The main financial intermediaries

Financial intermediaries include **banks** and **institutional investors** such as pension funds, investment trusts and unit trusts.

Having discussed the main financial markets and the instruments traded in those markets we can now turn in this section to the financial intermediaries.

7.1 Banks

Banks are major providers of credit. Banks create money when they give credit (through the 'credit multiplier' effect as we will see later), and so bank lending has two aspects which are important for the economy.

- The growth of credit and hence expenditure in the economy
- Increases in the money supply

Banks lend money that has been deposited with them by customers. A bank is effectively a go-between, or intermediary, between the initial lender and the ultimate borrower.

7.1.1 Types of bank

It is important to distinguish between **retail** banks and **wholesale** banks.

Retail banks (also known as commercial banks) are those that you are likely to be most familiar with. Retail banks are the 'high street' banks, such as HSBC and Barclays, which deal directly with individual households and businesses.

Wholesale banks (also known as investment banks) deal with high value transactions for large companies and institutions (such as pension funds). As well as managing large loans and deposits, they underwrite (guarantee the sale of) stock and bond issues, and advise corporations on capital market activities such as mergers and acquisitions.

Merchant banks are a type of wholesale bank that deal mostly in international finance, long-term loans for companies and underwriting share issues. Their knowledge of international finance often makes merchant banks specialists in dealing with multinational companies.

However, although we have highlighted the distinction between retail and wholesale banks it is important to note that some banking groups, such as Barclays contain an investment bank as well as a retail bank.

7.2 Building societies

The building societies of the UK have traditionally been **mutual** organisations whose main assets are mortgages of their members, and whose main liabilities are to the investor members who hold savings accounts with the society. However, since the 1980s and 1990s a number of former building societies have converted to become banks, and then became public companies owned by shareholders.

The distinction between building societies and banks has become increasingly blurred in the UK, following deregulation of the financial sector in the 1980s. Building societies have taken to providing a range of services formerly the province mainly of banks, and banks have themselves made inroads into the housing mortgage market. Some building societies now offer current accounts, cash cards and many other facilities that compete directly with the banks.

However, the traditional model of the building society is an example of **maturity transformation** in practice – they accept short term liquid deposits from savers and offer long term lending (mortgages) to borrowers. They make their profits from the differential interest rates between the two.

The building society sector has shrunk in size as a number of the major societies have either converted to public limited companies and therefore become banks or been taken over by banks or other financial institutions.

7.3 Institutional investors

There are also important groups of **institutional investors** which specialise in providing capital and act as financial intermediaries between suppliers and demanders of funds. Many financial services organisations now have diversified operations so they act as non-bank financial intermediaries offering a range of the following activities.

(a) **Pension funds**. Pension funds invest the pension contributions of individuals who subscribe to a pension fund, and of organisations with a company pension fund.

(b) **Investment trusts**. The business of investment trust companies is investing in the stocks and shares of other companies and the government. In other words, they trade in investments.

(c) **Unit trusts**. Unit trusts are similar to investment trusts, in the sense that they invest in stocks and shares of other companies. A unit trust comprises a 'portfolio' – that is, a holding of stocks or shares in a range of companies or gilts, perhaps with all the shares or stocks having a special characteristic, such as all shares in property companies or all shares in mining companies. The trust will then create a large number of small units of low nominal value, with each unit representing a stake in the total portfolio. These units are then sold to individual investors and investors will benefit from the income and capital gain on their units – ie their proportion of the portfolio.

(d) **Venture capital.** Venture capital providers are organisations that specialise in raising funds for new business ventures, such as 'management buy-outs' (ie purchases of firms by their management staff). These organisations are therefore providing capital for fairly risky ventures. However, venture capitalists are prepared to accept the risk of financing start-ups in the hope that some of the firms they support will become successful (as, for example, with Uber, Airbnb, or Flipkart).

(e) **Insurance**. See section 8 below.

(f) **Leasing and debt factoring**. Leasing companies lease out plant and equipment to businesses under either operating or finance leases. Factoring companies provide cash flows for businesses, using the businesses' receivables as security.

The role of financial intermediaries in capital markets is illustrated in the diagram below.

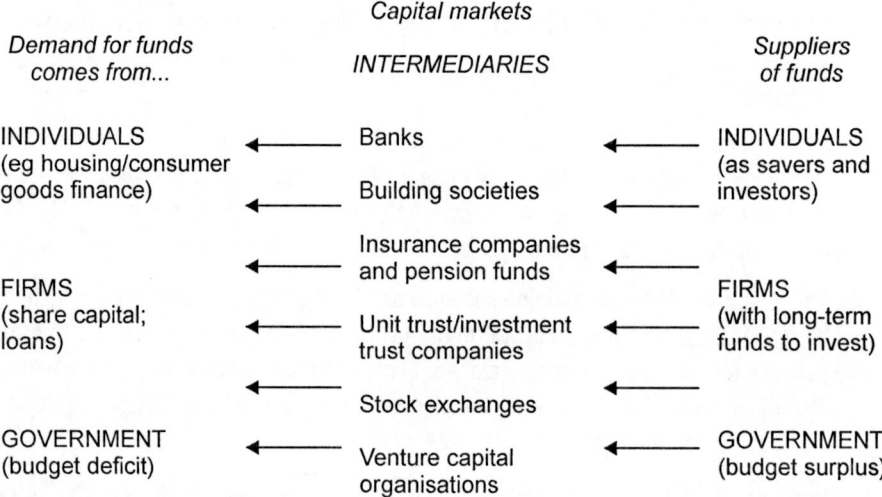

8 The insurance market

8.1 Insurance companies' intermediation role

We discussed above that the role of banks as financial intermediaries is to provide liquidity and bring together units with excess funds and units with a shortage of funds.

> **FAST FORWARD**
>
> Insurance companies act as **intermediaries** by bringing together units which want to **shed risk** and **uncertainty** together with units which are prepared to **take the risk** at a **price**.

Insurance companies, like banks, perform an intermediation role, but they **transfer risk** rather than funds.

The insurance market brings together units that want to shed risk (and uncertainty about future outcomes) and units which are prepared to take the risk at a price.

There are different types of risk that economic units face and like financial intermediaries insurance companies provide a range of risk transfer instruments to cater for these different types of risk.

Key term

An **insurance contract** or policy is an instrument through which risk is transferred from one unit to another, at a price which is determined to a large extent by demand and supply.

8.2 Risk and uncertainty

FAST FORWARD Risks associated with everyday life can be **mitigated** or eliminated through insurance.

Individuals, firms and governments face uncertainty in all spheres of their activity.

8.2.1 The risk facing individuals and businesses

Some of the major risks and uncertainties individuals face are:

- Uncertainty over how long they will live
- Their future earnings
- Their personal safety
- The state of their health
- The safety of their possessions

All the uncertainties relating to the above, (for example death, relating to longevity above), unemployment relating to uncertainty of earnings, can have serious repercussions on an individual's life.

The repercussions can be mitigated or completely eliminated by taking insurance.

There are two categories of insurable risk:

- Risk of events that will occur (eg death) – assurance (eg life assurance)
- Risk of events that may occur (eg fire) – insurance (eg fire insurance)

Question
Uncertainty

The use of a car involves uncertainty. Think of ways in which this uncertainty can be mitigated or eliminated.

Answer

By buying insurance we can mitigate or completely eliminate the uncertainty relating to our own use of the car.

If the car is stolen it will be replaced or, if it is damaged, insurance can cover the cost.

Whether we mitigate or completely eliminate the risk will depend on the premiums we will be prepared to pay.

Breakdown services mitigate risks of high recovery and roadside repair costs.

Businesses also face a number of risks they may wish to insure against, for example:

- Fire
- Flooding
- Consequential loss (ie the loss of earnings which result if a business's premises are damaged, for example, by fire or flooding)
- Public liability
- Employers' liability
- Theft

8.3 The nature of insurance contracts

FAST FORWARD

Insurance claims are **contingent claims**. The insured party benefits only if something adverse happens.

A business that provides insurance – known as the 'insurer' – agrees to take on a risk on behalf of the business or individual concerned – known as the 'insured'. The insurer does this by providing the insured with an insurance contract, also known as a policy. In this contract, the insurer will state what risks it has agreed to insure against, and how much it will pay to the insured party if the risk happens.

Insurance contracts will only benefit the insured party if something adverse happens for which he has taken cover. Because the insured party will benefit only if a particular contingency occurs, claims are referred to as **contingency claims**. This is why the level of insurance varies among individuals. The level of insurance that different individuals take depends on their degree of aversion to risk and the price of the insurance product. The task of **calculating risks** is complex, and is carried out by **actuaries**, who specialise in these risk analyses.

8.4 Organisation of the insurance industry

(a) General insurance companies cover all risks other than the risk of death. Examples include:

    (i) Motor insurance
    (ii) Household insurance
    (iii) Property
    (iv) Accident
    (v) Liability
        – Public liability
        – Employer's liability
        – Professional liability
    (vi) Marine
    (vii) Aviation

However, these are only examples and do not provide an exhaustive list.

(b) Life companies insure against the possibility of death. Life insurance is sometimes referred to as 'life assurance'.

Many large corporations which face a multitude of risks for which there is a regulatory obligation to insure have set up their own insurance companies. These companies are called **captive insurance companies**.

8.5 Insurance underwriters and insurance brokers

Key terms

An **insurance broker** acts as an intermediary between those seeking insurance and the insurers.

An **insurance underwriter** is the person who accepts the risk in exchange for a premium based on a calculation of the level of risk from the insured. The insurance company will then pay out compensation if a genuine claim is made on the policy.

8.6 Re-insurance

The nature of risk is such that the ultimate liability may be too big for an individual insurance company.

The costs involved in a large natural catastrophe for instance could completely wipe out the assets of a single insurance company. For this reason insurance companies themselves take insurance against their own exposure to the risk they undertake through what is referred to as re-insurance.

8.7 Lloyd's market

Lloyd's (previously known as Lloyd's of London) is the world's leading insurance market, where individual insurance companies or underwriters trade their risks. Lloyd's itself is not an insurance company, but acts as an **intermediary** between people and businesses all over the world who want to insure against various risks, and the Lloyd's members who will provide the insurance cover required.

8.8 The main life insurance (or assurance) contracts

(a) **Whole life contract**
A whole life contract pays a certain amount on death of the insured party. The premium is fixed when the policy is issued.

(b) **Universal life contract**
This contract is similar to a whole life contract but it allows the premiums paid to vary.

(c) **Term life**
This is a contract that insures against the risk of death for a specific period of time. This insurance product would benefit the insured party's beneficiaries if death happened during that specified period.

Diversification of life insurance contracts

Over recent years, the life assurance industry has launched a number of products to make this type of insurance more attractive.

Many life insurance products, although they retain an element of life cover, are essentially savings policies rather than protection policies. **Endowment assurance** pays out a sum on death or on maturity of the policy, and has often been used as a way of saving to pay off a mortgage. Such policies may be '**with profits**' – sharing in the long-term performance of the life company's funds – or the returns on the investment element of the policy may be linked to the performance of specific '**unit-linked**' funds.

With **single premium bonds**, a single lump sum is allocated to one or more funds.

8.9 Futures markets

In addition to standard insurance services, there are also specific ways which business can insure against financial risk, namely through the futures market.

A futures contract is a standardised contract, traded on a futures exchange, such as the London International Financial Futures and Options Exchange (LIFFE).

The futures contract gives the holder an obligation to buy or sell an underlying instrument at a certain date in the future at a specified price. For example, a business may use a futures contract to cover the potential foreign exchange risk arising from a long-term contract which will require payment in a foreign currency to an overseas supplier at a point in the future.

Chapter Roundup

- Money has four functions: to act as a medium of exchange; a store of value; a unit of account; and a standard for deferred payment.

- Within an economy, some people, firms and organisations will have money which is surplus to their needs, while others have less money than they need for their spending requirements. **Credit** involves lending money, and the transfer of money (usually in return for interest payments) from surplus units to deficit units.

- **Financial intermediaries** are institutions, such as banks and building societies, which help to provide credit, by channelling funds from savers (with surplus funds) to borrowers (who need additional funds).

- Credit for households comes from a variety of sources including credit agreements, bank loans and mortgages.

- A company must have **capital** to carry out its operations. Many companies start in a small way, often as family businesses, then grow to become **public companies**, which can invite the public to subscribe for shares.

- During any given period of time **governments** need to spend money on outlays of a **short**, **medium** and **long-term** nature. To pay for these outlays governments collect **taxes**.

- The government budget deficit is the **difference** between government **expenditures** and **revenues** in any one period, normally a year referred to as a fiscal year.

- The **government deficit** in any one fiscal year represents the **new borrowing** that the government needs to undertake.

- Finance can either be obtained directly, from **financial markets**, or indirectly, through **financial intermediaries**.

- Firms may obtain long-term or medium-term capital as **share capital (equity finance)** or as **debt finance**. Debentures, loan stock, bonds and commercial paper are all types of loan capital.

- **Financial intermediaries** include **banks** and **institutional investors** such as pension funds, investment trusts and unit trusts.

- Insurance companies act as **intermediaries** by bringing together units which want to **shed risk** and uncertainty together with units which are prepared to **take the risk** at a price.

- Risks associated with everyday life can be **mitigated** or eliminated through insurance.

- Insurance claims are **contingent claims**. The insured party benefits only if something adverse happens.

Quick Quiz

1. List the main sources of credit available to businesses.

2. What is meant by 'maturity transformation'?

3. In the global banking crisis of 2007–2010, some commercial banks needed injections of government funds to avoid them becoming insolvent. This was because the banks had loaned too much money to the property market and, when the property market collapsed, the banks could not recover the funds they needed to repay customers who had placed deposits with them.

    Which of the following functions of a financial intermediary had the banks failed to perform in this situation?

    A   Maturity transformation
    B   Risk transformation
    C   Aggregation
    D   Provision of a transmission mechanism

4. A 'money market' is best defined as:

    A   A market where organisations raise any form of finance
    B   A market where organisations raise long-term finance
    C   A market where organisations raise short-term finance
    D   A market where Treasury Bills are traded

5. Which of the following is NOT an advantage of obtaining a stock market listing?

    A   Better access to capital markets
    B   Ability to make share for share deals
    C   Ability to liquidate holdings
    D   Greater public scrutiny

6. Which TWO of the following are appropriate sources of long-term debt finance for an organisation?

    A   Mortgages
    B   Overdrafts
    C   Bonds
    D   Issuing shares
    E   Bills of exchange

7. In order for an asset to act as money, it must be:

    A   A note, coin or cheque
    B   Legal tender
    C   Generally acceptable
    D   A perishable commodity

8. What is the difference between insurance and assurance?

PART C HOUSEHOLD, CORPORATE AND FINANCE SECTORS

Answers to Quick Quiz

1   Short term credit may be had in the form of overdraft, trade credit and the issue of bills of exchange. Medium term credit often takes the form of term loans from banks, hire purchase and finance leases. Longer term credit may be obtained by issuing debentures and mortgages.

2   Maturity transformation describes the way financial intermediaries bridge the gap between lenders' desire for liquidity and borrowers' desires for loans over longer periods.

3   B   The process of risk transformation means that, typically, banks can spread the risks of lending by having a large number of borrowers. As such, if a few of these borrowers default on their loans, the bank can make good the shortfall from the interest they have earned on the remainder of the loans. However, in this case, the number of customers defaulting meant that the banks were unable to repay the money which had been invested with them by depositors.

Aggregation refers to the process where banks package up individual amounts invested by savers and lend them on to borrowers in larger amounts.

Maturity transformation refers to the fact that financial intermediaries typically lend for longer periods of time than they borrow. (In turn, this reflects the fact that savers typically want to invest funds for shorter periods of time than the periods over which borrowers want to borrow money.)

4   C   Money markets deal with short-term finance. Capital markets deal with long-term finance.

5   D   Greater public scrutiny may attract takeover bidders and will require the firm to pay more attention to public relations.

6   A, C   Long-term borrowing is usually in excess of 5 years.

Overdrafts are a form of short-term finance. Similarly, bills of exchange commonly have maturities of 3 months from the date of issue and so are also sources of short term finance. (As a guide, short-term sources of finance can be regarded as ones with a maturity of less than 1 year.)

Issuing shares can be a source of long-term finance, but constitutes equity finance, not debt finance.

7   C   Money is a medium of exchange and so an asset can act as money provided it is generally acceptable. It does not need to be legal tender, provided it is acceptable to both parties to the transaction.

8   Insurance provides cover against risks that **may** occur; assurance provides cover against risks that **will** occur.

End of chapter question

Capital markets

(a) Distinguish between the money market and the capital market, and identify the main institutions which operate in each market. **(10 marks)**

(b) Using examples, show how a business might need to use both the money and capital markets. **(12 marks)**

(c) Explain the circumstances under which the government might need to use the capital market. **(8 marks)**

(Total 30 marks)

PART C HOUSEHOLD, CORPORATE AND FINANCE SECTORS

Credit and banking

Topic list	Syllabus reference
1 Credit creation and the banking system	2.3
2 The role of the central bank	2.3
3 Yield on financial instruments	2.3
4 The global banking crisis 2007-2010	2.3

Introduction

In this chapter, we look more closely at three issues. First, we discuss the **role of the banks** in the **financial system** and in particular how they create **credit** and provide **liquidity**. Second, we discuss the role of the central bank, and how it influences the functioning of the financial system. Finally we discuss the structure of **yields** of the various instruments that trade in the financial markets.

The three areas are intertwined because the monetary policy of a government, operated through its central bank, influences the behaviour of banks by influencing their credit creation activities, and affects the level and structure of financial yields by setting short run interest rates. As both banks and financial markets are the major sources through which firms and individuals raise capital, the **central bank** can have a potent **impact on the financial markets** and the **real economy**.

PART C HOUSEHOLD, CORPORATE AND FINANCE SECTORS

1 Credit creation and the banking system

FAST FORWARD

Banks (and building societies) create **credit** when they lend or grant overdrafts, and their activities thus contribute significantly to the increase in the money supply. In practice, the size of the **credit multiplier** is restricted by 'leakages' and by central bank controls over the liquidity and capital structure of banks.

1.1 The banks and the banking system

As we have already discussed, banks are major financial intermediaries in a financial system. The term 'bank' is generic and there are different types of banks that operate within a banking system. We have already identified that there are different types of bank:

(a) **Clearing banks** operate the clearing system for settling payments (eg payments by cheque by bank customers).

(b) The terms **retail banks** or **commercial banks** are used to describe the traditional 'High Street' banks. The term **wholesale banks** refers to banks which specialise in lending in large quantities to major customers. The clearing banks are involved in both retail and wholesale banking but are commonly regarded as the main retail banks.

(c) **Investment banks** (which used to be referred to as **merchant banks**) offer services, often of a specialised nature, to corporate customers.

Question Bank's assets

In a retail bank's statement of financial position, which one of the following items do you think would constitute the largest asset?

(a) Customers' overdrafts and bank loans
(b) Customers' deposits
(c) Land and buildings

Answer

The answer is (a). Item (b) is not an asset of the bank – it is a liability (a sum of money owed by the bank to its customers). It might be tempting to choose item (c), if you think about the large number of branches owned by the retail banks, but in fact the value of this asset is dwarfed by the banks' lending.

1.2 The functions of the commercial banks

(a) **Providing a payments mechanism**. The **bank clearing system** is a way of transferring money between accounts within a branch of a bank, between different branches, and between different banks. The **clearing system** enables individuals and firms to make payments by cheque, and therefore acts as a system for **transferring money**. Banks also enable individuals and firms to make payments by using direct debits, standing order, and electronic transfers. Again, in these ways, the banks provide a money transmission service.

(b) **Providing a place for individuals, firms and government to store their wealth**. Banks compete with other financial institutions to attract the funds of individuals and firms. The banks then hold the money in two main types of account:

   (i) Current accounts
   (ii) Deposit accounts

(c) **Lending money** in the form of loans or overdrafts.

(d) **Acting as financial intermediaries** by accepting deposits and lending, and in doing so transforming the risk characteristics and maturity characteristics of the lending.

(e) **Providing customers with a means of obtaining foreign currency, or selling foreign currency**, whenever they require it. Banks play a central role in the foreign exchange markets.

The banks also provide a wide range of other **commercial services** to customers which facilitate trade for the banks' corporate customers.

(a) Advising and assisting companies, for example advising firms in a takeover bid and assisting companies to issue shares on the stock market.

(b) Providing assistance to exporters and importers, for example helping exporters to obtain payment from buyers abroad, and helping importers to pay for goods they buy from foreign suppliers

(c) Leasing

(d) Debt factoring services

(e) Executorship and trustee services

(f) Acting as insurance brokers for insurance companies by selling some insurance policies

(g) Selling insurance policies of their own, notably life assurance policies

(h) Selling pensions

(i) Share registration and share dealing services

(j) Unit trust business

(k) Giving investment advice

1.3 Wholesale banks

The second main type of bank, alongside commercial (retail) banks, is the **wholesale bank**. The most common of these banks are **investment banks**, but they also include **overseas banks** operating outside their home country.

Investment (merchant) banks are financial organisations that are primarily involved with accumulating the funds that businesses use for capital investment, mergers, and corporate start ups. By the nature of their business, they are dealing with very large amounts of money.

Investment banks help companies obtain funds through underwriting the issuance of new shares and bonds.

They often borrow from one another through the **inter-bank market**.

The banking activity of overseas banks mainly relates to financing international trade, and managing international capital movements and currency transactions.

1.4 Credit creation

Key terms

> The **bank multiplier** or **credit multiplier** is the name given to banks' ability to create credit, and hence money, by maintaining their cash reserves at less than 100% of the value of their deposits.

When someone deposits money in a bank, the banks are able as a result to 'create' credit of a much greater magnitude than the amount of money originally deposited, and thereby they can make profit for themselves.

Suppose, for example, that in a country with a single bank, customer deposits total $100,000. The bank, we will assume, re-lends all these deposits to other customers. The customers will use the money they have borrowed to buy goods and services and they will pay various firms and individuals for these purchases. If the firms and individuals receiving payment then put the money into their own accounts with the bank, the bank's deposits will have doubled.

It is because most additions to bank lending end up as money in someone's bank account, in turn adding to total customer deposits with the banks, that banks have this **ability to create credit**. They can do this because they know that not all of the cash that has been deposited with them will be withdrawn at the same time.

1.5 Illustration of credit creation

Illustrating the process with some figures may be helpful. We shall assume for simplicity that there is only one bank in the banking system, and that all money lent by the bank is re-deposited by various customers.

Let us assume a customer deposits $1,000 in cash in the bank.

Although this $1,000 is an asset for the customer, for the bank, this deposit is a **liability**. However, the deposit provides funds for the bank to acquire **assets**. We shall begin by assuming that the bank holds these assets entirely in the form of cash.

If the bank keeps the full $1,000 and does nothing with it, then it would simply operate as a 'safe' in which the client's money is deposited. However, if the bank believes that the client is unlikely to claim the full $1,000 for some time, there will be some incentive to use the money rather than to keep it idle. One possibility would be to lend it to another customer. The bank would be taking a risk that it will not have the cash when its first customer wants to have it back, but at the same time it would expect to make a profit by charging interest on the sum of money it had lent to the second customer.

On one hand, the deposit of the $1,000 creates the opportunity for the bank to make a profit in the form of the interest that it can charge on the money it lends (with this incentive being accentuated if the bank is paying interest on the deposits it accepts). On the other hand, however, there is a risk that when the money is out on loan the client may claim it back. The bank will then be unable to meet its obligation to repay the cash to the client unless it can recall the loan instantly, which is unlikely.

As long as the bank feels that the likelihood its depositors will demand a substantial proportion of their deposits in cash is small, then it faces an acceptable risk in lending some of the money. In other words, the bank strikes a balance between the desire to play safe by holding the cash and the desire to make profits by lending.

Let us assume that the bank has decided (on the basis of past experience and observation) to keep 20 cents in cash for every $1 deposited, and then lend out the other 80 cents. In other words, the bank in this example is operating a 20% cash ratio. At step (1) below, the bank has $1,000 in cash.

On the basis of the 20% cash ratio, the bank manager decides to keep $200 cash, and make a loan of $800 to a business (step 2).

This business in turn pays the $800 to another company, which banks at the same bank.

The second company then decides to pay the $800 into the bank (step 3).

So the bank is now holding $1,000 in cash, but has accepted total deposits of $1,800.

On the basis of the 20% cash ratio, the bank only needs to be holding $360 (20% × $1,800) as cash.

Accordingly (step 4), the bank lends $640 to another customer seeking a loan.

	Bank's liabilities (= customer deposits)	Bank's assets (= cash or loans to customers)
(1)	$1,000 deposit	$1,000 cash
(2)	$1,000 deposit	$200 cash
		$800 loans
(3)	$1,000 deposit	$200 cash
	$800 deposit	$800 loan
		$800 cash
(4)	$1,000 deposit	$200 cash
	$800 deposit	$800 loan
		$160 cash
		$640 loan

The bank can continue with this process of depositing and lending as long as the cash ratio is maintained. However, even by the end of step (4) in our simple example, we can see that, through the process of credit creation, the bank now has deposits of $1,800 compared to the initial deposit of $1,000. So, it has 'created' an extra $800.

Ultimately, if the bank kept on lending, applying the 20% cash ratio, total deposits would rise to $5,000 (the initial $1,000 plus an extra $4,000 'created').

1.6 The credit multiplier

If the bank decided that the 20% cash ratio was too conservative and reduced it to 10%, then for every $1,000 cash deposited with it, the bank would only need to hold $100, and could loan out the other $900. It is important to understand that banks, in the process of lending, are also potentially creating money because clients either borrowing or receiving the proceeds of borrowers' expenditure can use their deposits to make money transactions.

The fact that banks do not need to keep a 100% cash reserve ratio automatically implies that they have the capacity to create money out of nothing. The size of this credit expansion depends primarily on the size of their **cash reserve ratio**.

We can summarise the quantitative side of credit creation in banks as follows:

$$\text{Deposits} = \frac{\text{Initial cash deposit}}{\text{Cash ratio}} \quad \text{or} \quad D = \frac{c}{r}$$

The relationship of the total deposits resulting from an initial deposit to that initial deposit is known as the **credit multiplier** (or deposit multiplier).

The smaller the cash ratio or credit multiplier, the bigger the total of the deposits that a given amount of cash will be able to support and hence the larger the money supply.

If a bank decides to keep a cash reserve ratio of 10%, and it receives additional deposits of $1,000, the total increase in bank deposits will be $1,000 ÷ 10% = $10,000.

Key point

> Note, however, that this 'increase' of $10,000 includes the $1,000 initially deposited. Be careful not to double count the amount of the initial deposit.

PART C HOUSEHOLD, CORPORATE AND FINANCE SECTORS

Question — Cash reserve ratio

Suppose that all the commercial banks in an economy operated on a cash reserve ratio of 20%. How much cash would have to flow into the banks for the money supply to increase by $80 million?

Answer

Call the extra cash $C. Then:

$$\frac{C}{20\%} = 80 + C$$

$$C = 20\% \times (80 + C)$$

$$0.8C = 16$$

$$C = \$20 \text{ million}$$

If an extra $20 million is deposited, the total money supply will rise to $20 million ÷ 20% = $100 million. This includes the initial $20 million, so the increase is $80 million.

In practice, the amount of money a bank can create will be considerably less than the multiplier we have calculated.

There are constraints on the growth of a bank's deposits (and on the growth of the deposits of all banks in total).

(a) Cash leaks out of the banking system into less formal accumulations.
(b) Customers might not want to borrow at the interest rates the bank would charge.
(c) Banks should not lend to high-risk customers without good security.

A **cash ratio** or similar **fractional reserve system** might be imposed on banks by the government. The People's Bank of China (the central bank in China) uses changes in reserve requirements as a tool for helping to control inflation (by controlling the money supply in the economy).

1.7 Capital adequacy rules

We have seen how banks create credit through the credit multiplier. However, we also noted that the credit creation ratio is based on there being no leakages from the credit creation system.

However, in reality not all customers will repay the amounts they borrow and so banks will suffer irrecoverable debts.

Capital requirement rules state that credit institutions, like banks and building societies, must always maintain a **minimum amount of financial capital**, in order to cover the risks to which they are exposed. The aim is to ensure the financial soundness of such institutions, to maintain customer confidence in the solvency of the institutions, to ensure the stability of the financial system at large, and to protect depositors against losses.

The **Bank for International Settlements (BIS)** is the governing committee of central banks and is based in Basel, Switzerland. It hosts the quarterly meetings of the Basel Committee on Banking Supervision which lays down guidelines for banking supervision, the **Basel Accords.** The **Basel III Agreement** (or Basel 3) was developed in the wake of the worldwide collapse of banking in 2008 and the consequent bail-outs by governments and has added to the previous requirements that laid out banks' capital management, including the formalisation of a **capital adequacy ratio** and **minimum capital requirements** banks will be required to meet to cover credit, market and operational risk.

Basel III now requires that banks maintain the equivalent of 6% of their assets (weighted by risk) as top quality (Tier 1) capital – primarily share capital, share premiums and retained earnings. In addition, banks need to hold a further 2.5% of their assets as a (Tier 1) capital conservation buffer outside periods of stress, such that this buffer could be drawn down if losses are incurred in the future. So, in effect, banks now need to hold 8.5% of their risk-weighted assets as Tier 1 capital. This is a significant increase on the previous 4% requirement (under Basel II) and reflects the experience of regulators when, from 2008, they discovered that most banks were holding lots of worthless assets as reserves, so-called '**toxic debt**'.

As well as creating a framework to **control liquidity** and bad debt exposure, the Basel III agreement also sought to improve controls over the banking process. It introduced a new **supervisory review process** which required financial institutions to have their own internal processes to assess their capital needs and appoint supervisors to evaluate their overall risk profile, to ensure that they hold adequate capital.

It also aimed to improve **market discipline** by requiring banks to publish certain details of their risks, capital and risk management.

Question — Capital adequacy

A bank has a trigger ratio of 8% on its weighted risk assets. If the bank wants to support $150m of weighted risk assets, what is the minimum level of capital it must have?

Answer

$12m

Minimum level of capital required = weighted risk assets × trigger ratio

$150m × 8% = $12m

Exam focus point

You will not be required to calculate a bank's weighted risk assets. However, you need to be aware that there are controls in place to regulate how much it can lend.

1.8 Liquidity, profitability and security: aims of the banks

A commercial bank has three different and potentially conflicting aims which it must try to keep in balance. These are:

(a) **Profitability.** A bank must make a profit for its shareholders. The biggest profits come from lending at higher interest rates. These are obtained with long-term lending, and lending to higher-risk customers.

(b) **Liquidity.** A bank must have sufficient liquid assets. It needs enough notes and coin to meet demands from depositors for cash withdrawals. It also needs to be able to settle debts with other banks. For example, if on a particular day, customers of the Barclays Bank make payments by cheque to customers of Lloyds Bank totalling $200 million, and customers of Lloyds Bank make payments by cheque to customers of Barclays totalling $170 million, Barclays will be expected to pay Lloyds $30 million to settle the net value of transactions. This is done by transferring funds between the bank accounts of Barclays and Lloyds, which they keep with the Bank of England (as 'operational deposits'). A bank might also need to have some 'near liquid' assets which it can turn into liquid assets quickly, should it find itself with a need for more liquidity. Near-liquid assets earn relatively little interest. A bank will try to keep the quantity of such assets it holds to a safe minimum.

Note that, in general, the most profitable assets are the least liquid.

(c) **Security**. People deposit their money with banks because they are regarded as stable and secure institutions. A bank might lend to some high-risk customers, and suffer some bad debts, but on the whole, a bank will be expected to lend wisely and securely, with a strong likelihood that the loans will be repaid in full and with interest. If it did not, people might put their money somewhere else instead, not with the bank. This is why banks usually give careful consideration to the reliability of the borrower. Often, in doubtful cases, they will ask for security for a loan or overdraft. Security means that in the event of a default on loan repayments by the borrower, the bank can realise the security by selling the secured asset or assets and using the sale proceeds to pay off the debt.

1.9 Assets and liabilities of commercial banks

The triple aspects of bank lending – profitability, liquidity, and security – are evident in a commercial bank's **asset structure**.

(a) A small proportion of a retail bank's assets (< 5%) is likely to be till money (notes and coin) and deposits with the central bank (the Bank of England in the UK). Most of these assets are held to meet the need for immediate liquidity, but they earn no interest.

(b) Some assets are 'near-liquid' which means that they can quickly be converted into liquid deposits.

The most important near-liquid assets are loans to the money markets and other money market securities. But near-liquid assets also include bills of exchange and gilt-edged security investments.

Near-liquid assets – market loans, bills of exchange and gilt-edged security investments – might represent around 25% to 30% of a retail bank's assets.

(c) The biggest returns are earned by banks on their longer term **illiquid assets** – ie their loans to customers. Loans and advances to customers are the biggest proportion of a retail bank's assets (usually about 60 - 70%) and the rate of interest on the loans varies according to the perceived risk of the customer as well as current interest rates.

(d) Banks' assets also include the normal type of non-current (tangible) assets found in any large organisation – eg property and equipment. However, the value of these operational assets is small in relation to the size of loans, even for the big clearing banks.

In the UK, the **sterling sight and time deposits** of the retail banks account for most of their **liabilities**. Most sterling deposits are provided by the UK private sector (individuals and firms). **Other currency deposits** are the other main type of liability, consisting of deposits held by customers of UK banks in US dollars, euros and so on. In the UK, there are no exchange control regulations currently in operation, and so private individuals as well as commercial firms and financial institutions are allowed to maintain foreign currency accounts. The bulk of other currency deposits, however, are held by overseas customers of UK banks.

1.10 Definition of money

Although we have talked about money in the context of the flow of funds we have not used a precise definition of money so far. In the UK, the Bank of England uses two definitions of money, **narrow money** (known as M0) and **broad money** (known as M4). The precise definition of the two measures is as follows:

Key terms

> **M0** (narrow money): Notes and coins in circulation plus the commercial banks' operational deposits with the Bank of England (central bank).
> **M4** (broad money): M0 plus sterling deposit accounts with banks and building societies.

Other less important definitions used include M1, M2 and M3 which all contain M0 but are differentiated by the type of deposits they include.

Central banks, and other economic advisors, pay close attention to monetary aggregates for several reasons:

(a) **It is a good predictor of likely aggregate demand.** This is because if firms and households keep their wealth as money instead of bonds, equities or other precious assets, it means they are expecting to need it to spend soon.

(b) **It monitors the credit creating activity of banks.** If the stock of money is rising it suggests that banks are creating more credit. Moderate increases are regarded as signs of a healthy economy but rapid increases are feared because they may lead to rapid price inflation or bank instability.

(c) **An indicator of potential inflation.** If the amount of money increases faster than the value of what it can buy (ie aggregate supply) the consequence will be a rise in the level of prices.

2 The role of the central bank

The **central bank** has various functions. These include acting as a **banker to the central government** and to the **commercial banks**. In the UK, the Bank of England has responsibility for controlling sterling inflation by setting interest rates.

A central bank is a bank which acts on behalf of the government. The central bank for the UK is the Bank of England. The Bank of England ('the Bank') is overseen by a board of directors (known as the Court of Directors) and is accountable to Parliament through the House of Commons Treasury Committee.

Functions of the Bank of England (as the UK's central bank)

(a) **Monetary stability.** The Bank's most important function is maintaining monetary stability in the economy. Since May 1997, the Bank has had operational responsibility for **setting interest rates** at the level it considers appropriate in order to meet the government's **inflation target**.

The central bank can also control short-term interest rates by buying or selling government stock in the money market. Such activity is known as **open market operations**.

(b) The bank also has a key role in maintaining the **stability of the financial system**. In exceptional circumstances, this may require it to act as a lender to the banking system (**lender of last resort**). When the banking system is short of money, the Bank of England will provide the money the banks need – at a suitable rate of interest.

(c) It acts as a **banker to the commercial banks**. All commercial banks keep a bank account with the Bank of England. This enables the cheque clearing system to operate. At the end of each day the net balances on each bank's accounts with all the other banks are settled through their clearing accounts at the central bank. The funds which banks hold with the central bank act as a liquid reserve for the commercial bank, and are controlled by the fractional reserve ratio.

(d) It acts as **banker to the central government** and holds the 'public deposits'.

(e) It is the **central note-issuing authority** in the UK – it is responsible for issuing bank notes in England.

(f) It is the **manager of the National Debt** – ie it deals with long-term and short-term borrowing by the central government and the repayment of central government debt.

(g) It is the manager of the Exchange Equalisation Account (ie the UK's **foreign currency reserves**).

(h) It acts as advisor to the government on **monetary policy**.

The banking system in the UK is regulated by the Prudential Regulatory Authority (PRA) which is part of the Bank of England. A key part of the PRA's role is to protect the stability of the UK financial system; for example, ensuring that banks have sufficient capital to cover any business losses, and sufficient liquidity to meet customers' day-to-day requirements for cash.

2.1 The central bank as lender of last resort

In the UK, the short-term money market provides a link between the banking system and the government (Bank of England) whereby the Bank of England lends money to the banking system, when banks which need cash cannot get it from anywhere else. (Again, this is what happened when Northern Rock approached the Bank of England for funds.)

(a) The Bank will supply cash to the banking system on days when the banks have a cash shortage. It does this by buying eligible bills and other short-term financial investments from approved financial institutions in exchange for cash.

(b) The Bank will remove excess cash from the banking system on days when the banks have a cash surplus. It does this by selling bills to institutions, so that the short-term money markets obtain interest-bearing bills in place of the cash that they do not want.

The process whereby this is done currently is known as **open market operations** by the Bank. This simply describes the buying and selling of eligible bills and other short-term assets between the Bank and the short-term money market.

2.2 Open market operations and short-term interest rates

Key term

> **Open market operations**: a central bank's dealings in the capital market. The bank uses open market operations to control interest rates and to regulate the money supply in an economy.

Open market operations provide central banks (such as the Bank of England) with a method of control over **short-term interest rates**. They are thus an important feature of monetary policy, which central banks implement on behalf of the government.

When bills are bought and sold, they are traded at a discount to their face value, and there is an implied interest rate in the rate of discount obtained. Discounts on bills traded in open market operations have an immediate influence on other money market interest rates, such as the London Inter-Bank Offered Rate (LIBOR), and these in turn influence the 'benchmark' base rates of the major banks.

Because the eligible bills and other assets which the Bank of England acquires in its money market operations are short-term assets, a proportion mature each day. The market is then obliged to redeem these claims and must seek further refinancing from the bank. This continual turnover of assets gives the Bank of England the opportunity to determine the level of interest rates day by day.

2.3 Government stock and interest rates

When we look at macroeconomic policy later in this Text, we will look at how governments attempt to manage both economic growth and inflation. When we do so, we will see how interest rates are a vital part of economic policy.

However, for now, and in conjunction with looking at the open market operations of central banks, we should consider briefly what interest rates are.

In essence, interest rates reflect the **price of money**, or credit. And money is priced, like everything else, through the **supply and demand** for it.

We will look at what affects the demand for money later in this Text, but the key aspect to consider in connection with open market operations is how to **control the supply of money** and therefore determine the level of interest rates.

Through its open market operations, a central bank will either buy government stock from commercial banks or sell government stock to them.

If the central bank **buys government stock**, the commercial banks will get extra money in return for the stocks they have sold to the central bank. Therefore, the supply of money will increase, and the banks' ability to create credit through the credit multiplier will also increase. In effect, this increase in the supply of money should make money cheaper (reduce interest rates).

Conversely, if the central bank wants to reduce the supply of money through its open market operations (and thereby raise interest rates), it will look to **sell government stocks**. In buying the stocks, the commercial banks' money base will be reduced, as will the level of credit they can subsequently create through the credit multiplier.

2.4 The independence of the Bank of England in the UK

The Bank is an advisor used earlier to the government, but is not an agent of the government. But how much independence of action does the Bank actually have?

Proponents of **independence for central banks** argue that independence can prevent the worst government monetary excesses, which in some cases result in **hyperinflation**. High levels of existing public expenditure commitments combined with electoral pressures (along with other factors) build in strong underlying inflationary pressures. An independent central bank is seen as an essential counterweight to the potentially reckless decisions of politicians. As well as avoiding the worst excesses, a strong central bank is regarded as vital for the shorter term stability of domestic prices and of the currency, and so is important to overseas trade. Any government wishing to reduce an already high rate of inflation will, however, have to listen carefully to the advice of its central bank if it is to have any real success.

Those arguing against independence point out that the central bank is an unelected body and therefore does not have the open responsibility of politicians. However, the danger of having an unelected and unaccountable body is minimised by the formal publication of decisions and recommendations of the central bank.

Further, it is claimed that central bank views on monetary policy could be in conflict with other economic objectives of the government. For example, excessively strict pursuit of monetary policy in order to pursue an inflation target might result in prolonged recession and heavy under-utilisation of resources.

In May 1997, shortly after it had been elected, Tony Blair's Labour government in the UK announced important changes to the role of the UK central bank, the Bank of England. As already mentioned, the Chancellor of the Exchequer handed over to the Bank the power to set interest rates. Consequently, interest rates in the UK are now set by a **Monetary Policy Committee** of nine members, including the Governor of the Bank, the three Deputy Governors for Monetary Policy, the Bank's Chief Economist, and four external members appointed directly by the Chancellor. The appointment of independent, external members, who are experts in the field of economics and monetary policy, is designed to ensure that the committee benefits from their input as well as the knowledge already within the Bank.

The Committee sets interest rates with the aim of meeting the inflation target set by government.

The 1997 changes did not make the Bank of England fully independent, as the UK government can still override the Bank in an emergency. The role of the Bank of England also falls short of that of many other central banks in that responsibility for setting inflation or monetary targets rests with government.

One of the more independent central banks is the European Central Bank which is designed to be totally free of political interference.

3 Yield on financial instruments

FAST FORWARD

In practice, there is a variety of **interest rates**. To make a profit, institutions that borrow money to re-lend, or that accept deposits which they re-lend (eg banks) must pay lower interest on deposits than they charge to customers who borrow.

3.1 Interest rates and yields

Credit is a scarce commodity, priced through **interest rates**. Although there are many different interest rates in an economy, including banks' base rates, mortgage rates and yields on gilt-edged securities, they tend to move up or down together.

(a) If some interest rates go up, for example the banks' base rates, it is quite likely that other interest rates will move up too, if they have not gone up already.

(b) Similarly, if some interest rates go down, others are likely to follow them and move down too.

A central bank affects the general level of interest rates through its influence on short term interest rates.

A **yield** is a general term to describe the return from an investment. It is calculated by expressing the return as a percentage of the **market price** of the investment. Note this means that yields for bonds are inversely related to bond prices. That is, as the price of the bond falls, the yield % will rise.

For example, a $100 bond with a $10 return gives a yield of 10%. But if the bond price falls to $80, yield will be 12.5% (10/80). The yield will remain at $10 because it is referenced to the nominal value of the bond rather than the current price of the bond.

Exam focus point

You must remember that yields and interest rates are linked, and you should be able to calculate the impact that changes in interest rates have on changes in yields.

3.2 Nominal and real rates of interest

FAST FORWARD

The real value of income from investments is eroded by **inflation**. The real rate of interest can be calculated by using the formula below.

$$\frac{1 + \text{money rate}}{1 + \text{inflation rate}} = 1 + \text{real rate}$$

Nominal rates of interest are rates expressed in money terms. For example, if interest paid per annum on a loan of $1,000 is $150, the rate of interest would be 15%. The nominal rate of interest might also be referred to as the **money rate of interest**, or the **actual money yield** on an investment.

Real rates of interest are the rates of return that investors get from their investment, adjusted for the rate of inflation. The real rate of interest is therefore a measure of the increase in the real wealth, expressed in terms of buying power, of the investor or lender. Real rates of interest are lower than nominal rates when there is price inflation. For example, if the nominal rate of interest is 12% per annum and the annual rate of inflation is 8% per annum, the real rate of interest is the interest earned after allowing for the return needed just to keep pace with inflation.

The relationship between the inflation rate, the real rate of interest and the money rate of interest is:

(1+ real rate of interest) × (1+ inflation rate) = 1+ money rate of interest

We may rearrange this to find the real rate of interest in the example above.

$$\frac{1 + \text{money rate}}{1 + \text{inflation rate}} = 1 + \text{real rate}$$

$$\frac{1.12}{1.08} = 1.037$$

The real rate of interest is thus 3.7%.

The real rate of interest is commonly measured approximately, however, as the difference between the nominal rate of interest and the rate of inflation. In our example, this would be 12% − 8% = 4%.

FAST FORWARD Provision of finance brings **risk**, which will be reflected in the interest charged.

3.3 Interest rates and loans

The influences affecting interest rates in general will play a background part in determining the rate of interest for a particular loan. The main emphasis will be on specific factors concerning the nature of the borrowing and the status of the borrower.

The fundamental consideration in any lending decision is **risk**. The more **speculative** any borrowing proposal is believed to be, the higher will be the rate of interest. The lender is concerned not only with recovering the capital sum on the due maturity date, but also with earning a return on the money lent over the period of the loan. The time period of lending influences risk: the longer the time period, the greater the uncertainty about the ability of the borrower to repay the loan, or the greater the erosion in the value of money by inflation.

Borrowers and lenders will both take into account **real interest rates**. Consideration as to **future inflation levels** will therefore help determine the nominal rate of interest.

The **status of the borrower** will influence **perceived risk**. Those borrowers with a higher credit rating and moderate financial gearing will be granted more favourable borrowing terms and therefore relatively lower interest rates than those with a poor financial record. Whether a borrower can offer security for a loan and the quality of that security will be important: the better the collateral, the lower the rate of interest.

From both parties' points of view, but particularly that of the lender, the **type of any asset purchased by the loan is** important: is the security non-marketable on the one hand, or is it either marketable or redeemable on the other? In the latter case, there is possible escape from the financial commitment and risk, and means of adjustment to changed conditions. The more marketable/redeemable a security, the lower the interest rate.

The **amount** of any proposed loan will also be of some importance. Larger individual amounts will be less costly for a borrower to administer and this may be reflected in a marginally higher rate of interest on offer.

A lender will also be concerned in some instances with the **purpose** of any loan and the **competence of the borrower** in use of the funds. The reputation of a financial institution may be jeopardised by ill-considered lending which subsequently is adversely publicised. The greater the risk in this regard is considered to be, the higher will be the rate of interest.

3.4 Yields on short term money market instruments

Yield on commercial paper

Commercial paper (short term debts issued by a company) can be issued at a discount from the face value, or it can be issued in interest bearing form. The investor is getting the same rate of return regardless of whether the commercial paper is purchased on a discounted or interest bearing basis.

On a discounted basis, the investor pays less than the face value or principal amount of the commercial paper and receives the full face at maturity. The quoted discount rate of interest is the discount amount expressed as a percentage of the maturing face amount.

On a interest bearing basis, the investor pays for the full face value of the commercial paper and receives the face value plus accrued interest at the time of maturity. The quoted discount or interest rate is converted to a yield to calculate the interest at maturity. This conversion is simply a restatement of the discount rate as a percentage of the initial proceeds rather than the maturing amount.

Yield on Treasury bills

Treasury bills (T-bills) are purchased by investors at less than face value and are redeemed at maturity at face value. The difference between the purchase price and the face value of the bill is the investor's return.

The following formula is used to determine the discount yield for T-bills that have three- or six-month maturities:

$$y = \frac{F-P}{F} \times \frac{360}{M}$$

F = = face value

P = purchase price

M = maturity of bill. For a three-month T-bill (13 weeks) use 91, and for a six-month T-bill (26 weeks) use 182

360 = the number of days used by banks to determine short-term interest rates

3.4.1 Example

What is the discount yield for a 182-day T-bill, auctioned at an average price of $9,719.30 per $10,000 face value?

Solution

$$y = \frac{F-P}{F} \times \frac{360}{M} = \frac{10,000 - 9,719.3}{10,000} \times \frac{360}{182} = 0.0555$$

The discount yield is 5.55%

When comparing the return on investment in T-bills to other short-term investment options, the investment yield method can be used. This yield is alternatively called the **bond equivalent yield**, the coupon equivalent rate, the effective yield and the interest yield.

The yield on a Treasury bill varies according to the method of computation. The discount method relates the investor's return to the face value, while the investment method relates the return to the purchase price of the bill. The discount method tends to understate yields relative to those calculated using the investment method.

The following formula is used to calculate the investment yield for T-bills that have three- or six-month maturities:

$$\text{Investment yield} = y = \frac{F-P}{P} \times \frac{365}{M}$$

Note that the investment yield method is based on a calendar year: 365 days, or 366 in leap years.

3.4.2 Example

What is the investment yield of a 182-day T-bill, auctioned at an average price of $9,719.30 per $10,000 face value?

Solution

$$y = \frac{F-P}{P} \times \frac{365}{M} = \frac{10{,}000 - 9{,}719.3}{9{,}719.3} \times \frac{365}{182} = 0.0579$$

Investment yield = 5.79%

3.5 Yields on bonds

Yields on bonds

Yield calculations on bonds aim to show the return on a gilt or bond as a percentage of either its nominal value or its current price. There are three types of yield calculation that are commonly used, the **nominal or flat yield**, the **current or running yield** and the **yield to maturity** or **redemption yield**:

Nominal or flat yield

This is derived by dividing the annual coupon payment by the par value or nominal value of the bond.

$$\text{Nominal yield} = \frac{C}{F}$$

where C is the coupon and F is the nominal or par value.

3.5.1 Example

If the nominal value of a bond is $100 and the bond pays 4% what is the nominal yield on the bond?

Solution

$$\text{Nominal yield} = \frac{4}{100} = 0.04 \text{ or } 4\%$$

Current or running yield

This is calculated by dividing the annual coupon income on the bond by its current market price.

$$\text{Running yield} = \frac{C}{P}$$

where P is the market price.

3.5.2 Example

If the market price of the $100 bond dropped to $96, what is the current yield on the bond?

Solution

$$\text{Running yield} = \frac{4}{96} = 0.0417 \text{ or } 4.17\%$$

Redemption yield

The yield to maturity or redemption yield, is the rate of return investors earn if they buy the bond at a specific price (P) and hold it until maturity. Mathematically the yield to maturity (r) is the value that makes the present value of all the coupon payments equal to the purchase price.

PART C   HOUSEHOLD, CORPORATE AND FINANCE SECTORS

3.6 Variations in the general level of interest rates over time

FAST FORWARD

> Interest rates reflect a number of things, including **inflation, risk, demand for finance** and **government monetary policy**. A normal yield curve slopes upward.

Interest rates on any one type of financial asset will vary over time. In other words, the general level of interest rates might go up or down. The general level of interest rates is affected by several factors.

(a) **The need for a real return**. It is generally accepted that investors will want to earn a 'real' rate of return on their investment, that is, a return which exceeds the rate of inflation. The suitable real rate of return will depend on factors such as investment risk.

(b) **Uncertainty about future rates of inflation**. When investors are uncertain about what future nominal and real interest rates will be, they are likely to require higher interest yields to persuade them to take the risk of investing, especially in the longer term.

(c) **Changes in the level of government borrowing**. When the demand for credit increases, interest rates will go up. A high level of borrowing by the government, is likely to result in upward pressure on interest rates.

(d) **Higher demand for borrowing from individuals**. If individuals want to borrow more, for example because they feel confident about their level of future earnings, then interest rates will also tend to rise (as the demand for credit rises).

(e) **Monetary policy**. Governments (or the central banks acting on their behalf) control the level of interest rates in order to control inflation.

(f) **Interest rates abroad**. An appropriate real rate of interest in one country will be influenced by external factors, such as interest rates in other countries and expectations about the exchange rate.

3.7 The term structure of interest rates

The various interest rates can be grouped into three broad classes, according to the length of the loan period.

(a) Short-term interest rates
(b) Medium-term interest rates
(c) Long-term interest rates

Longer term financial assets should in general offer a higher yield than short-term lending. There are several reasons for this.

(a) The investor must be compensated for tying up his money in the asset for a longer period of time. If the government were to make two issues of 4% Treasury Stock on the same date, one with a term of five years and one with a term of 20 years (and if there were no expectations of changes in interest rates in the future) then the **liquidity preference** of investors would make them prefer the five-year stock.

The concept of **liquidity preference** is that, if all other things are equal, investors will prefer to hold money (liquidity) rather than bonds or other investments.

As an extension of this, it follows that investors will initially prefer short term (more liquid) investments over longer term ones.

(b) The only way to overcome the liquidity preference of investors is to compensate them for the loss of liquidity; in other words, to offer a higher rate of interest on longer dated stock.

(c) There is a greater **risk** in lending longer term than shorter term for two reasons.

  (i) **Inflation**. The longer the term of the asset, the greater is the possibility that the rate of inflation will increase, so that the fixed rate of interest paid on the asset will be overtaken by interest yields on new lending now that inflation is higher.

  (ii) **Uncertain economic prospects**. The future state of the economy cannot be predicted with certainty. If an organisation wishes to borrow money now for, say, 15 years, there is no certainty about what might happen to that organisation during that time. It might thrive and prosper or it might run into economic difficulties for one reason or another.

  Investors will require a higher return to compensate them for the increased risk.

(d) Note, however, that two other factors also affect the cost of borrowing.

  (i) The risk associated with the perceived ability of the borrower to fulfil the terms of the loan
  (ii) Whether or not the loan is secured by a mortgage on an asset

3.8 Yield curve

A yield curve shows the relationship between interest rates on similar assets with different terms to maturity. A normal yield curve will be upward-sloping, as shown in Figure 1, because of the higher interest rates which are likely to apply to longer terms of lending. Equally, as a stock nears maturity its market price will get closer to its nominal price, and therefore its yield will fall.

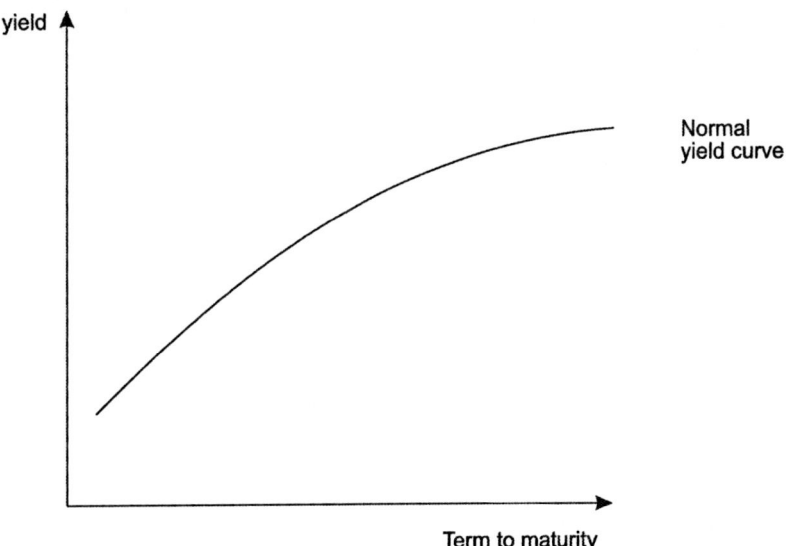

Figure 1 Yield curve

Notice that our yield curve in Figure 1 measures the percentage yield on an asset, and remember that yields rise when the market prices of the stocks falls.

One possible reason for the market prices of stocks falling is that markets for shares are bullish and so investors are looking to buy shares (either for capital growth or to earn dividends) instead of holding stocks.

3.9 Dividend yield

Dividend yield shows the return achieved from dividends as a percentage of the market price of the share.

$$\text{Dividend yield} = \frac{\text{Dividend per ordinary share}}{\text{Market price of the share}}$$

3.9.1 Example

Consider the following information on a share:

Current dividend per share	$0.2
Market price of share	$5.0

What is the dividend yield?

Solution

$$\text{Dividend yield} = \frac{\text{Dividend}}{\text{Market price}} = \frac{0.2}{5} = 0.04 = 4\%$$

Long term rates of return

As ordinary equities have no maturity and the dividend payments are not constant, it is difficult to calculate a return similar to the yield to maturity. However, approximate measures can be derived if we make assumptions about the dividends.

Two such assumptions are normally made: first, that the dividend paid is constant forever at level D. In this case if the price is P, the return on equities is given by the dividend yield since with no growth in dividend payments there will be no growth in the value of the firm.

The second assumption made is that dividends grow at a constant rate 'g'. In this case the rate of return is given by

$$K_E = \frac{D}{P}(1+g) + g$$

Where K_E = rate of return on equity
D = dividend paid
P = share price
g = dividend growth rate

3.9.2 Example

To illustrate, assume the following values for the expected growth, current dividends and current market price:

$g = 0.05$
$D = \$0.06$
$P = \$2$

Calculate the rate of return on equity.

Solution

$$K_E = \frac{0.06}{2}(1+0.05) + 0.05 = 0.0815 \text{ or } 8.15\%$$

3.9.3 Comparing yields

Being able to calculate a yield on equity is important for the rational investor. If all the markets are operating efficiently, then, *ceteris paribus,* the yield on equities (shares) will equal the yield on bonds (stocks). If they do not, the investor will reallocate their resources towards the **higher yielding instrument**. For example, if dividend yield is 4%, but the yield on bonds is 5%, rational investors will look to hold bonds rather than shares.

This also shows that interest rates can affect the price of shares. If interest rates rise, the yield on bonds will also be rising, and so holding bonds will become relatively more attractive than holding shares.

Therefore, in an efficient market, investors will seek to transfer their funds from shares to bonds. They will sell shares and buy bonds. Selling shares will reduce the price of shares, because it means there is an inward shift in the demand curve for shares (shift from D_0 to D_1, on Figure 2).

In turn, the fall in the price of shares will raise the dividend yield, so that investors are attracted back to holding shares.

This flux will continue until an equilibrium is reached whereby the yield on bonds is equal to the yield on shares.

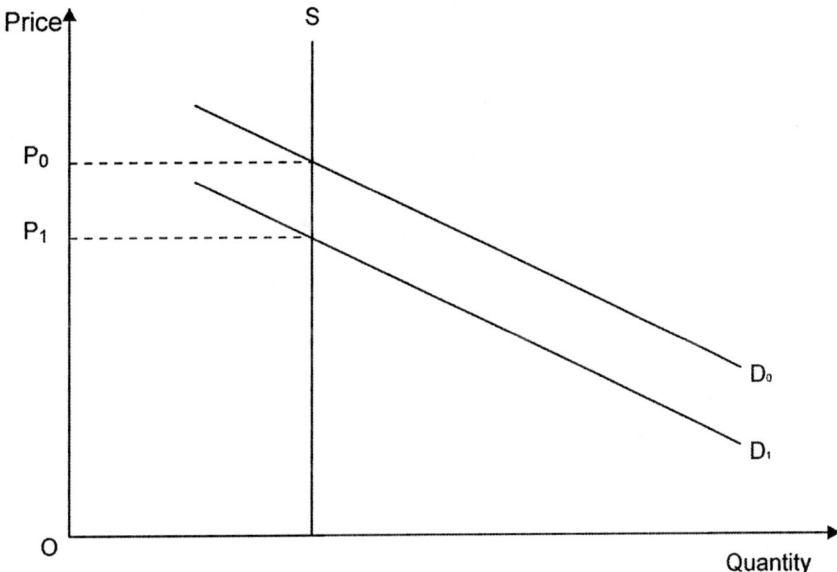

Figure 2 Impact of an increase in interest rates on demand for shares and the price of shares

3.10 Risk and return on financial assets

When investors invest in financial assets they receive in return an income as a compensation for giving up funds and therefore potential consumption. This income takes the form of a dividend or interest or a capital gain. Looking at the various instruments we have examined so far, we can make the following comments regarding the uncertainty surrounding the income and the capital gain element of compensation.

(a) A 91-day **Treasury bill** has no uncertainty regarding its income if it is held to maturity, since the compensation in the form of the discount yield is known at the beginning of the transaction.

(b) A **government bond** has no uncertainty regarding its income, since this is known at the time the bond is issued. It also faces no risk with regard to capital gains if it held to maturity. However, as we have noted earlier, if the bond is sold before maturity, it is possible however for the price of the bond to fall and a loss to incur.

(c) **Ordinary shares**, on the other hand, have uncertain dividend payments and uncertain selling prices, that makes the holding period return uncertain.

(d) Another aspect of risk that should be taken into account is **credit risk**. A corporate bond for example may pay fixed coupons but it may have a high risk of bankruptcy in which case even the coupon payment is rendered uncertain.

Taking these characteristics into account it is accepted that the ranking of securities in terms of risk is as follows.

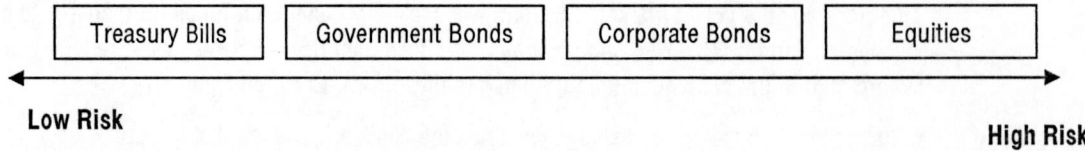

Since individuals are exposed to varying degrees of risk when invest in financial assets, it follows that investors will demand a higher compensation for the higher risk. The relationship between risk and return is thus positive and the determination of the precise relationship between risk and return is the object of financial theory. The accepted relationship between risk and return is shown in the diagram below.

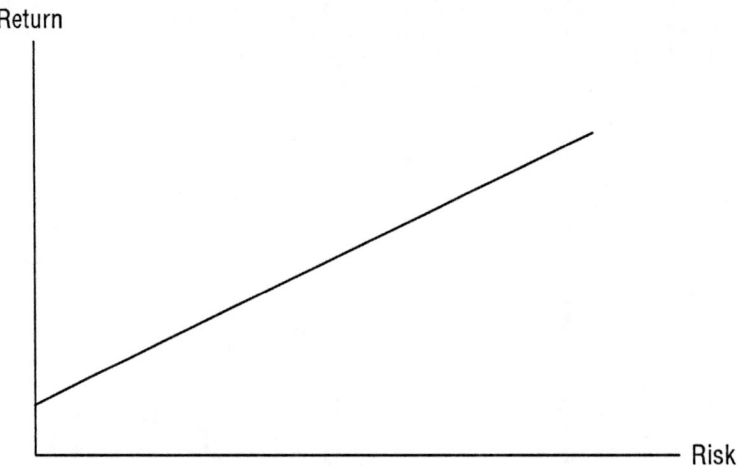

Figure 3 Risk return indifference curve

The return on any asset could be seen as made up of two components:

(a) The return from an **asset** which is **free of risk** such as government bond (a **risk free asset**) and

(b) An additional return, referred to as the **risk premium** which represents the compensation for bearing the risk.

3.11 The impact of the central bank on financial market yields

As discussed earlier, central banks may set short term interest rates. At the same time interest rates affect the yields on other financial assets. For example, an investor in equities will require a yield that would be at least equal to the prevailing short-term interest rates plus a risk premium appropriate to the equities held. If interest rates go up following an intervention by the central bank the required return by equity holders will go up and share prices will tend to fall.

Central banks can therefore play an important role in affecting yields and prices of financial assets.

4 The global banking crisis 2007-2010

The global financial crisis began with the collapse of the US sub-prime mortgage market in 2007 and then spread across the banking and financial sectors. The financial crisis led to a number of challenges in a world where confidence in banks and financial institutions fell to new lows, while at the same time banks and financial institutions were more careful about advancing credit to households and firms.

4.1 The causes of the 2007 – 2010 financial crisis

Economists offer a range of explanations for the crisis.

(a) **The US property boom of 1997 – 2006**. Prices of US houses rose 124% between 1997 – 2006, a trend echoed in some other countries. The cause initially was sub-prime mortgages, which allowed people with poor credit ratings to buy houses. The price of houses rose from 2.9 times average earnings in 1997 to 4.6 times in 2006. The rising house prices turned the market into one where buyers, and construction firms, speculated on house price rises by buying in at a low price using cheap credit and selling again soon after to make a capital gain. This was particularly attractive as such gains attracted no tax provided they did not exceed generous thresholds. Once the growth stopped, house prices fell sharply as people tried to pay back their borrowings.

(b) **The sub-prime mortgage crisis**. The effect of the collapse of the housing boom was to leave banks holding mortgages as assets which the borrowers had no way of paying back or paying the interest on. Sometimes the banks holding these were the original lenders, and sometimes they had been bought by other banks and financial institutions as bonds (or securitised debt) from the original lenders. Either way, the banks were holding worthless assets (termed 'toxic debt' by the media), having advanced too much credit without sufficient asset backing. Banks and financial institutions began to fail, and this forced rescue by governments which injected additional capital into them before they pulled the entire banking system down.

(c) **Low market interest rates**. Central banks followed a cheap money policy during the period before 2007. These low interest rates were mainly to help stabilise equity markets that had been falling and harming personal wealth and investments. This was the result of a fall in investor confidence following poor returns from investments in the internet shares boom of the late 1990s, and concerns over involvement in military action following the September 11th 2001 attack on the USA. These low rates encouraged borrowing by consumers, house buyers and property developers but left the economies fragile once the credit was no longer available.

(d) **Poor regulation of the financial sector**. Criticism has been made of the role of central banks and other regulatory bodies in not putting a stop to high risk lending. This has included a failure to understand the new institutions and assets of the **shadow banking sector** such as hedge funds and investment funds which gambled on the movements of asset prices and introduced instability into the markets. There were also examples of **predatory lending** in which borrowers were encouraged to borrow funds they could not repay using credit agreements, credit cards and very high mortgages.

(e) **Excessively complex financial assets**. The period saw the development of many new financial assets which were created using very complex mathematical models to establish the risks and returns on them. One such were credit default swaps which, the users believed, insulated them from the risks of defaults by the borrows behind the mortgages they held. The investor, regulators and even the creators did not fully understand these, with the effect that investors and financial institutions were exposed to risks that they had not anticipated.

(f) **Greed and poor governance**. Financial markets traditionally rely on the integrity and fair-dealing of the institutions and people involved in them. Regulation has been limited to allow them to be flexible and to develop. The payment of huge bonuses to management and traders encouraged them to expose their clients and the institutions they worked for to inappropriate risks.

We discussed corporate governance and its importance in Chapter 3 of this Study Text. However, this example reiterates the importance of corporate governance, and the potential consequences of failing to manage and control organisations effectively.

4.2 The consequences of the 2007 – 2010 financial crisis

The main consequences of the financial crisis were as follows:

(a) **Collapse of property sector.** Declining or stagnant prices of commercial and residential property in many developed countries, bringing the financial collapse of many construction and property development businesses.

(b) **Credit squeeze.** Tightened lending by banks reducing private sector investment and private consumption. This was a huge fall in injections with consequent downward multiplier effects through rising unemployment and business failures. (We will discuss multiplier effects in more detail in the next chapter).

(c) **Government intervention.** Large scale and co-ordinated intervention by governments to limit the crisis. The governments of developed economies individually and collectively took steps to reduce interest rates and also to provide funding to the banks to recapitalise them following the sharp fall in the values of their assets.

(d) **More regulation of banks and financial institutions.** A response in most countries has been to blame the banks and the financial sector and to seek to regulate them more closely. Banks also came under pressure from financial regulators to strengthen their balance sheets (statements of financial position) and improve their capital base, as indicated in the Basel III Agreement we discussed earlier.

(e) **Austerity budgets.** General nervousness about banks' exposure to toxic assets has led to increased scrutiny of the amount of government bills and bonds held by the banking sector. **Structural deficits** are fiscal deficits that are not run as a consequence of seeking to modify the recession and depression stage of the business cycle, but rather are perpetual. There is no possibility that the government will have the funds to pay back the borrowing in the future. Many governments were accused of running structural deficits and banks became nervous of lending to them. This forced the governments to take strong steps to eliminate the structural deficits, or at least convince the banks that they meant to, in order to keep the interest rates on their debts low and manageable. Such reductions of government spending and raising of taxation exerts a further downward multiplier effect, and further increases in unemployment.

Chapter Roundup

- Banks (and building societies) create **credit** when they lend or grant overdrafts, and their activities thus contribute significantly to the increase in the money supply. In practice, the size of the **credit multiplier** is restricted by 'leakages', and by central bank controls over the liquidity and capital structure of banks.

- The **central bank** has various functions. These include acting as a **banker to the central government** and to the **commercial banks**. In the UK, the Bank of England has responsibility for controlling sterling inflation by setting interest rates.

- In practice, there is a variety of **interest rates**. To make a profit, institutions that borrow money to re-lend, or that accept deposits which they re-lend (eg banks), must pay lower interest on deposits than they charge to customers who borrow.

- The real value of income from investments is eroded by **inflation**. The real rate of interest can be calculated by using the formula below.

$$\frac{1 + \text{money rate}}{1 + \text{inflation rate}} = 1 + \text{real rate}$$

- Provision of finance brings **risk**, which will be reflected in the interest charged.

- Interest rates reflect a number of things, including **inflation, risk, demand for finance** and **government monetary policy**. A normal yield curve slopes upward.

PART C HOUSEHOLD, CORPORATE AND FINANCE SECTORS

Quick Quiz

1. What is the credit multiplier?

2. What three aims must a commercial bank keep in balance?

3. List the likely functions of a central bank.

4. If the banking system has liquid reserves of $225bn and seeks to maintain a reserve ratio of 13%, what will broad money supply be?

    A $17bn
    B $1,731bn
    C $2,925bn
    D $292,599bn

5. The ability of the banks to create credit is constrained by all the following except:

    A   Leakages of cash out of the banking system
    B   A reduced reserve ratio
    C   Low demand for loans
    D   Prudent lending operations

6. What is the purpose of capital adequacy rules?

7. A $100 bond which pays 4% currently has a market price of $90. What is the current yield on the bond?

    A   3.6%
    B   4%
    C   4.44%
    D   5%

8. Which of the following would be likely to lead to a rise in share prices on a stock market?

    (i)   An expected rise in company profits
    (ii) A fall in share prices in other international stock markets
    (iii) A fall in interest rates

    A   (i) and (ii)
    B   (i) and (iii)
    C   (ii) and (iii)
    D   (i), (ii) and (iii)

Answers to Quick Quiz

1. The credit multiplier (or bank multiplier) is the name given to banks' ability to create credit, and hence money, by maintaining their cash reserves at less than 100% of the value of their deposits.

2. Liquidity, profitability and security.

3. Setting interest rates
   Banker to the government
   Central issuer of banknotes
   Manager of the national debt
   Manager of the nation's foreign currency reserves
   Banker to the clearing banks
   Lender to the clearing banks (lender of last resort)
   Supervision of the banking system

4. B $225bn × credit multiplier = total deposits (broad money) therefore $225bn × (1/0.13) = $1,731bn

5. B   A falling reserve ratio will increase the credit multiplier.

6. Capital adequacy rules are designed to ensure that banks have enough capital to cover their risk assets after allowing for the risk of potential debts.

7. C   Current yield = $\frac{4}{90}$ = 4.44%

8. B   A rise in company profits will encourage people to buy shares, so demand for shares will rise and their prices will also rise: meaning (i) is correct.

   A fall in share prices in one market tends to lead to falls in share prices in other markets around the world because stock markets are linked. So (ii) is not correct.

   Interest rates and share prices move in opposite directions. If interest rates are falling, people will look to buy shares instead of bonds, so this increased demand for shares will mean share prices rise. So (iii) is correct.

End of chapter question

Commercial banks

(a) Describe the functions of commercial banks and show how these meet the needs of business customers. **(10 marks)**

(b) With reference to the process of credit creation, explain briefly

   (i) how commercial banks can 'create credit' **(5 marks)**

   (ii) how the central bank can restrict the ability of commercial banks to create credit. **(5 marks)**

(Total 20 marks)

PART C HOUSEHOLD, CORPORATE AND FINANCE SECTORS

PART D

Public sector and macro-economy

Macroeconomic theory

10

Topic list	Syllabus reference
1 The Keynesian approach	2.4
2 The circular flow of income in the economy	2.4
3 Aggregate demand analysis: consumption, savings and investment	2.4
4 The multiplier and the accelerator	2.4
5 The business cycle	2.4

Introduction

In macroeconomics, we are looking not at individual spending decisions, investment decisions, pricing decisions, employment decisions, or output decisions but at spending, investment, price levels, employment, output and income in the economy as a whole.

Broadly speaking, macroeconomists can be divided into two camps when looking at macroeconomic decisions: the Keynesians and the monetarists. These two camps have had differing ideas about how national income can be made to grow, how full employment can be achieved, and how the booms and slumps of trade cycles can be smoothed out.

Keynes argued that the economy should be managed by controlling aggregate demand, and in this chapter we will study the basic elements of the Keynesian model for national income determination and equilibrium.

1 The Keynesian approach

1.1 Aggregate demand and aggregate supply

In Chapter 2, we identified how the price mechanism allows an equilibrium to be established between supply and demand.

However, this idea of equilibrium can also be applied at the macroeconomic level to the economy as a whole.

This similarity was highlighted by British Treasury advisor and academic economist John Maynard Keynes (1883 – 1946), who argued that demand and supply analysis could be applied to macroeconomic activity as well as that of individual producers and consumers. 'Keynesian analysis' – based around the interaction of aggregate demand and aggregate supply – has been a main pillar of economic theory and economic policy around the world since the middle of the 20th century.

> **FAST FORWARD**
>
> The **Keynesian model** provides a way of explaining how national income is determined, and how national income equilibrium is reached.
>
> **Aggregate demand** (AD) means the total demand for goods and services in the economy.
>
> **Aggregate supply** (AS) means the total supply of goods and services in the economy.

Aggregate supply (AS) depends on physical production conditions – the availability and cost of factors of production and technical know-how.

Keynes was concerned with short-run measures to affect the economy, and he also worked in a period of high unemployment when there was obviously no constraint on the availability of factors of production. His analysis therefore concentrated on the **demand side**.

'Supply side economics' (discussed later) describes the views of economists who do not subscribe to the Keynesian approach to dealing with the problem of national income and employment, and prefer instead to concentrate on supply side factors (in other words, the factors which affect the level of production in an economy).

The aggregate supply curve is upward sloping. This indicates that higher levels of national income and output can only be achieved at the expense of higher price levels. The main reason for this is a scarcity of factors of production causing prices in factor markets to rise (ie wages, rents, costs of materials and so on).

In the economy as a whole, supply will at some point reach a labour constraint, when the entire labour force is employed. When there is full employment, and firms cannot find extra labour to hire, they cannot produce more even when prices rise, unless there is some technical progress in production methods. The aggregate supply curve will therefore rise vertically when the full employment level of output is reached (AS in Figure 1). Notice that the horizontal axis of Figure 1 is labelled 'Real national income' and remember that national income equals total output in the economy. The axes of this diagram are therefore the same as in the microeconomic supply and demand diagrams we used in earlier chapters, but at the macro scale.

Aggregate demand (AD) is total planned demand in the economy for goods and services, including for capital goods, no matter whether the buyers are households, firms or government. Aggregate demand is a concept of fundamental importance in Keynesian economic analysis. Keynes believed that a national economy could be 'managed' by taking measures to influence aggregate demand up or down.

The AD curve will be downward sloping for two reasons:

(a) **Impact on competitiveness**. At higher prices, the demand for domestically produced goods will be less.

(b) **Impact on real purchasing power of money**. The aggregate demand curve shows 'real demand'. This means purchasing power with inflation removed. If the prices of goods rise the real purchasing power of money falls because a given amount of cash can buy less actual product. Therefore, the AD curve shows a decline in demand as the price level in the economy rises.

1.2 Equilibrium national income

The equilibrium national income can be defined as the level of income at which aggregate planned expenditure (aggregate demand) is equal to aggregate income and output. Keynes argued that a national economy will thus reach equilibrium where the aggregate demand curve and aggregate supply curve intersect.

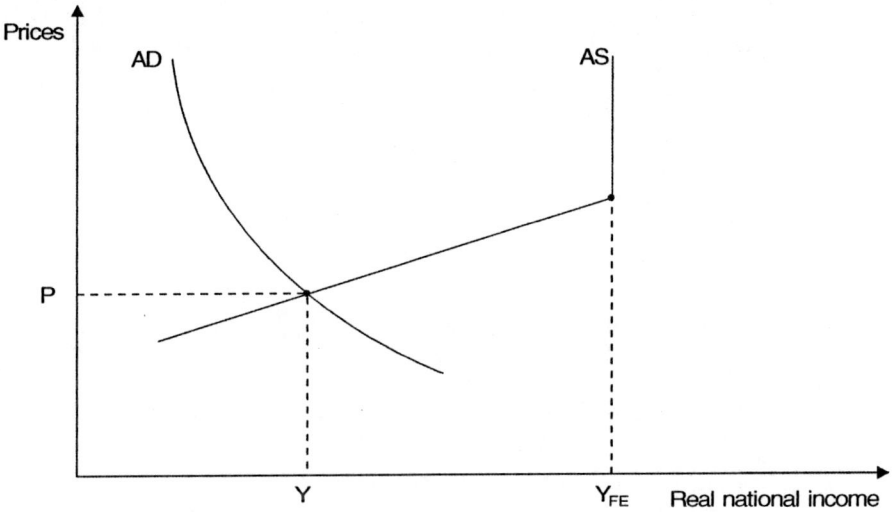

Figure 1 Equilibrium national income, using aggregate supply and aggregate demand analysis

The actual level of national income will be at the intersection of the AD curve and AS curves, ie at Y (Figure 1). The difference between the equilibrium national income Y and the full employment national income Y_{FE} shows how much national income could be increased with the resources at the economy's disposal. Price levels will be at P. Y therefore represents the level of satisfied demand in the economy. Note that the aggregate demand function assumes constant prices.

Two points follow on immediately from this initial analysis.

(a) Equilibrium national income Y might be at a level of national income below full employment national income Y_{FE}. This is the situation in Figure 1.

(b) On the other hand, the AD curve might cut the AS curve above the point at which it becomes vertical, in which case the economy will be at full employment, but price levels will be higher than they need to be. There will be inflationary pressures in the economy, as shown in Figure 2 below, if aggregate demand is AD_1.

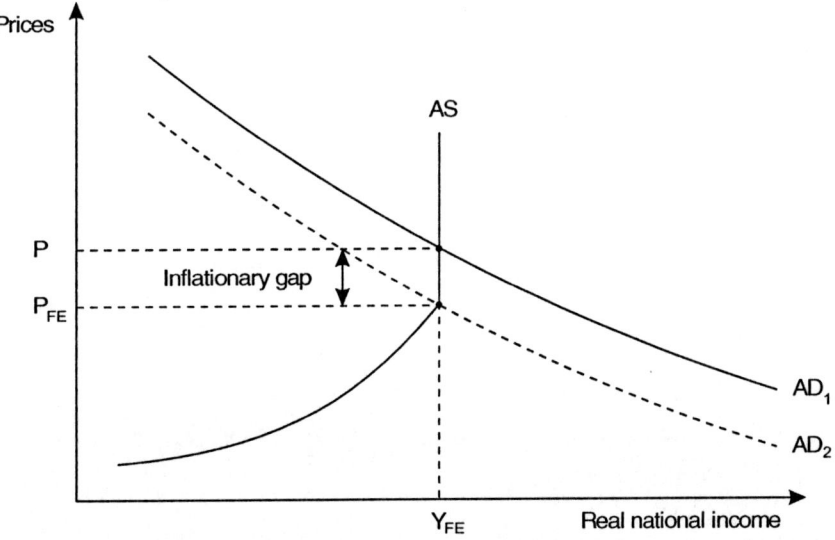

Figure 2 Equilibrium national income at full employment, but with inflationary pressures (an inflationary gap)

Shifts in the AD curve

As with demand and supply analysis in microeconomics, we can predict in macroeconomics that equilibrium national income can be increased by:

(a) shifting the AD curve to the right; or
(b) shifting the AS curve to the right;

thus expanding **either** AD or AS in the economy. As suggested already, Keynesian economists concentrate on shifts in AD.

You should also note that a shift in the AD curve or the AS curve will not only change the national income, it will also change price levels (P). In Figure 2, an inflationary gap can be removed by shifting the aggregate demand curve to the left, from AD_1 to AD_2.

The Keynesian argument is that if a country's economy is going to move from one equilibrium to a different equilibrium, there needs to be a shift in the aggregate demand curve. To achieve equilibrium at the full employment level of national income, it may therefore be necessary to shift the AD curve to the right (upward) or the left (downwards).

You should notice that the aggregate supply curve begins to slope upwards before full employment income is reached. This is because the employment of less easily employable and less efficient labour, competition by firms for labour, possibly lower plant efficiency as factories approach capacity output and so on, will raise prices as well as output. In other words, there can be some inflation when there is some unemployment.

The 'ideal' equilibrium national income

If one aim of a country's economic policy is full employment, then the 'ideal' equilibrium level of national income will be where AD and AS are in balance at the full employment level of national income, without any inflationary gap – in other words, where aggregate demand at current price levels is exactly sufficient to encourage firms to produce at an output capacity where the country's resources are fully employed. This is shown in Figure 3, where equilibrium output will be Y (full employment level) with price level P.

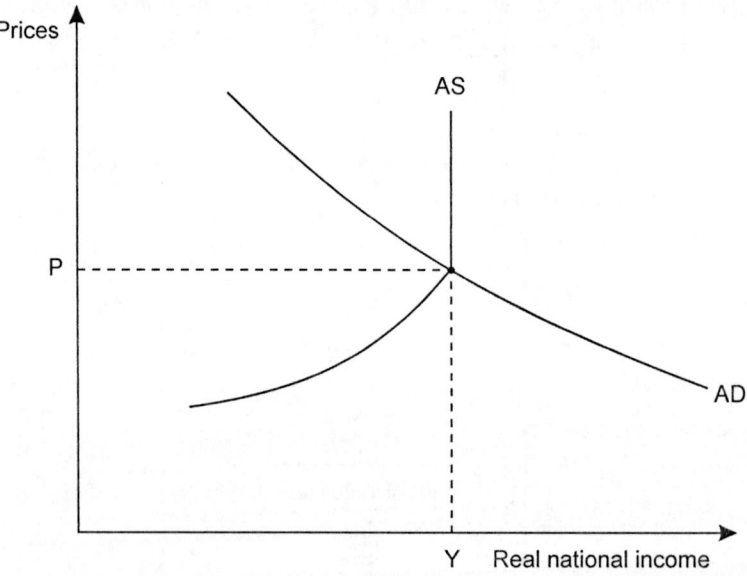

Figure 3 'Ideal' equilibrium national income

(A country will also seek economic growth, but to achieve a real increase in living standards, both AD and AS curves will now have to shift to the right.)

1.3 Determination of aggregate demand

The Keynesian approach states that the main influence on the level of macroeconomic activity, and therefore on national income, is variations in the level of aggregate demand.

This requires a more detailed account of the factors determining AD. These can be seen in the context of the model of the circular flow of income.

2 The circular flow of income in the economy

FAST FORWARD

There is a **circular flow of income** in an economy, which means that expenditure, output and income will all have the same total value.

There are **withdrawals** from the circular flow of income (**savings, taxation, imports**) and **injections** into the circular flow (**investment, government spending, exports**).

2.1 Income and expenditure flows

Firms must pay households for the factors of production, and households must pay firms for goods. The income of firms is the sales revenue from the sales of goods and services.

This creates a **circular flow** of income and expenditure, as illustrated in Figure 4. In Figure 4, we are describing a simple, **closed economy**, without foreign trade. This assumes the economy has only two sectors (firms and households), with no government intervention and no imports or exports. Equally, in this model, we assume all household income is spent on consumption, and all the firms' goods and services are sold to the households.

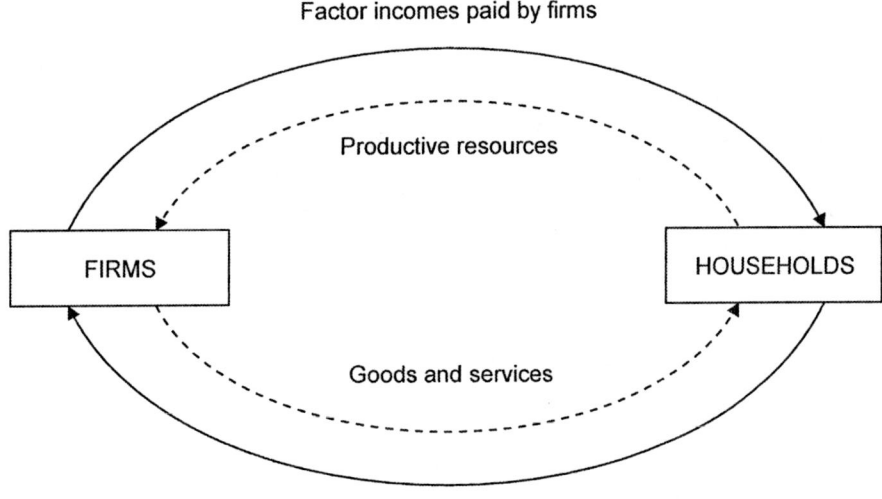

Figure 4 Circular flow of income

Households earn **income** because they have provided the factors of production which enable firms to provide goods and services. The income earned is used as **expenditure** on these goods and services that are made.

(a) The **total sales value** of goods produced should equal the **total expenditure** on goods, assuming that all goods that are produced are also sold.

(b) The amount of **expenditure** should also equal the **total income** of households, because it is households that consume the goods and they must have income to afford to pay for them.

Remember, at this stage we are assuming there are **no withdrawals** from, and **no injections** into, the circular flow of income.

2.2 The government and the circular flow of income

The government has several functions within the national economy, and so plays several different roles in the circular flow of income.

(a) It acts as the **producer** of certain goods and services instead of privately-owned firms, and the production of public administration services, education and health services, the police force, armed forces, fire services and public transport are all aspects of output. The government in this respect acts, like firms, as a producer, and must also pay wages to its employees.

(b) It acts as the **purchaser** of final goods and services and adds to total consumption expenditure. National and local government obtain funds from the firms or households of the economy in the form of taxation and then use these funds to buy goods and services from other firms.

(c) It **invests** by purchasing capital goods, for example building roads, schools and hospitals.

(d) It makes **transfer payments** from one section of economy to another, for example by taxing working households and paying pensions, and by paying unemployment benefits and social security benefits.

2.3 Withdrawals and injections into the circular flow of income

Our simplified diagram of the circular flow of income in Figure 4 assumes that an economy only includes two components (households and firms), and that households only consume domestically produced goods and services. However, that is not the case, so we need to extend the model to allow for two further elements:

(a) **Withdrawals** from the circular flow of income
(b) **Injections** into the circular flow of income

> **FAST FORWARD**
>
> **Withdrawals** are movements of funds out of the cycle of income and expenditure between firms and households, leading to reductions in the circular flow.
>
> **Injections** are movements of funds into the circular flow, leading to increases in the circular flow of income.

Withdrawals (W) from the circular flow of income

(a) **Savings (S).** Households do not spend all of their income. They save some, and these savings out of income are withdrawals from the circular flow of income.

(b) **Taxation (T).** Households must pay some of their income to the government, as taxation. Taxes cannot be spent by households.

(c) **Imports (M).** When we consider national income, we are interested in the economic wealth that a particular country is earning.

  (i) Spending on imports is expenditure, but on goods made by firms in other countries.

  (ii) The payments for imports go to firms in other countries, for output created in other countries.

  (iii) Spending on imports therefore withdraws funds out of a country's circular flow of income.

Be aware that **saving** is different from **investment**; saving simply means withdrawing money from circulation. Think of it as cash kept in a money box rather than being put into a bank to earn interest.

Injections (J) into the circular flow of income

(a) **Investment (I).** Investment is spending on creating new assets for the economy (in contrast to the expenditure in our initial model which relates to spending by households on goods and services).

Examples include firms' spending on new machinery or new buildings. Investment is an injection of funds into the circular flow of income, because it adds to the total economic wealth that is being created by the country.

Note that, in this context, investment does not mean buying financial assets such as shares. (That is classified as 'saving' by economists).

(b) **Government spending (G).** Government spending is also an injection into the circular flow of income. In most mixed economies, total spending by the government on goods and services represents a large proportion of total national expenditure. The funds to spend come from either taxation income or government borrowing.

(c) **Exports (X).** Firms produce goods and services for export. Exports earn income from abroad, and therefore provide an injection into a country's circular flow of income.

2.4 The open economy

Figure 5 shows a revised version of the circular flow of income, taking account of withdrawals and injections. This also now represents an **open economy**, since it participates in foreign trade.

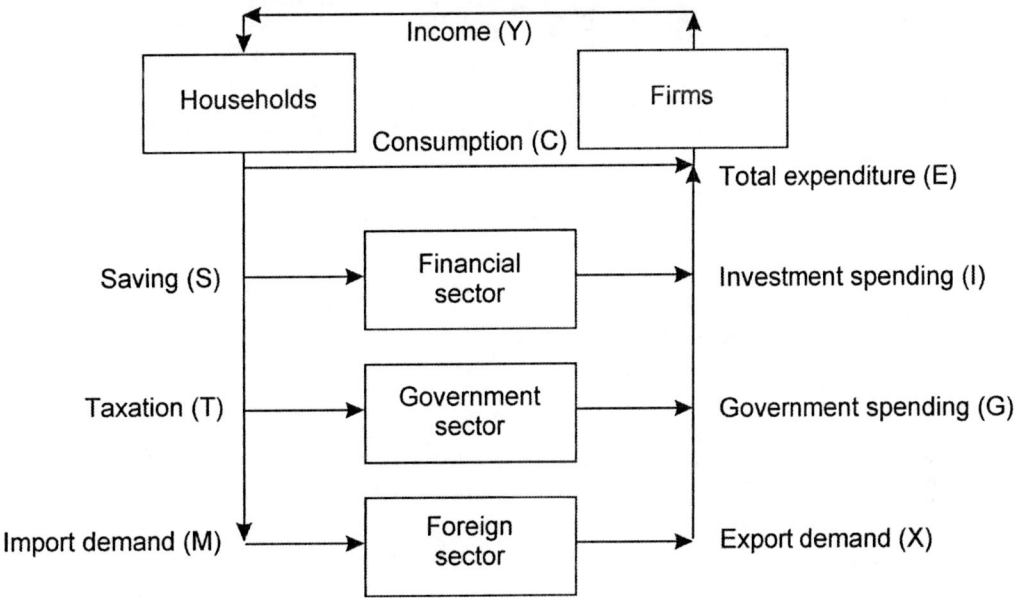

Figure 5 Circular flow of income showing withdrawals and injections

Key point

The economy is said to be in equilibrium when injections (J) equal withdrawals (W). So written out in full, equilibrium is reached in an economy when:

I	+	G	+	X	=	S	+	T	+	M
Investment	+	Government spending	+	Exports	=	Savings	+	Taxation	+	Imports

However, if injections are greater than withdrawals (J > W) the level of national income will rise.

Equally, if withdrawals are greater than injections (W > J) then the level of national income will fall.

2.5 Aggregate demand and national income

For Keynesian analysis to have practical value for the management of a national economy, it is necessary to establish how aggregate demand can be shifted.

To understand shifts in AD, we need to turn our attention to expenditure in the economy. A formula for total expenditure (gross national product) is:

$E = C + I + G + (X - M)$

where E is the total national expenditure   Gross national product (GNP)
       C is the total domestic consumption   (money spent on consumer goods)
       I is the total investment   (money spent by private sector firms and the public sector on capital items) *
       G is the total government spending   (government 'current' or 'consumption' spending)
       X is total exports   (including income from property abroad)
       M is total imports   (including money paid as income to residents in other countries for property they hold in the country)

* Alternatively, government investment spending on capital items can be included in G leaving I to represent investment by firms only.

FAST FORWARD

Demand management policies involve the manipulation of total national expenditure (E) by influencing C, I, G or net exports (X – M).

If we ignore capital consumption, we can equate GNP with national income. This is what we shall do in our analysis of the Keynesian model.

Gross National Product (GNP) is the total value of all final goods and services produced in a country, plus income earned by its citizens from foreign investments and possessions, less the income accruing to foreign residents from their investments in the country (including dividends, interest or profits).

However, national income can also be measured in relation to **Gross Domestic Product (GDP)**. GDP is a measure of the total value of goods and services produced by a country.

The key distinction between GNP and GDP is that GNP includes the income from investments owned abroad, whereas GDP only includes the value of goods and services produced in a country.

3 Aggregate demand analysis: consumption, savings and investment

3.1 Consumption and savings (C and S)

We will now look in a bit more detail at Keynesian analysis, and concentrate particularly on consumption, savings and investment. To simplify our analysis, we shall ignore government spending (G), taxation (T), exports (X) and imports (M) for the time being. By ignoring imports and exports, we are concentrating on a **closed economy** which is not in any way dependent on foreign trade.

If we ignore G, T, X, and M, we can look at a circular flow of income in which households divide all their income between two uses: consumption and saving. (Spending by households in the circular flow of income is known as consumption.)

Provided that national income is in equilibrium, we will have:

$Y = C + S$

where Y = national income
       C = consumption
       S = saving

This should seem logical to you. Income (Y) can only be either spent (C) or saved (S). Since we have a closed economy, consumption must be of goods produced by the economy itself.

3.2 Savings

There are two ways of saving. One is to hold the income as money (banknotes and coins, or in a current bank account). The other way is to put money into some form of interest-bearing investment. In the long run, there is no reason for people to hold banknotes or keep money in a current bank account, unless they intend to spend it fairly soon. If this is so, income that is not spent will be saved and income that is saved will, eventually, be invested. (The people who put their money into interest-bearing savings are not making any investment themselves in capital goods, but the institutions with whom they save will use the deposits to lend to investors and so indirectly there will be a real increase in investment when people save money in this way.)

Exercise: Influences on savings

What do you think are the main factors influencing the amount that people will save?

Solution

The amount that people save will depend on:

(a) How much income they are getting, and how much of this they want to spend on consumption

(b) How much income they want to save for precautionary reasons, for the future (for example, to pay unexpected bills)

(c) Interest rates. If the interest rate goes up we would expect people to consume less of their income, and to be willing to save and invest more.

3.3 The propensities to consume and save

Even when a household has zero income, it will still spend. This spending will be financed by earlier **savings** or from **welfare receipts** such as unemployment benefit. There is thus a constant, basic level of consumption which does not vary whatever the level of income. This is called **autonomous** consumption.

However, alongside this autonomous consumption there is also **non-autonomous consumption**, in which the amount spent will vary according to the income earned. When the household receives an income, some will be spent and some will be saved. The **proportion** of the income which is spent on non-autonomous consumption depends on the **marginal propensity to consume** (MPC) while the **proportion** which is saved is determined by the **marginal propensity to save** (MPS).

A household's marginal propensity to consume measures **the proportion of any change in income** which is spent (consumed.)

Formula to learn

$$\text{MPC is calculated as: MPC} = \frac{\text{Change in consumption}}{\text{Change in income}}$$

Exercise: MPC

A household's disposable income has increased from $200 to $250 per week, and consumption has increased from $180 to $£220.

What is the household's marginal propensity to consume?

Solution

0.8. $\dfrac{\text{Change in consumption}}{\text{Change in income}} = \dfrac{40}{50}$

In our analysis (ignoring G, T, X and M) saving and consumption are the only two uses for income, so MPC + MPS must = 1.

Taking autonomous and non-autonomous consumption together, we can say that a household's expenditure in a given period is made up of two elements:

(a) A fixed amount (a) which is the autonomous consumption.
(b) A further **constant** percentage of its income (b% of Y) representing the MPC.

Figure 6 shows how autonomous and non-autonomous consumption combine to give total consumption. The gradient of the consumption function (C) reflects the MPC.

The 45° line Y = C maps the points where income = consumption (expenditure), and therefore where average propensity to consume (APC) is 1.

If C > Y then we are witnessing **dis-saving**, and APC is greater than 1: ie $\dfrac{\text{Consumption}}{\text{Income}} > 1$.

Where Y > C then a household is making savings over and above their consumption. APC is less than 1.

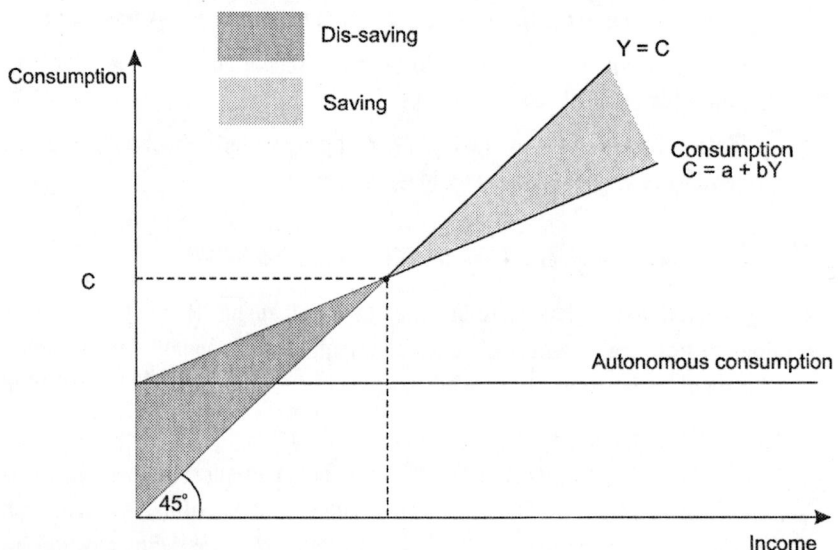

Figure 6 The consumption function

Similarly, a national economy as a whole will spend a fixed amount, 'a', plus a constant percentage (b%) of national income Y.

We can then state the overall consumption function as C = a + bY.

The marginal propensity to consume (MPC) will be represented by the gradient 'b', because it is the proportion of an extra $1 earned that is spent as consumption.

The **average propensity to consume** (APC) will be the ratio of consumption to income:

$\dfrac{C}{Y} = \dfrac{a + bY}{Y}$

For example, suppose an individual household has fixed spending of $100 per month, plus extra spending equal to 80% of its monthly income.

When its monthly income is $800, its consumption will be: $100 + 80% of $800 = $740

When its monthly income is $1,000 its consumption will be: $100 + 80% of $1,000 = $900

Because the household's marginal propensity to consume is 80%, consumption has increased by $160 following a rise in income of $200.

Exercise: Calculating APC

Using the above figures, calculate the household's average propensity to consume:

(a) When its income is $800
(b) When its income is $1,000

Solution

(a) $APC = \dfrac{740}{800} = 92.5\%$

(b) $APC = \dfrac{900}{1,000} = 90\%$

Note: If MPC < APC an increase in income will lead to a reduction in APC. But if MPC > APC an increase in income will lead to an increase in APC.

Changes in the marginal propensity to consume and the marginal propensity to save will involve a change of preference by households between current consumption and saving for future benefits. A cause of such a change might be a change in interest rates, which makes the investment of savings more or less attractive than before.

3.4 What factors influence the amount of consumption?

There will always be a minimum fixed amount of total consumption. Total consumption by households, however, is affected by six influences.

(a) **Changes in disposable income, and the marginal propensity to consume**. Changes in disposable income are affected by matters such as pay rises and changes in tax rates. An increase in household wealth, or expectations of a future increase in household wealth, may increase consumption levels.

(b) **Changes in the distribution of national income**. Some sections of the population will have a higher marginal propensity to consume than others, and so a redistribution of wealth might affect consumption. (A redistribution of wealth might be accomplished by taxing the rich and giving to the poor in the form of more government allowances.)

(c) **Government policy**. Government can influence consumption levels through taxation and/or public spending. For example, an increase in direct taxation will reduce disposable income and therefore will also reduce consumption.

(d) **The development of major new products**. When such developments happen, they can create a significant increase in spending by consumers who want to buy the goods or services.

(e) **Interest rates**. Changes in interest rates will influence the amount of income that households decide to **save**, and also the amount that they might elect to **borrow for spending**. High interest rates will make saving more attractive. Conversely, low interest rates will reduce the **cost of credit** and will therefore increase levels of consumption.

(f) **Price expectations**. Expectations of price increases may increase current consumption while expectations of price reductions may have the opposite effect.

Among the determinants of the MPC are **taste and attitude**. If a household believes that saving is a virtue it will save as much as possible and spend as little as possible. In the economy as a whole, a general belief in the value of thrift may mean that the MPC is low. Nowadays, however, the prestige attached to the possession of consumer goods may have overcome the admiration for thrift, making the MPC higher than it once was.

3.5 What factors influence the amount of saving?

Saving is the amount of income which is not consumed. Therefore, not surprisingly, the influences which affect savings are very similar to those that affect consumption – but in mirror image.

(a) **Income**. The level of income will be a key determinant in the level of savings. We have already noted that MPC + MPS = 1, but it is also true that APC + APS (average propensity to consume + average propensity to save) = 1.

(b) **Interest rates**. If interest rates rise, saving becomes more attractive relative to consumption.

(c) **Cost and availability of credit**. Similarly, as the cost of credit rises, consumption becomes less attractive, meaning that people will save more. As well as the cost of credit, the availability of credit is also important. When credit is easily available, people will be encouraged to spend on credit. In which case, they might acquire as much credit as they are saving, meaning that there is no net saving.

(d) **Inflation**. If inflation rates are high, then nominal interest rates are also likely to be high, even though the real rates (adjusted for inflation) may be low. Consumers may be attracted by the **money illusion** of high nominal interest rates into saving more.

(e) **Long term savings**. A large amount of household savings goes into long term, contractual savings, such as pension schemes. The savings may be less likely to vary with income than with the demographics – for example, the level of savings into pension schemes have risen alongside increases in life expectancy in developed countries.

3.6 Marginal propensity to withdraw

Remember that savings are not the only withdrawals from the circular flow of income. In a model that includes savings (S), taxes (T) and imports (M), the marginal propensity to withdraw (MPW) is given by:

MPW = MPS + MPT + MPM

The MPW is the proportion of national income that is withdrawn from the circular flow of income.

3.7 Investment

The total volume of desired investment in the economy depends on factors similar to those influencing 'micro-level' investment decisions by firms.

- The rate of interest on capital
- The marginal efficiency of capital (MEC) invested. (We will look at MEC in more detail later in this chapter, but it is the rate of return at which the net present value (NPV) of a project is zero.)
- Expectations about the future and business confidence, including expectations about future cash flows and profit flows arising from the investment
- The strength of consumer demand for goods
- Opportunity cost of investment

The demand for funds to invest by firms and the willingness of investors to lend their savings for investment (the supply of funds) should adjust to one another through the **price mechanism of the interest rate**.

(a) **Higher interest rates** should make firms less willing to invest, because the marginal efficiency of capital will have to be higher to justify the higher interest cost. However, firms cannot always cut their investment plans quickly and at short notice.

Higher interest rates should have two other effects.

(i) They will tempt individuals to consume less of their income and save more, with a view to investing it.

(ii) They will also tempt individuals to invest more of their savings – that is, to hold less cash and more interest-bearing investments.

(b) **Lower interest rates** should have the opposite effect.

An investment involves the acquisition of more fixed capital (buildings, machinery, plant and equipment) or inventories of goods and so on. The importance of the interest rate for investment should therefore be apparent in the marginal efficiency of capital. Firms should go on adding to their capital provided that the marginal efficiency of capital exceeds the interest rate, which is its marginal cost.

3.7.1 New technology and investment

When new technology emerges which changes methods of production (such as robotics) or provides opportunities to produce new types of good, there will be a boost to investment.

(a) New technology which reduces the unit costs of production will increase profitability. The supply curve for the goods that are affected by the new production methods will shift to the right. Firms will invest in the new technology in order to achieve lower costs and remain competitive.

(b) New technology which leads to new types of good will give a stimulus to consumption demand. Firms will invest to make the product and meet the consumer demand.

3.8 Investment and economic recovery

Investment represents one of the major injections in the circular flow of income. As we will see later when looking at the multiplier effect, variations in the level of investment can affect the level of national income and the level of aggregate demand in the economy. A major conclusion from Keynesian analysis is that in order to achieve economic recovery from a recession, there should be major investment.

Investment can be in either the public or the private sector of the economy, although the money to finance the investment might need to come from different sources.

(a) **Private sector investment** will come from retained profits, new issues of shares, or borrowing. However, in an economic recession profits might be low, and investors might lack confidence in a recovery, so that new share issues may be difficult on a large scale.

(b) **Public sector investment** might be financed by higher taxation, or by an increased deficit between government income and expenditure, that is, a higher **public sector net cash requirement (PSNCR)**. The PSNCR is the amount the government has to borrow each year to meet its expenditure commitments (because public sector revenue is less than expenditure).

(c) Public sector spending should have socially valuable spin-off effects, such as improved roads, sewers and public buildings.

(d) However, a high PSNCR, meaning large government borrowings, might force up interest rates in the capital markets and **crowd out** private sector investment, by making it too expensive for firms to borrow and invest profitably. (Keynesian economists deny that such crowding out takes place, however.)

There are two additional reasons why investment is very important.

(a) The act of investment represents consumption forgone now in order to increase the capacity to produce, and therefore to consume, in the future. It is through investment (or lack of it) that the future shape and pattern of economic activity is pre-determined.

(b) The growth rate of the economy is determined not only by the technological progress or the increases in the size and quality of the labour force but also by the rate at which the capital stock is increased or replaced. Investment represents an addition to the existing capital stock. If that addition is greater than the amount by which the capital stock depreciates, then the capital stock of the economy is growing and so is the capacity of the economy to produce more goods and services. Hence investment is an important determinant of the **long-term growth rate** of an economy.

We can illustrate the relationship between investment and national income as in Figure 7.

For the moment, we assume that we are dealing with a closed economy (no imports or exports) and with no government intervention (no taxation or subsidies).

We also assume that investment is constant (autonomous) and not related to national income levels.

Aggregate demand (AD) in the economy is represented by C + I.

The economy will be in equilibrium where aggregate demand equals the output of the economy, or aggregate supply (AS).

When AD > AS, national income will need to rise to restore the equilibrium position. This can be achieved through new injections into the economy – through investment.

We can see this at Y_1, where AD > AS, but I > S. However, the excess of investment over savings (I > S) will provide the injection necessary for the economy to grow and restore equilibrium, at Y_E. At this equilibrium point, savings and investment are equal. Because we are looking at a closed economy with no government intervention, saving is the only withdrawal and investment is the only injection. Therefore, at the equilibrium point injections equal withdrawals.

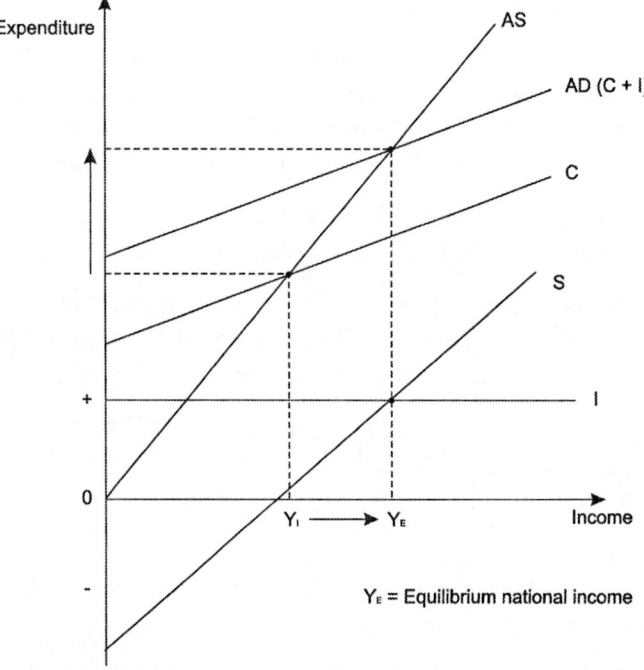

Figure 7 Equilibrium national income in a closed economy

3.9 Determinants of investment

In Figure 7 we have showed a constant level of investment. However, this is unrealistic because in practice investment will be determined by the levels of return firms expect to make from them.

3.9.1 Discounted cash flow and net present value

When considering an investment, a firm will be concerned with the net rate of return it will receive from its investment.

In this way, the firm will consider not only the values of future sales and costs, but also the timings of them and interest rate levels.

Interest rates are crucial to the investment decision, because if the funds used for the investment had not been invested they could have earned interest elsewhere.

Consequently, the future income stream which an investment is expected to generate has to be **discounted** to allow for the interest income forgone, and to convert it to its **net present value**.

Net present value (NPV) is the value obtained by discounting all cash outflows and inflows of a capital investment project by a chosen target rate of return or cost of capital.

The present value (PV) of a project can be shown as:

$$PV = \frac{Q}{1+r} + \frac{Q}{(1+r)^2} + \ldots + \frac{Q}{(1+r)^n}$$

where Q is the anticipated annual inflow, r is the interest rate, and n is the time period when the inflow will occur.

From this we can see that the PV will vary inversely to interest rates, meaning that if interest rates increase, the PV of the investment will fall, *ceteris paribus*.

3.9.2 Marginal efficiency of capital

Using the NPV method, present values are calculated by discounting at a target rate of return, and the difference between the PV of costs and the PV of benefits is the NPV.

In contrast, the marginal efficiency of capital approach (as introduced by Keynes) calculates the exact rate of return which a project is expected to achieve, in other words, the rate at which the NPV is zero.

This rate of return is termed the marginal efficiency of capital (MEC). If the MEC (or internal rate of return (IRR)) exceeds the current rate of interest, then an investment will be profitable.

Keynes used this concept to argue that there is a downward sloping MEC curve, that is levels of investment will be higher at lower rates of interest.

A change in interest rates is likely to induce a movement along the MEC curve and prompt a change in levels of investment (from Q to Q_1 in figure 8a below).

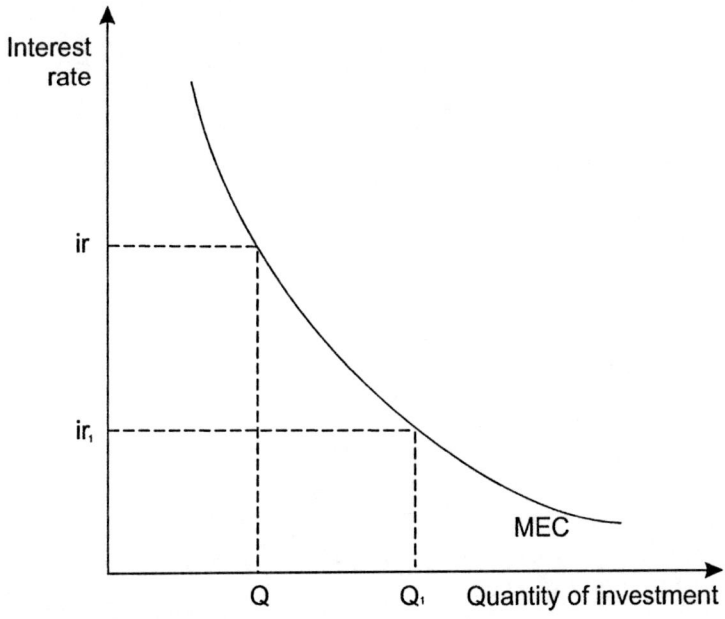

Figure 8a The marginal efficiency of capital

However, we could also witness shifts in the MEC curve, notably from changes in **business confidence**. If businesses are optimistic about the future they are more likely to invest. This would lead to an outward shift in the MEC curve (MEC to MEC_1 in Figure 8b). The MEC curve could also be shifted by **technological innovation** (making capital more productive) or **government policy** (for example, a reduction in taxes could encourage investment). A final factor which could lead to a shift in the MEC curve is the **substitution** of other factors of production. For example, if wage costs rise, a business may look to substitute capital for labour, in effect shifting the MEC curve to the right.

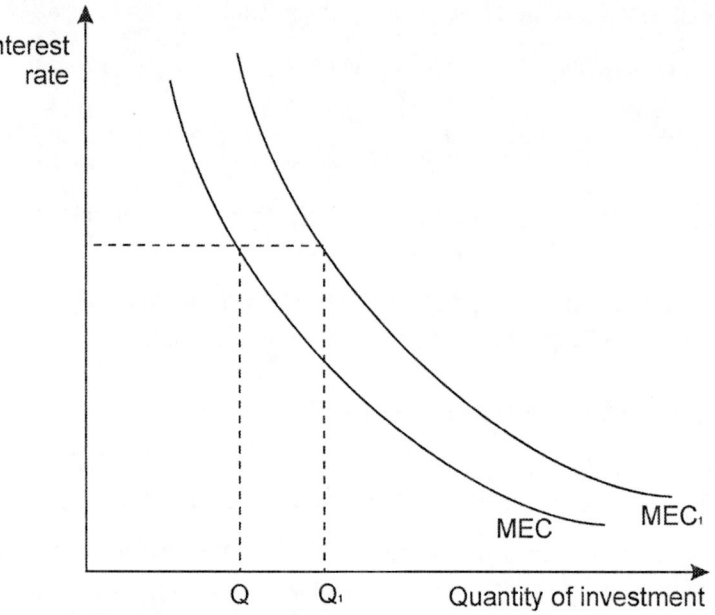

Figure 8b Shift in the marginal efficiency of capital

4 The multiplier and the accelerator

> **FAST FORWARD**
>
> The total change in the level of national income, following an injection into the economy, will be greater than the initial injection, due to the **multiplier effect**.
>
> The ratio of the **total increase** in national income to an **initial injection** is called the **multiplier**.
>
> Changes in national income can also be explained partially by the **accelerator principle**, which is the mechanism by which changes in investment spending are proportionally greater than changes in consumption spending, and therefore investment spending is more susceptible to bigger upturns and downturns.

4.1 The multiplier

The **multiplier** describes the **process of circulation of income** in the national economy, whereby an injection of a certain size leads to a much larger increase in national income. The firms or households receiving the injection use at least part of the money to increase their own consumption. This provides money for other firms and households to repeat the process and so on.

The level of national income might increase or decrease for a number of reasons; for example, there might be an increase in productivity or an increase in the country's exports. Keynes showed that if there is an **initial** change in expenditure due to an increase in exports, government spending, investment or consumer spending, a new equilibrium national income level will eventually be reached.

The eventual total increase in national income will be greater in size than the initial increase in expenditure. This is because of the continuing circulation of the funds concerned.

$$\text{Multiplier} = \frac{\text{Total increase in national income}}{\text{Initial increase in national income}}$$

The multiplier can be defined as a measure of the effect on total national income of a unit change in a component of aggregate demand: I, G or X.

Multiplier values can therefore be measured specifically for each of these separately.

$$\text{Investment multiplier} = \frac{\text{Eventual change in national income}}{\text{Initial change in investment spending}}$$

$$\text{Government spending multiplier} = \frac{\text{Eventual change in national income}}{\text{Initial change in government spending}}$$

$$\text{Export multiplier} = \frac{\text{Eventual change in national income}}{\text{Initial change in exports}}$$

4.2 Numerical illustration of the multiplier

A numerical illustration of the multiplier might help to explain it more clearly. In this example, we shall again ignore taxes, government spending, exports and imports, and assume a simple closed economy in which all income is either spent on consumption (C) or saved (S). Let us suppose that in this closed economy, marginal propensity to consume (MPC) is 0.9. This means that out of any addition to household income, 90% is consumed and 10% saved.

(a) If income goes up by $200, $180 would be spent on consumption, and $20 saved.

(b) Because of the circular flow, the $180 spent on consumption in turn increases the income of other people, who spend 90% of it ($162) and save $18.

(c) This $162 in turn becomes additional income to others. We can see that a snowball effect on consumption (and income and output) occurs, as follows.

			Increase in expenditure $	Increase in savings $
Stage	1	Income rises	200.00	–
	2	90% is consumed	180.00	20.00
	3	A further 90% is consumed	162.00	18.00
	4	90% of $162 is consumed	145.80	16.20
	5	90% is consumed	131.22	14.58
		etc	.....	.....
		Total increase in income	2,000.00	200.00

However, although we have identified that a 'snowball effect' has been created, it will not continue indefinitely, because at each stage a proportion of the extra income is lost through **withdrawals** (savings).

In this example, the initial increase in income of $200 will result in a final increase in national income of $2,000. The multiplier is 10.

4.3 The marginal propensity to save

In our example in section 4.2, the multiplier is 10, because in a closed economy, with no government intervention, the multiplier is the reciprocal of the marginal propensity to save. Since MPC = 0.9, MPS = 0.1.

$$\text{Multiplier} = \frac{1}{1-\text{MPC}} \text{ or } \frac{1}{\text{MPS}}$$

$$\text{Increase in national income} = \frac{\text{Initial increase in expenditure}}{\text{MPS}} = \frac{\$200}{0.1} = \$2{,}000$$

Note that at the new equilibrium, savings of $200 equal the initial increase in expenditure of $200 but national income has risen $2,000.

If the marginal propensity to consume were 80%, the marginal propensity to save would be 20% and the multiplier would only be 5. Because people have saved more of their extra income than they would have done if MPS had been 10%, the total increase in national income through extra consumption will be less.

4.4 The multiplier in the national economy

The multiplier in a national economy works in the same way. **An initial increase in expenditure will have a knock-on effect**, leading to further and further expenditures in the economy. Since total expenditure in the economy is one way of measuring national income, it follows that an initial increase in expenditure will cause an even larger increase in national income. The increase in national income will be a multiplier of the initial increase in spending, with the size of the multiple depending on factors which include the marginal propensity to save.

If you find this hard to visualise, think of an increase in government spending on the construction of roads. The government would spend money paying firms of road contractors, who in turn will purchase raw materials from suppliers, and sub-contract other work. All these firms employ workers who will receive wages that they can spend on goods and services of other firms. The new roads in turn might stimulate new economic activity, for example amongst road hauliers, house builders and estate agents.

Depending on the size of the multiplier, an increase in investment would therefore have repercussions throughout the economy, increasing the size of the national income by a multiple of the size of the original increase in investment.

If, for example, the national income were $10,000 million and the average and the marginal propensity to consume were both 75%, in equilibrium, ignoring G, T, X and M:

Y = $10,000 million

C = $7,500 million

I = S = $2,500 million

Since MPC = 75%, MPS = 25%, and the multiplier is 4.

An increase in investment of $1,000 million would upset the equilibrium, which would not be restored until the multiplier had taken effect, and national income increased by 4 × $1,000 million = $4,000 million, with:

Y = $14,000 million

C = $10,500 million (75%)

I = S = $3,500 million (25%)

A downward multiplier or **de-multiplier** effect also exists. A reduction in investment will have repercussions throughout the economy, so that a small disinvestment (reduction in expenditure/output) will result in a multiplied reduction in national income

4.5 The importance of the multiplier

The importance of the multiplier is that an increase in one of the components of aggregate demand will increase national income by more than the initial increase itself. Therefore if the government takes any action to increase expenditure (for example, by raising government current expenditure, or lowering interest rates to raise investment) it will set off a general expansionary process, and the eventual rise in national income will exceed the initial increase in aggregate demand.

This can have important implications for a government when it is planning for growth in national income through a demand management policy, using levels of taxation and government expenditure to influence levels of aggregate demand in the economy. By an initial increase in expenditure, a government can 'engineer' an even greater increase in national income, (provided that the country's industries can increase their output capacity), depending on the size of the multiplier.

4.6 The multiplier in an open economy

So far we have been considering a simplified economy in which income is either saved or spent on domestic production, and in which there is no government intervention. The real world is more complex, though, and we must now consider the effect of taxation and imports. Like savings, these are **withdrawals from the circular flow** and they therefore affect the multiplier. Thus, in an open economy, the value of the multiplier depends on three things.

(a) The marginal propensity to **save**.

(b) The marginal propensity to **import**, because imports reduce national income, and if households spend much of their extra income on imports, the snowball increase in total national income will be restricted because imports are a withdrawal out of the circular flow of income. One of the reasons for a low multiplier in the UK is the high marginal propensity to import.

(c) The level of **taxes**, because taxes reduce people's ability to consume and so are likely to affect the marginal propensity to consume and the marginal propensity to save.

Whereas the multiplier in a closed economy is the reciprocal of the marginal propensity to save, the multiplier in an open economy, taking into account government spending and taxation, and imports and exports, will be less. This is because government taxation and spending on imports reduces the multiplier effect on a country's economy.

For an open economy:

$$\text{Multiplier} = \frac{1}{s+m+t}$$

where s is the marginal propensity to save

m is the marginal propensity to import

t is the marginal propensity to tax – ie the amount of any increase in income that will be paid in taxes.

The multiplier as defined in this way may still be represented as below.

$\text{Multiplier} = \frac{1}{1-MPC}$, but this is now the same as $\frac{1}{MPW}$ (reflecting the impact of withdrawals as a whole).

For example, if in a country the marginal propensity to save is 10%, the marginal propensity to import is 45% and the marginal propensity to tax is 25%, the size of the multiplier would be:

$$\frac{1}{0.1+0.45+0.25} = \frac{1}{0.80} = 1.25$$

4.7 Changes in equilibrium national income and the multiplier: a graphical representation

It is possible to show the multiplier effect in the form of a diagram.

Exam focus point

The multiplier is a vital part of macroeconomic theory. You should understand the diagram in Figure 10 clearly and must also be confident you can apply the formula for calculating the multiplier.

In Figure 9, the horizontal axis represents national income (Y). The vertical axis represents planned or desired expenditure. The national economy is in equilibrium when actual output (which is the same as national income) is equal to desired expenditure. This occurs at any point along the 45° line Y=E.

On to this basic picture we have superimposed two other lines.

(a) The lower is the consumption function we described above. This consists of autonomous expenditure (a), which occurs even when income is zero, plus the proportion of income which is spent in accordance with the marginal propensity to consume (bY).

(b) Desired expenditure within the economy is not limited to consumption; we must also consider the **injections**, government spending (G), investment (I), and net exports (X-M). If we assume these are constant, total actual expenditure for any level of national income is shown by the upper line E = C + G + I + (X − M).

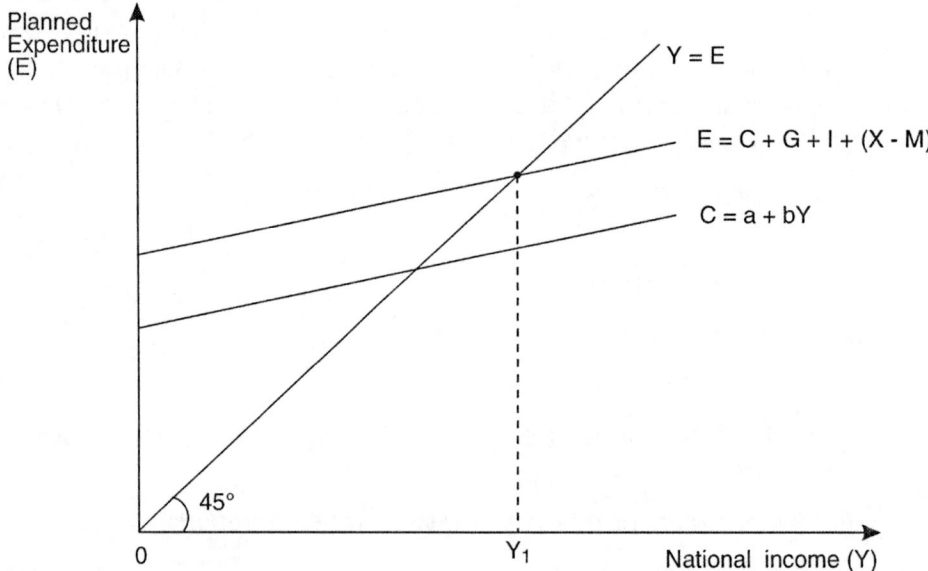

Figure 9 Equilibrium national income

Equilibrium national income in Figure 9 is at Y_1, where Y = E = C + G + I + (X − M).

But what will happen if the economy has unemployed resources at national income Y_1, and total expenditure is increased – that is, if C, G, I or (X − M) increases? By how much will national income increase? This is shown in Figure 10.

10: MACROECONOMIC THEORY

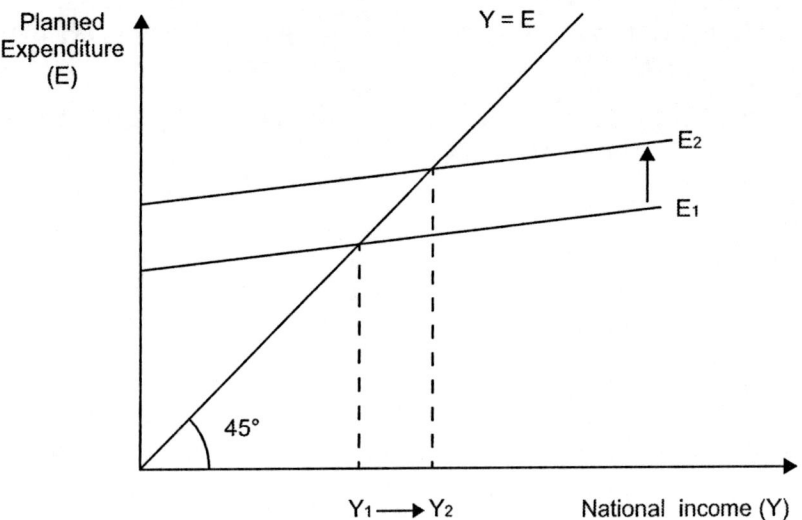

Figure 10 Multiplier effect

If injections increased (for example, through an increase in government spending or extra exports) then there would be a shift upwards in the E curve from E_1 to E_2. In Figure 10, the equilibrium level of income has now increased from Y_1 to Y_2. Notice however that the increase in the level of income from Y_1 to Y_2 is **greater than the increase in injections** (E_1 to E_2). In other words, total national income has increased by more than the amount of the initial increase in expenditure, and this is a portrayal of the multiplier effect.

4.8 Limitations of the multiplier

Keynes developed the concept of the multiplier in order to argue that extra government spending on public works, financed by a budget deficit, would have a stimulating effect on a demand-deficient economy:

(a) Demand would be increased, and national income would increase by more than the amount of the initial injection into the economy of the extra government spending.

(b) Because demand would be increased, unemployment would be reduced.

However, there are several important factors that limit the significance of the multiplier.

(a) It is relevant to a demand-deficient economy with high unemployment of resources. **If there is full employment, any increase in demand will lead to inflation** rather than a growth in the economy.

(b) The **leakages** from the circular flow of income might make the value of the multiplier very low. This is relevant to the UK, for example, where there is a high marginal propensity to import.

(c) There may be a **long period of adjustment** before the benefits of the multiplier are felt. If a government wants immediate action to improve the economy, relying on demand management and the multiplier could be too slow.

(d) The consumption function in advanced economies is probably more volatile than Keynes believed. If consumption is unpredictable, measures to influence national income through the multiplier will be impossible to predict too.

4.9 The accelerator principle

Accelerator principle: the theory that investment changes disproportionately in response to change in output.

The accelerator principle assumes that if there is a **small change** in the output of **consumer** goods, there will be a **much greater change** in the output of **capital** equipment required to make those consumer goods. This change in production of capital equipment (investment spending) speeds up the rate of economic growth, or slump.

A numerical example might help to illustrate this principle. Suppose that a firm makes biscuits and has 100 ovens in operation. The life of each oven is five years.

(a) If the demand for biscuits is constant, on average, 20 ovens must be replaced each year.

(b) If the demand for biscuits now rises by, say, 10% the firm will need 110 ovens in operation. During the first year of the increase, the demand for ovens will be 30 units (instead of the 20 which it would have bought under its usual replacement cycle). This is made up of replacement of 20 ovens and an extra requirement of 10 ovens to bring the total to 110.

So a 10% rise in demand for consumer goods results in a 50% rise in demand for capital goods in the short term. This is an example of the accelerator at work! The accelerator principle indicates how, when the demand for consumer goods rises, there will be an even greater proportional increase in the demand for capital goods. This speeds up growth in national income.

(a) If demand for biscuits now remains constant at the new level, annual replacement of capital equipment will average 22. There is consequently the danger that there will be over-capacity in the oven-making industry because the short-term peak demand of 30 ovens per annum is not maintained.

(b) This means that unless the rate of increase in consumer demand is maintained, over-capacity in capital goods industries is likely to occur.

4.10 The accelerator in reverse

The accelerator also works in reverse. A decline in demand for consumer goods will result in a much sharper decline in demand for the capital goods which make them.

The accelerator implies that investment, and hence national income, remain high only as long as consumption is rising.

So as income approaches the peak level dictated by available capacity, new investment will fall towards zero, reducing aggregate demand and hence national income. (The sharp fall in investment caused by the fall in consumption, due to the accelerator effect, will be compounded by the 'de-multiplier', so that the accelerator and the de-multiplier will combine to reduce national income more severely than the initial fall in consumption. The recovery in investment when demand stops falling will stimulate the economy again and cause income and thus demand to rise again.)

Note carefully that the accelerator comes into effect as a consequence of **changes in the rate of consumer demand**.

The extent of the change in investment depends on two things.

(a) The size of the change in consumer demand

(b) The **capital-output ratio**. This is the ratio of capital investment to the volume of output, in other words how much capital investment is needed to produce a quantity of output. For example, if the capital output ratio is 1:3, it would need capital investment of $1 to produce an extra $3 of output per year and so if demand went up by say, $3 billion, it would need an extra $1 billion of investment to produce the extra output to meet the demand. Accelerator theory assumes firms maintain a constant capital/output ratio.

Note: Accelerator theory also assumes that firms replace worn out capital each year (**replacement investment**).

Total investment therefore equals additional investment required to meet additional demand plus replacement investment.

5 The business cycle

5.1 What is the business cycle?

Business cycles or **trade cycles** are the continual sequence of rapid growth in national income, followed by a slow-down in growth and then a fall in national income (recession). After a recession, the economy starts to recover and grow again, prompting national income to rise again.

Four main phases of the business cycle can be distinguished.

- Recession
- Depression
- Recovery
- Boom

Recession tends to occur quickly, while recovery is typically a slower process. Figure 11 below can be used to help explain the phases of a business cycle.

5.2 Phases of the business cycle

At point A in Figure 11, the economy is entering a **recession**. In the recession phase, consumer demand falls and many investment projects already undertaken begin to look unprofitable. Orders will be cut, inventory levels will be reduced and business failures will occur as firms find themselves unable to sell their goods. Production and employment will fall. The general price level will begin to fall. Business and consumer confidence are diminished and investment remains low, while the economic outlook appears to be poor. Eventually, in the absence of any stimulus to aggregate demand, a period of full **depression** sets in and the economy will reach point B.

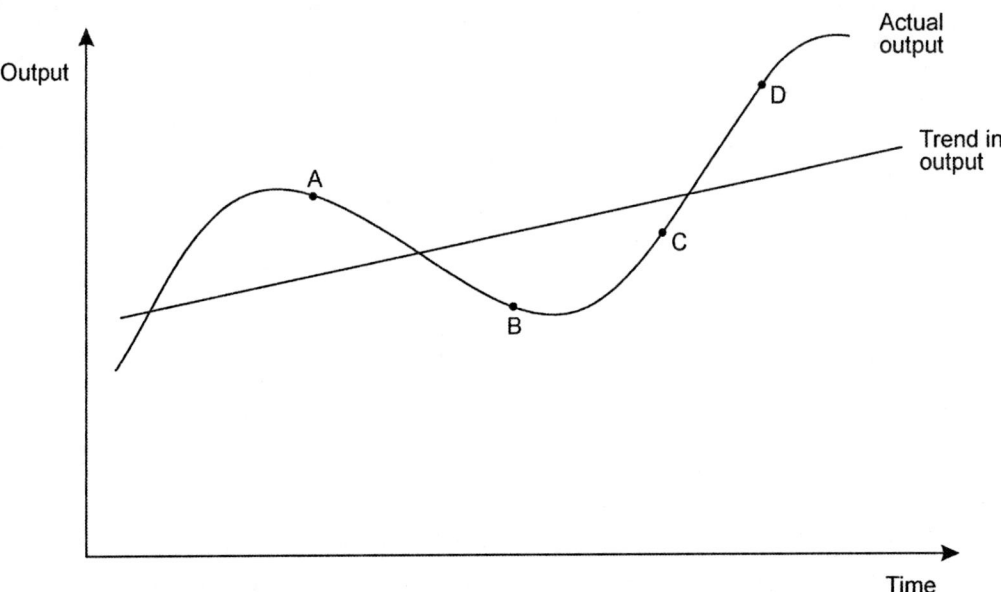

Figure 11 The business cycle

5.3 Analysis of the phases

Recession can begin relatively quickly because of the speed with which the effects of declining demand will be felt by businesses suffering a loss in sales revenue. The knock-on effects of destocking and cutting back on investment (accelerator theory) exacerbate the situation and add momentum to the recession. Public confidence is likely to be low, and aggregate demand across the economy will be falling. However, governments will try to limit the decline by boosting aggregate demand. They could do this through their fiscal policy: reducing taxation, lowering interest rates, or by raising public expenditure.

At point C in Figure 11 the economy has reached the recovery phase of the cycle. Once begun, the phase of recovery is likely to quicken as confidence returns. Output, employment and income will all begin to rise. Rising production, sales and profit levels will lead to optimistic business expectations, and new investment will be more readily undertaken. The rising level of demand can be met through increased production by bringing existing capacity into use and by hiring unemployed labour. The average price level will remain constant or begin to rise slowly.

In the recovery phase, decisions to purchase new materials and machinery may lead to benefits in efficiency from new technology. This can enhance the relative rate of economic growth in the recovery phase once it is under way.

As recovery proceeds, the output level climbs above its trend path, reaching point D, in the boom phase of the cycle. During the boom, capacity and labour will become fully utilised. This may cause bottlenecks in some industries which are unable to meet increases in demand, for example because they have no spare capacity or they lack certain categories of skilled labour, or they face shortages of key material inputs. Further rises in demand will, therefore, tend to be met by increases in prices (inflation) rather than by increases in production. In general, business will be profitable, with few firms facing losses. Expectations of the future may be very optimistic and the level of investment expenditure high.

Governments will be keen to prevent inflation becoming too high and may look to control aggregate demand by increasing taxes or raising interest rates.

It can be argued that wide fluctuations in levels of economic activity are damaging to the overall economic well-being of society. The inflation and speculation which accompanies boom periods may be inequitable in their impact on different sections of the population, while the bottom of the trade cycle may bring high unemployment. Governments generally seek to stabilise the economic system, trying to avoid the distortions of a widely fluctuating trade cycle.

Whereas in a recession they will try to bolster aggregate demand, during a boom they will try to keep it in check through raising taxation or interest rates, and by reducing public expenditure.

> **Exam focus point**
>
> It is important that you can not only recognise the characteristics of each phase of the business cycle, but also the appropriate policy for a government to employ at each stage.

5.4 Causes of the business cycle

According to the Keynesian approach to macroeconomics, the trade cycle is caused by fluctuations in aggregate demand and in particular by the interaction between the multiplier and the accelerator.

To see how this can happen, suppose that aggregate demand has increased. Because production is increasing, businesses have to invest more to keep up with their orders. This greater investment also has a multiplier effect, so it causes production to increase further – which requires a still higher rate of investment – which brings about still more increase in production via its multiplier effect – and so on.

Of course, this mutual reinforcement of the multiplier and the accelerator cannot go on forever, but it could explain why booms can go on for several years at a time. It can also explain why a recession occurs when production levels off. With production steady, businessmen only invest to replace their production capacity as it becomes obsolete. This means that investment could drop almost to zero, even though production is stable at a pretty high level.

This fall in investment demand will cause a reduction in aggregate demand and income. The Keynesian approach assumes that that economic fluctuations could be quite predictable and cyclical. This is where the term 'business cycles' comes from.

In practice, however, economic fluctuations may not be as predictable as the Keynesian approach assumes.

Chapter Roundup

- The **Keynesian model** provides a way of explaining how national income is determined, and how national income equilibrium is reached.
- **Aggregate demand** (AD) means the total demand for goods and services in the economy.
- **Aggregate supply** (AS) means the total supply of goods and services in the economy.
- There is a **circular flow of income** in an economy, which means that expenditure, output and income will all have the same total value.
- There are **withdrawals** from the circular flow of income (**savings, taxation, imports**) and **injections** into the circular flow (**investment, government spending, exports**).
- **Withdrawals** are movements of funds out of the cycle of income and expenditure between firms and households, leading to reduction in the circular flow.
- **Injections** are movements of funds into the circular flow, leading to increases in the circular flow of income
- **Demand management** policies involve the manipulation of total national expenditure (E) by influencing C, I, G or net exports (X – M).
- The total change in the level of national income, following an injection into the economy, will be greater than the initial injection, due to the **multiplier effect**.
- The ratio of the **total increase** in national income to an **initial injection** is called the **multiplier**.
- Changes in national income can also be explained partially by the **accelerator principle**, which is the mechanism by which changes in investment spending are proportionally greater than changes in consumption spending, and therefore investment spending is more susceptible to bigger upturns and downturns.
- **Accelerator principle**: the theory that investment changes disproportionately in response to change in output.
- **Business cycles** or **trade cycles** are the continual sequence of rapid growth in national income, followed by a slow-down in growth and then a fall in national income (recession). After a recession, the economy starts to recover and grow again, prompting national income to rise again.

PART D   PUBLIC SECTOR AND MACRO-ECONOMY

Quick Quiz

1   Which of the following is most likely to lead to an increase in aggregate demand in an economy?

   A   Increased saving
   B   Increased spending on imports
   C   Increased taxation
   D   Increased investment

2   What is meant by the terms marginal propensity to consume, and marginal propensity to save?

3   How might a government try to influence the volume of investment by firms?

4   Which of the following creates an injection into the circular flow of income?

   A   A firm increasing its inventories of finished goods, prior to a marketing campaign
   B   The purchase, by a pension fund, of shares in a newly privatised company
   C   Individuals depositing cash into an interest-bearing bank account
   D   The acquisition of one company by another company

5   The economy in a country is a closed economy with no government sector.

   Consumer expenditure = 50 + 0.6Y (where 'Y' = national income).

   Investment = 20

   What is the equilibrium level of national income in the country?

   A   50
   B   70
   C   125
   D   175

6   If the MPC is greater for the poor than the rich then a redistribution of national income in favour of the rich will:

   A   Raise savings out of a given income
   B   Increase the multiplier
   C   Decrease the MPS
   D   Stimulate import demand

7   If an economy has reached its equilibrium level of national income at full employment, which one of the following will lead to an inflationary gap occurring:

   A   Reducing government spending
   B   An expansion (rightward shift) in the aggregate supply curve
   C   An expansion of the workforce
   D   An expansion (rightward shift) in the aggregate demand curve

8   What is the multiplier effect?

9   In an aggregate demand and supply diagram, what would be the consequences if the aggregate supply curve shifted inwards?

   A   Prices would rise and national income would rise
   B   Prices would fall and national income would rise
   C   Prices would fall and national income would fall
   D   Prices would rise and national income would fall

10 In an economy, the marginal propensity to consume is 0.85. What is the multiplier in that economy?

Answers to Quick Quiz

1. **D** Investment is an injection into the circular flow of income in an economy, and therefore will be expected to increase aggregate demand.

    Saving, imports and taxation are all withdrawals, and so will reduce (rather than increase) aggregate demand.

2. When a household receives an increase in income, some will be spent and some will be saved. The proportion which is spent is the marginal propensity to consume, while the proportion which is saved is the marginal propensity to save.

3. Lower interest rates, investment grants and tax incentives may encourage investment. Governments can also stimulate demand by tax cuts or lower interest rates and improve business confidence by business friendly and growth enhancing policies like deregulation and controlling inflation. Policies to encourage technological development may also lead to increased investment.

4. **A** Increasing inventory levels is an investment in terms of the aggregate demand function (C + I + G + X), because the firm will have incurred expenditure to produce the extra items of inventory.

    Although the purchase of shares (Option B) or making a corporate acquisition (Option D) are both investments for the individuals or organisations concerned, they are merely the transfer of ownership of already-existing assets, and there is no creation of new non-current asset capital investment or inventories. From the point of view of the national economy as a whole, these do not count as investment and therefore do not provide an injection into the circular flow.

    The individual in Option C has chosen to save, rather than to spend, their cash. In economic terms, saving represents a withdrawal from the circular flow of income, rather than an injection into it.

5. **D** Equilibrium occurs when income = expenditure.

    In this case, expenditure comprises consumption plus investment (becase there are no imports or exports, and no government expenditure).

    So Y = 50 + 0.6Y + 20; which can be rearranged as 0.4 Y = 70

    70/0.4 = 175

6. **A** The rich will save more, not spend. The MPC is greater for the poor than the rich.

7. **D** If the economy is currently at its equilibrium level of national income at full employment, then increasing aggregate demand will lead to the creation of an inflationary gap (because aggregate demand will be now be greater than aggregate supply).

8. The multiplier explains how the increase in total national income will be much greater than an initial injection into an economy, due to the injection being recycled through the economy.

9. **D** If the aggregate supply curve shifts to the left, national income will fall. Because the aggregate demand curve is downward sloping, shifting the supply curve to the left will mean the intersection between supply and demand is at a higher price: prices will rise.

    This combination of rising prices and falling national income is characteristic of stagflation.

10. **6.67** The multiplier is $\dfrac{1}{1-\text{MPC}}$

    $$\dfrac{1}{1-0.85} = \dfrac{1}{0.15}$$

PART D PUBLIC SECTOR AND MACRO-ECONOMY

End of chapter question

Injections and withdrawals

(a) Explain what is meant by 'injections' and 'withdrawals' in the circular flow of income model **and** show their role in determining the level of national income. **(12 marks)**

(b) How might the business sector be affected if there were a rise in the savings rate in households? **(8 marks)**

(Total 20 marks)

Inflation and unemployment

Topic list	Syllabus reference
1 Inflation and its consequences	2.4
2 Unemployment	2.4
3 Unemployment and inflation	2.4

Introduction

Two of the key aims of macroeconomic policy are controlling price inflation and minimising the level of unemployment in a country.

In this chapter we will review the characteristics and consequences of inflation and unemployment, and then look at how they can be managed.

Not surprisingly, the Keynesians and monetarists differ in their views about the causes of inflation, the extent to which inflation creates unemployment and prevents economic growth, and the effectiveness of government measures to stimulate the economy.

1 Inflation and its consequences

FAST FORWARD — High rates of **inflation** are harmful to an economy. Inflation redistributes income and wealth. Uncertainty about the value of money makes business planning more difficult. Constantly changing prices impose extra costs.

1.1 Inflation

Key term

Inflation is a sustained increase in prices in an economy. It is also manifest in the decline in the purchasing power of money, because when the general price level rises each unit of currency buys fewer goods and services.

Historically, there have been very few periods when inflation has not been present in national economics. We discuss below why high rates of inflation are considered to be harmful. However, it is important to remember that **deflation** (falling prices) is normally associated with low rates of growth and even recession. It would seem that a healthy economy may require some inflation. This is recognised in the current UK inflation target of 2%, and the European Central Bank's target that inflation should be below 2% in the medium term. Certainly, if an economy is to grow, the money supply must expand, and the presence of a low level of inflation will ensure that growth is not hampered by a shortage of liquid funds.

If an economy's rate of inflation is higher than the target level, then the government will need to introduce disinflationary measures to reduce it.

In this context, it is very important to note the distinction between deflation and disinflation though.

Key term

Deflation is a sustained fall in prices in an economy; the opposite of inflation.

Disinflation is a slowdown in the rate of inflation in an economy. Unlike deflation (which refers to a fall in prices), prices continue to rise in a period of disinflation, but the rate at which prices are increasing slows down.

We can illustrate the distinction between the two using a simple example:

If the inflation rate in a country is 4% one year, 3% the following year, and 2% the year after that, this represents disinflation. Prices are still rising, but the rate at which they are rising is slowing down (4%, 3%, 2%.)

By contrast, if the inflation rate in another country is -2% over the same period, that country is experiencing deflation. The rate of inflation is negative, meaning that there is an absolute fall in prices.

1.2 Why is inflation a problem?

An economic policy objective which now has a central place in the policy approaches of the governments of many developed countries is that of stable prices. But why is a high rate of price inflation harmful and undesirable?

(a) **Redistribution of income and wealth**

Inflation leads to a redistribution of income and wealth in ways which may be undesirable. Redistribution of wealth might take place from suppliers to customers. This is because amounts payable or receivable lose 'real' value with inflation. For example, if you owed $1,000, and prices then doubled, you would still owe $1,000, but the **real value** of your debt would have been halved. In general, in times of inflation those with economic power tend to gain at the expense of the weak, particularly those on fixed incomes. Their nominal income will stay the same but the amount of goods and services they can buy with that income (its purchasing power) will fall.

(b) **Balance of payments effects**
If a country has a higher rate of inflation than its major trading partners, its exports will become relatively expensive and imports into it will be relatively cheap. As a result, the balance of trade will suffer, affecting employment in exporting industries and in industries producing import-substitutes. Eventually, the exchange rate will be affected.

(c) **Uncertainty of the value of money and prices**
If the rate of inflation is imperfectly anticipated, no one has certain knowledge of the true rate of inflation. As a result, no one has certain knowledge of the value of money or of the real meaning of prices. If the rate of inflation becomes excessive, and there is '**hyperinflation**', this problem becomes so exaggerated that money becomes worthless, so that people are unwilling to use it and are forced to resort to barter. In less extreme circumstances, the results are less dramatic, but the same problem exists. As prices convey less information, the process of resource allocation is less efficient and rational decision-making become much harder. Uncertainty about prices may also undermine business confidence because planning and forecasting may become less accurate.

(Remember, in Chapter 8 we identified that one of the functions of money is that it acts as a store value. However, it cannot fulfil this function during periods of hyperinflation.)

(d) **Wage bargaining**
Wage demands (particularly from trades' unions) will be increased in times of high inflation. If they are successful then a wage/price spiral will take hold, which will reinforce the problem.

(e) **Consumer behaviour**
People may stockpile goods fearing price increases later. This could create shortages for other people who haven't already stockpiled themselves.

1.3 Consumer price indices

We have already referred to the way in which inflation erodes the real value of money. In order to measure changes in the real value of money as a single figure, we need to group all goods and services into a single price index.

A **consumer price index** measures changes in the prices of goods and services which are bought by households. A weighting is decided for each item according to the average spending on the item by consumers.

Consumer price indices may be used for several purposes, for example as an indicator of inflationary pressures in the economy, as a benchmark for wage negotiations, and to determine annual increases in government benefits payments. Countries commonly have more than one consumer price index because one composite index may be considered too wide a grouping for different purposes.

Since 2003, the consumer price index (CPI) has been used as the basis for the UK's inflation target, so the 2% inflation target is measured against movements in CPI. Consumer prices are also used as the standardised index for measuring inflation across Europe. The standardised European measure is called the Harmonised Index of Consumer Prices (HICP).

As of 21 March 2017, the Consumer Prices Index started to include owner occupiers' housing costs (CPIH), which are excluded from CPI. Housing costs (in particular, mortgage payments and council tax) are a significant expense for many households, so CPIH has been developed to reflect that, and to provide a more comprehensive measure of inflation.

1.4 The RPI and the CPI

For many years, the rate of inflation in the UK used was measured with reference to the **Retail Prices Index (RPI)**. The RPI measures the percentage changes month by month in the average level of prices of the commodities and services, including housing costs, purchased by the great majority of households in the UK.

Unlike the RPI, the traditional CPI excluded most housing costs though (hence the move to introduce CPIH in March 2017).

1.5 The underlying rate of inflation

The term **underlying rate of inflation** is often used to refer to the retail price index (RPI) adjusted to exclude mortgage costs and sometimes other elements as well (such as the local council tax in the UK). The effects of interest rate changes on mortgage costs help to make the RPI fluctuate more widely than the underlying rate of inflation.

RPIX is the underlying rate of inflation measured as the increase in the RPI excluding mortgage interest payments. Another measure, called **RPIY**, goes further and excludes the effects of changes in sales tax (VAT) as well.

1.6 Causes of inflation

There are three main causes of inflation:

- Demand pull factors
- Cost push factors
- Excessive growth in the money supply (quantity theory of money)

1.7 Demand pull inflation

FAST FORWARD

> **Demand pull inflation** arises from an excess of aggregate demand over the productive capacity of the economy.

Key term

> **Demand pull inflation:** inflation resulting from a persistent excess of aggregate demand over aggregate supply, due to constraints on supply in the economy, for example if full employment levels have been reached.

Demand pull inflation occurs when the economy is buoyant and there is a high aggregate demand, in excess of the economy's ability to supply.

(a) Because aggregate demand exceeds supply, prices rise.

(b) Since supply needs to be raised to meet the higher demand, there will be an increase in demand for factors of production, and so factor rewards (wages, interest rates, and so on) will also rise.

(c) Since aggregate demand exceeds the output capability of the economy, it should follow that demand pull inflation can only exist when unemployment is low. A feature of inflation in the UK in the 1970s and early 1980s, however, was that high inflation occurred alongside high unemployment.

There are two main causes of demand pull inflation.

Fiscal. Government policies affect aggregate demand in an economy. For example, an increase in government spending or a reduction in taxes and interest rates will raise demand in the economy. However, if supply is relatively inelastic and expands to meet the increased demand, the result will be higher prices rather than the economic growth the government had intended.

Credit. If levels of credit extended to customers increase, expenditure is likely to follow suit. In this case, inflation is likely to be accompanied by customers increasing their debt burdens.

1.8 Cost push inflation

FAST FORWARD

Cost push inflation arises from increases in the costs of production, such as raw materials or wages.

Traditionally, Keynesian economists saw inflation as being caused by Demand pull factors. However, they now accept that Cost push factors are involved as well.

Cost push inflation occurs where the costs of factors of production rise regardless of whether or not they are in short supply, and where the rise in costs is not matched by an increase in productivity. This appears to be particularly the case with wages.

Key term

Cost push inflation: inflation resulting from an increase in the costs of production of goods and services, eg through escalating prices of imported raw materials or from wage increases.

In this context it is important to distinguish between **exogenous** and **endogenous** factors. Exogenous factors are things that cause inflation without being related to the level of aggregate demand in the economy. Endogenous factors are directly related to the level of aggregate demand in the economy.

Therefore, if wages rise even though the demand for labour has not increased, the wage rises are an exogenous factor which causes cost plus inflation.

1.9 Import cost factors

Import cost-push inflation occurs when the cost of essential imports rise regardless of whether or not they are in short supply. This has occurred in the past with the oil price rises of the 1970s.

Additionally, a fall in the value of a country's currency will have import cost-push effects since a weakening currency increases the price of imports. This has been the case in the UK following the so-called 'Brexit' referendum vote in June 2016 to leave the EU. A number of large-scale suppliers have increased the prices of the products (in the UK) as a result of a fall in the value of the pound (against the US dollar and the Euro).

This is another example of **exogenous** cost-push inflation, because the cost rise comes from outside the aggregate demand and aggregate supply in the country's economy.

1.10 Expectations and inflation

A further problem is that once the rate of inflation has begun to increase, a serious danger of **expectation-led inflation** will occur. This means that, regardless of whether the factors that have caused inflation are still persistent or not, there will be a perception of what inflation is likely to be, and so, to protect future income, wages and prices will be raised by the expected amount of future inflation. This can lead to the vicious circle known as the **wage-price spiral**, in which inflation becomes a relatively permanent feature, because of people's expectations that it will occur.

1.11 Money supply growth

In contrast to the cost push theory, monetarists argue that inflation is driven by cost factors, but rather it is caused by **increases in the supply of money** which lead in turn to excess demand for goods and services. There is a considerable debate as to whether increases in the money supply are a **cause** of inflation or whether increases in the money supply are a **symptom** of inflation.

Monetarists have argued that since inflation is caused by an increase in the money supply, inflation can be brought under control by reducing the rate of growth of the money supply.

Monetarism as a theory advocates that the level of national income and economic growth is determined by the quantity of money in circulation (the quantity theory of money). However, monetarism also argues that an **expansion of the money supply inherently leads to price inflation**, again as a result of the quantity theory of money.

> **Key term**
>
> **Quantity theory of money:** theory which argues that changes in the level of prices are caused predominantly by changes in the supply of money.

The **quantity theory of money** is expressed as: MV = PT (the **Fisher equation**)

where M = money supply
V = velocity of circulation (the average number of times money is used in a year)
P = the average price of each transaction
T = the number of transactions in a year

The equation is, in effect, restating the idea from national income accounting that national output must be equal to national income. MV must be equivalent to PT because they are two ways of measuring the same transactions.

However, monetarists also make some key assumptions when applying the quantity theory of money. Monetarists assume that the **velocity of circulation is constant** in the short run, and so are the **number of transactions** in a year. Therefore changes in price must be a function of money supply in the economy. In other words, P = f(M). Therefore if money supply grows at a faster rate than the level of output in the economy, then price levels will rise (inflation).

Keynesians, by contrast, challenge these assumptions. They do not accept that the velocity of circulation is constant or that the number of transactions remain constant, and argue that the relationship between the money supply and inflation is far more complex than the monetarists claim.

Question — Money supply and inflation

According to the Fisher equation, if an economy's money supply increases, what will happen to the level of prices in that economy?

Answer

The increase in the money supply will lead to an increase in price levels in the future.

1.12 Hyperinflation

The concept of 'hyperinflation' refers to an extreme and accelerating rate of inflation. In effect, hyperinflation means that inflation has become completely out of control.

The following table gives an indication of some real-world experiences of hyperinflation. You will note that the inflation rate is too high to be expressed in an annual rate, so it is expressed as a daily rate.

Country	Highest recorded month	Equivalent daily inflation rate	Time needed for prices to double
Hungary	July 1946	207%	15 hours
Zimbabwe	November 2008	98%	24.7 hours
Yugoslavia	January 1994	64.6%	1.4 days
Germany	October 1923	20.9%	3.7 days

The causes of hyperinflation are essentially monetary in origin:

1. Government seeks to maintain expenditure by compelling central banks to buy its bonds and to print additional currency despite there being nothing extra to buy with the money; or

2. Economic output has collapsed but the amount of money remains the same (or is rising) and so chases the goods available.

In the case of developing countries in Latin America and Africa some commentators have blamed the International Monetary Fund (IMF) for its willingness to keep lending money into countries where it increased demand in an economy unable to increase output.

The consequences of hyperinflation are such that the economy reaches the verge of collapse:

(a) **Flight from currency**: a rush to exchange money for any physical item that may hold it value better, or for a more stable currency. This causes prices to rise further and for the exchange rate to fall.

(b) **Unwillingness to use currency in exchange**: this leads to a collapse of normal trading and a return to direct exchange of goods for goods (sometimes called 'bartering').

(c) **Ad hoc policy responses**: the government seeks to fight the symptoms of hyperinflation by introducing price regulation to stop prices of foods rising, foreign exchange controls, and attempts to close banks to stop the further withdrawals of cash. Generally higher and higher denomination bank notes are issued, or the value of existing notes simply deemed to be 10, 100 or 1,000 times higher.

(d) **Impoverishment of lenders**: the real value of savings and loans collapse. This takes away the wealth of the saver and leads businesses to fail as the value of what they receive is not enough to keep their business going.

Policies to end hyperinflation include:

(a) **Launch a new currency with a fixed value:** this has the effect of restoring confidence

(b) **Allow use of foreign currency to conduct exchange:** this means people will switch to the stable currency and to stop using the domestic one until the inflation is ended.

2 Unemployment

> **FAST FORWARD**
>
> The monetarist concept of a stable equilibrium implies that with zero price inflation, there is a **natural optimal level of unemployment**, and a rate of economic growth and balance of trade position from which the economy will not deviate. Monetarism focuses on economic stability in the medium to long term, which can only be achieved by abandoning short-term demand management goals.

2.1 The rate of unemployment

The **rate of unemployment** in an economy can be calculated as:

$$\frac{\text{Number of unemployed}}{\text{Total workforce}} \times 100\%$$

The number of unemployed at any time is measured by government statistics. If the flow of workers through unemployment is constant then the size of the unemployed labour force will also be constant.

Flows into unemployment are:

(a) Members of the working labour force **becoming** unemployed

 (i) Redundancies
 (ii) Lay-offs
 (iii) Voluntary quitting from a job

(b) People **out** of the labour force **joining** the unemployed

    (i) School leavers or university graduates without a job
    (ii) Others (for example, carers) rejoining the workforce but having no job yet

Flows out of unemployment are:

- Unemployed people finding jobs
- Laid-off workers being re-employed
- Unemployed people stopping the search for work

In the UK, the monthly unemployment statistics published by the Office for National Statistics (ONS) count only the jobless who receive benefits.

The ONS also produce figures based on a quarterly survey of the labour force known as the International Labour Organisation measure (ILO measure) that provides seasonally adjusted monthly data. This figure is considered to be more useful because it is also an internationally comparable measure.

2.2 Consequences of unemployment

Unemployment results in the following problems.

(a) **Loss of output**. If labour is unemployed, the economy is not producing as much output as it could. Thus, total national income is less than it could be, because economic resources are not being fully used.

(b) **Loss of human capital**. If there is unemployment, the unemployed labour will gradually lose its skills, because skills can only be maintained by working.

(c) **Increasing inequalities in the distribution of income**. Unemployed people earn less than employed people, and so when unemployment is increasing, the poor get poorer.

(d) **Social costs**. Unemployment brings social problems of personal suffering and distress, and possibly also increases in crime such as theft and vandalism.

(e) **Increased burden of welfare payments**. This can have a major impact on government **fiscal policy**, because governments will have to pay out more in state benefits while collecting less through tax revenue.

2.3 Types and causes of unemployment

Unemployment may be classified into three major types, depending on the underlying causes.

Category	Comments
Frictional unemployment	It is inevitable that some unemployment is caused not because there are not enough jobs to go round, but because of the friction in the labour market (difficulty in matching quickly workers with jobs), caused perhaps by a lack of knowledge about job opportunities. These are imperfections in the labour market. In general, it takes time to match prospective employees with employers, and individuals will be unemployed during the search period for a new job. Frictional unemployment is temporary, lasting for the period of transition from one job to the next.
Structural	This occurs where long-term changes occur in the conditions of an industry. Structural unemployment is likely to result from either a long-term fall in demand for the good or service, or from changes in production methods which mean that labour-intensive production is replaced by capital-intensive production (technology). A feature of structural unemployment is high regional unemployment in the location of the industry affected.

11: INFLATION AND UNEMPLOYMENT

Category	Comments
Cyclical (or demand-deficient)	Past experience has shown that domestic and foreign trade go through cycles of boom, decline, recession, recovery, then boom again, and so on. (a) During recovery and boom years, the demand for output and jobs is high, and unemployment is low. (b) During decline and recession years, the demand for output and jobs falls, and unemployment rises to a high level. Keynes introduced the concept of 'demand-deficient' unemployment to illustrate that unemployment was a result of insufficient aggregate demand in the economy. Cyclical unemployment can be long-term, and a government might try to reduce it by doing what it can to minimise a recession or to encourage faster economic growth.

Frictional unemployment will be short-term. Structural unemployment and cyclical unemployment are longer term, and therefore more serious for an economy.

Exam focus point

A question on the May 2017 paper asked about these three types of unemployment.

To these three main categories we can add the following:

Seasonal unemployment occurs in certain industries, for example building, tourism and farming, where the demand for labour fluctuates in seasonal patterns throughout the year and where staff are often employed on temporary contracts.

Technological unemployment is a form of structural unemployment, which occurs when new technologies are introduced.

(a) Old skills are no longer required.
(b) There is likely to be a labour saving aspect, with machines doing the job that people used to do.

With automation, employment levels in an industry can fall sharply, even when the industry's total output is increasing.

Real wage unemployment is caused when the supply of labour exceeds the demand for labour, but real wages do not fall for the labour market to clear. This type of unemployment is normally caused by strong trade unions which resist a fall in their wages. Another cause of this type of unemployment is the minimum wage rate, when it is set above the market clearing level. Some people argue that real wage unemployment is a type of **voluntary unemployment**, which occurs when people are unwilling to work at existing wage rates.

The **causes of unemployment** can be summarised as follows.

Category	Comments
Demand-deficient	A fall in demand for goods and services means that the equilibrium level of output below the full employment position. The fall in aggregate demand could come from a fall in consumer expenditure; a fall in business investment (which will reduce aggregate demand); a decline in exports, or a fall in government expenditure.
Structural change	The demand for labour falls as a result of a significant change in the structure of an industry. This may result from: • Technological change (with machines and computers replacing people) • Shifts in the industry (for example, the decline in manufacturing industry in developed countries as it was relocated to cheaper, developing countries).

Category	Comments
	Note that service industries have now replaced manufacturing industries as the major source of employment in developed countries. This is indicative of structural change. New industries replace the declining ones, and provide new employment opportunities – provided the labour force have the skills required.
Supply side problems	In these situations, the aggregate supply curve shifts to the left, creating an equilibrium level of national income below the level of full employment.
	This shift could come from trade unions demanding higher wages for their members, labour market regulations such as minimum wage rates, or social security systems which allow workers to be better off by not working than working.
	Workers may also effectively be excluded from the labour market due to poor education and a lack of skills.
	It is possible that a rise in the cost of imported goods (particularly oil) could also lead to supply side unemployment. A steep rise in oil prices would raise production costs across an economy, and so could cause the aggregate supply curve to shift to the left. This leftward shift will lead to an increase in unemployment.

Exam focus point

You need to be familiar with all the different types and causes of unemployment for your exam.

2.4 Government employment policies

Job creation and reducing unemployment should often mean the same thing, but it is possible to create more jobs without reducing unemployment.

(a) This can happen when there is a greater number of people entering the jobs market than there are new jobs being created. For example, if 500,000 new jobs are created during the course of one year, but 750,000 extra school leavers are looking for jobs, there will be an increase in unemployment of 250,000.

(b) It is also possible to reduce the official unemployment figures without creating jobs. For example, individuals who enrol for a government-financed training scheme are taken off the unemployment register, even though they do not have full-time jobs.

A government can try several options to create jobs or reduce unemployment.

(a) **Spending more money directly on jobs** (for example, hiring more civil servants) or **funding public projects** (eg large-scale road or rail projects) which in turn will create demand for labour.

(b) **Encouraging growth** in the private sector of the economy. When aggregate demand is growing, firms will probably want to increase output to meet demand, and so will hire more labour.

(c) **Encouraging training in job skills**. There might be a high level of unemployment among unskilled workers, and at the same time a shortage of skilled workers. A government can help to finance training schemes, in order to provide a 'pool' of workers who have the skills that firms need and will pay for.

(d) **Offering grant assistance to employers** in key regional areas.

(e) **Encouraging labour mobility** by offering individuals financial assistance with relocation expenses, and improving the flow of information on vacancies.

Other policies may be directed at **reducing real wages to market clearing levels**.

(a) Abolishing '**closed shop**' agreements, which restrict certain jobs to trade union members

(b) Reviewing **minimum wage regulations**, to assess whether the level set for the minimum wage is preventing employers taking on new staff.

Question

Types of unemployment

Match the terms (1), (2) and (3) below with definitions A, B and C.

(1) Structural unemployment
(2) Cyclical unemployment
(3) Frictional unemployment

A   Unemployment arising from a temporary difficulty in matching unemployed workers with available jobs

B   Unemployment occurring in the downswing of an economy in between two booms

C   Unemployment arising from a long-term decline in a particular industry

Answer

The pairings are (1) C, (2) B and (3) A.

In recent years, the issue of unemployment has also become increasingly sensitive politically in the context of **migration**. Critics argue that immigrant workers displace domestic workers and therefore lead to an increase in unemployment.

However, supporters of immigration argue that migrant workers can relieve labour shortages, and therefore help to control wage inflation.

3 Unemployment and inflation

FAST FORWARD

There appears to be a connection between the **rate of inflation** and **unemployment**. The **Phillips curve** has been used to show the relationship between wage inflation and unemployment.

3.1 Unemployment and inflation

Managing unemployment and inflation are two of the key aspects that governments try to manage, and the two are often thought to be linked. It has been found that boosting demand to increase the level of employment can cause a higher rate of inflation. However, growth in unemployment can also be associated with a rising rate of inflation.

3.2 The meaning of full employment

The term full employment does not mean a situation in which everyone has a job. There will always be at least a certain **natural rate of unemployment**, which is the minimum level of unemployment that an economy can expect to achieve.

An aim of government policy might be to reduce unemployment to this minimum natural rate, and so get as close as possible to the goal of full employment. On the basis that unemployment cannot be kept below its natural rate without causing inflation, the natural rate of unemployment is sometimes called the **non-accelerating inflation rate of unemployment (NAIRU)**. But in order to understand the idea of a natural rate of unemployment more fully, we need to examine the **trade-off between unemployment and inflation** more closely.

3.3 Inflationary gaps and deflationary gaps

As we have seen where looking at national income, the equilibrium national income can be shown using an aggregate demand curve and an aggregate supply curve.

According to Keynes, **demand management** by the government could be based on government **spending and taxation policies** (fiscal policy). These could be used for two purposes.

(a) **To eliminate a deflationary gap** and create full employment. A small initial increase in government spending will start off a **multiplier-accelerator** effect, and so the actual government spending required to eliminate a deflationary gap should be less than the size of the gap itself.

(b) **To eliminate an inflationary gap** and take inflation out of the economy. This can be done by reducing government spending, or by increasing total taxation and not spending the taxes raised.

Keynesians accept that reductions in unemployment can only be achieved if prices are allowed to rise: reducing unemployment goes hand in hand with allowing some inflation.

3.3.1 Reflation

We noted in the previous chapter, that an inflationary gap arises if aggregate demand is at an equilibrium level in excess of the full employment level of output in an economy.

By contrast, a deflationary gap occurs where aggregate demand in an economy falls short of the level required for the equilibrium national income (AD = AS) to sustain full employment.

Under such circumstances, a policy of reflation may be necessary.

Reflation is a macroeconomic policy of **increasing aggregate demand** in an economy in order to reduce unemployment. Reflationary policies could include reducing taxes (fiscal policy), lowering interest rates (monetary policy) or increasing the money supply (so called 'quantitative easing' which we will discuss in the next year).

3.4 The Phillips curve

In 1958, A W Phillips found a statistical relationship between unemployment and the rate of money wage inflation which implied that, in general, **the rate of inflation falls unemployment rose and *vice versa***. A curve, known as a **Phillips curve**, can be drawn linking inflation and unemployment (Figure 1).

Key term

> **Phillips curve**: a graphical illustration of the inverse relationship which historically existed between the rate of wage inflation and the rate of unemployment.

Note the following two points about the Phillips curve.

(a) The curve crosses the horizontal axis at a positive value for the unemployment rate. This means that zero inflation will be associated with some unemployment; it is not possible to achieve zero inflation and zero unemployment at the same time.

(b) The shape of the curve means that the lower the level of unemployment, the higher the **rate of increase** in inflation.

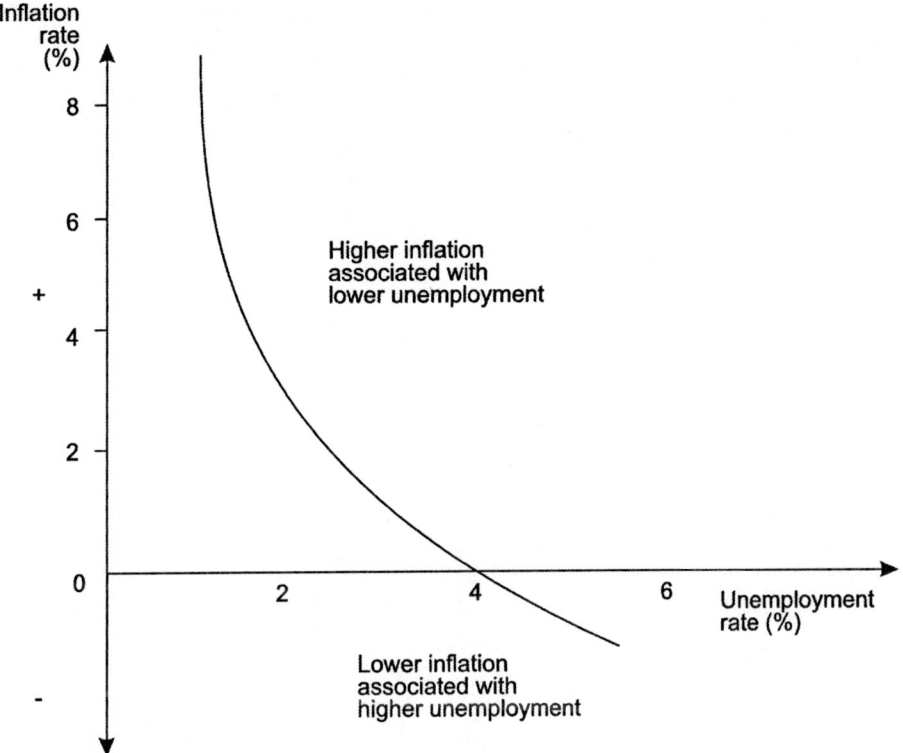

Figure 1 Phillips curve

The existence of a relationship between inflation and unemployment of the type indicated by the Phillips curve suggests that the government should be able to use **demand management policies** to take the economy to acceptable levels of inflation and unemployment.

This re-emphasises the argument of Keynesian economists that in order to achieve full employment, some inflation is unavoidable. If achieving full employment is an economic policy objective, a government must therefore be prepared to accept a certain level of inflation as a necessary evil.

The Phillips curve indicated that a government had to make a **choice between inflation or unemployment**. Price stability and full employment could not both be achieved together.

However, the Phillips curve relationship between inflation and unemployment broke down at the end of the 1960s when Britain began to experience **rising inflation at the same time as rising unemployment** (a phenomenon known as '**stagflation**').

But by the 1980s the relationship between inflation and unemployment had re-appeared, although at a higher absolute level of unemployment. The Phillips curve could be re-plotted, but it had shifted to the right. This was largely due to cost push pressures on inflation.

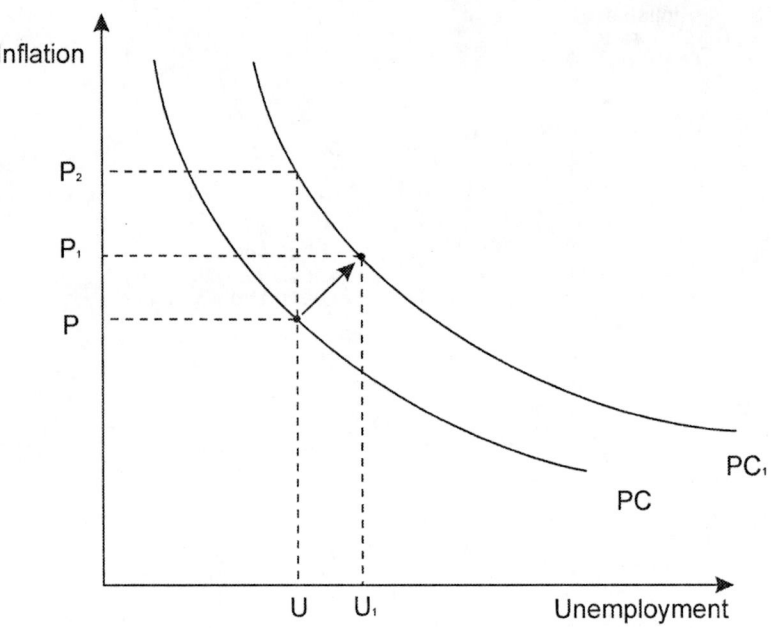

Figure 2 Shift in the Phillips curve

Cost push pressures had shifted the Phillips curve from PC to PC_1. If the government did not try to influence the level of aggregate demand, prices would rise to P_1 and unemployment to U_1. But if the government tried to bring down unemployment to U again, this would create **demand pull inflation**, increasing the general price level to P_2.

Once again though, this Phillips curve relationship appeared to break down in the 1990s where a number of Western countries enjoyed low unemployment alongside relatively low inflation.

Case Study

The UK, like many Western economies, enjoyed a sustained period of falling unemployment from the mid-1990s alongside low inflation rates. However, from 2006-7 this pattern began to change. Inflation began to rise, and CPI had reach 5.2% by October 2008, driven by a combination of rising fuel and commodity prices (which also directly affected food costs.) However, at the same time, unemployment started rising as the economy entered recession.

By 2008 (in the middle of the global financial crisis), the threat of **stagflation** loomed again, due to a combination of **weak economic growth, high inflation (cost-push inflation)** and **rising unemployment**.

3.5 The expectations augmented Phillips curve and NAIRU

The monetarist economist, Milton Friedman, developed an alternative approach to the Phillips curve to reflect the fact that **expectations** distort the inflationary process.

Friedman's model is known as the **expectations augmented Phillips curve**, and indicates that, although in the short run there may be trade-offs between inflation and unemployment, in the long run an economy is faced with a **vertical Phillips curve**, and there are inflationary expectations which reflect the rates of inflation that workers expect in the future.

Figure 3 illustrates why. The economy is initially in equilibrium with unemployment of U, and with very low inflation (PE_0).

The government tries to boost aggregate demand in the economy, and this reduces unemployment to U_1. However, it also creates excess demand in the labour market which prompts wage inflation.

This wage inflation in turn becomes price inflation, so workers are no better off in real terms than they were before the wage rise. In this case, the labour supply and hence unemployment returns to its previous level: U. Therefore the economy has found a new equilibrium with higher inflation (PE_1) and the original unemployment (U), because the price expectations in the market mean that the equilibrium rate of unemployment can now only be achieved at this higher rate of (wage) inflation. In effect, the short-run Phillips curve has shifted outwards from PC to PC_1.

These shifts in the **short-run** Phillips curves illustrate that a cycle of wage inflation has been created, but note that **long term** unemployment rate remains the same (at U on Figure 3). This means that governments can no longer base policies on the simple trade off between inflation and unemployment as proposed in the original Phillips curve.

Moreover, instead of trying to eradicate unemployment, governments need to accept that there is a natural rate of unemployment in the economy, and that this will also be the level at which inflation rates will be stable.

This natural rate of unemployment is called the **non-accelerating inflation rate of unemployment** (NAIRU), the level at which the rate of inflation is stable. (The NAIRU is also sometimes referred to as the **natural rate hypothesis**.)

NAIRU is a logical extension of the expectations-augmented Phillips curve, and is represented by U in Figure 3.

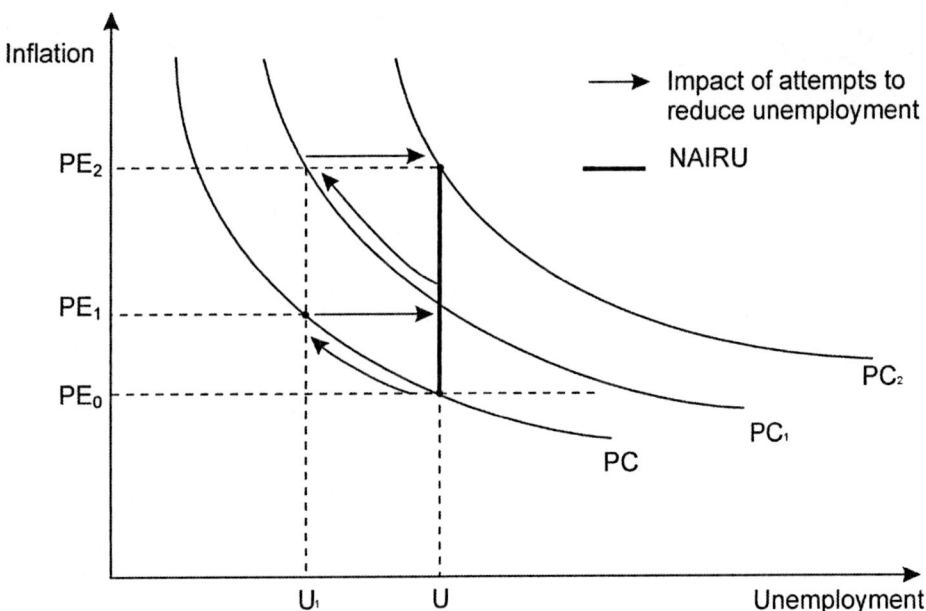

Figure 3 Expectations augmented Phillips curve

PART D   PUBLIC SECTOR AND MACRO-ECONOMY

Chapter Roundup

- High rates of **inflation** are harmful to an economy. Inflation redistributes income and wealth. Uncertainty about the value of money makes business planning more difficult. Constantly changing prices impose extra costs.

- **Demand pull inflation** arises from an excess of aggregate demand over the productive capacity of the economy.

- **Cost push inflation** arises from increases in the costs of production, such as raw materials or wages.

- The monetarist concept of a stable equilibrium implies that with zero price inflation, there is a **natural optimal level of unemployment**, and a rate of economic growth and balance of trade position from which the economy will not deviate. Monetarism focuses on economic stability in the medium to long term, which can only be achieved by abandoning short-term demand management goals.

- There appears to be a connection between the **rate of inflation** and **unemployment**. The **Phillips curve** has been used to show the relationship between wage inflation and unemployment.

Quick Quiz

1   What is the Phillips curve?

2   Name two types of short-term unemployment and two types of long-term unemployment.

3   Which one of the following is least likely to occur in a recession?

    A   An increase in inflation rates
    B   An increase in unemployment levels
    C   An increase in government spending
    D   An improvement in the balance of trade

4   Which one of the following is NOT an effect of inflation in an economy?

    A   Prices convey less information so rational decision making becomes harder
    B   The purchasing power of people on fixed incomes is reduced
    C   The balance of trade weakens as imports become more expensive
    D   Consumer behaviour will be distorted as consumers attempt to anticipate price changes

5   Structural unemployment is best defined as unemployment caused by:

    A   Lack of knowledge about job opportunities in the market
    B   The long term decline of particular industries
    C   Minimum wage rates being set above the market clearing wage
    D   The insufficient level of aggregate demand in the economy as a whole

11: INFLATION AND UNEMPLOYMENT

Answers to Quick Quiz

1. The Phillips curve is an illustration of the relationship between unemployment and inflation levels in an economy.

2. Short term unemployment: Seasonal, frictional
   Long term unemployment: two from: – Structural, technological, cyclical (demand-deficient), voluntary

3. A   Inflation rates are likely to fall due to the reduction in aggregate demand in the economy. The balance of trade position is likely to improve during a recession as demand for imports falls. Government spending will increase as government tries to bolster aggregate demand through public expenditure.

4. C   The balance of trade will weaken, but this will because **exports** become more expensive and imports become cheaper, leading to a decline in demand for exports and an increase in demand for imports.

5. B   Structural unemployment only affects certain industries. Option A describes frictional unemployment; C describes real wage unemployment; and Option D describes demand deficient (or cyclical) unemployment, because the problem is lack of aggregate demand in the economy as a whole.

End of chapter question

Macroeconomic environment (May 2008)

An economist has written to her Chief Executive who is thinking that the company should begin a significant programme of investment. The economist's letter is a warning of her concerns for the future macro-economic environment in which the business will be operating in the next few years. She has referred the Chief Executive to the diagram below:

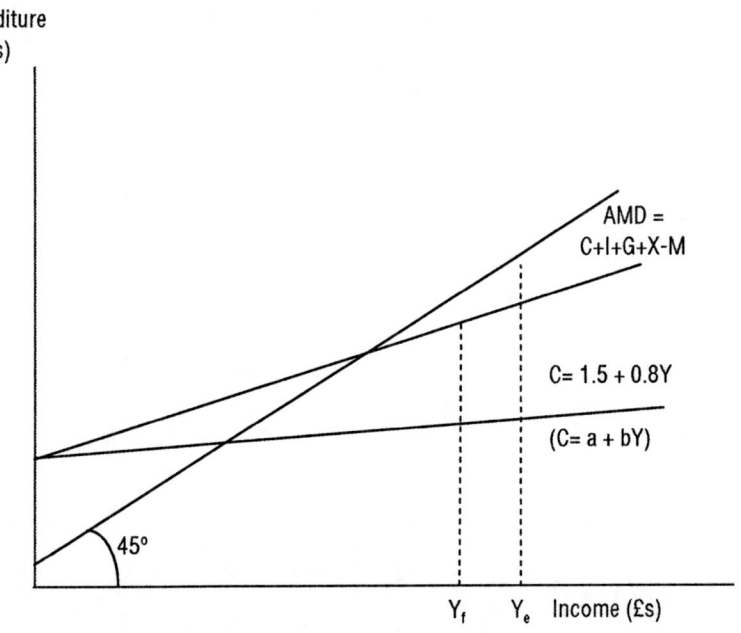

Y_e = LEVEL OF CURRENT NATIONAL INCOME

Y_f = NATIONAL INCOME AT FULL EMPLOYMENT

PART D   PUBLIC SECTOR AND MACRO-ECONOMY

Required

(a) Summarise the reasons why the diagram suggests an economy which may be in difficulty.

(6 marks)

(b) The economist in her letter mentions that she is particularly concerned that Government spending may be increased next year by a further £1billion.

   (i) From the diagram, why is this extra spending a concern? (2 marks)

   (ii) What is the expected increase in national income of this extra Government spending when the multiplier effect takes place? (4 marks)

   (iii) Why is this increased level of national income a worry for the economist? (4 marks)

(c) One concern for the economist in her letter is the longer term consequences for the company as a result of what the Government can be expected to do. What might the concerns of the economist be in this regard? (8 marks)

(d) Given the economist's concerns, what would you advise the Chief Executive to do about the planned programme of investment? (6 marks)

(Total 30 marks)

Managing unemployment and inflation (May 2016)

Managing unemployment and inflation are two of the key aspects that governments try to manage and the two are often thought to be linked. It has been found that boosting demand to increase the level of employment can cause a higher rate of inflation. However, growth in unemployment can also be associated with a decreasing rate of inflation.

Required

(a) Explain the meaning of 'unemployment' in the context of government policy. (5 marks)

(b) Explain 'demand management' by a government. List the two purposes of demand management in terms of dealing with unemployment based on government spending and taxation policies.

(6 marks)

(c) Draw and explain the Phillips curve. (9 marks)

(Total 20 marks)

Macroeconomic policy

Topic list	Syllabus reference
1 Government policies and objectives	2.4
2 Fiscal policy	2.4
3 Monetary theory	2.4
4 Monetary policy	2.4
5 Effectiveness of macroeconomic policy	2.4
6 Supply side policy	2.4
7 Summary of macroeconomic policies	2.4

Introduction

The previous chapter analysed the main macroeconomic phenomena such as inflation and unemployment. In this chapter we present an overview of the goals of macroeconomic policy in relation to these phenomena, and concentrate on three broad types of policy: fiscal policy, monetary policy and supply side policies.

First, we consider the role of fiscal policy in affecting aggregate demand, and we look at the different types of taxes which can be used as part of fiscal policy.

Next, we present alternative theories of how the money supply and interest rates affect the aggregate demand and we discuss the conduct of monetary policy.

Then, we examine the effectiveness of macroeconomic policy in controlling inflation and unemployment.

Finally, we discuss supply side policies which affect aggregate supply - in contrast to monetary and fiscal policies which affect aggregate demand.

PART D   PUBLIC SECTOR AND MACRO-ECONOMY

1 Government policies and objectives

> **FAST FORWARD**
>
> **Macroeconomic policy objectives** relate to economic growth, inflation, unemployment and the balance of payments.

1.1 Economic policy objectives

Nowadays, all governments are expected to manage their national economies to some extent. People generally suppose that government action can support or hinder the growth of prosperity in their country and look to their government for serviceable macroeconomic policies. There are four main objective of economic policy, though debate continues about their relative priority.

(a) **To achieve economic growth**, and growth in national income per head of the population. Growth implies an increase in national income in real terms. Increases caused by price inflation are not real increases at all.

(b) **To control price inflation** (to achieve stable prices). This has become a central objective of UK economic policy in recent years: to keep inflation (CPI) below the target figure of 2%.

(c) **To achieve full employment**. Full employment does not mean that everyone who wants a job has one all the time, but it does mean that unemployment levels are low, and involuntary unemployment is short-term.

(d) **To achieve a balance between exports and imports** (on the country's balance of payments accounts) over a period of years. The wealth of a country relative to others, a country's creditworthiness as a borrower, and the goodwill between countries in international relations might all depend on the achievement of an external balance over time.

Key terms

> **Fiscal policy** relates to government policy on taxation, public borrowing and public spending, and the impact these have on aggregate demand in an economy.
>
> **Monetary policy** - the way government or a central bank attempts to use money supply, interest rates, the availability of credit, or any other monetary variables, to achieve government objectives such as reducing inflation or reducing unemployment.
>
> Both fiscal and monetary policy attempt to attain the macroeconomic policy objectives by influencing **aggregate demand** in an economy.
>
> **Supply side** policies, on the other hand, attempt to the attain the macroeconomic policy objectives by shifting the aggregate supply curve in an economy.

2 Fiscal policy

> **FAST FORWARD**
>
> **Fiscal policy** provides a method of managing **aggregate demand** in the economy via **taxation** and **government spending**.

2.1 Fiscal policy and the Budget

Exam focus point

> Questions on fiscal policy often focus on the way government tax policy affects the level of aggregate demand in the economy.

A feature of fiscal policy is that a government must **plan** what it wants to spend, and so how much it needs to raise in income or by borrowing. It needs to make a plan in order to establish how much taxation

there should be, what form the taxes should take and which sectors of the economy (firms or households, high income earners or low income earners) the money should come from. This formal planning of fiscal policy is usually done once a year and is set out in **the Budget**.

The two components of the Budget which the government determines and through which it exercises its fiscal policy are:

(a) **Expenditure**. The government, at a national and local level, spends money to provide goods and services, such as a health service, public education, a police force, roads, public buildings and so on, and to pay its administrative work force. It may also, perhaps, provide finance to encourage investment by private industry, for example by means of grants.

(b) **Revenues**. Government expenditure must be financed, so the government must generate income. Most government income comes from **taxation**, although some income is obtained from **direct charges** to users of government services such as National Health Service charges.

A third element of the fiscal policy is:

(c) **Borrowing**. To the extent that a government's expenditure exceeds its income it must borrow to make up the difference. The amount that the government must borrow each year is now known as the **public sector net cash requirement (PSNCR)** in the UK. (Its former name was **public sector borrowing requirement (PSBR)**.) Where the government borrows from has an impact on the effectiveness of fiscal policy.

Key term

> The **public sector net cash requirement (PSNCR)** is the annual excess of spending over income for the entire public sector – not just the central government.

2.2 Budget surplus and budget deficit

If a government decides to use fiscal policy to influence demand in the economy, it can choose either expenditure changes or tax changes as its policy instrument. Suppose, for example, that the government wants to stimulate demand in the economy.

(a) **It can increase demand directly by spending more itself** – eg on the health service or education, and by employing more people itself.

   (i) This extra spending could be financed by higher taxes, but this would reduce spending by the private sector of the economy because the private sector's after-tax income would be lower.

   (ii) The extra government spending could also be financed by extra government borrowing. Just as individuals can borrow money for spending, so too can a government.

(b) **It can increase demand indirectly by reducing taxation** and so allowing firms and individuals more after-tax income to spend (or save).

   (i) Cuts in taxation can be matched by cuts in government spending, in which case total demand in the economy will not be stimulated significantly, if at all.

   (ii) Alternatively, tax cuts can be financed by more government borrowing.

Just as aggregate demand in the economy can be boosted either by more government spending or by tax cuts (in both cases leading to a higher PSNCR), so too can demand in the economy be reduced by cutting government spending or by raising taxes, and using the savings or higher income to cut government borrowing.

Expenditure changes and tax changes are not mutually exclusive options, of course. A government has several options.

(a) Increase expenditure and reduce taxes, with these changes financed by a higher PSNCR
(b) Reduce expenditure and increase taxes, with these changes reducing the size of the PSNCR
(c) Increase expenditure and partly or wholly finance this extra spending with higher taxes
(d) Reduce expenditure and use these savings to reduce taxes

When a government's income exceeds its expenditure, and there is a negative PSNCR or **public sector debt repayment (PSDR)**, we say that the government is running a **budget surplus**. When a government's expenditure exceeds its income, so that it must borrow to make up the difference, there is a PSNCR and we say that the government is running a **budget deficit**.

> **Budget deficit**: Government expenditure exceeds government revenue from taxation income.
>
> **Budget surplus**: Government expenditure is less than government revenue from taxation income.

2.3 Functions of taxation

Taxation has several functions.

(a) **To raise revenues for the government** and to finance the provision of public and merit goods such as defence, health and education.

(b) **To manage aggregate demand**. Aggregate demand could be boosted by lowering taxes, or it could be reduced by increasing taxes.

(c) **To provide a stabilising effect on national income**. Taxation reduces the effect of the multiplier, and so can be used to dampen upswings in a trade cycle – ie higher taxation when the economy shows signs of a boom will slow down the growth of money GNP and so take some inflationary pressures out of the economy.

The size of the multiplier, remember, is $\left(\dfrac{1}{s+m+t}\right)$ where 't' is the marginal rate of taxation.

(d) **To cause certain products to be priced to take into account their social costs**. For example, smoking entails certain social costs, including the cost of hospital care for those suffering from smoking-related diseases, and the government sees fit to make the price of tobacco reflect these social costs.

In a similar way, taxes could be used to discourage activities which are regarded as undesirable.

(e) **To redistribute income and wealth**. Higher rates of tax on higher incomes will serve to redistribute income. UK inheritance tax goes some way towards redistributing wealth.

(f) **To protect industries from foreign competition**. If the government levies a duty on all imported goods much of the duty will be passed on to the consumer in the form of higher prices, making imported goods more expensive. This has the effect of transferring a certain amount of demand from imported goods to domestically produced goods.

2.4 Qualities of a good tax

Adam Smith (in his seminal work *Wealth of Nations*) ascribed **four features to a good tax system**.

(a) **Equity**. People should pay according to their ability.

(b) **Certainty**. The tax should be well-defined and easily understood by all concerned.

(c) **Convenience**. The payment of tax should ideally be related to how and when people receive and spend their income (eg In the UK, PAYE is deducted when wages are paid, and sales tax (VAT) is charged when goods are bought).

(d) **Economy**. The cost of collection should be small relative to the yield.

Further features of a good tax can be identified.

(e) **Flexibility**. It should be adjustable so that rates may be altered up or down. For example, in the UK, the standard of sales tax (VAT) was reduced from 17.5% to 15% in 2008 to try to boost aggregate demand in the economy. The rate returned to 17.5% in January 2010, and was then increased to 20% in January 2011.

(f) **Efficiency**. A tax needs to achieve its objective efficiently, and avoidance should be difficult. However, the tax should not undermine other aims or taxes.

(g) It should attain its purpose **without distorting economic behaviour**.

2.4.1 Types of taxation

Taxation can be classified into three categories on the basis of what is being taxed.

(a) **Income** – income tax, corporation tax, national insurance
(b) **Expenditure** – sales tax (VAT), duties and levies.
(c) **Capital** – inheritance tax, capital gains tax

Taxes can also be categorised according to the percentage of income which is paid as tax by different groups in society.

(a) A **regressive tax** takes a higher **proportion** of a poor person's salary than of a rich person's. Television licences (the annual licence fee people have to pay in the UK to watch television) are an example of regressive taxes since they are the same for all people. Sales taxes (such as VAT) are also regressive because they are the same for all people, regardless of a person's income. Therefore, as their income rises, the tax represents a smaller percentage of a person's income.

(b) A **proportional tax** takes the **same proportion** of income in tax from all levels of income. So an income tax with a basic rate of tax at 20% is a proportional tax, (although it then becomes a progressive tax if higher income earners have to pay a higher rate than this basic rate).

(c) A **progressive tax** takes a **higher proportion** of income in tax as income rises. Income tax as a whole in the UK is progressive, since the first part of an individual's income is tax-free due to personal allowances and the rate of tax increases in steps from 20p in £1 (basic rate) to 40p in £1 (higher rate) and 45p in £1 (additional rate) as taxable income rises.

FAST FORWARD

> **Direct taxes** have the quality of being **progressive** or **proportional**. Income tax is usually progressive, with higher rates of tax charged on higher bands of taxable income. **Indirect taxes** can be **regressive**, when the taxes are placed on essential commodities or commodities consumed by poorer people in greater quantities.

2.5 Advantages and disadvantages of progressive taxation

Arguments in favour of progressive direct taxes

(a) **They are levied according to the ability of individuals to pay**. Individuals with a higher income are more able to afford to give up more of their income in tax than low income earners, who need a greater proportion of their earnings for the basic necessities of life. If taxes are to be raised according to the ability of people to pay (which is one of the features of a good tax suggested by Adam Smith) then there must be some progressiveness in them.

(b) **Progressive taxes enable a government to redistribute wealth from the rich to the poor in society**. Such a redistribution of wealth will alter the consumption patterns in society since the poorer members of society will spend their earnings and social security benefits on different types of goods than if the income had remained in the hands of the richer people. Poorer people are also likely to have a higher marginal propensity to consume than richer people, so leaving more income

in the hands of the poorer people is likely to increase aggregate demand in the economy as a whole.

(c) **Indirect taxes tend to be regressive and progressive taxes are needed as a counter-balance** to make the tax system as a whole more fair.

Arguments against progressive taxes

(a) **In an affluent society, there is less need for progressive taxes than in a poorer society.** Fewer people will live in poverty in such a society if taxes are not progressive than in a poorer society.

(b) **Higher taxes on extra corporate profits might deter entrepreneurs** from developing new companies because the potential increase in after-tax profits would not be worth the risks involved in undertaking new investments.

(c) **Individuals and firms that suffer from high taxes might try to avoid or evade paying tax** by transferring their wealth to other countries, or by setting up companies in tax havens where corporate tax rates are low. However, tax avoidance and evasion are practised whether tax rates are high or low. High taxes will simply raise the relative gains which can be made from avoidance or evasion.

(d) When progressive taxes are harsh, and either tax high income earners at very high marginal rates or tax the wealthy at high rates on their wealth, **they could act as a deterrent to initiative**. Skilled workers might leave the country and look for employment in countries where they can earn more money.

2.6 Proportional and regressive taxes

It is often argued that tax burdens should be **proportional** to income in order to be fair, although a proportional tax has the following disadvantages.

(a) A large administrative system is needed to calculate personal tax liabilities on a proportional basis. The costs of collecting income tax relative to tax revenues earned can be high, particularly in the case of lower income taxpayers.

(b) Such a tax does not contribute towards a redistribution of wealth among the population.

In the case of a **regressive** tax, a greater proportionate tax burden falls on those least able to afford it. The main disadvantage of a regressive tax is that it is not fair or equitable. The main advantage of a regressive tax is that it is often relatively easy to administer and collect.

Question   Taxation types

Below are details of three taxation systems, one of which is regressive, one proportional and one progressive. Which is which?

	Income before tax $	Income after tax $
System 1	10,000	8,000
	40,000	30,000
System 2	10,000	7,000
	40,000	28,000
System 3	10,000	9,000
	40,000	38,000

Answer

	Tax paid on low income %	Tax paid on high income %	Nature of tax
System 1	20	25	Progressive
System 2	30	30	Proportional
System 3	10	5	Regressive

2.7 Direct and indirect taxes

FAST FORWARD

A government must decide how it intends to raise tax revenues, from **direct or indirect taxes**, and what proportion of tax revenues will be raised from each source.

A **direct tax** is paid directly by the person or business on whom the tax is imposed. Examples of direct taxes in the UK are income tax, corporation tax, capital gains tax and inheritance tax. A direct tax can be levied on income and profits, or on wealth. Direct taxes tend to be progressive or proportional taxes. They are also usually unavoidable, which means that they must be paid by everyone.

An **indirect tax** is collected by an intermediary who then passes it on to the person who ultimately bears the economic burden of the tax. So, for example, when a consumer in the UK pays VAT on a product purchase, the retailer collects the tax as part of the purchase price, but the consumer bears the burden of the tax (because purchase price is higher than it would be if it didn't include VAT). Indirect taxes are taxes on spending.

There are two types of indirect taxes:

- A **specific tax** is charged as a fixed sum per unit sold.
- An **ad valorem tax** is charged as a fixed percentage of the price of the good.

2.7.1 Incidence of tax

We can also distinguish between the **formal** and **real incidence of a tax**. The formal incidence relates to the person **administering** the tax, the real incidence relates to the person who bears the **burden** of the tax. So, for VAT, the formal incidence lies with retailers, the real incidence passes to the consumer.

We can illustrate the impact of the incidence of taxation graphically in Figure 1.

The imposition of a sales tax causes the supply curve to shift to the left (S to S_t) because producers will reduce their supply at any given price due to part of the sales price being paid to the government. A new equilibrium will be reached, but this will be at a higher price and lower quantity than the pre-tax equilibrium.

The tax per unit is represented by the vertical distance between the supply curves ('a – b' on Figure 1). However, the burden of tax is split between the producer and the consumer.

The distribution of the tax burden between producer and consumer will depend on the **elasticity of demand**. When demand is **elastic**, the **producer** bears the greater burden of tax. When demand is **inelastic**, the **consumer** bears the greater burden of tax.

In Figure 1, demand is relatively inelastic, and we can see that the consumer bears a greater proportion of the burden of the tax than the producer.

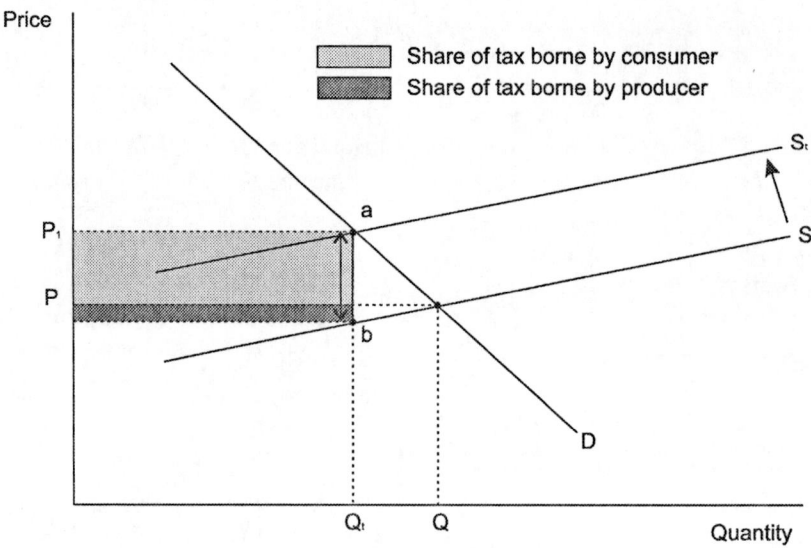

Figure 1 Incidence of taxation

2.8 Advantages of direct taxation on income

The main advantages of direct taxes on income are that they can be made **fair** and equitable by being designed as progressive or proportional to the degree desired. Because of their generally progressive nature they also tend to stabilise the economy, automatically taking more money out of the system during a boom and less during depression. Moreover, because they are more difficult to pass on, they are less inflationary than indirect taxes. Finally, taxpayers know what their tax liability is.

2.9 Disincentive effects

A direct tax on **profits might act as a disincentive to risk-taking and enterprise**. The tax will reduce the net return from a new investment and any disincentive effects will be greater when the tax is progressive. In addition, a tax on profits will reduce the ability to invest. A considerable part of the finance for new investment comes from retained profits, so any tax on corporate profits will reduce the ability of firms to save and therefore limit the sources of funds for investment.

High taxation acts as a disincentive to work for legitimate employees because if **marginal tax rates** (ie the proportion of additional income taken as tax) are high, individuals are likely to behave in one of two ways.

(a) They may forego opportunities to increase income through additional effort on the basis that the increase in net income does not adequately reward the effort or risk.

(b) They may resort to working in the parallel 'black' economy to avoid paying the tax.

2.10 The Laffer curve and tax yields

Key term

Laffer curve: a curve depicting the relationship between tax revenue and the average tax rate, designed to illustrate the thesis that there is an optimal tax rate at which tax revenues are maximised.

The **Laffer curve** (named after Professor Arthur Laffer) illustrates the effect of tax rates upon government revenue and national income.

In the hypothetical economy depicted in Figure 2 a tax rate of 0% results in the government receiving no tax revenue irrespective of the level of national income. If the rate is 100% then nobody will work because they keep none of their earnings and so once again total tax revenue is zero. In our example, at 25% tax rates the government will achieve a total tax take of $30bn; the same as the revenue they enjoy tax at rates of 75%. By deduction, the level of national income when taxes are 25% must be $120bn compared with only $40bn if taxes are 75%. High taxation appears to operate as a disincentive and reduce national income.

The government will be keen to identify the tax rate 'T_r' which maximises revenue, and it will not want to set taxes higher than that, because if it does the taxes become a disincentive to work.

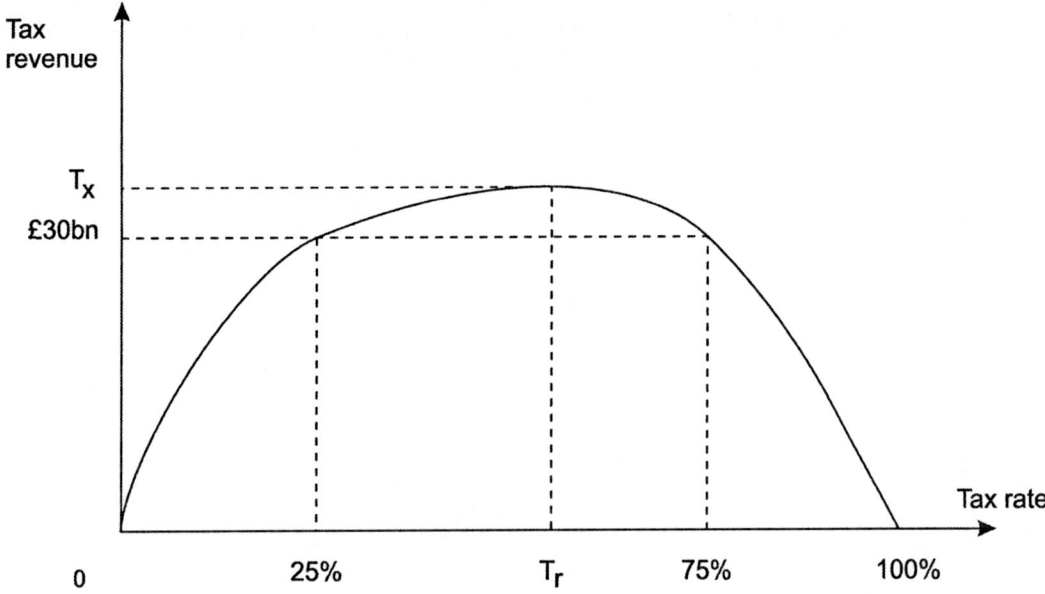

Figure 2 Laffer curve for a hypothetical economy

Three consequences flow from this Laffer curve analysis.

(a) **High rates of taxation act as a disincentive to work** and accordingly reduce output and employment, because people will substitute leisure for work. This is known as the **disincentive effect**.

(b) Governments cannot always expect to increase tax revenue by increasing tax rates. There appears to be a crucial tax rate beyond which the fall in national income resulting from the erosion of incentives and effort outweighs the increased tax rate. In Figure 2 the maximum tax revenue is T_x, at average tax rate T_r. If tax rates are above T_r, the government can increase tax revenues by cutting tax rates.

(c) There will always be two tax rates available which can yield the same total tax revenue: one associated with a high level of national income and another associated with a lower level. In consequence, governments committed to high government expenditure need not necessarily be associated with high rates of tax. Taxes could be set at the lower of the two rates and earn just the same amount of revenue as if they had been set at the higher amount.

In addition the following arguments can be made against high tax rates.

When income tax is levied at a high rate, it could act as a disincentive to work.

The idea of the **marginal tax rate** is important here. This is the rate of tax paid on an extra unit of income.

The marginal tax rates facing economic agents are often important in determining how tax affects a decision to work or not. For example, is it worth taking a higher paid job or working overtime if the majority of the additional income you earn will have to be paid over as tax?

The importance of this from a government's perspective is that if it sets the tax rate too high, tax yield will fall because workers will choose to have leisure time instead of working. In this case, the tax is no longer efficient.

Another danger of setting income tax too high is that it could encourage a '**brain drain**'. If a country has high marginal rates of taxation, this might cause a migration of highly skilled – and therefore highly paid – workers to countries with tax regimes that are more favourable for them. This means that the country with the high tax rates not only loses the potential tax revenue from these high earners, but it also loses their valuable skills.

High marginal tax rates, by narrowing the differentials in the after-tax pay of skilled and unskilled labour, may reduce the incentive to train and thereby cause a shortage of skilled labour.

High marginal tax rates may also be seen as creating a '**poverty trap**'. For example, if people are not working, they receive unemployment benefit. Once they find a job they will no longer receive their unemployment benefit, but will have to pay tax on their income instead. If tax rates are felt to be too high there would be little incentive for an unemployed worker to accept a low paid job. However, if direct taxes are lower, then workers will be more likely to accept the job because their post tax income will be higher.

High marginal rates of tax could **encourage tax avoidance** (finding legal loopholes in the tax rules so as to avoid paying tax). In the UK, high tax rates led to a growth of making income payments-in-kind by way of fringe benefits, for example, free medical and life insurance, preferential loans and favourable pension rights. The tax authorities responded to this by bringing an increasing number of fringe benefits into the tax net – for example, the private use of a company car.

In some cases individuals and companies may resort to **tax evasion**, which is the illegal non-payment of tax. Employed people have limited scope for tax evasion, because of the **pay as you earn** (PAYE) tax system in the UK. Undoubtedly, the self-employed have a greater ability to evade tax by failing to declare earnings. If evasion becomes widespread the cost of enforcing the tax laws may become very expensive.

Reductions in tax liability may encourage workers to accept lower wage increases, and this will mean there is less inflationary pressure from high wage claims.

2.11 Indirect taxation: advantages and disadvantages

Indirect taxes are hidden in the sense that the taxpayer is frequently unaware of the amount of tax he is paying, so that it is almost painlessly extracted (for example, in the high rate of tax on beer and spirits). This has considerable advantages from the government's point of view.

Indirect taxation can be used to encourage or discourage the production or consumption of particular goods and services and hence affect the allocation of resources. For example, the production of goods that produce environmental pollution may be taxed as a means of raising the price in order to reduce demand and output. Similarly, the consumption of cigarettes can be discouraged by high indirect taxation.

Question
Indirect tax

The burden of an indirect tax must either be borne by the producer or passed on by the producer to consumers. If a producer feels able to pass on the whole of the burden, what can you deduce about the elasticity of demand for his product?

Answer

Demand for the product must presumably be inelastic, at least in the opinion of the producer. Otherwise he would fear to pass on the tax burden by increasing his prices as this would lead to a fall in demand.

The effectiveness of indirect taxation is likely to depend on price elasticity of demand. If a good is price inelastic, then sales will not fall much when the tax is included in the price. By contrast, if a sales tax is added onto a good with elastic demand, demand will fall significantly following the increase in price.

Consequently, the amount of indirect tax revenue generated is likely to be higher when imposed on a good with inelastic demand than on one with elastic demand. This is another reason (alongside health issues) whey indirect taxes are imposed on alcohol and cigarettes – because they have price inelastic demand.

Indirect taxation is a relatively **flexible instrument of economic policy**. The rates of indirect taxes may be changed to take effect immediately. In the case of direct taxes, more notice must be given to the taxpayer.

Indirect taxes can be **cheap to collect**. Traders and companies are required to act as collectors of value added tax in the UK, thus reducing the administrative burden on government.

Indirect taxes do have disadvantages however.

(a) **They can be inflationary**. When prices are rising, the burden of *ad valorem* indirect taxes will naturally rise also. However, a specific indirect tax will only be inflationary if the rate at which it is applied is changed.

(b) **Indirect taxes also tend to be regressive**. A broadly levied indirect tax like VAT is likely to be quite regressive because the poorer members of the community spend a much larger proportion of their income than very rich people. A system of indirect taxes on luxury goods would not be regressive, however.

(c) **Indirect taxes are not completely impartial in their application in other ways**. For example, someone who seeks to relax with a drink in a pub is going to be much more heavily hit by indirect taxes than someone who likes walking (because of the taxes on alcohol). The differential taxes, moreover, prevent resources from being distributed optimally according to consumer preference. Unlike an income tax, indirect taxes change the relative price of goods. This means that consumers have to arrange their patterns of expenditure accordingly. This substitution may involve loss of satisfaction.

(d) Like taxes on incomes, **indirect taxes may be evaded by some**. The so-called 'black economy', in which cash payments are made and income is not declared for tax purposes, is undoubtedly large and widespread in the UK, particularly in the self-employed sector.

2.12 Fiscal policy and aggregate demand

Fiscal policy is concerned with **government spending** (an injection into the circular flow of income) and **taxation** (a withdrawal from the circular flow).

(a) If government spending is increased, there will be an increase in the amount of **injections**, expenditure in the economy will rise and so national income will rise (either in real terms, or in terms of price levels only; that is, the increase in national income might be real or inflationary).

(b) If government taxation is increased, there will be an increase in **withdrawals** from the economy, and expenditure and national income will fall. A government might deliberately raise taxation to take inflationary pressures out of the economy.

A government's **'fiscal stance'** may be **neutral, expansionary** or **contractionary,** according to its effect on national income.

(a) **Spending more money** and financing this expenditure by borrowing would indicate an expansionary fiscal stance.

(b) **Collecting more in taxes** without increasing spending would indicate a contractionary fiscal stance.

(c) Collecting more in taxes in order to **increase spending**, thus diverting income from one part of the economy to another would indicate a broadly neutral fiscal stance.

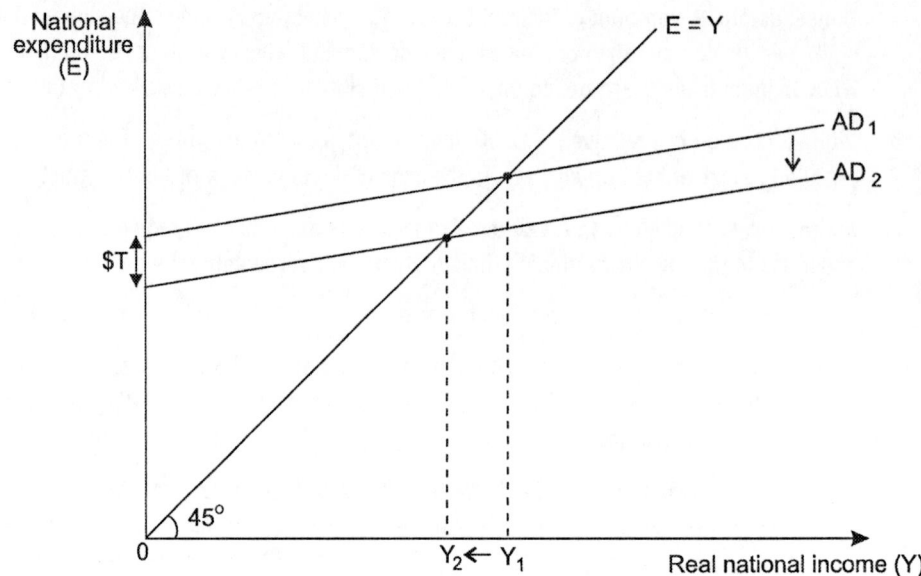

Figure 3 Increase in taxation

An increase in taxation by $T in Figure 3, without any matching increase in government expenditure, would **reduce** the aggregate expenditure in the economy from AD_1 to AD_2 and so the money value of national income would fall from Y_1 to Y_2. This would result in either a fall in real output or it would dampen inflationary pressures.

Similarly, a reduction in taxation without any reduction in government spending would **increase** the money value of national income. This would either cause real output to increase, or it would lead to price rises and inflation.

2.13 Fiscal policy and unemployment

Fiscal policy can be used to reduce unemployment and provide jobs.

(a) More government spending on capital projects would create jobs in the construction industries.

(b) Government-funded training schemes are a means of spending by government to improve training, so as to make people more qualified for jobs in private industry.

(c) A government might tax companies on the basis of the numbers and pay levels of people they employ (as with employers' national insurance contributions). Lower employment taxes would possibly make employers more willing to take on extra numbers of employees.

If government raises taxes and government spending by the same amount, so that the budget remains in balance, there will be an **increase in aggregate monetary demand**. This is because tax payers would have saved some of the money they pay in increased tax while the government spends all of its revenue within the economy. This effect is called the **balanced budget multiplier**.

Government spending, however, might create inflationary pressures. Fiscal policy must therefore be used with care, even to create new jobs.

2.14 Other effects

Since government spending or tax reductions might be inflationary, and higher domestic prices make imports relatively cheaper and exports less competitive in foreign markets, fiscal policy has possible implications for the **balance of payments** (which we will discuss in the chapter on international trade later in this Study Text).

The impact of changes in fiscal policy is not always certain, and fiscal policy to pursue one aim (eg lower inflation) might, for a while at least, create barriers to the pursuit of other aims (eg employment).

2.15 Crowding out

Deficit budgets have been criticised on the grounds that they '**crowd out**' private sector activity; that is, the government spending merely replaces private spending with no net increase in aggregate demand. In particular, it is suggested that increased government borrowing to finance government expenditure inevitably leads to higher interest rates, which, in turn, lead to a reduction in private borrowing for both consumption and investment. The Keynesian response to this criticism is to say that crowding out will not occur when there are **idle resources** within the economy, such as a large number of unemployed people.

2.16 The success of fiscal policy as a method of demand management

The success of fiscal policy as a means of influencing the economy sufficiently has been called into question.

(a) At the end of the 1970s, an analysis of fiscal policy in the UK concluded that the multiplier effect of various policies was quite small (perhaps less than 1.0 after the first year). The implication of this conclusion is that to increase government spending by borrowing more might have a disappointingly small effect on demand and employment in the UK.

(b) Expansion and contraction of the economy are both subject to the effect of **automatic stabilisers**. There are two types:

   (i) Tax revenues that rise as national income rises. Nearly all taxes fall into this category.

   (ii) Government expenditures that fall as national income rises. Welfare payments associated with unemployment and low incomes make up the bulk of this category.

The effect of automatic stabilisers is to reduce the value of the **multiplier**, thus dampening the rate of both expansion and contraction. When the economy is in the process of recovering from a recession the effect of the automatic stabilisers is called **fiscal drag**.

2.17 The National Debt

Key term

> The **National Debt** is the amount of debt owed by the **central government** of a country to its various creditors.

Creditors of the government may be nationals of the country (eg investors in government loan stock) or foreign nationals (perhaps foreign banks or even the International Monetary Fund (IMF)).

When the National Debt is high, interest repayments will account for a large proportion of central government expenditure. It is therefore important that when a government borrows money, it should be invested or spent in such a way as to ensure that sufficient income is eventually generated to repay the interest and debt capital. If a government is unable to do this (as in the case of many developing and less developed countries at the moment) it will lose its creditworthiness and find future loans much harder to come by.

Case Study

In late 2009, international confidence in Greece's economy plummeted when two rating agencies (Standard & Poor's; and Fitch) downgraded its credit ratings, concerned about the mounting public sector deficit in the country, and the government's ability to deal with the debt burden.

By the summer of 2015, Greece's debt burden (primarily to the EU and the IMF) was in excess of €300bn, and Greece's place in the EU was in jeopardy when it defaulted on a key debt repayment to the IMF. In July 2015, Eurozone leaders agreed a bailout deal to help Greece pay its arrears with the IMF, although that was widely viewed as a temporary fix rather than a way of starting to tackle Greece's underlying economic problems.

2.18 Servicing the National Debt and the burden on society

To service the National Debt, a government must pay interest on the debt and make capital repayments when they fall due. However, the problem of making capital repayments can be overcome, if required, by taking out new loans when old loans mature (eg to repay a loan of $100 million, a government can borrow a further $100 million).

If the loan is obtained from the private sector of the country's economy, the National Debt and servicing the debt involve the transfer of funds between different sections of society. When the government borrows, it takes money from one group and spends it on other sections of society. When the government pays interest, it will raise money in taxes from the rest of society and pay this money to its creditors. Once again, this involves a transfer of the funds.

Servicing the National Debt thus involves two processes.

(a) A redistribution of funds within society, through government borrowing and spending, or through taxation to pay debt interest.

(b) Borrowing to spend now and only repaying the debt with interest later. In other words, society benefits now, and the payment burden falls on society in later years, perhaps in some cases as long as a generation or so later.

When money is borrowed from abroad, the flow of funds in obtaining the money and in repaying the debt crosses national boundaries, and so there are implications for the balance of payments and the exchange rate of the domestic currency. Repaying a debt to foreign debtors also places a burden on society, because the money raised from taxes to service the debt must be paid abroad.

2.19 Public expenditure control

FAST FORWARD

If the government kept its own spending at the same level, but **reduced levels of taxation**, it would also **stimulate demand** in the economy because firms and households would have more of their own money after tax for consumption or saving/investing.

If the entire public sector had a balanced budget, the PSNCR would be nil. When there is an annual excess of income over expenditure, some of the National Debt can be repaid and so there is a public sector debt repayment (PSDR).

To reduce the size of the PSNCR, a government must either reduce its expenditure or raise its income from taxation. The sale of nationalised industries to the private sector is another source of funds.

Keynesian economists argue the need for **more government spending in a recession** to boost demand in the economy and create jobs. An argument put forward is that it makes sound financial sense to use current revenues from taxation to meet current expenditures and interest payments on debt, but to use borrowing for capital expenditure needs. Since taxation revenue exceeds current spending, the argument concludes that the government should borrow more for capital spending.

However, there needs to be a degree of caution here. If public expenditure is increased too much it is likely to place a considerable burden of taxation on companies and individuals in the future when the government looks to reduce the level of public debt.

Question — Government budget

Why might a government's budget vary from time to time, sometimes being in balance, sometimes in surplus and sometimes in deficit?

> **Answer**

A budget deficit occurs where expenditure exceeds income and a budget surplus occurs where expenditure is less than income.

In a mixed economy like that of the United Kingdom, the level of economic activity fluctuates depending upon where we are in the trade cycle. During the upturn in the trade cycle production is rising, firms and individuals earn more profits and wages so the government should collect more revenue. Unemployment should also fall during this period, and so government expenditure should fall. At this stage of the cycle, the budget may be in surplus.

During the downturn of a trade cycle, the reverse applies. Profits and incomes fall and government revenue falls, but unemployment rises and government expenditure on unemployment benefit rises. There is then more likely to be a budget deficit.

Keynes suggested that budget deficits should be used to help an economy out of recession. According to Keynes, unemployment was caused by a lack of aggregate demand in the economy. So if the government increased its expenditure, this would raise aggregate demand.

Using Keynesian policies, a government may plan a budget deficit to boost aggregate monetary demand. Increased government expenditure might be on infrastructure such as roads, schools or the health service. Alternatively, taxes could be cut to increase consumers' disposable incomes. The objective would be to close the 'deflationary gap' that is seen to be preventing the economy reaching a level of full employment. Thus, variations in the budget balance can be the result of deliberate government budgetary policy.

2.20 Government borrowing and budget deficits

There can be two elements to a budget deficit, a cyclical element and a structural element.

The **cyclical element** of a budget deficit reflects the phasing of the trade cycle. For example, a government may wish to run a budget deficit in time of recession to try to stimulate aggregate demand. The cyclical element is essentially short term.

However, the **structural element** is long term and reflects a permanent imbalance between government expenditure and government revenue (taxation) which occurs irrespective of the trade cycle. A structural deficit will imply continuous net borrowing by the government, and therefore an increase in the national debt.

A structural deficit could be caused by spending commitments on health, education and social security, and exacerbated by an ageing population. This would require greater government spending on **pensions** and **health care for the elderly**, but receipts from taxation would not be rising to pay for them.

Most governments seek to finance the public sector net cash requirement (PSNCR) through the sale of long term government debt to the private sector.

As with many other areas, the **Keynesians** and the **monetarists** have differing opinions of the effectiveness of government borrowing. Keynesians believe it can have a positive effect on the economy through boosting aggregate demand. Monetarists believe if merely increases money supply into the economy and causes inflation. Moreover, they argue that government spending merely replaces private spending (crowding out) with no real increase in aggregate demand.

However, whether they follow a Keynesian or a monetarist approach, governments acknowledge that it is important to keep the underlying level of budget deficit (national debt) under control because of the problems associated with having to pay interest on an ever-increasing level of national debt.

European Union countries wanting to join the euro have to satisfy criteria around the level of national debt and the level of current public sector borrowing in relation to national income.

In the UK, the government has specified two key fiscal rules that reinforce its adherence to prudence in public spending. These are:

(a) **The golden rule**: over the economic cycle, the government will borrow only to invest and not to fund current spending. In other words, all short-term government expenditure (on goods, services and transfer payments) must not exceed income from taxation, so that the government does not need to borrow to pay for it.

(b) **The sustainable investment rule**: over the economic cycle, public sector net debt as a proportion of GDP will be held at a stable and prudent level.

The fiscal rules provide benchmarks against which the performance of fiscal policy can be judged. The government will meet the golden rule if, on average over a complete economic cycle, the current budget is in balance or surplus.

Such restrictions on the level of debt which can be maintained ultimately mean that if a government wants to sustain the level of public expenditure which is creating a budget deficit it will need to increase tax revenue to fund it (and the decision to raise taxation may not be very popular politically).

Unfortunately, however, the recession which affected the UK from 2008/09 and the slow recovery which followed meant that the government has not been able to follow the golden rule, because short-term government spending has exceeded tax revenues and public debt has risen.

3 Monetary theory

> **FAST FORWARD**
>
> **Monetary theory** deals with the way changes in monetary variables affect the aggregate demand in the economy and its ultimate impact on **prices** and **output**. There are three theories of how the changes in the money supply are transmitted to the real economy: the quantity theory of money, the Keynesian theory, and the monetarist theory.

3.1 The classical quantity theory of money

Monetarism is based on the quantity theory of money which asserts that the level of prices in an economy are related to the **supply of money** in that economy, following the equation $MV = PT$ (where M = the supply of money, V = velocity of circulation, P = the level of prices, and T = the number of transactions).

This is the Fisher equation which we introduced in the previous chapter. Remember that Monetarists assume that 'V' and 'T' are constant, and therefore prices are a function of the supply of money in an economy.

3.2 The Keynesian demand for money

Keynes identified three reasons why people hold wealth as money rather than as interest-bearing securities.

Key terms

The **transactions motive**. Households need money to pay for their day-to-day purchases. The level of transactions demand for money depends on household incomes.

The **precautionary motive**. People choose to keep money on hand or in the bank as a precaution for when it might suddenly be needed.

The **speculative motive**. Some people choose to keep ready money to take advantage of a profitable opportunity to invest in bonds which may arise (or they may sell bonds for money when they fear a fall in the market prices of bonds).

There is an important contrast here with the classical quantity theory of money. The **quantity theory** assumes that the demand for money is governed by **transactions** only. By proposing two further reasons, Keynes strikes out into new territory.

The precautionary motive is really just an extension of the transactions motive. However, the **speculative motive** for holding money needs explaining a bit further.

(a) If individuals hold money for speculative purposes, this means that they are not using the money to invest in bonds. They are holding on to their savings for speculative reasons. Hence, savings and investment might not be in equilibrium, with consequences for changes in national income. (Remember that when we looked at national income accounting, we said that an economy would only be in equilibrium if savings equalled investments.)

(b) The reason for holding money instead of investing in bonds is that **interest rates are expected to go up**. If interest rates go up, bond prices will fall. For example, if the current market price of bonds which pay 5% interest on face value is $100, and interest rates doubled to 10%, the market value of the bonds would fall, perhaps to $50. This is because the interest paid on a bond is fixed at a percentage of face value. The ratio between the income paid and the market value adjusts to the current prevailing interest rate by means of changes in the market value. So, if interest rates are expected to go up, any bonds held now will be expected to lose value, and bond holders would make a capital loss. Thus, it makes sense to hold on to money, for investing in bonds later, after interest rates have gone up. Keynes called such money holdings **idle balances**.

(c) What causes individuals to have expectations about interest rate changes in the future? Keynes argued that each individual has some expectation of a **normal rate of interest**. This concept of a normal interest rate reflects past levels and movements in the interest rate, and expectations of the future rate level, obtained from available market information.

Question — Interest rates

Following this Keynesian analysis, how would you expect an individual to act if:

(a) They think that the current level of interest is below the 'normal' rate?
(b) They think that the current level of interest is above the 'normal' rate?

Answer

(a) If someone believes that the normal rate of interest is above the current level, he will expect the interest rate to rise and will therefore expect bond prices to fall. To avoid a capital loss the individual will sell bonds and hold money.

(b) Conversely, if an individual believes that the normal rate of interest is below the current market interest rate, he will expect the market interest rate to fall and bond prices to rise. Hence he will buy bonds, and run down speculative money holdings, in order to make a capital gain.

Key term

Liquidity preference describes people's preference for holding on to their savings as money (in liquid form) rather than investing it.

Keynes argued further that people will need money to satisfy the transactions motive and precautionary motive regardless of the level of interest. It is only the speculative motive which alters the demand for money as a result of interest rate changes.

(a) If interest rates are high, people will expect them to fall and will expect the price of bonds to rise. They will therefore purchase bonds in anticipation of a capital gain and will therefore have **low liquidity preference**. (That is, their demand for money is low because they prefer to hold bonds instead.)

(b) If interest rates are low but are expected to rise, this implies that bond prices are likely to fall. People will therefore hold liquid funds in order to be able to invest in bonds later on. Their **liquidity preference will be high**. (That is, their demand for money is high, because they would rather hold money than bonds.)

The conclusion is that the demand for money will be high (liquidity preference will be high) when interest rates are low. This is because the speculative demand for money will be high. Similarly, the demand for money will be low when interest rates are high, because the speculative demand for money will be low.

Taking Keynes' points about the demand for money together, we can see that there is a **minimum fixed demand** for money (transactions and precautionary motives) and **some demand** for money that varies with interest rates (speculative motive). This can be shown as a liquidity preference curve (Figure 4). A minimum quantity of money is needed, regardless of interest rate, to satisfy the minimum demand arising from the transactions and precautionary motives for holding money. Beyond that, demand for money increases as interest rates fall.

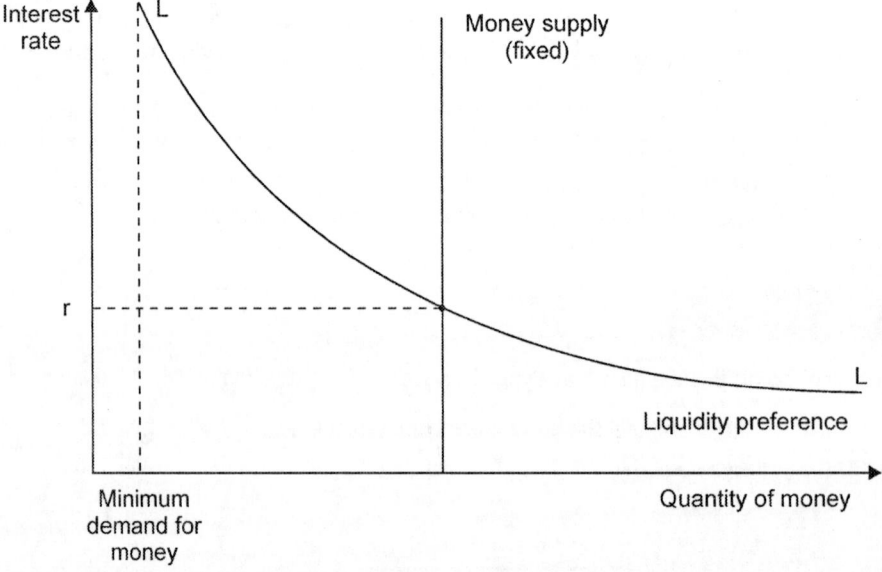

Figure 4 Interest rates, money demand and the money supply

Keynes' view on the determination of interest rates is, like the classical view, a market model. He argued that the level of interest rates is determined by the interaction of demand for and supply of money. While the liquidity preference curve may be thought of as a normal demand curve, with the rate of interest being the price of money, Keynes suggested that the money supply was fixed by government and therefore inelastic: a vertical supply curve, in other words, as shown in Figure 4.

The **quantity theory** assumes that an increase in the money supply will automatically lead to an increase in aggregate demand. Since the economy is assumed to be operating at full employment and therefore not able to produce more goods and services, this increase in aggregate demand will cause a rise in the level of prices generally. Keynes took a different view. He said that an **increase in the money supply** would lead to a **fall in interest rates**.

It is an important aspect of this theory, and a contrast with the quantity theory, that an increase in the money supply would not lead directly to an increase in aggregate demand.

If there is an increase in the money supply, (from MS_1 to MS_2 in Figure 5), money capital will become cheaper and interest rates will fall (from r_1 to r_2 in Figure 5). There will be some increase in the level of investment spending, since it now becomes more profitable for firms to invest in new capital because of the fall in the cost of borrowing. The increase in investment, being an injection into the circular flow of income, causes some increase in the level of national income through the multiplier process. According to the Keynesians, therefore, a change in the money supply only indirectly affects the demand for goods and services (and hence the level of income), via a change in the rate of interest. This is called an **indirect transmission mechanism**.

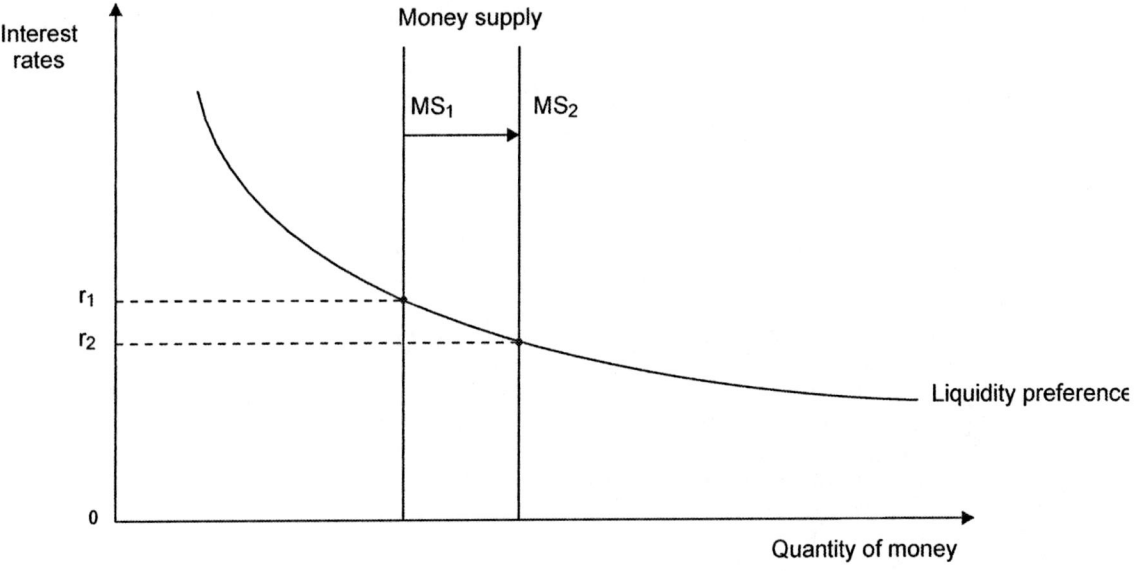

Figure 5 Consequence of an increase in the money supply

The impact on the economy of the increase in the money supply therefore depends on the effect that the fall in interest rates produces. According to the Keynesian view, both investment demand and consumer spending are **relatively insensitive** to interest rate changes, that is, they are relatively interest-inelastic. The **volume of investment** depends heavily, Keynes argued, on **technological changes** and **business confidence and expectations** too. It follows that the increase in the money supply will have only a limited effect on aggregate demand and consequently relatively little effect on output and employment or on price levels. This view implies that the velocity of circulation, V, is **not fixed**, since a varying amount of money is held as investment in bonds.

Keynesians therefore argue that monetary policy to control the money supply would have an effect on interest rates and changes in interest rates might in the longer term affect investment. In other respects, however, monetary policy would not really affect the economy and national income, because increases in the money supply would be neutralised by reductions in the velocity of circulation, leaving PT unaffected.

3.3 The new quantity theory of money

Friedman re-stated the quantity theory of money, as follows.

MV ≡ PQ

where
M is the **money supply**
V is the **velocity of circulation** of money
P is the **average price level**
Q is the physical quantity of **national output per period** (ie the real volume of economic output)

Thus, PQ is the **money value of national output** (ie national income, Y, at current prices). Remember that in the original Fisher equation, P was the **general level** of prices rather than a numerical average and T was the number of transactions. PT was therefore the money value of transactions and **proportional** to national income, **not equal** to it.

Monetarists argue that V and Q are independent of M. Therefore, an increase in money supply M will tend to raise prices P, via the direct transmission mechanism.

(a) Individuals will have more money than they want.

(b) They will spend this excess money, buying not just 'bonds' (as Keynes believed) but also equities and physical goods.

(c) The greater demand for physical goods will boost expenditure in the economy (and so the money value of national income).

(d) However, a rapid increase in the money supply will increase spending at a faster rate than the economy will be able to produce more physical output.

(e) A rapid increase in the money supply will therefore inevitably be inflationary.

In conclusion, for monetarists, changes in the money supply cause changes in the money value of national income. Remember that Keynes believed there was only a weak link between changes in the money supply and changes in aggregate demand.

Question
Money supply increases

According to monetarist economics, which of the following consequences will result from an increase in the money supply?

1. Households will have excess money.
2. Households will use this money to buy more bonds, equities and physical goods.
3. Interest rates will rise.
4. The demand for money will respond to the change in interest rates.
5. Expenditure in the economy will increase.

Answer

Consequences 1, 2 and 5 (but not 3 and 4) will result. According to monetarists, an increase in the money supply creates excess supply over demand. Households use the excess money to buy bonds (and so interest rates fall), equities and physical goods (and so expenditure in the economy rises). The demand for money is interest-rate inelastic, according to monetarists (but not according to Keynesians) and so this does not increase in response to any interest rate fall.

3.4 The monetarist view of money supply and inflation in the economy

Whereas Keynes argued that an increase in the money supply would merely result in lower interest rates, with no immediate effect on national income, Friedman and other monetarists argue that an increase in the money supply will lead directly and quickly to changes in national income and 'prices × transactions' (PT), with the velocity of circulation (V) remaining fairly constant.

In his analysis of the demand for money, Friedman argued that money is just one of five broad ways of holding wealth.

- **Money**
- **Bonds**
- **Equities**
- **Physical goods**
- **Human wealth**

(Human wealth here is a special concept and may be ignored for the purpose of our analysis.)

Each method of holding wealth brings some form of return or yield to the holder.

(a) The main yield from money is the **convenience** of having it when it is needed. This cannot be measured in money terms.

(b) The return on **bonds** is the interest plus any capital gain (or loss).

(c) **Equities** should provide dividends and capital growth which keep ahead of the rate of inflation.

(d) **Physical assets in this analysis,** do not waste away through use, because assets which are consumed cannot be a store of wealth. There might be an increase in their capital value but the yield also includes the non-monetary return, such as the use of furniture, the enjoyment from paintings and so on.

Friedman argued that the demand for money is related to the demand for holding wealth in its other forms. While Keynes believed that if people did not want to hold money, they would invest it to earn interest, monetarists believe that they might also use it instead to buy equities or physical assets.

Friedman argued that money gives a convenience yield but it is not an asset which is held for its own sake. It is a 'temporary abode of purchasing power' waiting to be spent on other types of financial or physical asset. The **demand for money** is therefore a function of the yield on money and the yield on other forms of holding wealth. **Yield** as defined here includes non-monetary yield such as convenience and enjoyment.

Monetarists would argue, further, that the demand for money is fairly interest-inelastic. The demand for money is related to a transactions motive, but not to any speculative motive. An expected rise in interest rates might persuade individuals to sell bonds and buy other assets, but not to hold speculative money.

Monetarists argue that, since money is a direct substitute for all other assets, an increase in the money supply, given a fairly stable velocity of circulation, will have a direct effect on demand for other assets because there will be more money to spend on those assets. If the total output of the economy is fixed, then an increase in the money supply will lead directly to higher prices.

Monetarists therefore reach the same basic conclusion as that identified by the old quantity theory of money. A rise in the money supply will lead to a rise in prices and probably also to a rise in money incomes. (It is also assumed by monetarists that the velocity of circulation remains fairly constant, again taking a view similar to the old quantity theory.) In the short run, monetarists argue that an increase in the money supply might cause some increase in real output and so an increase in employment. In the long run, however, all increases in the money supply will be reflected in higher prices unless there is longer term growth in the economy.

3.5 Weaknesses in monetarist theory

There are certain **complications with the monetarist views**, for example the following.

(a) The velocity of circulation is known to fluctuate up and down by small amounts.

(b) Increases in prices will not affect all goods equally. Some goods will rise in price more than others and so the relative price of goods will change. For example, the price of houses might exceed the average rate of inflation but the price of electronic goods might rise more slowly.

(c) A higher rate of inflation in one country than another might affect the country's balance of payments and currency value, thereby introducing complications for the economy from international trade movements.

(d) Prices in the economy might take some time to adjust to an increase in the money supply.

3.6 What makes the money supply grow?

We have looked at the demand for and supply of money without yet asking what it is that makes the money supply grow in the first place. If we define money broadly, to include bank deposits, **four main factors contribute to money supply growth.**

(a) Government short term borrowing has a direct effect on the money supply since the banks can use the Treasury bills they receive as part of their liquid reserves. Government borrowing thus releases cash into circulation that would otherwise be tied up in bank reserves.

(b) Who the government borrows from (whether it is banks or not) will affect the level of growth in the money supply since only banks have the ability to create money by lending.

(c) Bank lending generally.

(d) Flows of money between the country and foreign traders/investors.

Case Study

In the UK, the Bank of England has increased the money supply through a programme of **quantitative easing**: in effect, introducing **new money** into the financial system. In January 2009 it began a quantitative easing programme, designed to revive consumer spending and to provide a stimulus for growth in the economy. By the end of July 2012, the Bank had committed a total of £375 billion to quantitative easing, although that amount then remained unchanged until August 2016 when the Bank of England said it would buy £60 billion of UK government bonds and £10 billion of corporate bonds amidst uncertainty over 'Brexit' and concerns about economic growth.

In the US, the Federal Reserve has put over $2 trillion into quantitative easing since 2008.

3.7 Approaches to controlling the growth of the broad money supply

A government might take any of four broad approaches to controlling the growth of the money supply.

(a) To reduce or control government borrowing

(b) To finance as much government borrowing as possible by borrowing from the non-bank private sector, for example in the UK by encouraging National Savings in preference to issuing gilts

(c) To control the increase in bank lending

(d) To control external and foreign currency items, for example by keeping the balance of payments under control

3.8 The loanable funds theory of interest rates

According to Keynesians, the level of interest rates is determined by the interaction of the speculative demand for money and the money supply.

Monetarists hold the traditional view that the reasons for demanding money are for transactions only, not speculation about future investment. Monetarists argue instead that interest rates are determined by the demand and supply of **loanable funds**. An increase in the money supply, without any increase in demand for money (investment), will increase the amount of loanable funds available (savings). Interest rates will fall, and investment will rise.

3.9 The transmission mechanism and imbalances between money supply and demand

Monetarists say that the connection between the demand for money, the money supply and national income can be explained by **a direct transmission mechanism**.

Starting from a position of equilibrium holding of assets of all kinds, **an increase in the money supply** would leave individuals holding an excess of money balances. In order to restore the level of money holdings to its desired level, individuals will substitute assets of all kinds for money: the **demand for goods and services will increase**, not just demand for financial assets.

(a) The increase in the quantity of money means a fall in the rate of interest. This will not lead to an increase in the demand for money, according to the monetarists, because they believe that the **demand for money is interest-inelastic**.

(b) The increase in direct spending on goods and services will, however, lead to a **rise in the level of money national income**.

By assuming that money is a substitute for all assets, the monetarists conclude that variations in the money supply have a great influence on the level of national income. In terms of the classical quantity theory of money, if M goes up, and MV = PT, there will be an increase in PT, but this could mean an increase in either real output (T) or in prices and inflation (P).

Suppose that the demand for money goes up, but the authorities stop the money supply from increasing, so that there is an **excess demand** for money. The transmission mechanism will work the other way. Households will sell bonds and equities and reduce consumption on other goods in order to acquire more money. Interest rates will go up. There will be a decline in total spending in the economy until money supply and demand are again in equilibrium. Since MV = PT, a decline in PT will have one of two effects.

(a) If the economy is operating below its full employment national income level, there will be a decline in T leading to even less output and so more unemployment.

(b) If the economy has an inflationary gap, there will be a decline in P, and inflation will be brought under control.

3.10 Comparison of theories

	Classical Quantity Theory	Keynesian Theory	New Quantity Theory
Name	Fisher	Keynes	Friedman
Keyword/equation	MV≡PT	'Liquidity preference'	MV≡PQ
Uses for money	Transactions	Transaction motive Precautionary motive Speculative motive	Cash Bonds Equities Physical goods Human wealth
Assumptions	T, V constant; M independently determined	Only speculative demand varies; Money supply usually fixed	Demand for money is interest-inelastic
Effect of rise in money supply when economy at full employment	AD up, price rises	Price of bonds up, interest rate falls, small rise in AD and prices	Spending on assets of all kinds up, AD up, prices up
Transmission mechanism	Direct	Indirect, via interest rate	Direct
Determination of interest rate	Supply and demand for money	Since money supply is fixed, interest rate depends on speculative demand for bonds	Supply and demand of loanable funds

Question — Counter-inflation policies

(a) A government can help to counter Demand pull inflation by reducing interest rates. True or false?

(b) A government can help to counter Demand pull inflation by increasing sales taxes (such as VAT). True or false?

(c) A government can help to counter Cost push inflation by increasing income tax rates. True or false?

(d) A government can help to counter Cost push inflation by linking wage increases to productivity improvements. True or false?

Answer

(a) **False**. On the contrary, this would increase consumer borrowing and hence stimulate Demand pull inflation.

(b) **True**. This might increase total spending on goods and services inclusive of the tax, but spending net of tax will probably fall.

(c) **False**. Increasing direct taxation will reduce consumers' disposable income, but this is a measure aimed at countering Demand pull inflation, not Cost push inflation.

(d) **True**. This will reduce the unit costs of production.

3.11 Expectations and money supply growth

If the government controls the money supply without telling anyone what its planned targets of growth are, then people's **expectations** of inflation will run ahead of the growth in the money supply. Wage demands will remain at levels in keeping with these expectations and so the rate of increase in prices (P) will exceed the rate of increase in the money supply (M). If the government succeeds in its aim of limiting the growth of the money supply, but wages rise at a faster rate, then higher wages will mean less real income (Y) and less real output (T). In other words, the economy will slump even further.

It is for this reason that the government must announce its targets for growth in the money supply.

(a) Most monetarists argue that the government must give a clear announcement of its targets for monetary growth so as to influence people's expectations of inflation.

(b) Some economists might argue that an **incomes policy** should be imposed by the government to prevent wage rises in excess of government targets.

Monetarists pointed to the high inflation of the mid-1970s as evidence in support of their views since very rapid monetary growth preceded the price inflation. However, later research suggested that soaring oil and commodity prices were the culprits. Falling commodity prices helped subsequently to reduce inflation.

4 Monetary policy

Monetary policy focuses on the relationship between **interest rates** and the **supply of money** in an economy, and how the two of them together can influence aggregate demand.

4.1 Objectives of monetary policy

Exam focus point

Questions on monetary policy will often focus on its impact on the business sector. It is important that you understand how changes in interest rates could affect business decisions.

- Monetary policy can be used as a means towards achieving ultimate economic objectives for inflation, the balance of trade, full employment and real economic growth. To achieve these **ultimate objectives**, the authorities will set **intermediate objectives** for monetary policy.

- In the UK, the ultimate objective of monetary policy in recent years has been principally to reduce the rate of inflation to a sustainable low level. The intermediate objectives of monetary policy have related to the level of interest rates, growth in the money supply, the exchange rate for sterling, the expansion of credit and the growth of national income.

4.2 The money supply as a target of monetary policy

- To monetarist economists, the **money supply** is an obvious intermediate target of economic policy. This is because they claim that an increase in the money supply will raise prices and incomes and this in turn will raise the demand for money to spend.

- When such a policy is first introduced, the short-term effect would be unpredictable for three reasons.

- The effect on interest rates might be erratic.

- There might be a time lag before anything can be done. For example, it takes time to cut government spending and hence to use reduction in government borrowing as an instrument of monetary policy to control the growth in M0 or M4.

- There might be a time lag before control of the money supply alters expectations about inflation and wage demands.
- Growth in the money supply, if it is a monetary policy target, should therefore be a **medium-term target**. When the UK government set targets for the growth of the money supply as a main feature of its economic policy strategy, it is prepared to wait for some years to see any benefits from its policies and therefore sets out its policy targets in a **medium-term** financial strategy.

4.3 The effects of changing interest rates

While controlling the money supply is a key target of economic policy, the main feature of monetary policy is that of **controlling interest rates**. Governments will be particularly keen to use an interest rate policy if they consider there is a direct relationship between interest rates and the level of expenditure in the economy, or between interest rates and the rate of inflation. In other words, they will use interest rates to control the level of aggregate demand in an economy.

A rise in interest rates will raise the price of borrowing in the internal economy for both companies and individuals. If companies see the rise as relatively permanent, rates of return on investments will become less attractive and **investment plans may be curtailed**. Corporate profits will fall as a result of higher interest payments. Companies will reduce inventory levels as the cost of having money tied up in inventory rises. Individuals should be expected to reduce or postpone consumption in order to reduce borrowings, and should become less willing to borrow for major purchases, such as house purchases.

Although it is generally accepted that there is likely to be a connection between interest rates and investment (by companies) and consumer expenditure, **the connection is not a stable and predictable one**, and interest rate changes are only likely to affect the level of expenditure after a **considerable time lag**.

Other effects of raising interest rates

(a) High interest rates will keep the value of a country's current higher than it would otherwise be. This will keep the cost of exports high, and so discourage the purchase of exports. This may be necessary to protect the balance of payments and to prevent 'import-cost-push' inflation.

(b) High interest rates will attract foreign investors into capital investments, and so high interest rates in the UK could generate capital inflows which help to finance the large UK balance of payments deficit.

The impacts of a rise in interest rates

Impact	Comment
Spending falls	Higher interest rates increase the cost of credit and thereby deter spending. The higher interest rates are, the more attractive it is to hold money rather than to spend it.
Investment falls	The increased rate will increase the opportunity cost of investment and reduce the net present value of the investment. This will discourage firms from investing.
	The increased interest rates will make borrowing more expensive.
Foreign funds are attracted into the country	Interest rates are the reward for capital, so a rise in interest rates will encourage overseas investors because of the increased rate of return relative to other countries.

Impact	Comment
Exchange rate rises	The inflow of foreign funds (above) increases the demand for currency and therefore increases the exchange rate. A rise in exchange rates will make exports more expensive, and imports cheaper. The impact this will have on the balance of payments current account will depend on the relative price elasticities of imports and exports.
Inflation rate falls	This is the overall goal of an interest rate rise. The reduction in spending and investment will reduce aggregate demand in the economy. Higher exchange rates will force producers to make prices more competitive by cutting costs.
Bond prices fall	There is an inverse relationship between bond prices and the rate of interest.

An increase in interest rates will have a **disinflationary** (or possibly even a deflationary) impact on the economy.

Note, however, the potential conflicting objectives which monetary policy may face. A change in interest rates will have effects on both the domestic economy and on a country's international trade position (for example, through exchange rate movements). It may be the case that the interest rate movement required for the domestic economy conflicts with that required to achieve a balance on the external current account.

An important reason for pursuing an interest rate policy is that the authorities are able to influence interest rates much more effectively and rapidly than they can influence other policy targets, such as the money supply or the volume of credit.

4.4 The exchange rate as a target of monetary policy

Why the exchange rate is a target

(a) If the exchange rate falls, exports become cheaper to overseas buyers and so more competitive in export markets. Imports will become more expensive and so less competitive against goods produced by manufacturers at home. A fall in the exchange rate might therefore be good for a domestic economy, by giving a **stimulus to exports** and **reducing demand for imports**.

(b) An increase in the exchange rate will have the opposite effect, with dearer exports and cheaper imports. If the exchange rate rises and imports become cheaper, though there should be a reduction in the rate of domestic inflation. A fall in the exchange rate, on the other hand, tends to increase the cost of imports and adds to the rate of domestic inflation.

When a country's economy is heavily dependent on overseas trade, as the UK economy is, it might be appropriate for government policy to establish a target exchange value for the domestic currency. However, the exchange rate is dependent on both the domestic rate of inflation and the level of interest rates. Targets for the exchange rate cannot be achieved unless the rate of inflation at home is first brought under control.

4.5 Growth in money national income as a target of monetary policy

The authorities might set targets for the level of national income in the economy. For example, the policy might be for the growth in the national income (or GNP or GDP) to be X% per annum for a given number of years. However, it takes time to collect information about national income whereas targets of monetary policy should be items for which statistical data can be collected regularly and easily.

For this reason, although a target growth rate in national income itself is, in theory, probably the most suitable target of monetary policy, it is the least practical because the authorities would always be working with out-of-date information.

4.6 Targets and indicators

An economic indicator provides information about economic conditions and might be used as a way of judging the performance of government.

(a) A **leading indicator** is one which gives an advance indication of what will happen to the economy in the future. It can therefore be used to predict future conditions. For example, a fall in the value of sterling by, say, 2% might be used to predict what will happen to the balance of payments and to the rate of inflation in the UK.

(b) A **coincident indicator** is one which gives an indication of changes in economic conditions **at the same time** that these changes are occurring. For example, if the narrow money supply rises by 5%, this might 'confirm' that the rate of increase in GDP over the same period of time has been about the same, 5% in 'money' terms.

(c) A **lagging indicator**, not surprisingly, is one which 'lags behind' the economic cycle. Unemployment, to take an example, often continues to rise until after a recession has ended and only starts to fall again after recovery has begun.

Items which are selected as monetary targets will also be indicators, but not all indicators are selected by the authorities as targets. There are a number of monetary indicators.

(a) The size of the money stock
(b) Interest rates such as the banks' base rate of interest, the Treasury bill rate and the yield on long-dated government securities
(c) The exchange rate against the US dollar, or the trade-weighted exchange rate index
(d) The size of the government's borrowing
(e) Government borrowing as a percentage of Gross Domestic Product

4.7 The interrelationship between targets: the money supply and interest rate targets

The authorities can set intermediate targets for the growth of the money supply, but to achieve their targets of growth it will be necessary to allow interest rates to adjust to a level at which the demand for money matches the size of the money supply. For example, a policy to cut the growth of the money supply might result in higher real interest rates.

On the other hand, the authorities might set targets for the level of interest rates. If they do so, they must allow whatever demand for money there is to be met at that rate of interest by allowing the money supply to meet the demand. If they did not, interest rates would then rise above or fall below the target level.

This means that the authorities can set a target for the money supply or a target for interest rates, but **they cannot set independent targets for both at the same time**.

4.8 Instruments of monetary policy

There are a number of techniques or instruments which are available to the authorities to achieve their targets for monetary policies.

- Changing the level and/or structure of **interest rates** through **open market operations**
- **Reserve requirements**
- **Direct controls**, which might be either quantitative or qualitative
- **Intervention to influence the exchange rate**

4.9 Control over the level and structure of interest rates

When a government uses interest rates as an instrument of policy, it can try to influence either the general level of interest rates or the term structure of interest rates. It could do this by influencing either short-term interest rates or long-term interest rates. As we noted in Chapter 9, the Bank of England has had responsibility for setting short-term interest rates since 1997, and it can control interest rates through its open market operations – by buying or selling government securities in order to control their price, and consequently to control their interest rates. Long-term rates could possibly be influenced by increasing or reducing the PSNCR.

4.10 Reserve requirements on banks as a means of controlling the money supply

As another technique for controlling money supply growth, the government might impose **reserve requirements** on banks. A reserve requirement might be a compulsory minimum cash reserve ratio (ie ratio of cash to total assets) or a minimum liquid asset ratio.

You will recall that any initial increase in bank deposits or building society deposits will result in a much greater eventual increase in deposits, because of the credit multiplier.

Ignoring leakages, the formula for the credit multiplier is:

$$D = \frac{C}{r}$$

where C is the initial increase in deposits
r is the liquid assets ratio or reserve assets ratio
D is the eventual total increase in deposits

If the authorities wished to control the rate of increase in bank lending and building society lending, they could impose minimum reserve requirements – ie a minimum value for r. **The bigger the value of r, the lower size of the credit multiplier would be**.

There are drawbacks to reserve requirements as a monetary policy instrument.

(a) Unless the same requirements apply to all financial institutions in the country, some institutions will simply take business from others. For example, reserve requirements on UK banks but not on building societies would give the building societies a competitive advantage over the banks, without having any effect on the control of total credit/money supply growth.

(b) Similarly, restrictions on domestic financial institutions which do not apply to foreign banks would put the domestic financial institutions at a competitive disadvantage in international markets. This is one reason why international co-operation on the capital adequacy of banks (the Basel agreement) is an important step towards better regulation of financial markets.

4.11 Direct controls as a technique of monetary control

Another way of controlling the growth of the money supply is to impose direct controls on bank lending. Direct controls may be either quantitative or qualitative.

(a) **Quantitative controls** might be imposed on either bank lending (assets), for example a 'lending ceiling' limiting annual lending growth, or bank deposits (liabilities). The purpose of quantitative controls might be seen as a means of keeping bank lending in check without having to resort to higher interest rates.

(b) **Qualitative controls** might be used to alter the type of lending by banks. For example, the government (via the Bank) can ask the banks to limit their lending to the personal sector, and lend more to industry, or to lend less to a particular type of firm (such as, for example, property companies) and more to manufacturing businesses.

4.12 Quantitative controls

Controls might be temporary, in which case, in time, interest rates would still tend to rise if the money supply growth is to be kept under control. However, the advantage of a temporary scheme of direct quantitative controls is that it gives the authorities time to implement longer term policy. Quantitative controls are therefore a way of bridging the time-lag before these other policies take effect.

Quantitative controls might be more permanent. If they are, they will probably be unsuccessful because there will be financial institutions that manage to escape the control regulations, and so thrive at the expense of controlled institutions.

Direct controls on banks, for example, might succeed in reducing bank deposits but they will not succeed in controlling the level of demand and expenditure in the economy if lending is re-directed into other non-controlled financial instruments of non-controlled financial institutions. For example, large companies might use their own bank deposits to set up a scheme of lending themselves.

Direct controls are therefore rarely effective in dealing with the source rather than the symptom of the problem. Direct controls tend to divert financial flows into other, often less efficient, channels, rather than to stop the financial flows altogether, ie 'leakages' are inevitable.

4.13 Qualitative controls

Qualitative controls might be **mandatory** or they might be applied through **moral suasion**. Mandatory directives of a qualitative nature are unlikely in practice, because they are difficult to enforce without the co-operation of banks and other financial institutions. Moral suasion, on the other hand, might be used frequently. This is a process whereby the central bank appeals to the banks to do one or more things.

- To restrain lending
- To give priority to certain types of lending such as finance for exports or for investment
- Refuse other types of lending such as loans to private individuals

Moral suasion might therefore be a temporary form of control. For example, the Governor of the Bank of England might 'advise' the banks to be wary of lending to certain types of customer or to certain market sectors, thereby trying to influence banks' lending decisions without giving them directives or instructions.

4.14 Exchange rate control as an instrument of monetary policy

The exchange rate and changes in the exchange rate, have implications for the balance of payments, inflation and economic growth. The government might therefore seek to achieve a target exchange rate for its currency. We will look at exchange rates in more detail when we consider international trade in the final two chapters of this Study Text.

4.15 Monetary policy and fiscal policy

Monetary policy can be made to act as a subsidiary support to fiscal policy and demand management. Since Budgets are once-a-year events, a government must use non-fiscal measures in between Budgets to make adjustments to its control of the economy.

(a) A policy of **low interest rates** or the absence of any form of credit control might stimulate bank lending, which in turn would increase expenditure (demand) in the economy.

(b) **High interest rates might** act as a deterrent to borrowing and so reduce spending in the economy.

(c) Strict **credit controls** (for example, restrictions on bank lending) might be introduced to reduce lending and so reduce demand in the economy.

Alternatively, monetary policy might be given prominence over fiscal policy as the most effective approach by a government to achieving its main economic policy objectives. This might not however be possible:

from 1990 to 1992, for example, monetary policy in the UK was heavily constrained by the need to set interest rates at levels which maintained sterling's position in the European Exchange Rate Mechanism (ERM). (see Chapter 13, Section 4.5, for more details about the ERM.)

From 1997, the UK government has given the Bank of England the role of setting interest rates, although it is still the government which sets an inflation target.

4.16 Monetary policy, inflation control and economic growth

Monetarists argue that monetary control will put the brake on inflation, but how does this help the economy? We have already suggested that inflation seems to hinder economic growth, and so we could argue like this.

(a) High inflation increases **economic uncertainty**. Bringing inflation under control will restore business confidence and help international trade by stabilising the exchange rate.

(b) A resurgence of business confidence through lower interest rates (due to less uncertainty and lower inflation) will **stimulate investment** and **real output**.

(c) A **controlled growth in the money supply** will provide higher incomes for individuals to purchase the higher output.

5 Effectiveness of macroeconomic policy

FAST FORWARD

The **effectiveness of monetary policy** in influencing aggregate demand and unemployment is limited in the long-run.

Having discussed the way fiscal and monetary policies operate on aggregate demand, here we review their role in controlling inflation and affecting the level on unemployment.

5.1 The control of inflation

The best way of controlling inflation will depend on the causes of it. In practice, it may be difficult to know which cause is most significant. The table below sets out various policies designed to control inflation.

Cause of inflation	Policy to control inflation
Demand pull (high consumer demand)	Take steps to reduce demand in the economy • Higher taxation, to cut consumer spending • Lower government expenditure (and lower government borrowing to finance its expenditure) • Higher interest rates
Cost push factors (higher wage costs and other costs working through to higher prices)	Take steps to reduce production costs and price rises • De-regulate labour markets • Encourage greater productivity in industry • Apply controls over wage and price rises (prices and incomes policy)
Import cost push factors	Take steps to reduce the quantities or the price of imports. Such a policy might involve trying to achieve either an appreciation or depreciation of the domestic currency

PART D PUBLIC SECTOR AND MACRO-ECONOMY

Cause of inflation	Policy to control inflation
Excessively fast growth in the money supply	Take steps to try to reduce the rate of money supply growth • Reduced government borrowing and borrow from the non-bank private sector • Try to control or reduce bank lending • Try to achieve a balance of trade surplus • Maintain interest rates at a level that might deter money supply growth
Expectations of inflation	Pursue clear policies which indicate the government's determination to reduce the rate of inflation

5.2 High interest rates and inflation

A government (or a central bank acting on behalf of the government) may adopt a policy of raising **interest rates** as a means of trying to reduce the rate of inflation, when inflation is being caused by a boom in consumer demand (with demand rising faster than the ability of industry to increase its output to meet the demand).

If interest rates are high enough, there should eventually be a reduction in the rate of growth in consumer spending.

(a) People who borrow must pay more in interest out of their income. This will leave them less income, after paying the interest, to spend on other things. (The government would not want wages to rise, though, because if people build up their income again with high wage settlements, the consumer spending boom could continue and a wage-price spiral could be instigated.)

(b) High interest rates might deter people from borrowing, and so there would be less spending with borrowed funds.

(c) High interest rates should encourage more saving, with individuals therefore spending less of their income on consumption.

(d) High interest rates will tend to depress the values of non-monetary assets, such as houses, and the reduction in people's perceived wealth may make people feel 'poorer' and consequently reduce the amounts they spend on consumer goods.

5.3 Inflationary expectations

An explanation of rising inflation rates combined with rising unemployment was put forward, based on **inflationary expectations**. This **natural rate hypothesis** is supported by monetarist economists.

Inflationary expectations reflect the rates of inflation that are **expected** in the future. The inflationary expectations of the work force will be reflected in the level of wage rises that is demanded in the annual round of pay negotiations between employers and workers. This is the logic behind the **expectations augmented Phillips curve** which we looked at in connection with inflation and unemployment levels.

In the long run, unemployment will revert towards its natural level. The rate of inflation, however, will be determined by the short-run Phillips curve, which will shift upwards as inflationary expectations increase. The distinction between short and long-run Phillips curves can help explain the observation that, in the UK and other countries, unemployment and inflation have often both risen at the same time.

Key term

The **expectations augmented Phillips curve** shows that the expansion of aggregate demand to reduce unemployment below its natural rate will only produce inflation.

There is a non-accelerating rate of unemployment (NAIRU) at which the rate of inflation is stable.

Question: Natural rate hypothesis

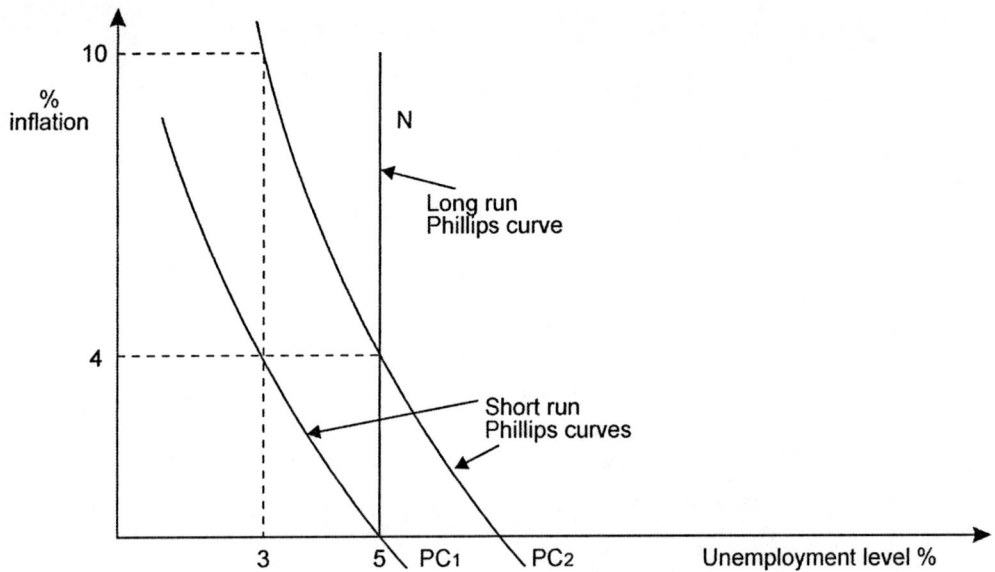

Suppose that the short-run Phillips curve is currently at PC_2, with unemployment at 5% and annual inflation at 4%. What would happen if the government now took measures to reduce unemployment to 3%?

Answer

Inflation would rise to about 10%, which is the rate of inflation on PC_2 associated with 3% unemployment. (Inflation and unemployment levels still follow PC_2, rather than shifting inwards to PC_1.) However, according to the natural rate hypothesis, in the longer run, unemployment would move back to 5%. A new short-run Phillips curve would be established, according to which an unemployment rate of 5% would be associated with 10% inflation.

Monetarist economists argue that the only way to reduce the rate of inflation is to get inflationary expectations out of the system. In doing so, excessive demands for wage rises should be resisted by employers. However a firm approach to reducing the rate of inflation could mean having to accept high levels of unemployment for a while.

5.4 New classical school

The **new classical school** of monetarists believe that the aggregate supply and Phillips curves are **vertical in the short run**. Therefore, they condemn any policy to expand demand as leading only to increased inflation. They suggest that human behaviour is governed by **rational expectations**; that is, by a rational assessment of all the information currently available. The implication is that the public will recognise inflation-producing policies as soon as they are introduced and adjust their expectations of inflation **immediately**. This will lead to increased wage demands and the expected inflation will ensue.

The new classical school sees unemployment as unrelated to inflation. They suggest that unemployment should be tackled by **supply-side measures** designed to reduce the NAIRU, while the sole aim of monetary policy should be to control inflation.

6 Supply side policy

> **FAST FORWARD** Fiscal policy and monetary policy both aim to manage aggregate demand in an economy. **Supply side policies** provide a method of managing **aggregate supply** in the economy.

6.1 The supply side approach

The Keynesian policy of demand management relies upon the proposition that the level of aggregate demand determines the level of national income and prices, since demand creates supply. Demand can be controlled either through fiscal or monetary policy. The **supply side approach**, on the other hand, focuses policy upon the **conditions of aggregate supply**, taking the view that the availability, quality and cost of resources are the long term determinants of national income and prices. Supply side economists argue that by putting resources to work, an economy will automatically generate the additional incomes necessary to purchase the higher outputs.

Key term

> **Supply side economics** can be defined as an approach to economic policymaking which advocates measures to improve the supply of goods and services (eg through deregulation) rather than measures to affect aggregate demand.

Supply side economics is characterised by the following propositions.

(a) The predominant long-term influences upon output, prices, and employment are the conditions of aggregate supply.

(b) Left to itself, the **free market** will automatically generate the highest level of national income and employment available to the economy.

(c) **Inflexibility in the labour market** through the existence of trade unions and other restrictive practices retain wages at uncompetitively high levels. This creates unemployment and restricts aggregate supply.

(d) The rates of **direct taxation** have a major influence upon aggregate supply through their effects upon the **incentive** to work.

(e) There is only a **limited role for government** in the economic system. Demand management can only influence output and employment 'artificially' in the short run, while in the long run creating inflation and hampering growth. Similarly state owned industries are likely to be uncompetitive and accordingly restrict aggregate supply.

6.2 Supply side economic policies

Supply side economists advise **against government intervention** in the economy at both the microeconomic and macroeconomic levels. **Microeconomic intervention** by government is disliked by supply side economists for a number of reasons.

(a) **Price regulation** distorts the signalling function essential for markets to reach optimal equilibrium.

(b) **Wage regulation** distorts the labour market's ability to ensure full employment.

(c) **Public ownership** blunts the incentive effects of the profit motive and leads to inefficiency.

(d) **Government grants and subsidies** encourage inefficient and 'lame duck' industries.

(e) **Public provision of services** may not encourage efficiency and can limit the discipline of consumer choice.

(f) **Employment legislation** such as employment protection limits market flexibility through discouraging recruitment and encouraging over-manning.

Macroeconomic intervention by government is regarded by supply side economists as harmful for several reasons.

(a) **Demand management** will be inflationary in the long run.

(b) High taxes will act as a **disincentive** to work (or as a disincentive to investment by firms).

(c) The possibility of **politically motivated policy changes** will create damaging uncertainty in the economy. This will discourage long-term investment.

Although most would accept the need for **expansion of the money stock** by government to accommodate increases in aggregate demand, some supply-siders have denied even this role to the government.

The main supply side policies are:

(a) **Reduction in government expenditure** and greater involvement of the private sector in the provision of services.

(b) **Increasing competition** through deregulation and privatisation of state-owned industries.

(c) **Reduction in direct taxes** in order to increase incentives to invest and to work.

(d) **Increasing flexibility** in the labour market by curbing the power of trade unions. Encouraging hiring of staff, through relaxing minimum wage legislation or employment protection legislation.

[Another way in which labour markets have become more flexible is through the increasing use of contractors and temporary staff, rather than firms only employing permanent, full-time members of staff.]

(e) Improvements in labour skills, for example through provision of training

(f) Reduction in disincentives for work, for example through reforming the benefit system.

6.3 The role of aggregate supply

The **central role of aggregate supply** is demonstrated in Figures 6(a) and (b).

(a)
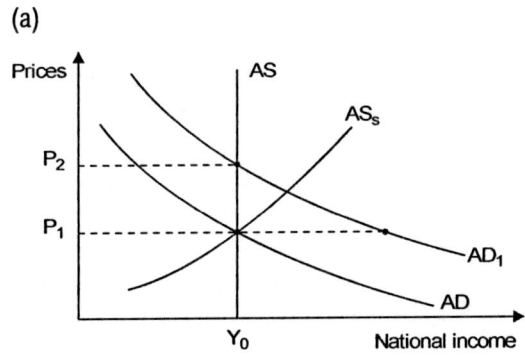

(b)
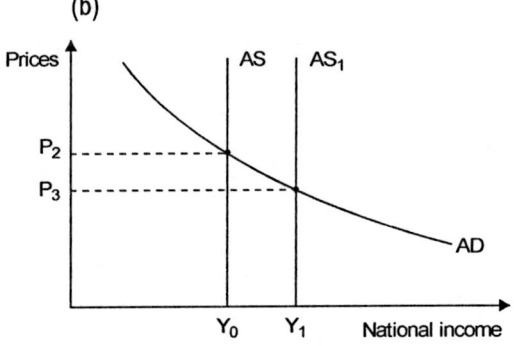

Figure 6 The importance of aggregate supply

Figure 6(a) shows the effect of a rise in aggregate demand, perhaps as the result of expansionary demand management policies. The aggregate demand schedule shifts from AD to AD_1, but in the long run national income remains at Y_0. AS_s is the short run supply schedule, so in the short run there will be a degree of expansion in national income. However, in the long run, aggregate supply is inelastic, represented by AS. The effect of the rise in aggregate demand will be to increase prices from P_1 to P_2. While supply side theorists accept that in the short run, national income may rise along the short-run aggregate supply curve AS_s, they contend that ultimately national income will fall to its long-run level of Y_0 because supply cannot be maintained above its long run level. Consequently, aggregate demand by itself is powerless to increase long-run output or employment.

Figure 6(b) illustrates a rise in aggregate supply from AS to AS_1. The income generated from the higher employment causes aggregate demand to extend and consequently national income rises from Y_0 to Y_1.

This demonstrates the supply side view that **only changes in the conditions of aggregate supply can lead to a sustained increase in output and employment**. The vertical aggregate supply curve suggests that changes in aggregate demand do not affect output but rather only influence prices.

The economy will self-regulate through the action of the price mechanism in each market. Flexible prices in goods and factor markets will ensure that at the microeconomic level each market tends towards a market-clearing equilibrium. At the macroeconomic level, the maximum attainable level of national income is at the level of full employment. Advocates of supply side economics argue that **flexible wages** will ensure the economy reaches this point.

6.4 Flexible wages

The importance of flexible wages is shown in Figure 7. When the wage rate is at W_0 the demand for labour is Q_d while the total supply of labour stands at Q_s. This creates involuntary unemployment of $(Q_s - Q_d)$ at the prevailing wage rate. By accepting lower wages workers can 'price themselves back into jobs' and consequently unemployment falls. If wages were perfectly flexible downwards then the market would restore full employment at wage rate W_1. This would leave unemployment at its natural rate.

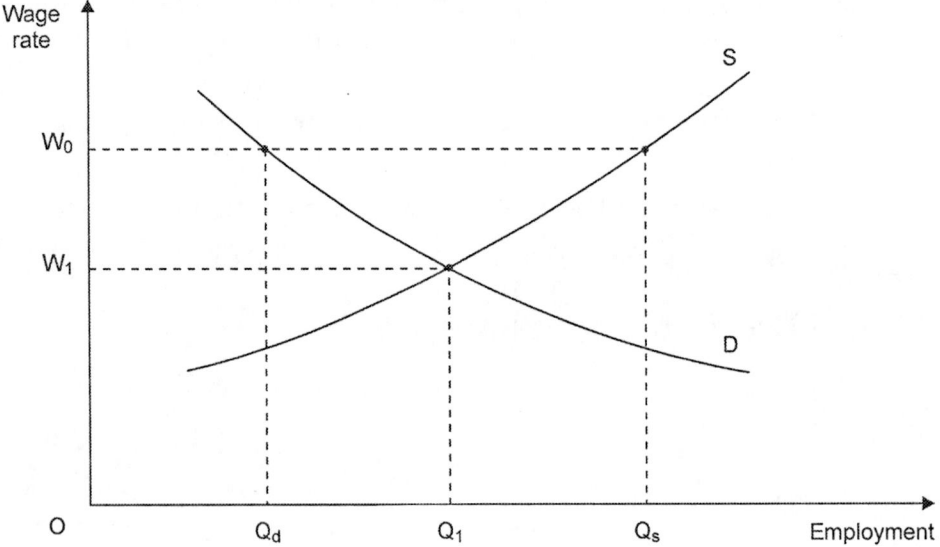

Figure 7 The labour market

7 Summary of macroeconomic policies

Throughout this chapter we have seen the ways Keynesian macroeconomic policy differs from monetarist economic policy.

The key differences in what Keynesians and monetarists think about economic policies are summarised in the following table:

Policy area	Keynesianism	Monetarism
Inflation	Caused by excess aggregate demand when economy is already at maximum output (full employment).	Caused by increases in the money supply, or excess money in the economy. Manage through measures to control the money supply – for example, interest rates.
Unemployment	Unemployment is involuntary and caused by weaknesses in the labour market, for example structural unemployment.	Unemployment is voluntary and caused by supply side weaknesses, for example workers not being prepared to work at the wage rates on offer.

Policy area	Keynesianism	Monetarism
Government spending	Government should intervene to bolster aggregate demand and reduce unemployment.	Should be minimised to avoid 'crowding out' of private sector spending.
Growth	Government should play an active role through fiscal policy.	Best promoted by supply side policies to stimulate markets

However, although the two schools' approaches on how to achieve the objectives vary, the underlying fact remains that the main objectives which most governments try to achieve through their domestic economic policies relate back to the objectives the Keynesians and monetarists discussed. They are:

(a) Price stability and low inflation
(b) Low unemployment
(c) Sustainable economic growth
(d) Balancing the balance of payments current account.

PART D PUBLIC SECTOR AND MACRO-ECONOMY

Chapter Roundup

- **Macroeconomic policy objectives** relate to economic growth, inflation, unemployment and the balance of payments.

- **Fiscal policy** provides a method of managing **aggregate demand** in the economy via **taxation** and **government spending**.

- **Direct taxes** have the quality of being **progressive** or **proportional**. Income tax is usually progressive, with high rates of tax charged on higher bands of taxable income. **Indirect taxes** can be **regressive**, when the taxes are placed on essential commodities or commodities consumed by poorer people in greater quantities.

- A government must decide how it intends to raise tax revenues, from **direct or indirect taxes**, and what proportion of tax revenues will be raised from each source.

- If the government kept its own spending at the same level, but **reduced levels of taxation**, it would also **stimulate demand** in the economy because firms and households would have more of their own money after tax for consumption or saving/investing.

- **Monetary theory** deals with the way changes in monetary variables affect the aggregate demand in the economy and its ultimate impact on **prices** and **output**. There are three theories of how the changes in the money supply are transmitted to the real economy: the quantity theory of money, the Keynesian theory, and the monetarist theory.

- **Monetary policy** focuses on the relationship between **interest rates** and the **supply of money** in an economy, and how the two of them together can influence aggregate demand.

- **The effectiveness of monetary policy** in influencing aggregate demand and unemployment is limited in the long-run.

- Fiscal policy and monetary policy both aim to manage aggregate demand in an economy. **Supply side policies** provide a method of managing **aggregate supply** in the economy.

Quick Quiz

1. What are the key differences between fiscal policy and monetary policy?

2. Outline how the government may use fiscal policy to influence aggregate demand.

3. What is:

    (a) A regressive tax?
    (b) A proportional tax?
    (c) A progressive tax?

4. Distinguish between direct taxation and indirect taxation.

5. The government of a certain country decides to introduce a poll tax, which will involve a flat rate levy of $200 on every adult member of the population. This new tax could be described as:

    A Regressive
    B Proportional
    C Progressive
    D Ad valorem

6. High rates of personal income tax are thought to have a disincentive effect. This refers to the likelihood that the high rates of tax will:

    A Encourage illegal tax evasion by individuals
    B Lead to a reduction in the supply of labour
    C Lead to a reduction in savings by individuals
    D Discourage consumer spending and company investments

7. The total yield from an indirect tax levied on a good is likely to be greatest when:

    A Demand is inelastic, supply is elastic
    B Demand is inelastic, supply is inelastic
    C Demand in elastic, supply is elastic
    D Demand is elastic, supply is inelastic

8. Which of the following will **not** be the immediate purpose of a tax measure by the government?

    A To discourage an activity regarded as socially undesirable.
    B To influence interest rates.
    C To influence the level of aggregate demand
    D To raise revenue to spend on public or merit goods

9. Which TWO of the following are suitable ways for a government to try to reduce the rate of demand pull inflation in an economy?

    A Reducing interest rates
    B Increasing direct taxes
    C Applying more stringent controls over bank lending
    D Increasing the budget deficit
    E Increasing the money supply ('quantitative easing')

10. What is the PSNCR?

11. According to Keynes, what are the three motives for wanting to hold money?

12. What will be the consequence for bond prices of an increase in interest rates?

PART D   PUBLIC SECTOR AND MACRO-ECONOMY

13 Which one of the following will be most likely to lead to a rise in aggregate demand in the economy?

   A   An increase in the level of income tax
   B   A decrease in government expenditure
   C   A decrease in interest rates
   D   An increase in the marginal propensity to save

14 What effect does an increase in interest rates have on the exchange rate?

15 What is the crowding-out effect?

16 According to Keynes, which one of the following is very sensitive to changes in interest rates?

   A   The money supply
   B   The speculative demand for money
   C   The precautionary demand for money
   D   Transactions demand for money

17 Other things remaining the same, according to Keynes, an increase in the money supply will tend to reduce:

   A   Interest rates
   B   Liquidity preference
   C   The volume of bank overdrafts
   D   Prices and incomes

18 According to monetarist economists, which of the following consequences will result from an increase in the money supply?

   1   Households will have excess money
   2   Households will use this money to buy more bonds, equities and physical goods
   3   Interest rates will rise
   4   The demand for money will respond to the change in interest rates
   5   Expenditure in the economy will increase

   A   1, 2 and 5 only will happen
   B   3 and 5 only will happen
   C   1, 2, 4 and 5 only will happen
   D   3, 4 and 5 will all happen

19 How do supply side policies affect inflation and unemployment?

   Answer in terms of the effect on the aggregate supply curve.

20 According to supply side theories, which of the following will be most likely to reduce unemployment in an economy?

   A   Increasing the money supply in the economy
   B   Increasing the levels of unemployment benefit
   C   Reducing the level of income tax
   D   Increasing vocational training and work skills for the unemployed

Answers to Quick Quiz

1. A government's fiscal policy is concerned with taxation, borrowing and spending; and their effects upon the economy. Monetary policy is concerned with money, the money supply, interest rates, inflation and the exchange rate.

2. A government can increase demand by spending more itself or by reducing taxation so that firms and households have more after-tax income to spend.

3. A regressive tax takes a higher proportion of a poor person's income than a rich person's. A progressive tax takes a higher proportion of a rich person's income and a lower proportion of a poor person's. A proportional tax takes the same proportion of all incomes.

4. Direct taxes are levied on income while indirect taxes are levied on expenditure. Indirect taxes are regressive. Direct taxes can be progressive.

5. **A**   A flat-rate poll tax, with no concession for the lower-paid, would take a higher proportion of the income of lower-income earners than of higher income earners. This is a regressive tax system.

6. **B**   The disincentive effect refers specifically to the disincentive of individuals to work.

7. **B**   The total yield from an indirect tax is likely to be greatest when (a) demand for the good is relatively unaffected by the addition of a tax on to the price and (b) supply is relatively unaffected, even though suppliers will be receiving the price net of the tax.

8. **B**   The main purpose of taxation will be to raise revenue for the government. Other aims might be to redistribute wealth or affect demand in the economy. Changes in rate of tax do not have a direct influence on interest rates, which can be influenced by a government's **monetary** policies.

9. **B, C**   Measures which could help to reduce the level of demand pull inflation will be ones which reduce the level of aggregate demand in an economy.

    Increasing direct taxes will reduce the amount of disposable income households have available for buying goods and services (which will reduce the 'consumption' element of aggregate demand).

    Imposing tougher controls over bank lending will reduce the amount of money banks lend. If there is less credit available to consumers (or firms), this will reduce the value of goods and services they can buy.

    Options A, D and E could all be used to try to increase demand in an economy, rather than to reduce it. Lowering interest rates (Option A) would be expected to lead to an increase in investment and consumer borrowing. Increasing the money supply (Option E) will lead to a fall in interest rates.

    Increasing government expenditure and/or reducing taxes (Option D) will provide an additional injection into the economy.

10. PSNCR (public sector net cash requirement) is the net amount borrowed by government when public sector spending is greater than tax revenues.

11. The transactions, precautionary and speculative motives.

12. Bond prices will fall until the fixed income they provide equates to the rate of interest.

13. **C**   If interest rates fall, people are more likely to spend rather than save. An increase in the level of income tax will mean people have less disposable income to spend. Government expenditure is an injection into the economy and a component of aggregate demand, so reducing government expenditure will deflate demand. An increase in the marginal propensity to save will mean increased levels of saving rather than demand (spending).

PART D PUBLIC SECTOR AND MACRO-ECONOMY

14   A rise in interest rates attracts foreign investment, thus increasing the demand for the currency. The currency typically strengthens as a result.

15   The crowding-out effect is the monetarist argument that public (government) expenditure merely displaces private sector spending in an economy rather than adding to it and boosting output.

16   B   According to Keynes, the money supply would be fixed by the authorities. The demand for money depends on three motives (transactions, precautionary and speculative) but it is the speculative demand for money that is sensitive to changes in interest rates, and this explains the liquidity preference schedule.

17   A   Lower interest rates should be a consequence of an increase in the money supply, with a movement along the liquidity preference curve rather than a shift in the liquidity preference curve.

18   A   The question describes the transmission mechanism, which is the link between an excess of money supply over demand (or money demand over supply) and changes in expenditure in the economy. According to monetarists, an increase in the money supply creates excess supply over demand. Households use the excess money to buy bonds (and so interest rates fall), equities and physical goods (and so expenditure in the economy rises). The demand for money is interest-rate inelastic, according to monetarists (but not according to Keynesians) and so this does not increase in response to any interest rate fall.

19   By shifting the supply curve to the right, a new equilibrium between aggregate supply and aggregate demand will be reached with levels of lower inflation and higher output (lower unemployment).

20   D   Supply side theories argue that unemployment results from problems with the supply of labour in an economy (rather the level of aggregate demand in an economy). Options A and C are measured designed to boost aggregate demand and so are not supply side policies. The availability of employment benefits (Option B) can be seen as encouraging unemployment rather than encouraging people to find work. On the other hand, providing unemployed people with new skills (Option D) should help them get jobs and boost the supply of labour in the economy.

End of chapter question

Main objectives

(a) Describe briefly the main objectives of macroeconomic policy in a mixed economy. **(8 marks)**

(b) Explain how fiscal policy can be used to achieve these objectives. **(12 marks)**

(c) Explain what is meant by 'supply side' economic policies. **(10 marks)**

(Total 30 marks)

PART D: PUBLIC SECTOR AND MACRO-ECONOMY

PART E

The external sector

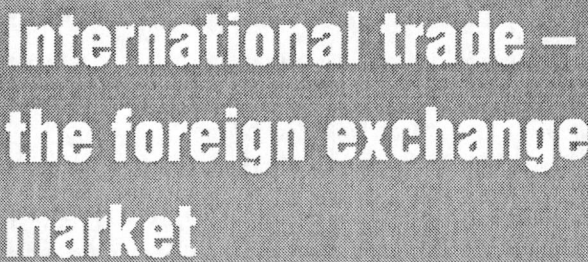

International trade – the foreign exchange market

Topic list	Syllabus reference
1 Exchange rates	2.5
2 Foreign exchange markets	2.5
3 Influences on exchange rates	2.5
4 Government policy	2.5
5 Risks of international trade	2.5

Introduction

In this chapter we look at how exchange rates are determined and how they impact on business. Before we see how the foreign exchange markets operate, we go through the terminology and basic calculations. The reason for doing this first is that the terminology is essential knowledge for all levels of your AIA studies.

In Section 2 we look at the operation of the foreign exchange markets and look at their impact on a business's competitiveness and ability to trade. An awareness of the factors that cause movements in the foreign exchange rates will help businesses predict what the effects are likely to be.

In Section 3 we consider the main influences on exchange rates. However, it is important to recognise that governments intervene to varying degrees to limit the fluctuations of exchange rate, and therefore in Section 4 we consider various exchange rate systems.

Fluctuations in exchange rates mean that businesses trading abroad will face some exchange risk and so in the last section we describe various methods firms use to counter foreign exchange risks, and also credit risks, which can also be significant when trading abroad.

PART E   THE EXTERNAL SECTOR

1 Exchange rates

The **spot rate** is the rate at which currencies are currently quoted on the foreign exchange markets. The **forward rate** is the rate at which currencies will be exchanged on a set future date.

1.1 Types of exchange rates

Key term

An **exchange rate** is the **price** of a currency expressed in terms of another currency.

An exchange rate is the rate at which one country's currency can be traded in exchange for another country's currency. It is the price of one currency expressed in terms of another currency.

This idea of an exchange rate being a price is important, because it indicates that an exchange rate (like any other price) may be set by the interaction of demand and supply – in this case the demand and supply for a currency compared to other currencies. An exchange rate determined solely by the interaction of demand and supply for a currency is known as a **floating exchange rate**. However, exchange rates may also be set by government intervention in order to maintain a constant rate of exchange (**fixed exchange rate**).

1.2 Dealing in foreign exchange

Dealers in foreign exchange make their profit by buying currency at one exchange rate (the **bid price**), and selling it at a more favourable rate for themselves (the **offer price**). This means that there is a **selling rate** and a **buying rate** for a currency.

1.2.1 Example: Buying and selling foreign exchange rates

Dan trades in the UK and wishes to purchase some machinery from a supplier in the United States. The transaction will be in dollars and the cost of the machinery is $500,000. Dan has also just received €100,000 on a contract and wishes to exchange the euros for pounds.

Assume the current exchange rates are:

$/£ 1.2700 – 1.2900
€/£ 1.1600 – 1.1800

Required

Calculate how much Dan will pay in sterling for the machinery and how much he will receive on the contract.

Solution

The key rule to remember is that Dan will always get the worse rate for the transaction and the foreign exchange dealers will always get the better rate.

(a) **The machinery**

Dan needs to **pay in dollars**, so needs to obtain or **buy dollars** with pounds. The rates quoted are how many dollars can be exchanged for each pound. Since Dan gets the worst of it, for each pound he pays to buy dollars, he will only obtain $1.2700, the **lower rate**.

Therefore to obtain $500,000, he needs to pay 500,000/1.2700 = £393,701

(b) **The contract payment**

Here Dan has **received euros** and wishes to **sell the euros** he has received in exchange for £. As Dan again gets the worse bargain, he has to sell more euros to obtain each pound, and so will have to hand over €1.1800 (the **higher rate**) to obtain each £.

Therefore, he will receive 100,000/1.1800 = £84,746

Question — Sterling receipts

Calculate how much sterling the exporter would receive, and how much sterling the importer would pay, in the following situations.

(a) A UK exporter receives a payment from a Danish customer of 150,000 kroners.
(b) A UK importer buys goods from a Japanese supplier and pays 1 million yen.

Assume current exchange rates are as follows.

	Bank sells		Bank buys
Danish Kr/£	8.3340	–	8.4380
Japan ¥/£	133.65	–	135.78

Answer

(a) The exporter is selling Danish kroners. The bank will buy Danish kroners and give

$$\frac{150{,}000}{8.4380} = £17{,}777 \text{ in exchange for the kroners}$$

(b) The importer is buying the yen from the bank. The bank will sell the yen to the importer, and will charge

$$\frac{1{,}000{,}000}{133.65} = £7{,}482$$

1.2.2 Mid-market price

Sometimes you will see a single exchange rate quoted which is the **mid-market price**. This is, unsurprisingly, the price midway between the bid and offer price. In the situation Dan is facing in the Example 1.2.1 above, the mid-market $/£ price would be 1.2800, mid-way between 1.2700 and 1.2900.

1.3 Direct and indirect currency quotes

Key terms

A **direct quote** is the amount of domestic currency that is equal to one foreign currency unit.

An **indirect quote** is the amount of foreign currency that is equal to one domestic currency unit.

Currencies may be quoted in either direction. For example, the US dollar and Euro might be quoted as €/$ = 0.9062 or $/€ = 1.1035. In other words €0.9062 = $1 and $1.1035 = €1. One rate is simply the reciprocal of the other.

A further complication to be aware of is that the selling rate in one country becomes the buying rate in the other. For example, Malaysian Ringgit (MR) are quoted in London as:

	Bank sells	Bank buys
MR/£	5.5655	5.5662

However, in Kuala Lumpur you would see:

	Bank sells	Bank buys
MR/£	5.5662	5.5655

Key term

> If a currency is quoted at $1.25:£, the $ is the **term currency** (the **reference currency**), and the pound sterling is the **base currency**.

1.3.1 Buying low and selling high

When considering the prices banks are using, remember that the bank will **sell the term (reference) currency low**, and **buy the term (reference) currency high**. For example, if a UK bank is buying and selling dollars, the bank's selling price may be $1.27 (the customer obtains fewer dollars for each pound he pays) and the bank's buying price may be $1.29 (the customer needs to give the bank $1.29 for the bank to pay each pound).

Exam focus point

> Always double-check which rate you are using. One sure method is to recognise that the bank makes money out of the transaction and will therefore offer you the worst of the two possible rates.

1.4 Spot and forward rates

Key terms

> A **spot rate** is the rate set for the immediate delivery of the currency.
>
> A **forward rate** is the rate set for the delivery of the currency at some future date.

A forward price is the **spot price** ruling on the day a forward exchange contract is made plus or minus the **interest differential** for the period of the contract. This differential reflects expectations of the movements in the various currencies between the current time and the date the forward rate becomes due. The expected exchange rate movements are likely to reflect interest rate differentials between the two countries, because as we will see later, interest rates can affect the demand for a currency.

The forward rate is **not a forecast** of what the spot rate will be on a given date in the future; it will be a coincidence if the forward rate turns out to be the same as the spot rate on that future date.

1.4.1 Discounts and premiums

Forward rates are not always quoted in full, but may be quoted at a discount or premium to the spot rates.

Forward rates as adjustments to spot rates	
Forward rate cheaper	Quoted at discount
Forward rate more expensive	Quoted at premium

A **discount** is therefore **added** to the spot rate, and a **premium** is therefore **subtracted** from the spot rate. (The mnemonic **ADDIS** may help you to remember that we ADD Discounts and so subtract premiums.) The longer the duration of a forward contract, the larger the quoted premium or discount will be.

1.4.2 Example: Discounts and premiums

The $/£ spot rate is currently quoted at 1.2700 – 1.2900 and the 1 month forward rate at 0.0006 – 0.0010 discount.

Required

Calculate the actual forward rate.

Solution

Because the forward rate is quoted at a discount, that means that more dollars can be obtained for each pound. The rate is therefore 1.2706 – 1.2910.

Question
Forward rate

The €/$ spot rate is currently quoted at 0.9000 – 0.9200 and the 3 month forward rate at 0.0012 – 0.0008 premium.

Required

Calculate the actual forward rate.

Answer

Because the forward rate is quoted at a premium, that means that fewer euros can be obtained for each dollar. The rate is therefore 0.8988 – 0.9192.

2 Foreign exchange markets

FAST FORWARD

Activity in foreign exchange markets partly depends on **currency demands** arising from **international trade**, but much dealing is done between banks.

If firms want to develop by doing business abroad, they will have to use foreign currency. However, their cash flows may be **threatened** by **adverse exchange rate movements** on the foreign currency markets.

Longer-term adverse exchange rate movements can threaten a firm's **competitiveness** in world markets.

2.1 Operation of foreign exchange markets

Currency markets exist to facilitate the **exchange of one currency** into another. Although demand to buy or sell foreign currencies arises from the demands of individuals (for example, tourists going abroad and firms doing business abroad), the main bulk buying and selling of foreign currencies is carried out by banks:

- Banks buy currency from customers and sell currency to customers
- Banks may buy currency from the government or sell currency to governments – this is how governments build up their official reserves
- Banks also buy or sell currencies between themselves

The foreign exchange markets are worldwide, and average daily turnover in global foreign exchange markets is thought to be over to $5 trillion.

PART E   THE EXTERNAL SECTOR

Weighted exchange rates

In its simplest form, an exchange rate can be measured as the value of one currency expressed in terms of another currency; for example, £1 = $1.28.

However, the value can also be expressed as a weighted average of exchange rates with a country's main trading partners, with the weightings being determined by the relative importance of the country as a competitor in export markets.

The weighted average of exchange rates is shown as an **index number**, and the weighted average is known as the **effective exchange rate**. A fall in the index shows an overall relative depreciation in a currency.

2.2 Dealing on foreign exchange markets

As we shall see later on in this chapter, some exchange rates are fixed, but many are allowed to vary. Rates are changing continually, and each bank will offer **new rates** for customer enquiries, according to how its dealers judge the market situation. Dealers are kept continually informed of rates at which deals are currently being made by means of computerised information services.

Exchange rates will often change by just small amounts up or down, but factors such as **speculation** may lead to more substantial movements.

2.3 Impact of foreign exchange markets on firms

2.3.1 Need for foreign exchange facilities

As we have mentioned, banks buy and sell foreign currency to their customers. Firms need to use banks because if they sell their products overseas, they will often not be able to price their products in their own currency, and will have to **price their products in the local currency** of the markets in which they are selling. They may, however, wish to convert the foreign currency earnings into their own currency, and so will have to use bank facilities to carry out this exchange. Similarly, if a firm buys from overseas, it may not be able to settle its account in its own currency, but may **require foreign currency to pay the supplier**.

Thus if firms wish to expand sales into new markets or use cheaper sources of production and supply, firms have to trade abroad and hence become involved in foreign exchange dealings.

2.3.2 Risks of exchange dealing

Although expending internationally and using foreign currencies may help a firm to grow, using foreign currency is also likely to expose a firm to **currency risk.** This is partly because doing business abroad does not just consist of a series of individual transactions settled instantaneously.

(a) A US company may agree in June to make a payment to a French company in September of €300,000. If the payment was made in June, the exchange rate could be 0.9200€/$ and hence the payment would have cost the company 300,000/0.9200 = $326,087. However by September the dollar may have weakened against the euro with the result that the company will, for each dollar it sells to the bank, obtain fewer of the euros that it needs. Say the rate has moved to 0.9000 by September. The payment will now cost the company 300,000/0.9000 = $333,333.

(b) A UK company may budget to receive $15,000,000 from sales in the USA over a year. If it expects the average exchange rate over the year to be 1.2500$/£, it will expect to obtain 15,000,000/1.2500 = £12,000,000 for the dollars it expects to earn and will budget accordingly. Suppose however that the value of the dollar falls, and the average exchange rate for the year turns out to be 1.2800$/£. Then the company will only earn 15,000,000/1.2800 = £11,718,750 and the actual value of sales will be less than budgeted, even though the quantities sold are the same as budgeted.

These examples illustrate how using foreign currencies in business can introduce a significant element of uncertainty into planning. We shall discuss how firms counter exchange risk later in this chapter.

2.3.3 Impact on competitiveness

For individual transactions, a company may be unlucky in being adversely affected by short-term currency movements. However, some currency movements may be longer-term. Over time, these movements may reduce the **longer-term competitiveness** of a firm. If its own local currency strengthens, then its products will become more expensive internationally and hence demand for them will decrease.

We can use a simple example to illustrate this. Suppose a UK company exports its product for sale in the US. The product price (in £) is £100. Initially the exchange rate is £1 : $1.3, so the selling price in the US will be $130. However, if the £ : $ exchange rate increases to £1 : $1.35, the selling price will become $135, so demand for the good in the US is likely to fall (*ceteribus paribus*).

As firms may both buy and sell overseas, it is possible that they may suffer adverse exchange rate movements in two ways. Suppose a UK company buys raw materials that are priced in US dollars. It converts these materials into finished products that it exports mainly to Spain. Over a period of several years, the pound depreciates against the dollar but strengthens against the euro. The **sterling value** of the **company's income declines** while the **sterling cost** of its **materials increases**, resulting in a double drop in the value of the company's cash flows.

A company need not even engage in any foreign activities to be subject to **longer-term currency exposure**. For example, if a company trades only in the UK but the pound strengthens appreciably against other world currencies, it may find that it loses UK sales to a foreign competitor who can now afford to charge cheaper sterling prices.

Case Study

Impact of Brexit

Following the UK's decision, in June 2016, to leave the EU ('Brexit'), the value of the pound fell significantly against the US dollar and the euro.

As such, the cost of imported commodities, priced in those currencies, increased and a number of suppliers, including Unilever, sought to increase their prices to offset these higher costs.

In October 2016, a dispute between Tesco and Unilever over who should bear the cost of the weakening pound led to Tesco briefly stopping the sale of dozens of Unilever products from its online store.

Although the dispute between Tesco and Unilever was quickly resolved, it nonetheless highlighted the potential impact that significant changes in exchange rates could have on businesses.

A significant decline in £ sterling will make imports of raw materials and commodities (which are often priced in US$) more expensive. Manufacturers then face a choice: they can either try to pass on the higher costs to consumers (by increasing their prices), or they keep prices unchanged and absorb the higher costs themselves (eg through lower profit margins).

In November 2016, a former boss of Sainsbury predicted that supermarket prices would rise by at least 6% in the following six months, as a result of the fall in the value of sterling. He highlighted that about half of the products UK supermarkets buy are sourced abroad, in currencies other than the pound. As such, he suggested that the fall in the value the pound could lead to 'profound change' for UK supermarkets, after years of broadly static grocery prices.

By contrast, however, the weaker pound could be a benefit to UK exporters.

For example, at an exchange rate of £1:€1.25, a product manufactured in the UK and sold for £5,000 would have a price, in euros, of €6,250. If the price in euros remains at €6,250 but the exchange rate falls to £1:€1.1, the UK company will receive £5,682 (6,250/1.1) from each unit of the product sold in Europe.

Alternatively, the UK company could reduce the price (in euros) at which the product is sold, making it more competitive and potentially increasing demand for it. At a rate of £1:€1.1, the selling price required for the manufacturer to receive £5,000 would be €5,500 (compared to 6,250 at the previous rate of £1:€1.25).

Question
Foreign trading

If a firm makes a lot of sales in one particular overseas countries, why might using suppliers within that country reduce its foreign exchange risk?

Answer

Because the firm is receiving monies and making payments in the same foreign currency, any adverse effect of an exchange rate movement on receipts will be countered by a beneficial effect on payments. This is the technique known as matching.

(There may well be other arguments for using suppliers in the same country that sales are made, and locating manufacturing facilities there as well: for example reduced transport and distribution costs.)

3 Influences on exchange rates

FAST FORWARD

Supply and demand for foreign currency are subject to a number of influences.
- The rate of inflation, compared with the rate of inflation in other countries
- Interest rates, compared with interest rates in other countries
- The balance of payments
- Speculation
- Government policy on intervention to influence the exchange rate

3.1 Factors influencing the exchange rate for a currency

In this section we will look at the major factors that influence movements on the foreign exchange markets, apart from government intervention, which we cover in section 4 of this Chapter.

Specifically, we will look here at how inflation, interest rates, the balance of payments and speculation affect exchange rates.

Generally economic conditions in a country can also affect the supply and demand for currency.

(a) **Total income and expenditure** (demand) in the domestic economy determines the demand for goods. This includes imported goods and demand for goods produced in the country which would otherwise be exported if demand for them did not exist in the home markets.

(b) **Output capacity and the level of employment** in the domestic economy might influence the balance of payments, because if the domestic economy has full employment already, it will be unable to increase its volume of production for exports.

(c) The **growth in the money supply** influences interest rates and domestic inflation. This is **monetarist** theory. The monetarist argument is that if a government restricts the growth of the money supply, it will be accompanied by high interest rates and consequently also a high exchange rate.

(d) A country's **economic prospects** can also affect its exchange rate. If the economic forecasts for the country are bullish, this might attract speculators' funds, thereby raising demand for the country's currency and increasing its exchange rate.

Moreover, since the 1980s, exchange rates have tended to reflect capital movements (driven by financiers buying and selling currencies) rather than the trading of goods and services between countries. Therefore, it could be argued that exchange rates do not accurately reflect real changes in an economy's competitiveness.

3.2 Inflation and the exchange rate

If the rate of inflation is higher in one country than in another country, the value of its currency will tend to weaken against the other country's currency.

3.2.1 Purchasing power parity theory

Purchasing power parity theory attempts to explain changes in the exchange rate as being a function of the relative rates of inflation in different countries. The theory predicts that the exchange value of a foreign currency depends on the relative purchasing power of each currency in its own country.

As a simple example, suppose that there is only one commodity, which costs £100 in the UK and €120 euros in France. The purchasing power parity exchange rate would be £1 = €1.2 (£100 = €120). If, as a result of inflation, the cost of the commodity in the UK rises to £120 but the cost in France remains unchanged, purchasing power parity theory would predict that the exchange rate would adjust to £1 = €1, because the same commodity now costs either £120 or €120.

If the exchange rate remained at £1 = €1.2, it would be cheaper in the UK to import more of the commodity from France rather than to produce it in the UK. If the commodity were bought in France for €120, at an exchange rate of £1 = €1.2 the equivalent cost in £ would be £100, whereas the cost of producing the commodity in the UK is now £120. As a result, the UK would have a balance of trade deficit in that commodity. This would only be corrected by an **alteration in the exchange rate**, with the pound weakening against the euro.

Purchasing power parity theory states that an exchange rate varies according to relative price changes, so that:

$$\text{'Old' exchange rate} \times \frac{\text{Price level in country A}}{\text{Price level in country B}} = \text{'New' exchange rate}$$

So, in our simple example we would see $1.2 \times \frac{100}{120} = 1$.

Unfortunately, the theory is not usually adequate in explaining movements in exchange rates **in the short term**, mainly because it ignores payments between countries (ie demand and supply transactions) and the influence of supply and demand for currency on exchange rates.

In addition, there are problems involved with measuring and comparing inflation across different countries: for example, that inflation figures include the price of some goods and services which are not traded internationally (eg housing), or that inflation figures include indirect taxes which only affect domestic prices. These issues can limit the validity of purchasing power parity theory.

3.3 Interest rates and the exchange rate

It would seem logical to assume that if one country raises its interest rates, it will become more profitable to invest in that country's currency, since the interest earned would be higher than if the investment were in a country with a lower interest rate. In this way, an increase in investment from overseas will push up the **spot exchange rate** because of the extra demand for the currency from overseas investors. In this way, governments could use high interest rates to sustain the external value of their currency.

However, while this may be true in the short-term, the **market adjusts forward rates** for this. If this were not so, then investors holding the currency with the lower interest rates would switch to the other currency for (say) three months, ensuring that they would not lose on returning to the original currency by fixing the exchange rate in advance at the forward rate. If enough investors acted in this way (known as **arbitrage**), forces of supply and demand would lead to a change in the forward rate to prevent such risk-free profit making.

3.3.1 Interest rate parity

The **interest rate parity** condition relates the forward and spot rates for two currencies to the interest rates prevailing in those two countries. Interest rate parity states that the spot price and the forward price of a currency incorporate any interest rate differentials between the two currencies.

We will illustrate this theory by looking at exchange rates for US$ and UK £, in which case the formula for calculating future exchange rates is:

$$\text{Forward rate US\$/£} = \text{Spot US\$/£} \times \frac{1 + \text{nominal US interest rate}}{1 + \text{nominal UK interest rate}}$$

The interest parity condition can also be expressed more generally as:

$$\text{Forward rate} = \text{Spot rate} \times \frac{1 + \text{domestic interest rate}}{1 + \text{foreign interest rate}}$$

This means that if domestic interest rates are greater than foreign interest rates, the forward price of the foreign currency will exceed its spot price.

Conversely, if domestic interest rates are below foreign interest rates, the forward price of foreign currency will be below the spot price.

3.3.2 Example: Interest rate parity

Assume the current exchange rate between the US and UK is $/£ 1.3000. Assume also that the current central bank lending rates in the two countries are 2% in the US, 1½% in the UK. What is the one-year forward exchange rate?

If we apply the formula we can calculate this as:

Forward rate US$/£ = 1.3000 × (1 + 0.02)/(1 + 0.015) = 1.3064

Question
Interest rate parity

Assume that the spot rate between the Japanese yen and the euro is currently 120.000 ¥/€. Assume also that the central bank lending rate in Japan is currently 1% and is 1½% in the Eurozone. What is the one-year forward exchange rate, using the interest rate parity condition?

Answer

Here we are dealing with two currencies that are not the dollar and the pound, but the logic of the formula remains the same. The exchange rate is quoted as the price in yen of one euro, which means the yen is the domestic currency so the Japanese interest rate goes on top of the interest rate parity equation.

Forward rate ¥/€ = 120.000 × (1 + 0.01)/(1 + 0.015) = 119.4089

3.4 The balance of payments and the exchange rate

If exchange rates respond to demand and supply for goods and services traded between countries and the balance of payments current account, then the balance of payments on the current account of all countries would tend towards equilibrium. This is not so, and in practice other factors influence exchange rates more strongly.

Demand for currency to invest in overseas capital investments, and supply of currency from firms disinvesting in an overseas currency have more influence on the exchange rate, in the short term at least, than the demand and supply of goods and services.

However, if a country has a **persistent deficit in its balance of payments current account**, international confidence in that country's currency will eventually be eroded. In the long term, its exchange rate will fall as capital inflows are no longer sufficient to counterbalance the country's trade deficit.

3.5 Speculation and exchange rate fluctuations

Speculators in foreign exchange are investors who buy or sell assets in a foreign currency, in the expectation of a rise or fall in the exchange rate, from which they seek to make a profit. Speculation could be destabilising if it creates such a high volume of demand to buy or sell a particular currency that the exchange rate fluctuates to levels where it is overvalued or undervalued in terms of what hard economic facts suggest it should be.

If a currency does become undervalued by heavy speculative selling, investors can make a further profit by purchasing it at the undervalued price and selling it later when its price rises.

Speculation, when it is destabilising, could **damage a country's economy** because the uncertainty about exchange rates disrupts trade in goods and services.

Keynesians point out that speculation distorts the market forces, by speculators 'selling' if the price of a currency is falling. (The normal economics of supply and demand suggests that demand for a good should increase if its price falls, but in this case, demand falls.) Keynesians suggest this is one illustration of the fact that exchange rates are not automatically adjusting, and therefore – contrary to the arguments of purchasing power parity theory – the 'real exchange rate' can remain in disequilibrium for a number of years.

4 Government policy

FAST FORWARD

Government policies on exchange rates might be to set **fixed exchange rates** or to allow **floating exchange rates**. Alternatively, governments may look for a policy somewhere between the two.

In practice, 'in-between' schemes have included:

- **Fixed rates**, but with provision for devaluations or revaluations of currencies from time to time ('adjustable pegs') and also some fluctuations ('margins') around the fixed exchange value permitted
- **Managed floating rates** within a desired range of values

Currency blocs and exchange rate systems enhance currency stability, but limit the ability of governments to pursue independent economic policies.

If several currencies adopt a single currency, then transactions between firms in different countries within the currency zone will become cheaper (no commission costs on currency dealings), and financial markets across the zone will become more flexible.

4.1 Free floating exchange rates

Sometimes governments will not intervene in the foreign exchange markets. Free floating or flexible exchange rates occur when **exchange rates are left to the interaction of market forces** and there is no official financing at all. In other words, the exchange rate will reflect the interaction of supply and demand for a currency.

(Note, however, the exchange rate theory assumes that currency is only demanded and supplied for the purpose of international trade.)

The demand curve for a currency shows how much of it will be demanded at a given rate of exchange. The shape of the curve will be downward sloping, like a normal demand curve.

Likewise, the supply of a currency shows how much of it will be supplied at a given price (rate of exchange) and this will be a normal, upward sloping supply curve.

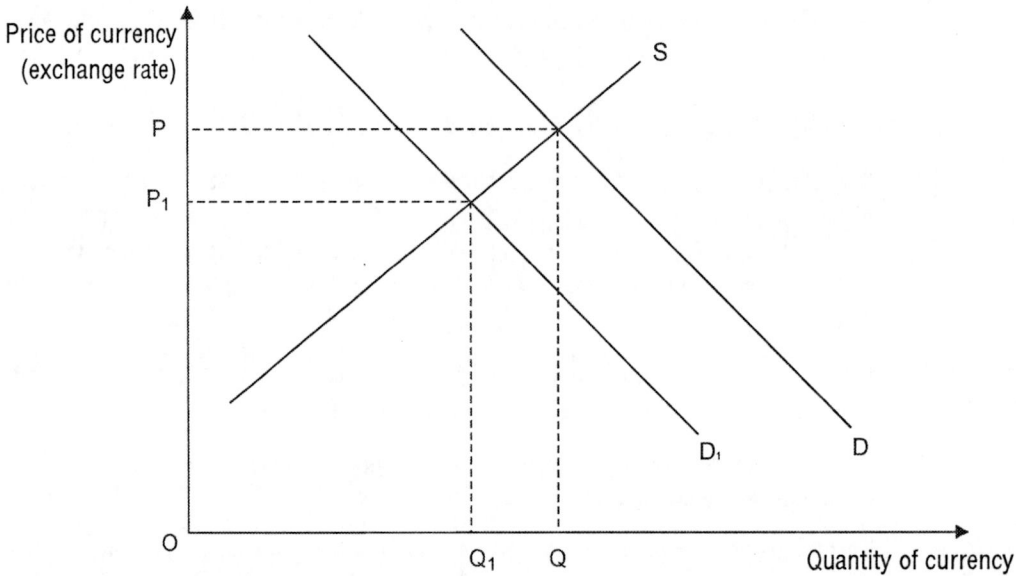

Figure 1 Floating exchange rate mechanism

It is important to remember that the demand for currency is a **derived demand**, reflecting the demand for exports from a country rather than simply the currency itself. For example, the demand for pounds sterling reflects the demand for British exports.

Therefore a fall in the demand for British exports would lead to an inward shift in the demand for GBP (D to D_1 on Figure 1). Consequently, the exchange rate for GBP would fall to P_1.

Equally, the supply of pounds is derived from the demand for imports into Britain. Pounds are needed to buy the foreign currency will which be required to pay for the imports.

Following the assumption that currency is only bought and sold for imports and exports, it follows that the exchange rate equilibrium also produces the balance of payments equilibrium; that is supply and demand for currency are equal at the point where imports are equal to exports.

It follows from this that a country with a deficit on its balance of trade (imports > exports) is likely to experience a fall in the exchange rate for its currency, because supply of it will exceed demand for it. *Vice versa*, a country with a balance of trade surplus (exports > imports) is likely to see an increase in its exchange rate because demand for its currency will exceed supply.

However, in practice, supply and demand of currency is not solely for imports and exports, and so exchange rates are subject to influences other than just trade.

As we have already mentioned, exchange rates are also affected by interest rates, inflation, and speculative motives.

Driver	Motive
Interest rates	As interest is the reward for capital, it follows that capital will tend to move towards the nation with the highest interest rate. This will increase the demand for that nation's currency, in turn pushing up its exchange rate.
Inflation	Currencies which suffer relatively high levels of inflation will be less attractive to depositors because their real value is depreciating against currencies with low inflation. So demand for a currency suffering high inflation will be relatively low, leading to a fall in its exchange rate.
Speculative	Sometimes investors may buy a currency simply to make a short-term capital gain, based on the appreciation of that currency. This will cause the currency to be overvalued relative to the equilibrium price which market forces would have generated.

These effects are also part of the logic which **Keynesian economists** use when they argue that exchange rates are not automatically adjusting. They believe that the 'real' exchange rate as determined by pure market forces can be in **disequilibrium** for a long time, precisely because of the distorting impact of external influences such as interest rates, and speculation.

Nonetheless, floating exchange rates are the only option available to governments when other systems break down and fail.

4.1.1 Advantages of floating exchange rates

(a) Governments do not have to spend or even hold foreign currency reserves.

(b) Balance of payments deficits or surpluses are automatically corrected. A deficit will result in the exchange rate falling; this will improve competitiveness, raise exports and restore equilibrium.

(c) Governments need not adopt economic policies that may be undesirable for other reasons to maintain exchange rates.

(d) Encourage efficient allocation of resources since exchange rates will reflect economic conditions.

4.1.2 Disadvantages of floating exchange rates

(a) If exchange rates **appreciate too much** under a floating rate system, then **firms' international competitiveness** may be reduced, and output and employment may fall across the economy.

(b) Uncertainty surrounding fluctuations in exchange rate could deter trade.

(c) If **exchange rates fall too much, import prices,** and hence **inflation**, will rise.

(d) **Currency risk** will be **maximised** under a system of floating exchange rates.

(e) The freedom afforded governments by (c) in the advantages above may mean governments do not pursue domestic policies which they should.

4.1.3 Managed floating

In practice, governments prefer generally to operate **managed floating** (or **dirty floating**) exchange rates for their currency, and a policy of allowing a currency to float entirely freely is rare. Under a system of managed floating exchange rates, governments will intervene in the market to buy or sell currency in order to achieve an exchange rate target. For example, they may wish to reduce the exchange rate to make exports more competitive, and they could, for example, achieve a reduction in the exchange rate by selling their own currency on the exchange markets.

4.2 Government intervention in foreign exchange markets

A government can intervene in the foreign exchange markets in two ways.

(a) It can **sell its own currency** in exchange for foreign currencies, when it wants to keep the exchange rate of its domestic currency low. The foreign currencies it buys can be added to the official reserves.

(b) It can **buy its own currency** and pay for it with the foreign currencies in its official reserves. It will do this when it wants to keep the exchange rate high when market forces are pushing it down.

The government can also intervene indirectly, by **changing domestic interest rates,** and so either attracting or discouraging investors in financial investments which are denominated in the domestic currency.

By managing the exchange rate for its currency, a government does not stop all fluctuations in the exchange rate, but it tries to keep the fluctuations within certain limits.

(a) **Unofficial limits**: a government might intervene in the foreign exchange markets and sell foreign currency from its official reserves to buy the domestic currency, and so support its exchange rate, even though there is no officially declared exchange rate that it is trying to support.

(b) **Official limits**: the country may be part of a system that allows its currency to fluctuate against the other currencies within the system only within specified limits.

4.2.1 Reasons for a policy of controlling the exchange rate

(a) To **rectify a balance of trade deficit**, by trying to bring about a fall in the exchange rate.

(b) To **prevent a balance of trade surplus** from getting too large, by trying to bring about a limited rise in the exchange rate.

(c) To **emulate economic conditions** in other countries, for example lower inflation.

(d) To **stabilise the exchange rate of its currency**. Exporters and importers will then face less risk of exchange rate movements wiping out their profits. A stable currency increases confidence in the currency and promotes international trade.

4.3 Fixed exchange rates

A policy of rigidly fixed exchange rates means that the government must use its **official reserves** to create an exact match between supply and demand for its currency in the foreign exchange markets, in order to keep the exchange rate unchanged. Using the official reserves will therefore cancel out a surplus or deficit on the current account and non-official capital transactions in their balance of payments. A balance of payments surplus would call for an addition to the official reserves, and a balance of payments deficit calls for drawings on official reserves.

For simplicity and convenience, the exchange rate is fixed against a standard. The standard might be one of the following.

- Gold
- A major currency
- A basket of major trading currencies

4.3.1 Advantages of fixed exchange rates

(a) A fixed exchange rate system removes exchange rate uncertainty and so encourages international trade.

(b) A fixed rate system also imposes economic disciplines on countries in deficit (or surplus).

4.3.2 Disadvantages of fixed rates

(a) There is inevitably **some loss of flexibility** in economic policy making once a country fixes its exchange rates. A government might be **forced to reduce demand** in the domestic economy (for example, by raising taxes and so cutting the demand for imports) in order to maintain a currency's exchange rate and avoid a devaluation.

(b) Countries regard **devaluation** as an indicator of failure of economic policy and often resist devaluation until long after it should have taken place.

4.4 Currency blocs

Currency blocs are where groups of countries **fix their exchange rates** against a major trading currency. The resulting stability is designed to help international trade, since the major currency used will be the currency of a country (countries) with whom members of the bloc carry out a lot of trade.

The currency may be a major world currency or it may be an artificial currency set up as part of a more formal exchange rate system.

4.5 Exchange rate systems

Exchange rate systems are systems where there is **stability** between the currencies of member currencies, even though there are fluctuations with the currencies of countries outside the systems. An example is the European Monetary System established in 1979. Part of this was the Exchange Rate Mechanism under which:

(a) Each country had a **central rate** in the system

(b) Currencies were only allowed to **fluctuate within certain levels** (bands)

(c) Within the bands, fluctuations of a certain limit should **trigger action** by governments to prevent fluctuations beyond the bands allowed.

The European Monetary System helped reduce exchange rate variability in Europe, and so acted as an important pre-cursor to the adoption of a single currency (the euro) in 1999.

4.5.1 Advantages of exchange rate systems

(a) **Reduction of inflation**

Exchange rate stability within an exchange rate system may help dampen inflation by preventing a government from allowing the currency to drift downwards in value to compensate for **price inflation**.

(b) **Expectations**

There are likely to be effects on people's expectations. In particular, the **perceived risk** of **exchange rate movements** between member currencies should be **low**. As well as allowing firms to plan and forecast with greater certainty, exchange rate stability ought to make a currency **less risky to hold**.

4.5.2 Problems with exchange rate systems

The UK joined the European Exchange Rate Mechanism (ERM) in 1990, with a rate set at £1 : 2.95 Deutschmarks (Germany's currency before the introduction of the Euro). However, UK was forced to withdraw from the ERM in 1992 because the UK's economic performance made the exchange rate unsustainable.

The UK's experience within the European Monetary System demonstrates a number of the potential problems of an exchange rate system.

(a) **Wrong initial rates**

In retrospect, it is clear that the UK entered the European Monetary System at **too high a rate**, leading to the UK becoming less competitive (as exports became too expensive for consumers in foreign countries), resulting in a deep recession and a significant deficit on the balance of payments.

(b) **Interest rate levels**

Interest rate policy must be consistent with keeping the currency stable. The problem the UK faced in the early 1990s was that it had to keep interest rates high to maintain the pound's value against the deutschmark because the German interest rate was also high. However, the two countries were facing different economic situations: Germany needed to keep interest rates high to counter continuing inflationary pressures caused by the unification of East and West Germany. The UK, though, had low levels of inflation but was suffering from recession and high unemployment, so what it needed were macroeconomic policies to stimulate growth.

(c) **Vulnerability**

Ultimately, the currency markets felt that the UK rate within the ERM was not sustainable, and **speculation proved self-fulfilling**. The UK's attempts to maintain the value of the pound by raising interest rates and spending foreign currency reserves to buy sterling proved in vain, and in September 1992 the UK devalued and left the ERM.

4.6 Single currency

A single currency is where a number of countries agree to adopt a single currency, for example, the euro. Twelve members of the European Union initially adopted a single currency, the euro, in 2002, but this has now risen to 19. The system is administered by the European Central Bank, which issues euros and sets interest rates across the Eurozone. The continuing success depends on **convergence of the economies** of the member economies. As we have seen with the UK's experience in the ERM, the system could run into serious difficulties if countries have different economic priorities.

The global economic slowdown from 2007-2010 also threatened to create a crisis in the Eurozone and exposed some fundamental imbalances between member countries – for example, between the economies of Greece, Portugal and Spain on the one hand, and Germany on the other.

4.6.1 Convergence criteria for joining EU

The convergence criteria are formally defined as a set of macroeconomic indicators which measure:

(a) **Price stability** – to show inflation is controlled. The potential Member State's consumer price inflation rate must be not more than 1.5 percentage points above the rate of the three best-performing Member States.

(b) **Soundness and sustainability of public finances**, through limits on government borrowing and national debt to avoid excessive deficit. The target figures are that the government deficit must be not more than 3% of GDP, and that government debt must be not more than 60% of GDP.

(c) **Exchange-rate stability**, through participation in the Exchange Rate Mechanism (ERM II) for at least two years without strong deviations from the ERM II central rate.

(d) **Long-term interest rates**, to assess the durability of the convergence achieved by fulfilling the other criteria. The potential Member State's long-term interest rate must be not more than 2 percentage points above the average rate of the three Member States which were the best performing in respect of price stability.

4.6.2 Advantages of a single currency

(a) The removal of exchange rate risk makes **cross-border trade and investment easier** and less risky.

(b) The removal of conversion fees paid by business and individuals to banks when converting different currencies makes **transactions** within the currency zone **cheaper**.

(c) **Financial markets** are **opened up** across the region and are more flexible and liquid than when there are many different currencies.

(d) **Price parity** or price transparency across borders is thought to **lower prices** across the area, because it allows consumers to compare prices across borders.

(e) **Funding** is **easier to obtain**, as there is greater cross-border borrowing.

(f) **Economic stability** within the zone is thought to benefit not just the member countries of the zone but also the **world economy** as a whole.

4.6.3 Disadvantages of a single currency

(a) **'One size fits all'** currency may **not be applicable** to countries with very different industrial structures and at very different levels of economic maturity.

(b) There is a **loss of national self-determination** in monetary matters.

(c) **Agreement and coordination** between the different countries using the currency may be **difficult to achieve**.

Question — Floating exchange rates

Which of the following is not a disadvantage of a government allowing a country's exchange rate to float freely?

A Floating may result in currency appreciation and a fall in competitiveness.
B Floating may result in currency depreciation and a rise in inflation.
C Floating will result in firms facing increased foreign exchange risk.
D Floating will mean that government economic policy becomes more restricted.

Answer

D Floating removes the restrictions on economic policy that are necessary to maintain exchange rates at fixed levels.

PART E THE EXTERNAL SECTOR

4.6.4 European Central Bank

The European Central Bank (ECB) is responsible for **monetary policy** in the eurozone (the countries using the euro), and its primary objective is to maintain price stability therein by managing interest rates.

The bank also seeks to **support the economic policies** of the European Union, which include maintaining a high level of employment, and achieving non-inflationary economic growth.

In addition, the ECB is responsible for conducting **foreign exchange operations**, and holding / managing the official foreign reserves of the eurozone countries.

Further tasks include **issuing banknotes** for the eurozone, (which ECB has the exclusive right to do) and promoting the smooth operation of payment systems.

5 Risks of international trade

5.1 Foreign exchange risk

> **FAST FORWARD**
>
> Basic methods of hedging risk include **matching receipts and payments, invoicing in own currency**, and **leading and lagging** the times that cash is received and paid.
>
> A **forward contract** specifies in advance the rate at which a specified quantity of currency will be bought and sold.
>
> **Money market hedging** involves borrowing in one currency, converting the money borrowed into another currency and putting the money on deposit until the time the transaction is completed, hoping to take advantage of favourable interest rate movements.
>
> More complex methods of hedging include use of derivatives such as **futures**, **options** and **swaps.**

Key terms

> **Foreign exchange (or currency) risk** is the risk that the value of a transaction will fluctuate due to changes in foreign exchange rates.

The main types of foreign exchange risk are as follows.

5.1.1 Transaction risk

Transaction risk is the risk of adverse exchange rate movements occurring in the course of **normal international trading transactions**. This arises when the prices of imports or exports are fixed in foreign currency terms and there is movement in the exchange rate between the date when the price is agreed and the date when the cash is paid or received in settlement.

We can illustrate this with a simple example.

Suppose a UK company has sold a product to a customer in the US, and the price the customer has agreed to pay was $1,200. At the time the sale was made, the exchange rate was £1 : $1.20. However, the company's payment terms meant the customer only had to pay one month later. By this time, the exchange rate has risen to £1 : $1.250.

This means the company will only receive £960 (1,200/1.25) for the sale rather than the £1,000 (1,200/1.2) it would have received if the rate had remained at £1 : $1.20.

5.1.2 Economic risk

This is the risk to the longer-term **international competitiveness** of a company. For example, a UK company might use raw materials that are priced in US dollars, but export its products mainly within the

EU. A depreciation of sterling against the dollar or an appreciation of sterling against other EU currencies will both erode the competitiveness of the company.

Economic exposure can be difficult to avoid, although **diversification of the supplier and customer base** across different countries will reduce this kind of exposure to risk.

5.1.3 Translation risk

This is the risk that the organisation will make exchange losses when the value of foreign assets or foreign liabilities is translated (converted) into the domestic currency. Translation losses can result, for example, from restating the book value of foreign assets at the exchange rate on the reporting date (year end) if the exchange rate rises. Such losses will not have an impact on the firm's cash flow unless the assets are sold though.

Movements in the exchange rate can also affect the value of a firm's foreign liability. For example, if the exchange rate falls, a business will have to pay more (in its domestic currency) to repay a foreign loan, than it had previously expected.

5.2 Dealing with foreign exchange transaction risk

5.2.1 Matching receipts and payments

A company can reduce or eliminate its foreign exchange transaction exposure by matching receipts and payments. Wherever possible, a company that expects to make payments and have receipts in the same foreign currency should plan to **offset** its **payments** against its **receipts** in that currency. Since the company will be setting off foreign currency receipts against foreign currency payments, it does not matter whether the currency strengthens or weakens against the company's 'domestic' currency because there will be **no purchase or sale of the currency**.

Since a company is unlikely to have exactly the same amount of receipts in a currency as it makes payments, it will still be **exposed to the extent of the difference**, and so the company may wish to avoid exposure on this difference by arranging forward exchange cover.

Offsetting (matching payments against receipts) will be cheaper than arranging a forward contract to buy currency and another forward contract to sell the currency, provided that:

- **Receipts occur before payments**, and
- The **time difference** between receipts and payments in the currency is **not too long**

5.2.2 Leads and lags

Companies might try to use:

- **Lead payments**: payments in advance, or
- **Lagged payments**: delaying payments beyond their due date

in order to take advantage of foreign exchange rate movements.

With a lead payment, paying in advance of the due date, there is a finance cost to consider. This is the interest cost on the money used to make the payment.

5.2.3 Currency of invoice

One way of avoiding exchange rate risk is for an exporter to invoice his foreign customer in his **domestic currency**, or for an importer to arrange with his **foreign supplier** to be invoiced in his **domestic currency**.

However, although either the exporter or the importer can avoid any exchange risk in this way, only one of them can deal in their own domestic currency. The other must accept the exchange risk, since there will be a period of time elapsing between agreeing a contract and paying for the goods (unless payment is made with the order).

5.3 Forward exchange contracts

Key term

A **forward exchange contract** is an agreement to exchange different currencies at a specified future date and at a specified rate. The difference between the specified rate and the spot rate ruling on the date the contract is entered into is the discount or premium on the forward contract.

Forward exchange contracts allow a trader who knows that he will have to buy or sell foreign currency at a date in the future to make the purchase or sale at a **predetermined rate of exchange**. The trader will therefore know in advance either how much **local currency** he will **receive** (if he is selling foreign currency to the bank) or how much local currency he must **pay** (if he is buying foreign currency from the bank).

5.3.1 Example: Forward exchange contracts

A UK importer knows on 1 April that he must pay a foreign supplier 16,500 Swiss francs in one month's time, on 1 May. He can arrange a forward exchange contract with his bank on 1 April, where the bank undertakes to sell the importer 16,500 Swiss francs on 1 May, at a fixed rate of say 1.2400 Swiss Francs:£.

The UK importer can be certain that, whatever the spot rate is between Swiss francs and sterling on 1 May, he will have to pay on that date, at this forward rate:

$$\frac{16,500}{1.2400} = £13,306$$

(a) If the spot rate is lower than 1.2400, the importer would have **successfully protected himself** against a weakening of sterling, and would have avoided paying more sterling to obtain the Swiss francs.

(b) If the spot rate is higher than 1.2400, sterling's value against the Swiss franc would mean that the **importer** would **pay more** under the forward exchange contract than he would have had to pay if he had obtained the francs at the spot rate on 1 May. He cannot avoid this extra cost, because a forward contract is binding.

Question

Forward exchange contracts

A German exporter is proposing to sell machinery to a UK customer worth £500,000 and is concerned about a change in the value of the euro against the £. The Finance Director therefore decides to take out a forward contract. The forward rates quoted are €/£ 1.1500 – 1.1550. How much in euros will the exporter receive under the contract?

Answer

The exporter in Germany will wish to sell the pounds sterling it anticipates that it will receive. The Finance Director takes out a forward contract maturing at the date of sale. The euro here is the **term** currency (X units) in the exchange rate quoted, therefore we have to **multiply** by the exchange rate.

Receipts = £500,000 × 1.1500 = €575,000.

5.4 Money market hedges

An exporter who invoices foreign customers in a foreign currency can hedge against the exchange risk by using the money markets.

5.4.1 Setting up a money market hedge for a foreign currency payment

Suppose a British company needs to pay a Swiss supplier in Swiss francs in three months' time. It does not have enough cash to pay now, but will have sufficient in three months' time. Instead of negotiating a forward contract, the company could:

Step 1 Borrow the appropriate amount in pounds now

Step 2 Convert the pounds to Swiss francs immediately

Step 3 Put the francs on deposit in a Swiss franc bank account

Step 4 When the time comes to pay the company:
  (a) Pay the supplier out of the Swiss franc bank account
  (b) Repay the pound loan account

5.4.2 Setting up a money market hedge for a foreign currency receipt

A similar technique can be used to cover a foreign currency **receipt** from a customer. To manufacture a forward exchange rate, follow the steps below.

Step 1 Borrow an appropriate amount in the foreign currency today

Step 2 Convert it immediately to home currency

Step 3 Place it on deposit in the home currency

Step 4 When the customer's cash is received:
  (a) Repay the foreign currency loan
  (b) Take the cash from the home currency deposit account

5.5 Derivatives

Derivatives are more complex methods of hedging foreign exchange risk. You only need a basic idea of how these work.

5.5.1 Futures

Futures are similar to forward exchange rate contracts in that they represent an **obligation to buy or sell currency** at a predetermined price at the end of the contract. However, unlike forward contracts, futures are **traded on organised exchanges** in contracts of standard size carrying standard terms and conditions. They are only available for a limited number of major currencies.

Futures are often '**closed out**' before they are due to be settled by undertaking a second transaction that reverses the effect of the original commitment. The profit or loss on closing out is set against the company's original requirement to buy or sell currency at whatever the spot rate is on the day that the contract is settled.

5.5.2 Options

Options allow businesses to **benefit from favourable movements** in exchange rates while allowing them protection if rates move adversely.

Currency options give the holder the **right** but **not the obligation** to buy or sell foreign currency on or before a specified date at a particular price (the exercise price).

(a) If exchange rates move adversely over time, so that buying or selling at the new spot rate is a worse deal than using the option, then the option will be exercised, and the company will deal at the **exercise price**.

(b) On the other hand if exchange rates have moved favourably, so that using the new spot rate is better for the business than using the option, then the option can be allowed to **lapse**.

The main disadvantage with options is that the **premium** that has to be paid to purchase them can be quite expensive. This means that if exchange rates move adversely, it will often be cheaper to have used an alternative method of hedging.

5.5.3 Swaps

In a **currency swap** arrangement, parties agree to swap equivalent amounts of currency for a period, effectively swapping debt between currencies. At the end of the swap, the original amounts are swapped back at an exchange rate agreed at the start of the swap.

Currency swaps can provide a **hedge** against **exchange rate movements** for longer periods than the forward market. If A Ltd gives £1 million to B Inc in return for $1.25 million, and the amounts are repaid after five years, then the effective exchange rate both at the beginning and at the end of the period is $1.25 = £1. Currency swaps can be similarly useful when using currencies for which no forward market is available.

Currency swaps can also be used to **restructure the currency base** of the company's liabilities. This may be important where the company is **trading overseas** and **receiving revenues** in **foreign currencies**, but its borrowings are **denominated** in the **currency of its home country**. Currency swaps therefore provide a means of **reducing exchange risk exposure**.

5.6 Credit risks

FAST FORWARD

> Management of **credit risk** is of particular importance to exporters, and various instruments and other arrangements are available to assist in this, such as letters of credit, export credit insurance and export credit guarantees.

Key term

> **Credit risk** is the possibility that a loss may occur from the failure of another party to perform according to the terms of a contract.

Credit means allowing customers to pay for their purchases in the future rather than immediately. Most often therefore credit risk means the failure of customers who have been allowed credit to pay for goods within a reasonable time, or even to pay at all.

5.7 Managing credit risk

Whether or not a firm trades overseas, there are certain basic things it can do to reduce the level of credit risk.

(a) Assess the **creditworthiness** of new customers before extending credit, by obtaining trade, bank and credit agency references and making use of information from financial statements and salesmen's reports.

(b) Set **credit limits** and **credit periods** in line with those offered by competitors, but taking account of the status of individual customers.

(c) Set up a system of **credit control** that will ensure that credit checks and terms are being adhered to.

(d) Set out clear **debt collection procedures** to be followed.

(e) **Monitor** the efficiency of the system by the regular production and review of **reports** such as age analysis, credit and bad debt ratios and statistical analyses of incidences and causes of default and bad debts amongst different types of customer and trade.

(f) **Debt factoring**. Consider the use of a debt factor to assist in the management, collection and financing of debts where this is cost effective. Debt factors may be employed solely on export sales.

5.8 International credit risk management

Where a company trades overseas, the risk of bad debts is potentially increased by the lack of direct contact with, and knowledge of, the overseas customers and the business environment within which they operate. While the basic methods of minimising foreign credit risk will be the same as those for managing credit risk domestically, there are additional options available to the exporter.

5.8.1 Letters of credit

Letters of credit (documentary credits) provide a method of payment in international trade which gives the exporter a risk-free method of obtaining payment.

At the same time, letters of credit are a method of obtaining **short-term finance** from a bank, for **working capital**. This is because a bank might agree to discount or negotiate a letter of credit.

(a) The exporter receives **immediate payment** of the amount due to him, less the discount, instead of having to wait for payment until the end of the credit period allowed to the buyer.

(b) The buyer is able to get a **period of credit** before having to pay for the imports.

The buyer and the seller first of all agree a contract for the sale of the goods, which provides for payment through a documentary credit. The **buyer** then requests a bank in his country to issue a **letter of credit** in favour of the exporter. The issuing bank, by issuing its letter of credit, **guarantees payment** to the exporter. The buyer does not have to pay for the goods until the end of the period specified in the documentary credit.

Letters of credit are slow to arrange, and are administratively cumbersome. However, they might be considered essential where the risk of non-payment is high, or when dealing for the first time with an unknown buyer.

5.8.2 Export credit insurance

Key term

Export credit insurance is insurance against the risk of non-payment by foreign customers for export debts.

You might be wondering why export credit insurance should be necessary, when exporters can pursue **non-paying customers** through the courts in order to obtain payment. The answer is that:

(a) If a credit customer defaults on payment, the task of pursuing the case through the courts will be lengthy, and it might be a long time before payment is eventually obtained.

(b) There are various reasons why non-payment might happen, for example, the foreign customer could go out of business, or file for bankruptcy. (Export credit insurance provides insurance against non-payment for a variety of risks in addition to the buyer's failure to pay on time.)

Not all exporters take out export credit insurance because premiums are very high and the benefits are sometimes not fully appreciated.

5.8.3 Export credit guarantees

Export credit guarantees are aimed at helping to **finance the export of medium-term capital goods**. These exports often involve long credit periods that could adversely affect the exporter's cash flow. In the UK, the Export Credit Guarantees Department (operating as UK Export Finance) arranges these facilities.

The export credit guarantee gives **security to banks** providing finance to exporters if that finance is threatened by the foreign customer defaulting. The finance made available to the exporter is for the majority (85% for example) of contract values, often at preferential rates. If the exporter complies with the terms of the loan, then they will not suffer any risk of loss on the amounts financed. The banks are prepared to take the risk because of the security provided by the export credit guarantee.

Chapter Roundup

- The **spot rate** is the rate at which currencies are currently quoted on the foreign exchange markets. The **forward rate** is the rate at which currencies will be exchange on a set future date.

- Activity in foreign exchange markets partly depends on **currency demands** arising from **international trade**, but much dealing is done between banks.

- If firms want to develop by doing business abroad, they will have to use foreign currency. However, their cash flows may be **threatened** by **adverse exchange rate movements** on the foreign currency markets.

- Longer-term adverse exchange rate movements can threaten a firm's **competitiveness** in world markets.

- Supply and demand for foreign currency are subject to a number of influences.
    - The rate of inflation, compared with the rate of inflation in other countries
    - Interest rates, compared with interest rates in other countries
    - The balance of payments
    - Speculation
    - Government policy on intervention to influence the exchange rate

- Government policies on exchange rates might be to set **fixed exchange rates** or to allow **floating exchange rates**. Alternatively, governments may look for a policy somewhere between the two.

- In practice, 'in-between' schemes have included:
    - **Fixed rates**, but with provision for devaluations or revaluations of currencies from time to time ('adjustable pegs') and also some fluctuations ('margins') around the fixed exchange value permitted
    - **Managed floating rates** within a desired range of values

- **Currency blocs** and **exchange rate systems** enhances currency stability, but limit the ability of governments to pursue independent economic policies.

- If several currencies adopt a **single currency**, then **transactions** between firms in different countries within the currency zone will become **cheaper** (no commission costs on currency dealings), and **financial markets** across the zone will become **more flexible**.

- Basic methods of hedging risk include **matching receipts and payments**, **invoicing in own currency**, and **leading and lagging** the times that cash is received and paid.

- A **forward contract** specifies in advance the rate at which a specified quantity of currency will be bought and sold.

- **Money market hedging** involves borrowing in one currency, converting the money borrowed into another currency and putting the money on deposit until the time the transaction is completed, hoping to take advantage of favourable interest rate movements.

- More complex methods of hedging include use of derivatives such as **futures**, **options** and **swaps**.

- Management of **credit risk** is of particular importance to exporters, and various instruments and other arrangements are available to assist in this, such as letters of credit, export credit insurance and export credit guarantees.

PART E THE EXTERNAL SECTOR

Quick Quiz

1 A UK trader is due to receive today a sum of $750,000 in settlement of a contract.

   Assume the $/£ spot rate is 1.2000 – 1.2200.

   How much in £ will the UK trader receive?

2 A German firm is due to receive £25,000 from a UK customer. Assume the €/£ exchange rate is 1.1650 – 1.1700. How much in € will the German firm receive?

   A € 21,368
   B € 21,459
   C € 29,125
   D € 29,250

3 The current mid-market spot rate for $/£ is 1.2500. Over the next year inflation is expected to be 2% in the UK, 4% in the US. Assuming that purchasing power parities hold, what would be the $/£ rate in one year's time?

4 The current mid market spot rate for £/€ 0.9100. Over the next year interest rates in the euro bloc are expected to be 2%, in the UK 1%. If the interest rate parity condition holds, what is the £/€ one-year forward rate?

5 What is the main advantage of a system of free floating exchange rates?

   A Currency risk will be minimised
   B Imposes policy discipline on governments
   C Balance of payments deficits or surpluses are automatically corrected
   D Consumers can compare prices across borders more easily

6 If a country has a freely floating exchange rate, which one of the following would lead to a rise (appreciation) in the rate of exchange for its currency?

   A A decrease in the level of exports
   B A decrease in the country's interest rates
   C A decrease in the country's inflation rate
   D A decrease in the level of capital inflows into the country

7 What is foreign currency hedging by means of borrowing the foreign currency converting it to the home currency, and placing the home currency on deposit known as?

   A Forward rate hedging
   B Money market hedging
   C Matching
   D Leading and lagging

8 Which of the following would normally result from a fall (depreciation) in a country's exchange rate?

   A A fall in the country's rate of inflation
   B A rise in the volume of exports
   C A worsening in its balance of payments
   D A rise in the volume of imports

Answers to Quick Quiz

1. 750,000/1.2200 = £614,754

2. **C**   25,000 × 1.1650 = €29,125. Note that we are given the €/£ exchange rate. If you chose 'A' you divided rather than multiplied, and used the rate that was more favourable to the firm rather than the rate that was more favourable to the bank. If you chose B you divided rather than multiplied. If you chose D you used the rate that was more favourable to the firm.

3. Using the purchasing power parity formula

    $$\text{Future US\$/£} = \text{Spot US\$/£} \times \frac{1 + \text{US inflation rate}}{1 + \text{UK inflation rate}}$$

    $$= 1.2500 \times 1.04/1.02$$

    $$= 1.2745$$

4. The interest rate parity formula for the currencies given in the question is:

    $$\text{Forward rate £/€} = \text{Spot £/€} \times \frac{1 + \text{nominal UK interest rate}}{1 + \text{nominal Euro interest rate}}$$

    $$= 0.9100 \times 1.01/1.02$$

    $$= 0.90101$$

    Note that the spot price expresses the prices of 1 euro in terms of £. So £ is the domestic currency and € is the foreign currency. This means that the UK interest rate goes on top of the interest rate parity equation.

5. **C**   Free floating exchange rates mean that market forces restore equilibrium in the market. A balance of payments deficit will mean that supply > demand for a country's currency, and so its exchange rate will fall. This will improve competitiveness of the country's exports so exports will increase and restore equilibrium in the balance of payments. (Answers A and D are benefits of a single cross-border currency such as the euro.)

6. A decrease in a country's inflation will make its exports cheaper, and therefore more attractive. The increase in demand for exports will lead to an increase in demand for the country's currency (for customers to pay for the exports) and this will lead to its exchange rate rising.

    Conversely, a decrease in the level of exports (A) will lead to a fall in demand for a country's currency, so this will lead to its exchange rates falling.

    Likewise if interest rates fall (B) it will be less attractive to invest money in a country's banks, so again there will be less demand for the country's money, from foreign investors looking to invest in it.

    A decrease in the level of capital inflows will also mean demand for the currency falls, and so, again, the exchange rate will fall.

7. **B**   This is money market hedging

8. **B**   The fall in the exchange rate will make a country's exports cheaper, therefore the volume of **exports will increase**. Conversely, the currency depreciation will make imports more expensive, so demand for **imports will fall**. The net of these two will lead to an improvement in the country's balance of payments. The rising price of imports will increase domestic inflation.

Devaluation policy

(a) Explain why a government might wish to reduce the exchange rate for its currency (devaluation) **and** discuss those factors that will determine the success of such a policy. **(12 marks)**

(b) Describe the possible effects on domestic companies of a significant devaluation of the currency.
(8 marks)
(Total 20 marks)

International trade – the international economy

Topic list	Syllabus reference
1 The balance of payments	2.5
2 The terms of trade	2.5
3 International trade and its economic advantages	2.5
4 Free trade agreements	2.5
5 Globalisation of markets	2.5
6 Global financial institutions	2.5

Introduction

In this final chapter, we examine three main things:

- The balance of payments and the economic policies affecting it
- Arguments for and against free trade
- Globalisation

The balance of payments is a statistical 'accounting' record of a country's international trade transactions (the purchase and sale of goods and services) and capital transactions (the acquisition and disposal of assets and liabilities) with other countries during a period of time.

Considering economics looks at how we use scarce resources, we need to consider how resources and trade are managed at an international level, rather than just within a single country.

Internationalisation and globalisation can have important consequences for businesses and national economies.

PART E THE EXTERNAL SECTOR

1 The balance of payments

FAST FORWARD

The **balance of payments accounts** consist of a **current account** with visibles and invisibles sections and transactions in **capital** (external assets and liabilities including official financing). The sum of the balances on these accounts must be zero, although in practice there is a balancing figure for measurement errors.

1.1 The nature of the balance of payments

Exam focus point

Students often confuse the balance of payments with the government budget. Make sure that the distinction is clear in your mind. A government cannot correct a balance of payments current account deficit through its own budget. The two are quite separate.

Receipts in the balance of payments (external balance) come from **exports** of goods and services and inflows of capital.

Payments in the balance of payments come from **imports** of goods and services and outflows of capital.

The balance of payments accounts have three parts:

(a) Current account
(b) Capital account
(c) Financial account

1.1.1 Current account

The **current account** can be subdivided as follows:

Visibles	Invisibles
• Trade in goods	• Trade in services • Primary income (interest, profit, dividends) • Secondary income (transfers)

Trade in goods relates to exports and imports of tangible goods, such as oil, machinery, transport equipment, electrical goods, clothing and so on.

Trade in services relates to exports and imports of services, and includes such things as international transport, travel, financial services and business services.

Primary income is divided into two parts.

(a) **Employment income** - Income from employment of UK residents by overseas firms

(b) **Investment income** - Income from capital investment overseas (such as dividends and interest earned)

Secondary income is also divided into two parts:

(a) Public sector payments to, and receipts from, overseas bodies such as the EU. Typically these are interest payments

(b) Non-government sector payments to and receipts from bodies such as the EU

1.1.2 Capital account

The **capital account** balance is made up of public sector flows of **capital** into and out of the country, such as government loans to other countries.

1.1.3 Financial account

The balance on the **financial account** is made up of flows of capital to and from the non-government sector, such as direct investment in overseas facilities; portfolio investment (in shares, bonds and so on); and speculative flows of currency ('hot money'). Movements on government foreign currency reserves are also included under this heading.

If a multinational company invests in Britain this would be shown as an inflow under the investment section of the financial account.

Similarly, if speculators buy up £ sterling in response to interest rate or exchange rate movements, these 'hot money' movements will still be shown as inflows in the financial account even though they are short-term capital movements.

1.2 Net errors and omissions

A balancing item appears in the balance of payments accounts because of errors and omissions in collecting statistics for the accounts (for example, sampling errors for items such as foreign investment and tourist expenditure and omissions from the data gathered about exports or imports). A positive balancing item indicates unrecorded net exports: a negative one, net imports.

The sum of the balance of payments accounts must always be zero (ignoring statistical errors in collecting the figures). This is for the same reason that a statement of financial position must always balance: for every debit there must be a credit.

So if the current account is in **deficit** it must be matched by a **surplus** on the capital or financial accounts.

If a country is suffering a current account deficit, it will need to attract additional capital and financial inflows into it. It can do this either by attracting **foreign direct investment** from multinational companies, or attracting foreign funds. It will achieve the latter through having a more attractive level of interest rates than other countries. This could lead to conflict between a domestic need for low interest rates and the need for higher interest rates to attract foreign funds.

1.3 The UK balance of payments accounts

The UK balance of payments account is summarised below, showing how the deficit on the current and capital accounts is matched by the surplus on the financial accounts.

UK balance of payments accounts

	2016 £m	2015 £m
Current account		
Trade in goods	(135,391)	(118,626)
Trade in services	92,378	86,256
Primary income	(50,417)	(42,937)
Secondary income	(22,025)	(22,838)
Current balance	**(115,455)**	**(98,145)**
Capital account	(1,344)	(1,978)
Financial account	119,562	90,892
	2,763	(9,231)
Net errors and omissions	(2,763)	9,231
	0	0

[*Source:* Office for National Statistics (ONS), Balance of Payments]

Given that the balance of payments in principle sums to zero, you may wonder what is meant by a surplus or deficit on the balance of payments. When journalists or economists speak of the balance of payments they are usually referring to the deficit or surplus on the current account, or possibly to the surplus or deficit on trade in goods only (this is also known as the **balance of trade**).

A surplus on the current account is generally regarded as desirable, because the **current account affects national income**. If a country has a current account deficit this represents a net withdrawal from the circular flow of income, and so a deficit on a country's current account will be **deflationary**.

Question
Balance of payments

'If the balance of payments always balances, why do we hear about deficits and surpluses?'

Answer

The sum of the three balance of payments accounts must always be zero, because every transaction in international trade has a double aspect. Just as accounting transactions are recorded by matching debit and credit entries, so too are international trade and financing transactions recorded by means of matching plus and minus transactions.

If a UK exporter sells goods to a foreign buyer:

(a) The value of the export is a plus in the current account of the balance of payments

(b) The payment for the export results in a reduction in the deposits held by foreigners in UK banks (a minus in the assets and liabilities section)

When we use the phrases 'deficit' or 'surplus on the balance of payments' what we actually mean is a deficit or surplus on the current account. If there is a surplus (+) on the current account we would expect this to be matched by a similar negative amount on the assets and liabilities section. This will take the form of:

(a) Additional claims on non-residents (for example, overseas loans)
(b) Decreased liabilities to non-residents (paying off our loans abroad)

This will involve not only banks and other firms but it may also involve the government too, since it is responsible for the 'reserves'.

If there is a deficit (-) on the current account the result will be a similar positive amount on the assets and liabilities section. This will consist of inward investment and/or increased overseas indebtedness, representing how the deficit has been 'financed'. This means that banks and other firms will owe more money abroad and the government may also be borrowing from abroad.

1.4 Foreign currency and international trade

With international trade, there is often a need for foreign currency for at least one of the parties to the transaction.

(a) If a UK exporter sells goods to a US buyer, and charges the buyer £20,000, the US buyer must somehow obtain the sterling in order to pay the UK supplier. The US buyer will do this by using some of his US dollars to buy the £20,000 sterling, probably from a bank in the USA.

(b) If a UK importer buys goods from Germany, he might be invoiced in euros, say €100,000. He must obtain this foreign currency to pay his debt, and he will do so by purchasing the euros from a UK bank in exchange for sterling.

(c) If a UK investor wishes to invest in US capital bonds, he would have to pay for them in US dollars, and so he would have to sell sterling to obtain the dollars.

Thus **capital outflows**, such as investing overseas, not just payments for imports, cause a demand to sell the domestic currency and buy foreign currencies. On the other hand, exports and capital inflows to a country cause a demand to buy the domestic currency in exchange for foreign currencies.

Exporters might want to sell foreign currency earnings to a bank in exchange for domestic currency, and importers may want to buy foreign currency from a bank in order to pay a foreign supplier.

1.5 Exchange rates and the UK balance of payments

As in any other market, the market for foreign exchange is a market in which buyers and suppliers come into contact, and 'prices' (exchange rates) are set by supply and demand. Exchange rates change continually. Significant movements in the exchange rate for a country's currency can have important implications for the country's balance of payments.

1.6 Equilibrium in the balance of payments

A balance of payments is in equilibrium if, over a period of years, the exchange rate remains stable and autonomous credits and debits are equal in value (the annual trade in goods and services is in overall balance). However, equilibrium will not exist if these things require the government to introduce measures which create unemployment or higher prices, sacrifice economic growth or impose trade barriers (eg import tariffs and import quotas).

1.7 Surplus or deficit in the current account

FAST FORWARD

> When newspapers and the press talk about a surplus or deficit on the balance of payments, they usually mean a **surplus or deficit on the current account**.

A problem arises for a country's balance of payments when the country has a deficit on its current account year after year, although there can also be problems for a country which enjoys a continual current account **surplus**.

The problems of a **deficit** on the current account are probably the more obvious though. When a country is continually in deficit, it is importing more goods and services that it is exporting.

The table below summarises the main reasons why a country might be suffering a current account deficit.

Increased import penetration	Poor export performance
Lower production costs mean overseas competitors can produce goods more cheaply than domestic producers.	Exports are not competitively priced and so overseas demand will fall.
Over-valuation of domestic currency makes imports relatively cheaper than domestic products.	Over-valuation of domestic currency makes exports relatively more expensive.
High income elasticity of demand for imports increases demand for imports as national income grows.	Low income elasticity of demand in foreign markets, so demand for exports only grows slowly despite foreign national incomes growing.
	Equally a country might have low exports because its own domestic market is growing, hence its producers will concentrate on domestic sales rather than looking to export.
Non-price features of imported goods (eg performance, service care) better than domestic goods.	Non-price features of exported goods (eg performance, service care) worse than those of home-produced goods in target markets.

Many of these situations characterise British industry in recent years, and explain why Britain has been experiencing a structural deficit in its balance of payments current account, with a high demand for imports alongside a weak performance in manufacturing exports. Productivity in Britain languishes a long way behind other developed countries, while a consumer boom and a strong currency have increased demand for imports.

A current account deficit leads to three possible consequences.

(a) A country may borrow more and more from abroad, to build up external **liabilities** which match the deficit on its current account, for example encouraging foreign investors to lend more by purchasing the government's gilt-edged securities.

(b) A country may sell more and more of its **assets**. This has been happening in the USA in the early 2000s, for example, where a large deficit on the US current account has resulted in large purchases of shares in US companies by foreign firms.

(c) **Reserves** of foreign currency held by the central bank may be run down.

Note, however, that none of these three can continue indefinitely, for example because reserves and assets will eventually run out and if liabilities increase too far foreigners will become unwilling to lend fearing their loans will be irrecoverable.

A current account deficit will also mean the demand to buy the country's currency in the foreign exchange markets will be weaker than the supply of the country's currency for sale. As a consequence, there will be pressure on the exchange rate to **depreciate in value**.

If a country has a **surplus** on current account year after year, it might invest the surplus abroad or add it to official reserves. The balance of payments position would be strong. There is the problem, however, that if one country which is a major trading nation (such as Japan) has a continuous surplus on its balance of payments current account, other countries must be in continual deficit. These other countries can run down their official reserves, perhaps to nothing, and borrow as much as they can to meet the payments overseas, but eventually, they will run out of money entirely and be unable even to pay their debts. Political pressure might therefore build up within the importing countries to impose tariffs or **import quotas**.

1.8 How can a government reduce a current account deficit?

The government of a country with a balance of payments deficit will usually be expected to take measures to reduce or eliminate the deficit. A deficit on current account may be rectified by one or more of the following measures.

(a) A **depreciation of the currency** to make exports more attractive and imports less attractive. This is called a **devaluation** when deliberately instigated by the government, for example by changing the value of the currency within a controlled exchange rate system.

(b) Direct measures to **restrict imports**, such as tariffs or import quotas or exchange control regulations.

(c) **Domestic deflation** to reduce aggregate demand in the domestic economy, and hence reduce the level of imports.

The first two are **expenditure switching** policies, which transfer resources and expenditure away from imports and towards domestic products, while the last is an **expenditure reducing** policy.

1.9 Depreciation/devaluation of the currency

A rising (ie appreciating) exchange rate may reflect relatively low inflation and strong trade and general economic performance in a country. Conversely, poor economic performance and high inflation will result in **currency depreciation** (devaluation).

[Note: A devaluation occurs when the value of a currency is lowered in a fixed exchange rate system. A depreciation occurs when an exchange rate is reduced under a floating exchange rate system.]

As a result of a fall in the value of the currency, exports would become relatively cheaper to foreign buyers, and so the demand for exports would rise.

The extent of the increase in export revenue would depend on several factors.

(a) The price elasticity of demand for the goods in export markets.

(b) The extent to which industry is able to respond to the export opportunities by either producing more goods, or switching from domestic to export markets.

(c) It may also depend on the price elasticity of supply. With greater demand for their goods, producers should be able to achieve some increase in prices (according to the law of supply and demand), and the willingness of suppliers to produce more would then depend on the price elasticity of supply.

[Note: An appreciation of a currency will have the opposite effects to those of a depreciation.]

The cost of imports would rise as a result of **currency depreciation** because more domestic currency would be needed to obtain the foreign currency to pay for imported goods. The volume of imports would fall, although whether or not the total value of imports fell too would depend on the elasticity of demand for imports.

(a) If demand for imports is inelastic, the volume of demand would fall by less than their cost goes up, so that the total value of imports would rise.

(b) If demand for imports is elastic, the total value of imports would fall since the fall in volume would outweigh the increase in unit costs.

If a country imports raw materials and exports manufactured goods which are made with those materials, the cost of imported raw materials will rise, and so producers will have to put up their prices to cover their higher costs. There will be a net fall in export prices, as explained above, but perhaps not by much.

1.10 Effects of a fall in exchange rate on the balance of payments

The effects of a fall in the exchange rate (for example, due to a government policy of devaluation) are likely to vary in the short term and the long term. The immediate effects will depend on the elasticity of demand for imports. Demand is likely to be fairly inelastic in the short term and so total expenditure on imports will rise. Exports will be cheaper in overseas markets (in foreign currency) but in the short term exporters might be unable to increase their output to meet the higher demand.

Until domestic industry adjusts to the change and increases its output of exported goods and home produced substitutes for imported goods, there will be a deterioration in the current account of the balance of payments.

After a time lag, production of exports and import substitutes can be expected to rise, so that the volume of exports will rise, thereby increasing the value of exports (despite the domestic currency's lower exchange rate) and the volume of imports will fall further. This will improve the current account balance.

The improvement in the balance of payments will have some limit, and the current balance should eventually level off. The effect of the falling exchange rate on the current balance through time has been portrayed in the form of the so-called **J curve** (Figure 1).

Key term

> **J curve effect**: the effect on the balance of payments of a falling exchange rate. Inelasticity of both supply and demand means that the current account will deteriorate at first but then improve.

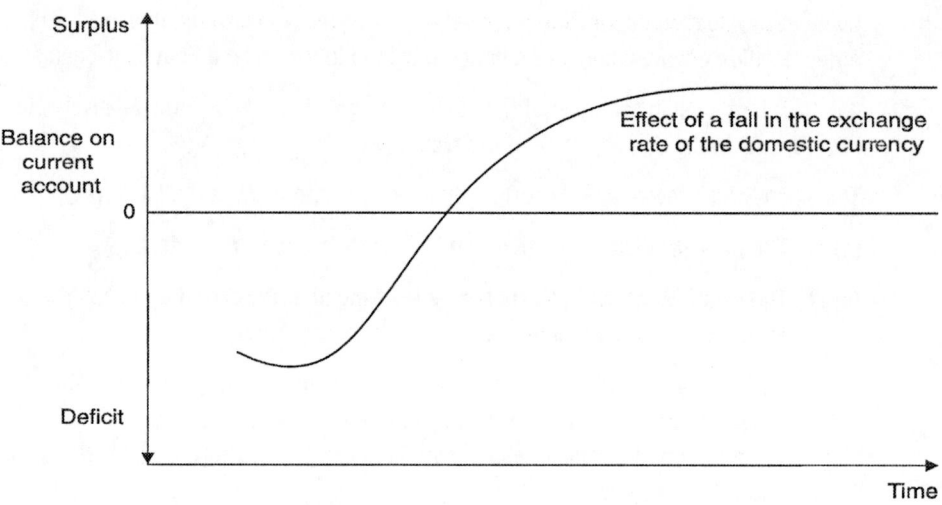

Figure 1 J curve

The upside in the J curve is based on the **Marshall-Lerner conditions** being met. These state that provided the sum of the price elasticity of demand coefficients for **exports and imports is greater than one**, then a fall in the exchange rate will reduce a balance of payments deficit. If demand for both imports and exports is inelastic (which it will be in the short run) then a currency depreciation will lead to a worsening of the balance of payments position. This is why the J curve falls initially.

1.11 Effects of currency appreciation

As we have noted, an increasing (**appreciating**) **exchange rate** may reflect relatively low inflation and strong trade and general economic performance, as in the case of Japan in the 1970s and 80s. (Conversely, poor economic performance and high inflation will result in currency depreciation.) To consider the implications for an economy such as Japan's of a rise in the value of the currency in more detail, we will look first at the effects on exports and then on imports.

As the yen rises in value, so other currencies weaken relatively. Over the years, the number of dollars, pounds, marks and so on required to buy 100 yen rises. The result is to increase the effective price of Japanese goods abroad, so that with price elasticity of demand, the volume of exports would be depressed. The diminished volume of exports would have domestic consequences.

- Inventories would gradually build up, leading to a curtailment of production.
- In turn, this could result in higher unit costs as fixed costs are less effectively spread.
- Short-time working and possibly labour redundancies might follow.
- Some investment decisions might be deferred or even cancelled altogether.

These reductions in the level of economic activity would have negative multiplier effects.

A strong currency means that imports become cheaper. Therefore costs of imported raw materials and foodstuffs fall. Input costs for industry therefore fall and any rises in retail prices are restrained. Inflationary pressures in the system are thus lessened. This may be used to advantage on exports to offset partially the effect of the rising currency: firms may be able to hold down their ex-factory price and so enable the net price overseas to rise very little. Any advantage on the import side of a stronger currency would depend on the relative importance of imports: a country having to import much of its raw materials and fuel could find this a useful advantage.

With a strong currency, there will also be an increased attraction for buying foreign consumer goods. Invisible imports may begin to rise: more Japanese residents might venture abroad on holiday, so increasing the supply of yen in currency markets and raising the demand for other currencies. This would exert some downward pressure on the yen. Any recessionary effects on industry would, of course, tend to lessen these import pressures.

The overall effect would depend on the balance between export and import effects – some unfavourable, some favourable. Any significant decline in the net inflow of capital as economic expansion slows could have a de-stabilising effect. The overall effect would also depend upon the ability of the economy to adjust to the changed conditions, for example through improved efficiency, so enabling ex-factory prices to be reduced. The overall effect would also depend upon economic conditions in the rest of the world.

1.12 Protectionist measures

Another way of attempting to rectify a balance of payments deficit is to take direct protectionist measures as if trying to **reduce the volume of imports**. These measures might include import **tariffs** or import **quotas**.

(We will look at protectionist measures in more detail later, in Section 3.8).

1.13 Domestic deflation

Deflation can be used to adjust a balance of trade deficit. When the total volume of expenditure and demand for goods in a country's economy is too high, the government can take steps to reduce it, by reducing its own expenditure, raising interest rates to deter borrowing, and cutting private consumption by raising taxes. This fall in demand should lead to a fall in prices or at least to a reduction in the rate of domestic inflation. Unfortunately, it might also lead, in the short term at least, to a reduction in industrial output and a loss of jobs in the country's economy. Certainly, the country must accept a lowering of its standard of living if severe deflationary measures are taken. The effect of deflation is not only to dampen domestic inflation rates, but to force domestic manufacturers, who will be faced with lower domestic demand for their goods, to switch more effort into selling to export markets.

Deflationary measures include cutting government spending, increasing taxation and raising interest rates. They have three purposes.

(a) To reduce the demand for goods and services at home, and so to reduce imports

(b) To encourage industry to switch to export markets, because of the fall in domestic demand

(c) To tackle domestic inflation, which might be undermining the beneficial effect for exports of a depreciating domestic currency by raising the prices of exported goods in terms of the domestic currency

Sometimes, a government's domestic economic policies are not deflationary, despite a balance of payments deficit, and on the contrary, the government's economic policies might encourage increasing demand, which will both boost demand for imports, and cause more inflation and a falling exchange rate. Economic policies which boost demand in the economy in spite of a balance of payments deficit will worsen, rather than improve, the deficit.

1.14 The balance of payments and the domestic economy

You should try to view any country's balance of payments position in the context of its domestic economy.

(a) When a country's exports exceed its imports, or *vice versa*, there may be a lack of equilibrium between **withdrawals** from the circular flow of income in the domestic economy (remember that these withdrawals include imports) and **injections** into the circular flow of income (which include exports). Equilibrium in the balance of payments (external equilibrium) will also help a country to achieve equilibrium in its circular flow of income (internal equilibrium).

(b) If a country's international trade is only small in size compared with its domestic economy, problems with any balance of payments deficit will be much less than for a country which relies heavily on international trade.

1.15 Interest rates and the balance of payments

Comparative interest rates between one country and another, and changes in interest rates, affect the balance of payments in two ways.

(a) Directly, by stimulating or discouraging foreign investment, and so inflows and outflows of capital.

(b) Indirectly, through the exchange rate. Foreign investment creates a demand for the currency and keeps the exchange rate at a high level.

Is a high interest rate policy a good solution to the problem of a deficit on the balance of payments current account?

(a) If a country relies on inflows of capital to finance a continuing balance of trade deficit, the country's balance of payments will never get into equilibrium. High interest rates will keep the exchange rate high for the country's currency, and this will make it more difficult to export (high export prices to foreign buyers) and encourage imports (cheaper prices). The country might therefore be unable to rectify its balance of trade deficit if it maintains a high interest rate.

(b) If there is a continuing balance of trade deficit, there will always be a threat that the country's currency will eventually depreciate in value. In turn, if there is an expectation that a country's currency will fall in value, this is also likely to deter investors – meaning that there is likely to be low demand for the country's currency. (As a result, its exchange rate will fall – meaning that the 'expectation' comes true).

Investors will only put money into capital investments abroad if they have satisfactory expectations about what the exchange rate for the foreign currency will be. However, interest rates alone are not the only factor on which to base an investment decision. After all, what is the value to an investor of high interest rates from investments in a foreign currency when the exchange value of the currency is falling?

1.16 External debt

A country's external debt is the total amount that the country owes to foreign creditors. It can include several elements.

(a) Loans from specialist international lending organisations, in particular the International Monetary Fund (IMF) and the World Bank

(b) Loans from foreign governments

(c) Loans from private foreign investors, in particular foreign banks

Question
External debt

Identify what the effects of a balance of payments current account deficit could be on a country's external debt.

Answer

A country's external debt increases whenever it has a balance of payments deficit on current account.

(a) A deficit on current account must be balanced (that is, equalled) by a matching surplus in transactions in external assets and liabilities, in other words, by:

   (i) Borrowing from abroad
   (ii) Selling assets that are owned abroad

(b) If a country's balance of trade deficit is very high, it must borrow heavily from abroad. Borrowing could be:

 (i) Borrowing by the government

 (ii) Borrowing by the private sector

 (iii) Increasing investments in the country's private sector by foreign firms, eg takeovers of domestic companies by foreign companies

(c) There would be fears of a depreciation in the exchange rate of the country's currency, as a consequence of the balance of trade deficit. How can a country succeed in attracting foreign investors if they fear that the value of their investment might fall because of a currency depreciation?

Interest rates will probably have to remain high to compensate foreign investors for this risk.

(d) If the country's external debt becomes very high, the cost of servicing the debt by meeting interest payment schedules could become a severe burden on the country's economy.

2 The terms of trade

FAST FORWARD

The balance of trade depends not only on the volumes of goods traded, but on the **relative prices** of exports and imports (ie on the **terms of trade**).

2.1 What are the terms of trade?

The **balance of trade** for any country depends on two things.

- The volume of goods exported and imported
- The relative prices of exports and imports

Key term

Terms of trade: a measure of the relative prices of a country's exports to its imports.

In effect, the **terms of trade** are an 'export : import' price ratio, which measures the relative prices of a country's exports and imports. The terms of trade for a country continually change as export prices and import prices change.

The terms of trade determine the volume of exports necessary to pay for a given volume of imports or, meaning the same thing, the volume of imports that can be purchased with the proceeds of a given volume of exports.

Other things being equal, if the price of exports falls relative to that of imports (a fall in the terms of trade) the trade balance will deteriorate, or *vice versa*.

Note that trade balance depends not just on the physical volume of exports and imports, but on the prices at which they are traded.

Exam focus point

Note that the 'terms of trade' and the 'balance of trade' are two distinct measures. Make sure you know what each is, and do not confuse the two.

PART E   THE EXTERNAL SECTOR

Trade effects

A country's electronics industry, which is its major export industry, switches from the production of mass low cost, low profit margin microchips to the production of more high powered, high cost, high profit margin custom-built microchips. Which one of the following effects would you expect to occur?

A   An improvement in the balance of trade
B   A deterioration in the balance of trade
C   An improvement in the terms of trade
D   A worsening in the terms of trade

Answer

The answer is C. This is one example of how a country's terms of trade might improve. By switching from low priced to high priced products in a major export industry, unit export prices will go up and the terms of trade will improve. The change in the balance of trade depends on changes in the volume of exports and imports, as well as changes in export and import prices. The question doesn't give any indication about the expected volume of exports, so we cannot tell what the likely effect of this change in the balance of trade will be.

2.2 Measuring the terms of trade

The terms of trade are measured as:

$$\frac{\text{Unit value of exports}}{\text{Unit value of imports}}$$

In practice, economists are usually concerned not with a measurable value for the terms of trade but with a measure of changes in the terms of trade, (eg from one year to the next).

Using indices for the average prices of imports and exports, the movement in the terms of trade between 2016 and 2017 would be computed as:

$$\frac{\text{Price of exports 2017/Price of exports 2016}}{\text{Price of imports 2017/Price of imports 2016}}$$

2.3 Changes in the terms of trade

Change in a country's terms of trade occur for two reasons.

(a)   A change in the composition of exports or imports.
(b)   Lower or higher prices of imports/exports.

A government has limited powers to influence its country's terms of trade, since it cannot directly influence the composition nor the prices of imports and exports – although it can affect the terms of trade through a revaluation or devaluation of the currency which would alter relative import/export prices.

(a)   If a country's terms of trade **worsen**, the unit value of its imports will rise by a bigger percentage than the unit value of its exports. The terms of trade will worsen when the exchange rate of the currency depreciates in value against other currencies.

(b)   If a country's terms of trade **improve**, the unit value of its exports will rise by a bigger percentage than the unit value of its imports. The terms of trade will improve when the exchange rate of the country's currency appreciates in value against other currencies.

It would seem logical to assume that an improving terms of trade is good for a country and a worsening terms of trade is bad for it. But this is not necessarily the case.

2.4 Terms of trade and the balance of payments

The effect of a change in the terms of trade should be considered in the context of the country's balance of payments. If the terms of trade worsen for a country, the country will be unable to afford the same volume of imports, or else its balance of payment position will deteriorate. By contrast, a country with improving terms of trade will be able to afford more imports or will improve its balance of payments.

Changes in the terms of trade affect a country's balance of payments via the price elasticity of demand for the goods traded. If a country's terms of trade improve, so that the price of its exported goods rises relative to the price of its imported goods, there will be a relative fall in the volume of goods exported and a rise in the volume of imports. The size of this fall in exports and increase in imports will depend on the price elasticities of demand for exported goods in foreign markets and imported goods in the country's domestic markets.

Note, however, that the terms of trade only measure trade in goods and not trade in services. So while the terms of trade can give an indication of a country's competitive position and balance of payments, it is not a definitive indicator.

Question — Terms of trade and balance of trade

From your knowledge of the theory of elasticity of demand, analyse what will happen to the current balance of trade when the terms of trade improve, on the assumptions that:

(a) Demand for exported goods and demand for imported goods are both inelastic
(b) Both demands are elastic

Answer

(a) If the demand for exported goods is inelastic the total value of exports will rise if their price goes up.
(b) If the demand for imported goods is inelastic the total value of imports will fall if their price falls.

Provided that price elasticity of demand for both exports and imports is inelastic, an improvement in the terms of trade will result in an improvement in the current balance of trade.

On the other hand if the price elasticity of demand for both exports and imports is elastic, an improvement in the terms of trade will lead to a worsening current balance of trade, because:

(a) A rise in export prices would reduce total export revenue
(b) A fall in import prices would increase total payments for imports

An improvement in the terms of trade might therefore result in a better or a worse balance of payments position. The same applies to worsening terms of trade.

3 International trade and its economic advantages

FAST FORWARD

World output of goods and services will increase if countries **specialise** in the production of goods or services in which they have a **comparative advantage**. Just how this total wealth is shared out between countries depends on circumstances.

3.1 International trade in goods and services

Economists distinguish the concepts of **comparative advantage** and **absolute advantage** in international trade. Our explanation of this distinction makes the following assumptions.

- There are only two countries, country X and country Y
- Only two goods are produced (in our example, these are trucks and wheat)
- There are no transport costs and no barriers to trade
- Resources within each country are easily transferred from one industry to another

3.2 Absolute advantage

A country is said to have an absolute advantage in the production of a good when it is more efficient than another country in the production of that good; that is, when that country can produce more of a particular good with a given amount of resources than another country. It is a fairly common situation for one country to be more efficient than another in the production of a particular good.

Assuming that Y produces wheat more efficiently than country X, while country X has an absolute advantage in producing trucks, a simple arithmetical example can illustrate the potential gains from trade. The table below shows the amounts of trucks and wheat that each country can produce per day, assuming that each country has an equal quantity of resources and devotes half of its resources to truck production and half to wheat production.

Daily production	Trucks	Wheat (tons)
Country X	20	100
Country Y	10	150
World total	30	250

The relative cost of truck production is lower in country X than in country Y, because X gives up 5 tons of wheat for every truck produced, while Y forgoes 15. The situation is reversed in the case of wheat production, however. For every truck Y forgoes it can produce an extra 15 tons of wheat, but X can only produce an extra 5. Country X has an absolute advantage in truck production and country Y has an absolute advantage in wheat production. Greater specialisation will, however, also increase total output.

Question — Absolute advantage

Suppose that each country devotes its entire production resources to the product for which it enjoys an absolute advantage. What will be the total output of trucks and wheat?

Answer

Total world output will be 40 trucks (produced by country X) and 300 tons of wheat (produced by country Y).

By specialising, total world output is now greater. In the simple example we have just looked at, there are ten more trucks and 50 tons more wheat now available for consumption. In order to obtain the benefits of specialisation countries X and Y in our example can exchange some part of their individual outputs. It is not possible to specify the exact rate of exchange but the limits of the exchange rate must be somewhere between the domestic opportunity cost ratios of the two countries. These are: for country X, 5 tons of wheat per truck and for country Y, 15 tons of wheat per truck. One country will not benefit from international trade if the 'exchange rate' is not between these ratios.

3.3 Comparative advantage

Key term

> The law of **comparative advantage** (or comparative costs) states that two countries can gain from trade when each specialises in the industries in which it has lowest opportunity costs.

The theory of **comparative advantage**, introduced by David Ricardo, is based on the idea of **opportunity cost** and the **production possibility frontier**. Within a country, the opportunity cost for any category of product may be established in terms of the next most advantageous use of national resources. If two countries produce different goods most efficiently and can exchange them at an advantageous rate in terms of the comparative opportunity costs of importing and home production, then it will be beneficial for them to **specialise** and **trade**. Total production of each good will be higher than if they each produce both goods. This is true even if one country has an absolute advantage in both goods.

3.4 Illustrative example

The principle of comparative costs can be shown by an arithmetical example. It is now assumed that country X is more efficient in the production of both trucks and wheat. If each country devotes half its resources to each industry the assumed daily production totals are as shown below.

Daily production	Trucks	Wheat (tons)
Country X	20	200
Country Y	10	150
World total	30	350

In terms of resources used, the costs of production in both industries are lower in country X. If we consider the opportunity costs, however, the picture is rather different. In country X the cost of one truck is ten tons of wheat, which means that devoting resources to the production of one truck in country X there is a sacrifice in terms of ten tons of wheat forgone. The opportunity cost of one truck in country Y is fifteen tons of wheat. Country X therefore has a comparative advantage in the production of trucks.

In country X the opportunity cost of a ton of wheat is now $1/10$ of a truck, while in country Y the opportunity cost is $1/15$ of a truck. In terms of the output of trucks forgone, wheat is cheaper in country Y than in country X. Country Y has a comparative advantage in wheat. It would now be possible for country Y to buy 10 trucks from country X in exchange for 200 tons of wheat. Country X would transfer some of its resources from the production of wheat to the production of trucks, while country Y would put all of its resources into the production of wheat. Total production would now look like this.

Daily production	Trucks	Wheat (tons)
Country X	30	100
Country Y	0	300
World total	30	400

There is an increase in the world output of wheat.

Alternatively, country X might buy 150 tons of wheat form country Y in exchange for 15 trucks. Country X would transfer even more resources to the production of trucks and the total production figures would change again.

Daily production	Trucks	Wheat (tons)
Country X	35	50
Country Y	0	300
	35	350

There has now been an increase in the world output of trucks.

Clearly, the two countries could adjust their trade between these extremes, achieving overall increases in **both** types of good. However, the key point is that total production is increased if each country specialises in producing the good for which it has a comparative advantage.

3.5 Other advantages of free international trade

Other advantages of free international trade are as follows.

(a) Some countries have a surplus of **raw materials**, and others have a deficit. A country with a surplus can take advantage of its resources to export them. A country with a deficit of a raw material must either import it, or accept restrictions on its economic prosperity and standard of living.

(b) International trade increases **competition** among suppliers in the world's markets. Greater competition reduces the likelihood of a market for a good in a country being dominated by a monopolist. The greater competition will force firms to be competitive and so will increase the pressures on them to be efficient, and also perhaps to produce goods of a high quality. So international trade should bring lower prices and greater choice for the consumer.

(c) International trade creates **larger markets** for a firm's output, and so some firms can benefit from **economies of scale** by engaging in export activities. Economies of scale improve the efficiency of the use of resources, reduce the output costs and also increase the likelihood of output being sold to the consumer at lower prices than if international trade did not exist.

(d) There may be **political advantages** to international trade, because the development of trading links provides a foundation for closer political links. An example of the development of political links based on trade is the European Union.

> **Exam focus point**
>
> Make sure that you are clear about the concept of comparative advantage. Fundamentally, the comparative advantage model explains trade in terms of the benefits of international specialisation. Note that it is trade that leads to specialisation and not the other way round.

3.6 Practical limitations to international trade

In our simple examples, one of the assumptions we made was that transport costs in international trade are negligible. High transport costs, however, can negate the advantages of specialisation and international trade.

Similarly, the theory of comparative advantage assumes that factors of production are mobile and can be shifted between different uses. However, in reality factors are often immobile in the short run.

3.7 Free movement of capital

Free trade is associated with the free movement of goods (and services) between countries. Another important aspect of international trade is the free movement of capital.

(a) If a UK company (or investor) wishes to set up a business in a different country, or to take over a company in another country, how easily can it transfer capital from the UK to the country in question, to pay for the investment?

(b) Similarly, if a Japanese company wishes to invest in the UK, how easily can it transfer funds out of Japan and into the UK to pay for the investment?

Some countries have allowed a fairly free flow of capital into and out of the country. Other countries have been more cautious, mainly for one of the following two reasons.

14: INTERNATIONAL TRADE – THE INTERNATIONAL ECONOMY

(a) The free inflow of foreign capital will make it easier for foreign companies to take over domestic companies. There is often a belief that certain key industries should be owned by residents of the country.

(b) Countries are reluctant to allow the free flow of capital out of the country. This applies particularly to less developed countries, but some more advanced economies have similar views. After all, they need capital to come into the country to develop the domestic economy.

For countries with a large and continuing balance of trade deficit, such as the UK and the USA, it is **essential** that capital should flow into the country to finance the deficit. The deficit country's currency may need to decline in value to attract funds in.

3.8 Barriers to free international trade

In practice, many barriers to free trade exist because governments try to protect home industries against foreign competition.

Protectionism can be practised by a government in a number of different ways.

(a) **Tariffs** or customs duties

(b) Import **quotas**

(c) A **total ban** or embargo on imports from a certain country

(d) Placing **administrative burdens** on importers (for example, increasing the documentation required or safety standards that imported goods must comply with)

(e) Exchange control regulations which make it difficult for importers to obtain foreign currency to buy goods from abroad

(f) Providing **subsidies to domestic producers**, to make the price of their products relatively more competitive compared to those of foreign competitors

(g) Public procurement (government departments deliberately buying from domestic firms in preference to overseas ones)

However, import restrictions and other protectionist measures can give rise to counter-measures by other countries. They are therefore potentially dangerous measures for a country whose economy relies heavily on external trade.

Exchange control regulations might be essential, however, for a country with a balance of payments deficit, low official reserves or one which has great difficulty in borrowing capital from abroad.

3.9 Tariffs or customs duties

Tariffs or customs duties are taxes on imported goods. The effect of a tariff is to raise the price paid for the imported goods by domestic consumers, while leaving the price paid to foreign producers the same, or even lower. The difference is transferred to the government sector.

However, the potential problem for one country of introducing a tariff on imports, is that other countries will retaliate by imposing their own tariffs on that country's exports.

3.10 Import quotas

Import quotas are restrictions on the **quantity** of a product that is allowed to be imported into the country. The quota has a similar effect on consumer welfare to that of import tariffs, but the overall effects are more complicated.

(a) Both domestic and foreign suppliers enjoy a higher price, while consumers buy less at the higher price.

(b) Domestic producers supply more.

(c) There are fewer imports (in volume).

(d) The government collects no revenue.

An **embargo** on imports from one particular country is a total ban, ie effectively a zero quota.

In the 1980s, Voluntary export restrictions or Voluntary export restraint agreements (VERAs) were introduced as an alternative to formal quota agreements. VERAs are an arrangement whereby an exporting country agrees to restrict exports without the importing country having to enact import controls. These agreements avoid the friction between the two countries which tariffs and quotas can create.

3.11 Hidden export subsidies and import restrictions

There has been an enormous range of **government subsidies** and assistance for exports and deterrents against imports. Some examples are given below.

(a) **For exports** – export credit guarantees (insurance against bad debts for overseas sales), financial help (such as government grants to the aircraft or shipbuilding industry) and state assistance via government departments.

(b) **For imports** – complex import regulations and documentation, or special safety standards demanded from imported goods and so on.

When a government gives grants to its domestic producers (for example, regional development grants for new investments in certain areas of the country or grants to investments in new industries) the effect of these grants is to make unit production costs lower. These give the domestic producer a cost advantage over foreign producers in export markets as well as domestic markets.

3.12 Arguments in favour of protection

Protectionist measures may be taken against imports of cheap goods that compete with higher-priced domestically produced goods, and so **preserve output and employment** in domestic industries. In the UK, advocates of protection have argued that UK industries are declining because of competition from overseas, and the advantages of more employment at a reasonably high wage for UK labour are greater than the disadvantages that protectionist measures would bring.

(a) Measures might be necessary to **counter dumping of surplus production** by other countries at an uneconomically low price, in other words preventing unfair competition. For example, if the European Union (EU) were to over-produce, it might decide to dump the surpluses on other countries. The losses from overproduction would be subsidised by the EU governments, and the domestic industries of countries receiving dumped goods would be facing unfair competition from abroad. Although dumping has short-term benefits for the countries receiving the cheap goods, the longer term consequences would be a reduction in domestic output and employment, even when domestic industries in the longer term might be more efficient.

(b) Protectionist measures by one country are often implemented in **retaliation** against measures taken by another country that are thought to be unfair. This is why protection tends to spiral once it has begun. Any country that does not take protectionist measures when other countries are doing so is likely to find that it suffers all of the disadvantages and none of the advantages of protection.

(c) There is an argument that protectionism is necessary, at least in the short term, to protect a country's **infant industries** that have not yet developed to the size where they can compete in international markets. Less developed countries in particular might need to protect industries against competition from advanced or developing countries.

(d) Protection might also help a country in the short term to deal with the problems of a **declining industry**. Without protection, the industry might quickly collapse and there would be severe problems of sudden mass unemployment. By imposing some protectionist measures, the decline in the industry might be slowed down, and the task of switching resources to new industries could be undertaken over a longer period of time.

(e) Protection is often seen as a means for a country to **reduce its balance of trade deficit**, by imposing tariffs or quotas on imports. However, because of retaliation by other countries, the success of such measures by one country would depend on the demand by other countries for its exports being inelastic with regard to price and its demand for imports being fairly elastic.

(f) Protective tariffs can also raise revenue for the government if they are imposed on goods with an inelastic demand.

3.13 Undesirable effects of protection

As well as reducing the benefits brought by trade, protection can have direct disadvantageous effects on a country's businesses.

Higher costs. Protection is likely to raise costs to domestic business for three reasons.

(a) Imports of raw materials, components, fuel and so on will be more expensive.
(b) Domestic producers of inputs will take advantage of the reduction in competition to raise their prices.
(c) Rising prices of both imports and domestic goods will lead to increased wage demands.

Reduced demand. Domestic producers will face reduced demand for two reasons.

(a) Foreign trading partners are likely to retaliate with protective measures of their own, thus reducing export demand.

(b) Home consumers will find their real income declines as costs rise (see above) and thus domestic demand will decline.

As well as these direct effects on domestic businesses, we can also argue that protectionism has undesirable impacts on the overall economy.

(a) The theory of **comparative advantage** shows that international free trade achieves the **optimal use of resources**. By definition, protectionism prevents this from happening.

(b) Because firms are protected from competition they will not strive for innovation and cost reduction. In this way, protectionism will **encourage inefficiency**.

(c) Factors of production will remain in 'declining' industries, whereas under free market economics they would move to other industries. Therefore, protectionism leads to a **misallocation of resources**.

(d) If protection is achieved through imposing taxes on imported goods, then consumers will suffer through **higher prices**.

(e) Protection by one country preventing imports may lead to **retaliation** by the other country. This may provoke a trade war.

For example, in September 2009, China started imposing tariffs on American exports of automotive products in retaliation to the US's decision to levy tariffs on tyres imported from China. In December 2011, China subsequently imposed additional duties on cars imported from the US – accusing America's car industry of 'dumping and subsidising' and causing substantial damage to China's domestic car industry as a result.

Similarly, in 2016, in response to the EU and US imposing tariffs on imports of Chinese steel into their economies, China retaliated by imposing its own tariffs on steel imported into China from the EU and the US.

4 Free trade agreements

FAST FORWARD — Free trade agreements include free trade areas, customs unions and common markets.

4.1 The World Trade Organisation

The World Trade Organisation (WTO) was formed in 1995 as a successor to the General Agreement on Tariffs and Trade (GATT). At the time of writing, the WTO has 164 countries as members.

The main objective of the WTO is to encourage free trade by policies such as the reciprocal dropping of tariffs between trading countries and the elimination of other forms of protectionism. It is also a forum for governments to negotiate trade agreements and to settle trade disputes.

In addition to the forum provided by the WTO, a group of leading industrialised countries have established their own forum. **The G8 Group** (US, Britain, France, Germany, Italy, Japan, Canada and Russia) meets on an informal basis to discuss a wide range of economic and social issues – including international trade, macroeconomic management and relationships with developing countries.

[Note: Russia was suspended from the G8 in 2014, following its annexation of Crimea from Ukraine, meaning that the forum became the Group of 7 (or **G7**).]

As is the case with the WTO, the G8 does not have any formal powers or resources, but it provides a forum for its member countries to discuss international issues.

The WTO has not made much progress with its objectives. For example, in 1999, WTO talks were terminated after rioters protested against the policies of some of the wealthier member nations. Recession in some economies has also encouraged an increase in protectionism.

4.2 The European Union

The European Union (EU) (formerly the European Community) is one of several international economic associations. It was formed in 1957 by the Treaty of Rome and currently consists of 28 nations, with a combined population of over 500 million people.

[Note: In June 2016, the UK voted to leave the EU in the so-called 'Brexit' referendum. However, the procedure for the UK to leave the EU is not expected to be complete until March 2019; until that point, the UK remains part of the EU while negotiations about the terms of its exit continue.]

The European Union has a **common market** combining different aspects, including **a free trade area** and a **customs union**.

(a) A **free trade area** exists when there is no restriction on the movement of goods and services between countries although individual member countries can impose their own restrictions on non-member countries.

(b) A free trade area may be extended into a **customs union** when there is a free trade area between all member countries of the union, and in addition, there are **common external tariffs** applying to imports from non-member countries into any part of the union. In other words, the union promotes free trade among its members but acts as a protectionist bloc against the rest of the world.

(c) A **common market** encompasses the idea of a customs union but has a number of additional features. In addition to free trade among member countries there are also free markets in each of the **factors of production**. A French citizen has the freedom to work in any other country of the European Union, for example. A common market will also aim to achieve stronger links between member countries, for example by harmonising government economic policies and by establishing a closer political confederation.

The European Union extends these features into an **economic and monetary union** by harmonising national economic policies, such as financial regulations, and by introducing its own central bank and currency (euro).

The **European Central Bank (ECB)** is the central bank for Europe's single currency (the euro). Its main task is to maintain price stability in the euro area.

However, this means the ECB has to balance the two potentially conflicting objectives in Article 2 of the Treaty on European Union: a high level of employment, and sustainable and non-inflationary growth.

In addition, as prescribed by Article 105.2 of the Treaty, the ECB's tasks are to:

- Define and implement **monetary policy** for the eurozone area
- Conduct **foreign exchange operations**
- Manage the official **foreign reserves** of the eurozone countries
- Promote the smooth operation of **payment systems** within the eurozone countries

4.3 The single European market

The EU set the end of 1992 as the target date for the removal of all existing physical, technical and fiscal barriers among member states, thus creating a large multinational European Single Market. This objective was embodied in the Single European Act of 1985. In practice, these changes have not occurred overnight, and many of them are still in progress.

Elimination of trade restrictions covers the following areas.

(a) **Physical barriers** (eg customs inspection) on good and services have been removed for most products. Companies have had to adjust to a new sales tax (VAT) regime as a consequence.

(b) **Technical standards** (eg for quality and safety) should be harmonised.

(c) Governments should not discriminate between EU companies in awarding **public works contracts**.

(d) **Telecommunications** should be subject to greater competition.

(e) It should be possible to provide **financial services** in any country.

(f) There should be **free movement of capital** within the community.

(g) **Professional qualifications** awarded in one Member State should be recognised in the others.

(h) The EU is taking a co-ordinated stand on matters related to **consumer protection**.

There are many areas however where harmonisation is a long way from being achieved. Here are some examples.

(a) **Company taxation**. Tax rates, which can affect the viability of investment plans, vary from country to country within the EU.

(b) **Indirect taxation** *(*eg sales tax, like VAT*)*. While there have been moves towards harmonisation, there are still differences between rates imposed by member states.

(c) **Differences in prosperity**. There are considerable differences in prosperity between the wealthiest EU economy (Germany), and the poorest (eg some of the newly enrolled Eastern European members).

(d) **Differences in workforce skills**. Again, this can have a significant effect on investment decisions. The workforce in Germany is perhaps the most highly trained, but also the most highly paid, and so might be suitable for products of a high added value.

(e) **Infrastructure**. Some countries are better provided with road and rail than others. Where accessibility to a market is an important issue, infrastructure can mean significant variations in distribution costs.

4.4 The European Free Trade Association (EFTA)

The European Free Trade Association (EFTA) was established in 1959, with seven member countries, one of which was the UK. The UK, Denmark and Portugal have since transferred to the EU, while Finland and Iceland joined the other original Member States, Sweden, Norway, Austria and Switzerland. More recently, Finland, Sweden and Austria have also joined the EU leaving the only four remaining Member States as Iceland, Liechtenstein, Norway and Switzerland. There is free trade between EFTA member countries but there is no harmonisation of tariffs with non-EFTA countries.

4.5 The European Economic Area (EEA)

On 1 January 1993, EFTA forged a link with the EU to create a European Economic Area (EEA) with a population of 465 million, so extending the benefits of the EU single market to the EFTA member countries (excluding Switzerland, which stayed out of the EEA). The membership of the EEA now comprises the EU countries (less Croatia whose accession into the EEA has not yet been ratified) plus Norway, Liechtenstein and Iceland.

4.6 The Trans-Pacific Pact (TPP)

The Trans-Pacific Pact (TPP) was signed in 2015 by 12 countries with a combined population of around 800 million people: US, Japan, Malaysia, Vietnam, Singapore, Brunei, Australia, New Zealand, Canada, Mexico, Chile and Peru. Collectively, the TPP countries have a population approaching twice that of the EU, and are responsible for about 40% of the world's trade.

Alongside aims to strengthen economic ties between themselves, reducing tariffs and promoting trade in order to increase growth, the member states also hoped to foster a closer relationship on economic policies and regulation. In this respect, the deal was seen as a remarkable achievement because of the significant differences between the member countries; for example, in relation to environmental protection and workers' rights.

However, shortly after his inauguration as US President in January 2017, Donald Trump withdrew the US from the agreement, throwing its future into doubt.

4.7 The North American Free Trade Agreement (NAFTA)

Canada, the USA and Mexico formed the North American Free Trade Agreement (NAFTA) in 1993. This free trade area is similar in size (of population) to the European Economic Area. However, its future is also in doubt following the election of Donald Trump, who has openly criticised it as 'bad for America' and has indicated that terms may have to be renegotiated.

4.8 Opinions on trading blocs

Not surprisingly, opinion on regional trading blocs is divided. Proponents of it argue it encourages trade creation by removing restrictions to trade. Opponents argue it leads to trade diversion and uneconomic behaviour, as member countries buy within that bloc when goods and services may be cheaper elsewhere. Critics also argue trading blocs will foster a fortress mentality and encourage protectionism worldwide, contravening the logic of free trade.

5 Globalisation of markets

The growth of **multinational enterprises** has taken place in an environment of increasing **globalisation of markets**.

5.1 Globalisation

Globalisation may be defined as the interdependence and integration of different national economies. It reflects the tendency of markets to become global rather than national and for it to be difficult to view any national economy as a stand-alone entity.

Factors driving globalisation

(a) Improved communications, for example the speed of access to the Internet
(b) Reduction of transport costs.
(c) Political realignments, for example the collapse of the former Soviet bloc
(d) Growth of global industries and institutions
(e) Break down of some trade barriers by free trade organisations and treaties

5.2 Multinational enterprises

A **multinational company** is one that has production or service facilities in more than one country. Multinational enterprises range from medium-sized companies having only a few facilities (or subsidiaries or 'affiliates') abroad to giant companies such as Exxon Mobil, Royal Dutch Shell, or WalMart whose annual revenues of hundreds of billions of dollars are greater than the GDPs of many of the countries in the world.

5.3 International expansion

Firms may be **pushed** into international expansion by domestic adversity, or **pulled** into it by attractive opportunities abroad. Some of the main reasons firms expand into new countries are the following:

(a) **Life cycle.** There may be little opportunity to increase sales in the company's existing country because its products are in the mature or decline stages of their life cycles. International expansion may allow sales growth, since products are often in different stages of the product life cycle in different countries. For example, if a product is at the mature stage of its life cycle in a firm's home market, it could be beneficial to expand into an emerging market where the product may be at the introductory or growth stages of its life cycle.

(b) **Competition.** Intense competition in an overcrowded domestic market sometimes induces firms to seek markets overseas where rivalry is less keen.

(c) **Reduce dependence.** Many companies wish to diversify away from an overdependence on a single domestic market. Increased geographical diversification can help to **spread risk**.

(d) **Economies of scale.** Technological factors may be such that a large volume is needed either to cover the high costs of plant, equipment, R&D and personnel or to exploit a large potential for economies of scale and experience. For these reasons firms in the aviation, ethical drugs, computer and automobile industries are often obliged to enter multiple countries.

(e) **Cheaper sources of raw materials.** Access to cheaper raw materials, or cheaper labour, could be a source of competitive advantage for an organisation, particularly if it is pursuing a cost leadership strategy.

(f) **Financial opportunities**. Many firms are attracted by favourable opportunities such as:

- The development of lucrative emerging markets (such as India and China)
- Depreciation in their domestic currency values (increasing the value of exports)
- Corporate tax benefits offered by particular countries
- Lowering of import barriers or other restrictions (such as tariffs and quotas)

(g) **Chance**. Firms may enter a particular country or countries by chance. A company executive may recognise an opportunity while on a foreign trip or the firm may receive chance orders or requests for information from potential foreign customers.

In addition, more people now travel internationally and they often want to purchase brands they recognise even when they are in foreign locations. This encourages companies (such as McDonalds for example) to operate in multiple countries around the world.

5.4 Impact of MNCs and FDI on national economies

For	Against
Improve economic welfare by introducing new capital.	Inward investment may not create new investment, but displace existing domestic investment.
Introduce new technologies (**technology transfer**).	Technology transfer may only be at a low level.
MNCs will provide **direct employment**, and may also create additional indirect employment through supplier firms. Possible multiplier effect resulting from new investment.	May not be new employment; may displace existing employment if MNCs displace existing firms.
Local producers establish direct linkages with MNCs and supply to them. Improve productivity of local producers.	Profits from the investment are repatriated to the host country of the MNC.
Balance of payments gains from inflows of FDI. Governments can get **tax revenue** from MNC profits.	MNCs likely to minimise tax liability through **transfer pricing**. Government offer grants and subsidies to attract MNC investment so may end up worse off.

5.5 Globalisation of production

Transnational companies are tending more and more to take a global view of production facilitated by technological advances which make it easier to do business internationally. Production facilities may be located in particular countries for a variety of reasons.

- To give access to markets protected by tariffs
- To reduce transport costs
- To exploit national or regional differences in demand for goods, and thereby expand sales
- To take advantage of low labour costs, and thereby reduce production costs. (Equally, production may need to be located in particular countries because specialised expertise and skilled labour is more readily available there than in other countries)
- To secure supply through backward vertical integration

Centralisation of manufacturing can bring important **economies of scale**. These must be balanced against transport costs and barriers to trade. And the companies must have a suitably developed organisational structure to control their operations overall.

5.6 Globalisation of capital markets

Globalisation describes the process by which the capital markets of each country have become internationally integrated. The process of integration is facilitated by improved telecommunications and the deregulation of markets in many countries (for example, the UK stock market's so-called Big Bang of 1986). Securities issued in one country can now be traded in capital markets around the world. This trend can only increase as stock exchanges are linked electronically as has happened with the London and Frankfurt markets.

For companies planning international investment activities (also known as foreign direct investment (FDI)), easy access to large amounts of funds denominated in foreign currencies can be very useful. Such funds are available in the eurocurrency markets. The eurocurrency markets can also help to bypass official constraints on international business activities.

6 Global financial institutions

The principal institutions of the global economy include the **World Bank** and the **International Monetary Fund**.

6.1 Role of global financial institutions

A number of institutions are central to the process of globalisation and the stability of the world economy including the World Bank Group (WB), the International Monetary Fund (IMF), and the Group of Twenty (G-20)

Together these seek to provide:

(a) Short-term stabilisation measures for particular countries or the world economy as a whole;

(b) Medium and long term financial help to countries seeking to restructure and invest in their economies

(c) Co-ordination of policies of member countries on financial regulation and economic policies to avert crises and simulate world economic growth.

6.2 The World Bank Group

The World Bank was formed in 1945 initially to help affected countries recover and rebuild after the damage of the Second World War.

It comprises five agencies although generally the term 'World Bank' is used to refer to just the IBRD and IDA together.

1. **International Bank for Reconstruction and Development (IBRD):** Its mission is to reduce poverty in middle-income countries and credit-worthy poorer countries by promoting sustainable development in them. It borrows funds from commercial banks by issuing bonds. The IBRD's credit rating is very high and so it can get these funds at much lower rates of interest than could the central bank of a developing country. It loans these funds to governments and public enterprises in developing countries at a low rate of interest to help them invest in development projects. Generally the IBRD lends using tight criteria that ensure the investment can be repaid. The IBRD requires a 'sovereign charge' – ie that the government of the country undertakes to repay the loan.

2. **International Development Association (IDA):** a sister agency to IBRD using same staff and premises. Its focus is on helping the world's poorest countries by issuing no-interest loans and grants (called 'credits') to local governments and public enterprises. These loans are long term (25

to 40 years). These help restructuring and also tackling environmental and health issues. Its funds come from donor countries, ie richer developed countries. A sovereign charge is taken for these too.

3. **International Finance Corporation (IFC):** in effect a consultancy and introducer to assist private sector investment projects. It has funds of its own to provide initial investment but also relies on encouraging private capital to invest. Where funds are raised by IFC they issue bonds and pass them on with a slight margin for administration to the private borrower. Any guarantees to repay are taken from the borrow and not a sovereign charge.

4. **Multilateral Investment Guarantee Agency (MIGA):** this insures investors against political risk of investing in developing countries. It also provides reports and a forum for sharing information on the risks of investing in particular countries.

5. **International Centre for Settlement of Investment Disputes (ICSID):** this resolves disputes on investments between member countries.

6.3 The International Monetary Fund

The IMF was formed in 1946. At the time of writing, it had 189 member countries.

The IMF's overall aims are: to foster global monetary cooperation, secure financial stability, facilitate international trade, promote high employment and sustainable economic growth, and reduce poverty around the world.

The IMF supports its membership by providing

- policy advice to governments and central banks based on analysis of economic trends and cross-country experiences;
- research, statistics, forecasts, and analysis based on tracking of global, regional, and individual economies and markets;
- loans to help countries overcome economic difficulties;
- concessional loans to help fight poverty in developing countries; and
- technical assistance and training to help countries improve the management of their economies.

Unlike the World Bank, which focuses on eliminating poverty in poor and middle income countries, the IMF provides its services equally to developed countries. Following the global economic crisis in 2007-2010, Greece, Portugal and the Republic of Ireland (which are all members of the EU) received bail outs from the IMF.

6.4 Nature of IMF intervention

The IMF focuses on helping countries which have balance of payments problems and need more foreign exchange to pay their way.

The IMF members deposit sums of their local currencies with the IMF and in return enjoy Special Drawing Rights (SDRs) that enable them to call on these funds to pay foreign debts.

A nation may become unable to raise foreign currency by issuing bonds to foreign banks. This is because the investment community is having doubts about the ability of that country to repay its debt and fears default. They will either refuse to lend or will charge very high rates of interest to lend. These high rates of interest deepen the problem because the country will require foreign currency to pay them and so they make the balance of payments deficit, and the need to borrow, deeper.

The IMF will lend at a much lower rate. However it will normally do so subject to the borrowing government agreeing to implement a Structural Adjustment Programme designed by the IMF to bring public finance into better order.

Typical cases where the IMF become involved are:

(a) **Temporary cyclical problems** where the boom stage of a trade cycle has led a country to run temporary balance of payment deficits. Normally drawing down on SDRs is sufficient to deal with this problem

(b) **Structural deficits** where the government of the country has been borrowing heavily to fund the growth of the economy but the growth is delayed or not likely to come about. The government has huge external interest payments and a bad credit rating such that it cannot borrow to pay the interest.

(c) **Sectoral problems** such as a threatened collapse of the banking and financial system that requires huge sums to recapitalise the balance sheets of the banks.

6.5 The Group of 20

The **Group of Twenty Finance Ministers and Central Bank Governors (G-20)** is a group of finance ministers and central bank governors from 20 economies: USA, Japan, China, Germany, France, UK, Italy, Russia, Brazil, Canada, India, Mexico, Australia, South Korea, Turkey, Indonesia, Saudi Arabia, Argentina, South Africa, and the rest of the EU represented, collectively, by the European council president.

Together these 20 economies (the 19 countries plus the remainder of the EU collectively) are home to two-thirds of the World's population, and account for around 80% of the World's GDP.

The G20 holds annual summits, or meetings, to discuss global financial issues. These have included

- Dealing with financial crises
- Harmonisation of taxation policies across countries to reduce tax avoidance
- Agreeing policies to detect and reduce illegal transfers of money from the proceeds of crime, terrorism and so on

The G20 has become very influential since it was formed in 2008 and has essentially replaced other groupings of rich countries such as the G7 and G8.

6.6 Impacts of globalisation

Globalisation used to be the unquestioned model for economic growth and stability but there are now many critics of the phenomena.

For globalisation

(a) Emergence of new growth markets, for example in the less developed countries
(b) Enhanced competitiveness as more producers and customers make up the global marketplace
(c) Growth of previously poor economies, such as China
(d) Cross-national business alliance and mergers
(e) International support for poorer nations and assistance provided in development of their economies
(f) World economic equalisation

Criticisms of globalisation

(a) The main institutions of globalisation follow the collective will of the G8 countries (USA, Japan, Germany, Canada, Italy, France, the UK and Russia) and are more concerned therefore in aiding the economic wealth of these countries.

(b) IMF, WB and G20 along with powerful multinational organisations dictate economic policy in countries but do not include real representation of these countries within their organisations. This lack of accountability has been called 'global governance without global government' (*Joseph Stiglitz*, Globalisation and its Discontents).

(c) World poverty is still an issue and many fear that the policies adopted by WB, IMF and others, for example in restricting subsidy in Africa and opening up their markets for Western imports that are produced under subsidy, actually makes some nations poorer.

(d) There is no enduring political and economic stability in the world and the collapse of one part of the economy, for example in South America, could have disastrous knock on effects for the rest of the world.

(e) Not all countries are included in global activity. Instead there is an increasing tendency for groups of counties, usually located in the same region to become involved in each others economies, for example the countries in the eurozone.

Chapter Roundup

- The **balance of payments accounts** consist of a **current account** with visibles and invisibles sections and transactions in **capital** (external assets and liabilities including official financing). The sum of the balances on these accounts must be zero, although in practice there is a balancing figure for measurement errors.

- When newspapers and the press talk about a surplus or deficit on the balance of payments, they usually mean a **surplus or deficit on the current account**.

- The balance of trade depends not only on the volumes of goods traded, but on the **relative prices** of exports and imports (ie on the **terms of trade**).

- World output of goods and services will increase if countries **specialise** in the production of goods or services in which they have a **comparative advantage**. Just how this total wealth is shared out between countries depends on circumstances.

- **Free trade agreements** include free trade areas, customs unions and common markets.

- The growth of **multinational enterprises** has taken place in an environment of increasing **globalisation of markets**.

- The principal institutions of the global economy include the **World Bank** and the **International Monetary Fund**.

Quick Quiz

1. What does the J curve describe?

2. How do deflationary measures help to eliminate a balance of payments deficit?

3. According to the theory of purchasing power parity, how are inflation rates and exchange rates related?

4. How may the government intervene in the foreign exchange markets?

5. What is the balance of trade?

    A   The balance of payments on current account
    B   Net visible trade
    C   Net visible and invisible trade
    D   The theory of gains from trade

6. Which of the following statements concerning international trade are true?

    (1) The J curve effect will work in reverse if there is a depreciation when the current account is in deficit.
    (2) Protectionism could reduce exports.
    (3) Devaluation of the domestic currency could reverse a current account deficit.

    A   (1) and (3) only
    B   (1), (2) and (3)
    C   (1) and (2) only
    D   (2) and (3) only

PART E   THE EXTERNAL SECTOR

7   From a given base year, a country's export prices rise by 8% and import prices rise by 20%. During this period, the terms of trade will have:

   A   Risen from 100 to 111.1
   B   Risen from 100 to 112
   C   Fallen from 100 to 90
   D   Fallen from 100 to 88

8   A devaluation will only benefit the UK balance of payments if:

   A   The sum of the price elasticities of demand for imports and exports is less than 1
   B   The sum of the price elasticities of demand for imports and exports is greater than 1
   C   The sum of the price elasticities of demand for imports and exports is less than 0
   D   The sum of the price elasticities of demand for imports and exports is greater than 0

9   Which one of the following best describes the theory of comparative advantage in relation to the production of cars?

   A   A country can produce cars at a lower opportunity cost than any of its trading partners
   B   A country can produce cars more cheaply than any other country can
   C   A country can produce more cars than any other country can
   D   A country has a higher opportunity cost of producing cars than any of its trading partners

10 What is meant by:

   (a) A free trade area
   (b) A customs union
   (c) A common market?

11 Assume that two small countries, X and Y, produce two commodities P and Q, and that there are no transport costs. One unit of resource in Country X produces 4 units of P or 8 units of Q. One unit of resource in Country Y produces 1 unit of P or 3 units of Q. Which one of the following statements is true?

   A   Country X has an absolute advantage over Country Y in producing P and Q, and so will not trade.
   B   Country X has a comparative advantage over Country Y in producing Q.
   C   Country Y has a comparative advantage over Country X in producing Q.
   D   Country X has a comparative advantage over Country Y in producing both P and Q.

12 The balance of payments current account will include which of the following items?

   (i)   Expenditure in a country by overseas visitors
   (ii) The inflow of capital investment by multinational companies
   (iii) Exports of manufactured goods

   A   (i) and (ii)
   B   (i) and (iii)
   C   (iii) only
   D   (i), (ii) and (iii)

13 Outline the main problems encountered in managing international business operations.

14 What are the main factors driving globalisation?

15 Which of the following is not an argument in favour of protection?

   A   Protect employment in domestic industries
   B   Prevent unfair competition from surplus production in other countries
   C   Reduce balance of trade deficit
   D   Promote innovation and cost reduction

Answers to Quick Quiz

1. The J curve shows the effect on the balance of payments of a falling exchange rate. A falling exchange rate will eventually reduce demand for imports and increase demand for exports. However, in the short term, both domestic and export demand are likely to be inelastic and the ability of domestic industry to meet any increase in export demand will be limited. The volume of goods and services traded is therefore unlikely to change in the short term, but imports will cost more in foreign currency and exports will sell for less. It is therefore likely that there will be a deterioration in the balance of payments in the short term.

2. Domestic deflation cuts demand, including demand for imports. Industry is therefore encouraged to switch to export markets.

3. Purchasing power parity theory suggests that exchange rates are determined by relative inflation rates. The currency of the country with high inflation will tend to weaken against those of countries with lower inflation rates, since more of its currency will be required to buy any given good.

4. Governments may intervene directly by buying and selling currency. They may also influence exchange rates by adjusting their interest rates and by direct currency controls such as limiting the amount of foreign currency which individuals are allowed to buy.

5. **B** Learn this definition. The balance of trade is the surplus or deficit on trade in goods only.

6. **D** The J curve would work in reverse if there were a surplus and the currency appreciated, so (i) is not true. Protectionism could reduce exports if other countries react hostilely to a country introducing import restrictions. Devaluation of the domestic currency should make exports cheaper, and so should help reduce a current account deficit.

7. **C** $108/120 \times 100 = 90$.

8. **B** In order to benefit, internal demand must react to a rise in the price of imports and external demand must react to a fall in the price of UK exported goods.

9. **A** The law of comparative advantage states that two countries can gain from trade when each specialises in the industries in which it has the lowest opportunity costs. The crucial factor is the opportunity cost of production not the absolute cost of production though. Therefore, the correct answer is A, not B.

10. A **free trade area** exists when there is no restriction on trade between countries. This is extended into a **customs union** when common external tariffs are levied on imports from non-member countries. A **common market** adds free movement of the factors of production, including labour and may harmonise economic policy.

11. **C** Country X has an absolute advantage over Country Y in making both P and Q, because 1 unit of resource in Country X will make more of either P or Q than one unit of resource in Country Y. However, international trade should still take place because of comparative advantage in producing P and Q. The opportunity costs of producing a unit of P is 2 units of Q in Country X and 3 units of Q in Country Y. Similarly, the opportunity cost of producing a unit of Q is 1/2 a unit of P in Country X and 1/3 of a unit of P in Country Y. Country X has a comparative advantage in producing P and Country Y has a comparative advantage in the production of Q. International trade should be beneficial for both countries, with country X exporting P and Country Y exporting Q.

12. **B** Exports of manufactured goods are part of the balance of trade element of the current account. Expenditure by tourists is part of the trade in services in the 'invisibles' part of the current account. Foreign investment by multi-national companies is part of the financial account.

PART E THE EXTERNAL SECTOR

13
- Planning is complicated by the wide variation in conditions between countries.
- It is difficult to structure an organisation to meet the demands of operations in different countries.
- Multinationals have to achieve a balance between local and expatriate staff
- Successful management styles vary from country to country.
- Control by reference to monetary measures is complicated by varying inflation rates, exchange rates, taxation rates and financial reporting practices.

14 The main factors affecting globalisation are:
(a) Reduced transport costs
(b) Improved communications
(c) Emergence of multinational organisations
(d) Breakdown of barriers to trade

15 D One of the arguments against protectionism is that it removes the incentive for firms to innovate and reduce costs. Critics argue protectionism encourages inefficiency, and does not promote innovation or cost reduction.

End of chapter question

Globalisation (May 2013)

During the last 20 years, globalisation is one of the most important changes in the business regime.

Required

(a) Explain the phrase 'going global, thinking local', and identify the potential conflicts for a business in behaving in this way. **(8 marks)**

(b) Discuss the advantages and disadvantages of the following important ways that a company might expand its operations internationally: export, wholly owned subsidiary and joint venture.

(12 marks)

(Total 20 marks)

Free trade and protectionism (Nov 2015)

The free trade debate that used to be such a huge part of British politics is re-emerging because of the trade agreement being negotiated between the United States and the European Union, the Transatlantic Trade and Investment Partnership (TTIP). Inflatable white elephants with TTIP written on them have been appearing at by-election rallies.

Pressure groups on the left are increasingly agitated that the agreement is being negotiated in secret and contains clauses that might force competition on the National Health Service - a canard that Mr Shapps (Minister of State at the Department for International Development) exposed as nonsense. They couch their opposition almost entirely in terms of the risks to producers - farmers, health-service managers and small businesses fearful of American competition.

The trade barriers in the Atlantic cost consumers on both sides. Mr Shapps pointed out recently that every American pair of jeans costs you 12 per cent more than it should; every British pint of beer costs Americans 157 per cent more than it should. Americans are forbidden by law from buying British lamb or venison. TTIP is set to tackle some of these absurdities, to reduce nontariff barriers, harmonise standards and give people more freedom to buy from whomever they choose

[Source: The Times, Monday, February 16, 2015, by Matt Ridley].

(White elephants: something that requires a lot of care and money and that gives little profit).

Required

(a) If an American pair of jeans costs you £56 in the UK, how much would the equivalent be in US dollars (assuming $/£ 1.5)? If a British pint of beer costs you £3 in the UK, how much would the equivalent be in US dollars (assuming $/£ 1.5)? **(6 marks)**

(b) Suppose Figure 1 indicates the equilibrium domestic (US) beer demand at world supply (free trade allowed) vs. at domestic supply (US supply without free trade), when free trade is allowed, how many units will the US import? If the US moves from a no-free-trade market equilibrium to free trade, how would the price and the total amount of the good produced domestically change?

PART E   THE EXTERNAL SECTOR

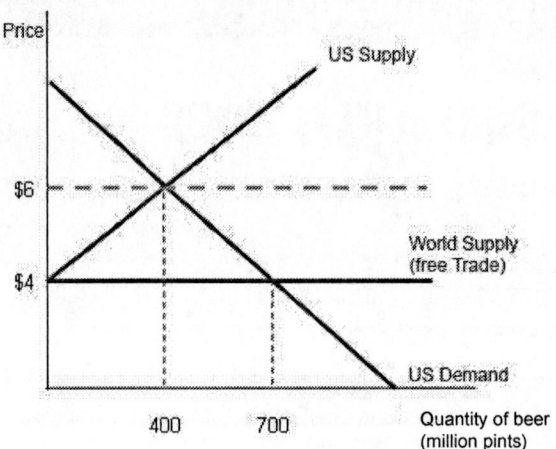

Figure 1 US equilibrium beer demands at different levels of supply

(9 marks)

(c)   In practice, many barriers to free trade exist because governments try to protect home industries against foreign competition. Protectionism has direct disadvantageous effects on a country's business, for example, higher cost and reduced demand. Please state **five** protectionism behaviours practised by a government and explain the indirect undesirable effects of protection.

(15 marks)

(Total 30 marks)

Answers to end of chapter questions

… ANSWERS TO END OF CHAPTER QUESTIONS

Chapter 1

Scarcity

From an economist's viewpoint, even very rich people face scarcity.

(1)   Scarcity occurs whenever people's wants exceed the ability of the available resources to meet these wants. Because people's wants are effectively infinite – it is always possible to imagine more things to want to have – wants will always exceed what can be produced with the available resources, and so scarcity will always be present.

(2)   A person faces scarcity whenever his or her wants exceed what he or she can obtain using his or her resources. Because the person cannot fulfil all of his or her wants, the person is forced to choose which wants will be satisfied and which wants will remain unsatisfied. The same results hold true for a society. All societies face scarcity because people's wants are essentially infinite, so that the resources available are not sufficient to fulfil everyone's wants. Because of this fact, societies must make choices about which (and whose) wants will be satisfied and which (and whose) wants will remain unsatisfied.

(3)   Even very rich people want things that they cannot have. An older rich person, for instance, might want to have all of his or her youthful energy, but medical science cannot (yet) provide this service. Alternatively, another rich person might enjoy life so much that he or she wants 25 hours in a day in order to have more time for more enjoyment. But, such a want is impossible. By way of another, perhaps more realistic example, Malcolm Forbes was the founder of Forbes magazine and was very rich. However, he did not obtain every piece of art that he bid for at auctions. Even though Mr. Forbes was very rich, he still passed on some art when the price got so high that he thought given his resources, the price exceeded what he was willing to pay. Mr. Forbes wanted the art, but he was not willing to bid higher in order to win it. Hence Mr. Forbes faced scarcity.

Chapter 2

Elasticity and pricing

The figures in the table indicate the price elasticity of demand for beef, which is the proportionate change in quantity of beef demanded, divided by the proportionate change in price. The higher the absolute figure, the more significant effect of the price change of beef on consumers' demand. From the data, it can be seen that the price elasticity of demand for most cuts of English beef is inelastic (roasting joint excepted); and the price elasticity of demand for English beef and Home-produced beef (including Scotland) is also low. Overall, it seems to indicate that, other things being equal, the change of demand for English beef is less than the change of price of English beef. Therefore, an increase in English beef price would lead to an increase in revenue for British farmers and the supermarkets. The increased price of English beef would encourage British farmers to produce more beef and would increase the supermarkets' sale revenue, thus, in turn, would make a contribution to the national economy and the English livestock sector in particular.

Candidates need to explain the effect of a price increase of a product on the demand for its competitive products. However, the price increase of English beef could have more effects than the data of price elasticity of English beef suggests because other competitive products, such as Irish beef and the other imported beef, are more price elastic. More British consumers (who used to buy English beef) may switch from UK beef in response to the price increase and buy more non-English beef than the NBA expects. Moreover, if beef farmers in other countries decide to reduce their prices of beef, some British consumers may purchase non-English-produced beef, resulting in a fall in demand for English beef. As a result, the price of English beef may be forced downwards, which, in turn, would reduce the production of English beef. This would negatively affect the English beef industry.

ANSWERS TO END OF CHAPTER QUESTIONS

Candidates need to mention the effect of other factors, such as the British attitude towards the consumption of English beef, tax effect, etc. The above situation may be exaggerated by other factors which may also affect the demand for English beef. For example, British people may prefer home-produced beef instead of imported beef despite the price rise of English beef; advertising campaigns may affect the demand for English beef, and tax changes may favour the supply of English beef.

Chapter 3

Performance and directors' remuneration

(a) The common performance measurements include:

- Market-based
    - Shareholder return
    - Share price (and other market based measures)
- Accounting-based
    - Profit based measures (e.g. Earnings Before Interest and Taxes (EBIT))
    - Return on capital employed
    - Earnings per share

(b) The above performance criteria will clearly be a key aspect of ensuring that directors' remuneration is perceived as fair and appropriate for the job and in keeping with the results achieved by the directors.

Problems with those performance criteria:

- Short-term performance of the management

    The use of performance indicators should incentivise directors but at the same time align their interests with those of shareholders, to the long-term benefit of the company. But the market-based indicators which are commonly used tend to bias to measure firm's short-term performance. Management is expected to perform over a short period of time and this is a clear mismatch with the underlying investor time horizons.

- EBIT induces high leverage

    EBIT is operating profit plus any other income earned on transactions not directly related to producing and/or selling the firm's products. The use of EBIT as the performance indicator can be problematic. It is argued that when EBIT becomes the definition of corporate earnings, it is a major incentive to expand a company by high debt (or high leverage) because the measure will reflect the flow of earnings from high leverage but not the service (interest) charge for that debt.

Suggested improvements

Academic research suggests situation would be improved if there were:

- Longer term tenures for corporate management.
- The cessation of stock options and in their place a generous basic salary and five-year restricted shares (shares that could not be cashed for five years).

In practice, the Association of British Insurers (ABI) (2002, 2005) guidelines recommend:

- Performance being measured over a period of at least three years to try to ensure sustained improvements in financial performance rather than the emphasis being placed on short-term performance.

- Share incentive schemes should be available to employees and executive directors but not to non-executive directors (although non-executive directors are encouraged to have shareholdings in the company, possibly by receiving shares in the company, at full market price, as payment of their non-executive director fees) because this may give them a rather unhealthy focus on the short-term share price of the company.
- Total shareholder return relative to an appropriate index or peer group is a generally acceptable performance criterion (reference point).

Chapter 4

Scale of operations

To: Local Entrepreneur
From: Trainee Accountant
Date: xxxxxx
Topic: Scale of operations

The **optimum size of the firm** is the size which minimises the average cost of production. In the long run, we can assume that all factors of production can be varied in quantity in order to reach the minimum of long run average costs. In the short run, returns to scale – ie economies arising from increasing the level of production – occur within a given production capacity limit. The **short-run average cost curves (SRAC)** and **long-run average cost curve (LRAC)** are illustrated in the diagram below.

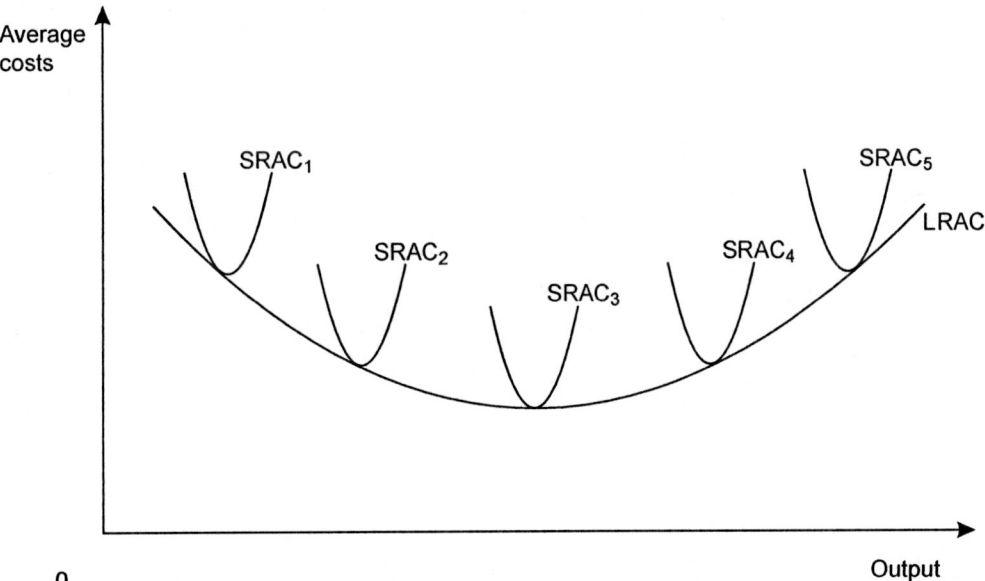

In most industries, as a firm grows in size, unit costs are reduced by producing greater volumes of output and thus producing on a larger scale. The reductions in long-run average cost that can be achieved by increasing production capacity are known as economies of scale. **Economies of scale** may be either internal, ie arising from within the firm, or external, is arising from the growth of the industry as a whole. Internal economies of scale can result from the specialisation and division of labour, and from the advantages of using larger or more specialised machinery. Economies may also be gained from administration and marketing cost savings and possibly reduced finance costs.

Eventually, the scope for making economies will diminish, and it may be that certain **'diseconomies' of scale** come into operation. Such diseconomies may arise from the bureaucratic inefficiencies of running a very large business. When diseconomies outweigh economies of scale, the long run average costs curve

LRAC begins to rise. The firm will be at optimum size at the minimum point of the LRAC. The LRAC may be flat over a range of outputs rather than there being a single minimum point.

There is considerable evidence that economies of scale occur, but less evidence of the operation of diseconomies of scale. It would however appear that economies of scale run out after a certain level of output, resulting in an L-shaped long run average cost curve, rather than a U-shaped one. This implies that there will be a range of optimum sizes for a firm above a certain level of output.

Chapter 5a

Perfect competition and market failure

(a) Perfect competition is a hypothetical market structure in which there are **a large number of buyers and sellers**. The quantity of the good bought by any buyer or sold by any seller is so small in relation to the total amount that changes in these quantities leave market prices unaffected.

Since consumers can choose to buy from any of a large number of suppliers, individual producers are under pressure to sell at the market price. If they try to enforce a higher price, consumers will merely buy from one of their competitors instead. There is no point in selling below the market price, as this would be unprofitable.

The model of perfect competition is based on a number of assumptions.

(i) Many buyers and sellers
(ii) Homogeneous product
(iii) Freedom of entry and exit
(iv) Perfect knowledge
(v) Lack of economic friction

Since the individual demand curve facing any one firm is completely elastic due to the intensive competition if the industry, the perfectly competitive firm would be in equilibrium where:

(i) MC = MR   Profits are being maximised
(ii) MC = AC   Cost per unit is minimised
(iii) MC = Price   The cost of the last unit produced is equal to the selling price at $Q^1 P^1$

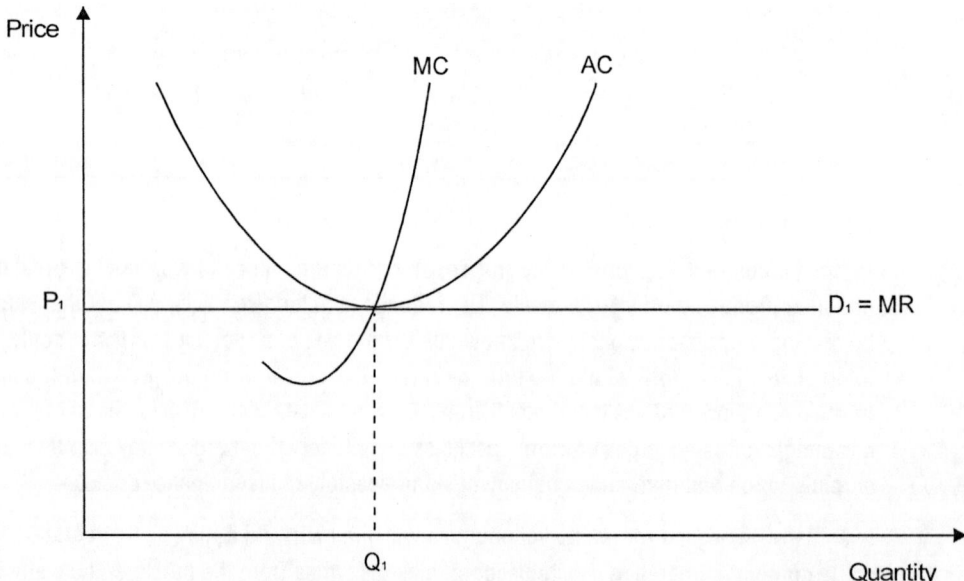

Figure 1 Perfect competition

(b) There are several reasons why market failure may occur. The most obvious is that in the real world perfect competition does not exist because some of the **assumptions** of perfect competition, such as homogeneous products and freedom of entry, **do not hold true in practice**.

A monopoly exists where one firm is able to dominate the market because there are **entry barriers** which prevent potential competitors from entering the market. In such a situation a dominant firm can charge market prices in excess of costs without fear of losing customers.

Another reason for market failure is the existence of **externalities**. Perfect competition theory does not take into account the social costs and benefits of individual choices. Left purely to market forces, a chemical company which pollutes the local river is not paying true environmental costs. Nor are the end users. Economic theory would suggest that this should result in the good being taxed, which would have the desired effect of raising price and reducing output.

For most good and services, the market process will work if the goods are mutually exclusive. For example, if an individual purchases and consumes a cup of coffee, no one else consume that coffee. However, something like street lighting can be enjoyed by everyone. This type of good is known as a public good. With public goods it is impossible to exclude others from benefiting. The market mechanism is not the best way to determine price and quantity of this type of good.

In a mature economy like the United Kingdom most people would agree that everyone should be entitled to an education and some kind of healthcare. Although these services may be free to the end user they are not free to produce. In a pure market economy, the consumer would have to pay for these services.

Finally, a market economy is likely to lead to an **uneven distribution of income and wealth**, which might be considered undesirable. A mixed economy combines the merits of an efficient economy with the more socially just public sector economy.

Monopolies and public interest

(a) A firm will **maximise its profits** when the price and output combination is such that the **marginal revenue** of an additional unit of output is equal to the **marginal cost** of producing it.

A market dominated by a single firm is called a **monopoly**. The monopolist can choose to set price at different levels and, as a **price-maker**, faces a downward sloping demand (average revenue) curve.

Because there are **barriers to the entry of new firms** to the industry, in a monopoly supernormal profits are not 'competed away' by other firms. The long-run equilibrium price and output of a monopoly firm is illustrated in the diagram below.

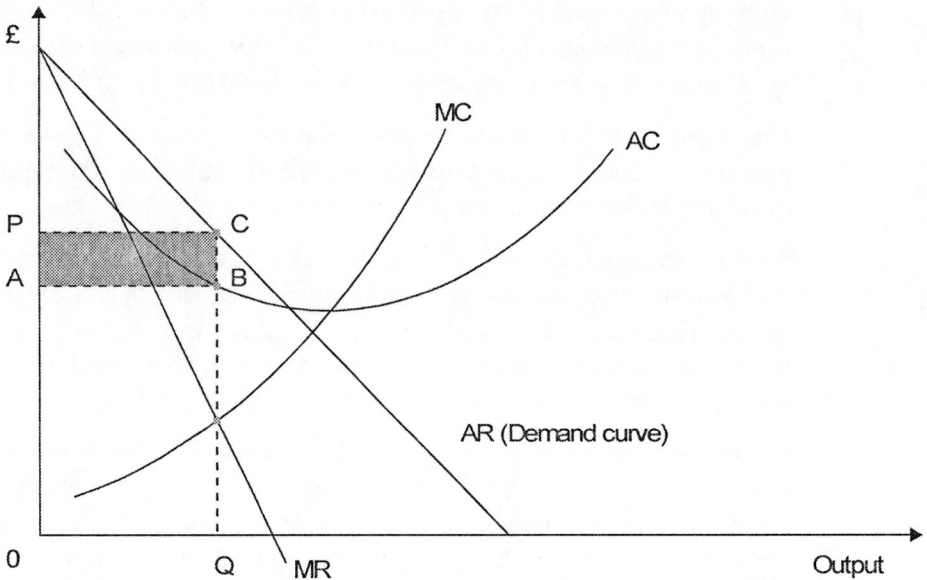

The **profit maximising position** for the firm is where MC = MR. This occurs at output Q in the diagram above, where the price paid by consumers is P. In this equilibrium position, the monopolist is achieving supernormal profits represented by the area of the rectangle PABC, which is the output quantity multiplied by the difference between average revenue (price) and total average costs (AC).

If demand for the firm's product is relatively inelastic, then the demand curve is more steeply downward sloping and the position of the monopolist is further removed from that of perfect competition: the monopolist is then more able to earn supernormal profits than if demand is more elastic.

The monopolist illustrated by the diagram is not producing at the lowest point of its average cost curve. This indicates a misallocation of resources since the firm is not operating as efficiently as it could be. Additionally, the earning of supernormal profits by the monopolist could be viewed as a failure in the distribution of income compared with perfect competition, with which all firms earn normal profits only.

(b) Monopoly conditions can clearly operate against the consumer's interest and against public policy, and can therefore be bad for an economy. For example, the profit maximising output of a monopolist is likely to be at a price and output level which leads to supernormal profits being earned. At the same time, such an output level can never coincide with the level at which average costs are minimised, so that monopolies are inherently inefficient. A monopolist is also free to carry out restrictive practices, such as price discrimination and the exploitation of **barriers to entry**.

Without government measures to control these problems the activities of a monopolist can operate against the public interest. Nevertheless, governments (including the present Conservative government of the UK in recent years) have sometimes encouraged the development of private monopolies relatively free from such controls. There are a number of possible reasons for this.

(i) The **minimum efficient plant size** may be such that the market is large enough only to accommodate a single firm. For example, it would clearly be a waste of resources for there to be two separate national systems for the distribution of electricity or gas to consumers.

(ii) **Competition from foreign firms** (sometimes benefiting from government subsidies) may threaten the existence of domestic producers. It may be that the only way to protect them is to confer on them the advantages of monopoly status.

(iii) Governments may believe that private enterprise is **more efficient** than public enterprise. In the case of the so-called natural monopolies a government might prefer to place the industry in the hands of a private organisation rather than a public one.

In practice, however, **supernormal profits** can be beneficial to an economy since they permit firms to invest for the longer term in both fixed capital (eg new equipment) and in other ways (eg expenditure on research and development). In some sectors, a monopoly may be necessary for profits to be achieved.

For example, in the pharmaceutical industry, the development of new drugs requires a high level of current profits to support current expenditure. There must also be an expectation that the development will, if successful, earn high profits in the future to recover its development costs and also the costs of those projects which fail (of which there will inevitably be some). Although the pharmaceutical industry is not an entire monopoly, some monopoly powers are available through patent legislation and the simple expedient of being first into the market with a new drug.

A monopoly may be able to exploit **economies of scale** by increasing its size and output to a scale which could never be achieved in a competitive market because of the entry of new firms into the market. This could result in lower prices to the consumer even though the monopolist still earns good profits. On the other hand, the lack of competition means that the monopolist does not necessarily have to be efficient to earn a satisfactory profit. Competitive markets do, in general, produce more efficient producers.

These two features (economies of scale and inefficiency) can, of course, exist simultaneously, making it very difficult to judge the overall impact of the monopoly.

There are certain sectors which operate on an **international basis** (eg aerospace) and an apparent monopoly in the home market does not have any impact in practice. Indeed, there may be other reasons (such as **national security**) why certain sectors need to be particularly strong and the creation of a monopoly may achieve this.

Chapter 5b

Oligopoly

(a) The actions of firms in an oligopolistic industry are dominated by **interdependence** of possible actions/reactions of competitors. Because individual firms must consider the effects of their actions on rival producers, there is **uncertainty** because they cannot be certain how rivals will react. Each of the oligopolists is faced by a downward sloping demand curve, commonly portrayed in the form of a **kinked demand curve**.

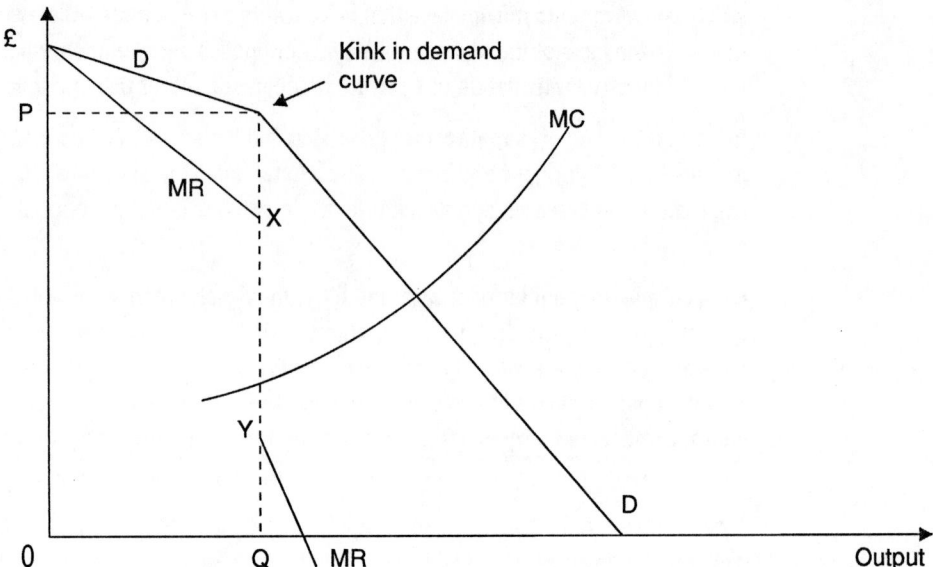

It is assumed that the market is relatively mature, in the sense that the firms are well established in the market, and that the present market position is the outcome of much interaction between them. Price is now at point P because any attempt in the past to raise the price would have been followed by rivals. Owing to the **elasticity of demand** above that point, any price raiser, through loss of sales, would soon have been forced back to price P. The relevant consideration is therefore possible price cuts below P. Throughout that lower part of the demand curve, demand is inelastic.

On the assumption that elasticity of demand in the aggregate market (the combined output of oligopolists X_1, X_2 and X_3) is fairly low, then a price cut by X_1 would soon be followed by equivalent price cuts by X_2 and X_3, as each strives to maintain its market share. All would be worse off as total revenue would fall. Indeed, there could be the added disadvantage for all (though not necessarily in equal proportions) of the advertising and promotional costs which might be necessary to make any price cut effective, apart from any decline in buyer confidence in the product.

The kink in the demand curve is due to the nature of the marginal revenue curve, MR. At price P, the MR curve falls vertically because at higher prices the curve corresponds to the elastic section of the demand curve, and at prices below P it reflects the inelastic section of demand.

The greater the **cross elasticities of demand** between the products of X_1, X_2 and X_3, ie the more they are substitutes for one another, the more the model on pricing response will hold and the sooner, initially, will the sales of X_2 and X_3 drop as customers switch to buying from X_1. At the same time, the higher the level of 'committed costs' of X_2 and X_3, the greater their need to maintain revenue through market share. However, the more effectively X_2 and X_3 have differentiated their products and the greater the loyalty of their customers, the slower will be the switch of sales to X_1. As time goes by, though, the basic similarity of the products will be increasingly recognised and demand will switch to X_1.

Awareness of this **switching process** leads oligopolists to avoid intra-industry price warfare where possible and to compete on points other than price eg by product. Nevertheless, price cutting does take place. If X_1 were to cut prices to exploit a growth in total demand for the industry product, the others would follow in order to hold market share as well as to exploit possible economies of scale. Alternatively price cutting could take place in the later stages of a product's life cycle, as demand declines, or in the later stages of a recession. Stocks might be liable to deterioration, or the firms might be facing cash flow problems.

(b) Oligopolistic industries are characterised by **heavy advertising expenditure** in part because advertising forms a very effective barrier to entry. If we consider the soft drinks industry, this is a special type of oligopoly, a duopoly where the market is dominated by two key players, Coca-Cola and Pepsi. Both companies spend heavily in advertising in order to keep up the brand image and consumers built up a certain amount of loyalty to their brands which makes it difficult for new firms such as Virgin to penetrate this market. Firms in oligopolistic markets often enjoy large profits which can be invested in further advertising, which can make it very difficult for new firms to come into the market.

Heavy advertising is also an example of **non-price competition**. Although the products of different firms may be very similar, the firms seek to differentiate their own product by building up a strong brand through advertising, or by emphasising small distinctive features of their products.

Advertising may increase the size of the overall market without affecting the revenues of individual firms adversely. This can help firms to reduce the uncertainty of what will happen if prices are raised. If brand loyalty can be established, the demand curve for rises in price will become less elastic.

Chapter 6

Labour mobility

(a) **Factors of production are not wanted for their own sakes but for what they can actually produce.** The demand for labour therefore is a derived demand. A firm's demand for labour will depend on how much each particular worker can produce and, more importantly, on the price for which that output can be sold.

Assume a farmer with a field of potatoes can sell his produce at $1 per kilo. Labour is the only cost in the production process and the farmer can employ as many homogeneous potato pickers at a wage rate of $200 per week as he wants. Assuming that he is seeking to maximise profits, this will be where marginal cost of employing the last worker is equal to their marginal revenue product. In other words, provided the farmer can sell the produce at a price greater than unit labour cost, he will continue to hire workers until profits cannot be increased. The demand for labour derives from the fact that the workers are needed to pick potatoes which can then be sold for a profit. The labour itself does not make the profit; what it produces does.

(b) **Labour immobility takes place when individual workers are either unable or unwilling to take on jobs in other industries or other geographical areas of the country.**

Trade unions and professional associations play an important part in determining the number of individuals coming into a particular trade or profession. In recent years, the powers of trade unions have been greatly reduced in many countries on the grounds that the efficiency of the labour market has been improved.

Geographical unemployment may result from poor knowledge of jobs in other parts of the country or a lack of affordable accommodation in the areas with the jobs. Family ties can also cause geographical immobility of labour.

Imperfections in the labour market are also caused by **lack of knowledge of employment opportunities**. However, the growth of private sector employment agencies has helped to bring buyers and sellers of labour closer together.

Discrimination in the work place is another cause of labour immobility but various forms of legislation against discrimination have helped to improve mobility of labour.

A **lack of basic education and training** will also increase labour immobility but the number of individuals entering higher education has continued to rise in recent years.

… Governments can also try to bring employment to the workers by encouraging **inward investment**. This is done by offering companies various financial **incentive schemes** to set up in particular areas.

Chapter 7

Takeover declined

(a)

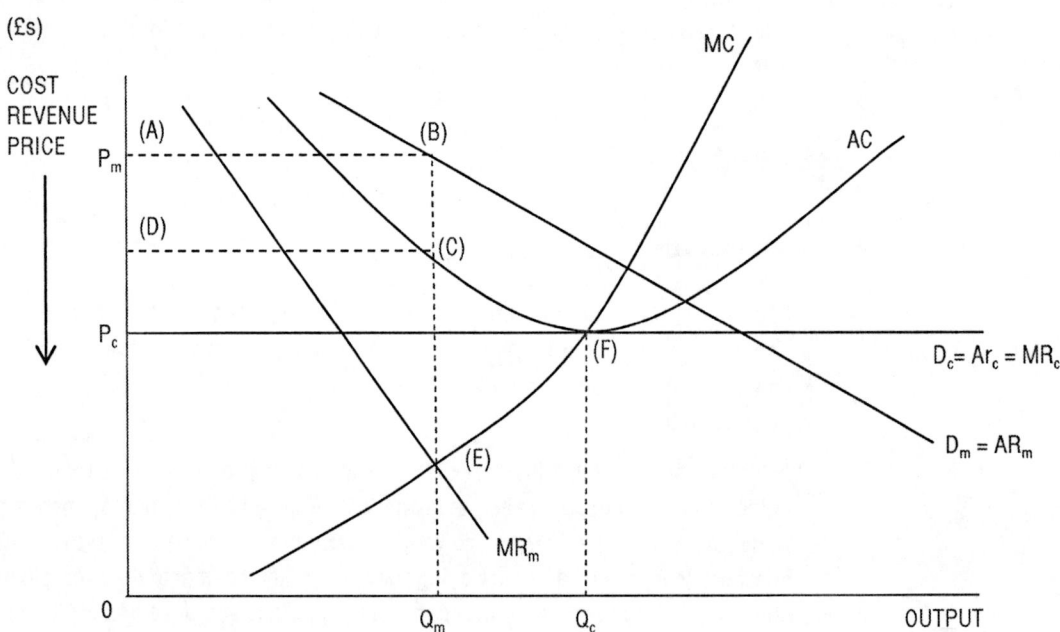

(The diagram above is complex in that it includes two sets of market conditions which generate two different demand and revenue curves.)

In the diagram, the perfectly competitive demand curve is labelled by the suffix (c) and that for monopoly by (m). This demonstrates a number of points:

- that prices for a perfectly competitive firm will always be lower than if the firm was a monopoly (on the diagram this is shown as Pm to Pc).
- that output will always be lower for the monopoly (shown as Qc to Qm)
- the demand curve in perfect competition is a horizontal line, but for a monopoly it is downward sloping (Dc and Dm respectively)

The monopoly will make supernormal profits which are shown in the diagram by the area (ABCD).

(b) X-inefficiency can be defined as the inefficiency that arises from output falling to Qm from Qc. In the diagram this is represented by points (F) to (C). The inefficiency arises because the company is not producing at its lowest point on the AC curve (F). X-inefficiency is a loss of technical efficiency due to reduced scale economies.

(c) This is a horizontal merger. This is the case because the merger will increase market share which means the company is trying to merge with a competitor. This is the definition of a horizontal merger.

(d) The Government agency will be aware of the economic concerns about increased price, abnormal profit, reduced output and X-inefficiency to do with monopolies. The only circumstances in which mergers that create monopoly would be allowed are either because of national security needs which mean the monopoly is needed to serve the national interest, or because of scale efficiencies.

The former view could be used for companies in the military defence sector who might be able to offer this argument if the merger was about protecting the national need to maintain dominance in a particular technology for example. This is a rarely used argument. The more realistic argument is that the merger is required to gain scale economies that overall will bring average costs and prices down below what they would be in a competitive market. This argument is the basis on which so called 'natural' monopolies are supported. The costs, for example, of having a number of water companies piping water into one region would be onerous. Having one monopoly supplier is much more efficient and it is then the role of a regulator to ensure this efficiency is utilised and passed on to the consumers through lower prices.

Chapter 8

Capital markets

(a) Both the money market and the capital market are sources of credit for borrowers. Each is made up of a number of financial intermediaries, some of whom operate in both markets. The principal distinction between the two markets is the period for which finance is provided; money market dealings would extend from overnight up to one year, while capital market funds would normally have a much longer period to maturity.

Dealing on the money market is principally in the form of wholesale lending and borrowing by the commercial banks, usually for sums in excess of $50,000. The financial instruments used are extremely liquid and there is a very narrow margin between lending and borrowing rates. The Central Bank deals on the money market when it carries out open market operations to influence interest rates. Other institutions using the money market include finance houses, larger commercial companies of all types and local authorities.

The principal institution in the capital market is likely to be a Stock Exchange, where longer term securities are issued and traded. Long term capital can be raised either by the issue of equity in the form of shares or by borrowing by issuing debentures. Major financial institutions, such as insurance companies and pension funds, provide most of the capital.

(b) Companies which deal directly with these financial markets would use the money market for short term finance and the capital market for longer term funds.

Short term funds are required in varying amounts from day to day as working capital, for instance to smooth the irregular flow of receipts and allow payments to be made when required. Working capital is also required to finance stock and to allow the provision of credit to customers.

The capital market is used to raise longer term capital, particularly to fund investment in land, buildings, plant and machinery. Regular investment in equipment is necessary if a firm is to obtain the benefits of new technology. The capital market can be used to obtain new capital by a fresh issue of securities to all investors or a rights issue to existing shareholders. The tradability of listed securities means that investors may be able to take some of their income in the form of capital growth: this permits the firm to retain cash for re-investment. Finally, many takeovers are financed by share exchanges rather than money payments.

(c) The government will use the capital market to fund part of its public sector borrowing Longer term government financial instruments are known as Government Bonds (or in the UK also as 'gilt-edged' stock or simply as 'gilts').

Government borrowing is due to current expenditure being greater than the amount raised in taxes and is a common method of raising aggregate demand in order to stimulate output and growth and reduce unemployment. It can also arise when the economy enters a recession. Receipts from taxes will fall as business turnover shrinks and incomes fall. At the same time, government spending on welfare will increase.

ANSWERS TO END OF CHAPTER QUESTIONS

Chapter 9

Commercial banks

(a) **Commercial banks** are often referred to as primary banks or retail banks but within the UK financial system, they are better known as **clearing banks**.

A very large amount of transactions pass through the **cheque clearing system** of these banks. Each day, a large number of cheques are written by individuals and companies on current account transactions, and accounts are debited and credited. The cheque clearing system is administered on every weekday through the Central Bank, where each commercial bank keeps an account in order that customers' transactions may be met.

Apart from cheque clearing, the commercial banks offer a **wide range of services** for business customers. It is now sometimes difficult to draw clear boundaries between the activities of commercial banks, merchant banks and building societies since they are each now moving into each other's territory to some extent.

The commercial banks provide money transmission services which assist a business in dealing with its receipts and payments.

As well as providing **current account** facilities, the banks offer **deposit accounts** or facilities for investing sums short-term on the **money markets**. Such facilities enable businesses to make best use of their cash surpluses.

Commercial banks provide **loans** to businesses, either in the form of an overdraft or a term loan (for a fixed period of time).

The banks offer various other services which can help a business to trade, including:

(i) provision of financial advice
(ii) acceptance of commercial bills
(iii) insurance services
(iv) foreign exchange facilities
(v) international payment facilities

(b) (i) Banks create money when they lend because most of the money lent will find its way back into the banking system as new customer deposits.

When a loan is made, the customer is likely to deposit the major part of his loan with the bank, and the firms to which the customer makes payments are similarly likely to deposit the payments with the banking system.

As a result, the bank only needs a relatively small cash reserve to support a given level of deposits. The proportion of the reserve that it is deemed to retain is known as the '**bank deposit multiplier**' (or credit multiplier) For example if 10% of the deposit is retained, this represents a multiplier of 10.

(ii) If it wishes to control commercial banks' ability to create credit, the central bank must control the banks' liquidity, as this forms the basis of the banks' ability to create credit. There are the following control methods.

Open market operations. This involves the central bank ('the Bank') selling government securities on the open market. The securities will be purchased with cheques drawn on the commercial banks. These transactions will be settled by reducing the operational deposits that the banks are obliged to keep with the Bank. As a result, the banks' cash reserves are diminished, and the growth in the money supply is inhibited.

Interest rate policy. A rise in interest rates – the cost of borrowing – will make customers less willing to take on loans, and so less money will be created.

Direct quantitative controls. The central bank might impose specified levels of liquid reserves that the commercial banks must keep. This will reduce the size of the monetary base for the purposes of lending. 'Special deposits' might be required from the banks, set at a specified proportion of the total liabilities of commercial bank. Such deposits must stay with the central bank, and so cannot form a part of the credit creation process.

Moral 'suasion'. The Bank may use exhortation or moral persuasion to discourage banks from engaging in particular kinds of lending.

Reserve ratio. Also, as we noted in part (b) (i), the amount of credit which commercial banks can create depends on the reserve ratio. Therefore, the central bank could reduce the credit multiplier by increasing the reserve ratio which commercial banks must hold.

Chapter 10

Injections and withdrawals

(a) The figure below is a simple model of the **circular flow of national income** showing only two groups, **firms** and **households**. Households earn their income from firms as **rent, wages, interest** and **profits** from selling to firms and households **land, labour, capital** and **entrepreneurship**. Firms earn their income from households as consumers' expenditure by selling goods and services to households.

The circular flow of income

Goods and services →

← Consumer expenditure

FIRMS ⇅ HOUSEHOLDS

Rents, wages, interest and profits →

← Land, labour, capital and entrepreneurship

The circular flow diagram illustrated presumes that households spend all the money they earn and that firms sell all of the goods and services (output) they produce.

The circular flow model shown will correspond more closely to reality if we include government and the external economy (ie international trade), and if we drop the assumption that all income is spent. To do this, we need to introduce the concept of injections into and withdrawals from the circular flow. An injection adds to the income of domestic firms not resulting from an increase in households' spending.

Injections into the economy comprise '**G**' for **government expenditure**, '**I**' for **investment** and '**X**' for **exports**. In other words, they consist of expenditure by government, business and foreigners. We can also refer to the **fiscal sector**, the **private sector** and the **foreign sector**. These are all supplementary to, that is they do not include, household expenditure.

Government spending. Something like 42p in each pound spent every day in the UK is spent by the government. That is £220 billion a year out of all spending or national income of £530 billion, on things like education, social services, defence, transport, trade and industry, environment and agriculture.

Investment. This is spending by business on things like office furniture, plant and equipment, vehicles and buildings. It involves adding to or replenishing capital stock.

Exports. These are goods and services sold overseas.

Sometimes called leakages, **withdrawals** comprise '**T**' for **taxation**, '**S**' for **savings** and '**M**' for **imports**. Withdrawals comprise income not passed into the circular flow of national income.

Taxation. Examples are **direct taxes** like income tax, corporation tax, capital gains tax, inheritance tax and petroleum tax, and **indirect taxes** like VAT oil duties, excise duties on alcohol and tobacco and oil duties. Included in other taxes are council taxes, road tax, television licence and airport taxes.

Savings consist of income not spent on consumption.

Imports. This is the purchase of goods and services from overseas.

Included in both exports and imports in the basic national income model are net capital transfers, overseas profits and speculative money flows.

The circular flow of income will be in **equilibrium** provided that **total injections equal total withdrawals**. If one is greater or less than the other national income will rise or fall accordingly. All of this affects the capacity of the nation's resources. For example, if injections exceed withdrawals, planned spending will now exceed available output, and producers will respond by expanding output. As national income rises, so will withdrawals, ie extra savings, taxes and imports. When the rise in withdrawals equals the original increase in injections, equilibrium will be restored but now at a higher income level.

(b) **Savings**, as we saw above, are a **withdrawal** from the circular flow of income. Therefore a **rise in the savings ratio** implies a lowering of the level of household consumption. With reduced consumer spending, the income of businesses falls and businesses find that demand does not match the output levels which they had planned. Firms will react by allowing their stocks to fall, which is equivalent to a dis-investment or lowering of investment.

All of this is exacerbated by the **multiplier effect**, that is the number by which a change in investment is multiplied to achieve the change in the equilibrium level of national income. The fall in output will result in a fall in employment and income levels.

The level of national income will continue to be driven down until equilibrium, that is the point at which planned withdrawals equal planned injections, is restored. With a new lower level of national income, firms will be operating in a downturn of the business cycle.

An increase in savings will also have the effect of putting more funds into the hands of **financial intermediaries**. The price of money, that is **interest rates**, will tend to fall, according to the **loanable funds theory**. A higher level of funds available more cheaply may boost investments. This may restore all or part of investments, depending on other determinants, including the confidence which businesses may have about the future, particularly the prospect of growth or otherwise of national income. Contraction of the national income may **lower business confidence**, so that the boost in investment does not occur.

Chapter 11

Macroeconomic environment

(a) The level of national income in the economy from the diagram has moved beyond the full employment position (Ye>Yf). This is a problem because it will lead to instability and is likely to result in inflation which will have longer term consequences for the economy and business in general. The term full employment should be explained as the full economic utilisation of all resources available, including land and labour resources. There are no extra resources available beyond this point that the economy can make use of, and thus the economy is unable to produce more goods and services if aggregate demand increases beyond this point.

(b) (i) The extra spending by the government at this time will shift the aggregate demand curve upwards resulting in an even greater increase in the equilibrium national income, thereby exacerbating the problems of an economy already operating at beyond the level of full employment.

    (ii) From the diagram, the relevant coefficient is 'b' which is the marginal propensity to consume (MPC). MPC is 0.8 which means the marginal propensity to save (MPS) is 0.2. The multiplier is 1/MPS. The multiplier is therefore 1/0.2 = 5.

    If the multiplier is 5 then the increase in government spending will result in an increase of national income of 5 × £1billion = £5billion.

    (iii) This level of national income is worrying because it is even further above the full employment level of national income. This extra income in the economy without a consequent increase in output will result in a period of instability. There is likely to be a further increase in inflation. There is a possibility that there may also be an increase in imports as some of this income will be spent on imports. Increased inflation may lead in time to a significant fall in exports and further rises in imports.

(c) The concerns of the economist are to do with the longer term consequences for an economy that is generating income above the level of actual output to support that income. The economist will be aware that the government will almost certainly need to make use of fiscal and monetary policy instruments to reduce demand in the economy.

The economist will be concerned that both policy instruments will be used. Fiscal policy in a neo-Keynesian sense will be focused on increasing taxes and/or reducing government spending. If the company is in markets with high income elasticities (such as luxury goods), any increase in personal taxes may have a deleterious effect on sales. If, on the other hand, the company is a supplier to government, any reduction in government spending might in time result in reduced revenue.

If the government sought to reduce demand by increasing interest rates, this could significantly affect the estimated investment returns for the company of any future projects, and interest payments on debt if the company is highly geared. These concerns, and the likely fall in consumption because of higher interest rates, would be the principal concerns of the economist.

(d) The Chief Executive will need to take account of how the likely change in the general macro economic environment will affect the company specifically. This will depend in part on the markets the company is in. The advice of the economist is essentially to be aware of the likely changes to taxation and interest rates, and to possible falls in high street spending.

The investment returns on the planned project are crucially affected by future interest rates. A key recommendation for the Chief Executive is thus to factor into the returns calculations for the planned investment, a higher rate of interest. In other words, increase the discount rate on future income from the project. The economist might also suggest that the estimates of future income might also be reduced to reflect reductions in the levels of real income (income after inflation) in future.

The Chief Executive may decide to postpone the project once these factors have been taken into account, or to reduce the level of spending on the proposed project in some way.

Managing unemployment and inflation

(a) The term full employment does not mean a situation in which everyone has a job. There will always be at least a certain natural rate of unemployment, which is the minimum level of unemployment that an economy can expect to achieve.

One of the aims of government employment policy might be to reduce unemployment to the minimum natural rate, and get as close as possible to the goal of full employment. On the basis that unemployment cannot be kept below its natural rate without causing inflation, the natural rate of unemployment is sometimes called the non-accelerating inflation rate of unemployment. But in order to understand the idea of a natural rate of unemployment more fully, we need to examine the trade-off between unemployment and inflation more closely.

(b) According to Keynes, demand management by the government could be based on government spending and taxation policies (fiscal policy). These could be used for two purposes.

(i) To eliminate a deflationary gap and create full employment. A small initial increase in government spending will start off a multiplier–accelerator effect, and so the actual government spending that is required to eliminate a deflationary gap should be less than the size of the gap itself.

(ii) To eliminate an inflationary gap and take inflation out of the economy. This can be done by reducing government spending (e.g., not spending the taxes revenue), or by increasing total taxation.

(c) The Phillips curve is an illustration of the relationship between unemployment and inflation levels in an economy.

Note the following two points about the Phillips curve:

(i) The curve crosses the horizontal axis at a positive value for the unemployment rate. This means that zero inflation will be associated with some unemployment; it is not possible to achieve zero inflation and zero unemployment at the same time.

(ii) The shape of the curve means that the lower the level of unemployment, the higher the rate of increase in inflation.

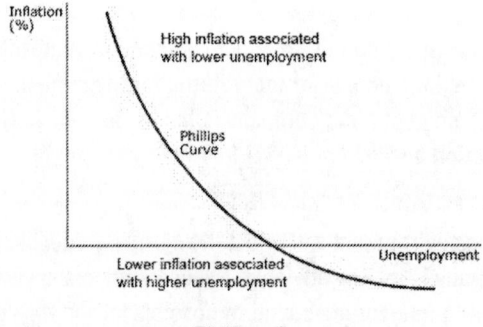

Phillips Curve

Chapter 12

Main objectives

(a) The overall fundamental objective of economic policy in a democratic country is to enhance the welfare or well-being of the community. Towards this end there are or need to be certain key objectives.

   (i) **The maintenance of 'full employment'.** Full employment may be defined as the full utilisation of all factors of production. The existence of persistently high unemployment of labour is objected to on the grounds of the resulting under-utilisation of national resources and the consequential loss of output and unnecessarily depressed living standards.

   It is now generally recognised that to be economically sustainable, the level of employment must be compatible with a low and stable level of inflation. Artificially maintaining or even raising employment levels, eg by over-manning or by public handouts, would only work against other economic objectives, for example through its effect on efficiency.

   An important aim is to improve the level and quality of training and therefore of skills, to overcome the common mis-match between job vacancies and the numbers unemployed.

   (ii) **Price stability.** The government is concerned not merely with stability of prices as such, but also with the level of inflation, the expectations of what the general level of prices will be in the future, and the effects of this on confidence. Major upsurges in inflation require government intervention and inevitably result in wasteful under-utilisation of resources in the ensuing period of deflation.

   (iii) **Equilibrium in the balance of payments over time.** A deficit on the balance of payments current account cannot be sustained indefinitely. The aim will not be to achieve the maximum possible surplus as this can work against the achieving of other economic objectives, through an exceptionally high exchange rate. In practice, the objective is likely to be to achieve a modest surplus on the balance of payments.

   (iv) **Economic growth.** The preceding objectives are really subsidiary to the prime objective of achieving and maintaining a reasonable, acceptable rate of growth, ie an increase in real national income. This can allow a widespread increase in living standards and makes possible the achievement of wider welfare objectives, eg maintaining the quality of the environment.

(b) **Fiscal policy** involves the direction of the economy through public financing and public expenditure. Public financing includes government borrowing and taxation. It is thus concerned with the overall relationship between government expenditure and income.

Governments may pursue a policy of **fiscal deficit**, with government expenditure exceeding its income. Often this is forced upon governments through high levels of expenditure commitments. When pursued out of choice, it could be in order to regenerate an economy later in a recession, ie to reduce unemployment and to get back on a path of economic growth. The aim would be to raise aggregate monetary demand, achieved possibly by means of tax cuts. A reduction in income tax, for instance, would have increased spending power in people's hands which the government would hope would be spent to add to the flow of national income. Increased spending within the economy on consumer goods could then raise the level of investment expenditure, so raising the level of national income. A problem there could be the high marginal propensity of consumers to buy foreign-made goods, resulting in harmful side-effects on the balance of payments.

Alternatively, a government could aim for a **budget surplus**. This would mean that revenue from taxation exceeds government expenditure. This would result in a fall in aggregate monetary demand. This could be applied at some stage in an attempt to deal with an over-heated economy and to combat a high level of inflation. Often, though, in such a condition there is already a large budget deficit and the immediate effort will be concerned with reducing that rather than actually moving into surplus.

A budget surplus could also have the intended effect of reducing a balance of payments deficit. It would be hoped that the reduction in consumer spending power would diminish the demand for foreign goods. The experience of some economies, however, shows general deflation to be a very blunt weapon to be used for this purpose.

Fiscal policy could be used more specifically to achieve economic objectives. Increases or reduction in taxes or government subsidies could be used to attempt to influence **employment** (eg reduction in employer national insurance contributions or the payment of an employment subsidy), to influence the level of **training** being provided (a subsidy to employers), or to raise the level of **private sector investment** (through investment allowances or less directly through a reduction in the tax on companies).

(c) The broad aim of **supply side policies** is to remove the obstacles which prevent or discourage people and firms from adapting quickly to changing conditions of market demand and changing techniques of production. The emphasis on supply side policies stems from a belief that if markets can be made to operate more efficiently, this will encourage economic growth and employment without adding to the risk of inflation.

There are various policies which the government might adopt in an attempt to improve the supply side of the economy. Measures to **improve training**, both for school leavers and for those already in work, can be used to assist the operation of the labour market, and labour mobility can be improved by providing better information on job opportunities and financial assistance to those people considering moving to take up a new job. Other measures may be aimed at trade unions and other restrictive practices which cause inflexibility in the labour market.

A number of policies can be implemented to **improve the efficiency of capital markets**. For example, the abolition of exchange controls removes the restriction on the flow of funds into and out of the country. The government can attempt to make its policies tax-neutral in respect of different savings schemes. The aim is to improve efficiency by allowing savings to go where the best combination of risk and return is deemed to be. Financial markets can be deregulated to encourage competition in the seeking and allocation of capital funds.

The government's **taxation policy** is regarded as an important aspect of supply side economics. It is claimed that cuts in the rates of personal taxation, for example, and increases in the tax threshold can be used as an incentive mechanism to encourage people to enter employment or to work harder. Similarly, it is claimed that dependence on state support can be reduced by cutting welfare and unemployment benefits or by making them taxable. The broad aim of all these measures is to ensure that, in general, people are better off in work than out of work. Cuts in corporation tax rates can also be introduced to encourage firms to invest in more productive capital by reducing the taxation of profits.

The government can make its **competition policy** more rigorous, remove unfair restrictions on trade and break up monopolies. This should encourage competition in the market place which, in turn, should improve economic performance.

In general, supply side measures concentrate on **encouraging entrepreneurship and self-reliance**. The aim of the government is then to create an **environment conducive to enterprise and risk-taking** in which individual initiative is rewarded as the basis for increasing economic efficiency.

Chapter 13

Devaluation policy

(a) If the UK was operating a **fixed exchange rate** and dropped the external price of its currency, eg if the rate moved from £1 = $2.50 to £1 = $1.75, this is termed devaluation of the pound sterling. This has the effect of making UK exports cheaper in US dollars and imports from the USA more expensive.

A government might consider **devaluation** if the country is experiencing a major and prolonged balance of payments deficit. This could be because the economy is uncompetitive with the economies of the country's main trading partners. Alternatively, it could be that the exchange rate has been set at too high a level to reflect purchasing power parity between countries. Devaluation would be intended to improve the relative price position of the country's products. As a result, export sales should rise, imports should fall, and the balance of payments deficit should be eliminated. Devaluation is an **expenditure switching measure**, directed to increasing the volume of exports and encouraging domestic buyers (industrialists and consumers) to switch out of imports into domestically produced substitutes.

For devaluation to be successful, certain conditions must be met. The total earnings from exports will rise only if the demand for exports is elastic; while expenditure on imports will be reduced only if demand for imports is elastic. However, that is not sufficient: the key point is how the relative elasticities of demand affect the balance of payments position. The **Marshall-Lerner criterion** states that devaluation will only improve the balance of payments if the sum of the elasticities of demand for exports and imports is greater than one.

In addition, **total domestic expenditure (C + I + G)** must not be absorbing the whole of the gross domestic product, ie there must be spare capacity in the domestic economy. Moreover, any consequential increase in exports will, through the multiplier, create an increase in national income which in turn will raise the demand for imports.

The **J-curve** effect also needs to be taken into account. According to this, shortly after the devaluation, a deterioration of the balance of payments would take place followed later by the recovery. This would be more likely to apply if insufficient capacity in the domestic system thwarts the effectiveness of the expenditure-switching measure.

In the absence of the necessary spare capacity, **aggregate monetary demand (AMD)** needs to be reduced through deflationary measures. It is preferable that these measures are taken some time before the devaluation as there is likely to be a delay before they become effective. The spare capacity needs to exist at the time the devaluation takes place.

It is essential that the downward adjustment of the exchange rate is sufficient to deal with the disequilibrium. To have to devalue a second time soon after the first one can be disastrous for confidence in both currency and business markets.

Devaluation may not be the appropriate measure. An excess of AMD could be the problem rather than the uncompetitiveness of producers or suppliers. **Deflation** would then be more suitable than devaluation.

The success of devaluation will, in part, depend upon economic conditions in the country's main trading partners being favourable. If some of those countries were undergoing a prolonged recession, this could impede any expansion of exports. Any advantage in importing terms might not compensate for the export disadvantage.

There is also the need to retain any advantage achieved through the devaluation. Rises in the prices of imports could diminish any apparent expenditure-switching advantages. The increased demand

ANSWERS TO END OF CHAPTER QUESTIONS

for labour and increased working time could increase the pressure for wage increases. These possibilities further underline the importance of the **spare capacity argument**. Appropriate deflationary measures might need to be applied for some while after the devaluation in order to keep inflation in check.

(b) The extent to which domestic companies would be affected by a significant devaluation of the currency would depend basically upon:

(i) their relative **dependence on imports**; and
(ii) the relative **importance to them of overseas markets** in which to sell their products.

Companies dependent upon imported raw materials, components or capital equipment would experience a **rise in costs**. Other companies able to purchase parts or equipment from home manufacturers would be less affected.

Companies with a major part of their output sold abroad could benefit markedly from the **fall in the exchange rate**, as this would enable them to lower their list prices. Any increase in sales volume, however, would depend upon the price elasticity of demand for the products. A company would also need to have the spare capacity to meet the extra demand. Instead of reducing list prices to overseas buyers by the extent of the devaluation, companies could take all or part of the advantage in the form of an increased margin of profit, so gaining an increased incentive to sell in these markets. The scope for doing this would, of course, depend upon the selling power in the given markets at the time. Some of the extra margin of profit could be used for improvements in product quality, marketing, or distribution, so strengthening the market position for the future.

Inevitably the effects of devaluation will **vary greatly** between companies, and sometimes even for companies within the same industry. Many companies now operate to a major extent through subsidiary companies abroad and this may insulate them from some of the effects of devaluation. Thus, for a company sourcing raw materials from overseas manufacturing subsidiaries, there might be no effect on input costs.

Devaluation by one country sometimes is followed by **devaluation by other countries**. This could eliminate any initial advantage/disadvantage in these particular markets. The different spread of overseas markets between companies would result in various effects on companies from the net devaluation process.

Some companies have **little or no involvement overseas**, whether through imports or exports. The consequences of devaluation for such companies could be very limited indeed and perhaps only indirect, from the adjustments that follow in the economic system as a whole.

Chapter 14

Globalisation

[Tutorial Note: Candidates need to discuss the benefits and costs of a business operating overseas. A good answer would weigh the benefits against the costs. It would explain the three expansion options with examples and understand that international expansion is a favoured option in many industries, but that there are risks and the decision needs to be properly managed.]

(a) By going global, the business generates a huge opportunity to create and benefit from economies of scale. However, in pursuit of such cost savings the business should not overlook the uniqueness of local market conditions. To do so may mean lost sales and hence profit. The problem with differentiating products for local markets, however, is that costs will rise. Hence a trade-off needs to be made between lowering costs and creating uniqueness.

(b) The simplest way of overseas expansion of a company is exporting products from the home market. This would be a relatively straightforward approach, but the company would have to deal with customers at a remote level. There may be tariffs to pay and there will be costs associated with travel for those involved.

Another option of expansion is to set up a subsidiary. This has the advantage of getting around the problems of tariffs and being remote from customers, but this is a much more significant investment with increased financial risk of failure and the risk of exchange rate fluctuation. Managing the operation is also a bigger task.

The next option is a joint venture. Here the main advantage is access to local knowledge and a reduction in risk, but there are practical questions about selection and the management of the venture and its direction.

Free trade and protectionism

(a) Theoretical US price for an American pair of jeans £56 / (1+12%) × 1.5($/£) = $75.

Theoretical US price for a British pint of beer £3 × (1+157%) × 1.5($/£) = $11.57.

(b) If free trade is allowed, this country will import 700 units;

If the US moves from a no-free-trade market equilibrium to free trade, the price that domestic buyers pay for this good would fall from $6 to $4;

If the US moves from a no-free-trade market equilibrium to free trade, the total amount of the good produced domestically would decrease from 400 million pints to 0.

(c) Protectionism can be practised by a government in several ways.

- Tariffs or customs duties
- Import quotas
- Embargoes: an embargo on imports from one particular country is a total ban, ie effectively a zero quota.
- Hidden subsidies for exporters and domestic producers
- Import restrictions
- Public procurement (government departments deliberately buying from domestic firms in preference to overseas ones)

Besides the direct effects, protectionism has undesirable impacts on the overall economy.

- The theory of comparative advantage shows that international free trade achieves the optimal use of resource. By definition, protectionism prevents this from happening.
- Because firms are protected from competition, they will not strive for innovation and cost reduction. In this way, protectionism will encourage inefficiency.
- Factors of production will remain in 'declining' industries, whereas under free market economics they would move to other industries. Therefore, protectionism leads to a misallocation of resources.
- If protection is achieved through imposing taxes on imported goods, then consumers will suffer through higher prices.
- Protection by one country preventing imports may lead to retaliation by another country. This may provoke a trade war. In this context, when the USA imposed 35% tariff on imports of Chinese tyres in September 2009, China responded by threatening to retaliate against US automobile parts, leading to concerns that these actions could escalate into a trade war although trade war is not provoked every time.

Exam question bank

1 Supply, demand and elasticity

November 2014

'Changes in the prices of crude oil and corn'

Changes in the prices of crude oil and corn, 2000 - 2006

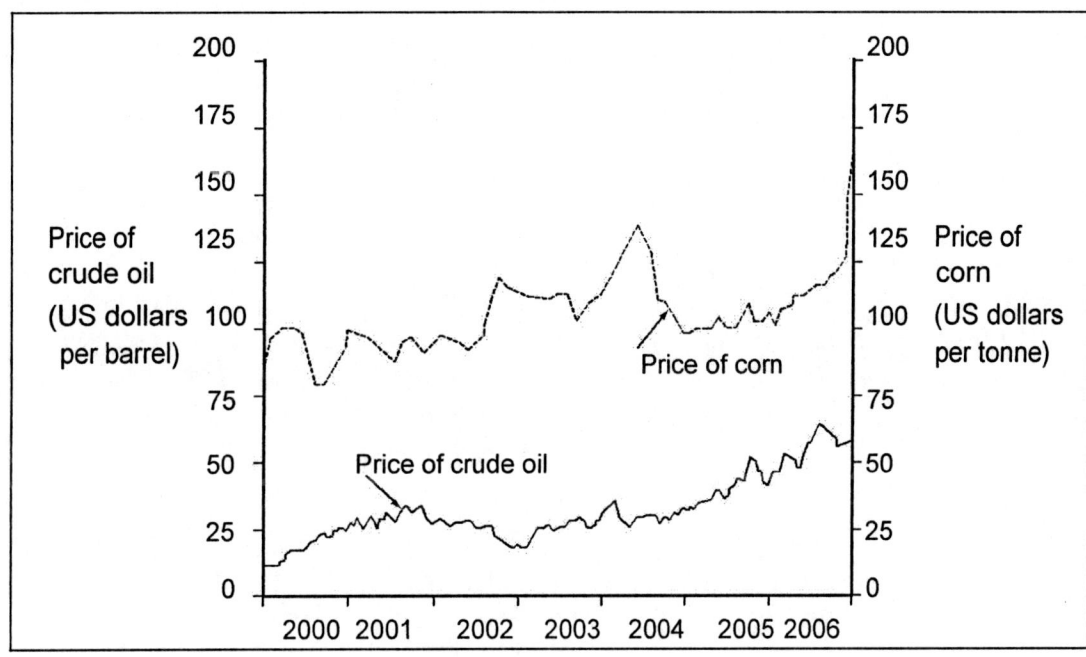

Source: Data compiled from various news reports.

In 2007, the prices of grains and crude oil hit ten-year highs. The rising price of oil stems partly from the fact that world oil supplies are running out. Farmers should be able to meet increased demand for grains such as corn (maize) and wheat simply by growing more. Indeed, more grains are being grown, but demand has grown even faster.

Grains are used as food, both for people and for livestock. In countries such as China incomes are rising. As incomes rise, people eat more meat. This in turn leads to an increase in demand for grains that are used for animal feed. It is also worth noting that the income elasticity of demand for grains is probably positive.

A second reason for rising grain prices lies in increased demand for bio-fuels such as ethanol. Bio-fuels made from corn, wheat, and from other crops are substitutes for petrol and diesel fuel. Since 2000, demand for corn used to make ethanol has risen by over 300 per cent in the USA. Over 20 per cent of US corn is now used as the raw material for ethanol. Governments in forty other countries are promoting the use of bio-fuels to reduce dependency on oil imported from countries such as Iran and Venezuela.

Source: Adapted from various newspapers/reports.

Required

(a) Compare the changes in the prices of crude oil and corn over the period. **(10 marks)**

(b) With the help of a demand and supply diagram, and using the information in the text, explain why the prices of grains such as corn and wheat were rising in 2007. **(15 marks)**

(c) Explain the statement in the text: 'It is also worth noting that the income elasticity of demand for grains is probably positive'. **(5 marks)**

(Total 30 marks)

2 Scarcity, elasticity and pricing

November 2013

The following is an extract from an article.

At the end of 2009 in which world oil prices have reached record highs, prices have once again surged past the $60 a barrel mark. This time the price rise was a result of snowstorms battering the North-Eastern states of America, which in turn caused American households to use more oil in heating their homes.

Over the past two years, the rise in oil prices has been attributed to two main factors. First, global economic expansion has led to a substantial rise in the demand for oil, especially from countries such as America and China. Second, violence and instability in countries such as Iraq has threatened oil production and has reduced the supply of oil on world markets. This factor has been worsened by natural disasters, such as Hurricane Katrina in September 2005, which significantly reduced oil production in America.

The impact of higher oil prices is much debated. Economists are concerned that higher oil prices will raise prices throughout the economy and lower world economic growth. Many economists would point out that the highly price inelastic demand for petrol means that this would not occur. Furthermore, as Table 1 shows, the actual production cost of petrol (which includes the cost of crude oil itself) is only a small part of the overall price which is charged to motorists. In addition, the small numbers of firms that dominate the petrol market are extremely wary of raising their prices in case they lose sales to their large rivals.

What is certain is that the government will continue to watch world oil prices very carefully. As the fuel protests of September 2000 showed, voters do not take kindly to having to pay more for their petrol.

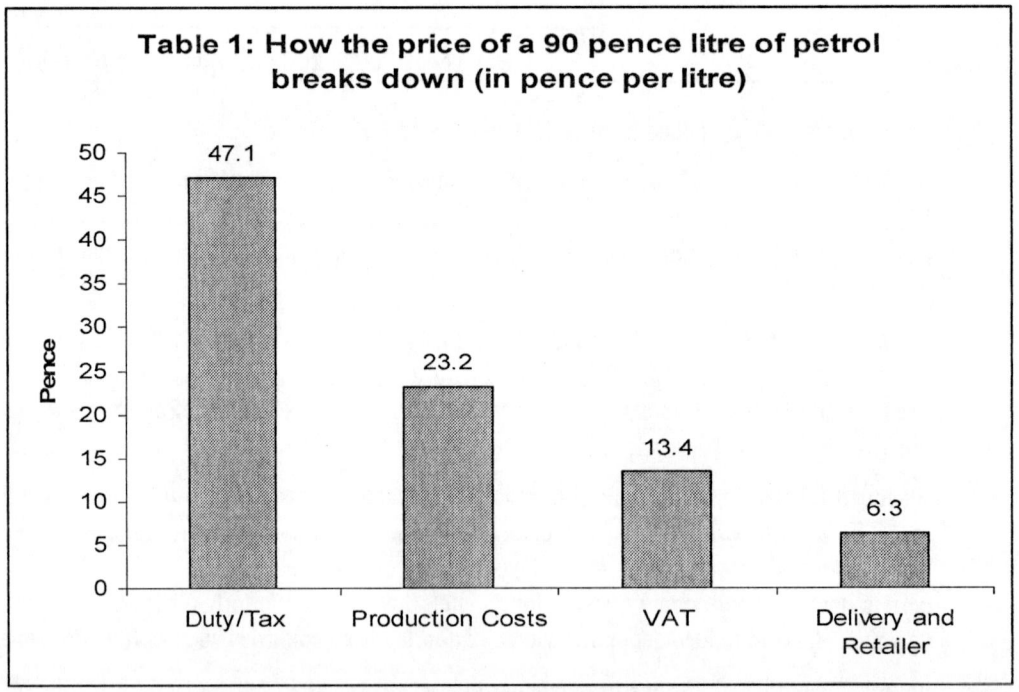

Source: The Automobile Association Motoring Trust, 2007

EXAM QUESTION BANK

Required

(a) Using the information provided, explain how the 'economic problem of scarcity' can be applied to the case of oil. **(4 marks)**

(b) (i) Line 13 of the article states that world petrol prices are "highly price inelastic". Explain the term 'inelastic price of a product'. **(2 marks)**

  (ii) State and explain two factors that will determine the price elasticity of demand for a product. **(6 marks)**

  (iii) Discuss the relevance of price elasticity of demand estimates for businesses. **(6 marks)**

(c) Lines 5 to 10 of the article explain some of the reasons why world oil prices have increased in recent years. Using diagrams show how world oil prices have been affected by the following:

  (i) Global economic expansion and economic growth in countries such as China. **(3 marks)**

  (ii) The impact of natural disasters such as Hurricane Katrina. **(3 marks)**

(d) Using the information provided, discuss 'whether a rise in the cost of crude oil would always lead to companies increasing retail petrol prices for motorists'. **(6 marks)**

(Total 30 mark)

> **Note:** The extract from the article in Question 2 also provides the scenario for Question 3.

3 Market failure

November 2013

In the Oil Price Case in Question 2, the impact of higher oil prices is much debated. Economists are concerned that higher oil prices will raise prices throughout the economy and lower world economic growth. In contrast, environmentalists see the higher oil prices as actually doing some good. Environmentalists argue that motorists cause negative externalities. They claim that by raising petrol prices motorists will be forced to make fewer journeys and therefore the resulting negative externalities will be reduced.

Required

(a) Explain why negative externalities arising from increased car use are an example of market failure. **(10 marks)**

(b) Discuss whether using indirect taxation is an effective solution to the market failure arising from the negative externalities of car usage. **(20 marks)**

(Total 30 marks)

4 Elasticity
May 2015

(a) Briefly explain what is meant by the term 'cross elasticity of demand'. **(2 marks)**

(b) State and explain two characteristics of an oligopolist market. **(4 marks)**

(c) The income elasticity of demand of two goods is as follows:

Jewellery: + 1.4

High specification cameras: + 3.5

  (i) Define the term income elasticity of demand. **(2 marks)**

  (ii) Explain what each of these values mean. **(4 marks)**

  (iii) Discuss the significance of these values for suppliers of Jewellery and High specification cameras respectively. **(8 marks)**

(Total 20 marks)

5 Externalities and market failure
November 2014

'Campaigners take on industry over airport expansion'

Environmental campaigners have revealed how they are preparing to lobby a public inquiry into plans to expand Stansted Airport in Essex. The owner of the airport is hoping to gain permission to increase the number of passengers using the airport, from 25 million to 35 million a year, through expansion.

Campaigners against the expansion claim that the plans directly contradict the government's target to reduce carbon dioxide emissions by 20% by 2010. They have already won the backing of the local council, which has thrown out the expansion plans, and they are also supported by pressure groups including Friends of the Earth and the National Trust.

The National Trust argues that Hatfield Forest, which is on the edge of the airport, will be negatively affected by increased noise and air pollution. Uniquely, the Forest has more than 800 trees which are over 500 years old. The National Trust's experts say that increases in nitrogen oxides in the air, as a result of the airport expansion, could put some of these trees in danger. Keith Turner, the National Trust's area manager, commented that "the expansion of the airport could damage the historic and scientific values of the Forest". Others point out that the 200,000 visitors to the Forest every year will no longer be able to enjoy the peace and quiet which the area provides.

The Airport's owner insists that environmental factors have already been taken into account when drawing up the expansion plans. As a result, the amount of land required for the Stansted expansion has been reduced by a third. Other supporters point to the fact that the economy will benefit to the tune of over £13 billion if airports are allowed to expand.

Required

(a) Explain why air travel is classified as a private good. **(6 marks)**

(b) Using the article, identify one possible external cost which might arise from the expansion of Stansted Airport. Explain how the existence of external costs causes allocative inefficiency. **(4 marks)**

(c) Explain the effectiveness of subsidies to producers as a solution to the market failure arising from positive externalities. **(6 marks)**

(d) One form of government intervention to correct market failure is regulation. Explain how effective this policy might be in correcting market failure. **(14 marks)**

(Total 30 marks)

EXAM QUESTION BANK

6 Remuneration and performance

May 2015

EasyJet is accused of stealth pay bonanza.

EasyJet founder Sir Stelios Haji-Ioannou has launched a blistering attack on the bosses of the budget airline for pocketing huge pay rises.

Yesterday [5 December 2013], the no-frills flyer slipped out details of a £4.6m package for chief executive Carolyn McCall, double what she received last year. The details were released minutes before the Chancellor George Osborne finished delivering his Autumn Statement speech. Campaigners last night accused the airline of trying to 'bury bad news' as it also revealed finance chief Chris Kennedy's package double to £3.7m.

The runaway pay enraged EasyJet's largest shareholder Haji-Ioannou, who warned of a bruising showdown with investors at next month's annual general meeting. He said: "although the share price has gone up roughly three times since this management took over, their take-home pay has multiplied in the order of 20-30 times."

McCall's package includes her £665,000 basic salary, a £1.15m annual bonus, and a £4.57m long-term performance related shares bonus. This was awarded in 2011 but McCall will be able to cash it in March next year [March 2014]. She opted to receive the maximum of 83pc of her bonus in shares which she can pocket in three years. Kennedy's £3.7m package included a £533,000 bonus and a £2.7m long-term shares award from 2011. Some 70 per cent of top executives' bonuses is linked to profits, with just 10 per cent linked to customer satisfaction, and 10 per cent to flights being on time.

The firm pointed out that investors have shared in its success. Its share price has also jumped by 120 per cent in the year to the end of September. A spokesman said: "EasyJet financial performance in 2013 set new records for revenue, profit and returns. Our remuneration strategy is to pay a basic salary with other compensation weighted towards variable pay dependent on performance. This ensures there is a clear link between the value created and the amount paid to EasyJet's directors."

[Source: Daily Mail, Friday, December, 6, 2013, Article by James Salmon]

Required

(a) What is the focus of the debate on executive directors' remuneration in the last decade? To what extent is the debate reflected in EasyJet's CEO remuneration case? **(8 marks)**

(b) What are the key elements of directors' remuneration? **(8 marks)**

(c) It is argued that executive directors' remuneration packages should be fairly and appropriately constructed, taking into account long-term objectives. Identify four common corporate performance measurements, including two market-based and two accounting-based indicators. **(4 marks)**

(d) Critically discuss those performance criteria identified in (c) that may be used in determining executive directors' remuneration. **(10 marks)**

(Total 30 marks)

7 Corporate social responsibility
November 2014

Corporate social responsibility (CSR) is of growing importance in many countries. A number of stock market indices of companies with developed CSR have been launched in recent years.

Required

(a) Define corporate social responsibility. **(6 marks)**

(b) Explain why organisations should be socially responsible. **(6 marks)**

(c) Describe what CSR involves. **(8 marks)**

(Total 20 marks)

8 Auditors and corporate governance
May 2013

(a) What are the main roles played by an external auditor and a firm's audit committee? **(12 marks)**

(b) What is the relationship between the external auditor and the firm's audit committee? **(6 marks)**

(c) Critically discuss the importance of the external auditor in corporate governance. **(12 marks)**

(Total 30 marks)

9 Monopolistic competition
May 2014

Cosmetic Luxury plc is considering entering a market which is currently dominated by monopolistic competition market and is trying to use this knowledge to inform their strategic decision-making.

Required

(a) Explain the most important characteristics of a monopolistic competition structure. **(10 marks)**

(b) Explain to what extent Cosmetic Luxury plc should be equally conscious of potential newcomers to the market. **(10 marks)**

(Total 20 marks)

10 The role of a central bank
May 2013

Discuss the following three issues regarding the roles of a central bank:

(a) What are the main roles of a central bank? **(8 marks)**

(b) Would it be possible for an economy to function without a central bank? **(2 marks)**

(c) Does increased bank competition necessarily make it harder for a central bank to force through changes in interest rates (i) by decree; (ii) by dealings in the money market? **(10 marks)**

(Total 20 marks)

11 Unemployment and minimum wages May 2015

Unemployment is regarded as one of the world's major macroeconomic problems. In many developed economies, such as the UK and the US, there has been a minimum wage debate among various economists and different political parties over the last several decades. Take the UK for example, the National Minimum Wage Act (NMW) was introduced by the Labour Government in 1998 and came into force in 1999, when the hourly NMW rate was set to £3.60 for workers aged 22 and over. In October 2010, this rate rose to £5.93, and the age at which one can qualify for this rate became 21 for the first time. From October 2014, the hourly NMW rate will increase to £6.50.

Although the national minimum wage act has been in effect for more than 10 years, differences of opinion from economists and political parties exist about the benefits and drawbacks of a minimum wage. Supporters of the minimum wage say the minimum wage could redistribute income from businesses towards low wage workers, reducing inequality and poverty. It also could boost the economy as low wage workers spend almost all of the money rather than saving it as richer people do. To the contrary, opponents of the minimum wage argue that an increase in the minimum wage would pose more burdens on employers, particularly when the economy is down and employers are slashing costs. In consequence, raising the minimum wage would impair job creation, increasing unemployment and poverty and damaging businesses.

Required

(a) Explain, with the aid of diagrams, the concept of disequilibrium unemployment and equilibrium unemployment. **(18 marks)**

(b) Explain the economic principle underlying the minimum wage debate. **(12 marks)**

(Total 30 marks)

12 Macroeconomic policy and the economy November 2012

Germany overtook the US in 2003 to become the world's largest exporter. In 2005 German firms exported a higher value of goods than the UK, France and the Netherlands combined.

Other components of Germany's aggregate demand grew more slowly. In particular, consumer expenditure was held back by low consumer confidence. This partially offset the good export record and adversely affected German economic growth. In turn, low economic growth kept the German unemployment rate high in historical terms. In 2005 the unemployment rate was particularly high among the low skilled, over a third of whom had been out of work for more than a year. To reduce such unemployment and increase aggregate demand, the German government considered a number of fiscal policy measures including cutting the rate of income tax.

Despite concerns about the slow growth in German aggregate demand, German aggregate supply continued to increase at a relatively rapid rate. This results in German potential economic growth exceeding its actual economic growth, giving rise to a negative output gap.

Required

(a) Define the terms: fiscal policy and the unemployment rate. **(4 marks)**

(b) State and explain two possible economic reasons why Germany was so successful at exporting. **(4 marks)**

(c) Explain the likely relationship between economic growth and unemployment. **(5 marks)**

(d) Comment on the effectiveness of a cut in the rate of income tax as a way of increasing aggregate demand. **(7 marks)**

(e) Discuss the extent to which an increase in exports will improve an economy's performance.
(10 marks)

(Total 30 marks)

13 Exchange rates   May 2016

Free floating or flexible exchange rates occur when exchange rates are left to the interaction of market forces and there is no official financing at all. In other words, the exchange rate will reflect the interaction of supply and demand for a currency.

Required

(a) Explain the floating exchange rate mechanism with a graph. **(9 marks)**

(b) If there is a fall in the demand for the export of a country with a floating exchange rate (eg the UK), explain the consequence on the exchange rate. **(2 marks)**

(c) Describe the advantages and disadvantages of floating exchange rates. **(9 marks)**

(Total 20 marks)

14 Global strategy   Nov 2014

Explain why corporations pursue a global strategy. List any 6 main 'Pull' factors and any 2 main 'Push' factors of corporations' overseas expansion. **(20 marks)**

15 Comparative advantage   May 2015

Discuss the following issue: 'If a developing country has a comparative advantage in primary products, to what extent should the government allow market forces to dictate the pattern of trade?' **(20 marks)**

Exam answer bank

EXAM ANSWER BANK

1 Supply, demand and elasticity

(a) The prices of both crude oil and corn increased over the whole period, e.g. from $11 to $60 a barrel in the case of oil, and from about $90 to about $162 dollars a tonne in the case of corn.

The prices of both crude oil and corn fluctuated up and down during the whole period.

The price of both crude oil and corn reached their peaks in 2006.

The price of both goods reached their lowest points at roughly the same time in 2000, though the price of corn fell and rose significantly in 2000.

The price of crude oil ranged from a high of about $68 a barrel to a low of about $11 a barrel whereas the price of corn ranged from a high of just over $165 a tonne to a low of about $77 a tonne.

Both prices were rising towards the end of the period, though the crude oil price dipped for a time in 2006.

(b) The diagram shows a rightward shift in the demand curve for grain.

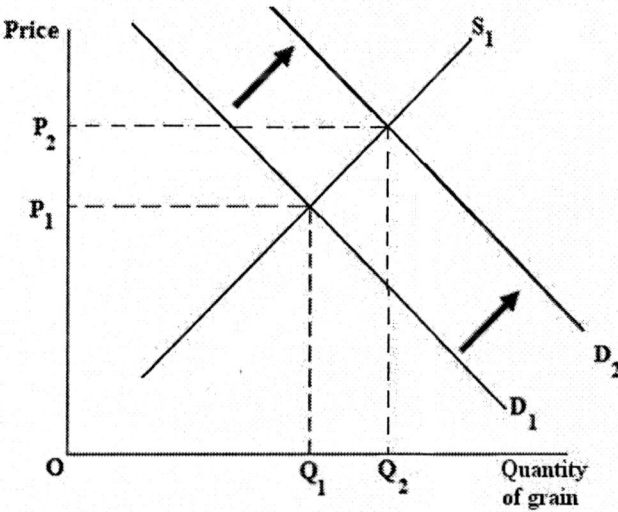

- Axes labelled (price and quantity or P and Q will do)
- Original demand and supply curves correctly labelled
- Co-ordinates drawn in at the initial equilibrium and labels such as P_1 and Q_1. Rightward shift of the demand curve
- Co-ordinates drawn in at the new equilibrium and labels such as P2 and Q2
- Any other relevant feature of the diagram (e.g. the amount of excess demand at the original equilibrium after the demand curve has shifted)

The following points need to be covered:

- The demand curve for grains shifts rightward because of the increased use of grain in bio-fuel.
- The demand curve for grains shifts rightward because richer consumers are eating more food.
- The demand curve for grains shifts rightward because richer consumers are eating more meat which requires increased use of grain as an animal feed.

- The adjustment to the new equilibrium price.
- Any other relevant point, e.g. the rightward shift of demand must have been greater than the rightward shift of supply for the prices of grains to rise.

(c) The income elasticity of demand measures the proportionate or percentage change in quantity demanded following an initial change in income.

$$\text{Income elasticity of demand} = \frac{\text{proportionate or percentage change in quantity demanded}}{\text{proportionate or percente change in income}}$$

The statement 'It is also worth noting that the income elasticity of demand for grains is probably positive' can have two meanings. Firstly, as incomes rise, people eat more meat and this leads to an increase in demand for grains that are used for animal feed. Secondly, the increased demand for bio-fuels, those are made from more corn, wheat and other crops leads to an increase of demand of grains.

2 Scarcity, elasticity and pricing

(a) The 'economic problem of scarcity' is that where there are only limited resources to meet unlimited wants of a good. Oil is a scarce resource and will eventually run out. The demand for oil largely outweighs the amount of scarce resources available as both motorists and producers have infinite wants for oil. This is scarcity.

(b) (i) Price inelasticity of a product is the demand for the product insensitive to a change in price.

(ii) The amount of substitutes for a product. The substitutes means that an increased competition for and a rise in the price of a product would drive consumers to consume more of its substitute, since consumers now have alternatives and are not forced to buy only one product. The existence of its substitutes makes the demand for a product elastic. The more substitutes exist, the higher price elastic the product will be.

The proportion of income that a product takes up. The larger the proportion of income that a product takes up, the higher price elastic a product will be. This is because consumers have a finite real disposable income; therefore, they will allocate their money in the most efficient way. A product that takes up a large proportion of income means consumers may consider more of their actual needs for that product since this product tends to be a luxury good rather than a necessity. Moreover because of its high price, the opportunity cost that arises from its purchase would tend to be high.

(iii) The value of price elasticity for a good shows how elastic a good is for a firm that produces that good. A good use of price elasticity indicator would guide the firm into making the right pricing strategies and forecasting revenue. An inelastic good normally means, in order to increase revenue, the price needs to be increased since the demand is insensitive to the rise in price and the quantity will not decrease by so much, thus, revenues would increase. However, the opposite price and revenue trends hold for an elastic good, that is, a fall in price would increase firm's revenue.

However, the value of price elasticity for a good is only an estimate, and is dependent on many factors, such as the rival's price changes, seasonal fluctuations in demand, recent one-off events that could bias the values, etc. The price elasticity is therefore not always a true representation of the actual demand. Businesses need to increase the time period that a good is monitored for as well as look at alternative indications.

(c) (i) The impact of China's economic expansion and growth.

Figure 1: Demand and supply of petrol

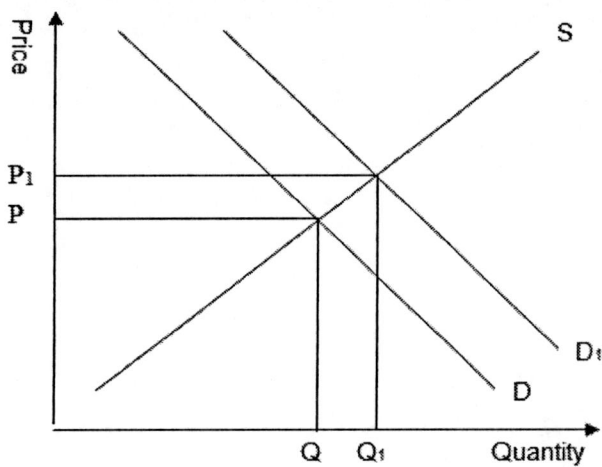

At the original equilibrium, the quantity of Q oil are traded at the price of P. Expansion and economic growth indicate increased productivity and increase in demand for oil (a factor of production), from D to D_1. This increases the price from P to P_1 and the quantity traded from Q to Q_1.

(ii) The impact of natural disasters such as Hurricane Katrina

Figure 2. Demand and Supply of Petrol

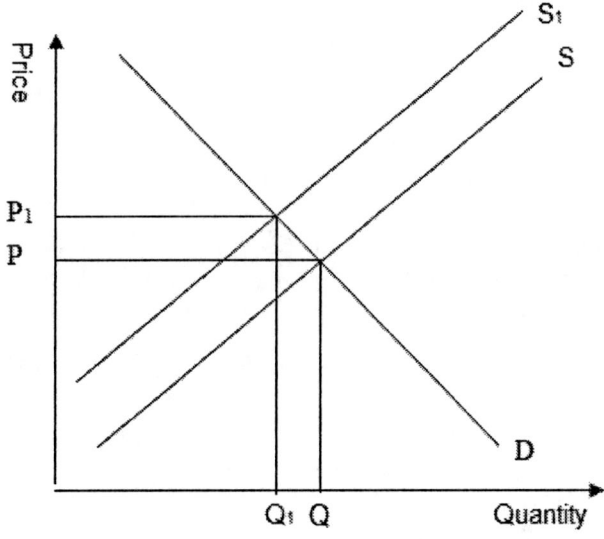

Natural disasters decrease the supply of oil from S to S_1 and the price rises from P to P1 and quantity decreases from Q to Q_1; the whole equilibrium moves from PQ to P_1Q_1.

(d) The increase in the cost of crude oil would often lead to a decrease in supply since the costs of petrol production go up. The petrol production costs take up around 25% of the total petrol costs, and this increase could affect petrol producers' revenue which depends on whether the petrol producers could pass the increase of costs on to the consumers (motorists).

Petrol firms face severe market competition, so the pricing strategy is important in order to keep and sustain their shares in the petrol market. Petrol firms also need to take into account the values of cross elasticity for petrol as well as price elasticity of the demand for petrol when working out the pricing strategies since a price increase could lead to unexpected larger consumer losses due to the fierce competition. Although demand for petrol is inelastic, the demand for petrol from individual firms is much more elastic. This is because the competition of petrol retail market that firms face is high. In order to win over consumers to fight off competition, petrol firms might sometimes reduce petrol prices in the short term. If the crude oil prices remain consistently high in the long run, petrol firms will eventually be forced to increase prices in order to keep sustained revenue.

3 Market failure

(a) Negative externalities are costs imposed on a third party through a decision/production of a firm. The car users do not need to take into account the external costs (pollution, traffic etc) that arise from petrol production and consumption unless they are taxed by the government.

Figure 3. Demand and Supply of Cars on the Road

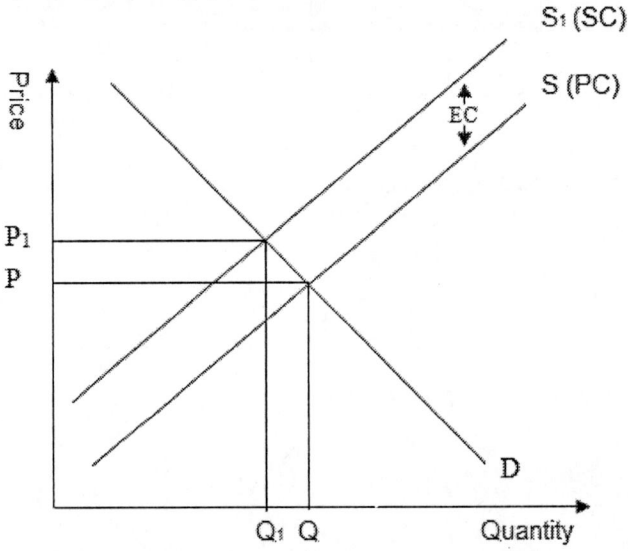

At the price equilibrium, PQ, without the inclusion of externalities, the prices of the cars on the road do not include the costs of externalities. When the costs of externalities are included in the prices, the prices of the cars would increase from P to P_1, however, the supply and demand of the cars may decrease to S_1 and Q_1 respectively. The difference between Q-Q_1 indicates the inefficiency of resource allocation which is an indication of market failure.

(b) An indirect tax is a tax that is levied on goods and services sold on the market, such as VAT, custom duties. One of the main aims of this tax is to reduce the consumption of goods that cause negative externalities, i.e. to make consumers pay for the external cost (EC indicated in Figure 3) caused by externalities and selling price reflect the true economic costs (P_1).

However, the value of the tax is not always equal to the costs of externalities since the amount of negative externalities is difficult to measure accurately. In a market of many substitutes, an unequally weighted tax on certain good would just lead to the increase in demand for a less taxed substitute. This means the total consumption of this type of goods has not actually decreased and this indicates the failure of government indirect tax.

Also, an indirect tax may not be always fully passed on to consumers but may be partially absorbed by producers, especially when productivity increases where supply increases and shifts to the right from S_1 back to S. The large quantity produced has a faster effect on supply than the change in tax that could reflect the increased productivity. The actual supply and demand for the product has, once again, not decreased.

Furthermore, the elasticity of a product may have an effect on the effectiveness of indirect tax, since more price inelastic products would still be subject to high demand that consumers are willing to pay extra (VAT) for that product. This is an example of information failure although the government could slowly correct this in the long term. The government could use the revenue collected from the tax and also use the revenue to subsidise better substitutes for those goods that allows the price of substitutes to be lower (thereby increasing the demand for it). This would in turn lead to a decrease in demand for the other goods and in the long term would make those goods more price elastic.

Overall, the main concern is the level of the indirect tax. Under-indirect-taxation would fail to correct market failure whilst over-indirect-taxation could have a large impact on the productivity of smaller firms as larger firms can absorb the effects of the tax. In extreme cases, the incorrect level of indirect tax could lead to smaller firms going out of business thus decreasing competition and induce X-inefficiency (the difference between efficient behaviour of firms assumed or implied by economic theory and their observed behaviour in practice). The optimum tax size is very difficult to achieve. It's best for the government to subsidise substitutes and alternatives in order to drive demand for the good that causes negative externalities away from it.

4 Elasticity

(a) Cross elasticity of demand is the responsiveness of the demand for a good to a change in the price of another good.

(b) The characteristics of an oligopolistic market:

- High or substantial barriers to entry - collusion
- A few large firms dominate the market – price rigidity
- Firms may not be profit maximisers – long run abnormal profits
- Firms are price makers – price leadership
- Product differentiation/branding – non price competition
- Interdependence

(c) (i) Income elasticity of demand is the responsiveness of demand to a change in income.

　　(ii)
- Both Jewellery and High specification cameras are elastic normal goods.
- High specification cameras are a more superior good.
- As incomes increase more of each is demanded.
- The change in demand for High specification cameras will be relatively much greater.

　　(iii)
- Business significance – good news for both when income increases.
- Markets can be expected to continue to grow in the future.
- Could be seen as an opportunity to invest.
- Takes out some of the risk and uncertainty.
- Markets could become more competitive.
- Helps to plan ahead.
- Possible comments are to relate to quality and reliability of data, historical data might change over time; businesses cannot really influence income changes.

EXAM ANSWER BANK

5 Externalities and market failure

(a) Air travel is a private good because it is 'rival', 'excludable' and 'rejectable'.

Air travel is rival because the consumption of this product by one consumer will reduce the amount available for others. This effectively means that consumers are rivals/competitors for the seat on the flight. In other words, consumption by one person does diminish the amount of the good available to others.

Air travel is excludable because those who are unable to afford the tickets will be stopped from consuming/using the flights; passengers without passports will be unable to board flights and, in this sense, will be excluded from flying. There will be an absence of free riders as non-payers can be stopped from using the flights.

Air travel is a matter of choice (ie 'rejectable') because consumers do not have to fly if they do not want to. This means that they can avoid consuming the product if they so wish.

(b) The possible factors could include the following:

- Increase in noise pollution/loss of peace and quiet
- Increase in carbon dioxide/greenhouse gas emissions (accept "air pollution")
- Increase in nitrogen oxide emissions
- Greater chemical emissions
- Damage to ancient trees
- Damage to the "historic and scientific values of the forest"

The explanations for why this might be the case:

- Consumers fail to take into account their external costs OR consumers fail to take into account the full costs OR the full costs are not paid.

- Therefore consumers effectively receive the product for a lower price than they would if the full social costs were taken into account, i.e. the good will be cheaper than ideally it should be/it is under-priced. In turn, this means that too many scarce resources are devoted towards the production of these goods/services which results in allocative inefficiency. (Accept the idea that there is an over allocation of resources but do not accept vague references to the fact that scarce resources are not being used in the best possible way)

(c) Comment on the effectiveness of subsidies to producers as a solution to the market failure arising from positive externalities.

A simple analysis of why subsidies will be effective:

- Subsidies to producers will lower firms' costs of production. This, in turn, will raise the supply of goods and services OR output increases OR more is produced OR the supply curve shifts to the right. This will lead to a fall in price and results in an extension of demand (which corrects the under-consumption).

- Accept relevant diagram showing a shift to the right of the supply curve for relevant analysis.

Evaluation/discussion. Possible evaluative comment may include:

- In order to fully correct the under-consumption, the subsidy must be set at the correct level. This is very difficult to do as, often, it is extremely difficult to measure the external benefits accurately. In other words, the effectiveness of the subsidy often depends upon the level at which it is set.

- The impact of the subsidy will depend upon the price elasticity of demand for the product. If PED is inelastic, then a huge subsidy will be needed in order to have any significant impact upon demand.

- The cost of the subsidy to the government may well be so large that it outweighs any possible benefit gained. Hence there will also be an opportunity cost to the government of funding such subsidies.

- If producers fail to pass on the subsidy in the form of lower prices, then there will be no extension of demand and hence market failure will remain.

- Subsidies may encourage (productive) inefficiency if firms become too reliant upon them.

- Time lag – a subsidy may have less impact in the short run if it takes time for firms to develop, produce and supply new products.

(d) Accept a wide interpretation of 'regulation' to include government competition policy (e.g. the work of the Competition and Markets Authority) and also price controls.

In order to be effective, regulations must be policed and this will involve government expenditure. This, in turn, implies the existence of opportunity cost.

- Regulation may also result in significant bureaucracy which may incur additional costs.

- The effectiveness of regulation depends upon the size of fines/action taken against firms which are found to be breaking the law. Two aspects: fine and the chance of detection.

- If output is not banned completely, then what is the optimum level of regulation? How can the government actually measure this? There is the possibility of government failure if regulation is introduced at the wrong level.

- If they are only the UK introduces regulations, then it will be very easy for companies to relocate overseas. Therefore, the effectiveness of such regulation depends upon whether other countries introduce regulations/laws as well.

- Regulation is not a market based solution. Regulation may fail if there is the possibility of illegal supplies available through the shadow economy.

- Possible time lag – there could be legislative delay or delay in implementing the regulation.

6 Remuneration and performance

(a) The debate on executive directors' remuneration has rumbled on through the last decade. The focus is well and truly on curtailing excessive and undeserved remuneration packages but left shareholders with little reward compared with what the executives received in terms of company's performance. It is argued that directors are overpaid to the detriment of the shareholders, the employees, and the company as a whole. In the case of Easyjet, the shareholder's concern lies in that although the share price has gone up roughly three times since this management took over, their take-home pay has multiplied in the order of 20-30 times, which clearly reflects the focus of the recent debate mentioned above.

The emphasis of the debate is to ensure that executive directors' remuneration packages are fairly and appropriately constructed, taking into account long-term objectives. Central to this aim is the use of performance indicators which will incentivise directors but at the same time align their interests with those of shareholders, to the long-term benefit of the company. It is argued that there should be a clear link between the remuneration top managers receive and the performance of the business. However, this correlation between reward and performance is far from clear. The introduction of remuneration committee does not appear to have controlled or restricted the rapid expansion of executive pay.

(b) Base salary

Base salary is received by a director in accordance with the terms of his contract. This element is not related either to the performance of the company nor to the performance of the individual director. The amount will be set with due regard to the size of the company, the industry sector, the experience of the individual director, and the level of base salary in similar companies.

Bonus

An annual bonus may be paid, which is often linked to the accounting performance of the firm or the share price performance.

Stock options

Stock options give directors the right to purchase shares (stock) at a specified exercise price over a specified time period. Directors may also participate in long-term incentive plans (LTIPs). UK share options generally have performance criteria attached, and much discussion is centred on these performance criteria, especially as to whether they are appropriate and demanding enough.

Restricted share plans (stock grants)

Shares may be awarded with limits on their transferability for a set time (usually a few years), and various performance conditions should be met.

(c) The common performance measurements include:

Market-based:

- Shareholder return
- Share price (and other market based measures)

Accounting-based:

- Profit based measures (e.g. EBIT)
- Earnings per share

(d) The above performance criteria will clearly be a key aspect of ensuring that directors' remuneration is perceived as fair and appropriate for the job and in keeping with the results achieved by the directors.

Problems with those performance criteria:

- Short-term performance of the management

    The use of performance indicators should incentivise directors but at the same time align their interests with those of shareholders, to the long-term benefit of the company. But the market-based indicators that are commonly used tend to bias to measure firm's short-term performance. Management is expected to perform over a short period of time and this is a clear mismatch with the underlying investor time horizons.

- EBIT induces high leverage

    The use of EBIT as the performance indicator can be problematic. It is argued that when EBIT becomes the definition of corporate earnings, it is a major incentive to expand a company by high debt (or high leverage) because the measure will reflect the flow of earnings from high leverage but not the service (interest) charge for that debt.

7 Corporate social responsibility

(a) Definitions of corporate social responsibility (CSR):

- A corporation should be held accountable for any of its actions that affect people, their communities and their environment (also known as their stakeholders). It implies that negative business impacts on people and society should be acknowledged and corrected if at all possible.

- A commitment by business to behave ethically and contribute to economic development while improving the quality of life of the workforce and their families as well as of the local community and society at large.

(b)
- A growing belief amongst many people that organisations have a duty to society greater than simply providing goods and services.

- Commercial organisations should have a role in society alongside that of non-commercial entities such as the family and religion.

- This links back to
  - the microeconomic environment, which includes the stakeholders;
  - the macroeconomic environment, which considers the national and global impact.

(c) CSR involves making sure:

- Goods and services meet customer requirements, and are provided in a fair way.

- Employees are given responsibility and opportunities to work with the organisation in supporting community projects.

- The organisation is involved in activities and programmes that support the development of the whole community.

- All members of society are involved by being provided with opportunities rather than being marginalised (eg disabled people).

8 Auditors and corporate governance

(a) The role of external auditor and firm's audit committee.

An external auditor is a professional audit firm who is independent from its clients and provides assessment and evaluation of financial statements of its clients and/or performs other agreed financial advice for its clients. The main role played by an external auditor is to produce an opinion on its clients' financial statements which must follow required accounting standards. An external auditor evaluates person, organisation, system, process, project or product to ascertain the validity and reliability of available information, and also provides an internal control assessment of its clients' financial system. As with accounting auditors have to comply with certain standards.

An audit committee serves to safeguard and advance the interests of shareholders. The literature regards an audit committee as a monitoring mechanism intended to reduce information asymmetries between insider and outsider since its key functions are to review financial information and control management's opportunistic behaviour. The literature further argues that the independence of audit committee is the key for effective monitoring. Most countries' corporate governance codes require that publicly listed companies must have an audit committee consisting of sufficient numbers of independent directors. The most important feature of a firm's audit committee is the independence of its members.

(b) Relationship between external auditor and audit committee.

A firm's audit committee consists of non-executive directors who are able to view a company's affairs in a detached and independent way and liaise effectively between the main board of directors and the external auditor. There is a close relationship between external auditor and firm's audit committee. The audit committee recommends the board on appointment, re-appointment or removal of external auditors. It oversees the selection process when any new auditor is appointed. It also approves the terms and remuneration of the external auditor and ensures the independence and objectivity of external auditor. The audit committee and the external auditors together review the scope of audit and make sure that appropriate plans are in place.

(c) The importance of external auditor in corporate governance.

Corporate Governance is a tool by which a company is operated and controlled for the interest of the stakeholders. Financial statements which provide almost all important information to all the concerned parties of the company are assessed and evaluated by an external auditor. The aim of corporate governance is to resolve the problems which arise from the relationship between the principal and the agents. Owners of a company have an interest in maximising the value of their shares but the managers are more interested in private consumption of firm resources along with the growth of the firm. The monitoring cost can be reduced when an external auditor provides an efficient audit service. An external auditor can facilitate a situation whereby managers are encouraged or compelled to be held more accountable. An external auditor could help in finding financial fraud, effectively control managerial opportunistic behaviour so that could make management more accountable for shareholders for its stewardship of a company. Prior to various corporate governance reforms in many jurisdictions, the pressures faced by external auditors from directors in many firms constituted the focus of several major issues. Furthermore playing with numbers (earnings management) became widespread. But the changes in selection criterion of external auditors, their roles and new reforms in corporate governance norms make the information available to the stakeholder more reliable. The objectivity, integrity and independence are the main factors related to the responsibilities of external auditors. Moreover, external auditors could also provide effective monitoring and control of the Board which enhance the capacity of the companies to comply with higher quality corporate governance.

9 Monopolistic competition

(a) [Tutorial note: A good answer might comment that in a monopolistic competition market, companies have a market advantage over their own brands which gives them some market power (the ability to influence their own price in relation to marginal cost based on the strength of their brand).]

The characteristics of monopolistic competition structure include a large number of relatively small suppliers, product differentiation and few, if any, barriers to entry. These characteristics need to be contrasted with other forms of competition. Monopolistic competition does exit in the retail sector where there are a large number of small firms with their own brands who are subject to the entry at any time of new competitors. No single company in a monopolistic competition market has a high market share, but each normally has a brand that forms the basis of the monopolistic nature of the market.

(b) [Tutorial note: Freedom of entry is a key feature of monopolistic competition structure thus both potential and existing competitors would be the company's threats. A good answer would mention also that firms process monopolistic power need always to be looking at reducing costs in response to the competition they face.]

Freedom of entry into monopolistic competition is the key threat incumbent firms face. This is a market that is termed 'contestable' in the sense that a firm may choose, for example, to make luxury brand lipsticks if it sees luxury lipsticks prices in this market increasing and incumbent firms making abnormal profits. Thus, any firm in a monopolistic market that is thinking of a way of increasing profits above the normal level is likely to face increased competition from both existing and potential competitors. The company needs to be able to see this threat and respond by trying to distance its products or services from the potential threats from substitute suppliers outside the market.

10 The role of a central bank

(a)
- It issues notes for the country.
- It acts as a bank for the government.
- It manages the government's borrowing programme.
- It oversees the activities of banks and other financial institutions.
- It provides liquidity, as necessary, to banks.
- It operates the government's monetary and exchange rate policy.

(b) No. The functions listed above have to be carried out in a modern money-based economy.

(c) (i) Yes. If all banks abide by a simple rule relating their base rates to the central bank's minimum lending rate, then a simple change in minimum lending rate will bring the desired effect on banks' interest rates. The more competition there is, however, the more difficult will it be for the central bank to enforce its decrees (even if they are statutory), partly as a result of competition from institutions not affected by the decrees, especially foreign banks, and partly as a result of banks seeking to circumvent the decrees.

(ii) No. There will be a knock on effect through the various markets. Nevertheless, it is possible that any interest rate changes may have to be more significant, if increased competition indicates the lifting of any statutory reserve requirements.

11 Unemployment and minimum wages

(a) The unemployment can be classified as
- disequilibrium unemployment
- equilibrium unemployment

Disequilibrium unemployment:

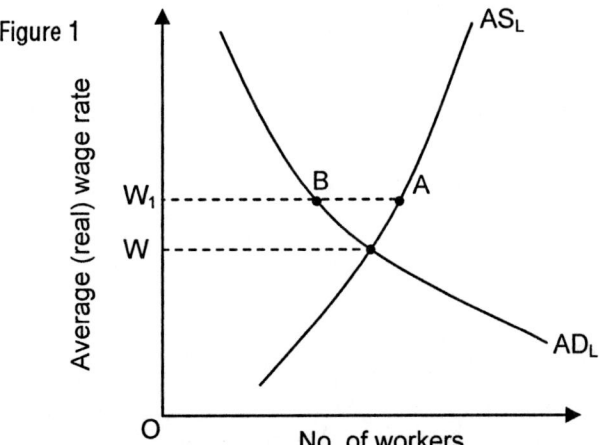

Figure 1

At W_1 the supply of labour exceeds the demand of labour. This kind of unemployment is disequilibrium unemployment.

Two conditions of disequilibrium unemployment:
- the supply of labour exceeding the demand
- stickiness in wages

Types of disequilibrium unemployment:

- Real wage unemployment
- Demand-deficient unemployment (cyclical unemployment)
- Growth in the labour supply

Equilibrium unemployment (natural unemployment)

Figure 2

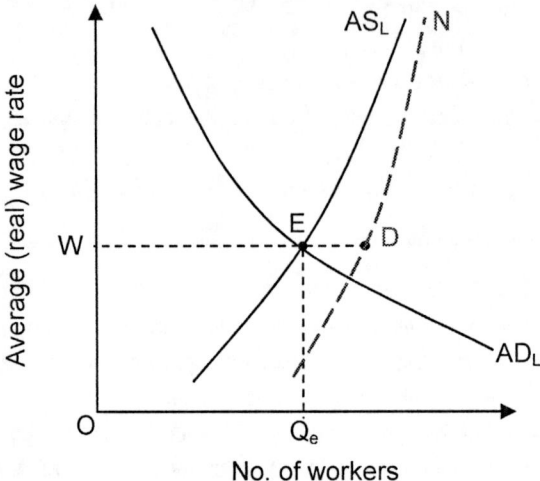

Even if the labour market is in equilibrium, not everyone looking for work will be employed. Some people will hold out, hoping to find a better job. Therefore, the aggregate supply of labour exceeds the aggregate demand for labour. DE represents the excess of people looking for work over those actually willing to accept jobs that represents the equilibrium level of unemployment (natural level of unemployment).

Types of equilibrium unemployment:

- Frictional (search) unemployment
- Structural unemployment
- Seasonal unemployment

(b) This is where trade unions use their power to drive wages above the market-clearing level. In the Figure, the wage rate is driven up above WE.

Excessive real wage rates were blamed by the Thatcher and Major governments for the high unemployment rate of the 1980s and the early 1990s and were one of the reasons for the rejection of a minimum wage by the Conservative Party in the UK.

The political debates on minimum wages have been going on in the UK since the 1980s. However, this kind of debate is not confined to the UK, and occurs in many countries, including in some emerging markets, such as China.

The solution to real wage unemployment would seem to be a reduction in real wage rates. However, it may be very difficult to prevent unions pushing up wages. Even if the government did succeed in reducing the average real wage rate, there would still be a problem of reduced consumer expenditure and a reduced demand for labour, with the result that unemployment might not fall at all. That is one of the reasons for the implementation of a minimum wage by the Labour Party in the UK.

12 Macroeconomic policy and the economy

(a)
- Fiscal policy includes: changes in/decisions on government spending and taxation.
- Unemployment rate: The number unemployed expressed as a percentage of the labour force.

(b)
- Reasons: innovation, low price, low exchange rate, good marketing, income growth in major export markets.
- Explain: Innovation will increase the quality of German products and make people, both at home and abroad, more willing to buy them. Low prices will make products competitive. Low exchange rate will reduce the prices of exported products. Good marketing will promote exporting sale. Income growth in major export markets will increase the demand for German products.

(c)
- There is an inverse relationship between economic growth and unemployment.
- Rise in real GDP is likely to increase demand for products.
- Higher demand for products will increase demand for labour.
- A fall in unemployment will move an economy closer to its production possibility curve.
- Possibilities of a time lag.
- Output could rise with no change in unemployment if productivity rises.
- Production possibility curve could move out without a fall in unemployment.

(d)
- Reasons for how a cut in the rate of income tax may raise aggregate demand:
  - An increase in disposable income will enable consumers to spend more.
  - Higher consumer expenditure may cause a rise in investment, further increasing aggregate demand.
- Evaluating the effect of the cut of rate of income tax
  - How much aggregate demand rises depends on the size of the cut; some of the extra income may be saved rather than spent.
  - If public confidence is low, consumption and investment may not rise.
  - Cut the lower rate of income tax is likely to be more effective.
  - Households and firms may expect that the cut will be reversed in the future.
  - There may be a time lag before households and firms react.

(e)
- The impact that an increase in exports will have on the economy depends on whether it lasts. A small increase of a short duration will have less of an impact than a large increase which lasts for some time. A rise in exports resulting from, for example, an increase in quality of products produced, may last longer than one resulting from a fall in the exchange rate.
- If the economy was initially operating well below full capacity, the effect of an increase in exports is likely to be more beneficial than if it was initially at or close to full capacity. In the former case, a rise in aggregate demand is likely to have more impact on employment and growth than on the price level. In the latter case, the impact is more likely to be inflationary.
- A rise in exports may be accompanied by a rise in imports or may be exceeded by a rise in imports. Exports raise income and some of the extra income is spent on imports, the effect on aggregate demand may be neutral.
- An increase in exports may result in a current account surplus. If the country is exporting more than it is importing, the country's citizens are enjoying a lower than possible living standard.

13 Exchange rates

(a) The demand curve for a currency shows how much of it will be demanded at a given rate of exchange. The shape of the curve will be downward sloping, like a normal demand curve.

Likewise, the supply of a currency shows how much of it will be supplied at a given price (exchange rate) and this will be a normal, upward sloping supply curve.

The demand for currency is a derived demand, reflecting the demand for exports from a country rather than simply the currency itself.

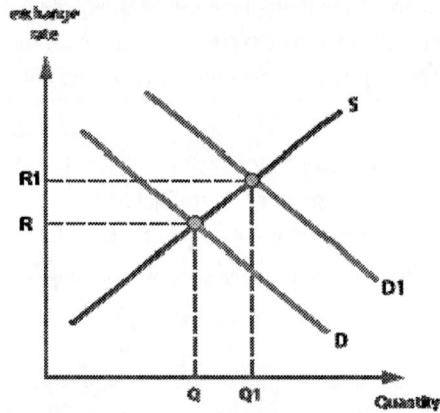

Floating exchange rate mechanism

(b) The demand for pounds sterling reflects the demand for British exports. Therefore a fall in the demand for British exports would lead to an inward shift in the demand for GBP D1 to D (see Figure 4). Consequently, the exchange rate of GBP would fall from R1 to R (see Figure 4).

(c) **Advantages of floating exchange rates**

(i) Governments do not have to spend or even hold foreign currency reserves.

(ii) Balance of payments deficits or surpluses are automatically corrected. A deficit will result in the exchange rate falling; this will improve competitiveness, raise exports and restore equilibrium.

(iii) Governments need not adopt economic policies that may be undesirable for other reasons to maintain exchange rates.

(iv) Encourage efficient allocation of resources since exchange rates will reflect economic conditions.

Disadvantages of floating exchange rates

(i) If exchange rates appreciate too much under a floating rate system, the firm's international competitiveness may be reduced, and output and employment may fall across the economy.

(ii) Uncertainty surrounding fluctuations in exchange rate could deter trade.

(iii) If exchange rates fall too much, import prices, and hence inflation, will rise.

(iv) Currency risk will be maximised under a system of floating exchange rates.

(v) The freedom afforded governments by (iii) in the advantages above may mean governments do not pursue domestic policies which they should.

14 Global strategy

(i) The 'pull' factors are those which come from an organisation recognising potential in global markets, attracting it to go overseas for this opportunity.

(ii) The 'push' factors are those which force an organisation to look globally for new markets when their domestic one is less attractive, so as to hopefully sustain their business.

(iii) Examples of pull factors:

- Reduce risk reliance on domestic market by operating overseas.
- Organisations beginning to trade overseas lead to a demand for other services to work on an international basis, such as accounting, advertising.
- Demand for clearly identifiable international goods, despite higher prices, such as the European and Japanese cosmetics.
- More people are travelling and they want to purchase recognisable domestic brands in overseas locations, such as McDonalds, Starbucks.
- Apart from accessing new markets, organisations may enter international trade to get new or better (cheaper or in higher quality) suppliers.
- Raw materials, labour and manufactured goods may be cheaper from other countries.
- Specialised expertise and skilled labour may be more readily available in other countries.

(iv) Examples of 'push' factors:

- Saturation of the domestic market, leads to organisations looking to sell elsewhere, e.g. fast-food, mobile handsets.
- In a specialised market, the number of domestic customers may be so small that it is impossible to achieve economies of scale. International markets need to be exploited to improve economies of scale and so that you can become more competitive both domestically and internationally.
- Reduction in availability of resources, e.g. raw materials from domestic market.

15 Comparative advantage

Given that markets are imperfect and factors are immobile, government intervention would normally be justified (unless governments themselves were even more imperfect than the market forces!).

Even though a country may have an initial comparative advantage in primary production (the production and extraction of natural resources, plus agriculture), the gains from specialising in primaries and exporting them may be offset by other disadvantages – disadvantages that build over time.

Note that a comparative advantage means if a country can produce a good at a lower opportunity cost, ie if it has to forgo less of other goods in order to produce it.

On the other hand, an absolute advantage means if a country can produce a good with fewer resources than the other country. With a low world income elasticity of demand for primary products, with the development of synthetic substitutes for minerals and with the protection of agriculture in developed countries, the demand for primary exports from developing countries has grown only slowly.

At the same time, the demand for manufactured imports into developing countries has grown rapidly.

The result has been a worsening balance of trade problem; and with a price-inelastic demand for both imports and exports, the terms of trade have worsened too.

In addition to these problems, there is also the danger that comparative costs may change over time; that most of the benefits from primary exports may accrue to foreign owners of mines and plantations, or to wealthy elites in the domestic population; that mines and plantations can involve substantial environmental and other external costs; and that export earnings can fluctuate, given instabilities in supply and unstable world prices.

Even if it is agreed that government intervention is warranted, the method of intervention is highly controversial. Some argue that the whole focus of intervention should be to make the private sector more responsive to market forces, so that it can respond quickly to changing market opportunities. For example, the country could be opened to international financial markets, regulations could be dismantled and there could be a programme of privatisation.

Others argue that the focus ought to be on improving the country's infrastructure – transport, communications, education, etc. This will require government expenditure, but it could still be seen as the government working with the market by helping to increase factor mobility, both occupationally and geographically.

Others argue that the problems with trade are so great that the country's exposure to international market forces ought to be minimised and the country should pursue an active policy of import substitution (the replacement of imports by domestically produced goods or services).

Mock exam 1 questions and answers

MODULE A

FOUNDATION EXAMINATION

PAPER 2 – BUSINESS ECONOMICS

TUESDAY 28th NOVEMBER 2017

Time allowed – 3 hours

SECTION A
Answer ALL questions

SECTION B
Answer ALL questions

You are allowed an additional 15 minutes reading time before the exam begins, during which you should read the question paper and, if you wish, make notes on the question paper. You are **not** allowed to open the exam script booklet and start writing or use your calculator during the reading time.

Section A

Answer ALL questions

Question 1

Say on pay

The 'say on pay' proposals were introduced in the UK in 2002 by the Directors' Remuneration Report Regulations. It has become increasingly important as a tool of governance activism in the context of expressing dissent on executive remuneration awards. Many countries including the USA, Australia, and various countries in Europe have introduced 'say on pay' proposals as a mechanism for voting against executive remuneration. In some countries, such as the UK, the 'say on pay' vote is an advisory one (at least for the time being), whilst in other countries it is a binding vote on which the board must take action.

In the USA, the Dodd-Frank Wall Street Reform and Consumer Protection Act (2010), under new 'say on pay' provisions, requires that at least once every three years there is a shareholder advisory vote to approve the company's executive compensation as disclosed pursuant to Securities and Exchange Commission rules. The 'say on frequency' provision requires companies to put to a shareholder advisory vote every six years as to whether the 'say on pay' resolution should occur every one, two, or three years.

Required

(a) What factors have influenced the executive directors' remuneration debate? **(6 marks)**

(b) List the four areas the executives' remuneration debate has tended to focus on. **(4 marks)**

(c) Describe the concept of 'say on pay'. **(2 marks)**

(d) Describe the main components of executive directors' remuneration packages. **(6 marks)**

(e) Explain the role of the remuneration committee. **(6 marks)**

(f) Describe and summarise how the Greenbury Report contributed to the existing UK Corporate Governance Code with regards to directors' remuneration. **(6 marks)**

(Total 30 marks)

Question 2

Demand for private universities in the U.S.

Private universities are not operated by governments, although many receive tax breaks, public student loans and grants. Depending on their location, private universities may be subject to government regulation. This is in contrast to public universities and national universities.

In the US, many universities and colleges are private, mostly operating as educational and research non-profit organisations, while there are also for-profit universities. About 20% of American college students attend private colleges.

Suppose the market demand function for four-year private universities is given by the equation

$$Q^d_{pr} = 84 - 3.1 P_{pr} + 0.8 I + 0.9 P_{pu}$$

where Q^d_{pr} is the number of applicants to private universities per year in thousands, P_{pr} is the average price of private universities (in thousands of USD), I is the household monthly income (in thousands of USD), and P_{pu} is the average price of public (government-supported) universities (in thousands of USD). Assume that P_{pr} is equal to 38, I is equal to 100, and P_{pu} is equal to 18.

Required

(a) Determine the price elasticity of demand for private universities. **(6 marks)**

(b) Calculate the income elasticity of demand for private universities. **(6 marks)**

(c) Explain the term 'normal goods' and 'inferior goods'. Are private universities a normal or an inferior good? Why? **(6 marks)**

(d) Calculate the cross-price elasticity of demand for private universities with respect to the price of public universities. **(6 marks)**

(e) Explain the term 'substitutes' and 'complements'. Are private universities and public universities substitutes or complements? **(6 marks)**

(Total 30 marks)

Section B

Answer ALL questions

Question 3

GDP and GNP

Gross domestic product (GDP) measures the market value of all final goods and services produced by factors of production (such as labour and capital) located within a country/economy during a given period of time, generally a year or a quarter. Gross national product (GNP), however, measures the market value of all final goods and services produced by factors of production (such as labour and capital) supplied by residents of a country, regardless of whether such production takes place within the country or outside of the country.

Required

(a) Explain the difference between GDP and GNP. **(4 marks)**

(b) Explain whether the following items should be in a comprehensive measure of GNP: (i) time spent by students in lectures; (ii) the income of criminals; (iii) the wages paid to traffic wardens; (iv) dropping litter. **(16 marks)**

(Total 20 marks)

Question 4

Exchange Rates

A French company has recently finalised a sale of goods to a UK-based client and expects to receive a payment of GBP50 million in 32 days. The corporate treasurer at the French company wants to hedge the foreign exchange risk of this transaction and receives the following exchange rate information from a dealer:

GBP/EUR spot rate	0.8752
One-month forward points (basis points)	−1.4

Required

(a) Interpret the forward discount shown. **(2 marks)**

(b) Given the above data, should the treasurer buy or sell EUR to hedge the foreign exchange risk? Please calculate the forward rate for the treasurer. **(4 marks)**

(c) If the 12-month forward rate is 0.87295 GBP/EUR, determine the 12-month forward points based on the data. **(4 marks)**

(d) If a second dealer quotes GBP/EUR at a 12-month forward discount of 0.30 percent on the same spot rate, explain whether the French company could lock in a profit in 12 months. **(6 marks)**

(e) Describe the factors that may influence the company's decision to make riskless arbitrage. **(4 marks)**

(Total 20 marks)

MODEL ANSWERS

MODULE A

FOUNDATION EXAMINATION

PAPER 2 – BUSINESS ECONOMICS

TUESDAY 28th NOVEMBER 2017

MOCK EXAM 1 ANSWERS

Section A

Question 1

This question relates to the corporate governance. (Syllabus reference 2.3 Household, Corporate and Finance Sectors, Corporate Governance 4th Edition Chapter 9).

Candidates need to show their understanding of the executive directors' remuneration and related corporate governance practice.

(a) The debate on executive directors' remuneration has rumbled on through the last decade, but with the increase in institutional investor activism, and the scandals and subsequent collapses associated with a number of large corporations in the UK, USA, and elsewhere, the focus is well and truly on curtailing excessive and undeserved remuneration packages. The global financial crisis and the collapse of various high profile banks and financial institutions has left the market reeling. There is a lack of public confidence in the boards of banks, and disbelief at some of the executive remuneration packages and ad hoc payments that have been made to executive directors, particularly when not linked to performance. There is now an emphasis on payment for performance in a way that theoretically was present before the global financial crisis but, in practice, all too often was not. The remuneration committees, comprised of independent non-executive directors, will come under increased scrutiny as they try to ensure that executive directors' remuneration packages are fairly and appropriately constructed, taking into account long-term objectives. Central to this aim is the use of performance indicators that will incentivise directors but at the same time align their interests with those of shareholders, to the long-term benefit of the company. Shareholders in many countries now have a 'say on pay', either in the form of an advisory or a binding vote, and seem increasingly active in expressing their dissent on executive remuneration.

(b) The last decade has seen considerable shareholder, media, and policy attention given to the issue of directors' remuneration. The debate has tended to focus on four areas: (i) the overall level of directors' remuneration and the role of share options; (ii) the suitability of performance measures linking directors' remuneration with performance; (iii) the role played by the remuneration committee in the setting of directors' remuneration; (iv) the influence that shareholders are able to exercise on directors' remuneration.

(c) The 'say on pay' is a mechanism for investors to express their approval or dissent in relation to executive remuneration packages and has become widely adopted. The concept of 'say on pay' enables shareholders to vote on executive remuneration matters.

(d) Directors' remuneration can encompass six elements:

- base salary;
- bonus;
- stock or share options;
- restricted share plans (stock grants);
- pension;
- benefits (car, healthcare, etc.).

However, most discussions of directors' remuneration will tend to concentrate on the first four elements listed earlier.

(e) The remuneration committee should make recommendations to the board, within agreed terms of reference, on the company's framework of executive remuneration and its cost; it should determine on their behalf specific remuneration packages for each of the executive directors, including pension rights and any compensation payments.

The establishment of a remuneration committee (in the form recommended by the Corporate Governance Code) prevents executive directors from setting their own remuneration levels. The remuneration committee mechanism should also provide a formal, transparent procedure for the setting of executive remuneration levels, including the determination of appropriate targets for any.

MOCK EXAM 1 ANSWERS

(f) There has been much discussion about how much disclosure there should be of directors' remuneration and how useful detailed disclosures might be. The Greenbury Report, issued in the UK in 1995, was established on the initiative of the Confederation of British Industry (CBI) because of public concern about directors' remuneration. Whilst the work of the Greenbury Report focused on the directors of public limited companies, it hoped that both smaller listed companies and unlisted companies would find its recommendations useful.

Central to the Greenbury Report recommendations were the strengthening of accountability and enhancing the performance of directors. These two aims were to be achieved by (i) the establishment of remuneration committees comprised of independent non-executive directors who would report fully to the shareholders each year about the company's executive remuneration policy, including full disclosure of the elements in the remuneration of individual directors; and (ii) the adoption of performance measures linking rewards to the performance of both the company and individual directors, so that the interests of directors and shareholders were more closely aligned.

Additional areas where credit might be given, note this is not an exhaustive list:

- **The Code (2016) states that 'the board should establish a remuneration committee of at least three, or in the case of smaller companies, two independent non-executive directors'.**
- **Turnbull Committee recommendations (1999, revised 2005)**
- **Directors' Remuneration Report Regulations 2002 (DTI)**

Question 2

This question relates to choice and the demand and supply principles. (Syllabus reference 2.1 Introduction to Economics and 2.2 Consumption, Production and Distribution, AIA e-book Chapter 1 and 2).

Candidates need to show their understanding of the economic problem of supply and demand, price determination, and price elasticity and income elasticity of supply and demand.

(a) From the demand function:

Solve for Q_{pr}^d:

$$\frac{\Delta Q_{pr}^d}{\Delta P_{pr}} = -3.1 \text{ (the coefficient in front of own price)}$$

$Q_{pr}^d = 84 - 3.1 P_{pr} + 0.8 I + 0.9 P_{pu}$

$= 84 - 3.1(38) + 0.8(100) + 0.9(18)$

$= 62.4$

At $P_{pr} = 38$,

price elasticity of demand $= \left(\dfrac{\Delta Q_{pr}^d}{\Delta P_{pr}} \right) \left(\dfrac{P_{pr}}{Q_{pr}^d} \right)$

$= (-3.1)(38/62.4)$

$= -1.9$

Hence, the price elasticity of demand for private universities is close to -1.9. Such negative value shows the inverse nature of the relationship between price and quantity demanded, indicating that if the price of private universities increases by 1%, the number of applicants to private universities per year will decrease by 1.9%.

MOCK EXAM 1 ANSWERS

(b) From the demand function:

Solve for Q_{pr}^d:

$$\frac{\Delta Q_{pr}^d}{\Delta I} = 0.8 \text{ (coefficient in front of the income variable)}$$

$$Q_{pr}^d = 84 - 3.1P_{pr} + 0.8I + 0.9P_{pu}$$

$$= 84 - 3.1(38) + 0.8(100) + 0.9(18)$$

$$= 62.4$$

At $I = 38$,

the income elasticity of demand $= \left(\dfrac{\Delta Q_{pr}^d}{\Delta I}\right)\left(\dfrac{I}{Q_{pr}^d}\right)$

$$= (0.8)(100/62.4)$$

$$= 1.3$$

Hence, the income elasticity of demand for private universities is close to 1.3. Such positive value shows that an increase in income by 1% will lead to a rise in demand for private universities by 1.3%, implying that private universities are normal goods.

(c) For most goods and services, an increase in income would cause consumers to buy more. These goods with positive income elasticity are called "normal" goods.

There are goods that consumers buy less of when their income rises and goods that they buy more of when their incomes fall. These goods with negative income elasticity are called "inferior" goods.

Private universities are a normal good as the income elasticity of demand for private universities is positive.

(d) From the demand function:

Solve for Q_{pr}^d:

$$\frac{\Delta Q_{pr}^d}{\Delta P_{pu}} = 0.9 \text{ (the coefficient in front of } P_{pu})$$

$$Q_{pr}^d = 84 - 3.1P_{pr} + 0.8I + 0.9P_{pu}$$

$$= 84 - 3.1(38) + 0.8(100) + 0.9(18)$$

$$= 62.4$$

At $P_{pu} = 18$,

the cross-price elasticity of demand $= \left(\dfrac{\Delta Q_{pr}^d}{\Delta P_{pu}}\right)\left(\dfrac{P_{pu}}{Q_{pr}^d}\right)$

$$= (0.9)(18/62.4)$$

$$= 0.3$$

Hence, the cross-price elasticity of demand for private universities with respect to the price of public universities is close to 0.3. Such a positive, cross-price elasticity denotes that private universities and public universities are substitute products, suggesting that an increase in the demand for public universities accompanies a decrease in the quantity demanded for private universities.

MOCK EXAM 1 ANSWERS

(e) If the cross-price elasticity of two goods is positive, they are substitutes, irrespective of whether someone would consider them "similar".

Alternatively, two goods whose cross-price elasticity of demand is negative are said to be complements.

Private universities and public universities are substitutes since the cross-price elasticity of demand for private universities with respect to the price of public universities is positive.

> **Additional areas where credit might be given, note this is not an exhaustive list:**
> - **Giffen goods, Veblen goods**
> - **Substitution effect, income effect**

MOCK EXAM 1 ANSWERS

Section B

Question 3

This question relates to the national income. (Syllabus reference 2.4 Public Sector and Macro Economy, AIA e-book Chapter 10).

Candidates need to show their understanding of national income and analyse the measures of national income.

(a) The difference between a country's GDP and its GNP is that GDP includes, and GNP excludes, the production of goods and services by foreigners within that country, whereas GNP includes, and GDP excludes, the production of goods and services by its citizens outside of the country.

(b) (i) This is not included unless the students are in paid employment (e.g.: apprentices on day release.) The grants of full time students, where they exist, are transfer payments, not earned income. However, a case could be made for including the time even of full-time grant-less students, since investment in human capital occurs.

(ii) No – this is simply a "transfer" payment, though if the mugged person claimed on the insurance that would be counted.

(iii) Yes, they are earnings.

(iv) Environmentalists argue that pollution should ideally be subtracted from GNP. Paradoxically, however, the wages paid to those who pick it up are counted, so in this way pollution actually adds to GNP (as, for example, does the cost of preventing crime).

> Additional areas where credit might be given, note this is not an exhaustive list:
> - Countries that have large differences between GDP and GNP generally have a large number of citizens who work abroad (for example, Pakistan and Portugal), and/or pay more for the use of foreign-owned capital in domestic production than they earn on the capital they own abroad (for example, Brazil and Canada).
> - GDP is more widely used as a measure of economic activity occurring within the country, which, in turn, affects employment, growth, and the investment environment.

Question 4

This question relates to the balance of payments, fixed and floating exchange rates, policies and effects (Syllabus reference 2.5 The External Sector, AIA e-book Chapter 13).

Candidates need to show their understanding of different exchange rate systems and how the exchange rate impacts to the supply and demand for currencies.

(a) A forward discount indicates that interest rates in the base currency country (France in this case, which uses the euro) are higher than those in the price currency country (the United Kingdom). One-month forward points of -1.4 indicates that one-month Eurozone interest rates are higher than those in the United Kingdom.

(b) The French company would want to convert the GBP to its domestic currency, the EUR (it wants to sell GBP, buy EUR).

The forward rate would be equal to: $0.8752 + (-1.4/10,000) = 0.87506$.

Forward points are the number of basis points (BPS) added to or subtracted from the current spot rate of a currency to determine the forward rate for delivery on a specific value date. One basis point is equal to 1/100th of 1%, or 0.01% (0.0001). In the example of one-month forward points, -1.4 means -1.4 basis points. We thus calculate the forward rate by firstly dividing -1.4 by 10000.

(c) The number of forward points is equal to the scaled difference between the forward rate and the spot rate. In this case: 0.87295 – 0.87520 = –0.00225. This is then multiplied by 10,000 to convert to the number of forward as one basis point is equal to 1/100th of 1%, or 0.01% (0.0001).

Hence, the 12-month forward points is -22.5.

(d) If a second dealer quotes GBP/EUR at a 12-month forward discount of 0.30 percent on the same spot rate, the French company could lock in a profit in 12 months by buying EUR from the second dealer and selling it to the original dealer. A 0.30 percent discount means that the second dealer will sell euros 12 months forward at $0.8752 \times (1 - 0.0030) = 0.87257$, a lower price per euro than the original dealer's quote of 0.87295. Buying euros at the cheaper 12-month forward rate (0.87257) and selling the same amount of euros 12 months forward at the higher 12-month forward rate (0.87295) means a profit of (0.87295 – 0.87257 = GBP 0.00038) per euro transacted, receivable when both forward contracts settle in 12 months.

(e) The spot exchange rate, the forward exchange rate, and the domestic and foreign interest rates must jointly satisfy an arbitrage relationship that equates the investment return on two alternative but equivalent investments. Given the spot exchange rate and the foreign and domestic interest rates, the forward exchange rate must take the value that prevents riskless arbitrage.

> **Additional areas where credit might be given, note this is not an exhaustive list:**
> - **Forward price, forward rate, forward rate agreements**
> - **Dirty floating**
> - **Exchange rate peg**

MOCK EXAM 1 ANSWERS

Mock exam 2 questions and answers

MODULE A

FOUNDATION EXAMINATION

PAPER 2 – BUSINESS ECONOMICS

TUESDAY 28th MAY 2018

Time allowed – 3 hours

SECTION A
Answer ALL questions

SECTION B
Answer ALL questions

You are allowed an additional 15 minutes reading time before the exam begins, during which you should read the question paper and, if you wish, make notes on the question paper. You are **not** allowed to open the exam script booklet and start writing or use your calculator during the reading time.

MOCK EXAM 2 QUESTIONS

Section A

Answer ALL questions

Question 1

Hotel versus Airbnb

> Ever since Airbnb entered the short term lodging business scene in 2008, the hotel industry have been monitoring it. In 2015 hotels had a strong year with occupancy abd rates breaking records.
>
> Airbnb, the largest home sharing network with over two million listings worldwide, is newly targeting business travellers, the typical clientele of hotels.
>
> Phocuswright, the travel research firm, noted that one in three leisure travellers in 2015 used private accommodation, up from one in 10 in 2011.
>
> "This is a more challenging event in the history of the lodging industry than almost any other," said Bjorn Hanson, clinical professor of the Jonathan M. Tisch Center for Hospitality and Tourism at New York University.
>
> How, and even whether, hotels are responding to the competition is a matter of debate. Only AccorHotels, the French hotel company whose brands include Sofitel and Raffles, has invested directly in the sharing economy, in its acquisition of Onefinestay, (a London-based home sharing service) that focuses on the high-end market.
>
> Extract adapted from:
>
> GLUSAC, E, 2016. Hotels vs. Airbnb: Let the Battle Begin. *New York Times*, 20 July 2016. https://www.nytimes.com/2016/07/24/travel/airbnb-hotels.html.

The company does not own any premises. It receives a commission from both guests and hosts.

Required

(a) Identify whether hotels and lodgings provided by Airbnb are complements or substitutes. Define substitutes and complements with two examples for each of them. **(7 marks)**

(b) Assume a rise in the price of an Airbnb lodging from £20 to £25 reduces quantity demanded from 250 to 100 nights. Calculate the price elasticity of demand. **(3 marks)**

(c) For each of the following cases, select the condition that characterises demand: elastic demand, inelastic demand, or unit elastic demand, and explain your selection.

　(i)　Total revenue decreases when price increases.

　(ii)　The additional revenue generated by an increase in quantity sold is exactly offset by revenue lost from the fall in price received per unit.

　(iii)　Total revenue falls when output increases.

　(iv)　Producers in an industry find they can increase their total revenues by coordinating a reduction in industry output. **(12 marks)**

(d) Identify four factors that determine the price elasticity of demand. **(8 marks)**

(Total 30 marks)

Question 2

Unitary Board versus Dual Board

> The Prime Minister (Theresa May) has ruled out forcing companies to appoint workers to boards or create continental-style dual boards, despite her earlier complaint that too many directors are drawn from the same narrow social and professional circles.
>
> Speaking at the Confederation of British Industry (CBI) Annual Conference, Theresa May said that the Government would publish a Green Paper within weeks that will set out reforms to shareholder accountability, executive pay and employee representation.
>
> She told business leaders: "I can categorically tell you that this is not about mandating works councils, or the direct appointment of workers or trade union representatives on boards.
>
> This is not about creating German-style binary boards which separate the running of the company from the inputs of shareholders, employees, customers or suppliers. Our unitary board system has served us well and will continue to do so."
>
> Source: Christopher Williams, Theresa May backtracks on putting workers on company boards, The Telegraph, 21 November 2016. [Adapted].

Required

(a) Define the unitary board system mentioned by Theresa May and identify two countries in which the unitary board structure is predominant. **(4 marks)**

(b) Define the binary boards (dual board) mentioned by Theresa May and identify two countries in which the dual board structure is predominant. **(4 marks)**

(c) Describe the commonalities between unitary and dual board structures and identify the advantages of these two board structure. **(8 marks)**

(d) 'Employees, customers or suppliers' mentioned by Theresa May are stakeholders of a company. Define the term 'stakeholder' and identify different stakeholder groups. **(5 marks)**

(e) Employees are a company's most important stakeholders. Some corporate governance systems provide for employee representation at board level. Explain the interest that employees might have as a stakeholder. **(9 marks)**

(Total 30 marks)

Section B

Answer ALL questions

Question 3

Germany overtook the U.S. in 2003 to become the world's largest exporter. For the first time, in 2005, Germany exported a higher value of goods than the U.K., France and the Netherlands combined.

Other components of Germany's aggregated demand grew more slowly. In particular, consumer expenditure was held back by low consumer confidence. This partially offset the good export record and adversely affected German economic growth. In turn, low economic growth kept the German unemployment rate high in historical terms. In 2005, the unemployment rate was particularly high among the low skilled, over a third of whom had been out of work for more than a year. To reduce such unemployment and increase aggregate demand, the German government considered a number of fiscal policy measures including cutting the rate of income tax.

Despite concerns about the slow growth in German aggregate demand, German aggregate supply continued to increase at a relatively rapid rate. This resulted in German potential economic growth exceeding its actual economic growth, giving rise to a negative output gap.

Required

(a) Define the terms: fiscal policy and the unemployment rate. **(4 marks)**

(b) Explain two possible economic reasons why Germany was so successful at exporting. **(4 marks)**

(c) Describe the likely relationship between economic growth and unemployment. **(5 marks)**

(d) Describe the effectiveness of a cut in the rate of income tax as a way of increasing aggregate demand. **(7 marks)**

(Total 20 marks)

Question 4

The G20 leaders met in Hamburg, Germany, on 7-8 July 2017. European Council President Donald Tusk and European Commission President Jean-Claude Juncker represented the EU at the summit. The theme of this year's summit was 'shaping an interconnected world'.

Required

(a) Describe the Group of Twenty and the issues discussed in G20 summits, or meetings. **(4 marks)**

(b) Describe the impact of globalisation and the criticisms of globalisation. **(16 marks)**

(Total 20 marks)

MODEL ANSWERS

MODULE B

FOUNDATION EXAMINATION

PAPER 2 – BUSINESS ECONOMICS

TUESDAY 28th MAY 2018

Section A

Question 1

This question relates to the price theory. (Syllabus reference 2.1 Entrepreneurship and 2.2 Consumption, Production and Distribution, AIA e-Book Chapter 1 and 2).

Candidates need to show their understanding of the price elasticity of demand, the calculation of price elasticity of demand, and the determinants of the price elasticity of demand.

(a) Hotels and Airbnb are substitutes.

Two goods are called substitutes if an increase in the quantity consumed of one cuts the quantity demanded of the other, all other things remaining constant.

Examples of substitute goods and services:

(i) Rival brands of the same commodity, like Coca-Cola and Pepsi-Cola

(ii) Supermarket 'ownbrand' products and branded products (e.g. supermarket 'own brand' Cola, as an alternative to either Coca-Cola or Pepsi-Cola)

(iii) Self-catering holidays and hotel accommodation

(iv) Tea and coffee

Two goods are called complements if an increase in the quantity consumed of one increases the quantity demanded of the other, all other things remaining constant.

Examples of complements:

(i) Cars and petrol
(ii) Tennis rackets and tennis balls
(iii) DVDs and DVD recorders
(iv) Washing machines and soap powder and fabric conditioner

(b) Using the formula, (change in quantity/change in price) times (price/quantity), where price and quantity are the average of the beginning and ending values, the elasticity is $(150/5) \times (22.5/175) = 3.857$.

(c) (i) Elastic demand. Consumers are highly responsive to changes in price. For a rise in price, the quantity effect (which tends to reduce total revenue) outweighs the price effect (which tends to increase total revenue). Overall, this leads to a fall in total revenue.

(ii) Unit-elastic demand. Here the revenue lost to the fall in price is exactly equal to the revenue gained from higher sales. The quantity effect exactly offsets the price effect.

(iii) Inelastic demand. Consumers are relatively unresponsive to changes in price. For consumers to purchase a given percent increase in output, the price must fall by an even greater percent. The price effect of a fall in price (which tends to reduce total revenue) outweighs the quantity effect (which tends to increase total revenue). As a result, total revenue decreases.

(iv) Inelastic demand. Consumers are relatively unresponsive to price, so the percent fall in output is smaller than the percent rise in price. The price effect of a rise in price (which tends to increase total revenue) outweighs the quantity effect (which tends to reduce total revenue). As a result, total revenue increases.

(d) (i) Percentage of income spent on the good;
(ii) the availability of close substitutes;
(iii) whether the good is a necessity or a luxury;
(iv) time horizon.

> Additional areas where credit might be given, note this is not an exhaustive list:
> - Cross elasticity of demand
> - Definition of the market, competitor pricing, habit forming
> - Other examples of substitutes
> - Other examples of complements

Question 2

This question relates to stakeholders and board structure. (Syllabus reference 2.1 Introduction to Economics and 2.3 Agency Theory, Stakeholder Theory and Dependency Theory, and Corporate Governance, Board of Directors and Sub-Committees of the Board, Audit, Remuneration, and Nomination Committees, Corporate Governance Chapter 4 and Chapter 8).

Candidates need to show their understanding to the stakeholders of a company and the different board structures.

(a) Unitary board

A unitary board of directors is characterized by one single board comprising both executive and non-executive directors. The unitary board is responsible for all aspects of the company's activities, and all the directors are working to achieve the same ends. The shareholders elect the directors to the board at the company's annual general meeting (AGM).

The unitary board structure is predominant in the UK and the USA.

(b) Dual board

A dual board system consists of a supervisory board and an executive board of management. However, in a dual board system, there is a clear separation between the functions of supervision (monitoring) and that of management. The supervisory board oversees the direction of the business, whilst the management board is responsible for the running of the business. Members of one board cannot be members of another, so there is a clear distinction between management and control. Shareholders appoint the members of the supervisory board (other than the employee members), whilst the supervisory board appoints the members of the management board.

In Austria, Germany, the Netherlands, and Denmark, the dual structure is predominant.

(c) Commonalities between unitary and dual board structures

There are many similarities in board practice between a unitary and a dual board system. The unitary board and the supervisory board usually appoint the members of the managerial body: the group of managers to whom the unitary board delegates authority in the unitary system and the management board in a dual system. Both bodies usually have responsibility for ensuring that financial reporting and control systems are operating properly and for ensuring compliance with the law. Usually, both the unitary board of directors and the supervisory board (in a dual system) are elected by shareholders (in some countries, such as Germany, employees may elect some supervisory board members). Whether the structure is unitary or dual, many codes seem to have a common approach to areas relating to the function of boards and key board committees, to independence, and to the consideration of shareholder and shareholder rights.

Advocates of each type of board structure identify their main advantages as: in a one-tier system, there is a closer relationship and better information flow as all directors, both executive and non-executive, are on the same single board; in a dual system, there is a more distinct and formal separation between the supervisory body and those being 'supervised', because of the separate management board and supervisory board structures.

MOCK EXAM 2 ANSWERS

(d) The term 'stakeholder' can encompass a wide range of interests: it refers to any individual or group on which the activities of the company have an impact.

There are various stakeholder groups: some directly related to the company, such as employees, providers of credit, suppliers and customers; others more indirectly related to the company, such as the local communities of the towns or cities in which it operates; environmental groups; and the government.

(e) The employees of a company have an interest in the company because it provides their livelihood in the present day and, at some future point, employees will often also be in receipt of a pension provided by the company's pension scheme. In terms of present-day employment, employees will be concerned with their pay and working conditions, and how the company's strategy will impact on these. Of course, the long-term growth and prosperity of the company is important for the longer term view of the employees, particularly as concerns pension benefits in the future. Most companies include, in their annual report and accounts, a statement or report to the employees stating in what ways they are looking after the employees' interests. The report will usually mention training programmes, working conditions, and equal opportunities.

Many companies have employee share schemes that give the employees the opportunity to own shares in the company, and feel more of a part of it; the theory being that the better the company performs (through employees' efforts, etc.), the more the employees themselves will benefit as their shares increase in price.

Companies need also to consider and work with the employees' trade unions, recognizing that a good relationship with the unions is desirable. The trade unions may, amongst other things, act as a conduit for company employee information dissemination, or be helpful when trying to ascertain the employees' views. Increasingly, trade unions are exerting their influence, via the pension funds, pressing for change by use of their voting rights.

Companies need also to consider and comply with employee legislation, whether related to equal opportunities, health and safety at work, or any other aspect. Companies should also have in place appropriate whistle-blowing procedures for helping to ensure that if employees feel that there is inappropriate behaviour in the company, they can 'blow the whistle' on these activities whilst minimizing the risk of adverse consequences for themselves as a result of this action.

> **Additional areas where credit might be given, note this is not an exhaustive list:**
> - **Agency theory, stakeholder theory, other corporate governance theories**
> - **Other stakeholders**
> - **Other countries in which the unitary board system is adopted**
> - **Other countries in which the dual board system is adopted**

Section B

Question 3

This question relates to the macroeconomic policy. (Syllabus reference 2.4 Public Sector and Macro Economy, AIA e-book Chapter 12).

Candidates need to explain the concept of fiscal policy and unemployment rate, identify and explain the reasons of a country's success at exporting, explain the relationship between economic growth and unemployment and explain how a cut in the rate of income tax may, or may not, raise consumer expenditure, then aggregate demand.

(a) Fiscal policy includes: changes in/decisions on government spending and taxation. Unemployment rate: the number unemployed expressed as a percentage of the labour force.

(b) (i) Innovation will increase the quality of German products and make people, both at home and abroad, more willing to buy them.

 (ii) Low prices will make products competitive.

 (iii) Low exchange rate will reduce the prices of exported products. Good marketing will promote exporting sale.

 (iv) Income growth in major export markets will increase the demand for German products.

(c) (i) There is an inverse relationship between economic growth and unemployment.
 (ii) Rise in real GDP is likely to increase demand for products.
 (iii) Higher demand for products will increase demand for labour.
 (iv) A fall in unemployment will move an economy closer to its production possibility curve.
 (v) Possibilities of a time lag.
 (vi) Output could rise with no change in unemployment if productivity rises.
 (vii) Production possibility curve could move out without a fall in unemployment.

(d) Reasons for how a cut in the rate of income tax may raise aggregated demand:

 (i) An increase in disposable income will enable consumers to spend more.

 (ii) Higher consumer expenditure may cause a rise in investment, further increasing aggregate demand.

Evaluating the effect of the cut in rate of income tax:

 (i) How much aggregate demand rises depends on the size of the cut; some of the extra income may be saved rather than spent.

 (ii) If public confidence is low, consumption and investment may not rise.

 (iii) Cut in the lower rate of income tax is likely to be more effective.

 (iv) Households and firms may expect that the cut will be reversed in the future.

 (v) There may be a time lag before households and firms react.

Additional areas where credit might be given, note this is not an exhaustive list:
- **Possibilities of a time lag.**
- **Rise in real GDP is likely to increase demand for products.**

Question 4

This question relates to the international trade – the international economy (Syllabus reference 2.5 The External Sector, AIA e-book Chapter 14).

Candidates need to show their understanding of international financial institution and critically discuss the impacts of globalisation.

(a) The Group of Twenty Finance Ministers and Central Bank Governors is a group of finance ministers and central bank governors from 20 economies: USA, Japan, China, Germany, France, UK, Italy, Russia, Brazil, Canada, India, Mexico, Australia, South Korea, Turkey, Indonesia, Saudi Arabia, Argentina, South Africa, and the rest of the EU represented, collectively, by the European council president.

Together these twenty economies (the 19 countries plus the remainder of the EU collectively) are home to two-thirds of the World's population, and account for around 80% of the World's GDP.

The G20 holds annual summits, or meetings, to discuss global financial issues. These have included:

(i) Dealing with the financial crises such as the banking crisis of 2007-2010

(ii) Harmonisation of taxation policies across countries to reduce tax avoidance

(iii) Agreeing policies to detect and reduce illegal transfers of money from the proceeds of crime, terrorism and so on

The G20 has become very influential since it was formed in 2008 and has essentially replaced other groupings of rich countries such as G7 and G8.

(b) Globalisation used to be the unquestioned model for economic growth and stability but there are now many critics of the phenomena.

For globalisation

(i) Emergence of new growth markets, for example, in the less developed countries;

(ii) Enhanced competitiveness as more producers and customers make up the global marketplace;

(iii) Growth of previously poor economies, such as China;

(iv) Cross-national business alliance and mergers;

(v) International support for poorer nations and assistance provided in development of their economies;

(vi) World economic equalisation.

Criticisms of globalisation

(i) The main institutions of globalisation follow the collective will of the G8 countries (USA, Japan, Germany, Canada, Italy, France, the UK and Russia) and are more concerned therefore in aiding the economic wealth of these countries.

(ii) The International Monetary Fund (IMF), the World Bank Group (WB) and G20 along with powerful multinational organisations dictate economic policy in countries but do not include real representation of these countries within their organisations. This lack of accountability has been called 'global gvoernance without global government' (*Joseph Stiglitz*, Globalisation and its Discontents).

(iii) World poverty is still an issue and many fear that the policies adopted by WB, IMF and others, for example, in restricting subsidies in Africa and opening up their markets for Western imports that are produced under a subsidy, can actually make some nations poorer.

(iv) There is no enduring political and economic stability in the world and the collapse of one part of the economy, for example in South America, could have disastrous knock on effects for the rest of the world.

(v) Not all countries are included in global activity. Instead, there is an increasing tendency for groups of countries, usually located in the same region to become involved in each others economies, for example the countries in the eurozone.

Additional areas where credit might be given, note this is not an exhaustive list:

- **Short-term stabilisation measures for particular countries or the world economy as a whole;**
- **Medium and long term financial help to countries seeking to restructure and invest in their economies;**
- **Co-ordination of policies of member countries on financial regulation and economic policies to avert crises and simulate world economic growth.**

Index

Note. **Key Terms** and their page references are given in **bold**.

Absolute advantage, 416
Accelerator principle, 303
Accounting profits, 124
Ad valorem tax, 335
Advantages of floating exchange rates, 387
Agency theory, 90
Aggregate demand, 284, **330**
Aggregate demand and national income, 289
Aggregate supply, 284
Aggregation (in financial intermediation), 239
Aims of the banks, 261
Allocative efficiency, 156, 213
Allocative inefficiency, 166, 216
Alternative investment market (AIM), 234, 242
Arbitrage, 384
Arc elasticity of demand, 38
Audit and auditors, 108
Audit committee, 107
Automatic stabilisers, 341
Average cost, 121
Average fixed cost (AFC), 121
Average propensity to consume, 292
Average revenue, 146
Average variable costs, 121

Backward vertical integration, **136**
Balance of payments, 313, 404
   and the exchange rate, 385
   Capital account, 404
   Current account, 405
   Financial account, 405
Balance of trade, 405
Balanced budget multiplier, 340
Balancing item, 405
Bank multiplier, 258
Bank of England, 263, 265
Bank overdraft, 232
Banks, 244, 256
Barriers to entry, 160, **166**
Base currency, 378
Basel III agreement, 261
Baumol's sales maximisation model, 92
Benchmark, 264
Big bang, 214
Bills of exchange, 232
Black marketeers, 56
Board of Directors, 100
Bond markets, 244
Bonds, 233
Borrowing, 233

Breakeven analysis, 150
Broad money, 262
Budget, 330
Budget deficit, 331, **332**
Budget surplus, 331, **332**
Building societies, 245
Business confidence, 347
Business cycles, 305
Business expansion, 137

Capital, 7, 190
Capital account, 404
Capital adequacy, 260
Capital markets, 239
Capital-output ratio, 304
Cartels, 177
Cash reserve ratio, 357
Causes of unemployment, 318
Central bank, 263, 264
Central government, 341
Centrally planned economy, 4
Certificates of deposit, 241
Ceteris paribus, 27
Charities, 84
Choice, 7
Circular flow of income, 287
Clearing banks, 256
Clearing system, 256
Coincident indicator, 356
Collective bargaining, 198
Collusion, 177
Collusive oligopoly, 181
Command economy, 4
Commercial banks, 256
Commercial paper, 232, 233
Common Agricultural Policy (CAP), 54
Common market, 422
Comparative advantage, 416, **417**
Competition and Markets Authority (CMA), 221
Competition Commission, 222
Competition policy, 221
Complements, 27
Compulsory competitive tendering, 214
Conditions of demand, 29
Conglomerate diversification, 136, **137**
Constant returns to scale, 130
Consumer price index (CPI), 229
Consumer watchdog bodies, 219
Consumption, 290
Consumption function, 292
Contestable markets, 183

INDEX

Corporate governance, 94, 101
Corporate Social Responsibilty (CSR), 87
Cost accounting, 124
Cost of production, 120
Cost push inflation, 315
Credit agreements, 232
Credit controls, 358
Credit creation, 258
Credit multiplier, **258**, 259
Credit risk, **396**
Cross elasticity of demand, 48
Crowding out, 295, 341
Currency blocs, 389
Currency of invoice, 393
Currency risk, 380
Current account, 404, 405
Current account deficit, 408
Customs duties, 419
Customs union, 422
Cyclical or demand-deficient unemployment, 319

Dead weight loss, 161
Deadweight burden, 164
Debentures, 233
Deficit on current account, 407
Deficit units, **230**
Definition of money, 262
Deflation, **312**, 408
Deflationary gap, 322
Demand curve, 25
Demand deficient unemployment, 319
Demand for factors of production, 190
Demand for labour, 194
Demand management, 289, 322
Demand pull inflation, **314**
Demand schedule, 25
Demerit good, 62
De-multiplier, 300
Deregulation, 213
Derived demand, **190**
Dimensional economies of scale, 132
Direct quote, **377**
Direct tax, 335
Disadvantages of floating exchange rates, 387
Discrimination, 197
Diseconomies of scale, 130, 133, 134
Disincentive effect, 337
Disinflation, **312**
Documentary credits, 397
Domestic deflation, 411
Dumping, 57, 420
Duopoly, 181

Economic exposure, 392
Economic growth, 330
Economic indicator, 356
Economic policy objectives, 330
Economic profits, 124
Economic rent, **203**
Economic system, 4
Economic value, 13
Economic wealth, 14
Economies of scale, **130**, 131, 134
Elasticity, 38
Elasticity of demand, 38
Elasticity of demand for imports, 409
Elasticity of supply, 48
Embargo on imports, 420
Endowment assurance, 249
Enterprise, 7
Enterprise Act (2002), 221
Entrepreneurship, 130, 190, 202
Equilibrium in the balance of payments, 407
Equilibrium price, 34
Equity, 233
Ethics, 88
Eurobonds, 233
Eurocurrency markets, 427
European central bank (ECB), 392
European economic area, 424
European free trade association (EFTA), 424
European union, 418, 422
Excess capacity theorem, 176
Exchange, 13
Exchange rate, 355, **376**
Exchange rate mechanism (ERM), 388
Exchange rate risk, 393
Exchange rate stability, 389
Exchange rate systems, 389
Exchange value, 13
Executive Committee, 102
Executive compensation committee, 103
Executive remuneration, 103
Expectational inflation, 315
Expectations augmented Phillips curve, 324, 360
Expenditure reducing, 408
Expenditure switching, 408
Explicit costs, 124
Export credit guarantees, 420
Export credit insurance, **397**
Export multiplier, 299
Export subsidies, 420
Exports, 289
External balance, 330
External debt, 412
External economies of scale, 133

Externalities, 58, 60

Factor markets, 190
Factor mobility, 197
Factor pricing, 203
Factors of production, 7, 120
Fiduciary responsibility, 97
Financial account, 404
Financial instruments, 230
Financial intermediaries, 230, 238, 245
Financial intermediation, 228, 230, 238
Firms, 24
Fiscal drag, 341
Fiscal policy, 330, 339
Fiscal year, 236
Fisher equation, 316
Fixed costs, 121, 126
Fixed exchange rates, 388
Floating exchange rates, 386
Floor price, 57
Flow of funds, 230
Footsie (FTSE 100) index, 242
Foreign currency, 406
Foreign exchange (or currency) risk, 392
Foreign exchange markets, 379
Forward exchange contract, 394
Forward rate, 378
Forward vertical integration, 136
Fractional reserve system, 260
Free floating exchange rates, 386
Free riders, 60, 61
Free trade area, 422
Frictional unemployment, 318
Full employment, 321, 330
Functions and qualities of money, 228

G8 group, 422
Game theory, 180, 181
GDP price deflator, 229
Geographical immobility of labour, 197
Globalisation, 425, 427
Gold, 389
Government bond, 273
Government intervention in foreign exchange markets, 388
Government payments, 235
Government receipts, 235
Government spending, 289
Government spending multiplier, 299

Horizontal integration, 136
Households, 24

Hyperinflation, 313

Implicit costs, 124
Import cost-push inflation, 315
Import quotas, 408, 419
Import restrictions, 420
Imports, 288
Incidence of tax, 335
Income elasticity of demand, 47
Incomes policy, 353
Indirect quote, 377
Indirect tax, 335
Indirect taxation, 45, 62, 338
Inequalities of wealth, 5
Infant industries, 420
Inferior goods, 28, 48
Inflation, 312, 321, 330, 349, 359
Inflation and the exchange rate, 383
Inflation and the value of money, 229
Inflationary expectations, 360
Inflationary gap, 322
Injections into the circular flow of income, 288
Institutional investors, 245
Insurance, 246
Insurance broker, 248
Insurance contract, 246
Insurance underwriter, 248
Interest, 7, 190, 191
Interest rate parity, 384
Interest rates, 191, 266, 354, 357, 360
Interest rates and the balance of payments, 412
Interest rates and the exchange rate, 384
Internal economies of scale, 133
International monetary fund (IMF), 412
International trade, 416
Investment, 288, 294
Investment banks, 256
Investment multiplier, 299
Investment trust, 245
Issued share capital, 233

J curve, 409
J curve effect, 409
Japan, 408

Keynesian demand for money, 345
Kinked oligopoly demand curve, 179

Labour, 7, 190
Labour immobility, 197
Labour productivity, 201
Laffer curve, 336

INDEX

Lagged payments, 393
Lagging indicator, 356
Land, 201
Land, 7, 190
Law of diminishing returns, 127
Lead payments, 393
Leading indicator, 356
Less developed countries, 420
Letters of credit, 397
Liberalisation, 213
Limited liability, 85
Liquidity, 261
Liquidity preference, 270, **346**
Loanable funds theory of interest rates, 351
London inter-bank offered rate, 264
Long run, 120
Long run, 51
Long run costs, 129

M0 (narrow money), 262
M4 (broad money), 262
Management accountability, 96
Management buy-outs, 246
Management discretion model, 92
Managerial economies, 132
Managerial model of the firm, 92
Managerial objectives, 92
Marginal cost, 121
Marginal efficiency of capital, 191, 297
Marginal productivity theory, 194
Marginal productivity theory of wages, 195
Marginal propensity to consume (MPC), 291
Marginal propensity to save (MPS), 291, 299
Marginal revenue, 146
Marginal revenue product (MRP), 195
Marginal tax rates, 336
Marginal utility, 68
Market clearing price, 35
Market concentration, 138
Market demand curve, 27
Market economy, 4
Market failure, 59, 212
Market period, 50
Market supply curve, 32
Marshall-Lerner conditions, 410
Matching receipts and payments, 393
Maximum prices, 55
Mergers, 136
Merit goods, 5, **59**, 61
Mezzanine finance, 233
Minimum efficient scale, 135
Minimum price legislation, 57
Minimum prices, 57

Minimum wages, 58
Mixed economy, 4
Monetarists, 315, 349
Monetary policy, 330, 353, 356, 358
Monetary theory, 344
Money market hedges, 395
Money markets, 239, 241
Money supply, 349, 353
Monopolies, 58
Monopolistic competition, 174
Monopoly, 157
Monopsony/monopsonists, 58
Moral suasion, 358
Multinational enterprises, 425
Multiplier, 298
Mutual organisations, 84

NAIRU (Non-accelerating inflational rate of unemployment), 321
Narrow money, 262
National Debt, 341
National income, 289
Nationalised industries, 219
Natural monopoly, 158
Natural rate hypothesis, 360
Natural rate of unemployment, 321
Net present value, 297
New classical school, 361
New quantity theory of money, 348
Nominal and real rates of interest, 266
Nominal rates of interest, 266
Nominations committee, 103
Non-price competition, 174
Normal goods, 28, 48
Normal profit, 120, 123, 152
North American Free Trade Agreement (NAFTA), 424

Objectives of firms, 86
Occupational immobility, 198
Oligopoly, 177
OPEC, 178
Open market operations, 264
Opportunity cost, 124, 417
Ordinary shares, 273
Organisational coalition, 92
Outsourcing, 140
Over the counter (OTC) markets, 240

Parallel markets, 242
Pension funds, 245
Perfect competition, 151

522

INDEX

Phillips curve, 322
Planned economy, 4
Point elasticity of demand, 39
Pollution, 6, 60, 62
Pollution policies, 63
Precautionary motive, 345
Price, 376
Price ceiling, 55
Price discrimination, 161
Price elasticity of demand, 38
Price leadership, 180
Price legislation, 62
Price mechanism, 33, 59
Price regulation, 55
Price theory, 24
Primary markets, 53
Principal sources of long-term capital, 233
Principal sources of short-term capital, 232
Principal-agent problem, 90
Private benefit, 59
Private cost, 59
Privatisation, 214
Product differentiation, **174**, 177
Production efficiency, 9
Production possibility curve, 8
Production possibility frontier, 8
Production quotas, 57
Productive inefficiency, 216
Professional associations, 197
Profit, 7, **120**, 123, 190, 203
Profit maximisation, 86, 146
Profit maximising position, 148, 149
Profit seeking organisations, 85
Profitability, 261
Progressive tax, 333
Proportional tax, 333
Protectionism, 419
Protectionist measures, 411
Public goods, 59
Public sector borrowing requirement (PSBR), 331
Public sector net cash requirement (PSNCR), 295, **331**
Public sector organisations, 85
Purchasing power parity theory, 383

Qualitative controls, 357
Qualities of money, 228
Quantitative controls, 357
Quantity theory of money, **316**, 344

Raising capital, 234
Raising finance, 234

Rate of interest, 191
Rationing, 56
Raw materials costs, 31
Real rates of interest, 266
Recession, 305
Redistribution of wealth, 62, 312
Reference currency, **378**
Reflation, 322
Regressive tax, 333
Regulation of markets, 212
Re-insurance, 248
Remuneration committee, 103
Rent, 7, 190, 201
Research and development, 132
Reserve requirements, 357
Resource dependency theory, 93
Retail banks, 256
Retail prices index, 314
Retained earnings, 234
Retained profits and other reserves, 233
Retraining schemes, 198
Risk, 267

Sales maximisation model, 92
Satisficing, 92
Savings, 288, 291
Scarcity, **6**
Scarcity of resources, 6, 7
Secular period, 51
Security, 261
Self-regulation, 212
Share price indices, 242
Share prices, 242
Shareholder activism, 105
Short run, 51, **120**
Short run average cost (SRAC) curve, 126
Short run costs, 121
Single currency, 390
Single premium bonds, 249
Skilled workers, 198
Small firms, 139
Social benefits, **59**
Social costs, **59**
Specialisation, 416
Specific tax, 335
Speculation, 382
Speculative motive, **345**
Spot rate, **378**
Stakeholder theory, 89
Statutory minimum wage, 200
Stock exchange, 214
Structural unemployment, 318
Subsidies, 62, 67
Substitute goods, 27

Sunk costs, 124
Supernormal profits, 160
Supply curve, 30
Supply curve for labour, 196
Supply of capital, 193
Supply schedule, 30
Supply side, 330
Supply side economic policies, 362
Supply side economics, 284, 362
Surplus on current account, 408
Surplus units, 230

Tariffs, 408
Tariffs, 419
Taxation, 288, 332, 333
Technical efficiency, 153
Technical inefficiency, 166, 216
Technological changes, 347
Technological developments, 32
Technological progress, 165
Term currency, 378
Term life, 249
Term structure of interest rates, 270
Terms of trade, 413
Total cost, 121
Total revenue, 146
Total revenue minus total cost, 120
Trade cycles, 305
Trade unions, 198
Transactions motive, 345
Transfer earnings, 203
Transfer payments, 204, 235, 288
Translation exposure, 393
Transmission mechanism, 351
Trans-Pacific Pact (TPP), 424
Treasury bill, 273
Types of unemployment, 318

Underlying rate of inflation, 314
Unemployment, 317, 318
Unit elasticity of demand, 42
Unit trusts, 245
Universal life contract, 249
Utility, 14

Variable costs, **121**, 126
Velocity of circulation, 316
Venture capital, 233, 246
Vertical integration, 136

Wage differentials, 198
Wage-price spiral, 315
Wages, 194
Wages, 7, 190
Wealth, 14
Whole life contract, 249
Williamson's management discretion model, 92
Withdrawals from the circular flow of income, 288
World Bank, 412
World Trade Organisation (WTO), 422

X-inefficiency, **134**, 166

Yield curve, 271
Yield on commercial paper, 267
Yield on equities (dividend yield), 271
Yield on financial instruments, 266, 274
Yield on treasury bills, 268
Yields on bonds, 269

NOTES

NOTES

NOTES

NOTES

NOTES

NOTES

NOTES

NOTES